THE
STRUCTURING
OF
ORGANIZATIONS

A Synthesis of the Research

Henry Mintzberg

McGill University

Prentice-Hall International, Inc.

The Theory of Management Policy Series
Henry Mintzberg, Editor

 © *1979 by Prentice-Hall, Inc., Englewood Cliffs, N.J. 07632*

Printed in the United States of America

10 9 8 7 6 5 4 3 2

ISBN 0-13-853771-2

Prentice-Hall International (UK) Limited, *London*
Prentice-Hall of Australia Pty. Limited, *Sydney*
Prentice-Hall Canada Inc., *Toronto*
Prentice-Hall Hispanoamericana, S.A., *Mexico*
Prentice-Hall of India Private Limited, *New Delhi*
Prentice-Hall of Japan, Inc., *Tokyo*
Simon & Schuster Asia Pte. Ltd., *Singapore*
Editora Prentice-Hall do Brasil, Ltda., *Rio de Janeiro*
Prentice-Hall, Inc., *Englewood Cliffs, New Jersey*

Foreword

The Theory of Management Policy Series

Management Policy has long been the stepchild of the management school. It had to be taught—the issues it dealt with were too important to ignore—yet it never quite attained the status of other fields, such as management science, organizational behavior, and marketing. The reason for this seems quite clear. While the other fields were developing substantial theoretical content throughout the 1960s and 1970s, Management Policy—having shed its long-standing "principles" orientation—was focusing its attention on the teaching of cases. Theory—systematic knowledge—was, and often remains, unwelcome in the Policy course.

I had the good fortune to study for a doctorate in Policy at a management school (the MIT Sloan School) that had no Policy area, not even a Policy professor. That enabled me to explore the field from a different perspective. Cases had no special place at MIT. Theory had. So my exploration became a search for Policy theory—specifically descriptive theory based on empirical research. And that search convinced me of one thing: that there in fact existed a large and relevant body of such theory, sufficient to put the field on a solid theoretical foundation. But that theory was to be found in no one place—no one textbook, for example; indeed a great deal of it was not recognized as Policy-related theory per se. In other words, the field lacked synthesis, even compendium—the bringing together of the useful theoretical materials. So by the time I completed my Ph.D. at the Sloan School in 1968, I had made up my mind to write a book called *The Theory of Management Policy*.

These ten years have been spent paying the price of that decision. What began as files on each chapter quickly became boxes, and then the boxes began to overflow, in some cases two and even three times. Convinced that the field needed a thorough publication, I let the chapters run to their natural lengths. In two cases, that came to over 400 pages of text! Hence this series.

The original outline of *The Theory of Management Policy* called for eleven chapters, eight of which are shown on the accompanying figure. Two (not shown) were introductory. The first, entitled "The Study of Management Policy," traced the development of the field, from its principles and case study traditions to contemporary approaches based on grand planning, eclectic and descriptive theory. This chapter concluded that the field should be built on descriptive theory, that this theory should be based on inductive research of the policy making process and be supported by research in underlying fields such as cognitive psychology, organizational sociology, and political science, and that the policy–making research should be rich in real–world description and not obsessed with rigor. The second chapter, "An Underlying Theory for Management Policy," combined the general systems theory of Ludwig von Bertalanffy with the decision theory of Herbert Simon to develop a framework in which to integrate the different topics of Management Policy. These two chapters actually exist as chapters, and may one day see the light of day in a single synthesized book. In the meantime, parts of them have been published as "Policy as a Field of Man-

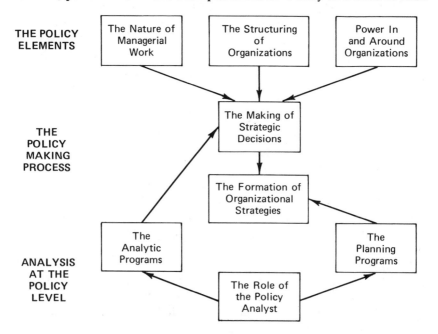

agement Theory" (in the *Academy of Management Review* of January, 1977), a paper that outlines my general views on the field.

Five chapters made up the core of the book—the descriptive theory. These will form this series, as it is presently conceived. The first three—the "policy elements"—were designed to synthesize the empirical research on three topics (generally considered in "organization theory") that I believe underlie the study of policy making—managerial work, organizational structure, and organizational power. *The Nature of Managerial Work*, based on my own doctoral research as well as related empirical literature, was published in 1973 and will be reproduced in this series. The current volume, *The Structuring of Organizations: A Synthesis of the Research*, is the original Chapter 3 having run a little long. And the next book to appear in the series, *Power In and Around Organizations*, is Chapter 5 having run even longer. Currently in draft form, the power volume should follow this one by about eighteen months. Both are based on the studies of large bodies of (mostly empirical) literature.

The two chapters on the "policy-making process" were intended to focus on the central core of the field of Management Policy. *The Making of Strategic Decisions* currently exists as a (not unreasonably) large Chapter 6; it will be expanded into a (not unreasonably) small volume three. Like the volume on managerial work, it combines a synthesis of the empirical literature with our own research, carried out at McGill University (and published in article form as "The Structure of 'Unstructured' Decision Processes," together with Duru Raisinghani and André Théorêt, in the *Administrative Science Quarterly* of June, 1976). This fourth volume considers the question of how organizations actually make single strategic decisions. The fifth volume, *The Formation of Organization Strategies*, is designed to look at how organizations combine such decisions over time to form strategies. This is the one book in the series that does not yet exist (although it has begun to take shape in two articles, "Strategy Making in Three Modes" published in the *California Management Review* in the winter of 1973, and "Patterns in Strategy Formation" published in the May, 1978 issue of *Management Science*). Here again, the empirical literature will be combined with our own research, except that in both cases the dimensions are much larger—four boxes of published materials coupled with the results of almost a decade of research. An appropriate publication date would seem to be 1984.

The prescriptive section of *The Theory of Management Policy*—three chapters on "analysis at the policy level" and a fourth on the future for Management Policy—remains a project on a dim horizon. A number of shorter items have been published on policy analysis (such as *Impediments to the Use of Management Information*, a 1975 monograph by the National Association of Accountants and the Society of Industrial Accountants of

Canada, "The Planning Dilemma" with James S. Hekimian in the May, 1968 issue of the *Management Review*, and especially "Beyond Implementation: An Analysis of the Resistance to Policy Analysis" in the proceedings of the 1978 Conference of the International Federation of Operational Research Societies). Perhaps these will one day be drawn together into a sixth volume on policy analysis, but more likely that volume will focus on the broader issue of organizational effectiveness.

And what of *The Theory of Management Policy?* In the not too distant future, I hope to draw the central concepts of all the books and articles into a single volume, a textbook along the lines of the original conception.

A few words about the title of the series are in order. "The" is meant to signify "the body" of theory in Management Policy, not "the one" theory of Management Policy. In fact, if one central theme runs through the series, it is an attempt to synthesize by seeking reconciliation among conflicting theories. The approach is essentially a contingency one—not which theory is correct, but under what conditions does each apply. Not planning versus muddling through, but when planning, when muddling through; not maximizing versus satisfying, but where maximizing, where satisfying.

"Theory" signifies that the series seeks to build conceptual frameworks. Theories are useful because they shortcut the need to store masses of data. One need not remember all the details one has learned about a phenomenon. Instead, one stores a theory, an abstraction that explains many of them. The level of that abstraction can vary widely. These volumes seek to present theory that is "middle range." In this sense, the series seeks to position itself between—and in so doing to reject both—Policy's case study tradition, which never sought to develop conceptual interpretation of its lower-range (concrete) descriptions, and Policy's principles tradition, whose high-range abstractions lost touch with the descriptive reality.

The attempt throughout this series is also to present theory that is "grounded"—that is rooted in data, that grows inductively out of systematic investigation of how organizations behave. I am firmly convinced that the best route to more effective policy making is better knowledge in the mind of the practitioner of the world he or she actually faces. This means that I take my role as researcher and writer to be the generation and dissemination of the best *descriptive* theory possible. I believe it is the job of the practitioner—line manager, staff analyst, consultant (including myself when in that role)—to prescribe, to find better approaches to policy making. In other words, I believe that the best prescription comes from the application of conceptual knowledge about a phenomenon *in a specific and familiar context*. To me, good descriptive theory in the right hands *is* a prescriptive tool, perhaps the most powerful one we have.

I use the word "Management," instead of the more common "Business," as the adjective for Policy to indicate that this series is about all kinds of organizations—to draw on the examples of this volume, not only automobile companies, banks, and consulting firms, but also cultural centers, penitentiaries, and space agencies. It is the focus on process rather than content—strategy making rather than strategies, the flow of power rather than the resulting goals—that enables us to take this broad perspective.

Finally the word "Policy," one that has been used in all kinds of ways. A government "policy" can range from having to use black ink on Form E5 to refusing aid to nonalligned nations. Here the word is used strictly as a label for a field of study—that one concerned with the management of the total organization, with particular emphasis on its decisional behavior. (I prefer Management Policy to Strategic Management—a term proposed in some quarters of the field—because the latter seems to me to have a narrower and more prescriptive orientation.)

I shall save specific acknowledgements for each of the volumes, with one exception. I began work on *The Theory of Management Policy* when I first taught the MBA Policy course at McGill University in 1968, doing the original detailed draft of its outline for my first students in that course. Over the years, nearly a thousand McGill MBAs have worked through various versions of this work, most of them too long. These students can take some solace in the fact that this series has benefited enormously from their inputs. Specifically, using the theory as the basis to study Montreal organizations, the students have—as will be evident in the pages that follow —applied, elaborated, modified, and rejected various parts of the theory, thereby grounding and enriching it as no other inputs could possibly have. I owe these students a large thank you. I can only hope that they learned something along the way.

HENRY MINTZBERG

To Tutyi

... beyond Adhocracy
(but still in the studio)

Contents

Preface

The Structuring of Organizations

I write first of all for myself. That is how I learn. As noted in the preceding Foreword to the Series, I wrote this book because I was interested in how organizations form their strategies, and thought I first had to learn how they structure themselves. So I set out to collect as much of the relevant literature as I practically could, and then to develop it into an explanation of the structuring of organizations.

That proved to be no easy task. Linearity is what makes all writing so difficult. This book contains about 175,000 words laid end to end in a single linear sequence. But the world is not linear, especially the world of organizational structuring. It intermingles all kinds of complex flows—parallel, circular, reciprocal.

I began with two full boxes, containing over 200 articles and book extracts. Were this to have been a traditional "textbook," I would simply have reviewed the literature, grouping the articles in some sort of clusters ("schools of thought"), and then recounting what each had to say, without a great deal of attention to the inconsistencies. But my intention was not to write a textbook—at least not in the usual sense of the term—nor to review the literature. I was here to answer a question: how do organizations structure themselves? And so I had to extract whatever bits and pieces seemed useful in each article and book, and then weld them all together into a single integrated answer. In other words, it was *synthesis* I was after, specifically synthesis of the literature that describes what organizations really do—the literature based on empirical research.

And so I read and piled up index cards, until they seemed to stand about a foot high. And then I tried to put them all together into one outline —into that single linear sequence. No task has ever frustrated me more, as those who ventured into my basement during those dark months can testify. (No small part of that frustration can be traced to the considerable body of research that unnecessarily complicates an already complex subject—arm's length studies that confuse vague perceptions of vague dimensions with the real world of structuring, and that mix organizations in ways that defy understanding of their context.) But gradually it all came together, into one outline of almost 200 pages. Not bad for what was supposed to be a chapter of another book!

In retrospect, I felt I had been working on a giant jigsaw puzzle, with many missing pieces. Some of the pieces I had seemed to fit in obvious places, and once enough of them were placed, an image began to appear in my mind. Thereafter, each new piece in place clarified that image. By the time I finished, I felt I had found a logical place for all the pieces available to me. In fact, the image had become so sharp that I felt confident in describing some of the missing pieces. (And in describing related images: in writing about structuring, as the reader will see, I learned a great deal about strategy formation, organizational democracy and alienation, and a number of other related topics. Structure seems to be at the root of many of the question we raise about organizations.) And so while no task has ever caused me more frustration, no result will likely ever give me more satisfaction. The image may be too sharp—the real world is not as clean as that one portrayed in this book. But that is how it came out. Besides, who wants a theory that hedges!

The reading and 200-page outline were essentially done alone in about six months of full-time work (if I can trust my poor memory). That was the hard part. All that remained was the writing, preparation of diagrams, insertion of quotations, preparation of bibliography, rewriting, typing, editing, circulating of rough draft, new reading (ninety-two more articles), rewriting, retyping, re-rewriting, and re-retyping, before the manuscript was ready for the publisher (and thereafter the permissions, review of copy editing, reading of galley proofs and then page proofs, and the preparation of index). That took a mere twenty-four months (plus twelve more in production). And it involved all kinds of other people, some of whom I would like to thank by name.

Half of the work was done in Aix-en-Provence, France, where I spent an extended sabbatical. Aix is no place to write a book. One of the truly delightful cities of the world—partly surrounded by rugged mountains, with the Alps a couple of hours up above, the sea an hour down below, Italy three hours off to the left and Spain six hours to the right—Aix does not make writing easy. For all those distractions and two wonderful years in

Aix, I must thank Maurice Saias and his "équipe" at the Centre d'Etude et de Recherche sur les Organisations et la Gestion of the Université d'Aix-Marseille, as well as the dean back home, Stan Shapiro, whose support and tolerance through these past years have been magnificent.

Between a computer in Montreal and a professor in Aix-en-Provence, joined by two mail systems that did not always work as the bureaucratic machines they were designed to be, sat Donna Jensen. That the twenty-nine hours of tape and two hundred odd scotch–taped quotations got typed at all was a feat; that they got typed quickly and accurately is a tribute to Donna's talent. Donna's mistake when she left McGill for better things was to leave her phone number behind. She agreed to do the minor corrections, and found herself virtually retyping the manuscript two full times. So Donna spent many long evenings at home over the typewriter, never complained (at least not to me), and finished the manuscript in record time. And I am forever grateful.

The support staff in Aix was Sylvia Niquet, who helped in a great many small ways, and later in Montreal was Nina Gregg who looked after permissions, while Cynthia Mulherin kept the more regular work flowing efficiently. Esther Koehn of Prentice–Hall recently joined this team as Prentice–Hall's pleasant and efficient production editor.

A number of colleagues, friends, and others provided many useful comments. My brother Leon went through the first draft very carefully, and cleaned up a lot of problems. Roger Gosselin gave a good deal of his time and help. Others who have influenced parts of the book constructively with their comments include Jim Waters, Don Armstrong, Maurice Boisvert, John Hunt, Derek Channon, Rosemary Stewart, Pierre Romelaer, Rich Livesley, as well as Gerry Susman, Craig Lundberg, and Herb Simon who commented on the first draft at the request of Prentice–Hall. Herb Simon should also be singled out as the one individual who in his own writings set up the conceptual framework without which this book could not have been written. And then I must thank Mattio Diorio pour le symbolisme des cinqs, Carson Eoyang for the suggestion of the sixth, and Bye Wynn for the short refresher course in geometry (though I still prefer hexagon).

Finally to Yvette, to whom this book is dedicated, and to Susie and Lisa, who still manage me (and still interrupt my writing in the basement), go my inadequate words of gratitude for a rich and loving home life which influences a book like this in so many profound but unexplainable ways.

HENRY MINTZBERG

A Note to the Reader

I like to think of this book, not as an American snack, nor a Swedish smör-gasbord, but a French banquet. What I mean is that it cannot be consumed on the run, nor can its many dishes be sampled at random. They are meant to be taken in the specific order presented. To reiterate a point stressed in its Preface, this book is not a review of the literature but a synthesis of its research findings.

The book has been written for all those interested in the structuring of organizations—managers who do it, specialists who advise them on it, professors who research it, and students who wish to understand it. I have tried to write the book in the belief that even the most difficult point can be made comprehensible for the novice without losing any of its richness for the expert. That of course does not mean that all readers have the same tastes and appetites. To cater to these differences is the purpose of this note.

First a brief review. This banquet consists of twenty-two chapters, in four sections. The first section is the introduction—the hors d'oeuvres—comprising Chapters 1 through 3, the first on five basic mechanisms for coordinating work in organizations, the second on five basic parts of organizations, the third on five fundamental systems of flows in organizations.

These three chapters are followed by the "analysis" of the book—consisting of Chapters 4 through 16—divided into two sections. Here the phenomenon of organizational structuring is taken apart, one element at a time. In effect, the reader is exposed to all of the tastes that make up a banquet on organizational structuring. Chapters 4 through 11 discuss each of nine design parameters of organizational design. The first four of these—job specialization (Chapter 4), behavior formalization (Chapter 5), training and indoctrination (Chapter 6), and unit grouping (Chapter 7)—are classic dishes served more or less in the classical manner. Unit size (usually called "span of control"), discussed in Chapter 8, is a classic dish too, but its manner of preparation is contemporary. Here the flavor of the synthesis can first be detected. Chapter 9 serves up planning and control systems in a new, light sauce, while Chapter 10 on the liaison devices will be new to anyone who has not already been to Jay Galbraith's banquet. And Chapter 11 offers that heavy dish called decentralization in a new, but necessarily rather thick sauce. Chapters 12 through 16, making up the third section of the book, then discuss the contingency factors, those conditions of the organization that most obviously influence its choice of design parameters. Chapter 12, on the effective structuring or organizations, serves as an important transition from the design parameters to the contingency factors, while the next four chapters discuss, respectively, the influence on structure of an organization's age and size, its technical system, its environment, and its power system. New flavors are mixed with old throughout this section.

The pièces de resistance of this banquet are found in the fourth section —the synthesis—comprising Chapters 17 through 22. Here all of the tastes of the early dishes are blended into five new ones, called "structural configurations"—Simple Structure, Machine Bureaucracy, Professional Bureaucracy, Divisionalized Form, and Adhocracy. In a sense, the first sixteen chapters prepare the palate for the last six, which are the real reasons for this banquet. Chapters 17 through 21 discuss each of these configurations, while Chapter 22—the "digestif"—takes a final look at some of their interrelationships.

Some people arrive at a meal hungrier than others, while some already familiar with the cuisine wish to save their appetites for the new dishes, hoping only to sample the classic ones to see how the chef prepares them. But no one should start without the hors d'oeuvres or end without the digestif. Moreover, those who proceed too quickly to the pièces de resistance risk burning their tongues on spicy dishes and so spoiling what could have been a good meal. And so I would suggest the following to the reader already familiar with the cuisine of organizational structuring.

Chapters 1 and 2 should be read in full since they set the framework for all that follows. So too should most of Chapters 17 to 21 since they constitute the essence of this book, the synthesis. Specifically, that synthesis is contained in the first two sections of each of these chapters, on the "description of the basic structure" and its "conditions." The last section of each of these chapters, on "some issues associated with" the structural configuration, can be considered as a dressing to be taken according to taste. And the short Chapter 22 serves as the digestif I believe necessary to ensure complete digestion of this large meal.

As for the chapters between the introduction and the synthesis, I would suggest that the reader already familiar with the literature read Chapters 11 and 12 in full, focus on whatever material he or she finds new in Chapters 8, 9, 10 and 13 through 16, and scan the rest of the book. **Note that scanning has been facilitated throughout by the use of bold face type (like this) for key sentences that, taken all together, serve to summarize all of the major points of the book.** As a bare minimum for the knowledgeable person in the field, the reading of all of these key sentences of the first sixteen chapters will provide a sense of the line of argument and the related vocabulary necessary to appreciate the last six chapters. Turning the pages, in order to read all these sentences, will also expose these readers to the diagrams, which have been made numerous in order to help explain this most nonlinear of phenomena, and enable these readers to explore the paragraphs around new and unexpected points. Those readers new to the field will not, however, get enough from these key sentences alone. For them, these sentences serve rather to highlight key points (no other summary being included in the book), perhaps enabling some to put aside their yellow markers.

So there you have it. Bon appétit!

1

The Essence of Structure

Ms. Raku made pottery in her basement. That involved a number of distinct tasks—wedging clay, forming pots, tooling them when semidry, preparing and then applying the glazes, and firing the pots in the kiln. But the coordination of all these tasks presented no problem: she did them all herself.

The problem was her ambition and the attractiveness of her pots: the orders exceeded her production capacity. So she hired Miss Bisque, who was eager to learn pottery. But this meant Ms. Raku had to divide up the work. Since the craft shops wanted pottery made by Ms. Raku, it was decided that Miss Bisque would wedge the clay and prepare the glazes, and Ms. Raku would do the rest. And this required coordination of the work, a small problem, in fact, with two people in a pottery studio: they simply communicated informally.

The arrangement worked well, so well that before long Ms. Raku was again swamped with orders. More assistants were needed, but this time, foreseeing the day when they would be forming pots themselves, Ms. Raku decided to hire them right out of the local pottery school. So while it had taken some time to train Miss Bisque, the three new assistants knew exactly what to do at the outset and blended right in; even with five people, coordination presented no problem.

As two more assistants were added, however, coordination problems did arise. One day Miss Bisque tripped over a pail of glaze and broke five

1

pots; another day Ms. Raku opened the kiln to find that the hanging planters had all been glazed fuchsia by mistake. At this point, she realized that seven people in a small pottery studio could not coordinate all of their work through the simple mechanism of informal communication. (There were 21 possible channels by which two people could communicate.) Making matters worse was the fact that Ms. Raku, now calling herself president of Ceramics Limited, was forced to spend more and more time with customers; indeed, these days she was more likely found in a Marimekko dress than a pair of jeans. So she named Miss Bisque studio manager, to occupy herself full-time with supervising and coordinating the work of the five producers of the pottery.

The firm continued to grow. Major changes again took place when a work study analyst was hired. He recommended changes whereby each individual performed only one task for one of the product lines (pots, ashtrays, hanging planters, and ceramic animals)—the first wedged, the second formed, the third tooled, and so on. Thus, production took the form of four assembly lines. Each person followed a set of standard instructions, worked out in advance to ensure the coordination of all their work. Of course, Ceramics Limited no longer sold to craft shops; Ms. Raku would only accept orders by the gross, most of which came from chains of discount stores.

Ms. Raku's ambition was limitless, and when the chance came to diversify, she did. First ceramic tiles, then bathroom fixtures, finally clay bricks. The firm was subsequently partitioned into three divisions—consumer products, building products, and industrial products. From her office on the fifty-fifth story of the Pottery Tower, she coordinated the activities of the divisions by reviewing their performance each quarter of the year and taking personal action when their profit and growth figures dipped below that budgeted. It was while sitting at her desk one day going over these budgets that Ms. Raku gazed out at the surrounding skyscrapers and decided to rename her company "Ceramico."

Every organized human activity—from the making of pots to the placing of a man on the moon—gives rise to two fundamental and opposing requirements: the *division of labor* into various tasks to be performed and the *coordination* of these tasks to accomplish the activity. **The structure of an organization can be defined simply as the sum total of the ways in which it divides its labor into distinct tasks and then achieves coordination among them.**

In Ceramico the division of labor—wedging, forming, tooling, glazing, firing—was dictated largely by the job to be done and the technical system available to do it. Coordination, however, proved to be a more complicated affair, involving various means. These can be referred to as *coordinating mechanisms,* although it should be noted that they are as much concerned with control and communication as with coordination.[1]

Five coordinating mechanisms seem to explain the fundamental ways in which organizations coordinate their work: mutual adjustment, direct supervision, standardization of work processes, standardization of work outputs, and standardization of worker skills.[2] These should be considered the most basic elements of structure, the glue that holds organizations together. From these all else follows—the structuring of organizations as well as the themes of this book. So let us look at each of them briefly before we see where this book is headed.

MUTUAL ADJUSTMENT

Mutual adjustment achieves the coordination of work by the simple process of informal communication. Under mutual adjustment, control of the work rests in the hands of the doers, as shown in Figure 1–1(a). Because it is such a simple coordinating mechanism, mutual adjustment is naturally used in the very simplest of organizations: for example, by two people in a canoe or a few in a pottery studio. Paradoxically, it is also used in the most complicated, because, as we shall see later, it is the only one that works under extremely difficult circumstances. Consider the organization charged with putting a man on the moon for the first time. Such an activity requires an incredibly elaborate division of labor, with thousands of specialists doing all kinds of specific jobs. But at the outset, no one can be sure exactly what needs to be done. That knowledge develops as the work unfolds. So in the final analysis, despite the use of other coordinating mechanisms, the success of the undertaking depends primarily on the ability of the specialists to adapt to each other along their uncharted route, not altogether unlike the two people in the canoe.[3]

DIRECT SUPERVISION

As an organization outgrows its simplest state—more than five or six people at work in a pottery studio, fifteen people paddling a war canoe—it tends to turn to a second coordinating mechanism. **Direct supervision**

[1]"Recent developments in the area of control, or cybernetics, have shown [control and coordination] to be the same in principle" (Litterer, 1965, p. 233).

[2]In part, this typology reflects the conclusions of Simon (1957), March and Simon (1958), and Galbraith (1973).

[3]For an extended theoretical treatment of the various ways in which independent decision makers can coordinate their actions, see Lindblom (1965, Chaps. 2–5). Chapter 14 of that book also discusses how mutual adjustment can sometimes achieve better coordination than direct supervision or certain forms of standardization.

achieves coordination by having one individual take responsibility for the
work of others, issuing instructions to them and monitoring their actions, as
indicated in Figure 1–1(b). In effect, one brain coordinates several hands, as
in the case of the supervisor of the pottery studio or the caller of the stroke
in the war canoe.

Consider the structure of an American football team. Here the division
of labor is quite sharp: eleven players are distinguished by the work they
do, its location on the field, and even its physical requirements. The slim
halfback stands behind the line of scrimmage and carries the ball; the squat

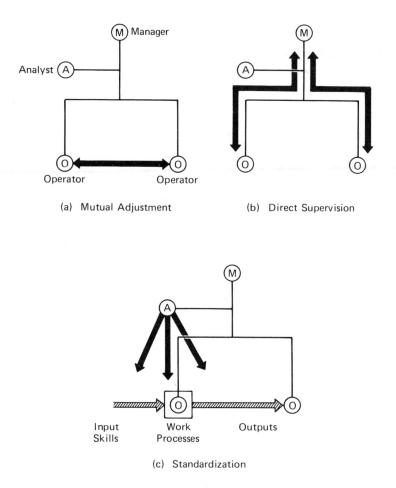

(a) Mutual Adjustment   (b) Direct Supervision

(c) Standardization

Figure 1-1.   *The Five Coordinating Mechanisms*

tackle stands on the line and blocks. Mutual adjustments do not suffice to coordinate their work, so a field leader is named, called the quarterback, and he coordinates their work by calling the plays.

STANDARDIZATION

Work can also be coordinated without mutual adjustment or direct supervision. It can be *standardized:* "The coordination of parts is incorporated in the program [for the work] when it is established, and the need for continuing communication is correspondingly reduced" (March and Simon, 1958, p. 162). Coordination is achieved on the drawing board, so to speak, before the work is undertaken. The workers on the automobile assembly line and the surgeons in the hospital operating room need not worry about coordinating with their colleagues under ordinary circumstances—they know exactly what to expect of them and proceed accordingly.

Figure 1–1(c) shows the three basic ways to achieve standardization in organizations. The work processes themselves, the outputs of the work, and the inputs to the work—the skills (and knowledge) of the people who do the work—can all be designed to meet predetermined standards.

STANDARDIZATION OF WORK PROCESSES

Work processes are standardized when the contents of the work are specified, or programmed. An example that comes to mind involves the assembly instructions provided with a child's toy. Here, the manufacturer in effect standardizes the work process of the parent. ("Take the two-inch round-head Phillips screw and insert it into hole BX, attaching this to part XB with the lock washer and hexagonal nut, at the same time holding. ...")

Standardization can be carried to great lengths in organizations, as in the four assembly lines in Ceramics Limited, or the pie filler I once observed in a bakery who dipped a ladel into a vat of pie filling literally thousands of times every day—cherry, blueberry, or apple, it made no difference to him —and emptied the contents into a pie crust that came around on a turntable. He required little direct supervision and no informal communication with his peers (except to maintain his sanity). Coordination of his work was accomplished by whoever designed that turntable. All the pie filler did was follow instructions, without concern for the workers on either side who placed the crusts under and over the filling. Of course, other work standards leave more room to maneuver: the purchasing agent may be required to get at least three bids on all orders over $10,000, but is otherwise left free to do his work as he sees fit.

STANDARDIZATION OF OUTPUTS

Outputs are standardized when the results of the work, for example the dimensions of the product or the performance, are specified. Taxi drivers are not told how to drive or what route to take; they are merely informed where to deliver their fares. The wedger is not told how to prepare the clay, only to do so in four-pound lumps; the thrower on the wheel knows that those lumps will produce pots of a certain size (his own output standard). With outputs standardized, the interfaces among tasks are predetermined, as in the book bindery which knows that the pages it receives from one place will fit perfectly into the covers it receives from another. Similarly, all the chiefs of the Ceramico divisions interfaced with headquarters in terms of performance standards. They were expected to produce certain profit and growth levels every quarter: how they did this was their own business.

STANDARDIZATION OF SKILLS

Sometimes neither the work nor its outputs can be standardized, yet some coordination is required. Antony Jay (1970) raises this issue in the context of the colonial empires. How were the kings to control and coordinate the activities of their governors, in charge of distant colonies, when direct supervision was impeded by communication channels that took months to run full cycle, and neither the work itself nor its outputs were amenable to standardization? The solution they adopted—that used by Ms. Raku to hire assistants in the pottery studio—was to standardize the worker who came to the work, if not the work itself or its outputs. **Skills (and knowledge) are standardized when the kind of training required to perform the work is specified.** The king trusted the governors because he trained them himself. More commonly, the individual is trained before he even joins the organization. Ms. Raku hired potters from school, just as hospitals do when they engage doctors. These institutions build right into the workers-to-be the work programs, as well as the basis of coordination. On the job, the workers appear to be acting autonomously, just as the good actor on the stage seems to be speaking extemporaneously. But in fact both have learned their lines well. So standardization of skills achieves indirectly what standardization of work processes or of work outputs does directly: it controls and coordinates the work. When an anesthesiologist and a surgeon meet in the operating room to remove an appendix, they need hardly communicate; by virtue of their respective training, they know exactly what to expect of each other. Their standardized skills take care of most of the coordination.[4]

A CONTINUUM AMONG THE
COORDINATING MECHANISMS

These five coordinating mechanisms seem to fall into a rough order. **As organizational work becomes more complicated, the favored means of coordination seems to shift, as shown in Figure 1–2, from mutual adjustment to direct supervision to standardization, preferably of work processes, otherwise of outputs, or else of skills, finally reverting back to mutual adjustment.**

An individual working alone has no great need for any of the mechanisms—coordination takes place simply, in one brain. Add a second person, however, and the situation changes significantly. Now coordination must be achieved across brains. Generally, people working side by side in small groups adapt to each other informally: mutual adjustment becomes the favored means of coordination.

As the group gets larger, however, it becomes less able to coordinate informally. Miller (1959) notes that coal mining groups with as many as 41 men have been found to function effectively. But with the advent of further growth or sharper divisions of labor—different shifts, different locations, more complex technical systems—supervision becomes a necessity:

> Postponement of differentiation of the management function beyond the optimum stage ... leads to a decline in the efficiency of the system. ... The energies of group members, instead of being devoted to the primary task, are increasingly diverted to the task of holding the group together ... (p. 88).

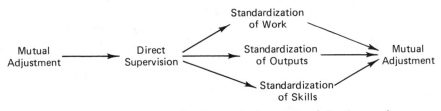

Figure 1–2. *The Coordinating Mechanisms: A Rough Continuum of Complexity*

---

[4]The same can, apparently, be said about much more complex operations. Observation of one five-hour open-heart surgical procedure indicated that there was almost no informal communication between the cardiovascular surgeons and the anesthesiologist (Gosselin, 1978).

Thus, there is a need for leadership. Control of the work of the group passes to a single individual, in effect, back to a single brain that now regulates others: direct supervision becomes the favored coordinating mechanism.

As the work becomes more involved, another major transition tends to occur. Whereas in the last one, some control of the work shifted from the worker to a supervisor, now there is a shift to standardization. As noted earlier, the organization has three choices here. When the tasks are simple and routine, the organization is tempted to rely on the standardization of the work processes themselves. But more complex work may preclude this, forcing the organization to turn to standardization of the outputs—specifying the results of the work but leaving the choice of process to the worker. In complex work, however, the outputs often cannot be standardized either, and so the organization must settle for standardizing the skills of the worker, if possible.

But should the divided tasks of the organization prove impossible to standardize, it may be forced to return full cycle, to favor the simplest, yet most adaptable coordinating mechanism—mutual adjustment. As noted earlier, sophisticated problem solvers facing extremely complicated situations must communicate informally if they are to accomplish their work.

Our discussion to this point implies that under specific conditions an organization will favor one coordinating mechanism over the others. It also suggests that the five are somewhat substitutable: the organization can replace one with another. These suggestions should not, however, be taken to mean that any organization can rely on a single coordinating mechanism. Most, in fact, mix all five. At the very least, a certain amount of direct supervision and mutual adjustment is always required, no matter what the reliance on standardization. Contemporary organizations simply cannot exist without leadership and informal communication, even if only to override the rigidities of standardization.[5] In the most automated (i.e., fully standardized) factory, machines break down, employees fail to show up for work, schedules must be changed at the last minute. Supervisors must intervene and workers must be free to deal with unexpected problems. Thus, Wren (1967) describes the Northeast Canada–United States Electric Grid System, which was fully automatic but lacked an effective override: "Technologically the systems were related for operating economies; organizationally, they were not. There were no, or few, provisions for linking the autonomous, yet interdependent, systems together" (p. 73). The result was the famous blackout of 1965.

---

[5]Emery and Trist (1960) argue that a work group is effective only when it can manage its own coordination (i.e., uses mutual adjustment). "The primary task in managing the enterprise as a whole is to relate the total system to its environment and is not on internal regulation per se" (p. 93). Here I take another position, arguing that while some units must rely on mutual adjustment, none exists without some recourse to direct supervision.

In general, beyond some minimum size, most organizations seem to rely on standardization where they can; where they cannot, they use direct supervision or mutual adjustment, these two being partly interchangeable. When direct supervision fails, perhaps because the task of coordination is too big for one brain, the organization will resort to mutual adjustment. Alternatively, when mutual adjustment breaks down, perhaps because there is a need for one brain to guide others that cannot agree among themselves, the organization will turn to direct supervision.[6]

WHERE TO FROM THE COORDINATING MECHANISMS

Films sometimes open with the important scene and then flash the title and credits. In a sense, the coordinating mechanisms are our most important scene. As noted earlier, these five mechanisms are the glue of structure, the basic elements that hold organizations together. They also hold this book together, serving as the foundation for the material that follows. So now let us turn to the credits: first a brief review of the literature and mention of one of its basic flaws, and then an outline of the book.

The Literature   The early literature focused on *formal structure*, the documented, official relationships among members of the organization. Two schools of thought dominated the literature until the 1950s, one preoccupied with direct supervision, the other with standardization.

The "principles of management" school of thought, fathered by Henri Fayol (1949, English translation), who first recorded his ideas in 1916, and popularized in the English-speaking world by Luther Gulick and Lyndall Urwick (1937), was concerned primarily with formal authority, in effect with the role of direct supervision in the organization. These writers popularized such terms as *unity of command* (the notion that a "subordinate" should have only a single "superior"), *scalar chain* (the direct line of this command from chief executive through successive superiors and subordinates to worker), and *span of control* (the number of subordinates reporting to a single superior).

[6]These conclusions have been adapted, with some significant modifications, from Galbraith (1973), who claims that organizations try to use rules and programs first, then hierarchical referral, then planning, as the amount of information to process increases. Should planning break down, Galbraith claims that the organization will go one of two ways: either eliminate the need for task interdependencies by creating resource buffer groups, extended deadlines, or self-contained units, or enhance the information processing capability of the structure by the use of sophisticated Management Information Systems (MIS) or by establishing lateral relationships—mutual adjustment devices such as liaison roles, task forces, and matrix structures.

The second school of thought really includes two groups that, from our point of view, promoted the same issue—the standardization of work throughout the organization. Both groups were established at the turn of the century by outstanding researchers, one on either side of the Atlantic Ocean. In America, Frederick Taylor (1947) led the "Scientific Management" movement, whose main preoccupation was the programming of the contents of operating work—that of pig iron handlers, coal shovelers, and the like. In Germany, Max Weber (Gerth and Mills, 1958) wrote of machine-like, or "bureaucratic" structures where activities were formalized by rules, job descriptions, and training.

And so for about half of this century, organization structure meant a set of official, standardized work relationships built around a tight system of formal authority.

With the publication in 1939 of Roethlisberger and Dickson's interpretation of a series of experiments carried out on workers at the Western Electric Hawthorne plant came the realization that other things were going on in organizational structures. Specifically, their observations about the presence of *informal structure*—unofficial relationships within the work group—constituted the simple realization that mutual adjustment served as an important coordinating mechanism in all organizations. This led to the establishment of a third school of thought in the 1950s and 1960s, originally called "human relations," whose proponents sought to demonstrate by empirical research that reliance on the formal structure—specifically on the mechanisms of direct supervision and standardization—was at best misguided, at worst dangerous to the psychological health of the worker (e.g., Likert, 1961).

More recent research has shifted away from these two extreme positions. In the last decade, there has been a tendency to look at structure more comprehensively, to study, for example, the relationships between the formal and informal, between direct supervision and standardization on the one hand and mutual adjustment on the other. The interesting work of the Tavestock Institute in the early 1950s set the pattern. Trist and Bamforth (1951), in a piece of research unsurpassed for detail and insight, studied the effect of technological change on work groups in coal mining and concluded that the technical and social systems of structure were inextricably intertwined. Later, Michel Crozier in *The Bureaucratic Phenomenon* (1964), showed how standardization and formal systems of authority impinge on, and are in turn affected by, unofficial power relationships. More recently, Jay Galbraith (1973) studied the structure of The Boeing Company and built a conceptual scheme to describe relationships among various coordinating mechanisms. Galbraith was really the first to explain clearly the role of modern mutual adjustment devices such as task forces and matrix forms in the formal structure.

These and similar studies have demonstrated that **formal and informal structures are intertwined and often indistinguishable.** The studies have shown, for example, how direct supervision and standardization have sometimes been used as *informal* devices to gain power and, conversely, how devices to enhance mutual adjustment have been designed into the *formal* structure. They have also conveyed the important message that formal structure often reflects official recognition of naturally occurring behavior patterns. Formal structures evolve in organizations much as roads do in forests—along well-trodden paths.

Another group of contemporary researchers, working under the title "contingency theory," have been investigating the relationships between structure and situation. They opposed the notion of the one best structural form; instead they sought to identify the particular alternative structural form—whether based on direct supervision, standardization of one kind or another, or mutual adjustment—that was most appropriate under a specific set of conditions. The path-breaking work here was that of Joan Woodward (1965), who in a study of industry in one region of England during the 1950s found pronounced evidence that a firm's structure was closely related to its technical system of production. Mass production firms seemed to require the formal type of structure favored by the early writers; firms in unit and process production seemed to require a looser structure, more reliant on mutual adjustment. Subsequently, two Harvard researchers, Paul Lawrence and Jay Lorsch (1967), found in a study of American firms in the container, food, and plastics industries that environmental conditions surrounding the organization affected its choice of structure significantly. Container firms in rather simple, stable environments relied upon direct supervision and standardization; the more dynamic and complex plastics industry favored mutual adjustment; the food companies fell in between.

Another group, led by Derek Pugh, working out of the University of Aston in England, found that the size of the organization best explained many of the characteristics of its structure (Pugh et al., 1963–64, 1968, 1969a, b; Hickson et al., 1969). For example, the larger the organization, the more important was standardization as a coordinating mechanism. The Aston results, based on large samples of varied organizations, were replicated a number of times (e.g., Inkson et al., 1970; Child, 1972b) and also stimulated a number of other studies of the relationships between structure and the contingency factors. For example, Khandwalla (1973a, b; 1974a) collected data on 79 U.S. firms and later on 103 Canadian firms and found rather more complex relationships among structure and technical system, size, and environment than had been indicated previously.

In sum, we have here a literature that is empirically based, large and growing rapidly, much of it recent. It is also a literature that has built on itself: by and large, the researchers have proceeded on the basis of an understanding of the previous work. Potentially, the literature has a great deal to tell us about how organizations structure themselves. What it lacks, however, is synthesis—the drawing together of the various findings into comprehensive theory. Everyone has been grinding in his own mill, to use an old Hungarian expression, conscious of the grinding of others, but unwilling to leave his own mill to blend the work of his colleagues. We do have a few literature reviews, but they are just that, many of them going "from topic to topic, without a clear view of organizations" or else reproducing various studies in the form of readers, "leaving students to sort it all out" (Perrow, 1973, p. 7). **This book has been written on the premise that the research on the structuring of organizations has come of age but the literature has not: there is the need to step back from the research, analyze it in context, and synthesize it into manageable theory.** This book seeks to provide that synthesis.

A Flaw   The book does not, however, begin straight away with the literature on organization structuring. That is because of a major flaw in the literature. **Most of the contemporary literature fails to relate the description of structure with that of the functioning of the organization.** The reader is seldom told what really goes on inside the structure, how work, information, and decision processes actually flow through it. Thus, we find Conrath (1973) concluding after an extensive search for literature that would link communication flows and organizational structure:

> Numerous concepts of organizational structure can be found in the literature. ... Unfortunately, few of these can be related to properties of communication, and those that can are primarily restricted to the study of small groups. ... In no cases were the communications data used directly to evidence properties of structure (p. 592).

The blame for this flaw can be placed largely on research "from a distance": research that records the perceptions of executives on questionnaires instead of their real behaviors, research of a cross-sectional nature that takes measures only at a point in time, research that uses abstract measures in too diverse an array of organizations (decentralization in parochial schools and post offices). None of this research has been able to come to grips with the complex flows that take place in organizations. Once we have a conceptual framework, we can extract some information from this research. But it should be noted that this research is of little use in generating such a framework in the first place.

A corollary flaw in the literature is that conclusions are often drawn for whole organizations when they clearly apply only to parts. One cannot, for example, call a company "decentralized" just because some decision-making power passes from the chief executive officer to the division vice presidents: how decentralized it is obviously depends also on what happens below the level of vice-president. Similarly, to find that the organization uses task forces to introduce new products is to describe not the whole structure but only one very limited part of it.

All of this is to say that the conclusions of the research often lack "context"—the type of organization and the part of it to which they apply, as well as the relationships between the structure and functioning of the organization. As a result, these conclusions often come across to the reader as detached from reality, devoid of real substance. After reading well in excess of 200 books and articles for the first draft of this book, I was not really sure what structure was. I found myself groping for a frame of reference. Finally, before I could begin to develop my own conclusions, I felt the need to collect a series of charts on organizations, many of which I knew intimately, in order to establish a personal context for all of the conceptual material I read.

The Outline   This book has been designed to try to avoid this problem, to ensure that the reader can put what he reads about structure into context. Thus, its first section deals not with organizational structure but with how the organization functions. The literature here is not very rich, but it is important to get whatever we know about organizational functioning on paper early so that it can serve as the foundation for the theory that follows.

Section I comprises two chapters. The first outlines five basic parts of the contemporary organization—the operating core, strategic apex, middle line, technostructure, and support staff—and discusses how they interrelate. The second chapter overlays five systems of flows on these component parts —in effect, five theories of how the organization functions: as a system of formal authority, as a system of regulated information flows, as a system of informal communication, as a system of work constellations, and as a system of ad hoc decision processes. These are treated as complementary: each describes part of what goes on inside the organization; in combination they begin to get at the complexity of the total system.

These two chapters (Chapters 2 and 3), as well as this introductory one, provide the foundation of the book. They are shown that way in Figure 1-3, which is designed to provide the reader with a conceptual overview of the book. This foundation consists of the five basic coordinating mechanisms, the five basic parts of the organization, and the five systems of basic flows in the organization. On this foundation is built the central core of the book—the analyses presented in Sections II and III. In these two sections, we take structure apart, first looking one by one at its component parts, and then looking at the factors that affect these parts, again one by one.

The chapters of Section II discuss nine *design parameters*, the basic elements used in designing organizational structures. We discuss in turn (1) job specialization, (2) behavior formalization, and (3) training and indoctrination, all three concerned with the design of individual positions; (4) unit grouping and (5) unit size, together constituting the design of the "superstructure"; (6) planning and control systems and (7) liaison devices, both concerned with the design of lateral linkages; and finally, (8) vertical and (9) horizontal decentralization, constituting the design of the decision-making

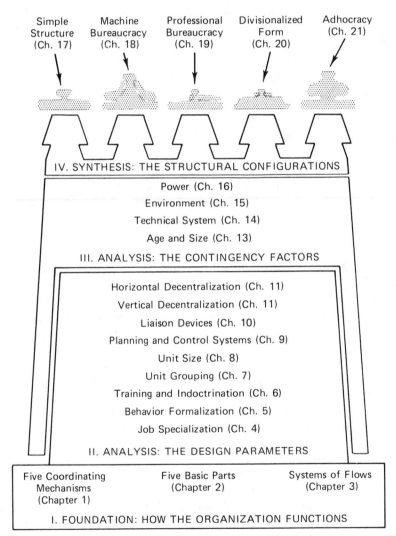

Figure 1-3. *A Conceptual Overview of the Book*

system. Each of these design parameters is discussed individually in its own chapter (except for the two aspects of decentralization, which are discussed together in Chapter 11). Each chapter ends with a discussion of the design parameter in each of the five parts of the organization; also, as we progress, we devote more and more attention to the links between the design parameters already discussed. But essentially, Section II presents analysis, not synthesis; it is more concerned with component parts than with integrated wholes.

Section III puts the design parameters into context, seeking to relate them to the various contingency factors, one at a time. Here we find most of the contemporary research. We look first, in Chapter 12, at the evidence on organizational effectiveness, which suggests that structural choices are dictated to a considerable extent first by organizational situation, and second by the need for the design parameters to form internally consistent sets. Taking this first point of view in Section III, we present sixteen hypotheses which review a good deal of the evidence on the relationship between structure and situation. Chapter 13 deals with the effect on structure of the age and size of the organization; Chapter 14 with the technical system it uses; Chapter 15 with the environment it faces; and Chapter 16 with its power conditions. Although the seeds of the synthesis are sown in this section, it again represents analysis. In fact, it seems more to divide than to unify. The hypotheses appear to stand independently, sometimes even to contradict each other. Nevertheless, they are a necessary step toward our ultimate goal.

That goal is synthesis, and it is pursued in Section IV. We noted earlier that effective organizations appear to achieve internal consistency among their design parameters; we also noted that different structures are associated with different situations. In Section IV we seek to show that the design parameters as well as the contingency factors configure into natural clusters, or "configurations." Five in particular seem to predominate: as a typology, they seem to explain a surprisingly large number of the findings of the research, including many of the contradictions; moreover, the five configurations fall into what seems to be a more than coincidental one-to-one correspondence with the five coordinating mechanisms, and one of the five parts of the organization emerges as preeminent in each of the five configurations. Together with the corresponding design parameter and preeminent part of the organization, the five configurations are: Simple Structure (direct supervision, strategic apex), Machine Bureaucracy (standardization of work processes, technostructure), Professional Bureaucracy (standardization of skills, operating core), Divisionalized Form (standardization of outputs. middle line), and Adhocracy (mutual adjustment, support staff). Each configuration is discussed in one chapter of Section IV, together with its design parameters, how it functions, and the contingency factors associated with it. In these five chapters I also take the liberty of discussing some of the major issues—managerial and social—that face each of the configurations. A final chapter of the book outlines in the context of a "pentagon" some of the examples, hybrids, and transitions among the five configurations, and speculates on a sixth.

PART I

HOW THE ORGANIZATION FUNCTIONS

To understand how organizations structure themselves, we should first know how they function. We need to know their component parts, what functions each performs, and how these functions interrelate. Specifically, we need to know how work, authority, information, and decision processes flow through organizations.

We do not have a profound understanding of these flows at the present time. There has simply been too little research on how organizations actually function. Nevertheless, it is important to put on paper what we do know, as a foundation on which to build the findings about organizational structure. In the first chapter of this section, the organization is described in terms of five basic parts. Then in the second chapter we look at a number of different views of how the organization functions—as a system of formal authority, regulated information flows, informal communication, work constellations, and ad hoc decision processes. These different views will appear to be at variance with one another, but, as we shall see throughout the book, every real organization in fact functions as a complex mixture of all five systems.

2

Five Basic Parts of the Organization

In Chapter 1 organizations were described in terms of their use of the coordinating mechanisms. We noted that, in theory, the simplest organization can rely on mutual adjustment to coordinate its basic work of producing a product or service. Its *operators*—those who do this basic work—are largely self-sufficient.

As the organization grows, however, and adopts a more complex division of labor among its operators, the need is increasingly felt for direct supervision. Another brain—that of a *manager*—is needed to help coordinate the work of the operators. So, whereas the division of labor up to this point has been between the operators themselves, the introduction of a manager introduces a first *administrative* division of labor in the structure—between those who do the work and those who supervise it. And as the organization further elaborates itself, more managers are added—not only managers of operators but also managers of managers. An administrative *hierarchy* of authority is built.

As the process of elaboration continues, the organization turns increasingly to standardization as a means of coordinating the work of its operators. The responsibility for much of this standardization falls on a third group, composed of *analysts*. Some, such as work study analysts and industrial engineers, concern themselves with the standardization of work processes; others, such as quality control engineers, accountants, planners, and production schedulers, focus on the standardization of outputs; while a few, such as personnel trainers, are charged with the standardization of skills (although most of this standardization takes place outside the organization, before the operators are hired). The introduction of these analysts brings a second kind of administrative division of labor to the organization, between those who do and who supervise the work, and those who standardize it. Whereas in the first case managers assumed responsibility from the operators for some of the coordination of their work by substituting direct supervision for mutual adjustment, the analysts assume responsibility from the managers (and the operators) by substituting standardization for direct supervision (and mutual adjustment). Earlier, some of the control over the work was removed from the operator; now it begins to be removed from the manager as well, as the systems designed by the analysts take increasing responsibility for coordination. The analyst "institutionalizes" the manager's job.

We end up with an organization that consists of a core of operators, who do the basic work of producing the products and services, and an *administrative* component of managers and analysts, who take some of the responsibility for coordinating their work. This leads us to the conceptual description of the organization shown in Figure 2–1. This figure will be used repeatedly throughout the book, sometimes overlaid to show flows, sometimes distorted to illustrate special structures. It emerges, in effect, as the "logo," or symbol, of the book.

At the base of the logo is the *operating core*, wherein the operators carry out the basic work of the organization—the input, processing, output, and direct support tasks associated with producing the products or services. Above them sits the administrative component, which is shown in three parts. First, are the managers, divided into two groups. Those at the very top of the hierarchy, together with their own personal staff, form the *strategic apex*. And those below, who join the strategic apex to the operating core through the chain of command (such at it exists), make up the *middle line*. To their left stands the *technostructure*, wherein the analysts carry out their work of standardizing the work of others, in addition to applying their analytical techniques to help the organization adapt to its environment. Finally, we add a fifth group, the *support staff*, shown to the right of the middle line. This staff supports the functioning of the operating core indirectly, that is, outside the basic flow of operating work. The support staff goes largely unrecognized in the literature of organizational structuring, yet a quick glance at the chart of virtually any large organization indicates that it is a major segment, one that should not be confused with the other four. Examples of support groups in a typical manufacturing firm are research and development, cafeteria, legal council, payroll, public relations, and mailroom.

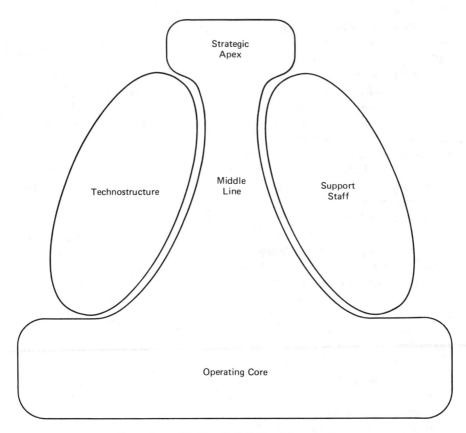

Figure 2-1. *The Five Basic Parts of Organizations*

Figure 2–1 shows a small strategic apex connected by a flaring middle line to a large, flat operating core. These three parts of the organization are shown in one uninterrupted sequence to indicate that they are typically connected through a single line of formal authority. The technostructure and the support staff are shown off to either side to indicate that they are separate from this main line of authority, and influence the operating core only indirectly.

It might be useful at this point to relate this scheme to some terms commonly used in organizations. The term "middle management," although seldom carefully defined, generally seems to include all members of the organization not at the strategic apex or in the operating core. In our scheme, therefore, "middle management" would comprise three distinct groups—the middle-line managers, the analysts, and the support staff. To avoid confusion, however, the term *middle level* will be used here to describe these three groups together, the term "management" being reserved for the managers of the strategic apex and the middle line.

The word "staff" should also be put into this context. In the early literature, the term was used in contrast to "line": in theory, line positions had formal authority to make decisions, while staff positions did not; they merely advised those who did. (This has sometimes been referred to as "functional" authority, in contrast to the line's formal or "hierarchical" authority.) Allen (1955), for example, delineates the staff's major activities as (1) providing advice, counsel, suggestions, and guidance on planning objectives, policies, and procedures to govern the operations of the line departments on how best to put decisions into practice; and (2) performing specific service activities for the line, for example, installing budgeting systems and recruiting line personnel, "which may include making decisions that the line has asked it to make" (p. 348). As we shall see later, this distinction between line and staff holds up in some kinds of structures and breaks down in others. Nevertheless, the distinction between line and staff is of some use to us, and we shall retain the terms here though in somewhat modified form. *Staff* will be used to refer to the technostructure *and* the support staff, those groups shown on either side in Figure 2–1. *Line* will refer to the central part of Figure 2–1, those managers in the flow of formal authority from the strategic apex to the operating core. Note that this definition does not mention the power to decide or advise. As we shall see, the support staff does not primarily advise; it has distinct functions to perform and decisions to make, although these relate only indirectly to the functions of the operating core. The chef in the plant cafeteria may be engaged in a production process, but it has nothing to do with the basic manufacturing process. Similarly, the technostructure's power to advise sometimes amounts to the power to decide, but that is outside the flow of formal authority that oversees the operating core.[1]

Some Conceptual Ideas of James D. Thompson   Before proceeding with a more detailed description of each of the five basic parts of the organization, it will be helpful to introduce at this point some of the important conceptual ideas of James D. Thompson (1967). To Thompson, "Uncertainty appears as the fundamental problem for complex organizations, and

---

[1]There are other, completely different, uses of the term "staff" that we are avoiding here. The military "chiefs of staff" are really managers of the strategic apex; the hospital "staff" physicians are really operators. Also, the introduction of the line/staff distinction here is not meant to sweep all of its problems under the rug, only to distinguish those involved directly from those involved peripherally with the operating work of organizations. By our definition, the production and sales functions in the typical manufacturing firm are clearly line activities, marketing research and public relations clearly staff. To debate whether engineering is line or staff—does it serve the operating core indirectly or is it an integral part of it?—depends on the importance one imputes to engineering in a particular firm. There is a gray area between line and staff: where it is narrow, for many organizations, we retain the distinction; where it is wide, we shall explicitly discard it.

coping with uncertainty, as the essence of the administrative process" (p. 159). Thompson describes the organization in terms of a "technical core," equivalent to our operating core, and a group of "boundary spanning units." In his terms, the organization reduces uncertainty by sealing off this core from the environment so that the operating activities can be protected. The boundary spanning units face the environment directly and deal with its uncertainties. For example, the research department interprets the confusing scientific environment for the organization, while the public relations department placates a hostile social environment.

Thompson and others who have built on his work describe various methods that organizations use to protect their operating cores. Standardization of work processes is, of course, a prime one. Others involve various forms of anticipation—planning, stockpiling, doing preventive maintenance, leveling production, conducting intelligence activities, and so on. Organizations also seek to dominate their environments, and so reduce uncertainty, by fixing prices, creating cartels, and integrating themselves vertically (i.e., becoming their own suppliers and customers).

Thompson also introduces a conceptual scheme to explain the *inter-dependencies* among organizational members. He distinguishes three ways in which the work can be coupled, shown in Figure 2–2. First is *pooled coupling,* where members share common resources but are otherwise independent. Figure 2–2(a) could represent teachers in a school who share common facilities and budgets but work alone with their pupils. In *sequential coupling,* members work in series, as in a relay race where the baton passes from runner to runner. Figure 2–2(b) could represent a mass production factory, where raw materials enter at one end, are sequentially fabricated and machined, then fed into an assembly line at various points, and finally emerge at the other end as finished products. In *reciprocal coupling,* the members feed their work back and forth among themselves; in effect each receives inputs from and provides outputs to the others. "This is illustrated by the airline which contains both operations and maintenance units. The production of the maintenance unit is an input for operations, in the form of a serviceable aircraft; and the product (or by-product) of operations is an input for maintenance, in the form of an aircraft needing maintenance" (Thompson, 1967, p. 55). Figure 2–2(c) could be taken to represent this example, or one in a hospital in which the nurse "preps" the patient, the surgeon operates, and the nurse then takes care of the postoperative care.

Clearly, pooled coupling involves the least amount of interdependence among members. Anyone can be plucked out; and, as long as there is no great change in the resources available, the others can continue to work uninterrupted. Pulling out a member of a sequentially coupled organization, however, is like breaking a link in a chain—the whole activity must cease to function. Reciprocal coupling is, of course, more interdependent still, since

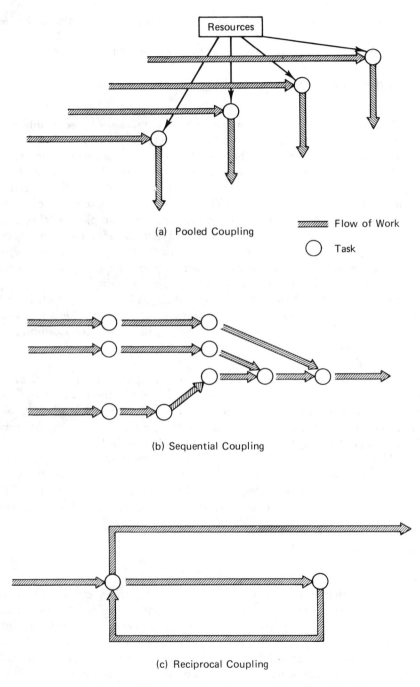

(a) Pooled Coupling

▨▨▨ Flow of Work

◯ Task

(b) Sequential Coupling

(c) Reciprocal Coupling

Figure 2-2. *Pooled, Sequential, and Reciprocal Coupling of Work*

23

a change in one task affects not only those farther along but also those behind.

Now let us take a look at each of the five parts of the organization.

THE OPERATING CORE

The operating core of the organization encompasses those members—the operators—who perform the basic work related directly to the production of products and services. The operators perform four prime functions: (1) They *secure the inputs* for production. For example, in a manufacturing firm, the purchasing department buys the raw materials and the receiving department takes it in the door. (2) They *transform the inputs into outputs.* Some organizations transform raw materials, for example, by chopping down trees and converting them to pulp and then paper. Others transform individual parts into complete units, for example, by assembling typewriters, while still others transform information or people, by writing consulting reports, educating students, cutting hair, or curing illness. (3) They *distribute the outputs*, for example, by selling and physically distributing what comes out of the transformation process. (4) They *provide direct support* to the input, transformation, and output functions, for example, by performing maintenance on the operating machines and inventorying the raw materials.

Since it is the operating core that the other parts of the organization seek to protect, standardization is generally carried furthest here. How far, of course, depends on the work being done: assemblers in automobile factories and professors in universities are both operators, although the work of the former is far more standardized than that of the latter.

The operating core is the heart of every organization, the part that produces the essential outputs that keep it alive. But except for the very smallest ones, organizations need to build *administrative* components. The administrative component comprises the strategic apex, middle line, and technostructure.

THE STRATEGIC APEX

At the other end of the organization lies the strategic apex. Here are found those people charged with overall responsibility for the organization—the chief executive officer (whether called president, superintendent, Pope, or whatever), and any other top-level managers whose concerns are global. Included here as well are those who provide direct support to the top managers—their secretaries, assistants, and so on.[2] In some organizations,

[2]Our subsequent discussion will focus only on the managers of the strategic apex, the work of the latter group being considered an integral part of their own.

the strategic apex includes the executive committee (because its mandate is global even if its members represent specific interests); in others, it includes what is known as the chief executive office—two or three individuals who share the job of chief executive.

The strategic apex is charged with ensuring that the organization serve its mission in an effective way, and also that it serve the needs of those people who control or otherwise have power over the organization (such as owners, government agencies, unions of the employees, pressure groups). This entails three sets of duties. One already discussed is that of direct supervision. To the extent that the organization relies on this mechanism of coordination, it is the managers of the strategic apex and middle line who effect it. Among the managerial roles (Mintzberg, 1973a) associated with direct supervision are resource allocator, including the design of the structure itself, the assignment of people and resources to tasks, the issuing of work orders, and the authorization of major decisions made by the employees; disturbance handler, involving the resolution of conflicts, exceptions, and disturbances sent up the hierarchy for resolution; monitor, involving the review of employees' activities; disseminator, involving the transmission of information to employees; and leader, involving the staffing of the organization and the motivating and rewarding of them. In its essence, direct supervision at the strategic apex means ensuring that the whole organization function smoothly as a single integrated unit.

But there is more to managing an organization than direct supervision. That is why even organizations with a minimal need for direct supervision, for example the very smallest that can rely on mutual adjustment, or professional ones that rely on formal training, still need managers. The second set of duties of the strategic apex involves the management of the organization's boundary conditions—its relationships with its environment. The managers of the strategic apex must spend a good deal of their time acting in the roles of spokesman, in informing influencial people in the environment about the organization's activities; liaison, to develop high-level contact for the organization, and monitor, to tap these for information and to serve as the contact point for those who wish to influence the organization's goals; negotiator, when major agreements must be reached with outside parties; and sometimes even figurehead, in carrying out ceremonial duties, such as greeting important customers. (Someone once defined the manager, only half in jest, as that person who sees the visitors so that everyone else can get their work done.)

The third set of duties relates to the development of the organization's strategy. Strategy may be viewed as a mediating force between the organization and its environment. Strategy formulation therefore involves the interpretation of the environment and the development of consistent patterns in streams of organizational decisions ("strategies") to deal with it. Thus, in managing the boundary conditions of the organization, the managers of the

strategic apex develops an understanding of its environment; and in carrying out the duties of direct supervision, they seek to tailor a strategy to its
strengths and its needs, trying to maintain a pace of change that is responsive to the environment without being disruptive to the organization. Specifically, in the entrepreneur role, the top managers search for effective
ways to carry out the organization's "mission" (i.e., its production of basic
products and services), and sometimes even seek to change that mission. In
a manufacturing firm, for example, management may decide what technical
system is best suited for the operating core, what distribution channels most
effectively carry the products to the market, what markets these should be,
and ultimately, what products should be produced. Top managers typically
spend a great deal of their time on various improvement projects, whereby
they seek to impose strategic changes on their organizations. Of course, as
we shall see later, the process of strategy formulation is not as cut and dried
as all that: for one thing, the other parts of the organization, in certain cases
even the operating core, can play an active role in formulating strategy; for
another, strategies sometimes form themselves, almost inadvertently, as
managers respond to the pressures of the environment, decision by decision. But one point should be stressed—the *strategic* apex, among the five
parts of the organization, typically plays the most important role in the
formulation of its strategy.[3]

In general, the strategic apex takes the widest, and as a result the most
abstract, perspective of the organization. Work at this level is generally
characterized by a minimum of repetition and standardization, considerable
discretion, and relatively long decision-making cycles. Mutual adjustment
is the favored mechanism for coordination among the managers of the strategic apex itself.

THE MIDDLE LINE

**The strategic apex is joined to the operating core by the chain of
middle-line managers with formal authority.** This chain runs from the
senior managers just below the strategic apex to the *first-line supervisors*
(e.g., the shop foremen), who have direct authority over the operators, and
embodies the coordinating mechanism that we have called direct supervision. Figure 2–3 shows one famous chain of authority, that of the U.S.
Army, from four-star general at the strategic apex to sergeant as first-line

---

[3]The preceding discussion on managerial roles is drawn from Mintzberg (1973a); that on
strategy formulation, from Mintzberg (1978).

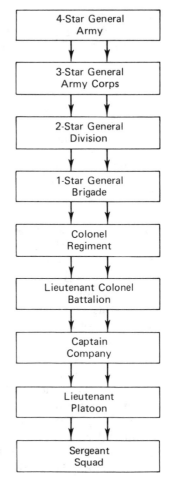

4-Star General Army
3-Star General Army Corps
2-Star General Division
1-Star General Brigade
Colonel Regiment
Lieutenant Colonel Battalion
Captain Company
Lieutenant Platoon
Sergeant Squad

Figure 2-3. *The Scalar Chain of Command in the U.S. Army*

supervisor. This particular chain of authority is *scalar*, that is, it runs in a single line from top to bottom. But as we shall see later, not all need be: some divide and rejoin; a "subordinate" can have more than one "superior."

What do all these levels of managers do? If the strategic apex provides overall direction and the operating core produces the products or services, why does the organization need this whole chain of middle-line managers? One answer seems evident. To the extent that the organization is large and reliant on direct supervision for coordination, it requires middle-line managers. In theory, one manager—the chief executive at the strategic apex— can supervise all the operators. In practice, however, direct supervision requires close personal contact between manager and operator, with the result that there is some limit to the number of operators any one manager

27

can supervise—his so-called "span of control." Small organizations can get along with one manager (at the strategic apex); bigger ones require more (in the middle line). As Moses was told in the desert:

> Thou shalt provide out of all the people able men, such as fear God, men of truth, hating covetousness; and place such over them, to be rulers of thousands, and rulers of hundreds, rulers of fifties, and rulers of tens: and let them judge the people at all seasons: and it shall be, that every great matter they shall bring unto thee, but every small matter they shall judge: so shall it be easier for thyself, and they shall bear the burden with thee. If thou shalt do this thing, and God command thee so, then thou shalt be able to endure, and all this people shall also go to their place in peace (Exodus 18:21-24).

Thus, an organizational *hierarchy* is built as a first-line supervisor is put in charge of a number of operators to form a basic organizational unit, another manager is put in charge of a number of these units to form a higher level unit, and so on until all the remaining units can come under a single manager at the strategic apex—designated the "chief executive officer"—to form the whole organization.

In this hierarchy, the middle-line manager performs a number of tasks in the flow of direct supervision above and below him. He collects "feedback" information on the performance of his own unit and passes some of this up to the managers above him, often aggregating it in the process. The sales manager of the machinery firm may receive information on every sale, but he reports to the district sales manager only a monthly total. He also intervenes in the flow of decisions. Flowing up are disturbances in the unit, proposals for change, decisions requiring authorization. Some the middle-line manager handles himself, while others he passes on up for action at a higher level in the hierarchy. Flowing down are resources that he must allocate in his unit, rules and plans that he must elaborate and projects that he must implement there. For example, the strategic apex in the Postal Service may decide to implement a project to sell "domestograms." Each regional manager and, in turn, each district manager must elaborate the plan as it applies to his geographical area.

But like the top manager, the middle manager is required to do more than simply engage in direct supervision. He, too, has boundary conditions to manage, horizontal ones related to the environment of his own unit. That environment may include other units within the larger organization as well as groups outside the organization. The sales manager must coordinate by mutual adjustment with the managers of production and of research, and he must visit some of the organization's customers. The foreman must spend a good deal of time with the industrial engineers who standardize the work processes of the operators and with the supplier installing a new machine in his shop, while the plant manager may spend his time with the production scheduler and the architect designing a new factory. In effect, each middle-line manager maintains liaison contacts with the other managers, analysts, support staffers, and outsiders whose work is interdependent with that of his own unit. Furthermore, the middle-line manager, like the top manager, is concerned with formulating the strategy for his unit, although this strategy is, of course, significantly affected by the strategy of the overall organization.

In general, the middle-line manager performs all the managerial roles of the chief executive, but in the context of managing his own unit (Mintzberg, 1973a). He must serve as a figurehead for his unit and lead its members; develop a network of liaison contacts; monitor the environment and his unit's activities and transmit some of the information he receives into his own unit, up the hierarchy, and outside the chain of command; allocate resources within his unit; negotiate with outsiders; initiate strategic change; and handle exceptions and conflicts.

Managerial jobs do, however, shift in orientation as they descend in the chain of authority. There is clear evidence that the job becomes more detailed and elaborated, less abstract and aggregated, more focused on the work flow itself. Thus, the "real-time" roles of the manager—in particular, negotiation and the handling of disturbances—become especially important at lower levels in the hierarchy (Mintzberg, 1973a, pp. 110–113). Martin (1956) studied the decisions made by four levels of production managers in the chain of authority and concluded that at each successively lower level, the decisions were more frequent, of shorter duration, and less elastic, ambiguous, and abstract; solutions tended to be more pat or predetermined; the significance of events and inter-relationships was more clear; in general, lower-level decision making was more structured.

Figure 2–4 shows the line manager in the middle of a field of forces. Sometimes these forces become so great—especially those of the analysts to institutionalize his job by the imposition of rules on the unit—that the individual in the job can hardly be called a "manager" at all, in the sense of really being "in charge" of an organizational unit. This is common at the level of first-line supervisor—for example, the foreman in some mass production manufacturing firms (see Figure 18–1) and branch managers in some large banking systems.

THE TECHNOSTRUCTURE

In the technostructure we find the analysts (and their supporting clerical staff) who serve the organization by affecting the work of others. These analysts are removed from the operating work flow—they may design it, plan it, change it, or train the people who do it, but they do not do it them-

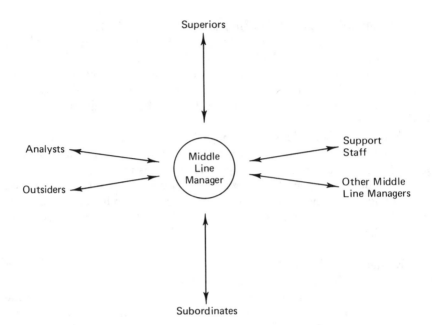

Figure 2-4. *The Line Manager in the Middle*

selves. Thus, the technostructure is effective only when it can use its analytical techniques to make the work of others more effective.[4]

Who makes up the technostructure? There are the analysts concerned with adaptation, with changing the organization to meet environmental change, and those concerned with control, with stabilizing and standardizing patterns of activity in the organization (Katz and Kahn, 1966). In this book we are concerned largely with the control analysts, those who focus their attention directly on the design and functioning of structure. **The control analysts of the technostructure serve to effect standardization in the organization.** This is not to say that operators cannot standardize their own work, just as everyone establishes his or her own procedure for getting dressed in the morning, or that managers cannot do it for them. But in general, the more standardization an organization uses, the more it relies on its technostructure. Such standardization reduces the need for direct supervision, in effect enabling clerks to do what managers once did.

We can distinguish three types of control analysts who correspond to the three forms of standardization: work study analysts (such as industrial engineers), who standardize work processes; planning and control analysts (such as long-range planners, budget analysts, and accountants), who

---

[4]This raises an interesting point: that the technostructure has a built-in commitment to change, to perpetual improvement. The modern organization's obsession with change probably derives in part at least from large and ambitious technostructures seeking to ensure their own survival. The perfectly stable organization has no need for a technostructure.

standardize outputs; and personnel analysts (including trainers and re-cruiters), who standardize skills.

In a fully developed organization, the technostructure may perform at all levels of the hierarchy. At the lowest levels of the manufacturing firm, analysts standardize the operating work flow by scheduling production, carrying out time-and-method studies of the operators' work, and institut-ing systems of quality control. At middle levels, they seek to standardize the intellectual work of the organization (e.g., by training middle managers) and carry out operations research studies of informational tasks. On behalf of the strategic apex, they design strategic planning systems and develop financial systems to control the goals of major units.

While the analysts exist to standardize the work of others, their own work would appear to be coordinated with others largely through mutual adjustment. (Standardization of skills does play a part in this coordination, however, because analysts are typically highly trained specialists.) Thus, analysts spend a good deal of their time in informal communication. Guetz-kow (1965, p. 537), for example, notes that staff people typically have wider communication contacts than line people, and my review of the liter-ature on managerial work (Mintzberg, 1973a, pp. 116–118) showed some evidence that staff managers pay more attention to the information proces-sing roles—monitor, disseminator, spokesman—than do line managers.

SUPPORT STAFF

A glance at the chart of almost any large contemporary organization reveals a great number of units, all specialized, that exist to provide support to the organization outside the operating work flow. Those comprise the *support staff*. For example, in a university, we find the alma mater fund, building and grounds department, museum, university press, bookstore, printing service, payroll department, janitorial service, endowment office, mailroom, real estate office, security department, switchboard, athletics department, student placement office, student residence, faculty club, guid-ance service, and chaplainery. None is a part of the operating core, that is, none engages in teaching or research, or even supports it directly (as does, say, the computing center or the library), yet each exists to provide indirect support to these basic missions. In the manufacturing firm, these units run the gamut from legal counsel to plant cafeteria.

The surprising thing is that these support units have been all but totally ignored in the literature on organizational structuring. Most often they are lumped together with the technostructure and labeled as the "staff" that provides advice to management. But these support units are most de-cidedly different from the technostructure—they are not preoccupied with standardization and they cannot be looked upon primarily as advice givers (although they may do some of that, too). Rather, they have distinct functions to perform. The university press publishes books, the faculty club provides a social setting for the professors, the alma mater fund brings in money.

Why do large organizations have so many of these support units? A great many of their services could be purchased from outside suppliers, yet the organization chooses to provide them to itself. Why? Following Thompson's logic, we can argue that the existence of the support staff reflects the organization's attempt to encompass more and more boundary activities in order to reduce uncertainty, to control its own affairs. By publishing its own books, the university avoids some of the uncertainties associated with the commercial houses; by fighting its own court cases, the manufacturing corporation maintains close control over the lawyers it uses; and by feeding its own employees in the plant cafeteria, it shortens the lunch period and, perhaps, even helps to determine the nutritiousness of their food.

Many support units are self-contained: they are mini-organizations, many with their own equivalent of an operating core, as in the case of the printing service in a university. These units take resources from the larger organization and, in turn, provide specific services to it. But they function independently of the main operating core; that is, they are coupled only in a pooled way. Compare, for example, the maintenance department with the cafeteria in a factory, the first a *direct* service and an integral part of the operating core, coupled reciprocally with it, the second quite separate from it, coupled only in the sharing of space and funds. Other support units, however, do exist in sequential or reciprocal relationships with units above the operating core.

The support units can be found at various levels of the hierarchy, depending on the receivers of their service. In most manufacturing firms, public relations and legal counsel are located near the top, since they tend to serve the strategic apex directly. At middle levels are found the units that support the decisions made there, such as industrial relations, pricing, and research and development. And at the lower levels are found the units with more standardized work, that akin to the work of the operating core— cafeteria, mailroom, reception, payroll. Figure 2–5 shows all these support groups overlaid on our logo, together with typical groups from the other four parts of the organization, again using the manufacturing firm as our example.

Because of the wide variations in the types of support units, we cannot draw a single definitive conclusion about the favored coordinating mechanism for all of them. Each unit relies on whatever mechanism is most appropriate for itself—standardization of skills in the office of legal council, mutual adjustment in the research laboratory, standardization of work pro-

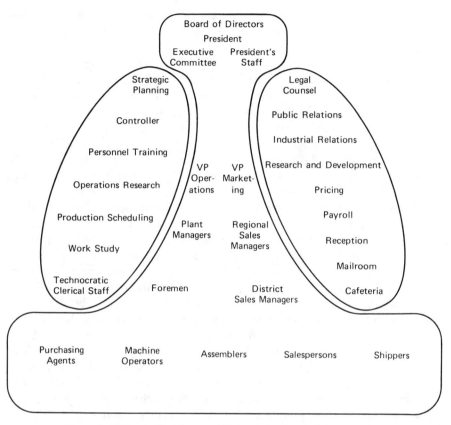

Board of Directors
President
Executive Committee   President's Staff

Strategic Planning

Controller

Personnel Training

Operations Research

Production Scheduling

Work Study

Technocratic Clerical Staff

VP Oper-ations   VP Market-ing

Plant Managers   Regional Sales Managers

Foremen   District Sales Managers

Legal Counsel

Public Relations

Industrial Relations

Research and Development

Pricing

Payroll

Reception

Mailroom

Cafeteria

Purchasing Agents   Machine Operators   Assemblers   Salespersons   Shippers

Figure 2-5. *Some Members and Units of the Parts of the Manufacturing Firm*

cesses in the cafeteria. However, because many of the support units are highly specialized and rely on professional staff, standardization of skills may be the single most important coordinating mechanism.

Do the staff groups of the organization—technocratic as well as support—tend to cluster at any special level of the hierarchy? One study of twenty-five organizations (Kaufman and Seidman, 1970) suggested that while the middle lines of organizations tend to form into pyramids, the staff does not. Its form is "extremely irregular"—if anything, inversely pyramidal (p. 446). Hence, while Figure 2-1 shows the middle line as flaring out toward the bottom, it depicts both the technostructure and the support staff as forming ellipses. Later we shall see that, in fact, the specific shape varies according to the type of structure used by the organization.

The most dramatic growth in organizations in recent decades has been in these staff groups, both the technostructure and the support staff. For example, Litterer (1973, pp. 584–585), in a study of thirty companies, noted the creation of 292 new staff units between 1920 and 1960, nearly ten units per company. More than half these units were in fact created between 1950 and 1960.

Organizations have always had operators and top managers, people to do the basic work and people to hold the whole system together. As they grew, typically they first elaborated their middle-line component, on the assumption in the early literature that coordination had to be effected by direct supervision. But as standardization became an accepted coordinating mechanism, the technostructure began to emerge. The work of Frederick Taylor gave rise to the "scientific management" movement of the 1920s, which saw the hiring of many work study analysts. Just after World War II, the establishment of operations research and the advent of the computer pushed the influence of the technostructure well into the middle levels of the organization, and with the more recent popularity of techniques such as strategic planning and sophisticated financial controls, the technostructure has entrenched itself firmly at the highest levels of the organization as well. And the growth of the support staff has perhaps been even more dramatic, as all kinds of specializations developed during this century—scientific research in a wide number of fields, industrial relations, public relations, and many more. Organizations have sought increasingly to bring these as well as the more traditional support functions such as maintenance and cafeteria within their boundaries. Thus, the ellipses to the left and right in the logo have become great bulges in many organizations. Joan Woodward (1965, p. 60) found in her research that firms in the modern process industries (such as oil refining) averaged one staff member for less than three operators, and in some cases the staff people actually outnumbered the operators by wide margins.[5]

[5]Woodward's tables and text here are very confusing, owing in part at least to some line errors in the page makeup. The data cited above are based on Figure 18, page 60, which seems to have the title that belongs to Figure 17 and which seems to relate back to Figure 7 on page 28, not to Figure 8 as Woodward claims.

3

The Organization as a System of Flows

Given the five parts of the organization—operating core, strategic apex, middle line, technostructure, and support staff—we may now ask how they all function together. In fact, we cannot describe the *one* way they function together, for research suggests that the linkages are varied and complex. The parts of the organization are joined together by different flows—of *authority*, of work *material*, of *information*, and of *decision processes* (themselves informational). In this chapter we look at these flows in terms of a number of schools of thought in the literature of organization theory. We begin with the view of the organization as a system of formal authority, and then we look at it as a system of regulated flows. Both represent traditional views of how the organization functions, the first made popular by the early management theorists, and the second, by the proponents of scientific management and later the control systems theorists. Today, both views live on in the theories of bureaucracy and of planning and information systems. Next, we look at the organization as a system of informal communication, a view made popular by the human relations theorists and favored today by many behavioral scientists. The two final views—the organization as a system of work constellations and as a system of ad hoc decision processes—although not yet well developed in the literature, are more indicative of contemporary trends in organizational theory, in part because they blend formal and informal relationships in organizations.

Each of these five views is depicted as an "overlay" on our logo. This notion of overlays is borrowed from Pfiffner and Sherwood (1960), who point out that, "The totality of these overlays might be so complex as to be opaque ..." (p. 19), but by treating them one at a time in relation to the totality, we can more easily come to understand the complexity of the whole system.[1]

THE ORGANIZATION AS A SYSTEM OF FORMAL AUTHORITY

Traditionally, the organization has been described in terms of an "organizational chart." (Borrowing from the French, I shall use the term *organigram* instead.[2]) The organigram shown in Figure 3–1—the first over-

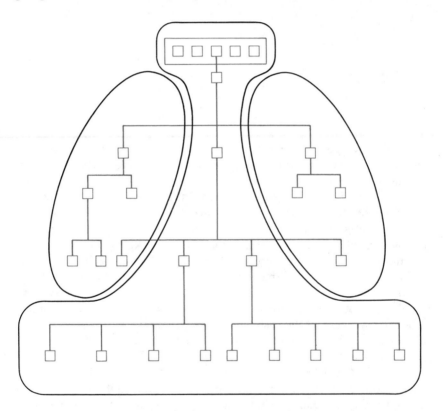

Figure 3-1.   *The Flow of Formal Authority*

[1]Pfiffner and Sherwood present five overlays on the "job-task pyramid" (which is really our overlay of formal authority): the sociometric network, the system of functional contracts, the grid of decision-making centers, the pattern of power, and the channels of communication.

[2]The correct French spelling is "organigramme."

lay—is symbolic, in that it is far too simple to represent any but the smallest organization that exists today.

The organigram is a controversial picture of the structure, for while most organizations continue to find it indispensable (the organigram is inevitably the first thing handed to anyone inquiring about structure), many organizational theorists reject it as an inadequate description of what really takes place inside the organization. Clearly, every organization has important power and communication relationships that are not put down on paper. However, the organigram should not be rejected, but rather placed in context: it tells us some useful things, even though it hides others. The organigram is somewhat like a map. A map is invaluable for finding towns and their connecting roads, but it tells us nothing about the economic or social relationships of the regions. Similarly, **while the organigram does not show informal relationships, it does represent an accurate picture of the division of labor, showing at a glance (1) what positions exist in the organization, (2) how these are grouped into units, and (3) how formal authority flows among them** (in effect, describing the use of direct supervision). Van de Ven (1976a, p. 70) appropriately refers to the organigram as the "skeletal configuration" of the organization.

While formal authority represents one very limited aspect of the complex organization, it must be studied and understood if the functioning of organizations is to be understood. As Melville Dalton (1959) notes in his insightful study of informal relationships in an American manufacturing plant, the formal structure restrains the informal in three basic ways: "First, the formal largely orders the direction the informal takes. Second, it consequently shapes the character of defenses created by the informal. And third, whether the formal is brightly or dimly existent in the blur of contradictions, it requires overt conformity to its precepts" (p. 237).

THE ORGANIZATION AS A SYSTEM OF REGULATED FLOWS

Figure 3–2, the second overlay, shows the organization as a network of regulated flows overlaid on the logo. The diagram is stylized, as these usually are, depicting the organization as a well-ordered, smoothly functioning system of flow processes. This view was not only a favorite of early organizational theorists, but remains the dominant one in the literature of planning and control systems today. Figure 3–3 shows one elaborate version of this view, taken from Stafford Beer's book, *Brain of the Firm* (1972).

The second overlay shows the flows of work materials, information, and decision processes, but only those aspects that are *regulated,* in other words, systematically and explicitly controlled. Thus, whereas the first view of the organization described the use of direct supervision as a

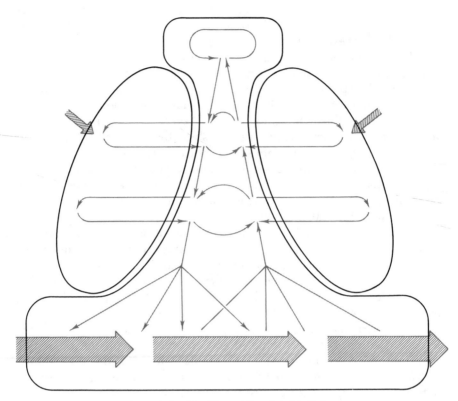

Figure 3-2. *The Flow of Regulated Activity*

coordinating mechanism, this one describes the use of standardization. Three distinct flows can be identified in the regulated system, the operating work flow, the flow of control information and decisions, and the flow of staff information.

The Operating Work Flow The flow of work through the operating core is shown in simplified form at the bottom of Figure 3–2 as three sequential arrows representing, symbolically, the input, processing, and output functions. Operating work flows involve the movements of materials and information in a variety of combinations. In manufacturing firms, the work flow centers on materials that are transformed—for example, the parts that move along the assembly line—backed up by information flows such as work documents and time sheets. In contrast, many service organizations transform information, which flows in the form of documents:

> In a life insurance company, for example, applications are received, examined, accepted or rejected, policies issued, policy-holders billed for premiums, premiums processed, and benefits paid. The file representing the individual policy is the focal center of the organization's work (Simon, 1957, p. 159).

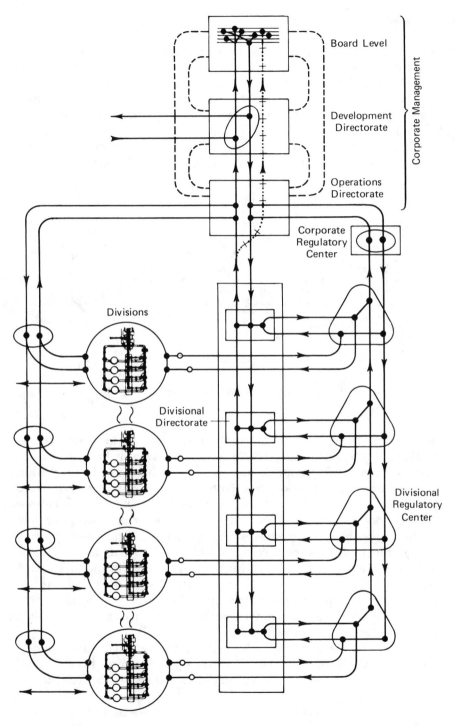

Figure 3-3. *One View of the Organization as a System of Regulated Flows (from Beer, 1972, p. 199)*

In retail firms, both materials and information—merchandise, cash, customer data, and so on—move in parallel systems, while in newspapers, information and materials move in separate systems—the information work flow in editorial feeds the material work flow (paper and ink) in printing. Sometimes the customer is the object of the work flow, as in hospitals and barbershops.[3]

The regulation of the operating work flow varies from one organization to another. Figure 3-4 shows the highly regulated flow of work, with

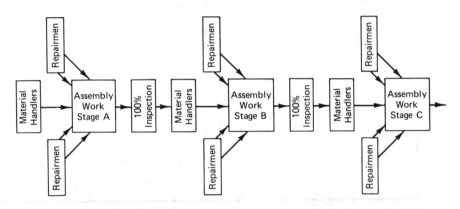

Figure 3-4. *A Highly Regulated Work Flow (from Chapple and Sayles, 1961, p. 30)*

sequential coupling, in a manufacturing assembly line. Less regulated are the flows Holstein and Berry (1970) recorded in what is known as a "job shop," a group of work stations (in this case, machines in a factory) which transfer work in a number of ways. Note in Figure 3-5 that no single transfer accounts for more than 4.4 percent of the total. Objects flow between work stations according to their individual needs for processing, as automobiles move about repair garages or people shop in department stores. In general, this leads to a more complex mixture of pooled, sequential, and reciprocal coupling. But one interesting finding of Holstein and Berry can be seen in Figure 3-5: there evolved "considerable work flow structure" (p. B325), that is, certain set patterns that most of the orders followed. In other words, as we shall see repeatedly in this book, patterns appear naturally in organizational flows and structures.

As a final note, it should be pointed out that regulated work-flow relationships, while most characteristic of the operating core, may also take place at other levels in the hierarchy. Figure 3-6 shows the regulated ex-

[3]See Argyris (1966) for a good description of the customer as "pacesetter" in the work flow of a trust department.

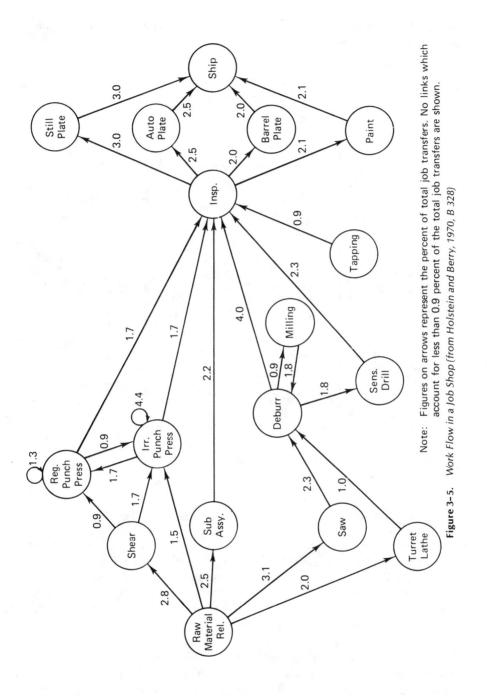

Note: Figures on arrows represent the percent of total job transfers. No links which account for less than 0.9 percent of the total job transfers are shown.

Figure 3-5. Work Flow in a Job Shop (from Holstein and Berry, 1970, B 328)

41

change of information among financial and production groups at four hierarchical levels of a manufacturing firm.

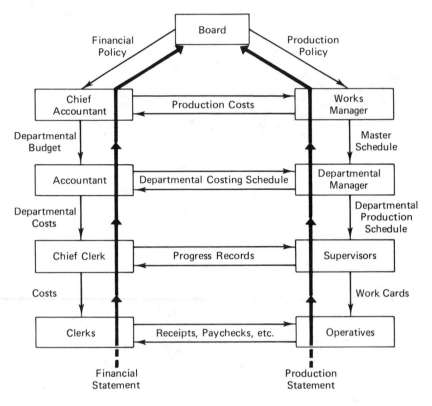

Figure 3-6.   *An Illustration of the Regulated Control Flows (from
Paterson, 1969, p. 49)*

The Regulated Control Flows   Officially, the formal control system
regulates the vertical flows of information and decision making, from the
operating core up the chain of authority. The regulated control flows are
shown in Figure 3-2 as vertical channels up and down the middle line. Flowing up is the feedback information on the operating work, while flowing
down are the commands and work instructions. In addition, at each level of
the management hierarchy are circular arrows, indicating the decision-
making role of the middle managers in the control system. Below we look at
each of these aspects in turn.

Commands and instructions are fed down the chain of authority,
emanating from the strategic apex or a middle-line position, and elaborated
as they flow downward. In the formal planning process, for example, general "strategic" plans are established at the strategic apex; successively,

these are elaborated into programs, capital and operating budgets, and operating plans (e.g., marketing and manpower plans), finally reaching the operating core as sets of detailed work instructions. In effect, in the regulated system the decisions made at the strategic apex set off ever-widening waves of implementational decisions as they flow down the hierarchy.

The upward control system exists as a "management information system," or MIS, that collects and codes data on performance, starting in the operating core. As this information passes each level in the hierarchy, it is aggregated until, finally, it reaches the strategic apex as a broad summary of overall organizational performance. Figure 3–6 shows some aspects of the regulated control flows in a manufacturing firm—the downward amplified planning system and the upward aggregated MIS in finance and production.

The regulated control system of the organization also includes a specification of the kinds of decisions that can be made at each level of the hierarchy. This represents, in effect, the vertical division of decision-making labor. For example, the spending authority of managers may be specified as $1000 for first-line supervisors, $10,000 for district managers, and so on up to the chief executive officer, who may be able to authorize expenditures of up to $100,000 without having to seek the approval of the board of directors. Figure 3–7 shows a more elaborate example of a regulated decision system.

When we combine this notion of vertical division of decision-making labor with those of the regulated flows of information aggregated up and commands elaborated down the hierarchy, we find that managers at different levels can interrupt these flows to make decisions appropriate to their own level. This is what the circular arrows in the middle line of Figure 3–2 are meant to describe. Commands coming down the hierarchy may be stopped at a given management level and handled there, as, for example, when a president receives a complaint by a customer and sends it down to the regional sales manager for action. And information on "exceptions"— decision situations that cannot be handled at a given level—are passed up the hierarchy until they reach a manager with the necessary formal authority to handle them. T. T. Paterson (1969) provides us with a number of interesting illustrations of this regulated decision system, the most graphic being in the British income tax office. Paterson speaks from experience:

> Faced by an income tax problem because I have an income from writing and broadcasting and the like in addition to a salary, I decide to take my problem to the local income tax office. A young clerk sees me come in and . . . comes towards the desk to receive me. I tell her I have problems and I bring out my income tax return form. She immediately answers by saying "Well, you fill this one in here, and fill that one in there" . . . This cannot solve my problem and she does not know how to solve it either, whereupon she lifts up the flap

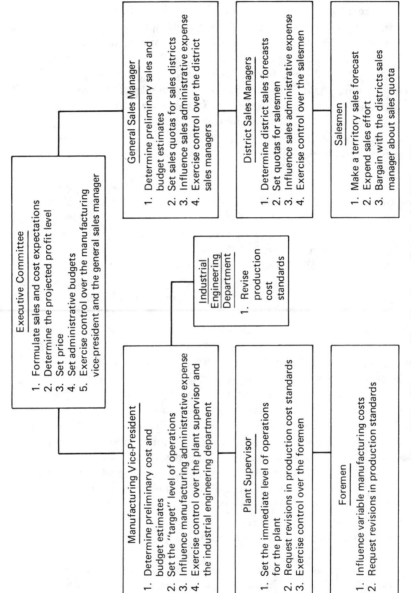

Figure 3-7. *A Regulated Decision System (from Bonini, 1967, p. 31)*

44

in the counter and takes me through the office into a room in which sits somebody I take to be a chief clerk, by reason of his oak desk and 10 square feet of carpet. He examines my problem and takes out a large book of rules governing income tax. I should give an answer on my return according to Section 23, paragraph A, but, unfortunately, this does not quite suit my particular case. . . .

I am then taken into a room which belongs to someone I assume to be a chief inspector because he has a mahogany desk and the carpet is fitted to the walls. He sees that my case is unique and the answers lie between paragraphs A and B; therefore he decides (because he has the right to) that I should answer somewhere in between. . . . he makes a decision lying between the limits set by the rules. Such rules have been laid out, in the first instance, by people in the Inland Revenue in London, so as to give limits within which chief inspectors may make such new, unique decisions, or regulations which the chief clerk can obey precisely (pp. 28–29).

The Regulated Staff Information Flows   A third aspect of the regulation system is the communication flow between line and staff, made for the purpose of feeding staff information and advice into line decision making. These flows are shown in Figure 3–2 as horizontal lines—between the line managers in the middle and the technocratic and support staff on either side. For example, a technocratic group may help a manager at a given level to elaborate plans for downward dissemination, while a support unit may help a manager to deal with an exception passed up the hierarchy. Figure 3–6 shows these types of contacts at different hierarchical levels, between accounting staff members in the technostructure and managers in the middle line.

It is, typically, the technostructure—notably the accountants and the like—who design and operate the management information system for the line managers. In addition, certain staff groups are specialized in the collection of *intelligence* information for the line managers, that is, information external to the organization. An economic analysis group may collect information on the state of the economy for the managers of the strategic apex, while a market research group may feed data on consumer buying habits to the marketing managers. The heavy arrows at the upper left and right of Figure 3–2 represent this flow of intelligence information.[4]

To conclude, the second overlay shows the organization as a regulated system characterized by orderly flows of materials, information, and decision processes. These include horizontal work flows in the operating core and elsewhere; upward aggregated flows of performance information and

[4]Boulding (1962) notes that, unofficially, intelligence can be an internal function as well, used to check on the formal information filtered up the hierarchy. March and Simon (1958, p. 167) note other, more routine informational tasks that staff members perform, such as carrying information (e.g., the messenger service), preparing reports (e.g., bookkeeping), and retaining information (e.g., archives).

exceptions; downward elaborated flows of commands, these last two interrupted according to the imperatives of the regulated decision system; and
horizontal information flows between staff specialists and line managers.

THE ORGANIZATION AS A SYSTEM
OF INFORMAL COMMUNICATION

Since the Hawthorne experiments, it has become increasingly clear
that organizations function in far more complex ways than those suggested
by overlays 1 and 2. In effect, considerable activity outside the systems of
formal authority and regulated flow processes has been uncovered in the research. **Centers of power exist that are not officially recognized; rich networks of informal communication supplement and sometimes circumvent
the regulated channels; and decision processes flow through the organization independent of the regulated system.**

> For centuries observers and leaders have remarked on the distinctions between
> expected and unexpected behavior in organizations. The fact that the distinc-
> tions continue to be made under various names points to an apparently univer-
> sal condition. From at least the time of Augustus Caesar, these dissimilarities
> were recognized and incorporated in the terms *de jure* (by right) and *de facto*
> (in fact), which are roughly equivalent to *legal* or *official* and *actual* but *unof-
> ficial.* In industry and business today one repeatedly hears the same general
> meaning phrased as "administration versus politics," "theory versus practice,"
> "red tape versus working relations," "fancy versus fact," etc. (Dalton, 1959,
> p. 219).

Dalton defines formal or official as "that which is planned and agreed upon"
and informal or unofficial as "the spontaneous and flexible ties among
members, guided by feelings and personal interests indispensable for the
operation of the formal, but too fluid to be entirely contained by it" (p.
219). Thus, whereas the first two views of the organization focus on the
formal use of direct supervision and standardization, this one focuses on
mutual adjustment as a coordinating mechanism.

Our third overlay is presented in Figure 3–8. This shows the flow of
informal communication in a municipal government, taken exactly as presented by Pfiffner and Sherwood (1960, p. 291) and overlaid on our logo. In
fact, Pfiffner and Sherwood's figure maps easily onto our five-part figure:
the two boxes at the strategic apex represent the city council and the city
manager; the middle-line position represents the assistant manager; the four
operating core units are building, police, parks, and fire; the four technocratic units on the left are the civil service commission, civil service department, engineer, and planning; while the three support units on the right are
attorney, library, and finance.

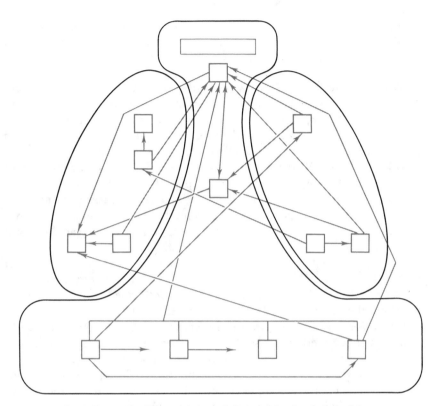

Figure 3-8. *The Flow of Informal Communication (adapted from Pfiffner and Sherwood, 1960, p. 291)*

Pfiffner and Sherwood refer to the diagram as a "Sociometric view of two (most frequent) contacts of the manager, his assistant, and department heads" (p. 291), implying that they are really exposing only the tip of the informal communications iceberg. A "sociogram" is simply a map of who communicates with whom in an organization, without regard to formal channels. This particular sociogram shows a number of interesting things. First, the top manager, as expected a central point in the flow of communication, is obviously prepared to bypass formal channels. Second, a glance at the contacts of the middle-line manager suggests that his formal rank in the hierarchy may be misleading. No contacts are shown with the operating units, even though this manager is shown in the organigram as being in charge of them. Third, the engineer at the base of the technostructure "is in a vital position, affecting organizational communication" (p. 291). This shows a further crack in the regulated system—a staff man, off to the side, occupies a position of major power.

... Hierarchical status is not the only factor of significance. The engineer is regarded as a high-status person in city governments principally because of his

professional identifications, his membership in a professional subculture. ...
his high status also comes from the centrality of his functional role to the work
of many other departments (pp. 290–291).

Trist and Bamforth's Coal Mine Study   Before attempting to explain
why informal communication is so important in the workings of the organization, it will be helpful to review one pathbreaking study of the complex
relationship between formal and informal communication. Trist and
Bamforth (1951), of the British Tavistock Institute, analyzed in great detail
the work situation in British coal mines before and after the introduction of
mechanization. In the premechanization period, the informal group was
responsible for the whole task of mining the coal seam. Tasks were multiple
and substitutable; the group used its own methods from beginning to end;
communication was informal and within the group. In effect, the dominant
mechanism for coordination was mutual adjustment.

With the advent of a new, advanced technical system, the division of
labor was formalized. Workers were now separated not only in terms of the
tasks they performed, but also the shift they performed them on and the
place along the seam where they performed them. The informal means of
communication and coordination were eliminated. Furthermore, the individual worker could no longer see his task carried to its natural completion;
rather he performed a single step isolated both in place and in time.

Unfortunately, no coordinating mechanism could replace mutual adjustment. Managers were designated, but direct supervision was ineffective
because of the physical distances separating of workers, the darkness, and
the dangerous conditions in the mines. Standardization of work process,
inherent in the new technical system, was insufficient for coordination,
while standardization of outputs of individual workers was not feasible because the outputs derived only from the coordinated efforts of the members
of the group. Hence, the new system destroyed the informal communication
system without setting up a formal one to take its place. The result was low
productivity and considerable worker alienation. Trist and Bamforth
describe four defenses that the coal miners used to cope with the new situation: the establishment of small, informal work groups; failing that, "the
development of a reactive individualism in which a reserve of personal
secrecy is apt to be maintained" (p. 31); mutual scapegoating between
people on different shifts in blaming each other for work problems; and
absenteeism.

Trist and Bamforth proposed a solution that recognized both the
informal social system and the formal technical system. (In a later paper,
Emery and Trist, 1960, write about the "sociotechnical" system.) Work
duties were reorganized to enable the new technical system to be used by
miners working in small, informal, self-managed groups. Jobs were shared,
informal communication took place, leadership emerged naturally within

the group when needed, and performance could be measured and therefore standardized. In effect, the formal and informal systems were brought back into accord with each other.[5]

The Importance of Informal Communication   There are two prime reasons for informal communication in organizations, both brought out clearly in the coal mine study. One is directly work-related, the other social.

In one study, Conrath (1973) found that 60 percent of the face-to-face communication in organizations was related directly to the tasks at hand. **Most work just cannot get done without some informal communication.** Life is simply too complicated to regulate everything. Standardization must be supplemented with mutual adjustment, even if only to deal with unexpected change. We saw a good example of this earlier, in the dramatic failure of the Northeast Electric Grid System for lack of an effective override. Even in highly simple and stable systems, the standards cannot cover all the requirements of the work. The best illustration of this is the work-to-rule strike, a favorite ploy of workers with the most standardized jobs (such as sorting mail). Here they follow the standards to the letter, and the result is chaos. The message is that a fully regulated system, devoid of recourse to informal communication, is next to impossible. Human organizations simply cannot be made so machinelike. (The example earlier of the assembly instructions for a child's toy is one we all understand well. It is amazing how difficult it can be to put even that simple task down on paper for the layman to understand; yet it can easily be explained by someone nearby who knows how to do it.)

At the managerial levels, study after study shows that managers of all kinds favor the verbal channels of the informal system over the documents of the formal (spending 65 to 80 percent of their time in verbal contact), and that they spend almost as much of their time (about 45 percent on average) communicating outside the chain of formal authority as inside it. The regulated channels are often slow and unreliable, frequently too limited in what they carry. The soft information, intangible and speculative, is simply ignored in the formal MIS despite clear evidence that managers depend on such information. And the MIS, because it must document and then aggregate hard facts, is often too slow for the manager, reporting the open barn door long after the cow has fled. Moreover, aggregation of information in the MIS often makes what finally reaches the strategic apex so abstract and vague as to be of limited use in the making of specific decisions. In contrast to the bland documents of the MIS, the verbal channels of communication —outside the regulated flow—are rich in the data they carry to the manager.

[5]For another, equally detailed study by the Tavistock Institute, see Rice's (1953) analysis of work in an Indian weaving mill (and Miller's, 1975, follow-up report). Both Tavistock studies are excellent examples of "action research," in which the researchers seek both to describe an organizational situation and to improve it.

The manager can "read" facial expressions, gestures, and tones of voice, and he can elicit immediate feedback.

The result is that managers bypass the MIS to get much of their own information. They build their own networks of informal contacts, which constitute their real information and intelligence systems. Aguilar (1967), in his study of external information that managers use, notes that personal sources exceeded impersonal sources in perceived importance—71 percent to 29 percent. He quotes a senior partner in an investment banking firm on the most important source of external information for the successful executive of the large corporation: "the informal network of contacts which he has outside the company" (p. 76).[6]

The second reason for the existence of informal communication in organizations is *social* in nature. People need to relate to each other as human beings, whether for purposes of friendship or to let off steam.

Much informal communication may be totally independent of the work of the organization, as in the case of the social grooming ("Good morning"; "Fine, thank you") that Desmond Morris (1967) talks about in *The Naked Ape.* Other social communication is decidedly "dysfunctional," actively interfering with the work to be done. In many organizations, people override the regulated systems to advance their personal needs. They leak sensitive information to outsiders and hold back critical information from their managers. But managers, too, use information "dysfunctionally." In his book *Organizational Intelligence,* Wilensky (1967) notes the existence of clandestine intelligence systems whereby leaders gather political and ideological information on their subordinates to maintain their authority. (Ironically, he finds these systems especially strong in the most democratic organizations, simply because the leaders must know the minds of those who elected them.)[7]

In many cases, however, social communication turns out to be vital to the success of the organization. Trist and Bamforth's study shows that social communication at the coal face was necessary to reassure the workers in their dangerous environment, while that in the pubs helped to achieve coordination across shifts.

In his study, Dalton (1959) describes vividly the intrigues, pressures, and distortions underneath the regulated system in a manufacturing plant. Dalton's theme is that the upper levels of the organization cannot impose regulations against the will of the groups lower down. Even the foremen sometimes aided the workers in resisting regulations imposed from above.

[6]The points in the last two paragraphs on the manager's use of formal and informal information are developed at length, together with references to the research literature, in Chapters 3 and 4 of *The Nature of Managerial Work* and in a monograph entitled *Impediments to the Use of Management Information* (Mintzberg, 1973a, 1975). See also Aguilar's book, *Scanning the Business Environment* (1967).

[7]Some dysfunctions of the system of regulated flows will be discussed in Chapters 5 and 18.

Changes could be made only through persuasion and bargaining—essentially through recognition of the relationships between the regulated and the social systems.

The Network of Informal Communication The system of informal communication in the organization is multichanneled and varied, a point Pfiffner (1960) expresses well:

> In place of the orderly information flow, step by step up the hierarchy, which we generally have accepted as a model, information really follows a grid of communications made up of overlapping, often contradictory and elusive channels, which really are not channels in the formal sense. Messages are mutual and compensatory, taking on the conformation of a galaxy ... (p. 129–130).

The network of informal communication may be thought of as a set of informal channels connected by "nerve centers"—individuals who stand at the crossroads of the channels. In these informal channels, individuals bypass the formal authority system in order to communicate directly. Figure 3–9 shows three cases of this. In the first, two peers communicate directly rather than through their bosses, in effect, replacing the direct supervision of the formal authority system by the mutual adjustment of the informal system. In the second case, of a diagonal nature, an individual at one level of the hierarchy communicates directly with the subordinate of a peer at a

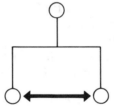

(a) Direct Peer Contact

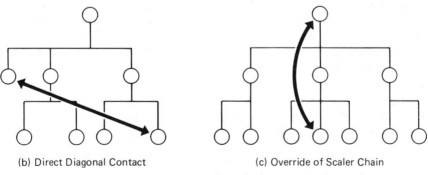

(b) Direct Diagonal Contact   (c) Override of Scaler Chain

Figure 3-9. *Some Bypass Channels of Communication*

lower level. In the third case, a manager is bypassed—and the scalar chain overrode—as his superior communicates directly with his subordinate, typically to avoid aggregation or distortion in the information transmitted. The use of those bypass channels is very common, at all levels in the hierarchy. Burns (1957), for example, in his study of the work of seventy-six senior and middle-level managers, concluded:

> The accepted view of management as a working hierarchy on organization chart lines may be dangerously misleading. Management simply does not operate as a flow of information up through a succession of filters, and a flow of decisions and instructions down through a succession of amplifiers (p. 60).

Strauss (1962–63), who studied the purchasing agents of the operating core, wrote a detailed article on their "Tactics of Lateral Relationships." He found that the effective and high-status purchasing agents favored mutual adjustment over direct supervision and standardization: in order to resolve conflicts they had with other departments (notably engineering), they were reluctant to appeal to the boss, to rely on the rules, or to require written acceptances; instead, "to oil the wheels of formal bureaucracy" (p. 173), they relied on friendship, the exchange of favors, and their own informal political power.[8]

One important informal network of communication, made up of a web of bypass channels, is the "grapevine." A study by Caplow (1966) of "Rumors in War" found the grapevine to be surprisingly fast, accurate, and comprehensive, while Davis (1953, 1968), who studied the grapevine in a 600-person firm, found it to be fast, selective, and discriminating. For one quality control problem initiated by a letter from a customer, he found that 68 percent of the executives received the information, but only three of the fourteen communications took place within the chain of command (Davis, 1953, p. 48).

At the crossroads, or "nodes," of the channels of informal communication are the "nerve centers," the individuals who collect information from different channels and switch it selectively into them. Certain staff specialists emerge in this capacity due to their access to a wide variety of line managers at different levels in the hierarchy (Davis, 1953; Strauss, 1962–63). Others so emerge because they are "gatekeepers," controlling the flows of important external information into the organization. Allen and Cohen (1969) found "technical gatekeepers" in the research laboratory, bringing in scientific information, while Strauss (1962–63) found them as purchasing agents, bringing in supplier information. Other staff nerve centers sit between departments, linking them together, as in the case of the engineer who carries information between the research and marketing departments.

[8]See also Landsberger (1961–62) for a thorough discussion of "The Horizontal Dimension in Bureaucracy."

Finally, managers themselves serve as nerve centers (and gatekeepers), since, as we saw in Figure 2-4 and in the data cited in this chapter, they stand not only in the vertical flow of formal information, but in the horizontal flow of informal information, between analysts, support staff, other managers, and outsiders. Thus, Sutton and Porter (1968) in a study of a government office found that all of the managers (as well as 10 percent of the rank and file) served as nerve centers (in their words "liaison individuals") in the flow of grapevine information.

To conclude, we see that in sharp contrast to the order and hierarchy of the first two overlays, the third suggests the existence of much more fluid, less orderly flow processes in organizations. But all three views of how the organization functions seem to dichotomize overly the distinction between the formal and informal systems. The two systems seem to be rather interdependent: at the very least, the formal appears to shape the informal, while the informal greatly influences what works in the formal, and sometimes even reflects its shape to come. Let us, therefore, consider two views that suggest a blending of the formal and informal.

THE ORGANIZATION AS A SYSTEM
OF WORK CONSTELLATIONS

In the last overlay, we viewed the organization as a rather random set of communication channels connected by nerve centers. Now we shall see a view that suggests that this informal network is patterned in certain ways and is related to the formal authority system.

To uncover some of these patterns, let us consider first some additional evidence on informal communication in organizations. In his review article on organization theory, Scott (1961) noted that where people work closely together and share common interests, they communicate extensively and informally with each other in "cliques." These cliques are commonly found in departments that are functionally specialized and in work flows that bring people into close physical contact. Similarly, in their study of a U.S. government tax office, Sutton and Porter (1968) found that 64 percent of the grapevine communication of the members (most of them nonmanagers) was destined for people within a functional group. In contrast, Davis (1953) found that for *managers* the prime flow of grapevine communication was across functions, not within. But Burns (1957) still found the presence of cliques for managers—they spent most of their time with a small number of peers:

> Perhaps the most striking of the results ... is the uniform segregation of a senior management group of three, usually, or four persons. Of the total time

spent in conversation with people within the concern (i.e., the factory), the general manager might spend half with the other two members of this group (p. 60).

What this evidence suggests is that people in organizations tend to work in cliques, or small peer groups, based on horizontal not vertical relationships: at the lower levels, these groups reflect functional specialization or work flow; at the managerial levels, they tend to cut across specialties or functions.

In a series of studies, Thomason (1966, 1967) supports this conclusion with the finding that the organization consists of various *distinct* communication networks, or cliques, at different levels of the hierarchy. Thomason found further that each served as the focal point for specialized information: ". . . the overall hierarchy becomes a composite of different subject-oriented communications networks, with the center of this network lying at the point in the hierarchy to which the subject is allowed or required to penetrate" (Thomason, 1967, p. 29).

So now a clear picture emerges: organizational members at a given level in the hierarchy deal with information that *differs in kind* from that dealt with at other levels. This is in sharp contrast with the regulated system view that all levels in the hierarchy deal with the *same* kind of information, only in a more aggregated or elaborated form: for example, the salesperson, the sales manager, and the marketing vice-president all deal with marketing information, the first with specific sales, the second with weekly totals, the third with quarterly reports. But the findings above suggest otherwise, that the issues each level addresses are fundamentally different. In effect, **the organization takes on the form of a set of work constellations, quasi-independent cliques of individuals who work on decisions appropriate to their own level in the hierarchy.** Thus, Landsberger (1961–62) concludes in his study of the flow of horizontal communication in organizations:

> . . . these flows, lying on top of each other, so to speak, may be relatively independent and qualitatively different from each other. A higher-level manager may admittedly spend some of his time arbitrating between subordinates, but at least as important is the time he spends in solving with colleagues roughly at his own level problems appropriate to his own level (p. 305).

In Weick's (1976) terms, these work constellations are "loosely coupled": "The imagery is that of numerous clusters of events that are tightly coupled within and loosely coupled between" (p. 14). In effect, each work constellation has responsibility for some decisional area of the organization— introducing new product lines, dealing with financial issues, bidding on contracts, scheduling production, or whatever. We would expect to find much of the informal communication and the decision making of the organization bounded within these work constellations, with the nerve centers

effecting much of the communication between them and the gatekeepers gathering in much of their external information.

Once this point is recognized, all kinds of illustrations of it appear in the literature. Perhaps the clearest is that of Lawrence and Lorsch (1967, pp. 55–56), who found that production problems in plastics companies were handled at the plant manager level, while scientific problems were handled by the scientists themselves or their immediate supervisors (such as group leaders), and marketing problems fell in between, being handled by product sales managers and the like, in the middle of the sales department hierarchy. And Sills (1957) found in his study of the National Foundation for Infantile Paralysis (which ran the famous March of Dimes campaign) a clear decision-making division of labor between the national headquarters and the local chapters: the chapters were responsible primarily for raising funds and financially assisting polio victims, while the headquarters focused directly on the sponsorship of scientific research. This was done to ensure the coordination of research activities on a national basis, and also to preclude "the possibility that Chapters might neglect the research program in favor of the more immediately rewarding patient care program" (p. 73). Furthermore, Gustavsen (1975) finds evidence that even the board of directors acts as a work constellation: "The boards seemed ... to act within certain fields rather than as a general managerial body at 'the top' of the enterprise" (p. 36), notably in the fields of investments, mergers, and the like.

Work constellations can range from the formal to the informal, from work groups shown as distinct units on the organigram, such as the payroll department, to those in which individuals from different units converse informally to deal with certain kinds of decisions, as when researchers, industrial engineers, production and sales managers meet to plan the introduction of new products. (Of course, this group could also be quasi-formal, for example, designated as an official "standing committee.") We would, in fact, expect most work constellations in the operating core to correspond to the work flow and to be reflected as formal units on the organigram. For example, as shown in Figure 3–10, newspapers comprise four distinct operating work constellations, each functioning relatively independently but feeding into one sequentially coupled work flow. The advertising constellation that sells the advertising space and the editorial constellation that writes the material both feed their outputs to a printing constellation that produces the newspaper, and this in turn feeds a circulation constellation that distributes it. (This example comes from a study carried out under the author's supervision by management students at McGill University.[9] A number of such examples will be used throughout this book.)

Similarly, in the support staff, we would expect to find a one-to-one correspondence between many of the formal work units and the work con-

[9]Based on a study submitted to the author in Management 420, McGill University, 1970, by Arthur Aron, Mike Glazer, Daniel Lichtenfeld, and Dave Saltzman.

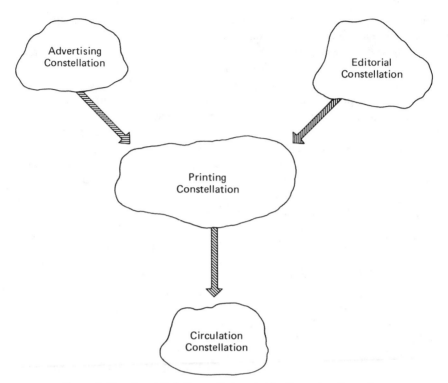

Figure 3-10. *Four Work Constellations in the Operating Core of a Newspaper*

stellations. Each of these support units in effect constitutes such a constellation, tightly coupled within but only loosely coupled with the rest of the organization. For example, the cafeteria or the public relations department provides a rather distinct, self-contained service.

In the case of the technostructure and middle line, however, according to the evidence of Davis, Burns, and Thomason cited earlier, we would expect the work constellations to be less formal in nature, often cutting across official departmental lines. The analysts, for example, accomplish their work only by changing the work of others; accordingly, we would expect to find them forming constellations with others, notably line managers, to effect these changes. And the line managers, as noted earlier, involve themselves in complex webs of relationships—in effect, work constellations —not only with analysts· but also with certain support staffers and with managers from other units.

Figure 3–11, our fourth overlay, illustrates some of the points we have been making about work constellations. It shows a manufacturing firm as a set of ten work constellations. In the operating core are three constellations coupled sequentially in the work flow and corresponding to the units on the organigram—a fabricating shop, an assembly operation, and a distribution

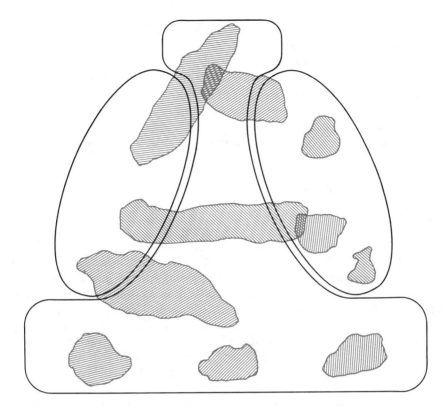

Figure 3-11. *The Set of Work Constellations*

department. Above and to the left of the operating core is the administrative production constellation, concerned with scheduling production, standardizing the manufacturing work, and handling the problems of the plant floor. It includes first-line production supervisors and analysts, such as industrial engineers and production schedulers. Immediately above this is the new product constellation, comprising middle-line marketing managers, analysts, and support staffers, such as marketing researchers and engineers from the research and development department. Off to the right, exclusively within the support staff ellipse and corresponding to the formal units on the organigram, are the plant cafeteria at the bottom, the research and development department in the middle (overlapping the new product constellation), and the public relations department near the top. Finally, two work constellations are shown connected to the strategic apex. The finance constellation links top managers and financial support staffers, while the long-range planning constellation links top managers, some board members, and high-level analysts of the technostructure.

Of course, this overlay—like the others—is highly simplified. It shows only a few of the many work constellations to be found in any fair-sized manufacturing firm, and it does not show the many nerve centers that

supply the needed coupling—however loose—between the different constellations or the gatekeepers that link each to the external environment.

To conclude, while the systems of formal authority and regulated
flows depict the organization as a kind of spiral spring, made up of one type
of material that gradually narrows as it rises to its apex, and the system of
informal communication depicts it as a marble cake with flows in every
direction, the system of work constellations describes it as a layer cake, less
orderly than the spiral spring but more orderly than the marble cake.

THE ORGANIZATION AS A SYSTEM OF
AD HOC DECISION PROCESSES

Authority and communication in organizations are not ends in themselves, but facilitating processes for the other two basic flow processes—the
making of decisions and the production of goods and services. In discussing
the regulated system, we dealt with the operating work flow and we looked
at the flow of regulated decision processes. Now we look at decision making
from a different perspective—as a rather more flexible flow of ad hoc
decision processes. Here we shall see how the formal and informal aspects
of organization—the formal authority, the regulated flow of information,
and the flow of informal communication—all blend together to determine
organizational behavior.

What is a "decision"? It may be defined as a *commitment to action*,
usually a commitment of resources. In other words, a decision signals an
explicit intention to act.

And how about a decision process? One thing it is *not* is just the selection of a course of action. Our research (Mintzberg, Raisinghani, and
Theorêt, 1976) indicates that selection is often the icing on the cake, one of
a series of steps leading to a decision, not necessarily the most important. A
decision process encompasses all those steps taken from the time a stimulus
for an action is perceived until the time the commitment to the action is
made. This research suggests that those steps draw on seven fundamentally
different kinds of activities, or "routines." Two take place in the *identification* phase of decision making: the *recognition* routine, wherein the need to
initiate a decision process is perceived, and the *diagnosis* routine, where the
decision situation is assessed. Two routines are associated with the phase of
development of solutions: the *search* routine, to find ready-made solutions,
and the *design* routine, to develop custom-made ones. The *selection* phase
includes three routines: the *screening* of ready-made solutions, the *evalua-
tion-choice* of one solution, and the *authorization* of this by people not
otherwise involved in the decision process. A single decision process can

encompass any and all of these routines, each in fact executed a number of times.

Categorizing Organizational Decision Processes There is no generally accepted "typology" based on empirical research of the kinds of decision processes organizations make. What we have instead are some rather general conceptual typologies. Organizational decision processes have, for example, been categorized as programmed and unprogrammed, and as routine and ad hoc. At one extreme we have the highly standardized decision made at regular intervals and at the other extreme, the highly unstructured ones made irregularly. Decision processes have also been categorized by their functional area—new product decisions in marketing, investment decisions in finance, hiring decisions in personnel, and so on.

Decision processes have also been categorized by their importance in the organization, most commonly as operating, administrative, and strategic.

1. *Operating* decisions are taken rather routinely in processes that are typically programmed and executed quickly, almost automatically, by operators or low-echelon support staffers working individually. A lathe operator makes an operating decision when he starts or stops his machine, as does a librarian when he is asked to find a simple reference. Such decision processes generally come under the purview of the regulated system. In these processes, recognition is clearly defined, not unlike the pigeon that darts for food when a bell is rung. There is little diagnosis, or design of custom-made solutions, only a highly circumscribed search for ready-made solutions. In effect, all the phases of operating decision making—identification, development, and selection —are largely predetermined, in such terms as "if *a*, do *x*"; "if *b*, do *y*."

2. *Administrative* decisions may be considered as coordinative or exceptional. *Coordinative* decisions guide and coordinate the operating decisions. Many of the decisions in the administrative levels of the regulated system fall into this group, including planning, scheduling, and budgeting decisions. These decision processes are typically routine, made on fixed schedules, and are sometimes even rather programmed, although typically less so than the operating decision processes. Some are forced into functional categories—for example, those related to marketing budgets, manpower plans, and production schedules. They are made by line managers or staff analysts—sometimes the two working together—although the most programmed of them can be made by clerks in the technostructure or even by computers. *Exception* decisions are those made on an ad hoc basis but with minor overall consequences. These are nonroutine and less programmed than the first two decision processes. As such, they involve

a distinct recognition step, and their steps of diagnosis, search, and selection are typically more elaborate than for the operating and many of the coordinative decisions. They may also include the design of custom-made solutions. Exception decisions also tend to cut across functional areas; indeed, many are evoked by an event that spills over a single function, as when marketing and production managers battle about the quality of a product. An exception decision can (a) emerge at a single level in the hierarchy, as when a regular supplier goes bankrupt and the purchasing department must initiate a decision process to find a new one; (b) rise up the hierarchy for resolution, as when a customer complaint to a salesperson is sent up to the sales manager for action; or (c) descend down the hierarchy for change, as when a decision made at the strategic apex to introduce a new product line requires the plant manager to purchase new machinery and the sales manager to hire new sales personnel. In effect, the type (a) exception decision is made within a single work constellation, whereas types (b) and (c) came under the regulated decision system. It should be noted, however, that the same exception decision may be evoked in any of three ways. A sales manager may decide to hire new salespeople because the managers above him decided to introduce a new product line, because the sales personnel below him complain of overwork, or because a salesperson resigns (forcing the making of a decision unique to his level).

3. *Strategic* decisions are also exceptions, but by definition they are significant in their impact on the organization. Examples of strategic decisions from our own research (Mintzberg, Raisinghani, and Théorêt, 1976) include the case of a consulting firm forced to merge after losing its biggest customer, an airport that decided to develop a runway extension, and a brokerage firm that decided to buy a seat on a major exchange in order to expand. It should be noted that no type of decision is inherently strategic; decisions are strategic only in context. The introduction of a new product is a major event for a brewery, but hardly worth mentioning in a toy company. In fact, we can label the same decision as strategic, exception, and operating in different contexts: the pricing decision for a company building giant oil tankers is strategic; that for a restaurant is an exception, taken only when costs go up; while that in a printing plant is operating, taken many times a day by clerks working with standard price lists. Strategic decisions are the least routine and programmed of all the decision processes, typically taking years and involving many members of the organization, from the strategic apex and other parts. Our research indicates that strategic decision processes involve very complex intermingling of the seven routines: recognition typically involves many stimuli, most of them difficult to interpret; diagnosis is a key routine,

but not very systematic; a great deal of effort goes into the development of solutions, especially design activity, since solutions must often be custom-made; and selection also turns out to be a complex, multistage process. To add to the complexity, single strategic decisions are typically factored into many smaller decisions which are made in processes that are continually being interrupted, blocked by political and other factors, delayed or speeded up by the decision makers themselves, and forced to recycle back on themselves. A strategic decision may be evoked by a change in the environment, as when a new technical system is developed; by an exception coming up the hierarchy, as when a customer complaint indicates a major problem with an important new product; or by individual initiative, as when a manager simply decides that it is time for a new product line. In general, strategic decisions set off waves of other decisions in the hierarchy. Many exception and coordinative decisions must be made to implement them, as when a new product line requires the hiring of new staff, the buying of new machines, and the preparation of new plans, budgets, and schedules. And ultimately they result in a host of changes in the operating decision processes: that is why they are strategic.

More important than a typology of decisions is an understanding of how decision processes flow through the organization. Specifically, **we need to understand how operating, administrative, and strategic decisions link together and what roles the different participants—operators, top and middle-line managers, technocratic and support staffers—play in the phases of the different decision processes.** We need to know who recognizes the need to make a given kind of decision, who diagnoses the situation, who develops the solution, who authorizes it, and so on. On these points we have little evidence. There has simply been too little research on the important question of how decision processes flow through organizations. Toward the end of the book, based on our findings, we shall speculate on the answer for different kinds of structures. But for the moment, we present an example below to illustrate the organization as a system of ad hoc decision processes.

An Ad Hoc Decision Process   The fifth overlay shown in Figure 3–12 presents a hypothetical example of an ad hoc decision process that involves a mix of the types of decisions discussed above. The example begins with a salesperson in the office of a customer, shown at point 1, in the operating core. The customer is dissatisfied with the product of the firm and suggests to the salesperson that it be modified. Finding merit in the recommendation, but lacking the authority to deal with it, the salesperson passes the idea up to the sales manager (2). He, in turn, sends it to the marketing vice-president (3), and the latter raises the issue at an executive meeting (4). In effect, the

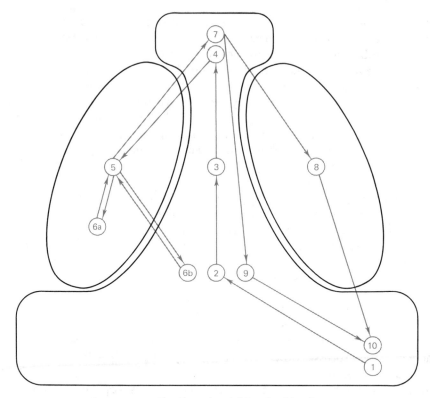

Figure 3-12. *The Flow of an Ad Hoc Decision Process*

stimulus for the decision, having originated at the operating core, has traveled as an *exception* through the regulated system, up the middle line to the strategic apex. There formal recognition takes place, and the president directs the head of the operations research department to form a task force to diagnose the situation and design a solution (5). The operations research manager draws his task-force members from various units and levels: the line sales manager, a member of the marketing research staff, an analyst from accounting. Together they design the new product, each one returning to his unit to evaluate specific details, for example, cost estimates (6a) and market potential (6b). Shortly thereafter, the operations research manager presents the group's findings to the executive committee (7). This group approves the recommendation, thereby authorizing the *strategic* decision. Now the implementational stage begins, with waves of *coordinative* and *exception* decisions affecting every corner of the organization. For example, the advertising department develops a promotional campaign for the new product (8), and the sales manager (together with analysts) prepares new plans and budgets, and specifies the staffing needs to effect the necessary changes in the sales department (9). One day, eighteen months after the process began, the original salesperson makes an *operating* decision—to return to the office of his customer, new product in hand (10).

Two important qualifications should be noted about this overlay. First, our story barely presents the skeleton of what really takes place when an organization introduces a new product. To show any reasonable part of the full implementation phase, for example, would make the fifth overlay hopelessly confusing. We would have lines going back and forth in every conceivable direction. A full description of the strategic decision process would take pages, not paragraphs. Little has been said about all the informal communication that necessarily accompanies such a strategic decision process, as well as the politics that inevitably result from a major change in an organization, and the many cycles, interruptions, and timing delays encountered along the way. Also, the fifth overlay only hints at the relationship between the work constellations and the decision process. In fact, that relationship is a rich one, with some parts of the process contained within particular constellations and others requiring complex interactions between them. In general, we would expect the strategic decision process to cut across many work constellations and the implementation process to be more neatly divided up among different ones.

The second qualification is that this overlay shows a "top-down" decision process, where the power for decision making remains at the top of the organization. The strategic decision process was guided from there and then implemented down the hierarchy. As we shall see later, this is one pattern of ad hoc decision processes among many. Strategic decisions may emerge anywhere in the organization, for example, in the operating core when a team of hospital psychiatrists decide to change their method of treatment. Furthermore, in some cases strategic decisions are not always so clearly delineated from implementational ones; later we shall see structures where decisions that appear to be operating in nature in fact lead to strategic change.

Despite these qualifications, the fifth overlay makes one important point which serves to conclude our discussion on how the organization functions. It shows the complex intermingling of the formal and informal flows of authority, communication, and decision processes. **Only by focusing on these real flows—of authority, work materials, information, and decision processes—can we begin to see how the organization really functions.** Such an understanding is an important prerequisite for a thorough understanding of organizational structure.

To conclude, we reiterate the point that each of the five systems overlays is an incomplete picture of how any real organization functions. But

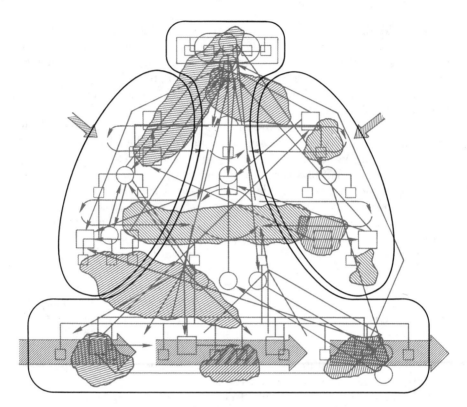

Figure 3-13. *A Combined Overlay: The Functioning of the Organization*

however incomplete, each system explains one important aspect. And taken all together—as is done in Figure 3–13—they suggest the true complexity of the functioning of the organization, and also serve as the basic framework on which we can now build our description of organizational structuring.

PART II

THE DESIGN PARAMETERS

In his book *The Sciences of the Artificial,* Herbert Simon (1969) discusses the sciences of man-made phenomena, such as engineering, medicine, and management. He identifies the major task of these sciences as *design:*

> Everyone designs who devises courses of action aimed at changing existing situations into preferred ones. The intellectual activity that produces material artifacts is no different fundamentally from the one that prescribes remedies for a sick patient or the one that devises a new sales plan for a company or a social welfare policy for a state. Design, so construed, is the core of all professional training; it is the principal mark that distinguishes the professions from the sciences. Schools of engineering, as well as schools of architecture, business, education, law, and medicine, are all centrally concerned with the process of design (pp. 55–56).

Design assumes discretion, an ability to alter a system. In the case of organizational structure, design means turning those knobs that influence the division of labor and the coordinating mechanisms, thereby affecting how the organization functions—how materials, authority, information, and decision processes flow through it. This section discusses these knobs— the essential parameters of organizational structure—and the ways in which each can be turned.

Consider the following questions:

- How many tasks should a given position in the organization contain and how specialized should each task be?
- To what extent should the work content of each position be standardized?
- What skills and knowledge should be required for each position?
- On what basis should positions be grouped into units and units into larger units?
- How large should each unit be; how many individuals should report to a given manager?
- To what extent should the output of each position or unit be standardized?
- What mechanisms should be established to facilitate mutual adjustment among positions and units?
- How much decision-making power should be delegated to the managers of line units down the chain of authority?
- How much decision-making power should pass from the line managers to the staff specialists and operators?

These are the basic issues of structural design we shall be discussing in this section. They suggest a set of nine *design parameters*—the basic components of organizational structure—that fall into four broad groupings. These are listed on the next page together with the most closely related concepts from Chapters 1-3.

Before proceeding with the discussion of each of the nine design parameters, two points should be noted. First, design parameters of a semiformal as well as formal nature have been included. Whereas, for example, the grouping of positions and units builds the formal authority system of the organization and the formalization of behavior serves as a pillar of the system of regulated flows, the use of liaison devices and of horizontal decentralization specifically encourages the flow of informal communication and the development of unofficial work constellations in the organization. In other words, to elaborate on our Chapter 1 definition, **in this book organizational structure encompasses those formal and semiformal means— in effect the nine design parameters—that organizations use to divide and coordinate their work in order to establish stable patterns of behavior.**

Second, it is sometimes assumed that structural change is a relatively simple matter, perhaps just the shift of a few boxes on the organigram. I recall the recommendation of a group of MBA students to a trucking company concerned about the low prestige of its safety department that it raise its position on the organigram, above that of the other departments report-

Group	Design Parameter	Related Concepts
Design of positions	Job specialization	Basic division of labor
	Behavior formalization	Standardization of work content
		System of regulated flows
	Training and indoctrination	Standardization of skills
Design of superstructure	Unit grouping	Direct supervision
		Administrative division of labor
		Systems of formal authority, regulated flows, informal communication, and work constellations
		Organigram
	Unit size	System of informal communication,
		Direct supervision
		Span of control
Design of lateral linkages	Planning and control systems	Standardization of outputs
		System of regulated flows
	Liaison devices	Mutual adjustment
		Systems of informal communication, work constellations, and ad hoc decision processes
Design of decision-making system	Vertical decentralization	Administrative division of labor
		Systems of formal authority, regulated flows, work constellations, and ad hoc decision processes
	Horizontal decentralization	Administrative division of labor
		Systems of informal communication, work constellations, and ad hoc decision processes

ing to the same manager. As if this change on a piece of paper would give the safety program its needed "boost" in the organization! Structural design is a difficult business, structure representing the established forces of habit and tradition, and of power as well. To tamper with these forces is often to invite strong resistance. There are times, of course, when the formal structure is so out of accord with the natural flows of work and communication, or with the social needs of the employees, that structural change is accepted readily. For example, Rice (1953) describes an Indian textile mill where the workers embraced a proposed change in structure to rid themselves of one that was far too rigid.

More commonly, however, structure reflects natural work and communication flows. Most structures represent real organizational needs, or at least those of the recent past; few structures are imposed artificially on the organization. As conditions change, of course organizational needs change, but changing the structure inevitably means interfering with established patterns of behavior. Thus, Paul Lawrence (1958) describes the reorganization of a food store chain that took years to effect:

> The researcher can testify that for the key people involved the making of these changes had not been easy. He witnessed their conscientious efforts to rethink their daily practices and change longstanding habit patterns....when one looks at the built-in, self-reinforcing persistence of the historical behavior patterns, it is remarkable that *any* discernible changes had occured (p. 204).

With this in mind, we now turn to our discussion of the nine design parameters. Each is considered in one of the following chapters, except for the two forms of decentralization that are discussed together in the final chapter. We begin with the smallest element of structure, the design of individual positions, discussing the specialization of jobs, formalization of behavior, and training and indoctrination successively in Chapters 4, 5, and 6. Then we look at the overall superstructure of the organization, in Chapter 7 the logic that underlies its bases for grouping and in Chapter 8 the size of its units. Then we turn to the question of how linkages of a lateral nature are used to fuse the elements of the superstructure together, first the planning and control system in Chapter 9 and then the liaison devices in Chapter 10. Finally, in Chapter 11, we see how all of this is tied together in a decision-making system, through the use of vertical and horizontal decentralization.

Section II of this book is analytic rather than synthetic; that is, it seeks to break structure down into its essential parts, rather than put it together as an integrated whole. Each chapter does describe the use of the particular design parameter in each of the five parts of the organization and links it to the design parameters already discussed. But the real synthesis comes later. We must first understand the basic elements of structure before we can put each of them into the context of the situation faced by a particular organization (in Section III), and, ultimately, see how all these elements cluster into specific configurations of structure (in Section IV).

4

Design of Positions: Job Specialization

We can consider three parameters in the design of individual positions in the organization: the specialization of the job, the formalization of behavior in carrying it out, and the training and indoctrination it requires. This chapter discusses the first of these.

Jobs can be specialized in two dimensions. First is its "breadth" or "scope"—how many different tasks are contained in each and how broad or narrow is each of these tasks. At one extreme, the worker is a jack-of-all-trades, forever jumping from one broad task to another; at the other extreme, he focuses his efforts on the same highly specialized task, repeated day-in and day-out even minute-in and minute-out. The second dimension of specialization relates to "depth," to the control over the work. At one extreme, the worker merely does the work without any thought as to how or why; at the other, he controls every aspect of the work in addition to doing it. The first dimension may be called *horizontal job specialization* (in that it deals with parallel activities) and its opposite, *horizontal job enlargement*; the second, *vertical job specialization* and *vertical job enlargement.*

HORIZONTAL JOB SPECIALIZATION

Job specialization in the horizontal dimension—the predominant form of division of labor—is an inherent part of every organization, indeed every human activity. For example, Filley et al. (1976, p. 337) note that work in the tenth-century English textile industry was divided into spinning, weaving, dying, and printing, while Udy (1959, p. 91) notes that on a seal hunt, the Gilyak eskimos divide their labor within the boat among harpooner, oarsman, and helmsman. In fact, the term "division of labor" dates back to 1776, when Adam Smith wrote *The Wealth of Nations*. There he presented his famous example which even by 1776 "the division of labor has been very often taken notice of, the trade of the pin maker":

> One man draws out the wire, another straights it, a third cuts it, a fourth points it, a fifth grinds it at the top for receiving the head; to make the head requires two or three distinct operations; to put it on is a peculiar business, to whiten the pins is another; it is even a trade by itself to put them into the paper; and the important business of making a pin is, in this manner, divided into about eighteen distinct operations, which, in some manufactories, are all performed by distinct hands, though in others the same man will sometimes perform two or three of them (Smith, 1910, p. 5).

Organizations so divide their labor—specialize their jobs—to increase productivity. Adam Smith noted that in one pin factory, 10 men specialized in their work were able to turn out about 12 pounds of pins in a day, about 4800 pins each. "But if they had all wrought separately and independently, and without any of them having been educated to this peculiar business, they certainly could not each of them have made twenty, perhaps not one pin in a day ..." (p. 5).

What are the reasons for such productivity increases? Smith notes three, the improved dexterity of the workman from specializing in one task, the saving in time lost in switching tasks, and the development of new methods and machines that come from specialization. All three reasons point to the key factor that links specialization to productivity: repetition. Horizontal specialization increases the repetition in the work, thereby facilitating its standardization. The outputs can be produced more uniformly and more efficiently. Horizontal specialization also focuses the attention of the worker, which facilitates learning. All individuals have limited cognition; in a world of technical and organization complexity, they can only deal effectively with comprehensible parts of the whole:

> By giving each [member] a particular task to accomplish, [the organization] directs and limits his attention to that task. The personnel officer concerns himself with recruitment, training, classification, and other personnel operations. He need not give particular concern to the accounting, purchasing, planning, or operative functions, which are equally vital to the accomplishment of the organization's task, because he knows they have been provided for elsewhere in the organization structure (Simon, 1957, p. 102).

Support for this argument comes from Charns et al. (1977) who found in a study of medical centers that doctors who performed concurrently the different roles of clinician, teacher, and researcher tended to confuse or "blurr" these tasks to the detriment of their performance.[1]

A final reason for specialization is that it allows the individual to be matched to the task. In Chapter 1 we noted that football teams put their slim players in the backfield, their squat players on the line. Likewise, Udy notes that the Gilyak eskimos put their best oarsmen toward the stern, their best shots in the bow. Even colonies of army ants find it appropriate to so divide their labor:

> ... the adult ants that differ in size and structure also exhibit contrasting patterns of behavior, with the result that there is a division of labor in the colony. Small workers ... spend most of their time in the nest feeding the larval broods; intermediate-sized workers constitute most of the population, going out on raids as well as doing other jobs. The largest workers ... have a huge head and long, powerful jaws. These individuals are what Verrill called soldiers; they carry no food but customarily run along the flanks of the raiding and emigration columns (Topoff, 1972, p. 72).

VERTICAL JOB SPECIALIZATION

Vertical job specialization separates the performance of the work from the administration of it. Litterer (1965) provides us with a useful way to describe this issue. Figure 4–1 shows his basic work control cycle, with the actual performance of an activity at the bottom left and the administration of it—the feedback and control system—above and to the right of it. In the vertically specialized job, the worker only performs the activity; as the job gets vertically enlarged, the worker gains more and more control over the activity—over the decisions involved and then over the goals and standards guiding these decisions.

Teaching offers a good example. Students who use workbooks or copy their lectures word for word have rather vertically specialized work—they simply carry out the activity. In contrast, when the students do projects, they assume control of much of the decision making in their work—their "jobs" become vertically enlarged and they shift from passive responders to active participants. In the case of the pie filler, discussed in Chapter 1, his job was highly specialized in the vertical (as well as the horizontal) dimen-

---

[1]Those doctors were, of course, specialized in terms of the medical knowledge they used (cardiovascular surgery, or whatever), if not in the roles they performed.

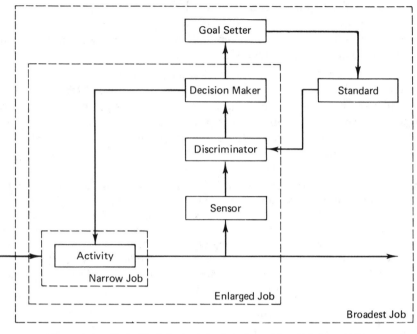

Figure 4-1. *Basic Work Control Cycle (adapted from Litterer, 1965, p. 237 ff)*

sion. Alternatively, were he told to bake a pie to sell for $1.50, he would have had responsibility for sensing, discriminating, and decision making, as well as part of the actual making of the pie, while if he owned the bakery, he would also have been able to decide on the price himself and whether he should have made pies at all, as opposed to, say, bread or bicycles.

Organizations specialize jobs in the vertical dimension in the belief that a different perspective is required to determine how the work should be done. In particular, when a job is highly specialized in the horizontal dimension, the worker's perspective is narrowed, making it difficult for him to relate his work to that of others. So control of the work is often passed to a manager with the overview necessary to coordinate the work by direct supervision or to an analyst who can do so by standardization. Thus, **jobs must often be specialized vertically because they are specialized horizontally.** That is, the very fact of having to perform a narrow task reduces the perspective of the worker and so robs him of control of it. Hence, we would expect to find a strong positive relationship between horizontal and vertical specialization: many jobs (although not all, as we shall soon see) tend to be either both or neither.

JOB ENLARGEMENT

Job specialization is hardly a panacea for the problems of position design; quite the contrary, **job specialization creates a number of its own problems, notably of communication and coordination.** Consider a simple example, the way in which orders are taken in French and American restaurants. In this respect, the work in many French restaurants is more specialized: the maitre d'hotel takes the order and writes it on a slip of paper and the waiter serves it. In the American restaurant, the waiter generally does both tasks. Thus, if the customer in the French restaurant has a special request, for example to have his coffee with his dessert instead of after it as is the norm in France, a communication problem arises. The maitre d'hotel must go to the trouble of telling the waiter or making a note on the slip of paper. (In fact, it is unlikely that he will do either and it is left to the customer to try, often in vain, to get his message across to the waiter directly.) In effect, specialization creates problems of coordination. (It is probably not coincidental that French diners seem generally more disciplined, Americans more fussy.) In more complex work, such as medicine, specialization has also been a mixed blessing. The great advances—for example, open-heart surgery, control of tuberculosis, transplants of various kinds—have been brought about by specialization in research and clinical work, but so too has specialization placed all kinds of artificial barriers across the practice of medicine. Few doctors treat the body as an integrated system; rather they treat clogged arteries, or emotional stress, or unhealthy diets.

High task specialization in the horizontal dimension also creates balancing problems for the organization. If a barbershop designates one man to cut only children's hair, it may face a situation where adult customers are forced to wait while a children's barber stands idle. Clearly, size is an important factor here: a high volume of work facilitates high horizontal specialization. Only the large barbershops can afford children's specialists.

Another serious problem, especially in the operating core, is what high specialization in both dimensions can do to the worker—to his feelings about his work and his motivation to do it well. With the rise of Taylor's Scientific Management movement after World War I, American industry (and, for that matter, Russian industry, too) became virtually obsessed with job specialization. "One has the feeling of division of labor having gone wild, far beyond any degree necessary for efficient production," wrote James Worthy, an executive of Sears, Roebuck, in 1950 (p. 174). For example, in the mid 1950s Davis et al. (1955) interviewed industrial engineers from seven manufacturing firms about what factors they normally took into account in assigning tasks to workers and in combining tasks to make specific jobs. Engineers from all the firms surveyed considered the following important.

1. Break the job into the smallest components possible to reduce skill requirements.
2. Make the content of the job as repetitive as possible.
3. Minimize internal transportation and handling time.
4. Provide suitable working conditions.
5. Obtain greater specialization.
6. Stabilize production and reduce job shifts to a minimum.
7. Have engineering departments, whenever possible, take an active part in assigning tasks and jobs (p. 6).

In a later book, *Big Business and Free Men*, Worthy (1959) traces the historical development of this mentality. He goes back to the rise of the factory, where he notes that specialization resulted in part from the scarcity of labor. "This scarcity encouraged the breaking down of complex skills into their simpler elements so that they could be learned more quickly by the inexperienced and unskilled workers industry found it necessary to employ" (this and all subsequent Worthy quotes from pp. 64–71). But this narrow specialization led to "crucial" problems of coordination and control, which gave rise to "management, as we know it today." Worthy gives credit to Taylor (1856–1915) as "one of the earliest and most creative of those concerned with thinking through these problems of organization and control." Taylor's work—involving everything from standardizing raw materials to minutely programming work processes, in effect, the planning of the production process in detail from beginning to end—"went a long way toward bringing production out of the confusion in which he found it, and in doing so laid the foundations for a phenomenal increase in the productivity of American industry."

But all was not well in the factory that emerged. Taylor's exhortations to specialize vertically—"All possible brain work should be removed from the shop floor and centered in the planning and laying out department"— led to the most machinelike of jobs, as engineers sought to "minimize the characteristics of workers that most significantly differentiate them from machines." Taylor himself "frequently referred to [the workers] as children and often used schoolroom analogies."

All of this, Worthy argues, "has been fantastically wasteful for industry and society," failing to make proper use of "management's most valuable resource: the complex and multiple capacities of people." Because "the meaning of work itself" was destroyed, people could only be treated as means; they could no longer exercise initiative. In place of intrinsic motivation, workers had "to be enticed by rewards and threatened by punishments."

Charlie Chaplin popularized the plight of these human robots in his pre-World War II film, *Modern Times*. But the problem has persisted to the present day. Here is how a felter in a luggage factory describes her job:

> In forty seconds you have to take the wet felt out of the felter, put the blanket on—a rubber sheeting—to draw out the excess moisture, wait two, three seconds, take the blanket off, pick the wet felt up, balance it on your shoulder —there is no way of holding it without it tearing all to pieces, it is wet and will collapse—reach over, get the hose, spray the inside of this copper screen to keep it from plugging, turn around, walk to the hot dry die behind you, take the hot piece off with your opposite hand, set it on the floor—this wet thing is still balanced on my shoulder—put the wet piece on the dry die, push this button that lets the dry press down, inspect the piece we just took off, the hot piece, stack it, and count it—when you get a stack of ten, you push it over and start another stack of ten—then go back and put our blanket on the wet piece coming up from the tank...and start all over. Forty seconds. (Quoted in Terkel, 1972, pp. 289–290).

Only recently, with increasing worker alienation posing a major threat to productivity itself, has there been a real thrust to change this situation. This has proceeded under the terms "job enlargement," for horizontal enlargement, and "job enrichment," for vertical coupled with horizontal enlargement (Herzberg, 1968);[2] more recently, all of this has been subsumed under the broader title "Quality of Working Life," now sufficiently in vogue to merit the acronym QWL. Here, for simplicity's sake and to contrast with job specialization, we shall stick with the term "job enlargement," whether horizontal or vertical.

In horizontal job enlargement, the worker engages in a wide variety of the tasks associated with producing products and services. He may either do more tasks in sequence, or he may do them one at a time, as before, but interchange tasks with his colleagues periodically so that his work becomes more varied. For example, in the assembly of the parts of a small motor, the assembly line may be eliminated and each worker may assemble the whole motor himself, or the workers may interchange positions on the assembly line periodically.

When a job is enlarged vertically, or "enriched," not only does the worker carry out more tasks, but he also gains more control over them. For example, a group of workers may be given responsibility for the assembly of the motor, a natural unit of work, including the power to decide how the

[2]In these types of jobs, it is unlikely that vertical job enlargement could proceed without some horizontal job enlargement.

work will be shared and carried out. In the Saab Motor Car Engine Assembly in Sweden:

> Seven assembly groups of four workers are arranged alongside an automatic conveyor. Apart from some pre-assembly work, finished engines are completely assembled in each group, the total work content of this final assembly being 30 minutes. Each group may choose to divide the work between them, each working on average for 7½ minutes on each engine, or each member may assemble a complete engine (Wild, 1976, p. 36).

Does job enlargement pay? The proponents say yes, and back up their conclusion with enthusiastic anecdotal reports. For example, returning to Worthy (1959):

> In [a California hospital for retarded children] half the patients were kept strapped to their cribs to keep them from hurting themselves. Older patients who were able to do simple chores aided in the care of the more helpless. Their work was organized on an assembly-line basis; some did nothing but scrub floors, others nothing but change diapers, others nothing but feeding. A new psychiatric technician, placed in charge of a cottage housing a hundred youngsters, changed all this. She unchained the children, she abolished the assembly line, and she put each helper in charge of three children with responsibility for doing all that was necessary for their care. "That's the way it's done in families," she said. "You don't have one person just washing diapers, another feed-the baby."
>
> This change in organization altered the entire atmosphere of the cottage and the people in it. The helpers began to take more interest in their jobs and in their charges. A sense of pride and of personal responsibility developed. And the younger, more helpless patients responded also, not only to the greater freedom they were allowed but to the warmer, more sympathetic, more human relationships that grew between themselves and the older helpers to whose care they were committed (pp. 86-87).

But more detached observers report failures as well as successes, and a series of recent reviews of the research studies suggest that while the successes probably predominate, the overall results of job enlargement are mixed (Pierce and Dunham, 1976; Dessler, 1976, pp. 79-84; Filley et al., 1976. pp. 343-357; Melcher, 1976, pp.72-83).

There seems, however, to be two clear problems with much of this research. First, the results of job enlargement clearly depend on the job in question. To take two extreme examples, the enlargement of the job of a secretary who must type the same letter all day every day cannot help but improve things; in contrast, to enlarge the job of the general practitioner (one wonders how ... perhaps by including nursing or pharmacological tasks) could only frustrate the doctor and harm the patient. In other words, jobs can be too large as well as too narrow. So the success of any job redesign clearly depends on the particular job in question and how specialized it is in the first place. The natural tendency has, of course, been to select for redesign the narrowest, most monotonous of jobs, some specialized to almost pathological degrees, of which there has been no shortage in this industrialized world left to us by the followers of Frederick Taylor. Hence, we should not be surprised to find more successes than failures reported in this research. That, however, should not lead to the conclusion that job enlargement is good per se.

Second is the question of trade-offs inherent in any attempt to redesign a job. What the writings of people like Worthy have done is to introduce the human factor into the performance equation, alongside the purely technical concerns of the time-and-motion study analysts. That has changed the equation: **job enlargement pays to the extent that the gains from better motivated workers in a particular job offset the losses from less than optimal technical specialization.** (Sometimes the two factors affect different performance measures. Dessler [1976, pp. 80–81] cites the case of one job redesign that resulted in lower productivity but higher quality.)

So to find out if job enlargement pays, we would first have to find out *for each particular job* where it stands in terms of technical efficiency and worker motivation, and then ascertain the trade-off of these two factors in the proposed modification. And that means an intensive probe into a single job, something that happens only rarely in the published research. Samples of one do not produce the correlation coefficients that many academic journals demand.[3] And so doubts can be raised about many of the published studies. Surveys of before and after performance measures tell us little in the absence of details on the jobs and workers in question and the changes made. Thus, like job specialization, job enlargement is hardly a panacea for the problems of position design; it is one design parameter among many, to be considered alongside the others, including job specialization, its obverse.

So far the question of whether job enlargement pays has been addressed solely from the point of view of the organization. But the worker counts, too, as a human being who often deserves something better than a monotonous job. But here the research literature throws a curve, with its evidence that **some workers prefer narrowly specialized, repetitive jobs.** For example, "Turner and Miclette interviewed 115 assembly-line operators over a two-year period. They found fewer than 20 percent who felt that their work was monotonous or boring ..." (Dessler, 1976, p. 83). Nowhere is this point made clearer than in Stud Terkel's fascinating book, *Working* (1972), in which all kinds of workers talk candidly about the work they do and their feelings about it. A clear message comes through: "One man's meat is

[3]Notable exceptions, discussed in Chapter 3, are Trist and Bamforth's (1951) study of work in British coal mines and Rice's (1953) study of work in an Indian textile mill.

another man's poison." Occasionally, Terkel juxtaposes the comments of two workers in the same job, one who relishes it and the other who detests it. Illustrative citations from Terkel's book will be used throughout this one.

Why should the same routine job motivate one individual and alienate another? The research suggests a number of reasons. Older workers and workers with more seniority show more tolerance for routine jobs (Dessler, 1976, p. 83; Pierce and Dunham, 1976, pp. 85, 91), presumably because as people age, they increasingly appreciate habit in their lives. All the reviewers cite the argument of Hulin and Blood (1968) that workers in large urban centers are more accepting of such work, or at least are less accepting of job enlargement. The explanation offered is that blue-collar workers raised in cities tend more than others to reject the Protestant work ethic—to feel less conscientious about their work and so prefer to remain as detached from it as possible. Monotonous jobs serve such needs splendidly!

But perhaps it is personality that best explains the differences between workers, notably a dimension that psychologists call "tolerance for ambiguity." Dessler (1976) cites evidence suggesting that "ambiguity is frequently associated with stress, tension, and dissatisfaction and that persons differ markedly in their tolerance for such ambiguity"; some personalities are simply "characterized by very high needs for structure and clarity" (p. 84). This can be put into the context of Abraham Maslow's (1954) "Needs Hierarchy Theory," which orders human needs into a hierarchy of five groups— physiological, safety or security, love and belongingness, esteem or status, and self-actualization (to create, to fulfill oneself). The theory postulates that one group of needs only becomes fully operative when the next lowest group is largely satisfied. In job design, the argument goes, people functioning at the lower end of the Maslow scale, most concerned with security needs and the like, prefer the specialized jobs, while those at the upper end, notably at the level of self-actualization, respond more favorably to enlarged jobs (Pierce and Dunham, 1976, p. 90). And this helps to explain why QWL has recently become such a big issue: with growing affluence and rising educational levels, the citizens of the more industrialized societies have been climbing up Maslow's hierarchy. Their growing need for self-actualization can only be met in enlarged jobs. The equation continues to change.

JOB SPECIALIZATION BY PART OF THE ORGANIZATION

We would expect to find some relationships between the specialization of jobs and their location in the organization. Productivity is more important in the operating core, where the basic products and services get produced; also, this is where the work is most repetitive. Hence, we would expect to find the most specialized jobs there, especially in the horizontal dimension. Operators generally carry out rather well-defined tasks in the operating work flow. We would, however, expect more variation in vertical specialization in the operating core. Many operators—such as those on assembly lines—perform the narrowest of jobs in both breadth and depth. These are the *unskilled* workers, on whom the job-enlargement programs have been concentrated. But other operators, because their specialized tasks are more complex, retain considerable control over them. In other words, their jobs are specialized horizontally but not vertically. Performing open-heart surgery, putting out fires in oil wells, or teaching retarded children all require considerable specialization, to master the skills and knowledge of the jobs. But the jobs are complex, requiring years of training, and that complexity precludes close managerial and technocratic control, thereby precluding vertical specialization.

Complex jobs, specialized horizontally but not vertically, are generally referred to as professional. And job enlargement is not an issue in these jobs, at least not from the perspective of the worker. Professionals seldom complain about monotony, since the complexity of the work and the satisfaction of applying accomplished skills keeps them motivated. Likewise, alienation is not a major issue, since it is the professionals who normally control their own work. Society tends to look very favorably on this kind of specialization; indeed, unskilled operators frequently try to have their jobs labeled "professional" to increase their status and reduce the controls imposed on them by the administrators.

Many of the same conclusions can be drawn for the staff units, both support and technocratic. Each support staff unit has a specialized function to perform—producing food in the plant cafeteria, fighting legal battles in the corporate legal office, and so on—with the result that support staff jobs tend to be highly specialized in the horizontal dimension. How specialized they are in the vertical dimension depends, as it does for the operator's jobs, on how complex or professional they are. In general, we would expect the support staffers of the lower echelons, such as those in the cafeterias, to have narrow, unskilled jobs subject to close control, while those at the high levels, such as in the legal office, would have more professional jobs, specialized horizontally but not vertically. As for the analysts of the technostructure, they are professionals, in that their work requires considerable knowledge and skill. Hence, we would also expect their jobs to be specialized horizontally but not vertically. However, the technocratic clerks—those who apply the systems routinely—would tend to be less skilled and therefore have jobs specialized in both dimensions.

Managers at all levels appear to perform a basic set of interpersonal, informational, and decisional roles; in that sense their work is specialized horizontally. But in a more fundamental sense, no true managerial job is specialized in the horizontal dimension. These roles managers perform are so varied, and so much switching is required among them in the course of any given day, that **managerial jobs are typically the least specialized in the organization.** Managers do not complain about repetition or boredom in their work, but rather about the lack of opportunity to concentrate on specific issues. This seems to be as true for foremen as it is for presidents.

There are, however, differences in vertical specialization in managerial jobs, according to level in the hierarchy. Managers near the bottom—notably first-line supervisors—are often subject to tight controls, both from the weight of the chain of authority above them and from the standards imposed on their units by the technostructure. These controls diminish as one climbs the hierarchy, until the strategic apex is reached: there, we find the least specialized jobs in the organization. The chief executive officer appears to perform the same broad set of roles as the other managers of the organization, but he applies them to the widest variety of problems. Attempts have, in fact, been made to specialize horizontally the work within the chief executive office, for example, by having one individual focus on external problems and another on internal matters, or by dividing responsibility for line and staff departments. But there is no conclusive evidence that such specialization is really more effective in the long run, and most organizations seem to keep the job of chief executive in tact, that is, enlarged. And, of course, the job of top manager is generally the least controlled—that is, the least vertically specialized—in the whole organization.[4]

To conclude our discussion, Table 4-1 shows the jobs of the different members of the organization categorized in a matrix of horizontal and vertical specialization. Highly specialized in both dimensions are the unskilled jobs in the operating core and staff units, while the professional jobs in both parts are specialized horizontally but not vertically. Managerial jobs are shown as not specialized in the horizontal dimension, but differing in the vertical dimension, according to their level in the hierarchy.

TABLE 4-1.   Job Specialization by Part of the Organization

		Horizontal Specialization	
		High	Low
Vertical Specialization	High	Unskilled Jobs (operating core and staff units)	Certain Lowest-Level Managerial Jobs
	Low	Professional Jobs (operating core and staff units)	All Other Managerial Jobs

[4]See Mintzberg (1973a) for further discussion and evidence of the points made in the last two paragraphs, specifically on the common roles managers perform, the daily work patterns for managers at all levels, and job sharing at the chief executive level.

5

Design of Positions: Behavior Formalization

In a paper entitled "A Convergence in Organization Theory," D.J. Hickson (1966–67) makes the interesting point that organizational theorists have been preoccupied with one parameter of organizational structure, which he labels "role specificity."[1] Hickson presents a table that lists various theorists in management who have focused on this parameter under one label or another. The table reads like a veritable who's who of writers in management—Taylor, Fayol, McGregor, Argyris, Simon, Whyte, Crozier, Thompson, and so on. At one point, by way of illustrating the diversity of their labels, Hickson refers to structure at one end of this dimension as "bureaucratic–mechanistic–closed–formalized–routinized–specific–dominant–well-defined–programmed–perceptually structured–habit–'scientific'–authoritative–rational" (p. 235). Here we shall refer to this design parameter simply as *formalization of behavior*, noting that it represents the organization's way of *pro*scribing discretion. Formalization of behavior is the design parameter by which the work processes of the organization are standardized. Behavior may be formalized in three ways, as follows:

1. *Formalization by job* In this case, the organization attaches the behavioral specifications to the job itself, typically documenting it in the formal job description. The incumbent may be told what steps

[1] More exactly, "the degree of specificity of the role prescription" and its opposite, "the range of legitimate discretion."

to take in his work, in what sequence, when, and where. March and Simon (1958) provide an example:

> 1. When material is drawn from stock, note whether the quantity that remains equals or exceeds the buffer stock. If not:
> 2. Determine from the sales forecast provided by the sales department the sales expected in the next k months.
> 3. Insert this quantity in the "order quantity formula," and write a purchase order for the quantity thus determined (p. 147).

2. *Formalization by work flow*   Instead of linking the specifications to the job, the organization can instead attach them to the work itself. Printing press operators receive dockets with instructions for each order, and orchestra musicians work from scores that specify each of their roles in a given symphony.

3. *Formalization by rules*   Finally, rather than formalizing behavior by job or work flow, the organization may instead institute rules for all situations—all jobs, all work flows, all workers. These may specify who can or cannot do what, when, where, to whom, and with whose permission. "Members of this advertising agency are expected to report for work in jacket and tie." "Grievances are to be reported to the industrial relations department on Form 94XZ, typed, single-spaced." "Expenditures of over \$1000 must be approved by the area manager." Such rules can cover a great variety of organizational behavior, from salaries paid to thicknesses of carpets. They are generally issued in written form and may be collected into a "policy manual," the bible of the formal organization.

No matter what the means of formalization—by job, work flow, or rules—the effect on the person doing the work is the same: his behavior is regulated. Power over how that work is to be done passes from him to that person who designs the specifications, often an analyst in the technostructure. Thus, formalization of behavior leads to vertical specialization of the job. Also, it stands to reason that formalization is closely related to horizontal specialization: the narrowest of the unskilled jobs are the simplest, the most repetitive, and the ones most amenable to high degrees of formalization. Bjork (1975) shows this link clearly in discussing the three principal "woes of mass production:"

> The principles are job simplification, repetition and close control. The worker is viewed as one more interchangeable part, programmed to perform a small task that is precisely specified on the basis of time and motion studies. He is assumed to be a passive element in the production process. ... In order to

energize and coordinate some dozens or hundreds of atomized human "parts" in a plant, a rigorous and highly detailed control system is called into play . . . (p. 17).

WHY BEHAVIOR IS FORMALIZED

As Björk suggests, **organizations formalize behavior to reduce its variability, ultimately to predict and control it.** One prime motive for doing so is to coordinate activities. As noted earlier, standardization of work content is a very tight coordinating mechanism. Its corresponding design parameter, behavior formalization, is used therefore when tasks require precise, carefully predetermined coordination. Firemen cannot stop each time they arrive at a new fire to figure out who will attach the hose to the hydrant and who will go up the ladder; similarly, airline pilots must be very sure about their landing procedures well in advance of descent.

The fully formalized organization, as far as possible, is the precise organization. There can be no confusion. Everyone knows exactly what to do in every event. Some organizations, in fact, come rather close to this kind of reliability: the Swiss train pulls out of the station as the second hand sweeps past its scheduled time of departure, and the post office delivers millions of pieces of mail each day with virtually no losses. These are the organizations that satisfy James Thompson's description to a tee—their operating cores have been almost perfectly sealed off: they operate under conditions as close to certainty as man can get.

Formalization of behavior is also used to ensure the machinelike consistency that leads to efficient production, as in the automobile factory Björk describes. Tasks are specialized in the horizontal dimension to achieve repetition; formalization is then used to impose the most efficient procedures on them.

Formalization is also used to ensure fairness to clients. The national tax office must treat everyone equally; that is why Patterson found so much formalization in it. Government organizations are particularly sensitive to accusations of favoritism; hence, they tend to proliferate rules and specifications. Some of these rules are instituted to protect the clients, others the employees. For example, promotion by seniority is used to preclude arbitrary decisions by managers (Crozier, 1964).

Organizations formalize behavior for other reasons as well, of more questionable validity. Formalization may reflect an arbitrary desire for order. For example, some tennis courts require all players to wear white. Yet it is difficult to understand what difference it would make if some appeared in mauve. The highly formalized structure is above all the neat one; it warms the hearts of people who like to see things orderly—everyone in his proper box on the organigram, all work processes predetermined, all contingencies accounted for, everyone in white.

BUREAUCRATIC AND ORGANIC FORMS OF STRUCTURE

Organizations that rely primarily on the formalization of behavior to achieve coordination are generally referred to as *bureaucracies*. It is appropriate at this point to take a close look at this important concept since it lies at the very heart of a great deal of discussion about organizational structure.

The word "bureaucracy" had an innocent-enough beginning—it derived from the French word "bureau," meaning desk or office. But since Max Weber, the great German sociologist, used it at the turn of the century to describe a particular type of organizational structure, it has had a rather tumultuous existence. Weber intended the term as a purely technical one, and it retains that sense today in the literature of organizational theory and sociology. But elsewhere, the word has taken on a decidedly pejorative meaning:

> "Bureaucracy" is a dirty word ... It suggests rigid rules and regulations ... impersonality, resistance to change. Yet every organization of any significant size is bureaucratized to some degree or, to put it differently, exhibits more or less stable patterns of behavior based upon a structure of roles and specialized tasks (Perrow, 1970, p. 50).

At this point the reader is asked to put aside the pejorative meaning and accept the word in its technical sense; that is how it will be used in this book.

Weber described bureaucracy as an "ideal type" of structure, "ideal" meaning not perfect but pure. He delineated the characteristics of this pure structural type as follows:

> I. There is the principle of fixed and official jurisdictional areas, which are generally ordered by rules, that is, by laws or administrative regulations.
> 1. The regular activities required for the purposes of the bureaucratically governed structure are distributed in a fixed way as official duties.
> 2. The authority to give the commands required for the discharge of these duties is distributed in a stable way and is strictly delimited by rules concerning the coercive means, physical, sacerdotal, or otherwise which may be placed at the disposal of officials.
> 3. Methodical provision is made for the regular and continuous fulfillment of these duties and for the execution of the corresponding rights;

only persons who have the generally regulated qualifications to serve
are employed.

II. The principles of office hierarchy and of levels of graded authority mean a
firmly ordered system of super- and subordinate in which there is a supervision
of the lower offices by the higher ones.

III. The management of the modern office is based upon written documents
("the files"), which are preserved in their original or draught form.

IV. Office management, at least all specialized office management—and such
management is distinctly modern—usually presupposes thorough and expert
training.

V. The management of the office follows general rules, which are more or
less stable, more or less exhaustive, and which can be learned. Knowledge of
these rules represents a special technical learning which the officials possess. It
involves jurisprudence, or administrative or business management (Gerth and
Mills, 1958, pp. 196–198).

Weber's description brings together a number of the concepts we have
already discussed—division of labor, specialization, formalization of behavior, hierarchy of authority, chain of command, regulated communication, and standardization of work processes and of skills. But how well do
all these defining characteristics hold together in real organizations? In
other words, does Weber's "ideal type" really exist or are there, in fact,
different types of bureaucratic structures, each exhibiting some but not all
of these characteristics?

It was only in the 1960s that this question began to be studied. The
initial work was carried out by Derek Pugh and his colleagues in a series of
studies at the University of Aston in England (Pugh et al., 1963, 1968, 1969a,
b;Inkson et al., 1970, Child, 1972b). In the main study, Pugh et al. (1963–
64) measured a variety of dimensions of forty-six organizations in the Birmingham area, "a random sample stratified by size and product or purpose"
including "firms making motor cars and chocolate bars, municipal departments repairing roads and teaching arithmetic, large retail stores, small
insurance companies, and so on" (p. 67). Three of their dimensions related
closely to those of Weber:

- *Specialization* was "concerned with the division of labor within the
  organization, the distribution of official duties among a number of
  positions" (pp. 72–73).

- *Standardization* related to the existence of procedures, events that
  occurred regularly and were legitimized by the organizations.

- *Formalization* was defined (more narrowly than in this chapter) as
  "the extent to which rules, procedures, instructions, and communications [were] written" (p. 75).

Pugh et al. found significant correlations between certain measures of these three dimensions, thus supporting Weber's description, in part at least. Role specification and overall standardization correlated at 0.80, role specialization and overall formalization at 0.68, and overall standardization and overall formalization at 0.83. Pugh et al. were, therefore, able to compress the three dimensions into a single factor, virtually identical to what we have here called formalization of behavior, which they called "structuring of activities":

> An organization that scores high on specialization, standardization, and formalization . . . would have gone a long way in the regulation of the work of its employees. . . . The intended behavior of employees has been structured by the specification of their specialized roles, the procedures they are to follow in carrying out those roles, and the documentation of what they have to do (p. 84).

These findings held up in replications of the original Aston study (Inkson et al., 1970, Child, 1972b). However, Pugh et al. also measured the extent to which authority over decision making was concentrated (that is, centralized), and here they found much smaller (and negative) correlations with the other dimensions. This led Pugh et al. (1969a) to conclude that there may, in fact, exist different bureaucratic structures, in effect, one where decisional power is centralized and another where it is not.[2] In any event, for our purposes at this point **we can define a structure as bureaucratic—centralized or not—to the extent that its behavior is predetermined or predictable, in effect, standardized.** This seems to be the main thread running through Weber's description.

We have so far talked only about bureaucratic structures. But if some organizations come out high on the Aston "structuring of activities" measure, obviously others must come out low, their patterns of behavior being neither highly specialized nor highly formalized. There exists, in other words, the inverse of the bureaucratic structure. In their study, Burns and Stalker (1966) found that bureaucratic-type structures worked well for organizations operating in stable circumstances but that others requiring innovation or adaptation to changing environments needed a very different

---

[2]Actually, centralization per se does not appear on Weber's five-point list. In fact, a debate has raged in the literature over whether these two kinds of bureaucracies do exist and, indeed, whether Weber meant to describe bureaucracies as centralized or decentralized in the first place. In his replication, with a more homogeneous sample of organizations, Child (1972b) also found a negative relationship, but a more pronounced one, between structuring of activities and centralization, leading him to conclude that the notion of one ideal type of bureaucracy is indeed viable, and that it is decentralized. We shall return to this debate in our discussion of the decentralization design parameters.

type of structure. This they labeled *organic,* and they identified it by the following characteristics:

(a) the contributive nature of special knowledge and experience to the common task of the concern;

(b) the "realistic" nature of the individual task, which is seen as set by the total situation of the concern;

(c) the adjustment and continual re-definition of individual tasks through interaction with others;

(d) the shedding of "responsibility" as a limited field of rights, obligations and methods. (Problems may not be posed upwards, downwards or sideways, as being someone else's responsbility);

(e) the spread of commitment to the concern beyond any technical definition;

(f) a network structure of control, authority, and communication. The sanctions which apply to the individual's conduct in his working role derive more from presumed community of interest with the rest of the working organization in the survival and growth of the firm, and less from a contractual relationship between himself and a non-personal corporation, represented for him by an immediate superior;

(g) omniscience no longer imputed to the head of the concern; knowledge about the technical or commercial nature of the here and now task may be located anywhere in the network; this location becoming the ad hoc centre of control authority and communication;

(h) a lateral rather than a vertical direction of communication through the organization, communication between people of different rank, also, resembling consultation rather than command;

(i) a content of communication which consists of information and advice rather than instructions and decisions;

(j) commitment to the concern's tasks and to the "technological ethos" of material progress and expansion is more highly valued than loyalty and obedience;

(k) importance and prestige attach to affiliations and expertise valid in the industrial and technical and commercial milieux external to the firm (pp. 121– 122).

In almost every dimension, this is the opposite of Weber's bureaucracy: organic structure is characterized above all by loose, informal working relationships—things are worked out as needs arise. In effect, whereas bureaucratic structure emphasizes standardization, organic structure as described by Burns and Stalker is built on mutual adjustment. However, **we shall here define organic structure by the absence of standardization in the organization** (allowing us later in the book to describe two types, one based on mutual adjustment, the other on direct supervision). In effect, we put bureaucratic and organic structure at two ends of the continuum of standardization.

Many other researchers have noted evidence of the organic type. For example, in her study of industrial firms in a region of England, Joan Woodward (1965, p. 24) found twice as many organic structures as bureaucratic ones. She noted that some of these were consciously intended to be organic; others simply turned out that way despite attempts to formalize them. And Wilensky (1967) drew attention to certain organizations that actually encouraged sloppy reporting relationships and competition among units in order to foster initiative. This was, for example, the approach of President Franklin D. Roosevelt, who devised an administrative structure for his welfare programs "that would baffle any conventional student of public administration. ... By any reasonable standard [it] was sloppy; by the same standard, it worked" (p. 53).

SOME DYSFUNCTIONS OF HIGHLY FORMALIZED STRUCTURES

Perhaps no topic in organizational theory has generated more heat than the consequences of extensive formalization of behavior in organizations. Early in this century, before the Hawthorne studies of the 1930s, industrial psychologists were concerned primarily with the physiological fatigue caused by monotonous work. This was, in fact, the original focus of the Hawthorne studies themselves. But there it became apparent that fatigue was only the tip of the iceberg, that such work—highly repetitive, formalized, and specialized horizontally and vertically—created psychological as well as physiological problems for many workers. Subsequently, a number of what have become the most well-known names in management—Argyris, Bennis, Likert, McGregor—built their careers on the analysis of the psychological dysfunctions of highly formalized structures. They point out man's inherent propensity to resist formalization and impersonalization, and they show the organizational "pathologies" that result from excesses in this direction. Each in one way or another describes a vicious circle in which rules are applied, workers resist, dysfunctional consequences arise, further rules are applied to control the resistance, the workers thereby lose more discretion in their work, they resist further, and so on. Figure 5-1 shows one well-known model of this vicious circle, that of R. K. Merton (as depicted by March and Simon, 1958[3]). These dysfunctional consequences take various forms: the ossification of behavior, with the automatic rejection of all innovative ideas, the mistreatment of clients, increases of absenteeism, turnover, strikes, and even the actual subversion of the operations of the organization.

[3]See Chapter 3 of their book for other models by Selznick and Gouldner.

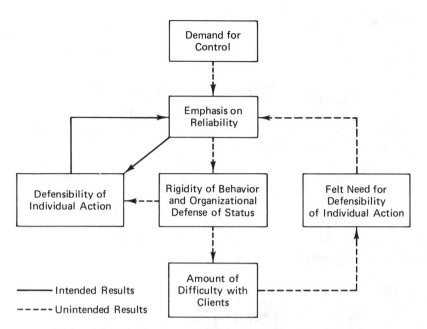

Figure 5-1. *The Consequences of Excessive Formalization of Behavior: "The Simplified Merton Model" (as presented by March and Simon, 1958, p. 41)*

Crozier's Study of Two French Government Bureaucracies In his book, *The Bureaucratic Phenomenon,* Michel Crozier (1964) describes many of the vicious circles of highly formalized structures, but he also casts doubt on some of the standard truths in this area. His important study merits a detailed review at this point.

Crozier studied two French government bureaucracies in depth, a clerical agency and a manufacturing monopoly (in the tobacco industry) with thirty plants throughout France. Both were very highly formalized and regulated at all levels:

> Impersonal rules delimit, in great detail, all the functions of every individual within the organization. They prescribe the behavior to be followed in all possible events. Equally impersonal rules determine who shall be chosen for each job and the career patterns that can be followed. ... The first rule is that open competitive examinations (*concours*) govern promotion from one main category to another. The second rule is that seniority determines job allocation, transfer, and promotions within each main category. ... nothing seems to be left of the arbitrary whim and individual initiative of an organization member (pp. 187–188).

Crozier discusses four basic points leading to a series of vicious circles. First, curiously enough, the reliance on rules serves to destroy the relationship of dependence between superior and subordinate. In effect, the rules delimit the power of both, including the power of the superior to issue arbitrary orders; he, too, becomes an applier of impersonal standards:

> Every member of the organization, therefore, is protected both from his superiors and from his subordinates. He is, on the one hand, totally deprived of initiative and completely controlled by rules imposed on him from the outside. On the other hand, he is completely free from personal interference by any other individual (p. 189).

In this first point Crozier describes a kind of "perverse democracy" (the term is ours, not Crozier's), where everyone is treated more or less equally because everyone is controlled by the same overwhelming set of rules. The workers in need of a special kind of security—protection from the whims of the boss—accept, even embrace, the rules, but at the price of doing exceedingly formalized work:

> They complain bitterly about the price they have to pay for it, but they are, in the last analysis, ready to pay that price. They adjust to it in a grumbling way but, one way or another, they adjust.
>
> As one very critical and skeptical girl states it: "I would not take another job and when I was younger I would not have done so either. I could not bear being at the boss's mercy" (p. 55).

The second point is that in order to preserve the climate of impersonality in the operating core, those decisions not covered by the rules (including the decisions to make the rules) tend to be made elsewhere, in effect, at central headquarters. Impersonality is thereby maintained, but at the price of separating the *power* for making decisions from the *knowledge* needed to make them:

> ... decisions must be made by people who have no direct knowledge of the field and of the relevant variables, and who must rely on the information given them by subordinates who may have a subjective interest in distorting the data. In this sense, one can state that the power of decision in this system tends to be located in a blind spot. Those who have the necessary information do not have the power to decide, and those who have the power to decide cannot get the necessary information (p. 51).

Third, communication rigidities develop, as a result of peer-group pressures within what Crozier calls "strata," or hierarchical levels. These minimize the interactions across strata:

> Deviant impulses will be severely sanctioned, and the discipline imposed by the peer group will be one of the main forces, apart from the rules, which regulate behavior. ... supervisors may not interfere ... (p. 191).

The effect of such forces is to focus the group's attention on its own goals at the expense of the broader goals of the organization.

Fourth, rules and central authority cannot regulate everything; a few areas of uncertainty must remain, and it is around these that informal power relationships develop. In effect, those people expert at dealing with these areas of uncertainty achieve great influence. Crozier so describes the maintenance men in the factories. Only they were able to handle machine breakdowns, the one major uncertainty in the highly regulated plants. Thus, they emerged as a highly privileged group. Crozier notes that, "Paradoxically, the more narrowly the organization is regulated, the greater the independence of the experts" (p. 193).

A number of Crozier's findings will be of interest at various points in this book. One that merits comment here is that the workers—obsessed with security—readily accepted the extreme formalization of behavior as a means of protecting themselves. In other words, Crozier shows another side to the arguments about the dysfunctions of highly formalized structures: that the workers sometimes see the standards as being in their best interest. Related to the conclusion of Chapter 4, workers with strong needs for security and with low tolerance for ambiguity prefer jobs that are highly formalized as well as highly specialized. These people find their way into bureaucratic structures; those who desire more flexibility and can tolerate the ambiguity seek out organic structures.

BEHAVIOR FORMALIZATION BY PART OF THE ORGANIZATION

One key relationship should be evident by now: **the more stable and repetitive the work, the more programmed it is and the more bureaucratic that part of the organization that contains it.** Thus, there can be considerable differences in formalization of behavior and bureaucratization across the various parts of a single organization. While we can (and will) characterize certain organizations as bureaucratic or organic overall, none is uniformly so across its entire range of activities. Thus, Hall (1962) divided departments in ten diverse organizations into those that performed uniform, easily routinized tasks and those that performed nonuniform or social tasks. He found that structures for the former were generally more bureaucratic, with more rigid divisions of labor and hierarchy of authority and more procedural specifications. Van de Ven and Delbecq (1974) found highly formalized work (many pacing rules, detailed work steps and output specifications, built-in quality control monitoring devices) where the work in the organization was low in variability.

In the operating core, the part of the organization that the others seek to protect, we would generally expect to find the most stable conditions and the most repetitive tasks, leading to the most bureaucratic structure. This should not be taken to mean that the work of the operating core is always formalized or bureaucratized. Some organizations, such as creative research centers and small entrepreneurial firms, tend to be rather organically structured even in their operating cores. Nevertheless, relatively speaking, **behavior formalization is most common in the operating core of the organization.**

As we leave the operating core and climb the chain of authority, we would expect the work to become increasingly less repetitive and so less formalized. The middle-line manager closest to the operating core would tend to be most influenced by the conditions there, while those farthest away would operate in the most organic conditions. Thus, we have the Martin (1956) finding, cited earlier, that the decision processes of manufacturing managers at four successively higher levels of the hierarchy—shift foreman, department foreman, divisional superintendent, and works manager—were successively less structured.

Of course, there can be variations in formalization at a given level of the hierarchy, depending on the work in the unit supervised and the boundary conditions it faces. Thus Lawrence and Lorsch (1967) found that managerial jobs in production were more formalized than those in either sales or research, presumably because while the production function is concerned with stabilizing the operating core, the sales department must remain flexible to deal with the variability of customer demands and the research department must remain flexible in order to innovate. In other words, a low-level research manager may find himself in a considerably more organic structure than a higher-level manufacturing manager. As Perrow (1970) notes in discussing the Lawrence and Lorsch study:

> ... the production manager complained that those responsible for coordinating production and R and D constantly came to him about matters that should have been handled by people several layers above him in the production hierarchy. But the coordinators, in this case identified with the research department, were accustomed to direct contact and on-the-spot problem solving in their department, regardless of formal rank. They could not understand why the production manager insisted upon going through channels. He, on the other hand, could not understand how he could be expected to violate rules and procedures so casually. The problem was not a matter of personality or daring, but one of coordinating two quite different structures (p. 70).

At the strategic apex, which typically comes face to face with the most fluid boundary—the environment at large—the work is the least programmed and so we should expect to find highly organic conditions. This conclusion became apparent in over fifty studies of different organizations carried out by the McGill student groups. Time and again, the organigrams were put on the blackboard and the students proceeded to explain why they were not accurate at upper levels of the hierarchy. The charts specified formal authority, but they did not describe the communication patterns and power relationships that really existed there. These relationships were simply too fluid to formalize; the structure had to evolve naturally and to shift continually; in a word, it had to be organic. This conclusion is supported in the more systematic research of Hall (1962). Comparing the work of executives with other members of the organization, he concluded:

> The executive levels operate in a less bureaucratic fashion in terms of the emphasis on hierarchy, division of labor, procedures, and impersonality. Since the executive is responsible for the behavior of his subordinates, the functional areas of work which he manages cover a wider range than the range of work of his subordinates. Similarly, since the executive is closer to the top of the hierarchy, such restrictions on decision making and rights to proceed without additional authorization as face the subordinates are not restrictive for the executive (pp. 305–306).

What we have, in effect, is support for the view of the organization as a system of regulated flows. There is a gradual formalization of work as it is passed down the hierarchy:

> This conception [ill-defined tasks at top, well-defined at bottom] seems consonant with the way in which tasks flow into and through organizations. They often enter at the top in ill-defined, new forms. The top works them over, defines and operationalizes them, and then, if they are to become continuing tasks, passes them down the hierarchy, where they are again converted from their now partially operational states into highly defined states, and again passed down to specially created or adapted substructures. Presumably the top, in the interim, has turned its attention to other new, ill-defined issues (Klahr and Leavitt, 1967, p. 112).

In the support staff, we would expect to find a range of structures, according to the work done and the boundary conditions faced. Support units that face little uncertainty and do repetitive work, such as the plant cafeteria, would tend to be highly formalized. In contrast, as noted above, in a research laboratory, where the need for creativity is high, or a public relations department, where there are significant work variations from day to day, little of the work can be formalized and so we would expect the structure to remain relatively organic, at least if the units are to be effective. Harrison (1974), for example, found in a study of 95 scientists in research laboratories that "the more organic the system of management, the higher the perceived role performance of the individual scientist" (p. 234).

Similarly, in the technostructure, we would expect that those units closest to the operating core, such as production scheduling, would have many rules and rather formalized work procedures. Others with more variable work, such as operations research, would likely adopt relatively organic structures. (It should be noted here that whatever its *own* structure, it is the technostructure that takes primary responsibility for the formalization of everyone else's work in the organization.)

Finally, organizations with strong orientations toward either bureaucratic or organic structure sometimes set up independent work constellations with the opposite kinds of structure to do special tasks. For example, Hlavacek and Thompson (1973) describe the new product or "venture" teams in highly bureaucratic manufacturing firms, created as pockets of organic structure isolated from the rest of the organization administratively, financially, spatially, and sometimes even legally. In this way, they are able to innovate, free of the restraints of bureaucracy.

6

Design of Positions:
Training and Indoctrination

The third aspect of position design entails the specifications of the requirements for holding a position. In particular, the organization can specify what knowledge and skills the jobholder must have and what norms he must exhibit. It can then establish recruiting and selection procedures to screen applicants in terms of those position requirements; alternatively, it can establish its own programs to develop them in the candidates it hires. In either case, the intention is the same—to ensure that the jobholder internalizes the necessary behaviors before he begins his work. Furthermore, the organization may later reinforce these behaviors with a host of personnel devices—job rotation, attendance at conferences, organizational development programs, and so on. **Training refers to the process by which job-related skills and knowledge are taught, while indoctrination is the process by which organizational norms are acquired.** Both amount to the "internalization" of accepted (i.e., standardized) patterns of behavior in the workers.

TRAINING

When a body of knowledge and a set of work skills are highly rationalized, the organization factors them into simple, easily learned jobs—that is, unskilled ones—and then relies on the formalization of behavior to achieve coordination. An automobile is a complex machine, its assembly an involved procedure. But over the years that procedure has been reduced to thousands of simple tasks, so that today workers with minimal skills and knowledge can assemble automobiles. Training is, therefore, an insignificant design parameter in the automobile assembly plant—it takes place in the first few hours on many jobs.

However, where a job entails a body of knowledge and a set of skills that are both complex and nonrationalized, the worker must spend a great deal of time learning them. For some jobs, of course, these requirements are not recorded as formal knowledge, and so they must be learned on the job: the worker assumes the role of "apprentice" under a "master," who himself earlier learned the job in the same way. Such work is generally referred to as *craft*. But where a body of knowledge has been recorded and the required skills have—in part at least—been specified, the individual can be trained before he begins his work. This kind of work—complex and nonrationalized, yet in part recorded and specified—is referred to as *professional*. Thus, **training is a key design parameter in all work we call professional.**

The "specification" of knowledge and skill is, of course, synonomous with the "standardization" of it. Thus, training is the design parameter by which the coordinating mechanism that we have called the standardization of skills is effected. Lest anyone doubt the relationship between professionalism and the standardization, we need only quote the words of a reputed professional about his most complex of professions. Writing about cardiovascular surgery, Frank Spencer (1976) discusses his "surgical cookbooks" as follows:

> The jargon term "cookbook" evolved from my loyal office staff, as this essentially describes "How I do this operation," somewhat analogous to "How I bake a cake." . . .
>
>   The components of a complex operation, such as repair of tetralogy of Fallot, may be divided into 10 to 15 sequential steps, with two to five essential features in each step. If each feature is symbolized by a single word, essential steps of an operation can be readily reduced to a series of chains of symbols, varying from six to ten chains containing 30 to 40 symbols. These are committed to memory, with review frequently enough so the essential 30 to 40 symbols representing key features of an operation can be reviewed mentally in 60 to 120 seconds at some time during the day preceding the operation. The sheer memorization feature is crucial, as opposed to simply scanning one's notes, with the ability to envision the chain of symbols rapidly, like quoting the alphabet. With these basic features firmly memorized, decision-making at operation, especially with unexpected events, is greatly augmented (p. 1182).

Professionals are trained over long periods of time, before they ever assume their positions. Generally, this training takes place outside the organization, often in a university. (There are, of course, exceptions. For example, police forces generally train their own personnel.) In effect, the training itself usually requires a particular and extensive expertise, beyond the capacity of the organization to provide. So the responsibility for it falls away from the technostructure, to some kind of professional association, which may use the university as its training ground. In the process, of course, the organization surrenders some control not only over the selection of its workers but also over the methods they use in their work.

Once the trainees have demonstrated the required behavior—that is, have internalized the standard skills and associated body of knowledge— they are duly certified by the professional association as appropriate for the job, and are subsequently hired by the organization to perform it.

Of course, the professional training program can seldom impart all the necessary skills and knowledge; some must always remain beyond specification and standardization. So professional training must generally be followed by some kind of on-the-job apprenticeship before the individual is considered fully trained. For example, after perhaps four years of postgraduate university training, the medical doctor must spend five years or more in on-the-job training, first as an intern, and then as a resident, before he is allowed to practice as a surgeon (Spencer, 1976, p. 1178).

INDOCTRINATION

Socialization "refers to the process by which a new member learns the value system, the norms, and the required behavior patterns of the society, organization, or group which he is entering" (Schein, 1968, p. 3). A good deal of socialization takes place informally in the organization; indeed some of it is carried out by the informal group in contradiction to the norms of the system of formal authority. **Indoctrination is the label used for the design parameter by which the organization formally socializes its members for its own benefit.**

Organizations allow some indoctrination to take place outside their own boundaries, as part of professional training. Law students, for example, learn more at the university than just legal precedent; they are expressly given clues about how a lawyer should behave. But much of the socialization is related to the "culture" of the specific organization, and so indoctrination is largely a responsibility of the organization itself.

Again, a good deal of this "in-house" indoctrination activity takes place before the person starts in the job, to ensure that he is sufficiently socialized to exhibit the desired behavior. Apprenticeship programs generally contain a good dose of indoctrination along with the training. Some organizations design programs solely for the purposes of indoctrination.

Freshly minted MBAs, for example, are often put through a "training" (read "indoctrination") program on first joining a large organization. They rotate through various departments for periods too brief to learn the work but not to sense the culture.

Often early indoctrination is supplemented by later programs designed to reinforce the employees' allegiance to the organization. For example, they are brought together for social events or inspiring speeches by the top managers, or they are rotated in their jobs so that they develop these allegiances to the whole organization rather than to any one of its parts. Galbraith and Edstrom (1976) note that in the multinational corporation, this latter practice creates informal communication networks that serve to integrate the goals of subsidiaries with those of the overall corporation.

As this last example suggests, **in-house indoctrination programs are particularly important where jobs are sensitive or remote**—managers of the foreign subsidiary, agents of the CIA, ambassadors of the nation, mounties of the R.C.M.P. In these cases, the need for coordination is paramount, particularly for the assurance that individuals working autonomously will act in the best interests of the organization. The nature and location of the work preclude the formalization of behavior and the use of direct supervision. So the organization must rely on training, especially on indoctrination. The U.S. Forest Ranger Service is a classic case of an organization with remote work. Commenting on Kaufman's (1960) study of the service, Wilensky (1967) demonstrates the use of a variety of indoctrinations as well as training devices—prejob as well as on-the-job:

> Only men with an ardent love of the outdoors, uniform professional training in forestry, and a strong commitment to a career in the Forest Service are recruited and survive the basic training period. Nine in ten of the approximately 4,000 employees of the Service are graduates of forestry schools; when in college, many held summer jobs in the forests. They share a common lore, similar technical knowledge, and identification even before embarking on ranger training. When they become rangers, they find themselves moving about from post to post, not necessarily upward; in fact, horizontal transfers, while not compulsory, are generally a prerequisite for advancement. Both rotation and the inculcation of the values of the Forest Service facilitate communication between headquarters and the field by keeping loyalties and career interests centrally directed. Rotation and indoctrination also keep the foresters independent of private interests in the regions or communities in which they serve ... (pp. 59–60).

Etzioni (1961) calls organizations that stress the use of indoctrination "normative," offering as illustrations the Communist Party and the Catholic Church. Antony Jay, in his book *Management and Machiavelli* (1970), provides us with an excellent illustration of the latter's use of indoctrination:

St. Augustine once gave as the only rule for Christian conduct, "Love God and do what you like." The implication is, of course, that if you truly love God, then you will only ever want to do things which are acceptable to Him. Equally, Jesuit priests are not constantly being rung up, or sent memos, by the head office of the Society. The long, intensive training over many years in Rome is a guarantee that wherever they go afterwards, and however long it may be before they even see another Jesuit, they will be able to do their work in accordance with the standards of the Society (p. 70).

TRAINING AND INDOCTRINATION
BY PART OF THE ORGANIZATION

No matter what the part of the organization, training is most important where jobs are complex, involving difficult, yet specified skills and sophisticated recorded bodies of knowledge—jobs essentially professional in nature. And indoctrination is most important where jobs are sensitive or remote, and where the culture and ideology of the organization demand a strong loyalty to it.

In some organizations—known as professional—a great deal of the work of the operating core involves complex skills and sophisticated knowledge. Examples are hospitals, law firms, social work agencies, and school systems. In each case, the organization relies extensively on training as a design parameter. Some organizations—sometimes the same professional ones—also make extensive use of indoctrination in the operating core because their operators do sensitive jobs or work in remote places. As noted in the earlier examples, the U.S. Forest Ranger Service and the R.C.M.P. stress both training and indoctrination for their operators.

Training and indoctrination is also used extensively in many of the staff units. Much of the technocratic work of the organization—for example, operations research and industrial engineering—is professional in nature; that is, it involves complex skills and knowledge that can be learned formally. So training is an important parameter in the design of their positions. Where the analysts have sensitive control responsibilities—for example, in the case of accountants who are sent out to divisions to keep watch over expenditures—indoctrination may be important as well. To ensure that their allegiances remain with the head office, job rotation from factory to factory is often used.[1] Similarly, many of the jobs in the support staff—legal council, researcher, industrial relations specialist—are professional in nature, requiring extensive training. Hall (1968, 1972) found in his

[1]For a thorough discussion of the divided loyalties of these accountants in the large manufacturing firm, see Simon et al. (1954).

research that professional units within organizations are not very different from professional organizations doing the same work: "The lawyer working in the trust department of a bank may actually be working in an organizational environment similar, and perhaps even identical, to the one he would find in a law firm" (1972, p. 191).

In the managerial ranks—the middle line and the strategic apex—the work is certainly complex, but it is not well understood, and so formal training is not paramount. True, there are skills and knowledge to be learned, and management schools to teach them, but so much of what managers do remains beyond recorded knowledge that management can hardly be called a profession. This is exemplified by the fact that the leaders of a great many of society's most important institutions—especially government—have had no management training whatsoever. Their work is craft: they learn it by observing and working with the masters. Thus, **training is not yet considered a major design parameter at the strategic apex or in the middle line**, although organizations do try to use brief "executive development" programs where specific managerial skills or knowledge can be taught. The growth in popularity of these in-house programs suggests that our base of understanding is widening, although it still has a long way to go.

Indoctrination plays perhaps a more important role in the managerial ranks, since the managers are, after all, the guardians of the organization's ideology. Thus, the newly hired MBA is put through the indoctrination program, and many large organizations rotate their managers frequently. Again, where managerial jobs are also sensitive or remote—ambassador, governor of a colony, manager of a foreign subsidiary—these indoctrination programs take on special importance. Jay (1970) provides us with an apt illustration:

> Like the Romans and the Jesuits, the British Army takes great pains to make sure that field commanders are really deeply ingrained with the thinking of the army as a whole: tours of duty abroad, spells at home, staff college, all tc ensure that when they take decisions on their own, they take the right ones, oɪ at least the best the army knows (p. 71).

TRAINING VERSUS FORMALIZATION

It has been evident throughout our discussion that specialization, formalization, and training and indoctrination are not completely independent design parameters. In essence, we have been describing two fundamentally different kinds of positions. One we have called *unskilled:* because the work is highly rationalized, it involves extensive specialization in both the horizontal and vertical dimensions, and it is often coordinated and controlled by the direct formalization of behavior. The other we have called *professional:* because the work is complex, it cannot easily be specialized in the vertical dimension or formalized by the organization's technostructure; it is, however, horizontally specialized—professionals are experts in well-defined fields—and the coordination is often achieved by the standardization of skills in extensive training programs, generally given outside the organization. (There are, of course, other kinds of work that are coordinated neither by formalization nor by training.)

This suggests that **formalization and training are basically substitutes.** Depending on the work in question, the organization can either control it directly through its own procedures and rules, or else it can achieve indirect control by hiring duly trained professionals. That is not to say that the one cannot supplement the other: hospitals rely on professional training to coordinate much of their operating work, yet they also use rules. But in general, most positions seem to stress one coordinating mechanism or the other, not both equally.

> ...formalization and professionalization are actually designed to do the same thing—organize and regularize the behavior of the members of the organization. Formalization is a process in which the organization sets the rules and procedures and the means of ensuring that they are followed. Professionalization, on the other hand, is a nonorganizationally based means of doing the same thing. From the organization's point of view, either technique would be appropriate, as long as the work gets done (Hall, 1972, p. 190).

Hall (1972) discusses the relationship between professionalism and formalization in some detail and cites considerable empirical evidence (including his own research; Hall, 1968) to support his conclusion that

> As the level of professionalization of the employees increases, the level of formalization decreases. ... The presence of professionals appears to cause a diminished need for formalized rules and procedures. Since professionals have internalized norms and standards, the imposition of organizational requirements is not only unnecessary; it is likely to lead to professional-organizational conflict (p. 121).[2]

The Hall comments raise a point about control of professional work. If these jobs are not specialized vertically, then control rests with the professionals. Yet Hall argues that professionalization "regularize[s] the behavior of the members of the organization." The point is that the professional's work is preprogrammed: in his training (or indoctrination for that matter) before he starts the job, he internalizes the required behavior:

[2]See also Becker and Neuhauser (1975, pp. 159–163) and Blau (1967–68).

> Buying and installing machines ... is one way of reducing the number of rules in an organization. The rules are built into the machine itself, and the organization pays for those rules in the price of the machine. A quite similar means of reducing the number of written rules is to "buy" personnel who have complex rules built into them. We generally call these people professionals. Professionals ... are trained on the outside, usually at the public expense, and a large number of rules are inculcated into them. They bring these into the organization and are expected to act upon them without further reference to their skills. ... Doctors know when they should give certain drugs or what kinds of drugs should not be given to certain kinds of people; medicine is a complex body of rather imperfect rules (Perrow, 1972, p. 27).

Once on the job, the professional appears to be autonomous, but he is, in fact, the product of his background, like the stage actor who has learned his lines well or even the bee who responds to innate programs. Melcher (1976) writes of the latter: "There's no need for formal authority systems, control systems, and little need for information systems, or leadership. Problems are solved by instinct that programs performance in a specific way" (p. 149). Of course, these analogies do an injustice to professional work. No matter how effective the training program, the inherent complexity of the work ensures that considerable discretion is left in it, far more than in unskilled jobs. Many important judgments must be made each day regarding at least which skills to apply in each situation.

A key point concerns where the control of professional work lies. The work of the unskilled employee is programmed by the analysts within the organization's technostructure; that of the professional, in large part by the professional association and school. So, the work is controlled, but not by the organization within which it is performed. **The professional organization surrenders a good deal of control over its choice of workers as well as their methods of work to the outside institutions that train and certify them and thereafter set standards that guide them in the conduct of their work.** With control passes allegiance: the professional tends to identify more with his profession than with the organization wherein he happens to practice it.

It may be recalled that Weber included training in his definition of bureaucracy: "Office management ... usually presupposes thorough and expert training" and "only persons who have the generally regulated qualifications to serve are employed." But we have just seen that training and formalization—the latter central to the Weber definition—are to some extent mutually exclusive. Could we have here the explanation of the Aston finding of two kinds of bureaucracy, one centralized and the other decentralized? Perhaps in one, because the operating work is unskilled, day-to-day control of it passes to the technostructure; in the other, because the work is professional, control of it remains with the operators themselves, and beyond them, with their associations. This is not the place to answer that question. Suffice it at this point to say that by our definition, **professionalism and bureaucracy can coexist in the same structure.** In Chapter 5 we defined bureaucracy as the extent to which organizational "behavior is predetermined or predictable, in effect standardized." Our discussion has certainly made clear that training and indoctrination are used to predetermine or standardize organizational behavior, specifically the skills and knowledge brought to the job. So to the extent that an organization relies on training and indoctrination in designing its structure, by our definition it can be called bureaucratic. Hence, we have an indication of two kinds of bureaucratic structure, one based on formalization of behavior (and the standardization of work processes), the other on training and indoctrination (and the standardization of skills).

7

Design of Superstructure: Unit Grouping

Given a set of positions, designed in terms of specialization, formalization, and training and indoctrination, two obvious questions face the designer of organizational structure: How should these positions be grouped into units? And how large should each unit be? Both questions—which pertain to the design of the *superstructure* of the organization—have received extensive consideration in the literature. In this chapter we take up the first one, in the next chapter the second.

It is through the process of grouping into units that the system of formal authority is established and the hierarchy of the organization is built. The organigram is the pictorial representation of this hierarchy, that is, of the results of the grouping process. Grouping can be viewed as a process of successive clustering, as shown in Figure 7-1, drawn from Conrath's work. Individual positions are grouped into first-order clusters, or units, these are, in turn, grouped into larger clusters or units, and so on until the entire organization is contained in the final cluster. For example, soldiers are grouped into squads, squads into platoons, platoons into companies, companies into battalions, and so on through regiments, brigades, and divisions, until the final grouping into armies.

Combining this process with those described in the last three chapters, we can describe organizational design as proceeding as follows, at least in principle. Given overall organizational needs—goals to be achieved, missions to be accomplished, as well as a technical system to accomplish

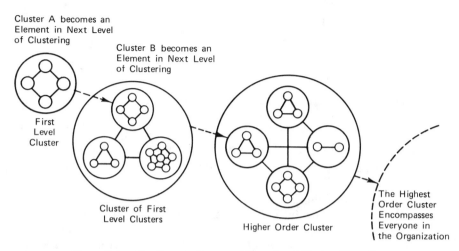

Cluster A becomes an Element in Next Level of Clustering

Cluster B becomes an Element in Next Level of Clustering

First Level Cluster

Cluster of First Level Clusters

Higher Order Cluster

The Highest Order Cluster Encompasses Everyone in the Organization

Figure 7-1. *The Organization as a Hierarchy of Clusters (from Conrath, 1973, p. 594)*

them—the designer delineates all the tasks that must be done. This is essentially a "top-down" procedure, from general needs to specific tasks. The designer then combines these tasks into positions according to the degree of specialization desired, and determines how formalized each should be as well as what kind of training and indoctrination it should require. The next step is to build the superstructure, first by determing what types and how many positions should be grouped into the first-order units, and then what types and how many units should be grouped into ever-more-comprehensive units until the hierarchy is complete. This last step is, of course, a "bottom-up" procedure, from specific tasks to the over-all hierarchy.

As noted, this is the procedure *in principle.* In practice, the organizational designer takes many shortcuts, reversing the top-down or bottom-up procedure. For example, the designer typically starts with a knowledge of specific structures and so can often move from missions to units directly. The designer of army structure need not work down to the level of soldier and then back up to the level of army. Instead, he shuffles divisions or armies around directly, as fixed blocks on the organigram. Likewise, he sometimes forms units from the top down, as when soldiers who were grouped into platoons for general training are later divided into squads for battlefield training. In other words, organization design is seldom carried out in a vacuum; in general, it proceeds with knowledge of past structures. In fact, organizational design is much less common than organizational redesign—incremental shifts from existing structures. In practice, **as goals and missions change, structural redesign is initiated from the top down; as the technical system of the operating core changes, it proceeds from the bottom up.**

105

Grouping is not simply a convenience for the sake of creating an organigram, a handy way of keeping track of who works in the organization. Rather, **grouping is a fundamental means to coordinate work in the organization.** Grouping can have at least four important effects.

1. Perhaps most important, **grouping establishes a system of common supervision among positions and units.** A manager is named for each unit, a single individual responsible for all its actions. (Litterer [1973], in fact, refers to units as "command groups.") And it is the linking of all these managers into a superstructure that creates the system of formal authority. Thus, **unit grouping is the design parameter by which the coordinating mechanism of direct supervision is built into the structure.**

2. **Grouping typically requires positions and units to share common resources.** The members or subunits of a unit, at the very least, share a common budget, and often are expected to share common facilities and equipment as well.

3. **Grouping typically creates common measures of performance.** To the extent that the members or subunits of a unit share common resources, the costs of their activities can be measured jointly. Moreover, to the extent that they contribute to the production of the same products or services, their outputs can also be measured jointly. Joint performance measures further encourage them to coordinate their activities.

4. **Finally, grouping encourages mutual adjustment.** In order to share resources and to facilitate their direct supervision, the members of a unit are often forced to share common facilities, thereby being brought into close physical proximity. This, in turn, encourages frequent, informal communication among them, which in turn encourages coordination by mutual adjustment. It is, for example, well known that members of groups or units tend to band together psychologically, and to treat others as "outsiders." A number of researchers have noted the presence of these relationships. Aguilar (1967), in his study of how managers scan their environments for external information, comments:

> Throughout the study, two factors were notable in their effect on the internal communication of external information; physical distance, and organizational structure. Generally, persons tended to communicate with others who were within easy reach, and also with others who were closely related in the organization.
> More striking than the inducements to communication provided by spatial and organizational *proximity* are the barriers erected by spa-

tial and organizational *distance*. The most severe and repeated failures of communication were noted between divisions of a company. Managers in all larger companies admitted to this problem (pp. 112–113).

Likewise, Scharpf (1977) finds in his study of a German government ministry that "organizational boundaries do matter. ... they seem to create semi-permeable walls which impede the flow of information ..." (p. 163). And Burns (1970) notes in his study of program offices for technologically advanced projects that results can depend on physical proximity: "The most successful of the offices studied had all but two of its members physically located in one large office. There were no partitions and members talked back and forth continually ..." (p. 148). This did not happen in the case of the poorest performer, where every member had an individual office and the laboratory was completely isolated from the office area.[1]

Thus, **grouping can stimulate to an important degree two important coordinating mechanisms—direct supervision and mutual adjustment—and can form the basis for a third—standardization of outputs—by providing common measures of performance.** Unit grouping is, as a result, one of the most powerful of the design parameters. (A prime characteristic of the two other coordinating mechanisms—standardization of work processes and of skills—is that they provide for the automatic coordination of the work of individuals; as a result, they can be used independently of the way positions are grouped.)

But for the same reason that grouping encourages strong coordination *within* a unit, it creates problems of coordination *between* units. As we have seen, the communication is focused within the unit, thereby isolating the members of different units from each other. In the well-known terms of Lawrence and Lorsch (1967), units become *differentiated* in their various orientations—in their goals, time perspectives, interpersonal styles of interaction, and degrees of formalization of their structures. For example, a production department might be oriented toward the goal of efficiency as opposed to that of creativity, have a short time perspective, exhibit an orientation to getting the job done rather than to the feelings of those who do it, and have a highly bureaucratic structure. In contrast, a research department may exhibit exactly the opposite characteristics on all four dimensions. Sometimes this differentiation is reinforced by special languages used in the different departments: there may actually be times when personnel in production and research simply cannot understand each other.

The result of all this is that each unit develops a propensity to focus ever more narrowly on its own problems while separating itself ever more

[1]See Melcher (1976, pp. 117–144) for an extensive review of the research on the effects of "spatial-physical" factors on organizational group processes.

sharply from the problems of the rest of the organization. **Unit grouping encourages intragroup coordination at the expense of intergroup coordination.** The management school that adopts a departmental structure soon finds that the finance professors are interacting more closely with each other but are seeing less of the policy and marketing professors, and all become more parochial in their outlook. Of course, this can also work to the advantage of the organization, allowing each unit to give particular attention to its own special problems. Earlier, we saw the example of the new venture team isolated from the rest of a bureaucratic structure so that it can function organically and therefore be more creative.

BASES FOR GROUPING

On what basis does the organization group positions into units and units into large ones? Six bases that have been discussed in the literature are listed below:

Grouping by Knowledge and Skill   Positions may be grouped according to the specialized knowledge and skills that members bring to the job. Hospitals, for example, group surgeons in one department, anesthetists in another, psychiatrists in a third. Figure 7–2 shows the organigram for the medical component of a Quebec teaching hospital, with the physicians grouped by knowledge and skill in two tiers. Grouping may also be based on the *level* of knowledge or skill; for example, different units may be created to house craftsmen, journeymen, and apprentices, or simply skilled and unskilled workers.

Grouping by Work Process and Function   Units may be based on the process or activity used by the worker. For example, a manufacturing firm may distinguish casting, welding, and machining shops, and a football team may divide into a line unit and a backfield unit for practice. Often, the technical system is the basis for process grouping, as in a printing shop that sets up separate letterpress and offset departments, two different processes to produce the same outputs. Work may also be grouped according to its basic function in the organization—to purchase supplies, raise capital, generate research, produce food in the cafeteria, or whatever. Perhaps the most common example of this is grouping by "business function"—manufacturing, marketing, engineering, finance, and so on, some of these groups being line and others staff. (Indeed, the grouping of line units into one cluster and staff units into another—a common practice—is another example of grouping by work function.) Figure 7–3 shows the organigram for a cultural center, where the grouping is based on work process and function.

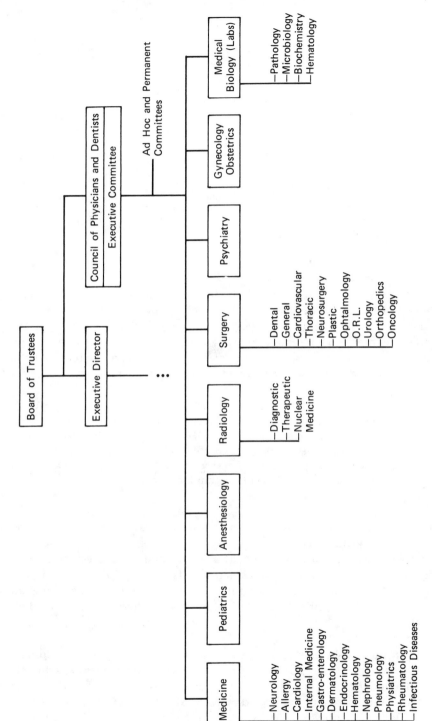

Figure 7-2. *Grouping by Knowledge and Skill: Medical Departments of the Teaching Hospital*

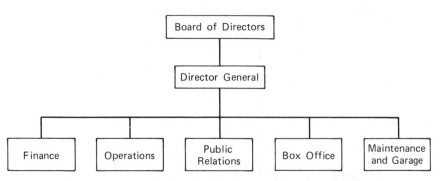

Figure 7-3. *Grouping by Work Process and Function: A Cultural Center*

Grouping by Time Groups may also be formed according to *when* the work is done. Different units do the same work in the same way but at different times, as in the case of different shifts in a factory. Rosemary Stewart (1970) discusses this basis of grouping and notes that it may also make sense to differentiate the work processes on different shifts. For example, a computer facility may run time-sharing applications by day, when there are many users, and batch jobs at night, when there are few. But she notes other cases where it is desirable to have different shifts to do identical tasks:

> Trist and Bamforth found that one of the troubles with the conventional long-wall method of coal-mining was that each shift was responsible for a different phase of coal getting, and that this contributed to the friction that existed between the shifts. Relations were much better when groups of workers, with members in each shift, were made responsible for a work cycle (p. 33).

Grouping by Output Here, the units are formed on the basis of the products they make or the services they render. A large manufacturing company may have separate divisions for each of its product lines, for example, one for chinaware, another for bulldozers; while a restaurant may separate organizationally as well as spatially its bar from its dining facilities. Figure 7-4 shows the product grouping by divisions in Imasco, a Canadian conglomerate firm (with two units—public relations and finance—based on function).

Grouping by Client Groups may also be formed to deal with different types of clients. An insurance firm may have separate sales departments for individual and group policies; similarly, hospitals in some countries have different wards for public and private patients. The Canadian Government Department of Industry was originally set up with ten branches—

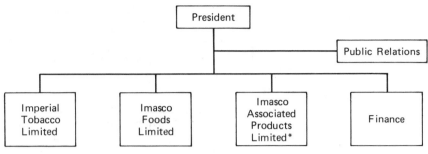

* retail chain stores, etc.

Figure 7-4. *Grouping by Product: Imasco Limited. Used by permission.*

food, machinery, motor vehicles, chemicals, etc.—each one designed to maintain contact with its own sphere of Canadian industry.

Grouping by Place Groups may be formed according to the geographical regions in which the organization operates. In May 1942, the U.S. War Department was organized in terms of seven "theaters"—North American, African Middle Eastern, European, Asiatic, Pacific, Southwest Pacific, and Latin American (Hewes, 1975, Chart 5). On a less global scale, a bread company may have the same baking facility duplicated in 20 different population areas to ensure fresh daily delivery in each. Figure 7-5 shows another example of geographical grouping—in this case two-tier—in the superstructure of the Canadian Post Office. A very different basis for grouping by place relates to the specific location (within a geographic area) where the work is actually carried out. Football players are differentiated according to where they stand on the field relative to the ball (linemen, backfielders, ends); aircraft construction crews are distinguished by the part of the airplane on which they work (wing, tail, etc.); and some medical specialists are grouped according to the part of the body on which they work (the head in psychiatry, the heart in cardiology).

Of course, like all nice, neat categorization schemes, this one has its own gray areas. Psychiatry was purposely included in two examples—one in grouping by place, the other in grouping by knowledge and skill—to illustrate this point. Consider, for example, the medical specialties of surgery and obstetrics. These are defined in the *Random House Dictionary* as follows:

- *Surgery:* the act, practice, or work of treating diseases, injuries, or deformities by manual operation or instrumental appliances.
- *Obstetrics:* the branch of medical science concerned with childbirth and caring for and treating women in or in connection with childbirth.

111

112

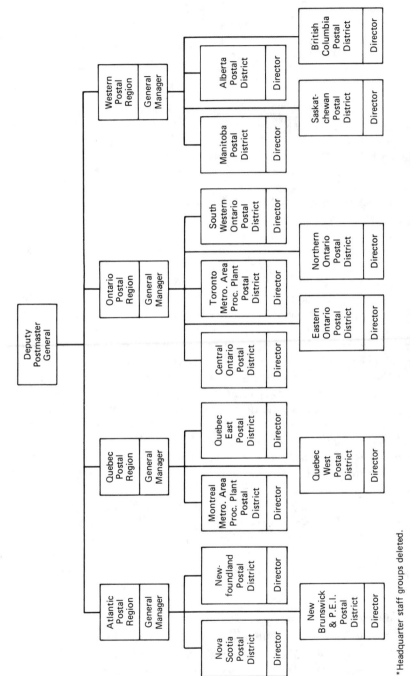

Figure 7-5. *Grouping by Place: The Canadian Post Office, circa 1978. * (Used with permission)*

*Headquarter staff groups deleted.

These definitions are not consistent in our terms. Obstetrics is defined according to client, while surgery is defined according to work processes. A closer look indicates that even within a medical specialty, the basis for specialization can be ambiguous. Obstetricians may deal with particular clients, but they also use particular work processes, and their outputs are also unique to their grouping (namely, delivered babies); surgeons treat special kinds of patients and they also have their own distinct outputs (removed or replaced organs). In the same vein, Herbert Simon (1957) points out that "an education department may be viewed as a purpose (to educate) organization, or a clientele (children) organization; the Forest Service as a purpose (forest conservation), process (forest management), clientele (lumbermen and cattlemen utilizing public forests), or area (publicly owned forest lands) organization" (pp. 30–31).

The notion of grouping by process, people, place, or purpose (output) is, in fact, one of the pillars of the classical literature on organization design, and Simon devotes some of his sharpest criticism of the classical principles to it (pp. 28–35). He is especially severe on the "ambiguities" of the terms, arguing as in the quotation above that the same group can often be perceived in different ways.

> A typist moves her fingers in order to type; types in order to reproduce a letter; reproduces a letter in order that an inquiry may be answered. Writing a letter is then the purpose for which the typing is performed; while writing a letter is also the process whereby the purpose of replying to an inquiry is achieved. It follows that the same activity may be described as purpose or process (p. 30).

Simon's basic point is that process and purpose are linked in a hierarchy of organizational means and ends, each activity being a process for a higher-order goal (typing a letter to answer an inquiry, manufacturing products to satisfy customers), and purpose for a lower-order one (moving fingers to type a letter, buying machines to manufacture a product). In the same sense, the *whole* organization can be viewed as a process in society—police departments for protection so that the citizens can live in peace, food companies to supply nourishment so that they can exist.

It is interesting to note that Simon's illustrations of ambiguities between process and purpose in specific organizational departments all come from organizations in which the operators are professionals. So, too, does our example of surgery and obstetrics. In fact, it so happens that their training differentiates the professionals by their knowledge and skills as well as the work processes they use, which leads them to be grouped on these two bases concurrently. In professional organizations clients select the professionals on these bases as well. One does not visit a cardiologist for an ingrown toenail; students interested in becoming chemists do not register in the business school. In other words, in professional organizations such as hospitals, accounting firms, and school systems, where professional operators serve their own clients directly, grouping the operators by knowledge, skill, work process, and client all amount to the same thing.

But is that true in other organizations? The purchasing department in a manufacturing firm is far removed from the clients; it merely performs one of the functions that eventually leads to the products being sold to the clients; thus, it cannot be considered to be a client-based or output-based group. Of course, in Simon's sense it does have its own outputs and its own clients—purchased items supplied to the manufacturing department. But this example shows how we can clarify the ambiguity Simon raises: simply by making the context clear. Specifically, we can define output, client, and place only in terms of the *entire* organization. In other words, in our context, purpose is defined in terms of the purpose of the organization vis-à-vis *its* clients or markets, not in terms of intermediate steps to get it to the point of servicing clients and markets, nor in terms of the needs of the larger society in which the organization is embedded.

In fact, we shall compress all the bases for grouping discussed above to two essential ones: *market* grouping, comprising the bases of output, client, and place,[2] and *functional* grouping, comprising the bases of knowledge, skill, work process, and function. (Grouping by time can be considered to fall into either category.) In effect, **we have the fundamental distinction between grouping activities by ends, by the characteristics of the ultimate markets served by the organization—the products and services it markets, the customers it supplies, the places where it supplies them—or by the means, the functions (including work processes, skills, and knowledge) it uses to produce its products and services.** For example, one study by Price (1968) found that while both the Fish and the Game Commissions in Oregon managed wildlife, the former was organized functionally and the latter was organized by markets. The Fish Commission was divided into four functional units representing the means used—research, fish culture, engineering, and administration. Research collected data on wildlife management and made recommendations about regulation; the fish culture department propagated salmon and steelhead trout; engineering looked after engineering, construction, and maintenance; while administration looked after purchasing, accounting, and recruiting. In contrast, the Game Commission was organized by the market areas served: these were northwest, southwest, central, northeast, and southeast regional units, each one carrying out all the functions required for wildlife management in its own region. Similarly, in a manufacturing plant, the activities may be grouped into assembly

[2]The term "market" is used expressly to refer to business as well as nonbusiness organizations. Every organization exists to serve some market, whether that consist of the citizens for a police force, the students for a school system, or the customers for a manufacturing firm.

lines, each representing a market unit producing its own distinct products, or into functional departments, such as casting, machining, and assembling, each doing one part of the process that eventually leads to the finished product. The management school may be organized into market-based programs —bachelor, master, doctor, executive—or into functional departments— policy, finance, marketing, and so on.

Each of these two bases for grouping merits detailed attention. But to better understand them, we would do well to consider first some of the criteria which organizations use to group positions and units.

CRITERIA FOR GROUPING

We can isolate four basic criteria that organizations use to select the bases for grouping positions and units—interdependencies in the work flow, in work process, of scale, and in social relationships.

Work-flow Interdependencies A number of studies that have focused on the relationships among specific operating tasks stress one conclusion: grouping of operating tasks should reflect natural work-flow interdependencies. This comes out most clearly in the Tavistock studies of British coal mines and Indian weaving sheds. Referring to the premechanized method of coal mining, Trist and Bamforth (1951) comment:

> A primary work-organization of this type has the advantage of placing responsibility for the complete coal-getting task squarely on the shoulders of a single, small, face-to-face group which experiences the entire cycle of operations within the compass of its membership. For each participant the task has total significance and dynamic closure (p. 6).

Miller (1959), referring to Rice's study in the Indian weaving mill, discusses "natural" and "unnatural" groupings in a sequential manufacturing process; his diagram is reproduced as Figure 7–7. Similarly, in a chapter entitled "Workflow as the Basis for Organization Design," Chapple and Sayles (1961) present a number of illustrations where tasks were regrouped in accordance with natural flows of work. In one, the work flow for the processing of orders in a manufacturing firm was divided among a number of supervisors, on the basis of business function, as shown in Figure 7–6. This resulted in differentiation within the work flow, which led to conflict. For example, in two cases the credit department canceled orders made by the sales department just after the general sales manager had expressly written to the customers thanking them for their confidence in the firm's product. The problems were solved by a reorganization, shown in Figure 7–6, that

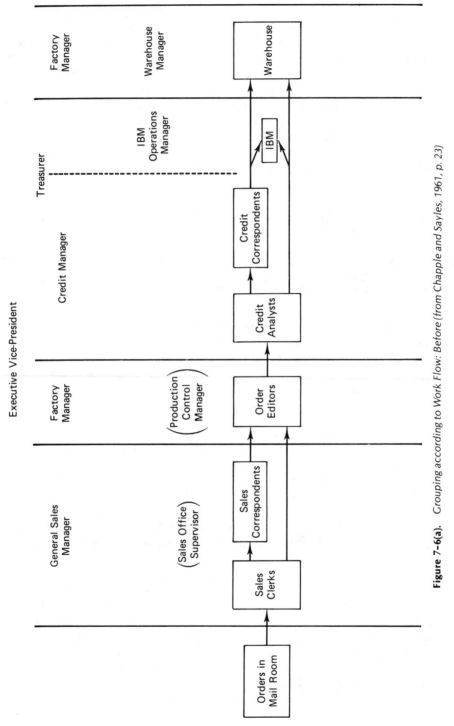

Figure 7–6(a). *Grouping according to Work Flow: Before (from Chapple and Sayles, 1961, p. 23)*

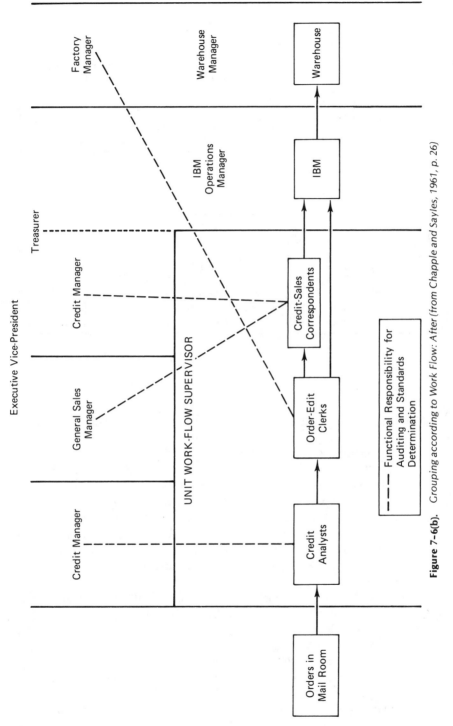

Executive Vice-President

Credit Manager   General Sales Manager   Credit Manager   Treasurer   IBM Operations Manager   Warehouse Manager

Factory Manager

UNIT WORK-FLOW SUPERVISOR

Orders in Mail Room → Credit Analysts → Order-Edit Clerks → Credit-Sales Correspondents → IBM → Warehouse

– – – Functional Responsibility for Auditing and Standards Determination

Figure 7-6(b). *Grouping according to Work Flow: After (from Chapple and Sayles, 1961, p. 26)*

117

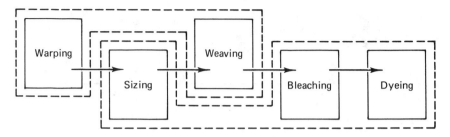

(a) Unnatural

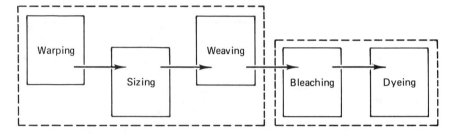

(b) Natural

Figure 7-7. *"Natural" and "Unnatural" Grouping in a Weaving Mill according to Work Flow (from Miller, 1959, p. 257)*

grouped the whole work flow into a single unit, under a "unit work-flow supervisor."

These examples show the advantages of what the Tavistock researchers call a "psychologically complete task": **in the market-based grouping, the members of a single unit have a sense of territorial integrity; they control a well-defined organizational process; most of the problems that arise in the course of their work can be solved simply, through their mutual adjustment; and many of the rest, which must be referred up the hierarchy, can still be handled within the unit, by that single manager in charge of the work flow.** In contrast, when well-defined work flows, such as mining a coal face or producing a purchase order, are divided among different units, coordination becomes much more difficult. Workers and managers with different allegiances are called upon to cooperate; since they often cannot, problems must be handled higher up in the hierarchy, by managers removed from the work flow.

James Thompson (1967) puts some nice flesh on the bones of these concepts, describing how organizations account for various kinds of interdependencies between tasks. It will be recalled that Thompson discusses three basic kinds of interdependence: pooled, involving only the sharing of resources; sequential, where the work is fed from one task to the next; and reciprocal, where the work is passed back and forth between tasks. Thompson claims that organizations try to group tasks so as to minimize coordination and communication costs. Since reciprocal interdependencies are the most complex and hence the most costly, followed by sequential, Thompson concludes that:

> The basic units are formed to handle reciprocal interdependence, if any. If there is none, then the basic units are shaped according to sequential interdependence, if any. If neither of the more complicated types of interdependence exists, the basic units are shaped according to common processes [to facilitate the handling of pooled interdependencies] (p. 59).

The question of grouping does not, however, end there, because "residual" interdependencies remain: one grouping cannot contain all the interdependencies. These must be picked up in higher-order groupings, thus necessitating the construction of a hierarchy. And so, "The question is not which criterion to use for grouping, but rather in which *priority* are the several criteria to be exercised" (p. 51). Thompson's answer is, of course, that the organization designs the lowest-level groups to contain the major reciprocal interdependencies; higher-order groups are then formed to handle the remaining sequential interdependencies, and the final groups, if necessary, are formed to handle any remaining pooled interdependencies.

Figure 7–8 illustrates this with a five-tier hierarchy of an apocryphal international manufacturing company. The first and second groupings are by work process, the third by business function, the fourth by output (product), and the top one by place (country). (Staff groups are also shown at each level; these will be discussed later in the chapter.) The tightest interdependencies, reciprocal in nature, would be between the turning, milling, and drilling departments in the factory. The next level contains the sequential interdependencies from fabricating to assembly. Similarly, the level above that, largely concerned with product development, contains important sequential interdependencies. In mass production, typically, the products are first designed in the engineering department, then produced in the manufacturing department, and finally marketed by the marketing department.[3] Above this, the interdependencies are basically pooled: for the most part, the product divisions and the national subsidiaries are independent of each other except that they share common financial resources and certain staff support services.

To say that grouping should be based on work-flow interdependencies does not solve the designer's problem. It only raises the difficult question of

---

[3]Woodward (1965) describes this sequence of product development activity in mass production, noting that different sequences occur in unit and process production. All three will be discussed in Chapter 14.

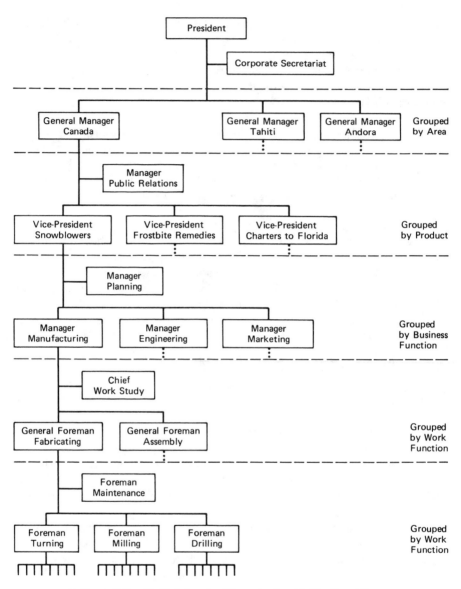

Figure 7-8. *Multiple Levels of Grouping in a Multinational Firm*

what those interdependencies are. For example, Gosselin (1978) spent months studying a cardiac surgery team in a teaching hospital—comprising cardiologists, cardioradiologists, and cardiac surgeons—just to establish what their work-flow interdependencies were. Figure 7–9, which shows only the flow of their patients, gives a good indication of the complexity of his results.

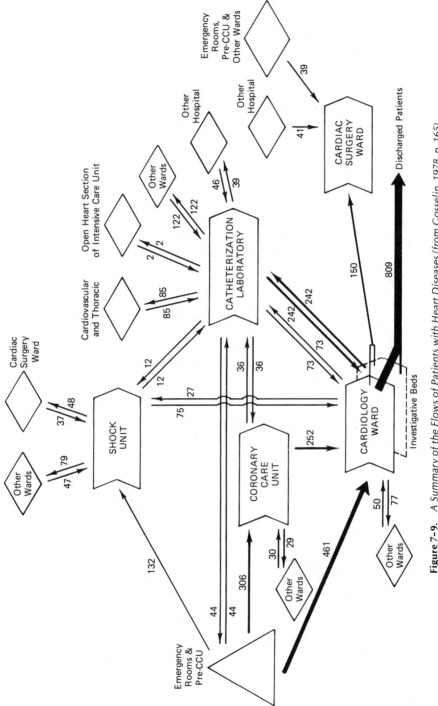

Figure 7-9. A Summary of the Flows of Patients with Heart Diseases (from Gosselin, 1978, p. 165)

Questions of interdependency in the flow of work do not only arise in the operating core. For example, Scharpf (1977) studied policy making in the West German Federal Ministry of Transport. Despite the logical grouping into seven "line" divisions by transportation sector—railroad, road transport, inland water transport, sea transport, air transport, road construction, and waterways—Scharpf suspected that important policy-making interdependencies existed across divisions, which would require structural reorganization. The results of three studies—of information exchanges, participation in a cross division of tasks, and the impact of specific tasks across units—overlaid on the organigram confirmed his suspicions. For example, the railroad division turned out to be "intensively" linked to units in the road transport division, while that latter division did not appear to be a simple "cohesive grouping." But if that was the case, Scharpf speculated, then perhaps the bases for the grouping did not really matter—that is, perhaps they did not impede coordination. Since the "soft" data suggested otherwise, Scharpf analyzed some more systematic interview responses on conflicts and information barriers across unit boundaries.

> These results are suggestive. They indicate that perceived deficits in information supply are four times as likely to occur in interactions across divisions than within divisions; that conflicts over policy substance are more than twice as frequent in inter-divisional interaction; and that even conflicts over jurisdiction (which can only be settled authoritatively by the central division and the leadership of the ministry) have a 50% higher probability of occurring in interactions between divisions than within divisions (p. 162).

And so Scharpf concluded that "organization boundaries do matter" (p. 162), and he proposed a reorganization of the ministry along the lines of the actual flow of policy making.

Process Interdependencies   Work-flow interdependencies are not, of course, the only ones to be taken into consideration by the designer of organization structure. A second important class of interdependencies relates to the *processes* used in the work flow. For example, one lathe operator may have to consult another, working on a different product line (i.e., in a different work flow), about what cutting tool to use on a certain job.

In effect, **we have interdependencies related to specialization, which favor functional grouping.** Positions may have to be grouped to encourage process interactions, even at the expense of work-flow coordination. Perhaps Gosselin's cardiovascular surgeons, or Scharpf's road transport policy makers, were grouped together to encourage high degrees of specialization in their respective fields. When like specialists are grouped together, they learn from each other and become more adept at their specialized work. They also feel more comfortable "among their own," with their work judged by peers and by managers expert in the same field.

Scale Interdependencies   The third criterion for grouping relates to economies of scale. **Groups may have to be formed to reach sizes large enough to function efficiently.** For example, every department in the factory requires maintenance. But that does not necessarily justify attaching one maintenance man to each department, in effect, grouping him by work flow. There may not be enough work for each maintenance man. So a central maintenance department may be set up for the whole factory.

This, of course, encourages process specialization: whereas the maintenance man in each department would have to be a jack of all trades, the one among many in a maintenance department can specialize, for example, in preventive maintenance. Similarly, it may make economic sense to have only one data-processing department for the entire company, so that it can use a large, efficient computer; data-processing departments in each division might have to use smaller, less efficient ones.

This issue, of the *concentration* or *dispersal* of services, arises in a great many contexts in the organization. Should secretaries be grouped into typing pools or assigned to individual users; should the university have a central library or a series of satellite ones attached to each faculty; should the corporation have a single strategic planning group at headquarters or one attached to each division (or both); should there be a central telephone switchboard or a centrex system, allowing the public to dial directly inside the organization? The issue lends itself well to mathematical formulation and has been so treated in the literature. For example, Kochen and Deutsch (1973; see also 1969) address the question for society as well as for organizations: how many facilities are needed and how dispersed and differentiated need they be? Kochen and Deutsch produce a continuum of twelve situations, some of the most concentrated being "the omnicompetent, aloof imperial ruler," the special-purpose batch-processing computer center, and the university telephone switchboard, and the more dispersed including drinking fountains, physicians in private practice, and private telephones. The authors then develop a mathematical formula to optimize the location of facilities, concluding that:

> Long-term trends may be toward [dispersal] when service loads and the costs of service time grow faster than capital costs and transport and adjustment speeds, as seems likely for the next several decades. Where the opposite conditions prevail, cost-effectiveness should favor [concentration] such as perhaps in some earlier periods, and possibly in the more distant future (p. 841).[4]

Social Interdependencies   A fourth criterion for grouping relates not to the work done but to the social relationships that accompany it. For example, the Trist and Bamforth study in the coal mines showed clearly the

[4]For a good discussion of the concentration or dispersal of intelligence staff units, see Wilensky (1967, pp. 58–62).

importance of these social factors. Here, for example, workers had to form groups to facilitate mutual support in a dangerous environment. To use a favorite Tavistock term, the system was *sociotechnical*.

Other social factors can enter into the design of units. For example, the Hawthorne studies suggested that when the work is dull, the workers should be close together, to facilitate social interaction and so avoid boredom. Personalities enter the picture as well, often as a major factor in organizational design. People prefer to be grouped on the basis of "getting along." As a result, **every superstructure design ends up as a compromise between the "objective" factors of work flow, process, and scale interdependency, and the "subjective" factors of personality and social need.** Organigrams may be conceived on paper, but they must function with flesh-and-blood human beings. "Sure, the sales manager should report to the area superintendent, but the fact is that they are not on speaking terms, so we show him reporting to the head of purchasing instead. It may seem screwy, but we had no choice." How often have we heard such statements? Scratch any structure of real people and you will find it loaded with such compromises.

In many cases, "getting along" encourages process specialization. Specialists get along best with their own kind, in part because their work makes them think alike, but also, perhaps more important, because in many cases it was common personality factors that caused them to choose their specialties in the first place. The extroverts seek out marketing or public relations positions, the analytic types end up in the technostructure. Sometimes it is best to keep them apart, at least on the organigram.

These four criteria—work flow, process, scale, and social interdependencies—constitute the prime criteria which organizations use to group into units. Now let us see how these apply to the functional and market bases for grouping.

GROUPING BY FUNCTION

Grouping by function—by knowledge, skill, work process, or work function—reflects an overriding concern for process and scale interdependencies (and perhaps secondarily for social interdependencies), generally at the expense of those of the work flow. By grouping on a functional basis, the organization can pool human and material resources across different work flows. Functional structure also encourages specialization, for example, by establishing career paths for specialists within their own area of expertise, by enabling them to be supervised by one of their own, and by bringing them together to encourage social interaction. Thus, in the functionally organized Fish Commission in Oregon, of the friends named by the employees, 55 percent came from other specialties, compared with 68 percent in the market-based Game Commission (Price, 1968, p. 364). Similarly, "Marquis found in a detailed study of thirty-eight firms working on U.S. government R and D contracts, while the existence of project [market-based] teams increased the likelihood of meeting cost and time targets, the presence of a strong functional base was associated with higher technical excellence as rated by both managers and clients" (Knight, 1976, pp. 115–116).

But these same characteristics indicate the chief weaknesses of the functional structure. The emphasis on narrow specialty detracts from attention to broader output. Individuals focus on their own means, not the organization's broader ends. It was in the Oregon Fish Commission that the hatcheryman more often ignored the biologists recommendations; in meetings and even in social activities the specialists stuck to themselves—only the biologists attended the research division picnic; in the Game Commission, the hatcherymen went along, too (p. 365).

Moreover, performance cannot easily be measured in the functional structure. When sales drop, who is at fault: marketing for not pushing hard enough or manufacturing for shoddy workmanship? One will blame the other, with nobody taking responsibility for the overall result. Someone up above is supposed to take care of all that:

> ... in a functionally organized electronics-goods manufacturing firm, the engineers were very competent but interested more in the elegance of design than the profitable marketability of their products. The manufacturing department wanted designs of products that would be easy to mass produce. The engineers often delayed giving designs to manufacturing for several months while working out the niceties of their blueprints. The manufacturing vice-president complained bitterly to the executive vice-president about this, saying that design engineers fiddled while the company got burned through lost orders and expensive and hurried retooling. Eventually, the executive vice-president had to step in to resolve the conflict (Khandwalla, 1977, pp. 490–491).

In effect, **the functional structure lacks a built-in mechanism for coordinating the work flow.** Unlike the market structures that contain the workflow interdependencies within single units, functional structures impede both mutual adjustment among different specialists and direct supervision at the unit level by the management. The structure is incomplete: additional means of coordination must be found, beyond the nearest unit.

The natural tendency is to let coordination problems rise to higher-level units in the hierarchy, until they arrive at a level where the different functions in question meet. The trouble with this, however, is that the level may be too far removed from the problem. In our Figure 7–8, for example, a problem involving the functions of both drilling and selling (e.g., a request by a customer to have a special hole drilled on his snowblowers for rear-view mirrors) would have to rise three levels to the vice-president in charge of snowblowers, the first individual whose responsibilities involve both functions.

Of course, functional structures need not rely on direct supervision for coordination. These are specialized organizations; where their jobs are unskilled, they tend to rely on formalization to achieve coordination. Thus, we can conclude that **the functional structures—notably where the operating work is unskilled—tend to be the more bureaucratic ones.** Their work tends to be more formalized, and that requires a more elaborate administrative structure—more analysts to formalize the work, and higher up the hierarchy, more managers, or, perhaps, as we shall see in Chapter 10, more liaison personnel, to coordinate the work across the functional units. So some of the gains made by the better balancing of human and machine resources are lost in the need for more personnel to achieve coordination.

To put this issue the other way around, bureaucratic structures (with unskilled operators) rely more extensively on the functional bases for grouping. That is, they tend to be organized by the function performed rather than the market served. (And where there are many levels of grouping, they tend to be organized on functional bases at higher levels in the hierarchy.) In seeking, above all, to rationalize their structures, such bureaucracies prefer to group according to the work processes used and then to coordinate by the formalization of work and the proliferation of rules. This way, on paper at least, all relationships are rationalized and coherent.

This conclusion on the relationship between bureaucratic structure and functional grouping was evident in a study by Walker and Lorsch (1970), who compared two plants, similar in many ways except that one was organized on a functional basis (called Plant F), the other on a market basis (called Plant P, for product). Plant F employees reported that their structure was more uniformly formal, "job responsibilities were well defined, and the distinctions between jobs were clear" (p. 45). There were more rules and procedures. In Plant P, while the production managers reported that their jobs were well defined and that rules and procedures were important, the plant and industrial engineers "were rather vague about their responsibilities ..." (p. 70). Furthermore, "In Plant P, communication among employees was more frequent, less formal, and more often of a face-to-face nature ..." (p. 46). The Plant F managers focused on short-term matters and were not adept at resolving conflict through mutual adjustment. But this was not so important, Walker and Lorsch suggest, since coordination was affected chiefly through plans, procedures, and the manufacturing technology itself. As long as the remaining problems were few, they could be handled effectively higher up in the hierarchy.

Lawrence and Lorsch (1967) provide us with an interesting illustration of the advantages of market grouping. They reproduce a memo from an advertising agency executive to his staff describing the rationale for a conversion from a functional structure (based on copy, art, and TV departments) to one of the market groups:

> Formation of the "total creative" department completely tears down the walls between art, copy, and television people. Behind this move is the realization that for best results all creative people, regardless of their particular specialty, must work together under the most intimate relationship as total advertising people, trying to solve creative problems together from start to finish.
>
> The new department will be broken into five groups reporting to the senior vice president and creative director, each under the direction of an associate creative director. Each group will be responsible for art, television, and copy in their accounts (p. 37).

In this case, market-based grouping is used to set up relatively self-contained units to deal with particular work flows. Ideally, these units contain all the important sequential and reciprocal interdependencies, so that only the pooled ones remain: each unit draws its resources and perhaps certain support services from the common structure and in turn contributes its surpluses or profits back to it. And because each unit performs all the functions for a given set of products, services, clients, or places, it tends to identify directly with them, and its performance can easily be measured in these terms. So markets, not processes, get the employees' undivided attention. Returning to the Walker and Lorsch study:

> The atmosphere at Plant P ... was well suited to the goal of improving plant capabilities, which it did very well. There was less differentiation between goals, since the functional specialists to a degree shared the product goals. ...
>
> Plant P managers were able to achieve the integration necessary to solve problems that hindered plant capability. Their shared goals and a common boss encouraged them to deal directly with each other and confront their conflicts. Given this pattern, it is not surprising that they felt very involved in their jobs (p. 50).

And, of course, with the necessary mutual adjustment and direct supervision contained right inside the unit, the organization need rely less on formalization for coordination, and so tends to emerge as less bureaucratic.

But, with the focus on coordination across specialties, there is, of course, less process specialization. Compare, for example, these two bases for grouping in a retail company, say, in hardware. The company can build one large downtown store that sells everything imaginable, organizing itself on the basis of specialist departments; in contrast, it can set itself up as a retail chain, a market-based structure with small stores throughout the city. In search of special items for his nail sculptures, the customer in the large specialized store would simply find the nail department and seek out a salesperson there who could tell him if copper roofing nails with crosshatched heads were available in the five-centimeter size or only in the seven-centimeter size. Should the nail sculptor find himself in the smaller branch store, almost certainly more conveniently located, he would probably find no copper nails of any kind in stock—nor a salesperson who could distinguish copper nails from brass-plated ones. But the salesperson in the chain store could better tell him where to find a hammer.

In general, the market structure is a less machinelike structure, less able to do a specialized or repetitive task well. But it can do more tasks and change tasks more easily, its essential flexibility deriving from the fact that its units are relatively independent of each other. New units can easily be added and old ones deleted. Any one store in a retail chain can easily be closed down, usually with little effect on the others. But closing down one specialized department in a large store may bankrupt it. There are chain stores that sell only bread or milk, but there is no supermarket that can afford to dispense with either.

But the market basis for grouping is no panacea for the problems of organizational design. We can see this most clearly in a study by Kover (1963–64). He, too, looked at an advertising agency that reorganized, in virtually the same way as the one cited earlier. But Kover found effects the first respondent did not mention: specialists had much less communication with colleagues in their own functions and even with the clients (communication with them now being restricted largely to the managers of the market units); their sense of professional worth diminished, in part because their work was judged by general managers instead of their specialist peers. Those who saw themselves as craftsmen became increasingly dissatisfied with their work and alienated from the firm; many, in fact, left within a year of the reorganization. In effect, the market-based structure detracted from an emphasis on specialization, apparently with a resulting decrease in the quality of the specialized work.

The market structure is also more wasteful of resources than the functional—at the lowest unit level if not in the administrative hierarchy—since it must duplicate personnel and equipment or else lose the advantages of specialization.

> ... if the organization has two projects, each requiring one half-time electronics engineer and one half-time electromechanical engineer, the pure project

[market] organization must either hire two electrical engineers—and reduce specialization—or hire four engineers (two electronics and two electromechanical)—and incur duplication costs (Galbraith; 1971, p. 30).

Moreover, the market structure, because of less functional specialization, cannot take advantage of economies of scale the way the functional structure can. The large hardware store can perhaps afford a lift truck at its unloading dock, whereas the small one cannot. Also, there may be wasteful competition within the market structure, as, for example, when stores in the same chain compete for the same customers.

What all of this comes down to is that **by choosing the market basis for grouping, the organization opts for work-flow coordination at the expense of process and scale specialization.** Litterer (1965) shows this well in his example of a factory, shown in Figure 7-10, where the work flows from points *A* to *B* to *C*. In Figure 7-10(a)—the market structure—work-flow coordination takes place within a single unit, while coordination related to work processes and methods (namely those associated with specialization) must take place across different units and, therefore, involve a higher level of management. The exact reverse occurs in the functional structure [Figure 7-10(b)], where coordination concerning process and method is contained within a single unit while work-flow interdependencies spill over it and require the involvement of the plant manager.

As this example makes clear, **if the work-flow interdependencies are the significant ones and if they cannot easily be contained by standardization, the organization will try to contain them in a market-based grouping to facilitate direct supervision and mutual adjustment** as it did in the example of the credit flow shown in Figure 7-6(b). However, **if the work flow is irregular (as in a job shop), if standardization can easily contain work-flow interdependencies, or if the process and scale interdependencies are the significant ones (as in the case of organizations with sophisticated machinery), then the organization will be inclined to seek the advantages of specialization and choose the functional basis for grouping instead.**[5]

GROUPING IN DIFFERENT PARTS OF THE ORGANIZATION

At this point it is useful to distinguish the first-order grouping—that is, individual positions into units—from higher-order grouping—units into larger units. In this way we can distinguish the grouping of operators, analysts, and support staffers as individuals into their basic working units,

[5]Choices must, of course, often be made between different functional or market bases for grouping. See, for example, Stopford and Wells (1972, Chaps. 3 and 4) for an extended discussion of product versus area groupings in the multinational firm.

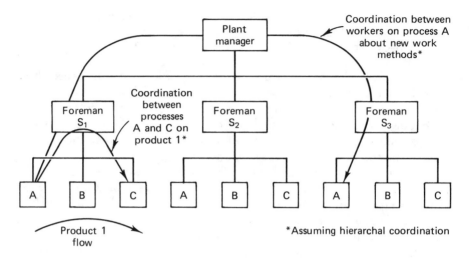

(a) Grouping by product (i.e., market)

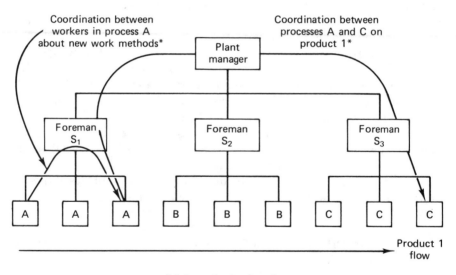

(b) Grouping by function

Figure 7-10. *Grouping to Contain Work-flow or Specialization Interdependencies (from Litterer, 1965, p. 328)*

from the construction of the managerial hierarchy that combines these into larger units.

A characteristic of these first-order groupings is that **operators, analysts, and support staffers tend to be grouped into their own respective units**

in the first instance. That is, operators tend to form units with other operators, analysts with other analysts, and staff support personnel with other staff support personnel. (Obviously, this assumes that the organization is large enough to have a number of positions of each. An important exception to this—to be discussed later—is the case where a staff member is assigned as an individual to a line group, as for example, when an accountant reports directly to a factory manager.) It is typically when the higher-order groups are formed that the operators, analysts, and support staffers come together under common supervision. We shall elaborate on this point in our discussion of each of these groups.

The examples cited in this chapter have shown that positions in the operating core can be grouped on a functional or a market basis, depending primarily on the importance of process and scale interdependencies as opposed to those of the work flow. Assembly lines are market-based groups, organized according to the work flow, while job shops, because of irregular work flows or the need for expensive machinery, group their positions by work process and so represent functional groupings. And as we noted earlier, in operating cores manned by professionals, the functional and market bases for grouping are often achieved concurrently: the professionals are grouped according to their knowledge and skills and the work processes they use, but since their clients select them on these bases, the groups become, in effect, market-based as well.

Which basis for grouping is more common in the operating core? The research provides no definite answer on this question. But ours is a society of specialists, and that is most clearly manifested in our formal organizations, particularly in their operating cores and staff structures. (As noted earlier, managers are in an important sense generalists, linking together the work of different specialists.) Thus, we should expect to find the functional basis for grouping the most common in the operating core. There are, of course, pressures to adopt the market basis for grouping: when the Tavistock researchers and Chapple and Sayles argue for both bottom-up organizational design and grouping according to the work flow, they are essentially making the case for market-based grouping in the operating core. But that flies in the face of very strong pressures for process specialization.

There is, by definition, only one level of grouping in the operating core—the operators grouped into units managed by the first-line supervisors. From there on, grouping brings line managers together and so builds the administrative superstructure of the middle line.

In designing this superstructure, we meet squarely the question that Thompson posed: not which basis of grouping but rather in which order of priority. Much as fires are built by stacking logs first one way and then the other, so organizations are often built by varying the bases for grouping units. For example, in Figure 7–8, the first grouping within the middle line is based on work process (fabricating and assembling) the next above on business function (engineering, manufacturing, and marketing), the one above that on market (snowblowers, etc.), and the last one on place (Canada, etc.). The presence of market-based groups in the upper region of the administrative hierarchy is probably indicative: although no research on the issue has been found, **the anecdotal evidence (published organigrams, etc.) suggests that the market basis for grouping is more common at the higher levels of the middle line than at the lower ones, particularly in large organizations.**

As a final note on the administrative superstructure, it should be pointed out that, by definition, there is only one grouping at the strategic apex, and that encompasses the entire organization—all of its functions and markets. From the organization's point of view this can be thought of as a market group, although from society's point of view the whole organization can also be considered as performing some particular function (delivering the mail in the case of the post office or supplying fuel in the case of an oil company).

Staff personnel—both analysts and support staff—seem, like wolves, to move in packs, or homogeneous clusters, according to the function they perform in the organization. (True, they provide their services to the line units, in a sense their "markets"; but bear in mind that "market" was defined earlier in terms of the entire organization—what it produces or provides its clients.) To put this another way, staff members are not often found in the structure as individuals reporting with operators or different staffers directly to line managers of market units which they serve. Instead, they tend in the first instance to report to managers of their own specialty—the accountant to a controller, the work study analyst to the manager of industrial engineering, the scientist to the chief of the research laboratory, the chef to the manager of the plant cafeteria. This in large part reflects the need to encourage specialization in their knowledge and skills, as well as to balance their use efficiently across the whole organization. The need for specialization as well as the high cost, dictate that there be only one research laboratory and economic forecasting unit in many organizations. Especially for the higher-level staff personnel, the use of the functional group to build and maintain expertise is crucial.

Sometimes, in fact, an individual analyst, such as an accountant, is placed within a market unit, ostensibly reporting to its line manager. But he is there to exercise control over the behavior of the line unit (and its manager), and whether de facto or de jure, his allegiance runs straight back to his specialized unit in the technostructure.

But at some point—for staff units if not for staff individuals—the question arises as to where they should be placed in the superstructure. Should they be dispensed in small clusters to the departments they are to serve—often market-based units—or should they be concentrated into larger single departments at a central location to serve the entire organization? And how high up in the superstructure should they be placed; that is, to line managers at what level should they report?

As for level, the decision depends on the staffers' interactions. A unit of financial experts who work with the chief executive officer would naturally report to him, while one of work study analysts might report to the manager at the plant level. As for concentration or dispersal, the decision reflects all the factors discussed above, especially the trade-off between work-flow interdependencies (namely, the interactions with the users) and the need for specialization and economies of scale. For example, in the case of secretaries, the creation of a pool allows for specialization (one secretary can type manuscripts, another letters, etc.) and the better balancing of personnel, while individual assignments allow for a closer rapport with the users (I cannot imagine every member of a typing pool learning to read my handwriting!). Thus, in universities, where the professors' needs are varied and the secretarial costs low relative to those of the professors, secretarial services are generally widely dispersed. In contrast, university swimming pools, which are expensive, are concentrated, while libraries may go either way, depending on the location and specific needs of the various users.

Referring back to Figure 7–8, we find staff units at all levels of the hierarchy, some concentrated at the top, others dispersed to the market divisions and functional departments. The corporate secretariat serves the whole organization and links closely with the top management; thus, it reports directly to the strategic apex. The other units are dispersed to serve more-or-less local needs. One level down, public relations is attached to each of the national general managers so that, for example, each subsidiary can combat political resistance at the national level. Planning is dispersed to the next level, the product divisions, because of their conglomerate nature: each must plan independently for its own distinct product lines. Other staff units, such as work study, are dispersed to the next, functional level, where they can serve their respective factories. (We also find our ubiquitous cafeteria here—one for each plant.) Finally, the maintenance department is dispersed down to the general foreman level, to serve fabricating or assembly.

8

Design of Superstructure: Unit Size

The second basic issue in the design of the superstructure concerns how large each unit or work group should be. How many positions should be contained in the first-level grouping and how many units in each successively higher-order unit? This question of unit size can be rephrased in two important ways: How many individuals should report to each manager; that is, what should be his *span of control?* And what *shape* should the superstructure be: *tall*, with small units and narrow spans of control, or *wide*, with large units and wide spans of control?

On this point, the traditional literature was firm: "No supervisor can supervise directly the work of more than five or, at the most, six subordinates whose work interlocks," said Colonel Lydal Urwick unequivocally (1956, p. 41). But subsequent investigation has made this statement seem rather quaint. Holden et al. (1968, p. 95) report that the span of control of the chief executive officers in the firms they studied averaged ten, with a range from one to fourteen. In Woodward's (1965) study of industrial firms, the median for chief executives was six, but in five "successful" firms the chief executives supervised more than twelve immediate subordinates. For first-line supervisors in mass production firms, she found an average span of control of close to fifty, in some cases ranging into the nineties. Worthy (1959) reports that the merchandising vice-president of Sears, Roebuck and Co. had forty-four senior executives reporting to him, while for the typical store manager the figure was "forty-odd" department managers (p. 109). And Pfiffner and Sherwood (1960) note the extreme example of "the Bank of America, which has over 600 branches throughout California, each of which reports directly to corporate headquarters at San Francisco. There is no intervening area structure with directive powers over the branch offices" (p. 161). In some of these cases, notably the Bank of America and perhaps also Sears, Roebuck, Urwick's qualification about interlocking work may apply. But certainly not in all.

About the concept of span of control, Pfiffner and Sherwood have commented:

> Much blood has been let to reduce the executive's span with inconsequential results to administrative performance. Yet span of control sails merrily on. There is much written about it. Most consultants tab this as an essential in reform proposals. Students sweat over its definition, mainly because they assume the concept should be more complicated than it really is. Thus, regardless of what its merits may be, span of control is so entrenched in the administrative culture that it must be accorded a prominent place in any book on organization (pp. 155–156).

There is no doubt that the concept merits a prominent place in this book. But there is reason to doubt Pfiffner and Sherwood's suggestion that it is a simple one (Ouchi and Dowling, 1974). Who should be counted as a subordinate: for example, what about the assistant to, or those whose work is reviewed by the manager even though they do not formally report to him? What about the nonsupervisory aspects of the manager's job—collecting information, developing liaison contacts, and so on: does a narrow span of control necessarily mean close "control," as the traditional literature suggested, or might it instead imply that the manager is busy doing these other things? What about the influence of the coordinating mechanisms other than direct supervision on the size of the work unit? As Worthy (1959) has noted, "The essential error of the generally accepted span of control theory is its implicit assumption that the superior must not only direct the work of his subordinates but must mediate many of the relationships between them. ... [Certain studies suggest] a skeptical attitude toward the ability of subordinates to cooperate spontaneously without the intervention of the superior" (p. 107).

What all of this suggests is that the issue is not a simple one and the focus on control is misplaced. Control—that is, direct supervision—is only one factor among many in deciding how many positions to group into one unit, or how many units to group in one larger unit, in both cases under a single manager. Hence, the term "unit size" is preferred in this chapter to "span of control." Let us now try to sort out some of this confusion and see what can be learned from the empirical studies, first those of tall versus flat structures and then those which relate unit size to the coordinating mechanisms.

STUDIES OF TALL VERSUS FLAT STRUCTURES

In essence, a tall structure has a long chain of authority with relatively small groups at each hierarchical level, while a flat structure has few levels with relatively large work groups at each. In one laboratory experiment, Carzo and Yanouzas (1969) contrasted the results of work performed by a tall structure (four levels with a span of control of two persons at each) with that of a flat one (one individual supervising fourteen individuals directly). These two structures are shown in Figure 8–1. The task involved estimating the demand for a hypothetical product in each of seven geographical areas and then deciding what quantity of goods to order from the suppliers. The "operators," specialized by geographical area, made the initial decisions, and ultimately the "president" had to finalize them. While Carzo and Yanouzas found no significant difference in the time taken to do the assigned task, they did find differences in how the two structures went about doing them. The greater number of levels in the tall structure interrupted the

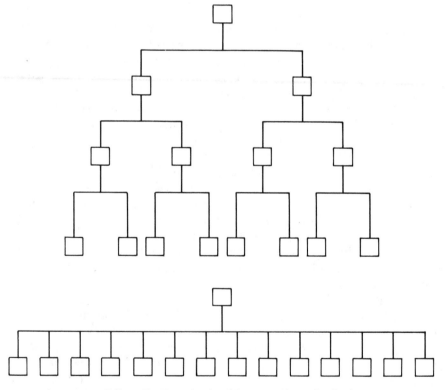

Figure 8-1. *Tall vs. Flat Organizational Structures (grouping in the Carzo and Yanouzas' Experiment, 1969)*

vertical flow of information more frequently. However, the flat structure required more discussion and consultation. In effect, "the greater time required for decisions to pass through several levels of a tall structure is offset by the time required to resolve differences and coordinate the efforts of many subordinates in a flat structure" (p. 189). Carzo and Yanouzas also found evidence of greater status differences in the tall structure, which impeded information flow and so required the managers to be more careful in their data collection. Nevertheless, in this experiment, on measures of profit and return on investment, the tall structures did better:

> The superior performance of the groups under the tall structure may be explained by the fact that their decisions were subjected to more analysis than the decisions of the groups under the flat structure. The intermediate supervisory levels ... provided the means for repeated evaluation of decisions. ...
>
> In addition, the narrow span of supervision in the tall structure permitted a much more orderly decision and communication process. Freed from the burdens that arise from having many subordinates, decision makers appeared to be able to develop a better understanding of the problem (p. 190).

So the plot thickens. A small unit can reduce the time the manager must spend on direct supervision and so provide more time for his other roles. In fact, Blau and Schoenherr (1971, p. 321) found the same thing in their study of employment security agencies, that the managers in the taller structures had more time for decision making and external work.

A number of findings have been put forward concerning the psychological impact of tall and flat organization structures. Some researchers have noted that tall structures better serve the individual's need for security, since a superior is always readily available (Porter and Lawler, 1964). Others argue that tall structures lead to supervision that can be too close, creating a frustrating situation for the employee in search of autonomy and self-actualization. Thus, Ivancevich and Donnelly (1975), in a study of trade salespersons, found that those in the flat structures (115 salespeople reporting to eight division managers reporting to a sales vice-president) claimed to be more satisfied on the dimensions of self-actualization and autonomy, indicated less anxiety and stress, and performed more efficiently than those in the medium and tall structures. (In the former, 142 salespersons reported to thirteen district operations managers, who reported to eight field sales managers, who reported to a president of marketing. In the latter, 210 salespeople reported to twenty-two district sales managers, who reported to twelve divisional sales managers, who reported to three regional sales managers, who reported to a field sales coordinator, who reported to a chief marketing executive.) Whereas the salespersons in the flat structures felt little supervisory pressure, planned their own schedules of visits, set their own monthly sales quotas, and perceived less emphasis on rules and policies, even about checking with the supervisors before closing big sales, a number of those in the medium and tall structures complained of being checked on constantly, which reduced their confidence in their ability to sell the product. Cummings and Berger (1976), in their review of the impact of organizational structure on attitude, note that top managers who do the controlling report being more satisfied in tall structures while lower-level managers—on the receiving end—report that they are happier in flat ones. As Argyris notes, tall structures "increase the subordinates' feelings of dependence, submissiveness, passivity, and the like" (quoted in Starbuck, 1971, p. 88).

Clearly, there can be more freedom in the flatter structure, where the absence of close contact between the manager and each of his employees forces the latter to succeed or fail on their own. This, in fact, was Worthy's (1959) explanation of Sears' wide spans of control:

> The limited span of control makes it difficult for subordinate executives to get too far off base or to stay off base too long. But precisely for this reason, subordinates in such a system are deprived of one of their most valuable means of learning. For people learn as much—perhaps more—from their mistakes as from their successes. . . .
>
> [In structures with wide spans of control] people are encouraged, even pushed, to reach to the limit of their capacities, and sometimes to develop capacities they never knew they had (pp. 110–111).

Similarly, Pfiffner and Sherwood (1960) explain how the Bank of America was able to tolerate an effective span of control of over 600:

> When officers of the bank are questioned about this seemingly unorthodox setup, their response is that they do not want to risk setting up an echelon that would take authority away from the branch managers. They want them to be self-reliant local businessmen with a maximum opportunity for making decisions on their own (p. 161).

UNIT SIZE IN RELATIONSHIP TO THE COORDINATING MECHANISMS

Much of the confusion in this area seems to stem from considering unit size, or span of control, only with respect to the coordinating mechanism of direct supervision, not standardization or mutual adjustment. The traditional management theorists set the tone by implying that control and coordination could be achieved only by direct supervision. What else would have prompted Urwick to insist on his "five, or at the most, six" formula?

As has been pointed out repeatedly since the start of our discussion, the five coordinating mechanisms are to some extent substitutable. For example, the manager's job can be "institutionalized" by standardization; and mutual adjustment within the work group can be used in place of direct supervision from above. We would, of course, expect such replacement of direct supervision by another coordinating mechanism to affect significantly the size of a unit. Thus, **we should be able to explain variations in unit size largely in terms of the mechanisms used to coordinate work.**

We can summarize our conclusions in terms of two basic hypotheses, one dealing with standardization, the other with mutual adjustment. First, **the greater the use of standardization for coordination, the larger the size of the work unit.** It stands to reason that the more coordination in a unit is achieved through the systems of standardization designed by the technostructure, the less time its manager need spend on the direct supervision of each employee, and so the greater the number of employees that can report to him. With this conclusion, we can rather easily explain Joan Woodward's (1965) finding about the very high spans of control encountered in the mass production firms. Bear in mind two points about her findings. First, the very wide spans of control were found at the first level of supervision, namely in those units containing the operators themselves. Second, as can be seen in Figure 8–2, reproduced from Woodward's book, the largest operating units—with an average of almost fifty employees—were found in the mass production firms. Those in unit and process production had units averaging less than twenty-five and fifteen operators, respectively. Indeed, they had virtually no units even as large as the *average* for the mass producers. Now, when we combine this with Woodward's findings that the mass production firms were the only bureaucratic ones, the other two being structured organically, we see an evident relationship. Unit size was largest where the work was the most standardized—in the operating cores of the most bureaucratic organizations.

So far, we have discussed only the standardization of work processes. However, our first hypothesis is not restricted to any special kind of standardization. In other words, standardization of skills and of outputs should also lead to larger unit size. In the case of skills, it stands to reason that the more highly trained the employees, the less closely they need be supervised, and so the larger can be their work units. We see this most clearly in general hospitals and universities. At the time of this writing, fifty of my colleagues and myself work in a single unit, which runs smoothly under a single dean with no department heads. Ouchi and Dowling (1974) tested this relationship by comparing four measures of the spans of control of the department managers of retail stores with two measures they considered related to the professionalism of the salespersons—the size of the store's training staff and

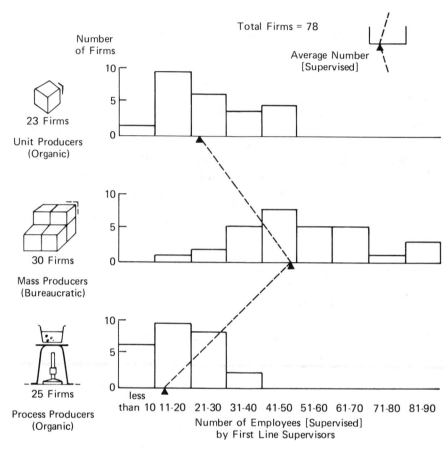

Figure 8-2. *Unit Size and Work Standardization (from Woodward, 1965, p. 62)*

its high-priced image. All the correlations were found to be positive, with what Ouchi and Dowling thought their most reliable measure of span of control correlating significantly with both measures of professionalism.[1]

Similarly, we would expect that the more standardized the outputs, the larger can be the size of the work unit. Thus, although the Bank of America justified its span of control of 600 on the basis of encouraging the initiative

[1]That measure accounted only for the time the department managers spent on the selling floor and included the time the buyers spent aiding the managers in day-to-day supervision. One of the other measures used full-time equivalent salespersons instead of the total number, with the preceding measure of supervision. The other two used the total number of salespersons and excluded the buyers, and one of these (the "raw" measure) did not adjust for the time the managers spent on the floor.

of its branch managers, we would be on safe ground in assuming that this enormous span of control would simply be impossible without a very tight system of performance (output) control, not to mention the use of all kinds of rules and regulations and of training and indoctrination programs for the branch managers. Similarly, those who shop at Sears well know how standardized that operation is. As Moore, referring implicitly to the role of indoctrination, commented, "Sears can decentralize [i.e., release the store managers from close supervision]; everyone thinks alike anyway" (quoted in Wilensky, 1967, p. 60). Chains of banks and retail stores frequently exhibit very wide spans of control precisely because each outlet is a carbon copy of all the others, thereby facilitating standardization.

Thus, we cannot conclude that being a member of a large unit automatically frees the individual from close control. Control from his boss perhaps, but not necessarily from the systems of the technostructure—or even from his earlier training and indoctrination. In fact, the most tightly controlled members of organizations are typically those in the largest units: the operators doing unskilled work in highly bureaucratic operating cores. Even their managers feel the same control: I once spoke to eighty branch managers of large Canadian banking firms on the nature of managerial work; the ensuing discussion period was dominated by one issue—their extreme frustration in being unable to act as full-fledged managers, because of the rules imposed on their branches by the corporate technostructures. Thus, we cannot, it seems, accept Cummings and Berger's conclusion without qualification: lower-level managers are more satisfied in flat structures only if extensive standardization has not replaced close direct supervision as the means of coordination.

Our second hypothesis is: **the greater the reliance on mutual adjustment (due to interdependencies among complex tasks), the smaller the size of the work unit.** A relationship between complex interdependent tasks and small unit size can be explained in two ways. The obvious one is that, all coordinating mechanisms (especially standardization) remaining equal, the more interdependent the tasks (complex or not) in a unit, the greater will be the need for contact between the manager and the employees to coordinate their work. Ostensibly, the manager will have to monitor and supervise the unit's activities more closely and to be more readily available for consultation and advice. Therefore, the manager requires a small span of control. This suggests yet another angle on the Sears and Bank of America stories, namely the absence of interdependence. Geographically dispersed retail branches, each serving its own customers, are neither reciprocally nor sequentially interdependent; far more of them can, therefore, be supervised than, say, the sequentially interdependent departments of a factory. That is why Urwick qualified his principle of span of control with the word "interlocks."

But there is a second, more subtle explanation for the hypothesized relationship between *complex* interdependent tasks and small unit size. These kind of tasks are difficult to supervise, so instead of an increase in direct supervision, they give rise to an increase in mutual adjustment to achieve coordination. The employees themselves must communicate on a face-to-face basis to coordinate their work. But for such communication to function effectively, the work unit must be small, small enough to encourage convenient, frequent, and informal interaction among all its members. For example, Filley et al. (1976, pp. 417–418) review a number of studies that demonstrate the relationship between the small size of the group and such factors as its cohesiveness and the participation of its members. One study indicated that beyond 10 members, groups tend to fraction into cliques, that is, smaller groups, and another found that five to seven members was optimal for consensus. Now, organizations, being what they are, designate a leader—a "manager"—for each of their units, no matter how small, even when that individual acts as little more than the unit's official spokesperson. And so, when the span of control of units doing interdependent complex tasks is measured, lo and behold it turns out to be small.

Let us reflect on this conclusion for a moment. On the surface, it is counterintuitive, since it could be restated as follows: the less the reliance on direct supervision, the *narrower* the manager's span of control. The confusion, of course, lies with the term used, for here span of control has nothing to do with "control"; it is merely an indication of the need to maintain a small face-to-face work group to encourage mutual adjustment when the work is complex and interdependent. In other words, while the restatement of the hypothesis may be technically correct, it is misleading to use terms like "direct supervision" and "span of control." We are better off to conclude that, because of the need for "mutual adjustment," "unit size" must be small.

This point suggests two lessons. First, in the area of structure (I am tempted to say management in general), things are not necessarily what they seem. We cannot rely on the pleasant conceptualizations of the armchair; we have to go out and research phenomena directly. Careful observation produces its own share of surprises. Second, we had better choose our terms (like "control") very carefully, and be quite sure of what we are measuring when we do empirical research.

One final point should be mentioned. Much of the evidence showing that complex interdependent tasks lead to small unit size comes from studies of professional groups. (See especially Hall, 1972, p. 153ff.) But how can we reconcile this finding with that of the first hypothesis, namely that professionalism (i.e., standardization of skills) leads to a large unit size? The answer lies in interdependence: professional work is always complex (by our definition), but it is not always interdependent. **There are, in effect, two** kinds of professional work—independent and interdependent—requiring two very different structural forms. In one case, the standardization of skills handles most of the interdependencies, so there is little need for mutual adjustment and the professionals can work independently, in large units. This is the situation we find in most accounting firms and educational systems, where individual professionals serve their own clients. In the other case, interdependencies remain which cannot be handled by the standardization of skills, so there must be considerable mutual adjustment. The professionals must work cooperatively in small, informal units. This happens, for example, in research laboratories and think-tank consulting firms. Thus, Meyer, who studied 254 finance departments of state and local governments and found the lowest spans of control in those with the highest expertise, was careful to qualify his result: "... it is not expertness in and of itself but rather the need for frequent consultations and communications that produces low spans of control in parts of organizations that employ highly qualified personnel" (quoted in Hall, 1972, p. 155).

To conclude our general discussion, we have seen that **unit size is driven up by (1) standardization of all three types, (2) similarity in the tasks performed in a given unit, (3) the employees' needs for autonomy and self-actualization, and (4) the need to reduce distortion in the flow of information up the hierarchy; and it is driven down by (1) the need for close direct supervision, (2) the need for mutual adjustment among complex interdependent tasks, (3) the extent to which the manager of a unit has nonsupervisory duties to perform, and (4) the need for members of the unit to have frequent access to the manager for consultation or advice.**

GROUP SIZE BY PART
OF THE ORGANIZATION

How does group size vary from one part of the organization to another? Generalizations are somewhat risky here, since as we have seen, group size is heavily influenced by many factors. Nevertheless, some general comments are warranted.

It is in the operating core that we would expect to find the largest units, since this part of the organization tends to rely most extensively on standardization for coordination, especially standardization of work processes. Thus, as can be seen in Figure 8–3, Woodward found the span of control of chief executive officers to be rather narrow on average—a median of six— while that for the first-line supervisors was in the high thirties.

Managerial work is generally complex, so we might expect the size of units in the administrative structure to depend heavily on the interdepen-

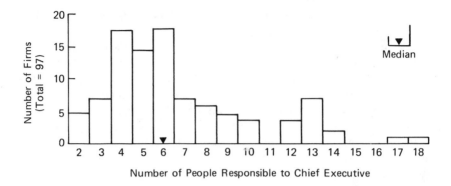

(a) Span of Control of Chief Executives

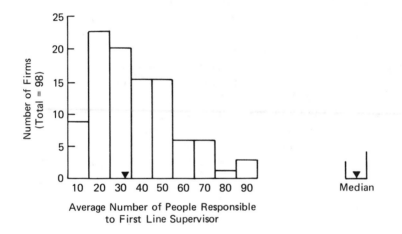

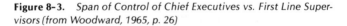

(b) Span of Control of First Line Supervisors

Figure 8-3. *Span of Control of Chief Executives vs. First Line Supervisors (from Woodward, 1965, p. 26)*

dence encountered at a given level of the hierarchy. As we saw in Chapter 7, interdependencies are closely related to the grouping of a unit. Specifically, market grouping is often selected because it contains the work-flow interdependencies within each unit (and because the process interdependencies are secondary), whereas functional grouping often does not, requiring either that a higher-level manager coordinate the work flow across different units or that the managers or members of each of the units in question do so themselves through mutual adjustment. In either event, the result is the same: **only a few functional units can be grouped into a higher-order unit, whereas, typically, many more market-based units can be so grouped.** A great many autonomous divisions can report to one company president, as can a great many schools to one superintendent; in contrast, the president of an integrated manufacturing firm or the manager of a television station can supervise only a few interdependent functional departments. (It will be recalled, further, that both Sears stores and Bank of America branches are market-based units.) And since, as discussed in Chapter 7, organizations vary the bases for grouping used at different levels in the administrative hierarchy, we would not expect the middle line of the large organization to be uniformly tall or flat, but rather to exhibit a wavy shape, flat where grouping is based on markets, tall where it is based on function.

Earlier we noted that as we move up the hierarchy, managerial decision making becomes more complex, less amenable to regulation. Therefore, holding interdependence constant, we would expect a greater need for mutual adjustment at the higher levels, with a resulting decrease in unit size. So **the overall managerial hierarchy should look like a cone—albeit it a wavy one—with progressively steepening sides.** Simon (1973a) makes this point in terms of what he calls "attention management":

> The information-processing systems of our contemporary world swim in an exceedingly rich soup of information, of symbols. In a world of this kind, the scarce resource is not information; it is processing capacity to attend to information. Attention is the chief bottleneck in organizational activity, and the bottleneck becomes narrower and narrower as we move to the tops of organizations, where parallel processing capacity becomes less easy to provide without damaging the coordinating function that is a prime responsibility of these levels (pp. 270–271).

Thus, holding all else constant, we should expect the chief executive officer to have the narrowest average span of control in the organization. In fact, we saw evidence of this earlier. What may not, however, remain constant is the basis for grouping. As noted earlier, the market basis is often used toward the top of the middle line. Where it is so used, and the people reporting to the chief executive supervise functional units, we would expect his span of control to be wider than theirs.

Another factor that confounds the span of control for the managers of the middle line is their relationship with the staff units. Coordination of line and staff activities typically requires mutual adjustment, that is, flexible communication outside the chain of authority. This, of course, takes a good deal of the line manager's time, leaving less for direct supervision. So we would expect that where there is much line/staff interdependence, spans of control in the middle line should be narrower. **Organizations with great**

proliferations of technocratic and support staff units should have rather small units in the middle line.

This leads us to an interesting conclusion about highly bureaucratic organizations heavily dependent on technocratic staff groups to formalize the operating work: while the spans of control of the first-line supervisors should be high because of the extensive standardization in the operating core, that of the managers higher up should be small because of the need for mutual adjustment with the staff members. In fact, this is exactly what comes out of the Woodward study. The first-line supervisors in the mass production firms (the bureaucratic ones) had the highest spans of control, but the middle-line managers above them had rather narrower ones. In contrast, the firms in process industries, with organic structures and the most extensively elaborated staff components, exhibited much narrower spans of control at both levels. And those in unit production, with organic structures and little staff—in essence, the opposite conditions of the mass producers— exhibited very narrow spans of control at the level of the first-line supervisor and rather wide ones at the middle levels of management. Woodward (1965) specifically attributes the small spans of control in unit and process production to "the breakdown of the labor force into small primary work groups," resulting in more intimate and informal relationships with supervisors (p. 60). All of this is shown in Figure 14–1 in the chapter on the technical system as a contingency factor where we shall return to this issue.

Finally, what about the size of the staff units themselves? How many staff members can a staff manager supervise? In those support units that do relatively unskilled work—the cafeteria and mailroom, for example—the structure would tend to be bureaucratic and the units therefore large. But what of the other units in the technostructure and support staff? **The factors we discussed earlier indicate small size for most of the professional-type staff units.** The work within these units is complex and, being of a project nature, typically creates interdependencies among the professionals. In other words, these staff members are professionals of the second type discussed earlier, namely those who must function in small interdependent units rather than as independent individuals attached to larger units. Furthermore, as noted earlier, the technocratic units accomplish their work only when they are able to change the work of others in the organization. Hence, the managers of technocratic units must spend a good deal of their time "selling" the proposals of their units in the middle line (Mintzberg, 1973a, pp. 116–117). Likewise, the support specialists do not work in a vacuum but serve the rest of the organization, and so their managers must spend a good deal of time in liaison with it. In both cases, this reduces the number of people the staff managers can supervise, and so shrinks the average size of staff units.

To conclude, in general we would expect the operating core of the organization to assume a flat shape, the middle line to appear as a cone with progressively steepening sides, and the technostructure and more professional support units to be tall in shape. That is, in fact, the design of our logo, as a quick glance back at Figure 2–1 will illustrate.

9

Design of Lateral Linkages: Planning and Control Systems

Organizational design is not complete when the positions have been established and the superstructure built. At one time, the literature on organizational design stopped here, but contemporary research has made clear the need to flesh out the bones of the superstructure with linkages that are lateral, as opposed to strictly vertical. Two main groups of these linkages have received extensive treatment in the contemporary literature on organizational design—planning and control systems that standardize outputs and liaison devices that grease the wheels of mutual adjustment. In this chapter we discuss the first of these.

The purpose of a plan is to specify a desired output—a standard—at some future time. And the purpose of control is to assess whether or not that standard has been achieved. Thus, planning and control go together like the proverbial horse and carriage: there can be no control without prior planning, and plans lose their influence without follow-up controls. Together plans and controls regulate outputs and, indirectly, behavior as well.

Plans may specify (standardize) the quantity, quality, cost, and timing of outputs, as well as their specific characteristics (such as size and color). *Budgets* are plans that specify the costs of outputs for given periods of time; *schedules* are plans that establish time frames for outputs; *objectives* are plans that detail output quantities for given periods of time; *operating plans* are those that establish a variety of standards, generally the quantities and costs of outputs. For example, an operating plan for a manufacturing firm would specify budgets as well as sales targets, production quantities, manpower requirements, and so on, for all the line departments near the operating core. Typically, planning systems, as well as the reporting systems that feed back the control information, are designed in the technostructure, by analysts with titles such as Planner, Budget Analyst, Controller, MIS Analyst, Production Scheduler, and Quality Control Analyst.

We can distinguish two fundamentally different kinds of planning and control systems, one that focuses on the regulation of overall performance and the other that seeks to regulate specific actions. Since the former is concerned primarily with *after-the-fact* monitoring of results, we shall call it *performance control*. The latter, oriented to specifying activities that *will* take place, is labeled *action planning*. In other words, as shown in Figure 9-1, the organization can regulate outputs in two ways. It can use performance control to measure the results of a whole series of actions, and use this information to make changes: "The profit rate should increase from 7 percent to 10 percent," or "The drilling of holes should be increased from fifty to sixty per day." Alternatively, it can use action planning to determine in advance what specific decisions or actions are required: "Blue widgets

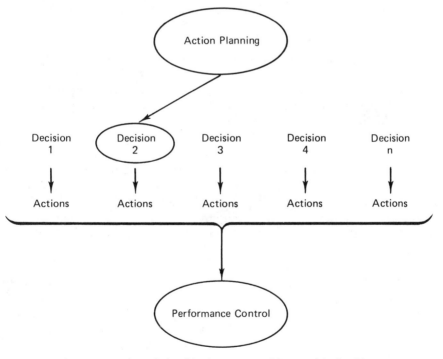

Figure 9-1. *The Relationships between Decisions and Action Planning and Performance Control*

should be sold to customers X, Y, and Z," or "The hole should be drilled 1.108 centimeters wide." As we shall see, while performance control is a pure means of standardizing outputs, action planning—because it specifies particular actions—resembles in some ways the design parameter of formalization of behavior.

PERFORMANCE CONTROL

The purpose of performance control is to regulate the overall results of a given unit. Objectives, budgets, operating plans, and various other kinds of general standards are established for the unit, and its performance is later measured in terms of these standards and is fed back up the hierarchy by the MIS. This suggests two important points. First, performance control systems map unto the bases for grouping in the organization. The planning system establishes output standards for each unit, and the control system assesses whether or not these have been met. Second, performance control is concerned with overall results for given periods of time, not with specific decisions or actions at specific points in time. For example, a performance plan may call for the production of 70,000 widgets in June, or the reduction of costs by 3 percent in July; it does not call for the shift from blue widgets to green ones or the achievement of cost reduction by the purchase of a more efficient machine. Thus, performance control only influences decision making and action taking indirectly, by establishing general targets that the decision maker must keep in the back of his mind as he makes specific decisions in the front.

Where is performance control used in the organization? To some extent, everywhere. Because cost control is always crucial and because costs—at least economic ones—are easily measured, virtually every organizational unit is given a budget, that is, a performance plan to standardize its expenditures. And where the unit's production is easily measured, its performance plan will typically specify this as well. The plant is expected to produce 400,000 widgets this month; marketing is expected to sell 375,000 of them.

But **performance control systems are most relied upon where the interdependencies between units are primarily of a pooled nature, namely where the units are grouped on a market basis.** Here the major concern is that the unit perform adequately, that it make an appropriate contribution to the central organization without squandering its resources. In other words, because there is little interdependency between units, coordination requires the regulation of performance, not actions. And this is facilitated in the market-based structure by the fact that each unit has its own distinct outputs. Thus, its overall behavior is regulated by performance controls; otherwise, it is left alone to do its own action planning.

Indeed, such performance controls are typically crucial for market-based units. Because they are self-contained, they are generally given considerable freedom to act, quasi-autonomy. Typically, as noted in Chapter 8, a great many such units report to a single manager. Without a performance control system, the manager may be unable to catch serious problems (e.g., those requiring replacement of a market unit manager) until it is much too late. A wayward Sears store or Bank of America branch could, for example, get lost for years, too small a part of the organization to be otherwise noticed. And, from the perspective of the market unit itself, the performance control system serves to preclude direct supervision and so to grant it the freedom it needs to determine its own decisions and actions. "Each manager in the organizational hierarchy is able, in the short run, to operate his department relatively free of direction by higher-level managers. The direction that does exist is of an aggregate, rather than a detailed, nature" (Emery, 1969, p. 32). Thus, the conglomerate corporation sets up each of its market units (its "divisions") as a profit or investment center, and holds it responsible for its own financial performance.[1]

One researcher who has looked at the use of planning and control systems in the context of organizational structure is Khandwalla (1974a). He is careful to note that, simple as they may seem, these systems are sophisticated and they can be expensive, requiring "substantial information processing skills on the part of managers who utilize them" (p. 86). Khandwalla found a strong relationship between the autonomy granted a manager down the chain of authority and the use of nine of these systems, most of them performance control: statistical quality control of operations, standard costing and analysis of cost variances, inventory control and production scheduling by operations research techniques, marginal costing, flexible or activity budgeting, internal audit, the use of internal rates of return or present values in evaluating investments, systematic evaluation of senior personnel, and performance or operational audit.

Performance control systems can serve two purposes: to measure and to motivate. On the one hand, they can be used simply to signal when the performance of a unit has deteriorated. Higher-level management can then step in and take corrective action. On the other hand, they can be used to elicit higher performance. The performance standards are the carrots that management places before the unit manager to motivate him to achieve better results. Whenever he manages a nibble, the carrot is moved a little

---

[1]That is not to say, of course, that a performance control system can never be tight. It can specify so many detailed performance standards that the unit is left little room to maneuver. (We shall see examples of this in Chapter 20.) But, in general, performance controls are used in the market-based structure to maintain only the most general regulation of outputs.

farther out and the manager runs faster. Systems such as management by objectives (MBO) have been developed to give unit managers a say in the establishment of these standards so that they will be committed to them and, therefore, the theory goes, strive harder to achieve them.

But this motivational aspect introduces a variety of problems. For one thing, given the right to participate in the setting of performance standards, the unit manager has a strong incentive to set the standards low enough to ensure that they can easily be met. And he also has an incentive to distort the feedback information sent up the MIS to make it look like his unit has met a standard it, in fact, missed.

A second problem arises with the choice of the planning period. There is, as noted, no direct link between the performance standards and specific decisions taken; it is only hoped that the manager will bear the standards in mind when he makes decisions. Long planning periods loosen the connection: the farther back the day of judgment, the less the manager is inclined to think about the standards. Besides, what is the use of rewarding or penalizing a manager for a decision he made a long time ago. Short planning periods, while keeping the performance standards front and center in the manager's mind, defeat a prime purpose of the system, namely giving him freedom of action. The "flash reports" on the tenth of every month used by some corporations certainly keep the manager hopping after short-term results. But do they let him think beyond thirty days?

A third problem of motivation arises with standards that cannot be realized for reasons beyond the manager's control. What to do when a major change in the environment, say the bankruptcy of a major customer, renders achievement of a performance standard impossible? Should the organization insist on honoring the agreement to the letter, and penalize the manager, or should it overrule the performance control system to determine rewards, in which case the system loses a good deal of its motivational punch?

ACTION PLANNING

As we have seen, performance control is a key design parameter in market-based structures. But what happens in functional structures? Functional work flows sequentially or reciprocally across them. This means that distinct organizational goals cannot easily be identified with any one unit. So aside from budgets and the like to control their expenditures, performance control systems cannot really cope with the interdependencies of functional units. As Worthy has noted:

... where the internal structure of the organization is broken down into a series of functional divisions, there are no "natural" standards of performance and management is forced to exercise considerable ingenuity in inventing controls which it can use for administrative purposes. Unfortunately, contrived controls such as these, so far from facilitating inter-divisional cooperation (which is one of their chief purposes) often become themselves a source of conflict (quoted in Chapple and Sayles, 1961, pp. 70–71).

In other words, something other than a performance control system must be found to coordinate work in the functional structure. As we saw in Chapter 7, direct supervision effected through the superstructure and standardization of work processes effected through behavior formalization emerge as key mechanisms to coordinate work in functional structures. They are preferred because they are the tightest available coordinating mechanisms. But sometimes they cannot contain all of the interdependencies. And so the organization must turn to planning and control systems to standardize outputs. Specifically, it uses action planning. Simon (1957) provides a dramatic example of what can happen when action planning fails to coordinate the remaining work-flow interdependencies:

In the first portion of the Waterloo campaign, Napoleon's army was divided in two parts. The right wing, commanded by the Emperor himself, faced Blucher at Ligny; the left wing, under Marshal Ney, faced Wellington at Quatre Bras. Both Ney and the Emperor prepared to attack, and both had prepared excellent plans for their respective operations. Unfortunately, both plans contemplated the use of Erlon's corps to deliver the final blow on the flank of the enemy. Because they failed to communicate these plans, and because orders were unclear on the day of the battle, Erlon's corps spent the day marching back and forth between the two fields without engaging in the action on either. Somewhat less brilliant tactical plans, coordinated, would have had greater success (p. 193).

Two points should be noted about action planning. First, unlike performance control, action planning does not necessarily respect unit autonomy, nor does it necessarily map onto the system of grouping. Action plans specify decisions that call for specific actions—to market new products, build new factories, visit different customers, sell old machines. Some of the proposed actions may be taken within single units, but others can cut across unit boundaries.

Second, by its imposition of specific decisions, action planning turns out to be a less than pure form of standardizing outputs; more exactly, it falls between that and standardizing work processes. This point can be expressed in terms of a continuum of increasingly tight regulation, as follows:

- *Performance control* imposes general performance standards over a period of time, with no reference to specific actions
- *Action planning* imposes specific decisions and actions to be carried out at specific points in time
- *Behavior formalization* imposes the means by which decisions and actions are to be carried out

So, whereas performance control says, "Increase sales by 10 percent this year [in any way you care to]," action planning says, "Do it by introducing blue widgets." It, too, specifies outputs, but in a way that constitutes the specification of means. At the limit, action planning becomes behavior formalization; specifically the specification of the work flow: "... the plan may control, down to minute details, a whole complex pattern of behavior. The completed plan of the battleship will specify the design of the ship down to the last rivet. The task of the construction crew is minutely specified by this design" (Simon, 1957, p. 231).

Action planning emerges as the means by which the nonroutine decisions and actions of an entire organization, typically structured on a functional basis, can be designed as an integrated system. All of this is accomplished in advance, on the drawing board so to speak. Behavior formalization designs the organization as an integrated system, too, but only for its routine activities. Action planning is its counterpart for the nonroutine activities, for the changes. It specifies who will do what, when, and where, so that the change will take place as desired.

*THE HIERARCHY OF PLANNING
AND CONTROL SYSTEMS*

How do these two planning and control systems relate to the superstructure and to each other? A great deal has been written on the hierarchical nature of each of them and a little bit about some of their interrelationships, but almost none of this is based on empirical evidence about how they really function. So let us try to build a picture from the conceptual literature.

Figure 9–2 shows performance control and action planning as two separate hierarchical systems, with certain "crossovers" between them. Performance control is shown as a system in which overall objectives at the top give rise to subobjectives, budgets, and other output standards, which in turn are elaborated into ever more detailed subobjectives, budgets, and standards until they emerge at the bottom of the structure as operating plans. The final outcome is, of course, organizational actions, but the con-

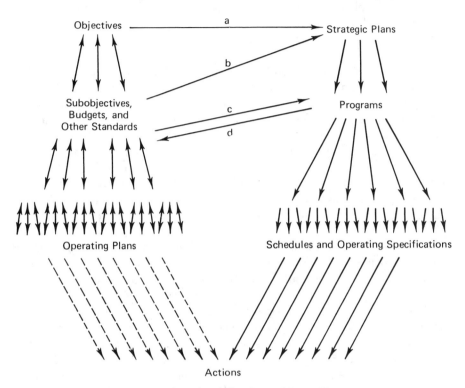

Performance Control System

Action Planning System

Objectives ——————— a ——————→ Strategic Plans

b

Subobjectives,
Budgets, and
Other Standards

c

d

Programs

Operating Plans

Schedules and Operating Specifications

Actions

Figure 9-2. *Hierarchy of Planning and Control Systems*

nection between the plans and the actions is shown as a series of dotted lines to indicate that it is only indirect: the operating plans only indicate the general results expected from all actions of a given type, for example, sales of 70,000 units in a year from all sales calls, 450 holes drilled in a week from all the efforts of a machine operator. As noted earlier, this whole performance control system—objectives, budgets, etc.—maps unto the superstructure.

The arrows in the diagram are two-sided, to indicate that the performance control system may be not only top-down—where objectives decided at the strategic apex are elaborated into ever more detailed performance standards as they pass down the hierarchy—but also bottom-up, where the units at the very bottom establish their own performance standards, and these are then aggregated up the hierarchy by unit, until they emerge at the strategic apex as composite standards, in effect, objectives for the whole organization. In actual practice, however, we would expect the performance control system to function most commonly, not in a purely top-down or bottom-up manner, but as a combination of the two. Some performance standards are elaborated down the hierarchy and others are aggregated up it; at each level, managers seek to impose standards on their employees, who propose less stringent ones instead. Through this kind of bargaining, there emerges a set of performance standards at all levels, composite and detailed.

The action planning system is essentially top-down. In theory it begins with strategic planning, wherein the organization systematically assesses its strengths and weaknesses in terms of trends in the environment, and then formulates an explicit, integrated set of strategies it intends to follow in the future. These strategies are then developed into "programs," that is, specific projects, such as introducing a new product line, building a new factory, reorganizing the structure. These programs are, in turn, elaborated and scheduled, perhaps in terms of a critical path (PERT or CPM) system, and eventually emerge as a set of specific operating specifications—to call on a customer, pour concrete, print an organigram—which evoke specific actions.

So far we have discussed the two planning and control systems as being independent of each other. In a conceptual sense they are, one being concerned with general results, the other with specific actions. But the literature also suggests a number of links or crossovers between the two, as shown in Figure 9–2. At the top (line a), there is a crossover from performance objectives to strategic plans. According to the conceptual literature, the whole action planning process must begin with the specification of the overall objectives of the organization: it is believed that only with a knowledge of what the organization wants—operationalized in quantitative terms—can strategic plans be generated.

The crossover from subobjectives or budgets to strategic plans (line b) is similar to that discussed above. Where there is unit autonomy, as in market-based structures, the strategic apex may develop overall objectives and then negotiate subobjectives and budgets with each of the units. These then become the objectives that initiate the action planning process in each unit. For example, top management tells the snowblower division that it expects a 10 percent increase in sales this year, and that $500,000 of investment money is available to it. That division, in turn, develops a strategic plan that calls for the introduction of a new aluminum frame on its models, the purchase of new machinery to produce it, and so on.

A crossover also takes place from subobjectives and budgets to programs directly, shown by line c. This is more common in a functional structure, where a budget given to a department evokes specific programs rather than overall strategies. Thus, when the research department is told that its budget will be increased by $300,000 next year, it proceeds with plans to build the new laboratory it has been wanting, just as when manufacturing is told its budget is to be reduced by 5 percent, it initiates a cost-cutting program.

The last crossover (line d) runs from programs to budgets and eventually to operating plans. This reflects the fact that the unit must assess the impact of all its proposed actions—the products to be marketed, machines to be bought, and so on—on its flow of funds (i.e., its budgets), the subobjectives it can reach, the manpower it must hire, and so on. In other words, the impact of specific actions on overall results must be assessed, hence the crossover from action planning to performance control.

Another crossover—perhaps the most important one, but not shown because of the nature of our diagram—is the overall feedback from performance control to action planning. As the organization assesses its performance, it initiates new action plans to correct the problems that appear.

We can better understand the linkages between the two systems by describing some specific examples of "hybrid" action planning and performance control systems. Figure 9–3 shows three of these. The first, shown in Figure 9–3(a), is the classic planning–programming–budgeting system

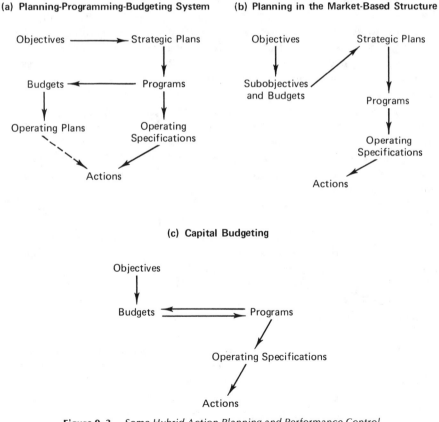

(a) Planning-Programming-Budgeting System

(b) Planning in the Market-Based Structure

(c) Capital Budgeting

Figure 9-3. *Some Hybrid Action Planning and Performance Control Systems*

(PPBS). Here overall performance control objectives lead to the development of overall strategic plans, which are converted into specific programs, which continue on down to generate operating specifications and also cross over again to be cumulated as budgets, which in turn lead to operating plans. This is the most fully developed of the planning and control systems.

The second hybrid system, shown in Figure 9–3(b), describes planning in the market-based structure. Here the strategic apex develops objectives, and from them negotiates subobjectives and budgets with each of the market units; these, in turn, initiate the full action planning process in each of the market units, which generates strategic plans which get elaborated as programs that give rise to operating specifications—and, normally, unit budgets and operating plans as well, although these are not shown in Figure 9–3(b). This particular example illustrates most clearly the need for crossovers due to a change in the basis of grouping, performance control being most appropriate to coordinate the work of market-based units, action planning better suiting the needs of functional units.

Figure 9–3(c) describes capital budgeting, a similar system except that the crossover is at the level of program instead of strategic plan. The strategic apex establishes objectives and converts these into a capital budget— in effect, a statement of the funds available for investment purposes. Meanwhile, the units propose specific programs to the strategic apex. It assesses each program in terms of benefit and cost criteria (return on investment if both are exclusively monetary), rank-orders them, and approves as many programs as its capital budget will allow. The approved programs are then sent back to the units for implementation. In effect, capital budgeting assumes only pooled interdependence among the programs—that they draw on common funds but produce independent benefits. Tighter interdependencies between programs require a strategic planning system instead of a capital budgeting one.

Systems such as these three are described in an extensive literature of planning and control systems. The problem with that literature, however, is that it is conceptual without being empirical: it describes the systems as highly ordered and regulated, as the theorists would like to see them operate. But the reader has no way of knowing if the reality really is like that, if formal plans and controls really influence decisions and actions as they are supposed to. How many organizations, for example, really do develop their strategies in the integrated, comprehensive process described above, instead of using a more flexible entrepreneurial or adaptive approach (Mintzberg, 1973b)? How many really develop their goals into systematic hierarchies of objectives, as opposed to letting them evolve naturally? Do capital budgeting and PPBS really work as they are described in the literature? Indeed, even in organizations that plan extensively, it is a fair question to ask how much of that is just going through the motions, and how much gets converted into specific actions. Observers of the management scene frequently come across examples of planning systems carried out almost ritualistically, unconnected to the day-to-day functioning of the organization. Every year on January 1, or whenever, subobjectives are duly established for all the units, and then filed in drawers so that the managers can get on with the real work of managing their units. Six months later, the strategic plans land on top of them, subject to the same fate. Clearly, some organizations do a lot of planning and take it seriously, while others do not (plan and/or take it seriously). What we need to know is who does what, when, how . . . and why.

PLANNING AND CONTROL SYSTEMS BY PART OF THE ORGANIZATION

We have already seen examples in this chapter of both action planning and performance control at all levels of the hierarchy. In the case of the former, we had strategic planning and capital budgeting at the strategic apex and upper levels of the middle line, programming and PERT/CPM scheduling techniques at the middle levels, and production scheduling at the level of the operating core. In the case of performance control, we saw that objectives, budgets, and standards can be set for units and positions at any level, from the strategic apex to the operating core. At the top is the setting of overall organizational objectives; high up in the middle line are commonly found the financial reporting systems that treat major market units as profit or investment centers; elsewhere in the middle line are the standard costing systems to control aggregated performance and MBO systems to motivate line managers; and near the bottom, we find the operating plans and the quality control systems.

However, our discussion also made clear that there are important differences by part of the organization. For example, while performance control can be used for individual positions—as when salespeople are given quotas or machine operators quality control standards—we would expect it to be more commonly applied to units (and, of course, to the managers who supervise those units). Not so for action planning. We would expect action planning to apply to individual operators, as when a machinist is given specifications for the products he is to make.

Higher up in the hierarchy, we would expect the situation to be reversed. **The more global the responsibilities of a unit, the greater the propensity to control its overall performance rather than its specific actions.** For market-based units, as noted earlier, the performance control system is a critical device for control, while action planning is not. And since, as noted in Chapter 7, the market basis for grouping is more common at higher than at lower levels in the structure, we find another reason why performance control would be favored over action planning in the upper reaches of the middle line. Thus, profit and investment centers, MBO, profit-sharing systems, and the like are all used extensively at the higher levels of the hierarchy. Of course, action planning systems may also be used at these levels where the basis for grouping is functional. As for the strategic apex, should it be subject to outside control (say, by a well-defined owner), it may also have to respond to a performance control system. And if the basis for grouping the highest-level units is functional, then action planning may very well start right in the strategic apex, as we already saw in some examples in this chapter.

As noted earlier, the technostructure is largely responsible for the design of all these planning and control systems. But that does not mean that its own work is regulated by them. In fact, owing to the difficulty of standardizing the outputs of analytic work, much of which is carried out on a project or ad hoc basis, we would expect little use of performance controls in the technosructure. As for action planning, again the technocratic units do a good deal of it, but seem to be only marginally affected by it themselves.

We would expect the use of planning and control systems to vary considerably in the support staff. Only those units which act as relatively autonomous entities and which have easily measured outputs—such as the cafeteria in the plant or the bookstore in the university—can be controlled primarily by performance standards. Some staff units with important interdependencies with other parts of the organization—such as the research department in the corporation—may be subject to action planning, at least to the extent that the line departments they serve are so subjected. And others, such as legal council, may experience little in the way of any planning and control system.

10

Design of Lateral Linkages: Liaison Devices

Often neither direct supervision nor all three forms of standardization are sufficient to achieve the coordination an organization requires. In other words, important interdependencies remain after all the individual positions have been designed, the superstructure built, and the planning and control systems set in place. The organization must then turn to mutual adjustment for coordination. A customer complaint about poor service may, for example, require the sales and manufacturing managers to sit down together to work out new delivery arrangements.

Until recently, this kind of mutual adjustment was left largely to chance: at best it took place informally, outside the formal organizational structure. But in recent years, **organizations have developed a whole set of devices to encourage liaison contacts between individuals, devices that can be incorporated into the formal structure.** In fact, these *liaison devices* represent the most significant contemporary development in organization design, indeed the only serious one since the establishment of planning and control systems a decade or two earlier.

Since the 1960s, the popular literature on organizational theory has heralded each new liaison device as a major discovery. First it was "task forces," then "matrix structure," later the "integrators." But the reader was left in confusion: were these just different names for the same phenomenon, or was each, in fact, a distinctly new contribution? And if so, did each bear any relationship to the others? The recent writings of Jay Galbraith (1973) has satisfactorily resolved these questions. Galbraith proposed a continuum of these liaison devices that explains how they differ as well as how certain ones are simply extensions of the others. Galbraith's seven-point continuum runs from the simplest device to the most elaborate: direct contact between managers, liaison roles, task forces, teams, integrating roles, managerial linking roles, and matrix organization. For purposes of our discussion, Galbraith's scheme has been reduced to four basic types of liaison devices—liaison positions, task forces and standing committees, integrating managers, and matrix structure.[1]

LIAISON POSITIONS

When a considerable amount of contact is necessary to coordinate the work of two units, a "liaison" position may be formally established to route the communication directly, bypassing the vertical channels. The position carries no formal authority, but because the incumbent serves at the crossroads of communication channels, he emerges as an organizational nerve center with considerable informal power.

In their study, Lawrence and Lorsch (1967) note that where the work of units is sharply differentiated, with interdependencies leading to problems of communication, organizations tend to create liaison positions. Lawrence and Lorsch found further that success in these positions derives from specialized knowledge, not from status, and that successful liaison individuals tend to develop time, interpersonal, and goal orientations midway between the differentiated units whose work they link.

Some liaison positions serve between different line units, for example, the engineering liaison man discussed by Galbraith (1973, p. 50) who is a member of the engineering department but is physically located in the plant. Landsberger (1961–1962) notes the case of the sales liaison person who mediates between the field sales force and the factory, while Strauss (1962–63) provides considerable detail on the purchase engineer who sits between purchasing and engineering.

> Some purchasing departments send out what are, in effect, ambassadors to other departments. They may appoint purchase engineers, men with engineering backgrounds (perhaps from the company's own engineering group) who report administratively to purchasing but spend most of their time in the engineering department. Their job is to be instantly available to provide in-

[1]Direct contact between managers was excluded here since it is not formal in nature. Galbraith's liaison role is maintained here as is his matrix organization. Task forces and teams are combined (with the addition of standing committees), as are integrating roles and managerial linking roles.

formation to engineers whenever they need help in choosing components. They assist in writing specifications (thus making them more realistic and readable) and help expedite delivery of laboratory supplies and material for prototype models. Through making themselves useful, purchase engineers acquire influence and are able to introduce the purchasing point of view before the "completion barrier" makes this difficult (pp. 180–181).

Other liaison positions join line and staff groups. Thompson (1967, p. 61) provides a number of examples of these, such as the personnel specialists and accountants who counsel line departments while remaining responsive to their technocratic homes. Dalton (1959) describes one such accountant, a man he called Rees, who, although assigned to a manufacturing plant called Milo, clearly saw his role as maintaining budgetary control on behalf of the company's head office. And his direct links with it gave him considerable informal power:

> For some time the most widespread struggle in Milo had been between line factions favoring and opposing the use of maintenance incentives. Otis Blanke, head of Division A, opposed the incentives and persuaded Hardy that dropping them would benefit Milo. At a meeting to deal with the problem Hardy stated his position and concluded, "We should stop using maintenance incentives. They cause us too much trouble and cost too much."
>
> Then as only a staff head, and one without vested interest in this issue or the formal authority to warrant threats or decisive statements, Rees arose and said: "I agree that maintenance incentives have caused a lot of trouble. But I don't think it's because they're not useful. It's because there are too many people not willing to toe the mark and give them a try. The (Office) put that system in here and by God we're going to make it work, not just tolerate it!" The surprise at these remarks broke the meeting up in embarrassment for everyone but Rees. ... Early the following day all line executives who had been approached by the staff supervisor telephoned apologies for their inability to aid him, and they asked him to please consider their position in view of Rees' stand. These and other less overt incidents led Milo executives to see Rees as an unofficial spokesman for the Office (pp. 24–25).

TASK FORCES AND STANDING COMMITTEES

The *meeting*, an "act of coming together" according to the *Random House Dictionary*, is the prime vehicle used in the organization to facilitate mutual adjustment. Some meetings are impromptu; people bump into each other in the hall and decide to have a "meeting"; others are scheduled on an ad hoc basis, as required. When the organization reaches the point of institutionalizing the meeting—that is, formally designating its participants, perhaps also scheduling it on a regular basis—it may be considered to have become part of the formal structure. This happens when extensive and fairly regular contact—at least for a period of time—is required between the members of various units to discuss common concerns. Two prime liaison devices are used to institutionalize the meeting. One is the *task force,* a kind of formal team; the other is the *standing committee.*

The task force is a committee formed to accomplish a particular task and then disband, "a temporary patchwork on the functional structure, used to short-circuit communication lines in a time of high uncertainty" (Galbraith, 1973, p. 51). Galbraith elaborates:

> These groups may arise informally or on a formal basis. In one company, when a problem arises on the assembly floor the foreman calls the process engineer, a member from the company laboratory, quality control, and purchasing if vendor parts are involved. This group works out the problem. When an acceptable solution is created, they return to their normal duties.
>
> On other occasions, the establishment of the group is more formal. An aerospace firm holds weekly design reviews. When a significant problem arises, a group is appointed, given a deadline, a limit to their discretion, and asked to solve the problem (p. 51).

The standing committee is a more permanent interdepartmental grouping, one that meets regularly to discuss issues of common interest. Many standing committees exist at middle levels of the organization. Lawrence and Lorsch (1967, p. 57) note the existence in plastics companies of cross-functional committees formed according to product lines, while Galbraith (1973, p. 53) cites the case in the Boeing Company of production planning committees corresponding to sections of the aircraft, which drew members from both line and technocratic functions. For example, the wing team consisted of representatives from Engineering, Industrial Engineering, Production Control, Manufacturing, and Quality Control. Other standing committees are formed at the strategic apex. Holden et al. (1968, pp. 104–105) found anywhere from one to six high-level standing committees in virtually every one of the firms they studied. The most common was the executive committee, typically used to advise the chief executive on decisions. Other standing committees at the strategic apex served more to transmit information and were variably called administrative committee, management council, executive council, and operations review committee. A chief executive described the functions of one of these as follows:

> Our administration committee meets monthly, at which time actions taken at the last board of directors meeting are reviewed and reports are made by group vice presidents and staff vice presidents; the committee is essentially a communications device and a medium for passing policy information to the organization (p. 105).

When more coordination by mutual adjustment is required than liaison positions, task forces, and standing committees can provide, the organization may designate an integrating manager, in effect a liaison position with formal authority. A new individual, sometimes with his own unit, is superimposed on the old departmental structure and given some of the power that formerly resided in the separate departments. That power is necessary "to integrate the activities of organizational units whose major goals and loyalties are not normally consistent with the goals of the overall system" (Sayles, 1976, p. 10).

Integrating managers may be brand managers in consumer goods firms, responsible for the production and marketing of particular products; project managers in aerospace agencies, responsible for integrating certain functional activities; unit managers in hospitals, responsible for integrating the activities of doctors, nurses, and support staff in particular wards; court administrators in governments who "tie together the diverse and organizationally dispersed elements that make up the criminal justice system—not only the courts themselves, but law enforcement, prosecution, defense, probation, jury selection, correctional institutions, and so on" (Sayles, 1976, p. 9).

The formal power of the integrating manager always includes some aspects of the decision processes that cut across the affected departments, but it never (by definition) extends to formal authority over the departmental personnel. (That would make him department manager instead of integrating manager.) To control their behavior, therefore, the integrating manager must use his decisional authority and, more important, his powers of persuasion and negotiation. Galbraith (1973) lists three stages in the extension of the decisional power of the integrating manager. First, he can be given power to approve completed decisions, for example, to review the budgets of the departments. Second, he can enter the decision process at an earlier stage, for example, to draw up the budget in the first place which the departments must then approve. Third, he can be given control of the decision process, as when he determines the budget and pays the departments for the use of their resources.

Consider the brand manager in a consumer goods firm. He is a kind of mini-general manager, responsible for the success of a single product. His performance is measured by how well it does in the marketplace. He must understand purchasing, manufacturing, packaging, pricing, distribution, sales, promotion, advertising, and marketing, and must develop plans for the brand, including sales forecasts, budgets, and production schedules. But the brand manager has no direct authority over the marketing or manufacturing departments. Rather, along with all the other brand managers of his firm, he negotiates with manufacturing to produce his brand and with marketing to sell it. If, however, he controls the budget for his brand, and has discretion in the use of it—for example, to contract its manufacture to different plants—he may have considerable power. This arrangement results in an overlay of a set of competing brand managers on a traditional functional structure, all of them using their power as well as the techniques of mutual adjustment (such as persuasion) to push their own products through the system. Sayles (1976) illustrates:

> Ellen Fisher is a product manager responsible for the introduction of new soap products. She works through several functional departments, including market research, the development laboratory's production, and sales. In designing the new product, market research usually conducts a test of consumer reactions. In this case, the market research head, Hank Fellers, wants to run the standard field test on the new brand in two preselected cities. Ellen is opposed to this because it would delay the product introduction date of September 1; if that date can be met, sales has promised to obtain a major chain-store customer (using a house-brand label) whose existing contract for this type of soap is about to expire.
>
> At the same time, manufacturing is resisting a commitment to fill this large order by the date sales established because "new-product introductions have to be carefully meshed in our schedule with other products our facilities are producing. . . ."
>
> Ellen's job is to negotiate with market research and manufacturing. This means assessing how important their technical criteria are, which ones are modifiable and, overall, what is best for the new product's introduction. . . . Her goal is to balance off the legitimate objections of manufacturing and sales as she perceives them against her need to get the new product off to a flying start (pp. 11–12).

While the brand manager is concerned with an existing or ongoing product, the project or program manager is concerned with bringing a new or embryonic undertaking to fruition. As Sayles notes in the case of organizational innovations:

> . . . the major impediment to implementation is the shock and disruption to the ongoing routines necessary to achieve reasonable efficiency. Each impacted department finds countless unanticipated costs of adaptation. A sponsor-facilitator exerting encouragement and pressure is essential if the innovation is not to flounder because one department or another finds it easier to slip back to its more comfortable and successful past routines (p. 10).

Sayles also describes the project manager as a "broker" who resolves stalemates between warring departments. Holden et al. (1968) note another reason for using project managers, in this case where organizations must deal with the government: that manager "is virtually a prerequisite to obtaining a contract of any appreciable magnitude. He is the principal contact with his counterpart in the procuring agency" (p. 99). Once the contract is signed, each side appoints a project manager to integrate its respective activities and to maintain liaison with the other side for the duration of the project.[2]

So far, our examples have illustrated the situation where integrating managers with market orientations are superimposed on functional structures to achieve work-flow coordination. But, although perhaps less common, there are cases where integrating managers with functional orientations are superimposed on market-based structures to encourage specialization. Galbraith (1973, pp. 137–141) discusses a data-processing department organized on a project (market) basis. The projects were delivered on time but with problems of technical quality. In addition, morale was low and turnover high among the programmers, and insufficient attention was paid to their specialized skills. (They suffered from the same problems as the "craft" employees of the advertising agency discussed in Chapter 10 that shifted to a project structure.) These were, of course, the very problems that functional structure attends to. So the solution was simply to overlay two functional integrating managers—"resource integrators"—on the project structure:

> The integrating departments became a home base for systems analysts and programmers respectively. The integrators were primarily concerned with skill mix, maintaining skill levels, and allocation across projects. The allocations were joint decisions between the integrator and project manager. Since the integrators were selected to be competent in their respective areas, they were respected in the allocation process and in the work evaluation process (p. 141).

The job of integrating manager is not an easy one, the prime difficulty being to influence the behavior of individuals over whom he has no formal authority. The brand manager, for example, must convince the manufacturing department to give priority to the production of his product and must encourage the sales department to promote his brand over the others. Galbraith outlines the means at hand to accomplish the job (all quotes from 1973, pp. 94–99). First, "The integrator has contacts": he has the ear of the general manager, and he "is at the crossroads of several information streams. ... He exercises influence based on access to information." Second, "The integrator establishes trust": ideally, being oriented to organizational

---

[2]Chandler and Sayles (1971), in *Managing Large Systems,* a book based largely on the experiences of the NASA of the Apollo era, discuss project management in considerable detail from the point of view of the government agency.

rather than parochial goals and having knowledge, he can build up confidence. Third, "The integrator manages decision making": he "manages the joint decision process, rather than making the decision himself. ... He must be able to listen to a proposal in 'marketing talk' and relate it in 'engineering talk.'" In this way, he "achieves coordination without eliminating the differences—languages, attitude, etc.—that promote good subtask performance." In decision making, the integrator is a formal embodiment of "expert power based on knowledge and information." He must "behave in ways that remove possible impediments to information sharing and problem solving. Such individuals are difficult to find and training technologies are not yet developed to create them." Nevertheless, some desirable personality characteristics have been identified, notably a high need for affiliation and an ability to stand between conflicting groups and gain the acceptance of both without being absorbed into either.

MATRIX STRUCTURES

No single basis for grouping can contain all the interdependencies. Functional ones pose work-flow problems; market-based ones impede contacts among specialists; and so on. Standardization effected through the formalization of behavior, training and indoctrination, or planning and control systems can sometimes alleviate the problem, but important interdependencies often remain.

In our discussion to this point, we have seen at least three ways in which organizations handle this problem. These are shown in Figure 10-1. The first, noted in Thompson's work and shown in Figure 10-1(a), is to contain the residual interdependencies at the next higher level in the hierarchy. For example, divisions of a multinational corporation can first be grouped by product line and then by country, as we saw in Figure 7-8. A second way, shown in Figure 10-1(b), is to deal with the residual interdependencies in the staff units: a dual structure is built, one line with the formal authority to decide, that contains the main interdependencies, the other staff with only the right to advise, that contains the residual interdependencies. For example, staff market researchers and financial analysts may advise the different product managers and so help to coordinate their activities functionally. The third way, of course, is to use one of the liaison devices already discussed. The organization in effect preserves the traditional authority structure but superimposes an overlay of liaison roles, task forces, standing committees, or integrating managers to deal with the residual interdependencies. The case of the task force is shown in Figure 10-1(c).

But each one of these solutions favors one basis of grouping over another. Sometimes, however, the organization needs two (or even three)

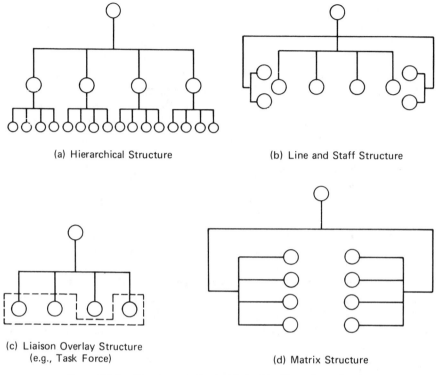

(a) Hierarchical Structure

(b) Line and Staff Structure

(c) Liaison Overlay Structure
(e.g., Task Force)

(d) Matrix Structure

Figure 10-1. *Structures to Deal with Residual Interdependencies*

bases of grouping in equal balance. For example, an international firm may not wish to favor either a geographical or product orientation in its structure, or a data-processing department or advertising agency may not wish to make a choice between a project orientation and an emphasis on specialization. Galbraith (1971) cites the case of the high-technology company whose products were undergoing continual change. Some managers argued for product divisions to deal with the complex problems of scheduling, replacing, and managing the new products, but others objected. The engineering manager felt that this would reduce the influence of his people just when he was experiencing morale and turnover problems. Management needed a product orientation as well as an improvement in the morale of the key specialists, both at the same hierarchical level. In these cases, organizations turn to the ultimate liaison device—*matrix structure.*

    By using matrix structure, the organization avoids choosing one basis of grouping over another: instead, it chooses both. "In the simplest terms, matrix structure represents the effort, organizationally speaking, to 'have your cake and eat it, too'" (Sayles, 1976, p. 5). But in so doing, the organization sets up a dual authority structure. As a result, **matrix structure sacri-**

fices the principle of unity of command. As shown in Figure 10–1(d), formal authority comes down the hierarchy and then splits, doing away with the notion of an unbroken chain of authority. To the classical writers, dual authority was an anathema; it violated the principles and destroyed the neatness of the structure.[3] But as Galbraith (1973) notes, dual authority is hardly foreign to us: "Almost all of us were raised in the dual authority system of the family..." (p. 144). Similarly, in the matrix structure, different line managers are equally and jointly responsible for the same decisions and are therefore forced to reconcile between themselves the differences that arise. A delicate balance of power is created. To return to our example of the advertising agency, if the specialists need to be oriented to projects, yet insist on being evaluated by their own kind, then matrix structure would have the evaluation decision made jointly by project and functional managers.

This balance of formal power is what distinguishes matrix structure from the other means of handling residual interdependencies, including the other liaison devices. It is one thing to have four product managers, each with a manufacturing, marketing, engineering, and personnel manager reporting to him, or to have four integrating managers each seeking to coordinate the work of four functional managers with the line authority, or even to combine the latter into market-based task forces, and quite another thing to force the product and functional managers to face each other, as in Figure 10–1(d), with equal formal power.

Nevertheless, Sayles (1976) notes in his review of matrix structure that in many contemporary organizations, the alternatives to it are simply too confusing:

> There are just too many connections and interdependencies among all line and staff executives—involving diagonal, dotted, and other "informal" lines of control, communication, and cooperation—to accommodate the comfortable simplicity of the traditional hierarchy, be it flat or tall. . . .
>
> Many companies, in fact, tie themselves in semantic knots trying to figure out which of their key groups are "line" and which "staff" (pp. 3, 15).

Sayles goes on to suggest that matrix structure is for organizations that are prepared to resolve their conflicts through informal negotiation among equals rather than recourse to formal authority, to the formal power of superiors over subordinates and line over staff. In effect, he seems to be telling us—picking up on Galbraith's point about the family—that matrix structure is for grown-up organizations.

---

[3]Frederick Taylor was a notable exception. His calls for functional authority of staff personnel were in this sense prophetic.

In fact, Sayles believes that many organizations have already adopted some form of matrix`structure, even if not in name. "... in looking at both contemporary government and contemporary business, we find that the matrix may be becoming the dominant form of structure, a finding with profound implications for modern management" (p. 5). Sayles cites a variety of examples to back up his point, even a state government conservation department that use it, in contrast to the Oregon Fish and Game Commissions described earlier.

Two kinds of matrix structures can be distinguished, a permanent form, where the interdependencies remain more-or-less stable and so, as a result, do the units and the people in them, and a shifting form, geared to project work, where the interdependencies, the market units, and the people in them shift around frequently.

One example of the *permanent matrix structure*, cited by Sayles, are in certain mass-market retail chains, such as J. C. Penney.

> They contain two sets of managers, with relatively equal power and some-what opposed interests, who are supposed to negotiate their differences. The systems managers are the store- or regional-level executives, responsible for operating a diversified department store that is responsive to the consumer tastes of particular communities and areas. They are dependent for their merchandise on equivalent functional managers—divisional merchandise managers. The latter identify, specify, and purchase the major categories of merchandise the stores will carry—furniture, for example, or tires or women's fashion apparel. These two sets of managers have separate performance responsibilities, report up separate lines of authority, and see the world from separate perspectives—the former from a store in a particular place or geographic area, the latter from the perspective of the overall market (p. 13).

Permanent matrix structures are also found in the administration of some cities, where the functional city-wide departments of parks, police, health, and so on, coordinate with the administrators of specific wards, and the two are jointly responsible for ensuring the quality of services to the city population.

Recently some international companies have also moved toward this type of structure, typically putting the managers of geographical regions face to face with the managers of worldwide product lines (Stopford and Wells, 1972, pp. 86–91). Reporting to both would be a regional product manager, to whom in turn would report the functional managers, as shown in Figure 10–2. Dow Corning has apparently gone one better, its chief executive officer (Goggin, 1974) describing it as having a three-dimensional matrix structure, with the functional as well as the regional and product managers all facing each other at the same level. Figure 10–3 shows this

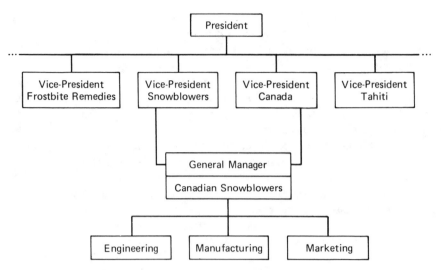

Figure 10-2. *A Permanent Matrix Structure in an International Firm*

structure as a graphical matrix of three dimensions. (This type of graphical representation, the common way to represent such structures, is, of course, the reason for the use of the term "matrix."[4])

A characteristic of the permanent matrix structure which can be seen in Figure 10-2 is that the chain of authority, once split, may reunite again, so that while one manager reports to two above him, his own subordinates report only to him.

The *shifting matrix structure* is used for project work, where the outputs change frequently, as in aerospace firms, research laboratories, and consulting think tanks. In these cases, the organization operates as a set of project teams or task forces (in effect, temporary market-based units) which draw their members from the functional departments. In Thompson's (1967) words, "Organizations designed to handle unique or custom tasks, and subject to rationality norms, base specialists in homogeneous [functional] groups for 'housekeeping' purposes, but deploy them into task forces for operational purposes" (p. 80). A well-known user of this type of structure is the National Aeronautics and Space Administration (NASA); Figure 10-4 shows a simplified version of its Weather Satellite Program. A fundamental characteristic of the task forces used in the shifting matrix structure is that their leaders are full-fledged managers (of the market units), with

[4]Actually, Goggin claims a fourth dimension, space and time, making the point that the structure is flexible and changes over time. He also notes the overlay of various task forces and standing committees on the matrix structure, as well as the use of planning systems and management by objectives.

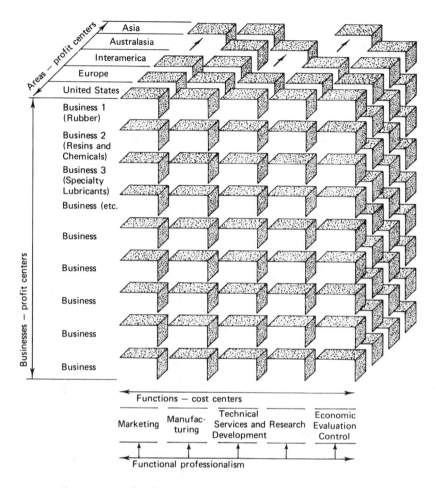

Asia
Australasia
Interamerica
Europe
United States

Areas — profit centers

Business 1
(Rubber)

Business 2
(Resins and
Chemicals)

Business 3
(Specialty
Lubricants)

Business (etc.

Business

Business

Business

Business

Business

Businesses — profit centers

Functions — cost centers

Marketing	Manufac-turing	Technical Services and Development	Research	Economic Evaluation Control

Functional professionalism

Figure 10-3. *The Three Dimensional Matrix Structure at Dow Corning (from Goggin, 1974, p. 57)*

formal authority (jointly shared with the managers of the functional units) over their members. That is what distinguishes them from the leaders of the task forces and the integrating managers described earlier. Those liaison devices were superimposed on traditional line structures. This structure is matrix precisely because the task-force leaders take their place alongside the functional managers, sharing power equally with them.

Finally, it should be noted that **matrix structure seems to be a most effective device for developing new activities and for coordinating complex multiple interdependencies, but it is no place for those in need of security and stability.** Dispensing with the principle of unity of command creates

173

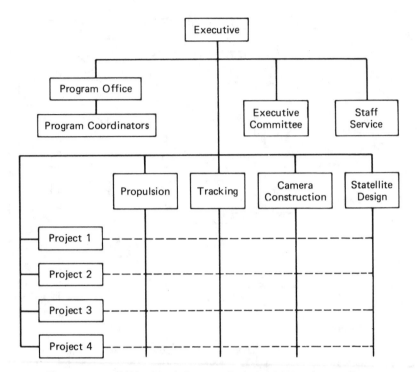

Figure 10-4. *Shifting Matrix Structure in the NASA Weather Satellite Program (modified from Delbecq and Filley, 1974, p. 16)*

relationships that require highly developed interpersonal skills and considerable tolerance for ambiguity. As Galbraith (1973) notes, "Rather than refer each circumstance to a general manager, the matrix design institutionalizes an adversary system" (p. 105). In his review of matrix structure, Knight (1976) discusses four main problems which it evokes. One is conflict: the matrix design structures and internalizes conflicts between organizational needs and environmental pressures, but it does not remove them. "... conflicting objectives and accountabilities, disputes about credit and blame, and attempts to redress an unequal power balance" (p. 123) all give rise to conflict among individuals. Matrix structure breaks down "those organizational 'boundaries' which normally act as protective walls for the individual manager, safeguarding his undisputed control over a given sphere of operations" (p. 123). The second problem Knight discusses is stress: "Matrix organizations can be stressful places to work in, not only for managers, for whom they can mean insecurity and conflict, but also for their subordinates" (p. 125). Reporting to more than one superior introduces "role conflict"; unclear expectations introduce "role ambiguity"; and too many demands placed on the individual (notably for meetings and discussions) introduces "role overload."

The third problem is the maintenance of the delicate balance of power between facing managers. A tilt in one direction or the other amounts to a reversion to a traditional single-chain hierarchy, with the resulting loss of the benefits of matrix structure. However, a perfect balance without cooperation between facing managers can lead to so many disputes going up the hierarchy for arbitration that top management becomes overloaded. And the fourth problem in matrix structure is the cost of administration and communication. "The system demands that people have to spend far more time at meetings, discussing rather than doing work, than in a simpler authority structure. There simply is more communicating to be done, more information has to get to more people ..." (p. 126). Moreover, as we shall soon see, matrix structure requires many more managers than traditional structures, thereby pushing up the administrative costs considerably.

A CONTINUUM OF THE LIAISON DEVICES

Figure 10-5 summarizes our discussion of these four liaison devices—liaison positions, task forces and standing committees, integrating managers, and matrix structure. Again the idea is borrowed from Galbraith and then modified. The figure forms a continuum, with pure functional structure at one end (i.e., functional structure as the single chain of line authority) and pure market structure at the other. (Again, any other basis for grouping could be put at either end.) The first and most minor modification to either of the pure structures shown next to each is the superimposition of liaison positions on it. Such positions generate a mild market orientation in the functional structure or a mild functional orientation in the market structure, thereby reducing slightly the informal power of the line managers (as shown by the diagonal line that cuts across the figure). A stronger modification is the superimposition of task forces or standing committees on either of the pure structures, while the strongest modification, short of dispensing with the principle of unity of command, is the introduction of a set of integrating managers. As we have seen, such managers are given some formal decisional power, for example, control of important resources, and acquire considerable informal power. But the other managers—whether functional or market—retain their traditional line authority, including that over the personnel. Finally, standing midway between the two pure structures of Figure 10-5 is matrix structure, which represents an equal balance of power between the two. Dual authority replaces unity of command.

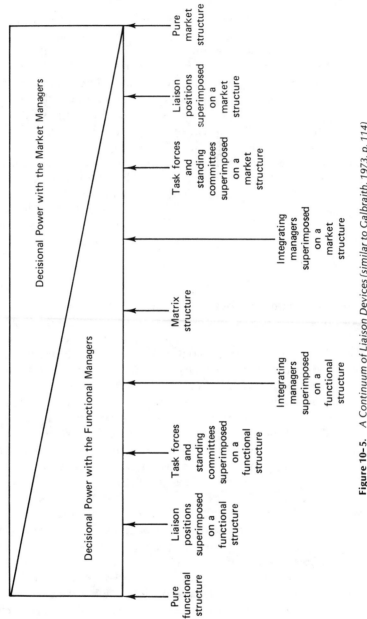

Figure 10-5. *A Continuum of Liaison Devices (similar to Galbraith, 1973, p. 114)*

THE LIAISON DEVICES AND
THE OTHER DESIGN PARAMETERS

At a number of points, our discussion has hinted at the relationships between the liaison devices and the design parameters we have already discussed. Now let us focus on these relationships, looking first at the superstructure and then at the individual positions.

It is clear that the liaison devices can be used with any basis for grouping, since they are designed to override the limitations of using only a single one. Nevertheless, a review of the examples in the literature suggests that these devices are most often superimposed on functional groupings to introduce an orientation to markets.

As for unit size, as we saw earlier, liaison devices are the tools to encourage mutual adjustment by informal communication, and as we noted in Chapter 8, such communication requires face-to-face work groups of small size. Hence, we would expect that **the greater the use of the liaison devices, the smaller the average size of organizational units.** This should be especially pronounced for task forces and standing committees, as well as for temporary matrix structures, where the essential work is carried out in groups. Some evidence for this comes from Middleton (cited in Kast and Rosenzweig, 1970, p. 234), who found that the introduction of project structure in several companies resulted in a significant increase in the number of departments, the number of vice-presidents and directors, and the number of second-line supervisors. Presumably, more communication required more smaller units, which required more managers. Were we to use span of control instead of unit size, the effect of the liaison devices should be even more pronounced. The addition of integrating managers ups the proportion of managers to nonmanagers significantly, while the switch to matrix structure means the doubling of managers, more or less,[5] since many employees now have two bosses. So **certain of the liaison devices, especially matrix structure, result in a proliferation of the managers in the organization.**

Turning to the design of the individual positions, we would expect the liaison devices to be used where the organization cannot standardize its behaviors but must instead rely on mutual adjustment to coordinate its activities. Hage et al. (1971, p. 868) found that the more programmed the organization's tasks, the fewer the departmental meetings; and the greater

---

[5]Assuming, that is, that nothing else changes. In the sense that those two managers must spend considerable time communicating with each other instead of supervising their employees, we might expect more rather than less. But in the sense that two individuals share the supervisory duties, we might expect less. To confound the issue, we shall see below and in Chapter 21 that matrix structure is associated with work that needs little direct supervision, but intimate managerial involvement.

the extent of job descriptions in the organization, the fewer the overall un-scheduled interactions, especially between individuals at the same status level in different departments. In other words, there is less need for informal communication in bureaucratic structure, which means that **the liaison devices are tools primarily of organic structures.** They are flexible mechanisms to encourage loose, informal relationships. No doubt the milder liaison devices—liaison positions, task forces, and standing committees, those toward the ends of the Figure 10-5 continuum—are sometimes super-imposed on bureaucratic structures to reduce their inflexibility in places; but the use of the stronger liaison devices—integrating managers and matrix structure—so upset the traditional patterns of formalized behavior that the resulting structure can no longer be thought of as bureaucratic.

The liaison devices are generally used where work is, at the same time, (1) horizontally specialized, (2) complex, and (3) highly interdependent. If the work were not both horizontally specialized and interdependent, close coordination would not be necessary and the liaison devices would not be used. And if the work were not complex, the necessary coordination could be achieved largely by direct supervision or the standardization of work processes or outputs. Complex work can, of course, be coordinated by standardizing the skills used to do it—but only as long as the interdepend-encies are not great. Past some point of interdependence among specialized complex tasks, mutual adjustment is mandatory for coordination. And so those are the tasks that call for the use of liaison devices to coordinate them.

Of course, specialized complex tasks are professional ones, and so we should find a relationship between professionalism (as well as training) and the use of the liaison devices. Indeed, many of our examples in this chapter have come from organizations that rely on professional expertise—aero-space agencies, research laboratories, and the like. Earlier it was suggested that there could be two kinds of professional organizations, one where the professionals function independently as individuals, and the other where they work together in groups. Now we see that the liaison devices are key design parameters in this second type of professional organization.

In their study, Lawrence and Lorsch (1967) highlight the relationship between horizontal specialization and the use of the liaison devices. They claim that the more "differentiated" the organization, the more emphasis it places on "integration." As we saw earlier, Lawrence and Lorsch use the term "differentiation" to describe the extent to which the units of an organi-zation differ on the dimensions of time, goals, and interpersonal orientation, as well as the formality of their structures—all of which reflect the extent to which their work is horizontally specialized. While Lawrence and Lorsch define "integration" broadly, as "the quality of the state of collaboration" (p. 11) among units that have to work together, in operationalizing this definition they place the greatest emphasis on the extent to which use is made of what we have called here the liaison devices. Thus, in their comparison of three high-performing firms in three industries, Lawrence and Lorsch note that the highly differentiated plastics firm used formal integrating departments (what we described under integrating managers) as well as permanent integrating teams (and had a ratio of liaison personnel to all managers of 22 percent); the slightly less differentiated food firm used liaison positions—less developed devices on our Figure 10-5 continuum (and these numbered 17 percent); while the relatively nondifferentiated container firm relied primarily on direct supervision for coordination and had 0 percent liaison personnel.[6]

As for the relationship between liaison devices and planning and control systems, to some extent at least the use of these two lateral linkages is likely to be mutually exclusive. Unable to contain task interdependencies by the design of both individual positions and the superstructure, the organization would rely either on the standardization of outputs or the use of the devices of mutual adjustment. Consider, for example, how Sayles (1976) describes the organization that uses matrix structure. Its introduction of multiple sources of authority presupposed that its decisions "cannot be made by a well-programmed computer or small, expert planning groups" (p. 15); its "goals are, at once, multiple and conflicting and changing" (p. 16); the nature of its work interdependencies are such that "no accounting model" (p. 15) can balance the range of forces present in it; rather, "The matrix forces decision making to be a constant process of interchange and trade-off, not only between the overall system and its specialized components and interest groups, but also between and among the specialists in the interest groups themselves" (p. 17). Clearly, planning and control systems cannot flourish in such an organization. In particular, performance control systems inappropriately require stable goals and units, with only pooled interdependencies. And while some action planning may be feasible to deal with unit interdependencies, it must be general enough to allow for considerable adaptation through mutual adjustment. NASA used action planning to lay out the general schedule of the Apollo project, but so much additional coordination and adaptation was required that the space agency emerged from the project as a leader in the use of the liaison devices.

LIAISON DEVICES BY PART
OF THE ORGANIZATION

The liaison devices appear to be best suited to the work carried out at the middle levels of the structure, involving many of the line managers as well as staff specialists. A standing committee may meet weekly to bring together the plant superintendent, sales manager, and head of purchasing;

---

[6]The relative measures of differentiation for these three firms, respectively, were 10.7, 8.0, and 5.7. This material is summarized in a table on page 138 of the Lawrence and Lorsch book.

an engineer may be designated to a liaison position between a staff group in research and the line marketing department; a task force may be created, drawing middle-level members from the accounting, manufacturing, engineering, and purchasing departments, to investigate the feasibility of purchasing new equipment. And matrix structure, especially of the permanent kind, is commonly used where the power of middle-line managers representing two different bases for grouping must be balanced.

In general, given the nature of the work of middle managers—largely ad hoc but somewhat amenable to structure—we would expect the set of liaison devices to be the single most important design parameter of the middle line. At the very least, meetings abound in this part of the organization, many of them bringing together task forces and standing committees. Similarly, within staff units doing specialized, complex, and highly interdependent work—both in much of the technostructure and the upper levels of the support staff—we would expect the set of liaison devices to be the prime design parameter. Task forces and shifting matrix structure are especially well suited to the project work that often takes place in the technostructure. For example, a management science department may base its specialists in homogeneous groups (cost analysts, statisticians, economists, etc.), but deploy them in project teams to do their studies. And as we shall see in Chapter 21, organizations with many staff groups in close contact with middle-line units make such heavy use of the liaison devices that the staff / line distinction virtually breaks down and their three middle parts emerge as one amorphous mass of mutual adjustment relationships.

As noted in earlier chapters, work in the operating core is coordinated primarily by standardization, with direct supervision as the backup coordinating mechanism. But in cases where the operating core is manned by professionals whose work interdependencies require them to work in teams—as in research centers and creative film companies—mutual adjustment is the key coordinating mechanism and task forces and shifting matrix structures the key design parameters.

Some use is also made of the liaison devices at the strategic apex. As noted earlier, standing committees are common among senior managers; task forces are also used sometimes to bring them together with middle-line managers as well as senior staff personnel; likewise, liaison positions are sometimes designated to link the strategic apex to other parts of the organization, as when a presidential assistant is designated to maintain contact with a newly acquired subsidiary. But wider use of the liaison devices at the top of the organization is probably restricted by the very fluid and unprogrammed nature of the work there. Even the flexible liaison devices are simply too structured. Top managers often seem to prefer the informal telephone call or the impromptu meeting to the task force with its designated membership or the standing committee that meets on a regular basis (Mintzberg, 1973a).

11

Design of Decision-Making System: Vertical and Horizontal Decentralization

The words *centralization* and *decentralization* have been bandied about for as long as anyone has cared to write about organizations. Yet this remains probably the most confused topic in organization theory. The terms have been used in so many different ways that they have almost ceased to have any useful meaning.

Here we shall discuss the issue of centralization and decentralization exclusively in terms of power over the decisions made in the organization. **When all the power for decision making rests at a single point in the organization—ultimately in the hands of a single individual—we shall call the structure centralized; to the extent that the power is dispersed among many individuals, we shall call the structure decentralized.**

Logically, the subject of decentralization would seem to belong with the discussion of the design of the superstructure. Once the units have been designed, it seems appropriate to address the question of how much power each should have. But it should be evident by now that all of this logic—beginning with the mission, determining the positions, their specialization, formalization, and requirements for training and indoctrination, then grouping the positions to build the superstructure, after that determining the distribution of decisional power within it, and finally fleshing the whole thing out with the lateral linkages—has little to do with the practice of organizational design. The relationships among the design parameters are clearly reciprocal, not sequential: **The design parameters form an integrated system in which each is linked to all the others as a dependent as well as**

independent variable: change any one design parameter and all the others must be changed as well. Decentralization is discussed last because it is the most complex of the design parameters, the one most in need of an understanding of all the others.

WHY DECENTRALIZE A STRUCTURE?

What prompts an organization to centralize or decentralize its structure? As with most of the issues of structure, this one centers on the question of division of labor versus coordination. **Centralization is the tightest means of coordinating decision making in the organization.** All decisions are made by one individual, in one brain, and then implemented through direct supervision. Other reasons have been given for centralizing structures—a well-known one being the lust for power—but most of the rest amount to the need for coordination.

Why, then, should an organization decentralize? Simply because all the decisions cannot be understood at one center, in one brain. Sometimes the necessary information just cannot be brought to that center. Perhaps too much of it is soft, difficult to transmit. How can the Baghdad salesperson explain the nature of his clients to the Birmingham manager? Sometimes the information can be transmitted to one center, but a lack of cognitive capacity (brainpower) precludes it from being comprehended there. How can the president of the conglomerate corporation possibly learn about, say, 100 different product lines? Even if a report could be written on each, he would lack the time to study them all. Sometimes a sophisticated MIS gives the allusion of knowledge without the capacity to absorb it. Simon (1968) cites a newspaper report to tell a common story:

> The U.S. State Department, drowning in a river of words estimated at 15 million a month to and from 278 diplomatic outposts around the world, has turned to the computer for help. Final testing is under way on a $3.5 million combination of computers, high-speed printers and other electronic devices. Officials say these will eliminate bottlenecks in the system, especially during crises when torrents of cabled messages flow in from world troubled spots.
>
> When the new system goes into full operation this Fall, computers will be able to absorb cable messages electronically at a rate of 1,200 lines a minute. The old teletypes can receive messages at a rate of only 100 words a minute (p. 622).

Simon concludes:

> A touching faith in more water as an antidote to drowning! Let us hope that

Foreign Ministers will not feel themselves obliged to process those 1,200 lines of messages per minute just because they are there (p. 622).

Perhaps the most common error committed in organizational design is the centralization of decision making in the face of cognitive limitations. The top managers, empowered to design the structure, see errors committed below and believe that they can do better, either because they believe themselves smarter or believe they can more easily coordinate decisions. Unfortunately, in complex conditions this inevitably leads to a state known as "information overload": the more information the brain tries to receive, the less the total amount that actually gets through (Driver and Streufert, 1969). In other words, past some point the top managers can be neither smarter nor better coordinators. They would have been better off to have left the decisional power with other brains, which together had the processing capacities—and the time—to assimilate the necessary information. As Jay (1970, p. 64) notes, excessive centralization requires those people with the necessary knowledge to refer their decisions up to managers out of touch with the day-to-day realities.

To sum up, having the power to make a decision gives one neither the information nor the cognitive capacity to make it. In fact, because so many organizations face complex conditions, decentralization is a very widespread organizational phenomenon. One individual can hardly make all the important decisions for a ten-person social work agency, let alone a General Electric. Decision-making powers are shared so that the individuals who are able to understand the specifics can respond intelligently to them. Power is placed where the knowledge is.

Another related reason for decentralization is that it allows the organization to respond quickly to local conditions. The transmission of information to the center and back takes time, which may be crucial. As the Bank of America once advertised, by having its "man-on-the-spot," presumably empowered to make decisions, it could provide better service to its clients.

And one last reason for decentralization is that it is a stimulus for motivation. Creative and intelligent people require considerable room to maneuver. The organization can attract and retain such people, and utilize their initiative, only if it gives them considerable power to make decisions. Such motivation is crucial in professional jobs (and since these are the complex jobs, the professional organization has two good reasons to decentralize). Motivation is also a key factor in most managerial jobs, so some decentralization down the middle line is always warranted. Giving power to middle-line managers also trains them in decision making so that some day one of them can take over the job of chief executive, where the most difficult decisions must be made.

SOME CONCEPTUAL CUTS AT
CENTRALIZATION/DECENTRALIZATION

So far, all of this seems clear enough. But that is only because we have not yet looked inside that black box called decentralization. The fact is that no one word can possibly describe a phenomenon as complex as the distribution of power in the organization. Consider the following questions:

- Which is more centralized: a library called "centralized" because it is in one place, although most of the decision-making power is dispersed to the department heads, or a "decentralized" library system, consisting of widely scattered satellite libraries, where the chief librarian of each guards all the power, sharing it with none of the other employees?

- How about the organization where decision-making power is dispersed to a large number of individuals, but because their decisions are closely monitored by a central individual who can fire them at a moment's notice, they make those decisions with careful assessment of his wishes? Or the case of the Jesuit priest or CIA agent who has complete autonomy in the field, except that he has been carefully indoctrinated to decide in a given way before he ever left the central headquarters? Are these organizations decentralized?

- In the United States, divisionalized corporations that rely on performance control systems for coordination are called "decentralized," whereas Americans are in the habit of calling the communist economies "centralized," even though they are organized like giant divisionalized corporations that rely on performance control systems for coordination. Which is it?

- Does standardization of work bring about centralization or decentralization? When a worker, because he is subject to a great many rules, is left free of direct supervision, can we say that he has power over his decisions? More generally, are bureaucracies centralized or decentralized? How about the one Crozier describes, where the workers force in rules that reduce the power of their managers over them, with the result that both end up in straightjackets?

- What about the case where a line manager has the authority to make a decision but his advisors, by virtue of their superior technical knowledge, lead him into his choices? Or the case where the manager decides, but in executing the choices, his subordinates twist the outcome to their liking? Are these organizations centralized by virtue of the distribution of the formal power, or decentralized by virtue of the distribution of the informal?

- Finally, what about the organization where some decisions—say those concerning finance and personnel—are made by the chief executive while others—say those in the areas of production and marketing—are dispersed to managers lower down? Is it centralized or decentralized?

The answer to these questions is that there is no simple answer, that unqualified use of the term "centralization" or "decentralization" should always be suspect. Yet a great deal of the research on organization structure has done just that, leading one recent handbook reviewer to question "the very concept": "... it seems that the decentralization literature is of limited usefulness from an organization design point of view" (Jennergren, 1974, p. 104).

So the waters of decentralization are dirty. But before spilling them away, it may be worthwhile to see if we can find a baby in there.

Our list of questions seems to indicate two major points about the concept. First, **centralization and decentralization should not be treated as absolutes, but rather as two ends of a continuum.** The Soviet economy is not "centralized," just more centralized than a capitalist economy; the divisionalized firm is not "decentralized," just more decentralized than some with functional structures. Second, much of the confusion seems to stem from the presence of a number of different concepts fighting for recognition under the same label. Perhaps it is the presence of two or even three babies in that bathwater that has obscured the perception of any.

Below we discuss three uses of the term "decentralization," and retain two for our purposes. Each is discussed at length in the body of this chapter, and together they are used in a summary section to develop a typology of five basic kinds of decentralization commonly found in organizations.

Three Uses of the Term "Decentralization"   The term "decentralization" seems to be used in three fundamentally different ways in the literature:

1. First is the dispersal of formal power down the chain of authority. In principle, such power is vested in the first instance in the chief executive at the strategic apex. Here it may remain, or the chief executive may choose to disperse it—"delegate" is a common synonym for this kind of decentralization—to levels lower down in the vertical hierarchy. **The dispersal of formal power down the chain of line authority will be called vertical decentralization.**

2. Decisional power—in this case, primarily informal—may remain with line managers in the system of formal authority, or it may flow to people outside the line structure—to analysts, support specialists, and

operators. **Horizontal decentralization will refer to the extent to which nonmanagers control decision processes.**[1]

3. Finally, the term "decentralization" is used to refer to the physical dispersal of services. Libraries, copying machines, and police forces are "centralized" in single locations or "decentralized" to many, to be close to their users. But this "decentralization" has nothing to do with power over decision making (the satellite library, like the copying machine, may not make the decisions that most affect it). Thus, this third use of the term only serves to confuse the issue. In fact, we have already discussed this concept in Chapter 7, using the terms *concentrated* and *dispersed* instead of "centralized" and "decentralized." In this book the term "decentralization" will not be used to describe physical location.

This leaves us with two essential design parameters: vertical and horizontal decentralization.[2] Conceptually, they can be seen to be distinct. Power can be delegated down the chain of authority and yet remain with line managers; the ultimate case of this vertical decentralization with horizontal centralization would give all the power to the first-line supervisors. The opposite—horizontal decentralization with vertical centralization—would occur when senior staff people, high up in the hierarchy, hold all the power. Centralization of both occurs when the strategic apex keeps all the power, while decentralization of both sees power pass all the way down the chain of authority and then out to the operators.[3]

[1]For purposes of our definition, managers of staff units are included among nonmanagers. Note that the term "horizontal" correctly describes this flow of power to analysts and support specialists as they are shown in our logo. The operators are, of course, shown below the vertical chain of authority, but for convenience are also included in our definition of horizontal decentralization.

[2]Van de Ven (1976b) introduces a similar conceptual scheme when he distinguishes three dimensions of decision-making authority: "(1) the degree of supervisory decision making (hierarchial authority), (2) the degree of individual decision making by nonsupervisory unit employees (personal authority), and (3) the degree of group or team decision making by unit personnel (colleagial authority)" (p. 256), the latter two being different forms of what we call horizontal decentralization.

[3]Some empirical support for their distinctiveness comes from Blau and Schoenherr (1971, p. 112) and from Reimann (1973, p. 466) in his review of the Aston studies. Both found that decentralization *to* a unit was not strongly correlated with decentralization *within* a unit, in other words, that vertical decentralization (to the unit manager) did not necessarily lend to further vertical decentralization (to his subordinate line managers) or to horizontal decentralization (to staff or operating personnel within the unit). And Beyer and Lodahl (1976, p. 125) found that physical science departments had more autonomy in the university (that is, were more vertically decentralized), but less internal autonomy for professors (i.e., were less horizontal decentralized), while the reverse held true for social science and humanity departments.

But decisional powers need not be dispersed consistently, which gives rise to two other kinds of decentralization. **In selective decentralization, the power over different kinds of decisions rests in different places in the organization.** For example, finance decisions may be made at the strategic apex, marketing decisions in the support units, and production decisions at the bottom of the middle line, by the first-line supervisors. **Parallel decentralization refers to the dispersal of power for many kinds of decisions to the same place.** For example, finance, marketing, and production decisions would all be made by the division managers in the middle line.

But one element is missing before we can begin our discussion of the kinds of decentralization found in organizations. As our questions implied, even within a single decision process, the power wielded by different individuals can vary. We need a framework to understand what control over the decision process really means.

CONTROL OVER THE DECISION PROCESS

What matters, of course, is not control over decisions but over actions: what the organization actually does, such as marketing a new product, building a new factory, hiring a new mechanic. And actions can be controlled by more than just making choices. Power over any step in the decision process—from initiating the original stimulus to driving the last nail in the final execution of it—constitutes a certain power over the whole process.

Paterson (1969) provides us with a useful framework to understand this issue. He depicts the decision process as a number of steps, as shown in modified form in Figure 11-1: (1) collecting *information* to pass on to the decision maker, without comment, about what can be done; (2) processing that information to present *advice* to the decision maker about what should be done; (3) making the *choice*, that is, determining what is intended to be done[4]; (4) *authorizing* elsewhere what is intended to be done; and (5) doing it, that is, *executing* what is, in fact, done. The power of an individual is then determined by his control over these various steps. His power is maximized—and the decision process most centralized—when he controls all the steps: he collects his own information, analyzes it himself, makes the choice, need seek no authorization of it, and then executes it himself. As others impinge on these steps, he loses power, and the process becomes decentralized.

[4]In terms of our discussion of Chapter 3, this step would include the recognition, screening, and choice routines. The diagnosis and development aspects (search and design) may be considered as the generation of advice for the final choice, although, as noted earlier, numerous intermediate choices are in fact made during development.

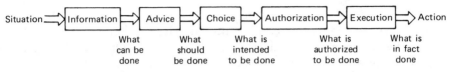

Figure 11-1. *A Continuum of Control over the Decision Process (similar to Paterson, 1969, p. 150)*

Control over input information enables another individual to select what factors will—and will not—be considered in the decision process. When information is filtered extensively, such control can be tantamount to control over the choice itself. More important still is the power to advise, since it directs the decision maker down a single path. Classical line/staff distinctions notwithstanding, there are times when the separation between giving advice and making the choice is fine indeed. History tells us of kings who were virtual figureheads, while their advisors—a Richelieu in France, a Rasputin in Russia—controlled the affairs of state. Likewise, the management of literature tells us of staff members—sometimes "objective" management scientists—who purposely distort their advice to managers to effect the outcomes they desire (e.g., Pettigrew, 1972; Cyert and March, 1963, p. 81).

Control over what happens after the choice has been made can also constitute power. The right to authorize a choice is, of course, the right to block it or even change it. And the right to execute a choice often gives one the power to twist or even distort it. Newspapers carry accounts every day of how the "bureaucrats" misdirected the intentions of the politicians and ended up doing what they thought best in the first place. In effect, the decisions ended up being theirs.

And so, **a decision process is most decentralized when the decision maker controls only the making of the choice (the least he can do and still be called decision maker): in the organizational hierarchy, he loses some power to the information gatherers and advisors to his side, to the authorizers above, and to the executers below.** In other words, control over the making of choices—as opposed to control over the whole decision process—does not necessarily constitute tight centralization. With this in mind, let us now look at vertical and horizontal decentralization.

VERTICAL DECENTRALIZATION

Vertical decentralization is concerned with the delegation of decision-making power down the chain of authority, from the strategic apex into the middle line. The focus here is on formal power, in Paterson's terms, to make choices and authorize them, as opposed to the informal power that arises from advising and executing. Three design questions arise in vertical decentralization:

1. What decision powers should be delegated down the chain of authority?
2. How far down the chain should they be delegated?
3. How should their use be coordinated (or controlled)?

These three questions turn out to be tightly intertwined. Let us consider first some evidence on selective decentralization down the chain of authority. Dale (cited in Pfiffner and Sherwood, 1960, p. 201) found that corporations tend to delegate power for manufacturing and marketing decisions farther down the chain of authority than power for finance and legal decisions. Later, Khandwalla (1973a) supported this finding in his research. Lawrence and Lorsch (1967) found that power for a decision process tends to rest at that level where the necessary information can best be accumulated. For example, in the plastics industry, research and development decisions involved very sophisticated knowledge which was at the command of the scientist or group leader in the laboratory but was difficult to transfer up the hierarchy. Hence, these decisions tended to be made at relatively low levels in the hierarchy. In contrast, manufacturing decisions tended to be made at higher levels (plant manager), because the appropriate information could easily be accumulated there. Marketing decisions fell in between these two.

These findings, in effect, describe the organization as a system of work constellations, our fourth overlay of Chapter 3. Each constellation exists at that level in the hierarchy where the information concerning the decisions of a functional area can be accumulated most effectively. Combining the findings of Dale, Khandwalla, and Lawrence and Lorsch in Figure 11-2, we have four work constellations overlaid on our logo—a finance constellation at the top, a manufacturing constellation below that, then a marketing constellation, and finally the research and development one. Thus, **selective vertical decentralization is logically associated with work constellations grouped on a functional basis.** (Note that the decentralization in this case can be horizontal as well as vertical: staff groups at different hierarchical levels are shown involved in the top three constellations, and the fourth is exclusively staff.)

But such selective decentralization leaves important interdependencies to be reconciled, which raises the question of coordination and control. Direct supervision may be used to some extent, specifically by having the decisions of each work constellation authorized, and therefore coordinated, by the managers at the strategic apex. But too great a reliance on this form of coordination would be tantamount to recentralizing the decision processes and thereby canceling the advantages of selective decentralization.

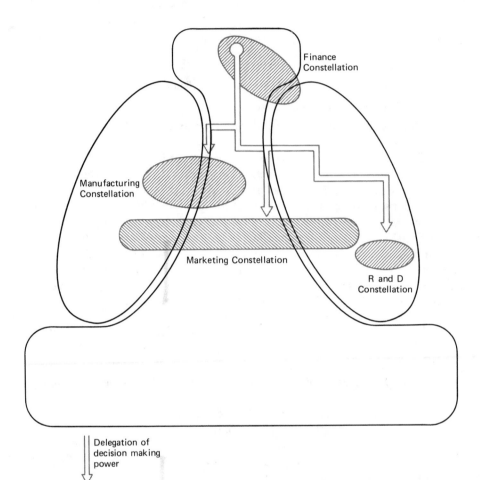

Figure 11-2. *Selective Decentralization to Work Constellations*

The same is true for the standardization of work processes or outputs, since that transfers power over the decision processes from all the constellations to the technostructure, which amounts to horizontal centralization instead of vertical decentralization. So, although it may make some use of activity planning, in the final analysis **the organization that is selectively decentralized in the vertical dimension will coordinate its decision making largely by mutual adjustment.** Specifically, it will place heavy emphasis on the use of the liaison devices.

The situation is quite different for parallel decentralization in the vertical dimension. This kind of decentralization does away with decision interdependencies: power for the different functional decisions is focused at a single level in the hierarchy, specifically within units grouped on the basis of market. This is the structure known as "divisionalized" in the corporate sector. Each unit or division is decoupled from the others and given the power necessary to make all those decisions that affect its own products, services, or geographical areas. In other words, **parallel vertical decentralization is the only way to grant market-based units the power they need to function quasi-autonomously.** (Of course, such vertical decentralization must always be *somewhat* selective. That is, some decision-making power is always retained at the strategic apex. The divisionalized corporation typically delegates marketing and manufacturing decisions to the divisions but keeps finance and acquisition decisions at the strategic apex.)

With the extensive autonomy of each market-based unit, there is no need to encourage mutual adjustment or action planning to coordinate work across them. What is important is to ensure that the autonomy is well used, that each market unit contributes to the goals considered important by the strategic apex. So the strategic apex faces the delicate task of controlling the behavior of its market units without restricting their autonomy unduly. Three coordinating mechanisms present themselves for such control—direct supervision and the standardization of skills and of outputs. (The standardization of work processes would obviously be too restrictive.) There is some room for direct supervision, notably to authorize their major expenditures and to intervene when their behavior moves way out of line. But too much direct supervision defeats the purpose of the decentralization: the strategic apex, instead of its own manager, comes to manage the unit. The standardization of skills, through training and indoctrination, can also be used to control the behavior of the manager of the parallel decentralized market unit. We have already seen an example of this in Jay's description of the colonial empire, where the governors were carefully indoctrinated and then sent out to run the colonies with virtually complete autonomy. But there typically remains the need to monitor behavior—to find out when it is out of line. And that is typically left to the performance control system. **Parallel decentralization in the vertical dimension (to market-based units) is regulated primarily by performance control systems.** The units are given performance standards and as long as they meet them, they preserve their autonomy. It is presumably this specific case—parallel vertical decentralization to market-based units coupled with performance controls—which explains why a number of researchers, such as Khandwalla (1974a), have found strong correlations between "decentralization" and the use of sophisticated planning and control systems.

But does parallel vertical decentralization to market-based units constitute "decentralization"? In the corporate world, the terms "divisionalization" and "decentralization" have been used synonomously ever since Alfred P. Sloan reorganized General Motors in the 1920s under the maxim "decentralized operations and responsibilities with coordinated control"

(Chandler, 1962, p. 160; see also Sloan, 1963). Faced with a structural mess left by William C. Durant, who had put the legal entity together through a series of acquisitions but had never consolidated it into a single organization, Sloan established product divisions with some operating autonomy but maintained tight financial controls at headquarters. A number of large corporations followed suit, and today the divisionalized structure is the most popular one among the largest American corporations (Wrigley, 1970; Rumelt, 1974). But does divisionalization constitute decentralization? Not at all: it constitutes the vesting of considerable decision-making power in the hands of a few people—the market unit managers in the middle line, usually near the top of it—nothing more. That is, **divisionalization constitutes a rather limited form of vertical decentralization.** These managers can, of course, delegate their power farther down the chain of authority, or out to staff specialists, but nothing requires them to do so. To paraphrase Mason Haire (1964, p. 226), "decentralization" can give a manager the autonomy to run a "centralized" show![5] Thus, we should not be surprised when the same structure in a different context—the communist economy—is called centralized. A structure—capitalist or communist—in which a few division managers can control decisions that affect thousands or even millions of people can hardly be called decentralized, although it is certainly more so than one in which these decisions are made by even fewer managers at the strategic apex.

HORIZONTAL DECENTRALIZATION

Now we turn to the question of horizontal decentralization, namely to the shift of power from managers to nonmanagers (or, more exactly, from line managers to staff managers, analysts, support specialists, and operators). An assumption in our discussion of vertical decentralization was that power—specifically formal power, or authority—rests in the line structure of the organization, in the first instance at the strategic apex. Vertical decentralization dealt with the delegation of that power down the chain of authority, at the will of the top managers.

When we talk of horizontal decentralization, we broaden the discussion in two regards. First, in discussing the transfer of power out of the line structure, we move into the realm of informal power, specifically of control

---

[5]But that raises a dilemma for the manager up above who prefers more decentralization. "Can he pull back the autonomy and order the subordinate to push decentralization down further? Or will this centralized intervention to further decentralization destroy the decentralization?" (Haire, p. 226)

over information gathering and advice giving to line managers and the execution of their choices, as opposed to the making and authorizing of these choices. And second, in discussing horizontal decentralization, we drop the assumption that formal power necessarily rests in the line structure, in the first instance at the strategic apex. Here formal power can rest elsewhere, for example with operators who are empowered to elect the managers of the strategic apex.

Assuming a two-tier hierarchy with a full complement of staff personnel, we can imagine a continuum of four stages of horizontal decentralization, shown in Figure 11-3 and listed below:

1. Power rests with a single *individual,* generally by virtue of the *office* he occupies.

2. Power shifts to the few *analysts* of the technostructure, by virtue of the influence their *systems* of standardization have on the decisions of others.

3. Power goes to the *experts*—the analytic and support staff specialists, or the operators if they are professional—by virtue of their *knowledge.*

4. Power goes to *everyone* by virtue of *membership* in the organization.

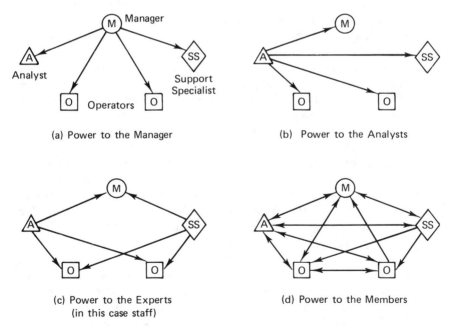

(a) Power to the Manager

(b) Power to the Analysts

(c) Power to the Experts
(in this case staff)

(d) Power to the Members

Figure 11-3. *A Continuum of Horizontal Decentralization*

Thus, in the most horizontally centralized organization, one individual holds all the power, typically the top manager. Of course, even here there can be variations according to how open that individual is to advice. There is a difference between the "omnicompetent aloof, imperial ruler," such as the Byzantine emperor, and the "omnicompetent but very accessible and responsive leader," such as a John F. Kennedy (Kochen and Deutsch, 1973, p. 843). Hereafter, we find different degrees of horizontal decentralization, first to a few analysts whose systems control the behavior of others, then to all the experts with knowledge, and finally to everybody just because they are members of the organization.

HORIZONTAL DECENTRALIZATION: POWER TO THE ANALYSTS

When an organization relies on systems of standardization for coordination, some power must pass out from the line managers to the designers of those systems, typically the analysts of the technostructure. How much power, of course, depends on the extent and the kind of standardization. Obviously, the more the organization relies on systems of standardization for coordination, the greater the power of the analysts. Soviet government planners have more power than their American counterparts; the work study analysts of an automobile company are more influential than those of a hospital. The tighter the kind of standardization the more powerful the analysts. By that token, job designers and work-study analysts—those who tell workers *how* to produce by standardizing their work processes—should typically have more power than production schedulers and planners—those who only tell them *what* and *when* to produce by standardizing their outputs. And trainers—those who teach people to produce by standardizing their skills—should have less power still. Thus, the factory worker would normally perceive the work-study analyst as the greatest threat to his autonomy, followed by the production scheduler and then the trainer. (However, to the extent that planners and trainers direct their efforts at people higher up in the structure—say, middle-line managers as opposed to operators—they can be more powerful. Moreover, we should not forget that much of the training takes place outside the organization, in professional schools and the like, thereby forcing the organization to surrender some power to these outside institutions. We shall return to this point later in the chapter.) Who surrenders power to the analysts? Obviously, those whose work is standardized, such as the operator who loses the power to choose his work process and the manager who loses the power to decide on his unit's outputs. But so, too, do the managers of these people: as noted earlier, their jobs became institutionalized, technocratic standardization replacing their power of direct supervision.

This leads us to two important conclusions. First, **power to the analysts constitutes only a limited form of horizontal decentralization.** Only a few nonmanagers—these designers of the technocratic system—gain some informal power, and that at the expense of the many operators and others whose behavior and outputs are standardized. And second, **this kind of limited horizontal decentralization in fact serves to centralize the organization in the vertical dimension, by reducing the power of the lower-line managers relative to those higher up.** In other words, **organizations that rely on technocratic standardization for coordination are rather centralized in nature, especially in the vertical dimension but also somewhat in the horizontal.**

Are Bureaucracies Centralized?   In fact, the issue raised in our last sentence is the subject of a major debate in the literature. Posing the question, "Are bureaucracies centralized?," many have drawn a conclusion opposite to ours, that they are not. It all began with the Aston studies (Pugh et al., 1963-1964). As noted earlier, these researchers found a strong relationship among a number of Weber's dimensions of bureaucracy, which they compressed into the single factor they called "structuring of activities," similar to our behavior formalization. But they found no strong relationship between this factor and another one which they called "concentration of authority" (or centralization). Pugh et al. concluded that there could not be one single "ideal type" of bureaucracy, as Weber implied, but different ones with different degrees of decentralization.

Then, along came John Child (1972b), using the same research instrument but with a sample that contained only autonomous organization, not subsidiaries, branch plants, and the like. Child believed that the inclusion of the latter in the Aston studies confounded their measure of centralization.[6] Child found a more pronounced and *negative* relationship between the two factors, especially for manufacturing firms, leading him to conclude that there could indeed be one ideal type of bureaucracy after all, formalized and *de*centralized. In fact, Child argued that Weber so described bureaucracy: the officeholders were given the power to make decisions within the confines of the standards. As Mansfield (1973), who came to Child's support, noted, the standards, or rules, "delimit" the authority of the boss.[7] But

---

[6]"In the twenty Aston branch organizations, branch managers, who were usually departmental or site heads, were scored as chief executives, as were the heads of whole units. This procedure tends to give branches relatively high scores on overall centralization, for a given reply on locus of decision making" (Child, 1972b, p. 168).

[7]Mansfield, however, points out that Weber never discussed the relationship between bureaucracy and centralization, although he cites one statement by Weber as implying that it was negative: "He indicated that the notion of authority within a bureaucratically administered organization does not mean 'that the 'higher' authority is simply authorized to take over the business of the 'lower.' Indeed, the opposite is the rule'" (p. 478).

while some researchers supported Child (e.g., Blau and Schoenherr, 1971; Inkson et al., 1970), others did not, finding no relationship between centralization and bureaucratization, or even a positive one (e.g., Holdaway et al., 1975; Manns, 1976; see also Jennergren, 1974). Donaldson (1975) even went back to the original Aston data, removed the nonautonomous organizations from the sample, and found that it made no difference. Thus, he concluded that "the Aston results cannot be explained away as an aberration produced by inconsistent measurement of centralization across units having different organizational status. And the resolution of this puzzle needs to be looked for elsewhere" (pp. 455–456). Child (1975) replied that elsewhere might be in the kind of organization, manufacturing firms being perhaps more efficient because of competition and, therefore, more careful to decentralize when they bureaucratize. Aldrich (1975) obliged, rerunning Donaldson's analysis of the Aston data without the government organizations but—you guessed it—that did not help: "In particular, 'formalization,' one of the original puzzles in Child's [data] emerges as even more of a mystery" (p. 459). Aldrich encouraged "all hands to get back to the data and look this question over a little more carefully" (p. 459). So Greenwood and Hinings (1976) did just that, and concluded that perhaps the data were not so good after all, that the measure all these researchers used for centralization could not be combined into a single factor—in effect, that centralization "is a more complex concept" than previously thought.

What were the Aston measures anyway? For each of 37 decisions (such as "Buying procedures," "New product or service") they asked, "Who is the last person whose assent must be obtained before *legitimate action* is taken—even if others have subsequently to confirm the decision?" (Pugh et al., 1968, p. 77). In terms of our continuum of control over decision processes, shown in Figure 11-1, this emerges as a confusing and inadequate question, perhaps identifying either the choice maker or the authorizer of the decision (who, is not clear) while ignoring all those who have power over the other steps (Jennergren, 1974, p. 16). As Perrow (1974) has noted:

> ... it is always possible to deny empirical generalizations, such as those by Blau and the Aston Group, on the grounds that the variables were not measured adequately. This is rightly called cheap criticism, but in an area as important as the centralization of the authority I think it is worth raising the point quite strenuously. We should not measure decentralization by the level at which people may hire, fire, or spend a few thousand dollars without proper authorization. We must also measure the unobtrusive controls (p. 40).

Perhaps we can sort out the confusion by turning to a very different kind of research—one where the researcher investigated a few specific power relationships fully, in only two organizations. In *The Bureaucratic*

Phenomenon, Crozier (1964) looked at power distribution in bureaucracies. But he never concluded that the organizations he studied were *de*centralized. Quite the contrary, he specifically argued that they were highly centralized. The key point is that using rules to reduce the power of the superior did not give power to the subordinate instead. Rather Crozier concluded that the rules weakened both:" . . . every member of the organization . . . [is] totally deprived of initiative and completely controlled by rules *imposed on him from the outside*" (p. 189, italics added). Where was this "outside" Crozier talked about? In other words, who controlled the decisions in these bureaucracies? Again Crozier is quite clear: the central headquarters. Power over rule making in particular and decision making in general was centralized there. Crozier does not discuss the role of the headquarters' technostructure, but it seems a fair assumption that the analysts there played an important role in developing these rules.

We can now begin to sort out much of the confusion by discussing centralization in terms of our five coordinating mechanisms. Child seems to take a restrictive view of centralization, implicitly equating it with direct supervision: an organization is centralized if direct supervision is close; to the extent that work standards replace direct supervision, the organization becomes decentralized. But calling a bureaucracy decentralized because work rules instead of managers control the workers is like calling puppets purposeful because computers instead of people pull their strings.

Direct supervision may be the tightest coordinating mechanism, and therefore close control by managers may constitute the tightest form of horizontal centralization. Any move the individual makes can bring a wrap on the knuckles from the boss: "That is not the way I expected you to do it." And standardization of work processes by rules may provide the employee with more autonomy, since he knows what he can and cannot do. But that does not mean that it is a loose coordinating mechanism. Of course, if the rules are few, the employee has considerable discretion. But we are discussing organizations where the rules are many—bureaucracies that rely on such rules for coordination, and so proliferate them. As Greenwood and Hinings (1976) found: "Organizations apparently routinize all activities rather than some and not others" (p. 154). The important point is that the reliance by the organization on any of the other coordinating mechanisms would yield its employees more freedom still in their work. That would happen if their outputs were standardized and they were allowed to choose their own work processes. Better still, if their work was coordinated by the standardization of skills, they would be trained and indoctrinated before they started to work and thereafter would be left alone to choose their work processes and determine their outputs as they saw fit. And best of all is the absence of standardization and direct supervision altogether: the employees would be completely free to work out their own coordination by mutual adjustment.

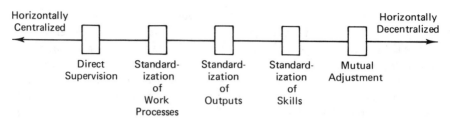

Figure 11-4. *The Coordinating Mechanisms on a Continuum of Horizontal Decentralization*

In other words, as shown in Figure 11–4, **the coordinating mechanisms form a continuum, with direct supervision the most horizontally centralizing and mutual adjustment the least, and with the three forms of standardization—first work processes, then outputs, finally skills—falling in between.** And because standardization of work processes falls next to direct supervision as the second most centralizing coordinating mechanism, we conclude that organizations that rely on this mechanism for coordination are relatively centralized. Specifically, decisional power rests largely at the top of the chain of authority as well as, to some extent, in the technostructure where the rules are formulated.

But to tie up a loose end, we cannot say that all bureaucracies are centralized. These particular bureaucracies are—the ones that rely on the standardization of work processes to coordinate the work of their unskilled operators. But earlier we came across a second kind of bureaucracy, one with professional operators who coordinate their work by the standardization of their skills. And because this coordinating mechanism falls near the decentralization end of our Figure 11-4 continuum, we can conclude that this second kind of bureaucracy is relatively *de*centralized in the horizontal dimension. In fact, mixing these two kinds of bureaucracies in the same research sample could lead to the kind of confusing results we witnessed earlier. In any event, we shall return to the discussion of the second kind of bureaucracy shortly.

HORIZONTAL DECENTRALIZATION: POWER TO THE EXPERTS

In this stage of horizontal decentralization, the organization is dependent on specialized knowledge. So it must put its power where its knowledge is, namely with the experts, whether they be in the technostructure, support staff, operating core, or, for that matter, middle line. "In the world of blind men, the one-eyed man is king." The surgeons dominate the operating rooms, the Werner von Brauns rule the space agencies. In the previous discussion there was only one recognized expert—the analyst—and his power was informal. But here the organization draws on the knowledge of a wider array of experts and begins to formalize more and more of the power it gives to them. The experts do not merely advise; they come to participate actively in making decisions.

How dependent the organization is on its experts and where they are found in its structure determine how much power they accumulate. We can identify at least three types of expert power.

1. *Informal expert power superimposed on a traditional authority structure* In the least horizontally decentralized type, the system of formal authority remains intact; that is, formal power remains in the hierarchy of line managers. But **to the extent that the organization has need of specialized knowledge, notably because certain decisions are highly technical ones, certain experts attain considerable informal power.** Thus, the maintenance men ruled the tobacco factories Crozier (1964) studied because only they could handle the one major source of uncertainty:

> ... machine stoppages are the only major happenings that cannot be predicted and to which impersonal rulings cannot apply. The rules govern the consequences of the stoppages, the reallocation of jobs, and the adjustment of the work load and of pay; but they cannot indicate when the stoppage will occur and how long it will take to repair. ... The people who are in charge of maintenance and repair are the only ones who can cope with machine stoppage. They cannot be overseen by anyone in the shop. No one can understand what they are doing and check on them. ...
>
> A supervisor cannot reprimand the mechanics who work in his shop. There is likely to be a perpetual fight for control, and the supervisors will usually be the losers (p. 109).

These experts made choices; others gain informal power by virtue of the advice they give managers before their choices are made, especially technical choices that the managers do not understand. Pettigrew (1972) describes a decision concerning data-processing equipment which became a power game among three experts, each vying to convince management to give the contract to his favored manufacturer. And experts can also gain power by twisting managerial choices when they execute them, as in the case of General McArthur in Korea, who ignored President Truman's commands to the point of insubordination.

The authorization step of decision making, often carried out as part of a capital budgeting process, lends itself to the manipulation of managers by experts. The sponsor of a decision or project, that person who first decided to proceed with it, has the expert knowledge of it but also has a strong commitment to see it authorized. The manager above, who must do the authorizing, can be more objective in his assessment of the project, but he lacks the detailed knowledge of it and the time to get it (Carter, 1971, p. 422). The situation is ripe for manipulation. The sponsor is encouraged to distort his analysis of the project, and the authorizing manager cannot easily see through such an analysis— market forecasts that are too optimistic, cost estimates that are too low, or even certain expenses conveniently forgotten. As one less-than-objective analyst told a researcher, "In the final analysis, if anyone brings up an item of cost we haven't thought of, we can balance it by making another source of savings tangible" (Cyert and March, (1963, p. 81). In effect, systems of capital budgeting often fail because they cannot put the formal power for authorization where the required knowledge of the project is.

2. *Expert power merged with formal authority*   **As expertise becomes increasingly important in decision making, the distinction between line and staff—between the formal authority to choose on one hand and the expertise to advise on the other—becomes increasingly artificial.** Eventually, it is done away with altogether, and line managers and staff experts join in task forces and standing committees to share decision-making power. A good example is the new product group that brings together marketing, manufacturing, engineering, and research personnel from the technostructure, middle line, and support staff. Power within the group is based not on position but on expertise: each individual participates according to the knowledge he can bring to the decision in question. This means a continual shift in the group's power relationships. For example, the marketing researcher may have a lot to say about the color of the product, while the engineer's role may be preeminent when the conversation turns to the product's structural characteristics.

   Thus, this situation of expert power merged with formal authority amounts to *selective* decentralization in the horizontal dimension, the experts having power for some decisions but not for others. In fact, a reference back to Figure 11-2, where various functional work constellations were overlaid on our logo, suggests a link to selective decentralization in the vertical dimension. In other words, **selective decentralization seems to occur concurrently in both the horizontal and vertical dimensions.**

3. *Expert power with the operators*   In this third and most decentralized case of expert power, the operators themselves are the experts. And

this expertise vests in them considerable power, which in turn decentralizes the organization in both dimensions: power rests in the operating core, at the bottom of the hierarchy with nonmanagers. Of course, expert operators are professional ones, which leads us to a rather important relationship, one that is well supported in the research: **the more professional an organization, the more decentralized its structure in both dimensions.** Hage and Aiken (1967), for example, found in a study of sixteen health and welfare organizations that the more highly trained the staff, the more their participation in decision making. In another study, Palumbo (1969) compared the work and attitudes of nurses and sanitarians of fourteen local public health departments. The work of the nurses was more professional, that of the sanitarians (involving tasks such as the inspection of eating places) was less skilled. For the sanitarians, morale was positively correlated with centralization ($+0.46$); for the nurses, it was negatively correlated (-0.17). In other words, the nurses preferred decentralized structures, presumably because they could better accomplish their professional work in them, whereas the less skilled sanitarians were happier in centralized structures.[8]

This brings the issue of bureaucracy and centralization into sharper focus. We can now see the two kinds of bureaucracy emerging clearly, one relatively centralized, the other decentralized. The first is bureaucratic by virtue of the work standards imposed by its own technostructure. Its operating work is specialized but unskilled. It is relatively *centralized* both vertically and horizontally, because most of its decision-making power rests with its senior managers and the small number of analysts who formalize the behavior of everyone else. In the second, the operating core is started with professionals. It is bureaucratic by virtue of the standards imposed on it from the outside, by the professional associations which train its operators and later impose certain rules to govern their behavior. But because the professionals require considerable autonomy in their work, and because coordination is effected primarily by the standardization of skills—a coordinating mechanism shown near the decentralization end of the Figure 11-4 continuum—this second bureaucracy is rather decentralized in both dimensions. That is, power rests with the operators at the bottom of the hierarchy.

---

[8]Interestingly, Palumbo also found that the more professional the nursing department, the higher the morale ($+0.65$), whereas the more professional the sanitation department, the *lower* the morale (-0.22). Professionalism was measured as years of professional or graduate school training. Extensive training presumably raises expectations, which are frustrated in an unskilled job.

HORIZONTAL DECENTRALIZATION:
POWER TO THE MEMBERS

The theme of our discussion so far has been that power in the hands of the managers constitutes horizontal centralization; that bureaucratization by the formalization of behavior puts some power into the technostructure and thereby constitutes a limited form of horizontal decentralization; and that the more that power is attracted to knowledge as opposed to position, the more the structure becomes horizontally decentralized, culminating in the professional organization whose operators control much of the decision making.

But, in theory at least, that is not the ultimate case of horizontal decentralization. Professional organizations may be meritocratic but they are not democratic. As long as knowledge is not uniformly dispersed, so too will power not be evenly distributed. One need only ask the orderlies (or even the nurses) of the hospital about their status vis-à-vis the doctors.

Horizontal decentralization is complete when power is based not on position or knowledge, but on membership. Everyone participates equally in decision making. The organization is democratic.[9]

Does such an organization exist? The perfectly democratic organization would settle all issues by something corresponding to a vote. Managers might be elected to expedite the members' choices, but they would have no special influence in making them. Everyone would be equal. Certain volunteer organizations—such as Israeli kibbutzim or private clubs—approach this ideal, but do any other organizations?

"Industrial democracy" has received considerable attention in Europe recently. In Yugoslavia, workers own many of the enterprises and elect their own managers. In France, there has been much talk of "autogestion" (self-management), as well as cases where workers illegally took over companies and managed them for short periods. In Germany one-half of the seats on the boards of directors of the larger corporations are by law reserved for workers' representatives.

Although experience has been too limited to draw any definitive conclusions, the early evidence suggests that these steps do not lead to pure democratization, or anything close to it. Thus, in their excellent review of worker participation in eight countries of Europe, Asia, and the Middle East, Strauss and Rosenstein (1970) conclude:

[9] I trust that the reader will accept a small logical inconsistency here. By our definition, full horizontal decentralization technically means that everyone shares power except the line managers. Full democracy, of course, grants them the same power as everyone else—no more, but no less.

1. Participation in many cases has been introduced from the top down as a symbolic solution to ideological contradictions;
2. Its appeal is due in large part to its apparent consistency with both socialist and human relations theory;
3. In practice it has only spotty success and chiefly in the personnel and welfare rather than in the production areas;
4. Its chief value may be that of providing another forum for the resolution of conflict as well as another means by which management can induce compliance with its directives (p. 171).

These reviewers suggest that workers are not really interested in issues that do not pertain directly to their work. Most surprising, they find in reviewing one study that participation may serve to strengthen the hand of top management at the expense of other groups, "to bypass middle management, to weaken the staff function, and to inhibit the development of professionalism" (p. 186; see also Bergmann, 1975). Paradoxically, industrial democracy seems to centralize the organization in both the vertical and horizontal dimensions. (A probable reason for this will be discussed in Chapter 16.)

Crozier (1964) describes another kind of organizational democracy, but it seems to have a similar effect. In this case, as noted earlier, the workers institute rules that delimit the power their superiors have over them. That renders the two equal—superior and subordinate are locked into the same straightjacket (except for the maintenance men of the tobacco factories, who exploited that last remaining bit of uncertainty). Power for decision making in turn reverts up to the organization's headquarters. The resulting structure is, in a sense, doubly bureaucratic—there being the usual rules to coordinate the work as well as special ones to protect the workers. And doubly bureaucratic means, in the same sense, doubly centralized. So what results is a perverse kind of democracy indeed, the organization emerging as more bureaucratic and more centralized than ever, its extreme rigidity rendering it less able to serve its clients or to satisfy the higher-order needs of its workers.

These movements in organizational democracy have barely touched the United States. What has received considerable attention there instead is "participative management." In discussing this concept, two of its propositions should be clearly distinguished. One, of a factual—that is, testable—nature, is that participation leads to increased productivity: "Involve your employees and they will produce more," management is told (e.g., Likert, 1961). The other, a value proposition and so not subject to verification, is that participation is a value worthy in and of itself: "In a 'democratic' society, workers have the right to participate in the organizations that employ them." The American debate over participative management has focused almost exclusively on the first, factual proposition (although the proponents seem really to be committed to the second, value position). In light of this focus, it is interesting that the factual proposition has not held up in much of the research. Studies by Fiedler (1966) and others have indicated that participation is not necessarily correlated with satisfaction or productivity. Those relationships depend on the work situation in question, for example, as the Palumbo study indicates, on the level of skills of the workers.

In any event, participative management can hardly be called democratization, since it is based on the premises that the line manager has the formal power and that he chooses to share it with his employees. He calls on them for advice and perhaps to share in the making of choices as well. But democracy does not depend on the generosity of those who hold formal power; instead, it distributes that power constitutionally throughout the organization. Charles Perrow (1974) is one of the few American organizational theorists who has faced this issue squarely:

> The term participative management ... includes the hygenic sprays that are supposed to reduce alienation, but it also deals with feelings of powerlessness. The lower orders are consulted on decisions and encouraged to make their own in some areas, subject to the veto of superiors. The veto is important; it is like saying we have a democratic system of government in which people elect their leaders, but subject to the veto of the incumbent leaders. Workers and managers can have their say, make suggestions, and present arguments, and there is no doubt this is extremely desirable. It presumably results in the superior's making better decisions—but they are still his decisions (p. 35).

So far we have found little to encourage the proponents of organizational democracy. It may work in small volunteer organizations, but attempts to achieve it in larger ones seem only to foster more centralization. But the evidence so far collected from actual practice is sparse. We do, however, have more evidence from the behavioral science laboratory, where the issue of leader versus member power, and its effects on efficiency and morale, have received considerable attention.

In 1950, Alex Bavelas published the first in what turned out to be a long series of "communication net" studies. The researchers placed their subjects in networks where the channels of communication were more or less restricted, gave them simple tasks to perform, and then studied the resulting flows of communication. For example, in one variation, each subject was placed in a cubicle and allowed to communicate with certain others by sending written messages between slots in the walls. Each was given a card with various symbols on it, only one symbol being common to all the cards. The object was to find out which one that was, in the shortest possible time. The five networks used most commonly in these experiments are shown in Figure 11–5—wheel, Y, chain, circle, and all-channel.

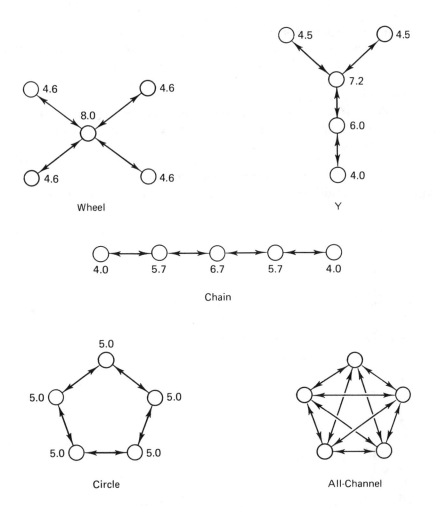

Wheel

Y

Chain

Circle

All-Channel

Note: Figures shown are the relative indices of centrality from the Smith and Leavitt study (cited in Glanzer and Glaser, 1961, p. 4). The All-Channel network was not included in this study, but its symmetrical shape would likely have produced the same results as the Circle.

Figure 11-5. *The Laboratory Communication Networks*

Certain relationships seem evident by sight. The wheel, Y, and chain clearly restrict communication the most; these also show clear "centralizing tendencies," especially the wheel, which passes all communication through a single individual. In contrast, the circle and all-channel networks show no centralizing tendencies, and the all-channel in particular has no communication restrictions. These two correspond most closely to democratic structures, in that the power to communicate is shared equally.

Many of the findings are not surprising.[10] There was a clear relationship between leadership and position in the networks with the leaders emerging at the center of the wheel and chain and at the junction of the Y, and not at all in the circle and all-channel networks. The centrality indices from one study are shown in Figure 11–5.

Understandably, the more decentralized networks tended to use more messages to accomplish their tasks and to make more errors. Not so obvious, however, at least in the Guetzkow and Simon (1954–55) experiments, was the finding that the decentralized, all-channel network eventually settled down to nearly the same operating efficiency as the centralized wheel. (These results are shown in Figure 11–6.) In other words, the two

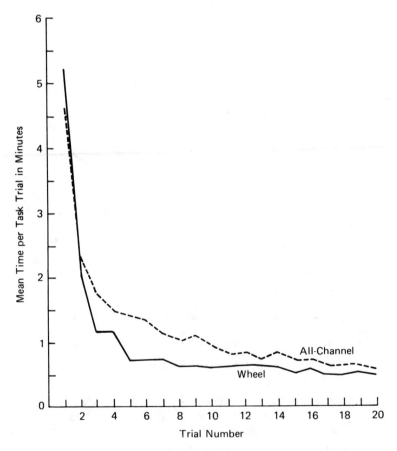

Figure 11-6. *Organizing and Operating Efficiency in Communication Networks (modified from Guetzkow and Simon, 1954–55, p. 241)*

[10]Glanzer and Glaser (1961), from whom the subsequent discussion is largely drawn, provide an extensive review of these studies.

differed not in their eventual operating efficiency, but in how fast they organized to reach it. The leaderless all-channel networks eventually found ways to organize themselves for efficient communication; in fact, most surprising, seventeen of the twenty of them in the Guetzkow and Simon sample developed hierarchies. Their real difficulty was in deciding which of their twenty possible one-way channels they would not use; as Guetzkow and Simon note, complete freedom can at times be more of a problem than restricted communication.[11]

Another researcher, Harold Leavitt (cited in the Glanzer and Glaser review, 1961, p. 4), found variations in motivation within those networks that had natural centrality (such as the wheel or Y): The individuals in central locations—the emergent leaders—enjoyed their jobs more than those at the periphery. Another researcher, Trow, questioned whether the leaders' satisfaction was based on centrality per se or on autonomy—the freedom to make independent decisions. He managed to separate these two factors experimentally and found that "autonomy produces a higher level of job satisfaction than does dependence; the effect of centrality upon satisfaction is not significant" (quoted in Glanzer and Glaser, pp. 7–8). But there were also indications that centrality evoked autocratic behavior. "In one group, the individual to whom the necessary insight occurred [to complete the tasks] was 'ordered' by the emergent leader to forget it '" (op. perd.). And finally, in one study where the leaders were explicitly told to be either autocratic or democratic, the autocrats produced higher efficiency but lower morale (Shaw, cited in Glanzer and Glaser, p. 13).

These findings suggest some interesting conclusions about horizontal decentralization. For one thing, the centralized organization may be more efficient under certain circumstances, particularly at early stages of the work. In contrast, the horizontally decentralized organization—the democratic one—seems better for morale. But the latter may sometimes be unstable, eventually reverting to a more hierarchical—and centralized— structure to complete its tasks. This, in fact, is exactly what the field studies indicate: that democratization leads, paradoxically, to centralization.

So the answer to our question about democracy seems to be negative. Attempts to make centralized organizations democratic—whether by having the workers elect the directors, encouraging them to participate in decision making, instituting rules to delimit the power of their managers, or establishing unrestricted communication channels—all seem to lead, one way or

---

[11]The circle was also included in this study, and proved to be the least efficient network. It organized more slowly and never reached the level of operating efficiency of the other two. Not only does the circle have the same leadership problem as the all-channel network, but it also has communication restrictions that interfere with its members' attempts to organize. Thus, only three of the twenty-one circle networks developed hierarchies. However, the communication restrictions of the circle are rather arbitrary, ones less likely to be found in practice than those of the wheel. (The data on the circle have been deleted from Figure 11–6.)

another, back to centralization. Note that all the experiments have taken place in organizations that do simple, repetitive, unskilled tasks.[12] A laboratory group cannot be asked to design a thermonuclear reactor, let alone deliver a baby. Likewise, organizational democracy has not been a burning issue in research laboratories or hospitals; the attention has been focused on automobile plants, tobacco factories, and the like, organizations staffed largely with unskilled operators. Here is where the workers have had the least decision-making power and have been the most alienated. And here, unfortunately, is where attempts to tamper with the power system—to make it more democratic—seem to have failed the most dramatically.

Other organizations come closer to the democratic ideal—namely, those with professional operators, such as research laboratories and hospitals. They distribute their power widely. But not because anyone decided that participation was a good thing. And not so widely that every member shares power equally. Power follows knowledge in these organizations, which itself is distributed widely but unevenly. Thus, it seems that, at best, **we shall have to settle for meritocracy, not democracy, in our nonvoluntee organizations, and then only when it is called for by tasks that are professional in nature.**

SUMMARY CONTINUUM OF TYPES OF DECENTRALIZATION

Five distinct types of vertical and horizontal decentralization seem to emerge from our discussion. These can, in fact, be placed along a single continuum, from centralization in both dimensions at one end to decentralization in both at the other. There are shown in Figure 11–7, as distortions of our logo (where, it should be noted, the inflated size of a shaded part represents its special decision-making power, not its size). Each of the five types of decentralization is discussed briefly below.

> **Type A: Vertical and Horizontal Centralization**   **Decisional power here is concentrated in the hands of a single individual, the manager at the top in the line hierarchy, the chief executive officer.** Power bulges in Figure 11–7(a) at the strategic apex. **The chief executive retains both formal and informal power, making all the important decisions himself and coordinating their execution by direct supervision.** As such, he has little need to share his power with staffers, middle-line managers, or operators.

[12]For organizations that do complex and creative tasks, we might expect the flexibility and motivation inherent in the less restrictive, more horizontally decentralized structures to render them more efficient (a finding, in fact, suggested in the studies of Leavitt and Shaw).

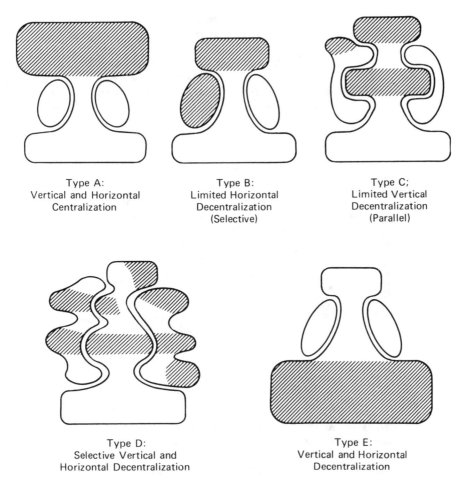

Type A:
Vertical and Horizontal
Centralization

Type B:
Limited Horizontal
Decentralization
(Selective)

Type C;
Limited Vertical
Decentralization
(Parallel)

Type D:
Selective Vertical and
Horizontal Decentralization

Type E:
Vertical and Horizontal
Decentralization

Note: The inflated size of the shaded parts indicates their special power in decision making, not their size

Figure 11-7. *A Continuum of Types of Decentralization*

Type B: Limited Horizontal Decentralization (Selective) In this type we find the bureaucratic organization with unskilled tasks that relies on standardization of work processes for coordination. (Here is where the experiments in democratization have been concentrated.) The analysts play a leading role in this organization by formalizing the behavior of the other members, notably the operators, who consequently emerge as rather powerless. Standardization diminishes the importance of direct supervision as a coordinating mechanism, thereby reducing the power of the middle-line managers as well, particularly at the lower levels. As a result, **the structure is centralized in the vertical dimension: formal power is concentrated in the upper reaches**

of the line hierarchy, notably at the strategic apex. (Should it be concentrated in the operating core as part of a program of democratization, it immediately reverts to the strategic apex by virtue of election procedures.) **Because of their role in formalizing behavior, the analysts are, however, able to gain some informal power, which means horizontal decentralization.** But the analysts are few relative to the other nonmanagers, and their actions serve to reduce the power of the other nonmanagers, notably the operators; thus, the horizontal decentralization, in fact, turns out to be of the most limited kind. It is selective, in any event, since the analysts are involved only in the decisions concerning work formalization. Figure 11-7(b) shows power bulging at the strategic apex and in the technostructure.

Type C: Limited Vertical Decentralization (Parallel)   Here we find the organization that is divided into market units, or divisions, to whose managers are delegated (in parallel) a good deal of formal power to make the decisions concerning their markets. But because that power need be delegated no farther down the chain of authority, the vertical decentralization is limited in nature. Likewise, because they need not necessarily share their power with staff personnel or operators, the organization can be described as centralized in the horizontal dimension. Of course, the strategic apex retains ultimate formal power over the divisions. And because it coordinates their behavior by the standardization of outputs, effected by performance control systems designed in the technostructure, a few high-level planners retain some power as well. Thus, Figure 11-7(c) shows the major bulge well up in the middle line and minor ones in the strategic apex and at the top of the technostructure.

Type D: Selective Vertical and Horizontal Decentralization   Here we see our findings about selective decentralization in the two dimensions coming together. In the vertical dimension, power for different types of decisions is delegated to work constellations at various levels of the hierarchy. And in the horizontal dimension, these constellations make selective use of the staff experts, according to how technical are the decisions they must make: for some, the experts merely advise the line managers, while for others, they join the managers on teams and task forces, sometimes even controlling the choices themselves. **Coordination within as well as between the constellations is effected primarily through mutual adjustment.** Power in Figure 11-7(d) bulges in various places (corresponding to Figure 11-2), notably in the support staff (especially as compared with the other four types), where a good deal of the organization's expertise lies.

Type E: Vertical and Horizontal Decentralization   Decision power here is concentrated largely in the operating core—the only bulge in Figure 11-7(e)—**because its members are professionals, whose work is coordinated largely by the standardization of skills.** The organization is strongly decentralized in the vertical dimension because this power rests at the very bottom of the hierarchy. And it is strongly decentralized in the horizontal dimension since this power rests with a large number of nonmanagers, namely the operators. If another power center were to be identified, it would have to be shown apart, since the organization is forced to surrender a good deal of its control over decision processes to the professional schools that train its operators and the professional associations that later control their standards.

DECENTRALIZATION AND THE OTHER DESIGN PARAMETERS

The relationship between our two forms of decentralization and the other seven design parameters has been discussed throughout this chapter; here we need merely review these findings briefly.

Decentralization is closely related to the design of positions. **The formalization of behavior takes formal power away from the workers and the managers who supervise them and concentrates it near the top of the line hierarchy and in the technostructure, thus centralizing the organization in both dimensions.** The result is Type A decentralization. **Training and indoctrination produces exactly the opposite effect: it develops expertise below the middle line, thereby decentralizing the structure in both dimensions** (Type E). Putting these two conclusions together, we can see that specialization of the unskilled type centralizes the structure in both dimensions, whereas specialization of the skilled or professional type decentralizes it in both dimensions.

We have also seen a number of relationships between decentralization and the design of the superstructure. **The use of market grouping leads to limited vertical decentralization of a parallel nature** (Type C): a good deal of power rests with the managers of the market units. No such definitive conclusion can be drawn for functional grouping. Types B and D are both typically functional structures, the first bureaucratic and rather centralized in both dimensions, the second organic—that is, reliant on mutual adjustment—and selectively decentralized in both dimensions. Similarly, Types A and E, at the two ends of our continuum, are often described as functional. Thus, we are led to the conclusion that **functional structure is possible with almost any degree of decentralization, in either dimension.**

The same conclusion can be drawn for unit size, or span of control. Too many other factors intervene. For example, large unit size may reflect extensive use of behavior formalization, in which case the structure is rather centralized in both dimensions (Type B). But it may also reflect extensive use of training and indoctrination, in which the structure is decentralized in both dimensions (Type E). It may also indicate the presence of market-based grouping, which results in limited vertical decentralization (Type C). Likewise, small unit size may indicate close supervision and centralization (of Type A), or the presence of small autonomous work teams and selective decentralization (of Type D).

As for the lateral linkages, we have seen that performance control systems are used primarily to control quasi-autonomous market units, and so are related to limited vertical decentralization (Type C). Activity planning enables the strategic apex to control the important organizational decisions, although it must surrender some of its power to the staff planners, which results in Type B decentralization. In general, therefore, planning and control systems emerge as design parameters to effect modest or extensive centralization. And finally, the liaison devices are used primarily to coordinate the work within and between the selectively decentralized work constellations (Type D).

DECENTRALIZATION BY PART OF THE ORGANIZATION

We have so far had little difficulty discussing each of the other design parameters by part of the organization. The same will not be true for the two kinds of decentralization, since the distribution of power is an organization-wide phenomenon. Nevertheless, some conclusions can be drawn.

By definition, vertical decentralization involves only the chain of authority, that is, the strategic apex and middle line. And here all kinds of patterns are possible. In some organizations, power remains at the strategic apex; in others, it is delegated to various levels in the middle line, sometimes selectively, sometimes in parallel; and in still other cases, power passes right to the bottom of the middle line, and perhaps beyond, to the operating core. If one generalization is in order, it is that classic authority patterns continue to dominate organizational power systems, that is, formal power resides in the first instance with the chief executive at the top of the hierarchy. From there it is delegated at his will. And formal power, vis-à-vis the informal, still matters a great deal in organizations. Thus, structures may be more centralized in the vertical as well as the horizontal dimension than their situations call for. In other words, **there may be a tendency to retain somewhat more power than is necessary in the line structure, especially at the strategic apex.**

Horizontal decentralization, by definition, brings the other three parts of the organization—namely the technostructure, support staff, and operating core—into the power system. Again we have seen all kinds of power distributions, from negligible staff groups to powerful ones, from weak operating cores to dominant ones. But one point is clear. All have informal power to the extent that they contain expertise. Staff groups do more than just advise when they have the knowledge needed to make technical decisions; operators accumulate power when they have the expertise needed to execute managerial decisions, and when they are professionals, that is, perform jobs based on complex knowledge and skills. As a final point, we might note that *within* the technocratic units and the higher-level support units, where the work is essentially professional, we would expect to find a good deal of decentralization, from the staff managers to the staff specialists themselves.

We have now discussed the nine design parameters in some detail. We have seen the various forms each can take in the structure as well as the relationship of each to the coordinating mechanisms. Direct supervision is effected through the design of the superstructure, notably the grouping into units, which creates the hierarchy of managerial positions. It is also strongly influenced by the design of the decision-making system, that is, by horizontal and vertical decentralization. Standardization of work processes is achieved through the formalization of behavior, standardization of skills through the establishment of training and indoctrination programs, and standardization of outputs through the use of planning and control systems. Finally, mutual adjustment is encouraged by the use of the liaison devices.

We have also begun to see some fundamental interrelationships among the nine design parameters. Some are mutually exclusive. For example, an organization may rely on prejob training or else it may formalize behavior through the use of on-the-job rules; but it seldom does a great deal of both. Other design parameters are clearly used concurrently, for example, performance control systems and market-based grouping, or the liaison devices and organic structure. But more important, we have seen a good deal of indication that it is the clustering or configuring of many of these design parameters, not the covarying of two, that seems to hold the key to understanding the structuring of organizations. But before we can discuss this clustering, we must add a final set of factors to our discussion.

PART III

THE CONTINGENCY FACTORS

Section II described each of nine design parameters. We saw that organizational structures are designed by combining these in various ways. But how does the organization select its design parameters: how does it decide when to use a market and when a functional basis for grouping in the middle line, when to formalize behavior in the operating core and when to rely on training or the use of the liaison devices to encourage mutual adjustment, when to decentralize horizontally and when vertically? In effect, we are in search of the conditions that will tell us why the organization designs its structure as it does.

In fact, most of the contemporary research on organizational structuring has focused on this very issue. This research has uncovered a set of what are called situational or *contingency factors,* organizational states or conditions that are associated with the use of certain design parameters. In this section we discuss these factors in four groups, one in each chapter: the *age* and *size* of the organization; the *technical system* it uses in its operating core; various aspects of its *environment,* notably stability, complexity, diversity, and hostility; and certain of its *power* relationships. But before we discuss each, we must first comment on the notion of effectiveness in structural design.

12

The Effective Structuring
of Organizations

A number of researchers have studied the relationship between structure and performance, typically by comparing the structures of high- and low-profit business firms. Four of these studies are of particular interest to us here.

In the mid-1950s, Joan Woodward (1965) isolated the manufacturing firms in one region of England, and studied the relationship between their structures and the production (technical) systems they used in their operating cores. This relationship turned out to be a strong one, especially so for the more successful firms in her sample:

> There were administrative expedients that were linked with success in one system of production and failure in another. For example, the duties and responsibilities of managerial and supervisory staff were clearly and precisely defined on paper in most of the successful large batch production firms studied and in none of the unsuccessful firms. In process production, however, this kind of definition was more often associated with failure. It was found too that as technology became more advanced, the chief executive seemed able to control an increasing number of direct subordinates successfully. All the successful firms in which the span of control of the chief executive was ten or more were process production firms (p. 71).

Woodward's general finding was that the structures of the successful firms were the most typical of their class of technical system; that is, their measures of the design parameters deviated least from the means. With these findings, Woodward introduced the notion of contingency theory, that organizational effectiveness results from a match between situation and structure.

Then in 1961 in Scotland, Burns and Stalker (1966) produced the first edition of their book, *The Management of Innovation*. These researchers found that structure—notably the design parameter of behavior formalization—varied according to another contingency factor, the predictability of the environment. Electronics firms were better able to handle their dynamic environments with organic structures, while textile firms functioned more effectively in their stable environments with bureaucratic structures.

Subsequently, two Harvard Business School researchers, Paul Lawrence and Jay Lorsch (1967), compared high and low performers in the plastics, food, and container industries. They, too, found structural differences, leading them, like Woodward and Burns and Stalker earlier, to conclude that there was no one best structure, but rather different best ones under different conditions. Like Burns and Stalker, Lawrence and Lorsch believed it was the environmental conditions—complexity as well as predictability in this case—that dictated structure, again with only the high performers finding the right fit. Firms in the complex and dynamic plastics industry required more extensive structural differentiation and use of the liaison devices for coordination, while those in the simpler and more stable container industry needed to differentiate themselves less, to rely on the hierarchy for coordination (that is, to coordinate by direct supervision in centralized structures), and to be more bureaucratic. (The food firms fell in between on all these dimensions, contingency as well as structural.)

Later, Pradip Khandwalla (1971, 1973b, c, 1974a) used a questionnaire to measure a variety of characteristics—contingency as well as structural—of seventy-nine American manufacturing firms. (He later repeated his study with 103 Canadian firms, with confirming results.) Khandwalla carefully divided his sample into two equal groups of firms matched for size, industry, and other factors, and mismatched for performance. The higher performers exceeded 12 percent profit on net worth (before tax, average of highest and lowest performance over a five-year period), while the others did not. (In fact, these measures gave an average profit figure of 30 percent for one group, 6 percent for the other.) Khandwalla found support for the Lawrence and Lorsch relationship among uncertainty, differentiation, and integration, and like Woodward, he noted that the measures for the high performers fell nearer the means, showing less variance than those for the low performers.

But Khandwalla reported another, more important finding in his 1971 paper. While he found *not a single* significant correlation between any single structural variable and performance (they ranged from 0.00 to 0.10), he uncovered a number of significant correlations within the set of structural variables, especially for the sample of high performers. In other words, success seemed to stem, not from the use of any single structural device, such as management by objectives, decentralization, or a planning system,[1] but from the combination of appropriate ones. For example:

> ... the data suggest that a firm whose top level decision making is highly centralized, provided that the centralized firm is relatively small, does not use formal management controls, is not very divisionalized, does not use participative or group decision making to a significant extent, does not invest much in specialized staff or EDP, and is not vertically integrated. Under opposite conditions, the decentralized firm is likely to be successful (1971, p. 7).

Let us take a closer look at the Khandwalla data. Figure 12–1 shows the results of the reported use of seven structural parameters for the high and low performers. Considering the publicity that techniques such as

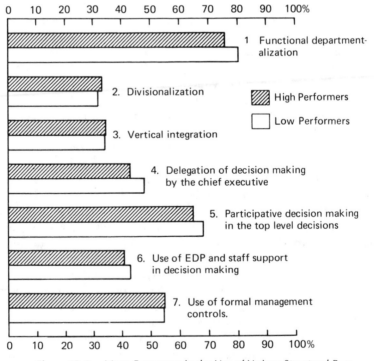

Figure 12-1. *Mean Responses in the Use of Various Structural Parameters in the High and Low Profit Firms (from Khandwalla, 1971, p. 3)*

[1]Khandwalla found the same thing for the contingency factors, suggesting, in other words, that success does not stem from being large, using a particular technical system, operating in a certain environment, or whatever.

participative management and formal control systems have received in the management press, the remarkable similarity in the use of such techniques by the high and low performers is very interesting. In contrast, Figure 12-2 shows the covariations among this same set of parameters for the two groups. Many of these are statistically significant. But while eight of the statistically significant relationships hold for both groups and only two for the low performers alone, eleven hold uniquely for the high performers.

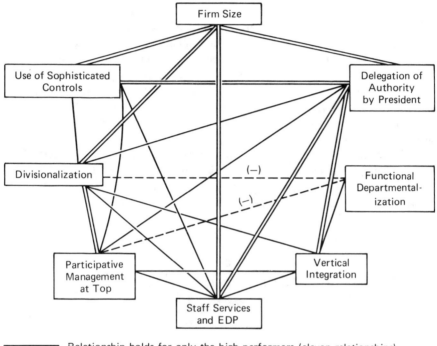

——————— Relationship holds for <u>only</u> the high performers (eleven relationships)

– – – – – Relationship holds for <u>only</u> the low performers (two relationships)

================= Relationship holds for both groups (eight relationships)

(−) Correlation is negative

Figure 12-2. *Covariations among the Structural Parameters (from Khandwalla, 1971, p. 6)*

Hypotheses of Structural Effectiveness   These studies lead to two important and distinct conclusions about structural effectiveness. The first we can label the *congruence* hypothesis: **effective structuring requires a close fit between the contingency factors and the design parameters.** In other words, the successful organization designs its structure to match its situation. And the second we can call the *configuration* hypothesis: **effective structuring requires an internal consistency among the design parameters.**

The successful organization develops a logical configuration of the design parameters.[2]

Do these two hypotheses contradict each other? Not necessarily. Not as long as an organization's major contingencies—for example, its size on the one hand and its technical system on the other—do not call for design parameters that are mutually inconsistent. Where they do, the organization would have to trade off situational fit for consistency in its internal structure. But where they do not, the organization would simply select the structural configuration that best matches its situation. This situation is not, however, something beyond the organization's control. That is, it can choose, not only its design parameters, but certain aspects of its situation as well: it designs its own technical system, decides whether or not to grow large, gravitates to an environment that is stable or dynamic, and so on (Child, 1972a). So the contingency factors can be clustered, too. That enables us to combine the two hypotheses into a single, *extended configuration* hypothesis: **effective structuring requires a consistency among the design parameters and contingency factors.**

This section of the book focuses on the congruence hypothesis. That is, it considers the evidence on the relationships between the contingency factors and the design parameters. The next and final section—the synthesis—looks at the configurations that emerge from our discussion of the research, not only among the design parameters, but with the contingency factors as well.

INDEPENDENT, INTERMEDIATE, AND DEPENDENT VARIABLES IN CONTINGENCY THEORY

Evidence of relationships between what we have called the contingency factors and the design parameters have appeared in a great many studies. Most of these studies have been cross-sectional in nature—that is, they took their measures at one point in time—and the relationships they generated were correlational. That meant that causation could not be deter-

---

[2]Support for Khandwalla's finding comes from John Child (1977), who found in a study of four airlines that the two high performers, operating in almost identical situations, were distinguished from each other by very different structures and from the lower performers in the internal consistency of their structures. Also, the Scandinavian Institutes for Administrative Research group of Sweden, in summarizing its experiences in many action research studies, concludes: "... the 'principle of consonance' is one of the most important ideas to emerge from our general programme of organization research. According to this postulate, a lack of fit or consonance between subsystems is the major source of inefficiency and conflict" (SIAR, 1973, p. 29).

mined: there was no way to know whether the contingency factor gave rise to the design parameter, or vice versa (or the two emerged together, as suggested in the extended configuration hypothesis). Nevertheless, since structure seems easier to change—it is one thing to decentralize, quite another to eliminate competition—causation was assumed to flow from situation to structure, from contingency factor to design parameter. That is, the contingency factors were treated as the *independent* variables, the design parameters as the dependent ones. The design of the structure was assumed to be "contingent" on the organization's situation.

In this section of the book (but not the next), we shall accept this assumption. Thus, Figure 12-3 shows the contingency variables at the left, as independent, and the structural variables at the right, as dependent. Eleven

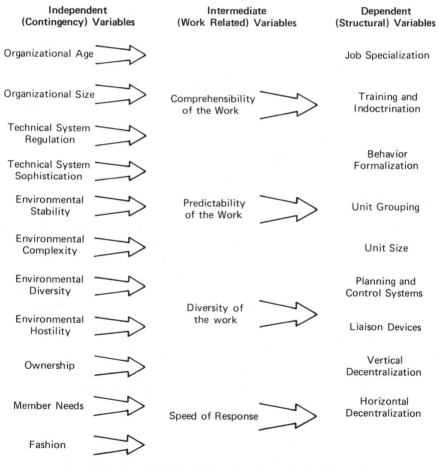

Figure 12-3.   *The Variables: Independent, Intermediate, Dependent*

contingency variables are shown: the organization's age and size (discussed in Chapter 13); the regulation and sophistication of its technical system (Chapter 14); the stability, complexity, diversity, and hostility of its environment (Chapter 15); and the power factors of ownership, member needs, and fashion (Chapter 16). The dependent variables are, of course, our nine design parameters.

In addition, it is helpful to include certain *intermediate* variables that stand between the independent and dependent ones. Galbraith (1973), for example, describes the impact of environment on structure by its effects on the information that has to be processed to make decisions. Perrow (1970) prefers to think of the impact of environment by its effects on the analyzability of search processes and the number of exceptions encountered. Here, we shall introduce four intermediate variables into our discussion, all of which concern the work to be done in the organization:

1. *Comprehensibility of the work*   The first intermediate variable concerns the ease with which the work of the organization can be understood. We shall see that this intermediate variable is most influenced by the independent variables of complexity of the environment and sophistication of the organization's technical system. Comprehensibility of the work, in turn, determines the intellectual load on the organization, which influences its use of experts and thereby most strongly affects the dependent variables of specialization and decentralization.

2. *Predictability of the work*   This second intermediate variable concerns the prior knowledge that the organization has of the work it must do. Age and size of the organization, stability as well as absence of hostility in its environment, and degree to which its technical system regulates activity all contribute importantly to making its work predictable. Predictable work lends itself to standardization, and so this intermediate variable has its greatest influence on the three design parameters that correspond to the three forms of standardization—behavior formalization, planning and control systems, and training and indoctrination.[3]

3. *Diversity of the work*   This describes how varied the work is that the organization need do. Environmental diversity affects it directly, and organizational size indirectly. In turn, work diversity influences the organization's choice of its bases for grouping, as well as its ability to formalize behavior and use the liaison devices.

[3]The interdependency of the work could be another intermediate variable, but as we shall see, it is not independent of predictability. Predictability allows for standardization, which reduces interdependency.

4. *Speed of response*   This intermediate variable describes the speed with which the organization must react to its environment. Environmental hostility affects it considerably, as do ownership and age to a lesser extent. Speed of response, in turn, influences the design parameters of decentralization, behavior formalization, and unit grouping.

CONFUSION IN CONTINGENCY THEORY

We are now ready to begin our discussion of the relationships between each of the four sets of contingency factors and the design parameters. But before proceeding, a few words of caution are in order. While some of these relationships are clear enough, others are surrounded by a great deal of confusion. There are cases, as we shall see, where different researchers present diametrically opposed findings, sometimes marshalling a half dozen or more competing arguments between them to explain their findings. Overall, the debate over which one of the contingency factors—notably organizational size, technical system, or environment—most influences structure continues to be hotly debated in the literature.

In large part, the confusion can be blamed on the research methodologies that have been relied upon to date, especially cross-sectional studies of two variables based on perceptual measures. These methodologies have generated a host of problems.

For one thing, there is the confusion introduced by the fact that structural change lags situational change (Stopford and Wells, 1972, pp. 66-67). A stable environment must become significantly dynamic before the organization will respond; likewise, a rapidly growing organization cannot change its formal structure every month. So it is somewhat a matter of luck whether a cross-sectional study manages to capture the structure that reflects today's situation, which it measures, or yesterday's, which it does not. As Kimberly (1976) notes in his review of the studies of size as a contingency factor, "Cross-sectional measures and conceptualizations have led to a static perspective" (p. 591).

Then there is the problem of multiple contingencies (Child, 1977), mentioned earlier. What if the technical system calls for a bureaucratic structure while the age of the organization calls for an organic one (the case, we shall see, of a young mass production organization)? The researcher takes measures of the technical system or the age but not both (and does not realize he must correct for the other). His correlation coefficients tend to be driven down, quite possibly below that level required for statistical significance, and he concludes—incorrectly—that the contingency factor has no relationship with the design parameter.

What about discontinuities in variables? Most of the statistical techniques used in the research assume linear relationships—more of the contingency factor always gives more (or less) of the design parameter. Yet the few studies that have looked for U-shaped relationships—more of one variable gives more of the other only to a point, after which it gives less—have typically found them. As we have seen repeatedly, many of the design parameters change not only in degree but in kind; like the moth, they metamorphose.

Perhaps most of the confusion has been brought about by the use of abstract concepts. **As soon as the researcher selects a variable that cannot be measured in the organization's own terms, he is reduced to using perceptual measures, which can distort the reality.** As we saw earlier, concepts such as "decentralization" or "participation" cannot be measured in terms of any single organizational activity. These are abstract concepts, invented by theorists to describe phenomena. But nothing happens in the organization to generate a single valid objective measure of them. The closest the researcher can come is to tabulate who plays what role in each of the steps involved in each decision process, and then to cumulate these findings across all decision processes. That will generate some impression of the true distribution of decisional power in the organization. But that also involves an enormous amount of work. And so there is a strong inclination to generate measures for abstract concepts directly, and that means relying on perceptions. The researcher must ask a manager or someone else for his perception of the concept, typically by getting him to rate it on a seven-point scale. What the researcher gets is answers, in the form of data that can be plugged into the computer. What he does not get is any idea of the relationship between the perceptions he has measured and the reality they purport to describe. There is no doubt that "the perceptions of the chief executive are important in understanding why organizations are structured as they are" (Pfeffer and Leblebici, 1973–74, p. 273). But that does not justify researchers—these and many others—in drawing conclusions about how the "environment"—as opposed to the "perception of the environment"—affects structure. In other words, we must distinguish clearly between links a and c of Figure 12–4. The problem is that distortions can enter into management's perception of the contingency factor—link b of Figure 12–4, which is seldom studied—such that the researcher ends up inadvertently describing an organizational pathology: how the management designs a structure to fit its misperceptions of the organization's situation. Tinker (1976, p. 507) is particularly critical of what he calls "actor-surrogate perceptual measures", which he sees as having reduced "organization theory to a problem of psychoanalysis of actors." He concludes: "... 'facts,' however many are accumulated, will never compensate for a bleak intellectual landscape such as that evidenced by our inadequate conceptualizations of organizational environments." To

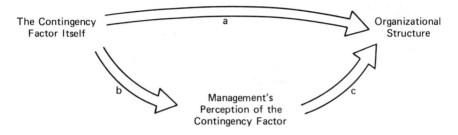

Figure 12-4. *The Contingency Factor–Perception–Structure Link*

conclude, the contingency theory literature is full of research from a distance, research that artificially forces the rich reality of organizational life into the sterile categories of the researcher, research that generates data too poor to explain anything new.

Last is the problem of context. In some research, the samples are so vast—"as different as a large tire manufacturing firm and the public baths in Birmingham" (Holdaway et al., 1975, p. 38, in reference to the first Aston study)—that they make it difficult to sort out the findings. Earlier we saw the problems caused by the inclusion of nonautonomous organizations in that Aston sample. In other research, the samples are very narrow—employment security agencies in one study, stock brokerage offices in another. That is fine, except when the researchers measure abstract concepts which hide the richness of reality and then proceed to extrapolate their findings to organizations at large. (Blau and Shoenherr, 1971, title their book based on a study of employment security agencies, *The Structure of Organizations.*) There is also the problem of context within the organization. As Van de Ven (1976a) has noted, "Attempts to compute composite scores on standardization, formalization, discretion, and other structural dimensions across all their data, some researchers have been less than careful about making clear what part of the organization they have studied."

If there is one theme that runs through these methodological problems, it is that a lack of attention to the building of a solid conceptual framework to understand what goes on in structures has impeded the serious researching of them. Take, for example, the question of unit size. We saw that a large unit can mean considerable worker autonomy, because the supervisor cannot keep close control, or little autonomy, because that control is effected instead by behavior formalization. Likewise, we saw that bureaucracies can be centralized and they can be decentralized, depending on what mechanism they rely on for standardization. Studies that isolate a few variables, in the absence of a solid conceptual framework to describe context, are bound to confuse. Here is what Kimberly (1976), in his thorough review of the studies of size as a contingency factor, has to say:

If one is concerned with understanding the structural configuration of organizations, size alone, as it has traditionally been conceptualized and measured, does not explain much of anything. It may be related empirically to other organizational characteristics, but the empirical findings are not easily translated into theory. What theory there is may be more a function of the multivariate techniques used than of an understanding of the phenomenon (p. 590).

Section IV, in its pursuit of the configuration hypothesis, seeks to develop a conceptual framework to help us understand the structuring of organizations. But we still need to gain some understanding of the contingency relationships. Despite all their problems, there are important things to be learned from the contingency studies, especially those that focused on tangible variables in clearly defined contexts. Let us, therefore, turn to our review of them.

use virtually no unpaid family workers. But they do employ many clerks, "a good indication of the development of files, regularized communication channels using written communication between designated officials" (p. 157). To Stinchcombe, this signified the birth of the bureaucratic form of structure. Much of the control, however, remains with self-employed owners.

The next period—called the railroad age, because it saw the rise of railroads and related industries such as coal mining—brought in professional managers to replace owner-managers (the proportion of self-employed and paid family workers fell below 3 percent for the first time, except for three industries of previous periods). Stinchcombe sees this as the second "crucial" stage of the "bureaucratization of industry" (p. 157). Finally, in what Stinchcombe calls the modern age—including the motor vehicle, chemical, electrical utility, and other industries—came the growth of staff departments and professionalism. Organizations of this founding period (with one exception) have professionals in more than 50 percent of what Stinchcombe refers to as their authority positions.[4]

Stinchcombe stops his analysis at this point. But the obvious question facing the reader is whether the industries of our day—aerospace, electronics, think-tank consulting—form a fourth period. In fact, later in the book we shall see clear evidence that they do. We shall also see that a number of the design parameters that Stinchcombe does not discuss—presumably for lack of evidence—fall into line with those that he does. In other words, we shall extend his findings to show the development of distinct structural configuration in specific periods of recent history.

What would cause structure to reflect the age of founding of the industry? That is, why should different industries of the same period have adopted similar structural forms in the first place, and why should these have perpetuated themselves into later periods, after the appearance of new structural forms? Why, for instance, should railroads operating in the late twentieth century have structures more like nineteenth-century coal mines than twentieth-century aerospace companies? Stinchcombe notes that industries develop because of the technical and economic conditions of their time. As long as these conditions do not change for them, there is no reason to expect them to change their structures. For example, "... railroads perhaps could not be 'invented' until the social forms appropriate to an inherently very large-scale enterprise had been invented, and railroads still being inherently a large-scale enterprise ... they still show the characteristics inevitably associated with size" (p. 160). In other words, to the extent that the

---

[4]Based on Woodward's (1965) findings of major structural differences between mass production and process firms, to be discussed in the next chapter, a case could probably be made to split this group into the early-twentieth-century mass producers and the middle-twentieth-century process producers.

conditions remain the same, the original structure may, in fact, continue to be the most appropriate.

But this explanation is not sufficient for Stinchcombe. Traditions and vested interests also play a role in preserving structural form: for example, indoctrination solidifies the structure around a set of values, an ideology. Stinchcombe notes that (at the time of his writing) fraternities retained their racial and religious exclusion clauses, as did European working-class parties their Marxist ideologies, and universities maintained certain traditional relationships with government.

To recapitulate, Hypothesis 1 describes an organization's structure as influenced by its age, its own date of founding, while Hypothesis 2 suggests that its structure is also influenced by the date of founding of the industry in which it happens to operate, regardless of the age of the organization itself.

Hypothesis 3: The larger the organization, the more elaborate its structure, that is, the more specialized its tasks, the more differentiated its units, and the more developed its administrative component.[5] The evidence for this hypothesis is overwhelming (Khandwalla, 1977; Blau et al., 1976; Reimann, 1973; Hall, 1972; Pugh et al., 1968; Udy, 1965; and others cited below).

This relationship would seem to spring from job specialization, from an organization's increasing ability to divide its labor as it adds employees and increases its volume of output. Thus, one study by a McGill MBA group found that while "grandpa" could do virtually everything in the family food store, when it became a full-fledged supermarket, there was a need to specialize: "... 'grandpa' handled the buying of produce. 'Grandma' supervised the store operations. 'Father' dealt with the procurement of the rest of the goods, whereas 'mother' handled the cash."[6] Likewise, with a greater division of labor, the units can be more extensively differentiated. In other words, increased size gives greater homogeneity of work within units but greater diversity of work between units.

But as Lawrence and Lorsch (1967) point out, the more differentiated the structure, the more emphasis it must place on coordination. Hence, the larger organization must use more, and more elaborate, coordination devices, such as a larger hierarchy to coordinate by direct supervision, more behavior formalization to coordinate by the standardization of work processes, more sophisticated planning and control systems to coordinate by

[5]Organization size can be measured by the number of employees, the amount of sales, the size of the budget, the size of the capital investment, and other factors. (Woodward, 1965, pp. 55–57, argues, for example, that the best indication of "bigness" is the size of the management group.) See Kimberly (1976) for a discussion of the measures of size. In this chapter size will generally mean the number of employees.

[6]From a paper submitted to the author in Management Policy 701, November 1969, by Selin Anter, Gilles Bonnier, Dominique Egre, and Bill Freeman.

output standardization, or more liaison devices to coordinate by mutual adjustment. All of this means a more elaborate administrative hierarchy, with a sharper administrative division of labor. That means that we should expect sharper lines drawn between the operators who do the work, the analysts who design and plan it, and the managers who coordinate it. Thus, while it is not uncommon for the president of a small company to roll up his sleeves and fix a machine, or to serve in the role of analyst in designing an inventory system (Choran, cited in Mintzberg, 1973a, pp. 104–107), we would be surprised to see the president of a large company doing these things.

There has been some research on how manufacturing firms elaborate their structures as they grow. Wickesberg (cited in Starbuck, 1965, p. 478) found that the production unit tends to be established first, followed by sales, then purchasing, and then quality control. According to Rosemary Stewart (1970), the establishment of these basic line units is followed by the elaboration of the technostructure:

> A study in the United States in the early 1950's of 211 manufacturing companies found that purchasing, shipping and receiving, accounting and engineering are usually completely differentiated by the time the company has 75 to 99 production workers. Production control, inspection, time-and-motion study and personnel become differentiated functions, if not actual departments, when the company employs 100 to 499 production workers. At first these jobs may be the responsibility of single individuals, but as the organization grows, some —such as accounting and personnel—may become major departments (p. 21).

Chandler (1962), Scott (1971), and others (to be discussed at length in Chapter 20) describe the typical structural elaboration that follow the establishment of the basic administrative hierarchy, as the firm continues to grow. First it integrates vertically, that is, takes over some of the activities of its suppliers and customers, and thereby further differentiates its structure along functional lines. And then it diversifies—introduces new product lines—and expands its geographical markets, first domestically and then internationally. These changes require the firm to further differentiate its structure, but this time along market lines: eventually, it superimposes a market grouping—product or geographical, or both—on its traditional functional structure. In fact, there is some early evidence that final structural elaboration sometimes occurs when those giant international firms faced with competing functional, product, and geographical orientations adopt the matrix form of structure to give two or three of them equal weight (Stopford and Wells, 1972).

In fact, this sequence of structural elaboration—development of the basic operating functions, followed by elaboration of the administrative hierarchy, particularly the technostructure, followed by the creation of more complex functional and later market-based forms—describes not only the individual business firm but also the whole of industrialized society. At the turn of the century, the typical American firm was small, functionally structured and with little administrative hierarchy; today U.S. industry is dominated by giant divisionalized corporations with very elaborate administrative structures. In effect, whole societies of organizations grow and elaborate their structures over time. And this, of course, is the very point that Stinchcombe was making. The forces of economic and technological development have brought new industries with new structures, as well as ever-larger organizations, and all these changes have caused increasing structural elaboration.

Hypothesis 4: The larger the organization, the larger the size of its average unit. Obviously, as an organization adds new employees, it must eventually form new units, each with a new manager, and it must also add more managers over these managers. In other words, it must elaborate its administrative hierarchy. Not so obvious is that this elaboration is moderated by an increase in average unit size. As organizations grow, they apparently call on their managers to supervise more and more employees. Dale (cited in Litterer, 1965, p. 311) found that the larger the business firm, the wider the span of control of its chief executive. And Blau and Schoenherr (1971) found in their study of employment security agencies that as the size of the overall organization increased, so also did the average size of its units and the average span of control of its managers, at all levels—at headquarters, in the local offices, and in their sections, from agency director to first-line supervisor.

We can explain this in terms of the relationship between size and specialization, discussed above. As positions in the organization become more specialized, and the units more differentiated, each becomes easier to manage. It is one thing to supervise twenty operators all sewing red sweatshirts, or even twenty managers running identical supermarkets, quite another to supervise a like number of couturiers, each making a different dress, or a like number of department store merchandise managers, with different and often overlapping product lines. Furthermore, not only is the work of like specialists more easily supervised, it is also more easily standardized. As a result, the manager's job can be partially institutionalized—replaced by technocratic systems of behavior formalizing or activity planning—thus reducing his workload and enabling him to supervise more people. Thus, to the extent that larger organization size means greater specialization, it also means larger unit size.

It should be noted that not only size itself but also rate of growth probably influences unit size. An organization grows more or less continuously, but its structure is changed only in discrete steps. The organization designer must go to the specific effort of adding a new unit, or splitting an old one in two. This he presumably does only when it becomes evident that the existing unit is overgrown, that it is too large to function effectively. In other words, we would expect to find a lag in the setting up of new units, especially where growth is rapid. And so we can conclude as a corollary of Hypothesis 4 that the faster the rate of growth of the organization, the larger the average size of its units (Indik, 1964).

Hypothesis 5: The larger the organization, the more formalized its behavior. Just as the older organization formalizes what it has seen before, so the larger organization formalizes what it sees often. ("Listen, mister, I've heard that story at least five times today. Just fill in the form like it says.") More formally: the larger the organization, the more that behaviors repeat themselves; as a result, the more predictable they become; and so the greater the propensity to formalize them.

Furthermore, as Litterer (1965, p. 410) notes, with increased size comes greater internal confusion. Morale also suffers. "Absenteeism and accident rates increase and job satisfaction decreases.... Severity of disputes between unions and management rises ...," spatial barriers increase, individuals feel more and more isolated. The formal group breaks down and informal ones arise in its place (Melcher, 1976, pp. 409, 412). Management must find the means to make behavior lower down more predictable and so it turns to rules, procedures, job descriptions, and the like, all devices that formalize behavior.

Finally, the findings of the last two hypotheses also suggest increasing formalization with increasing size. With their greater specialization, more unit differentiation, greater need for coordination (particularly by formal means), more elaborate administrative hierarchies, and sharper distinctions between operators, analysts, and managers, it follows that larger organizations will be more regulated by rules and procedures, make greater use of formal communication, and in general, be more impersonal.

There is a good deal of support for this hypothesis. For example, Samuel and Mannheim (1970) found that larger size meant less control by direct supervision, more by rules and procedures. Udy (1965, p. 669) and Guetzkow (1965, p. 539) in their handbook reviews and Pugh et al. (1968) in their own research found a relationship between size and formality and impersonality. Guetzkow cites one study which suggested that the relationship holds even in volunteer organizations: as the size of the local unit of the U.S. League of Women Voters increased, more information flowed down the hierarchy and less up; in other words, the executives became more detached from the volunteers. Finally, Choran (cited in Mintzberg, 1973a, pp. 105–107) found that in smaller companies, the presidents tended to be closer to the work flow, to rely less on staff specialists, to spend less time in formal roles, such as figurehead, and to engage in less formal activity, such as meetings that were scheduled.

The relationships that we have been discussing in the last three hypotheses are summarized in the path diagram of Figure 13-1, which is similar to that suggested in the Blau and Schoenherr (1971) study. Increased size leads to greater job specialization *within* units, and both of these factors lead to more differentiation *between* units, then to more levels in the hierarchy. Job specialization reduces the need for intraunit coordination, which

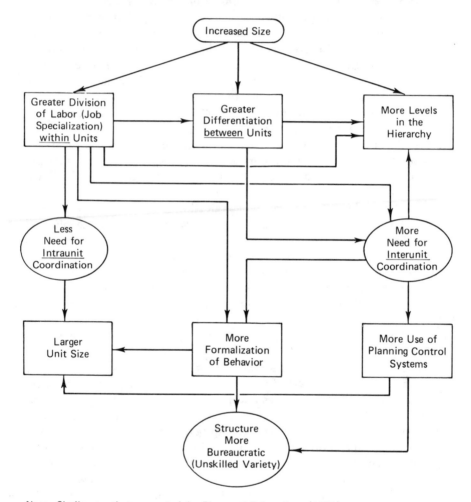

Note: Similar to that suggested in Blau and Schoenherr (1971); assumes conditions of technical system and environment held constant.

Figure 13-1.   *Path Diagram of the Relationship between Organizational Size and Structure*

allows for an increase in unit size. But job specialization, together with unit differentiation also increase the need for interunit coordination, which causes the organization to formalize its behavior and make greater use of planning and control systems (both of which enable units to increase further in size). Finally, more formalized behavior and greater use of planning and control systems mean more standardization, which means increased bureaucratization of the structure (of the unskilled, not professional, variety).

It is worth noting at this point that all these relationships can be mitigated by other factors. Woodward (1965), for example, found that some of the smaller firms in her sample, with process technical systems, had fully developed administrative structures—line as well as staff—while at least one large firm, with a simpler technical system, had no personnel function— the foremen hired their own workers. And Hall (1972, p. 119) concludes that large size breeds formalization only in organizations with routine technical systems, ones that produce standard products and services.[7] Likewise, very rapid growth may so disrupt a structure that it becomes organic even though large. This is not to say that the relationships of Hypotheses 3, 4, and 5 are absent in these cases, only that other factors overwhelm them. Large, rapidly growing organizations are probably somewhat more bureaucratic than medium ones growing at the same rate, even though both may be considerably less bureaucratic than slow-growth organizations of either size.

The A/P Studies   There has been a great deal of research on the relationship between the size of an organization and the relative size of its administrative component, that is, the proportion of its staff and line administrative personnel (A) to operating or production personnel (P), hence the term A/P. A sixth hypothesis would normally be in order, except that this research has produced more confusion than insight. Let us go back to the beginning.

In 1957, with his tongue firmly planted in his cheek, C. Northcote Parkinson published his famous first law, the law of "the rising pyramid": "Work expands so as to fill the time available for its completion" (p. 33). Parkinson argued that, in government at least, "there need be little or no relationship between the work to be done and the size of the staff to which it may be assigned" (p. 33). This conclusion derived from "two almost axiomatic statements, thus (1) 'An official wants to multiply subordinates, not rivals' and (2) 'Officials make work for each other'" (p. 35). Parkinson elaborated:

---

[7]Thus, Hall et al. (1967), who studied a wide range of organizations and did not control for technical system, found that the larger organizations were only slightly more complex and formalized. See Kast and Rosenzweig (1970, p. 227) for further discussion of the relationship between size and formalization.

To comprehend Factor 1, we must picture a civil servant, called A, who finds himself overworked. ... For this real or imagined overwork there are, broadly speaking, three possible remedies. He may resign; he may ask to halve the work with a colleague called B; he may demand the assistance of two subordinates, to be called C and D. There is probably no instance in history, however, of A choosing any but the third alternative. By resignation he would lose his pension rights. By having B appointed, on his own level in the hierarchy, he would merely bring in a rival for promotion to W's vacancy when W (at long last) retires. So A would rather have C and D, junior men, below him. They will add to his consequence and, by dividing the work into two categories, as between C and D, he will have the merit of being the only man who comprehends them both. ... Subordinates must thus number two or more, each being thus kept in order by fear of the other's promotion. When C complains in turn of being overworked (as he certainly will) A will, with the concurrence of C, advise the appointment of two assistants to help C. But he can then avert internal friction only by advising the appointment of two more assistants to help D, whose position is much the same. With this recruitment of E, F, G, and H the promotion of A is now practically certain.

Seven officials are now doing what one did before. This is where Factor 2 comes into operation. For these seven make so much work for each other that all are fully occupied and A is actually working harder than ever. An incoming document may well come before each of them in turn. Official E decides that it falls within the province of F, who places a draft reply before C, who amends it drastically before consulting D, who asks G to deal with it. But G goes on leave at this point, handing the file over to H, who drafts a minute that is signed by D and returned to C, who revises his draft accordingly and lays the new version before A (pp. 35–37).

To drive home his point, Parkinson cited the case of the British Royal Navy, which between the years 1914 and 1928 increased its officer corps by 78 percent and its on-shore officials and clerks by 40 percent although its total manpower dropped by 32 percent and its number of capital warships in commission dropped by 68 percent!

What Parkinson said half in jest (but only half) set off a flurry of excitement among deadly serious sociologists. The result has been a stream of research on the relationship between organizational size and administrative ratio, or A/P, that ranks second to none in this literature for utter confusion (and perhaps stands as the best testimonial to Parkinson's first law). Some of the research samples have been of the grossest sort, with all kinds of organizations mixed together. The measures of A and P have hidden a multitude of sins (how, for example, to classify the chef in the corporate cafeteria—certainly not an administrator, but hardly involved with the production of the organization's outputs, either).

Nevertheless, let us consider the evidence on whether or not organizations add nonoperating personnel faster than operators as they grow, in other words, whether they show positive or negative "administrative economies of scale."

Mason Haire (1959) threw out an appropriately whimsical, but nevertheless appealing, argument: that as they grow, organizations—like bridges and giants—need more and more structure just to support themselves. In the physical world at least, linear growth in each dimension results in cubic growth in the volume to be supported but only square growth in the surface doing the supporting. Hence, the pressure on the support members increases with growth. Haire notes that while a plank of ten feet by one foot by one inch can lie flat, supported at each end, one of 100 feet by ten feet by ten inches would bend or break. And, of course, the Jolly Green Giant would collapse under his own weight unless he were shaped like an elephant! So Haire concluded that organizations must change their shape as they grow. Specifically, he hypothesized that organizations must grow fastest where the pressures are the greatest, notably in units dealing with communication, organization design, labor relations, accounting, and marketing. He even presented some data—that for one firm is reproduced in Figure 13-2— suggesting an area/volume relationship: As size changed, the square root of the number of external employees (those primarily concerned with things outside the firm, including purchasing agents, shippers, receptionists, and so on—those on the surface so to speak) covaried with the cube root of the

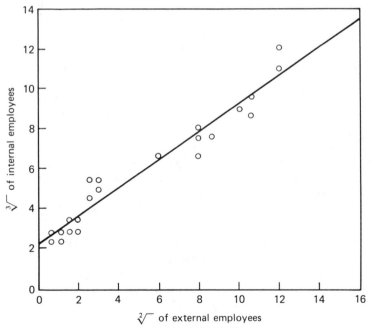

Figure 13-2. *Area-Volume Relationship with Size in One Firm* *(from Haire, 1959, p. 286)*

number of internal employees (those that constituted the firm's volume).

Despite the appeal of Haire's argument, McWhinney (1965) came along to challenge it. He reanalyzed Haire's data, and together with other evidence, concluded that the "biological-growth analogy" could not be supported. "Such analogies may provide some ideas on which a geometry of organizations might be constructed ... [But the] essential connection to the empirical world ... is still missing" (p. 362).

What then, about the evidence from the more conventional studies, where statistical tests were run on measures of A, P, and size for large samples of organizations? Right from the outset, there were problems: two of the first studies showed diametrically opposed results. Terrien and Mills' 1955 analysis of California school districts showed an A/P increasing with size, while Anderson and Warkov's 1961 follow-up in veteran's hospitals showed it to decrease. When Rushing (1967–68, p. 274) reviewed 12 studies six years later, he found two that showed increasing administrative ratios, six that showed decreasing ratios, and four that found no significant change.

Then along came Blau and Schoenherr in 1971, who, in their study of employment security agencies, provided some important clues to the mystery. They found two opposing forces in the administrative component of a growing organization. As can be seen in Figure 13-1, on the one hand, growth leads to specialization, which facilitates intraunit coordination, which results in larger unit size, proportionately fewer managers, and a smaller A/P. On the other hand, growth also leads to greater differentiation between units, which makes interunit coordination more difficult, which requires more supervisory staff, which results in a larger A/P. Thus, the forces of specialization (of jobs) and differentiation (of units) create opposing forces in the administrative structure.

Furthermore, Rushing (1967–68) found in his own research that organization growth affected two separate components of the administrative structure differentially: the managerial component decreased while the clerical component increased. (The clerical component is in large part the technocratic one, clerks manning the systems of the technostructure.) Thus, it appears that specialization within units, while it reduces the need for managers, in promoting standardization increases the need for technocratic staff. In effect, increasing size causes a shift within the administration from managers of the middle line to analysts and clerks of the technostructure. "... as industrial firms grow larger, clerical personnel increasingly become functional alternatives for managerial personnel in the performance of essential organizational functions" (Rushing, 1976, p. 38).[8]

So now the question becomes: as organizations grow, do they become more efficient administratively because of decreases in the proportion of

---

[8] Child (1973) supported Rushing's conclusion with his finding that line managers and staff employees were clearly distinct groups; controlling for size, he found a significant negative correlation between the number of line managers and staff employees.

line managers, or less so because of increases in the proportion of staff specialists? Which force predominates? In the employment security agencies that Blau and Schoenherr studied, the former apparently did, because A/P correlated negatively with organizational size, although less so as size increased. This result led them to hypothesize that "Organizations exhibit an economy of scale in management overhead" (p. 309), and that it proceeds at a decelerating rate.

But is such a blanket conclusion warranted? Might the relationship not depend on other factors, including the actual size of the organization? The Blau and Schoenherr hypothesis indicates that no matter how large grows an employment security agency—or barbershop, automobile company or government—its administrative efficiency could only increase or at worst remain constant, never decrease. Clearly, like Haire's plank—or the dinosaur—there must be some point at which an organization grows too large to be able to support itself. And that size would surely vary with its situation: small for barbershops, large for automobile companies. But infinity for no organization—there must be a limit even to what the General Motors administration can handle.

Thus, Pondy (1969, p. 47) found A/P to range in a study of forty-five different industries from 9 percent in logging to 131 percent in drugs, with a mean of 38 percent and a standard deviation of 29 percent. Assuming that organizations that survive cluster around the optimal administrative ratio, these findings suggest very different optima under different conditions. And Child (1973) in his excellent review of the A/P studies—he analyzes them on a variable-by-variable basis, including size, complexity, spatial dispersion, technology, ownership and control, membership of a large group—was able to explain some of the discrepancies in the findings in terms of industry. Positive relationships between size and A/P seemed to come from service and voluntary organizations, and negative ones from manufacturing firms.

Child introduces other factors that influence A/P in his own study of 54 British manufacturing firms, wherein he probably did more than any other researcher to break down the administrative component. (He isolates sixteen different functional groups in all. Child does not mention the chef in the corporate cafeteria, but he does have a category called "office services"!) Child finds that spatial dispersion, technological complexity, and the number of work-flow divisions all influence the administrative ratio. Most important, he finds that the relationships do not hold uniformly for all groups of administrative personnel: different factors are required to explain the rate of growth of different administrative groups.[9]

---

[9]Starbuck (1965) hypothesizes relationships between A/P and the volume of production output, the size of total employment, technological complexity, and time (i.e., time over the course of decades, a relationship we saw earlier in the Stinchcombe study). But Starbuck eventually concludes. "These four hypotheses are virtually impossible to disentangle empirically because, in typical data, the variables are all correlated with one another" (p. 506).

All of this suggests two conclusions. First, there is some range of organization size where the administrative component reached its optimum size. Second, that range varies from one industry, and one set of conditions, to another. As Klatzky (1970) and others (Starbuck, 1965; Hall, 1972) have suggested, the relationship between size and A/P is probably not linear, but curvilinear: as it grows, the organization formalizes its behaviors and replaces managers by technocratic personnel; in so doing, its administrative ratio decreases (perhaps after an initial increase when it first introduces technocratic systems) until some point of optimality; after that the A/P increases as the organization becomes too large for its situation, with a top-heavy and inefficient administration struggling in vain to coordinate its activities.

Where does all of this leave Parkinson? On the sidelines to be sure. Parkinson never talked about A/P, differentiation, or holding technology constant; all he said was that managers prefer to multiply subordinates, not rivals, and in government, where efficiency measures are absent, they are able to do so. Debating how many administrators sit on the head of a plant does not address his point. Only one study seems to. Louis Pondy (1969) found that as management was increasingly separated from ownership, the A/P increased. Pondy suggests that this could be explained by the owner-manager being reluctant to hire staff people with whom he must share power or by his tendency to work longer hours and therefore having less need for staff people. Pondy, however, finds a more compelling explanation for his finding: that professional managers are more interested in adding redundant staff to build up the size of their units in order to satisfy their personal need for power in the impersonal organization. And that, of course, was Parkinson's very argument, namely that, in the absence of direct performance measures, managers build empires.

If there is one lesson to be learned from all of this, it has nothing to do with administrative ratios. Rather it is that we shall never understand the complex reality of organizations if we persist in studying them from a distance, in large samples with gross, cross-sectional measures. We learn how birds fly by studying them one at a time, not by scanning flocks of them on radar screens.

In fact, as soon as we isolate distinct organizational types, we begin to clear up a good deal of confusion in organization theory. We shall see this with regard even to administrative ratio in our final section on structural configurations. But even on the issue of age and size, we clarify a good deal when we begin to look at distinct stages of structural development, at how organizations change as they age and grow. By considering the contingency variables over time, and by focusing on discontinuous changes in the structural variable, the stages of development theory provides an effective summary and synthesis of the relationships we have been discussing in this chapter.

Above, we found reason to believe that much of the confusion in the *A/P* research stemmed from the search for continuous relationships that turned out to be discontinuous. Specifically, there appears to be strong evidence that **as organizations grow, they go through structural transitions, changes in kind rather than degree.**

In a review of the literature on organizational growth, Starbuck (1965) discusses what he calls "metamorphosis models," ones that view growth not as "a smooth continuous process" but as one "marked by abrupt and discreet changes" in organization conditions and structures (p. 486). So just as the pupa sheds its coccoon to emerge as a butterfly, so also does the organization sheds its organic structure to emerge as a bureaucracy (hardly as delightful, but nevertheless a metamorphosis).

These models are more commonly referred to as stages of growth or development theories. A number of them have been proposed in the literature, but all seem to describe different aspects of the same sequence. Below, we shall discuss the sequence in five stages, the first a starting point only for certain kinds of organizations, the last a tentative ending point so far reached by only a few, the three in the middle being common to many. Organizations generally begin their lives with nonelaborated, organic structures. Some begin in the *craft* stage and then shift to the *entrepreneurial* stage as they begin to grow, although more seem to begin in the entrepreneurial stage. (These are designated as stages 1a and 1b, respectively.) As organizations in the entrepreneurial stage age and grow, they begin to formalize their structure and eventually make the transition to a new stage, that of *bureaucratic* structure. Further growth and aging often drive stage two bureaucracies to superimpose market-based grouping on their functional structure, thus bringing them into the new stage, *divisionalized* structure. Finally, some recent evidence suggests that there may be a final stage, that of *matrix* structure, which transcends divisionalization and causes a reversion to organic structure. Of course, not all organizations need pass through all these stages, but many seem to pass through a number of them in the sequence presented. The reader will recall the story of Ms. Raku and Ceramico, a typical one, introduced on page 1 of this book.

A good deal of our discussion is drawn from Filley and House (1969, 1976), who describe the first three of these stages in sequence, and from Chandler (1962) and Scott (1971), who describe the three middle stages in sequence. Litterer (1965) and Whyte (1969) also describe the transition from the small, informal organization to that coordinated by managers, followed by that coordinated by a line and staff hierarchy, with a final transition to the divisional structure. Other sources are also referenced in the text. For the most part, these writers describe the stages of structural development in business firms. But they seem to hold in other kinds of organizations as well. Filley and House, in fact, base their description on the "remarkable similarity" (1969, p. 411) in the growth of businesses, nations, unions, political and economic institutions, and mass movements.[10]

Our discussion focuses on the stages of development themselves, but the reader should note that the transitions are at least as important, because they are seldom smooth.[11] An organization may remain in one stage for half a century and then be required to make a transition to another all of a sudden, as when the autocratic leader of an overgrown entrepreneurial firm passes away. Sometimes the world does change smoothly; but seldom does the structure; so, almost inevitably, when the transition finally does come, it creates disruption in the organization.

Stage 1(a): Craft Structure   As Filley and House (1969, 1976) describe the smallest and youngest of organizations **in the craft stage, there is but one group, informally organized.** A natural division of labor can be found in it, based on craft skills, but that is not sharp, and jobs are easily interchanged. **Most of the coordination is effected by the standardization of skills—the result of apprenticeship training—with whatever interdependencies remaining coordinated by mutual adjustment among the craftsmen.** There is little need for direct supervision: "... management is inherent in relationships within the group: either there is no recognized leader at all (as in the case in some mining groups), or, if there is one, he spends all or most of his time working alongside the other members of the group on tasks comparable to theirs" (Miller, 1959; p. 244). With little standardization of work processes or outputs, there is little need for a technostructure. So **the administrative component of the craft organization is small and nonelaborated, comprising a few managers who work alongside the operators.**

The craft stage of structural development is typical of small proprietorships—pottery studios, barbershops, and service stations—including Stinchcombe's prefactory industries, such as construction and farming.

Stage 1(b): Entrepreneurial Structure   When craft organizations grow, informal face-to-face communication becomes increasingly inadequate for coordination. To quote Miller again: "The energies of group members, instead of being devoted to the primary task, are increasingly diverted to the task of holding the group together ..." (p. 249). So new levels of management must develop and direct supervision be more relied upon for coordination. This signals the arrival of the entrepreneurial stage.

---

[10]In the 1969 edition, p. 441n, they cite a number of empirical and theoretical studies of stages of growth in these spheres.

[11]Numerous practical books and articles discuss these; see, for example, Greiner (1972) and Buchele (1967).

More commonly, however, organizations begin their lives in the entrepreneurial stage. An aggressive entrepreneur founds a new organization to promote a new idea, whether he be a businessperson seeking to promote a new product, a union leader seeking to organize a new group of workers, or an ideologue seeking to express a new political philosophy.

The entrepreneurial stage brings a vertical division of labor, with the entrepreneur making all the important decisions himself, coordinating their execution by direct supervision, and everyone else carrying out his orders. The structure, however, remains informal and organic: entrepreneurs typically abhor formalization as limiting their flexibility to innovate and impinging on their power to rule autonomously. Hence they discourage structural elaboration: **the entrepreneurial organization has no technostructure or middle-line hierarchy to speak of.**

This was the dominant form of structure until late in the nineteenth century (Rogers, 1975, p. 82); today it is typical of young and small organizations. The entrepreneurial organization generally focuses its efforts on a single market and emphasizes a single function (such as marketing or manufacturing). The organization is efficient within its niche; its structure is well suited to rapid growth.

Stage 2: Bureaucratic Structure   The corporate landscape is littered with the wrecks of entrepreneurial firms that were *too* successful. Each started out with a small, informal structure, attracted clients and grew quickly, but then failed to make the transition that larger size required. Wishing to maintain central control despite the increased size of his organization, the entrepreneur allowed his span of control to increase to the point of overload, and then became a bottleneck in the flow of information and decision making. The informal procedures became increasingly burdensome and the employees—now more numerous and specialized, each with less access to the chief executive—never received the new means of coordination and the sharper job descriptions they required.

Survival for such organizations would have meant the adoption of formal patterns of behavior and coordination and the construction of a more elaborate administrative component, in other words, the significant shift from organic to bureaucratic structure. Such a transition is, in fact, typical of most organizations that are able to survive beyond their formative years and to leave small-scale operations behind, public agencies and institutes as well as business firms:

> For example, the innovating psychiatric clinic gains a reputation and attracts both patients and personnel. Its novel techniques, created by one or a few people, are viewed as the reason for its success. Thus, the same techniques are prescribed for new personnel to follow. As a result, these techniques must be explicated and broken down into steps, and checkpoints must be provided

along the way. Soon the new approaches are frozen into convenient dogma, and the clinic has become a factory (Perrow, 1970, p. 66).

The transition to bureaucratic structure seems to be set off by the specialization of jobs, and proceeds as follows: Job specialization requires the elaboration of the hierarchy of authority to effect coordination through direct supervision. Then, as work becomes more specialized and the units larger, the organization turns to standardization for coordination. This introduces a major division of administrative labor, between designing the work and supervising it: a technostructure is added to plan and formalize the work. In Bos's (1969) words, this stage is the antithesis of the previous one: "rational instead of intuitive, mechanistic instead of organic, impersonal instead of personal" (p. 21).

William F. Whyte (1969, pp. 571–576) describes this elaboration of structure graphically in his well-known story of Tom Jones' short-order restaurant. Jones begins in the craft stage, shown in Figure 13–3(a), with two employees and no division of labor: all three cook, serve, and wash dishes. With expansion, the restaurant quickly moves into the entrepreneurial stage: Jones hires new personnel and divides their labor into the three functions, as shown in Figure 13–3(b). But coordination rests in his hands: "he keeps track of everything and frequently pitches in to work when he is needed at one of the stations." Relationships remain close and personal, the formal controls few. The customers come, not so much because the food is good—they believe some of the competitors serve equally good food—but "because they enjoy the familiar, friendly atmosphere of the place and because they are personally loyal to the owner-manager."

But with more expansion, intermediate levels of supervision are required. As shown in Figure 13–3(c), supervisors of service, food production, and dishwashing are added. Jones "also employs a checker to total checks for his waitresses and to see that the food is served in correct portions and style." With more customers, Jones sets up a service pantry between the kitchen and the waitresses, to carry the orders into the kitchen and the food out. This requires yet another level of supervision, shown in Figure 13–3(d). At this point, Jones can no longer keep in close touch with his customers: there are too many of them and they come and go too fast. Nor can he maintain close rapport with his employees. "With those who were with him in the early days, he manages to maintain a cordial personal relationship even though he has much less time for them than before. But those more recently hired are little more than names and faces to him." In the earlier days, when Jones worked behind the counter, "he did not need to worry about elaborate financial controls. He knew his workers and he trusted them. He knew, from day-to-day experience, just about how much business he was doing, so that if the cash register was ever short, he could check up

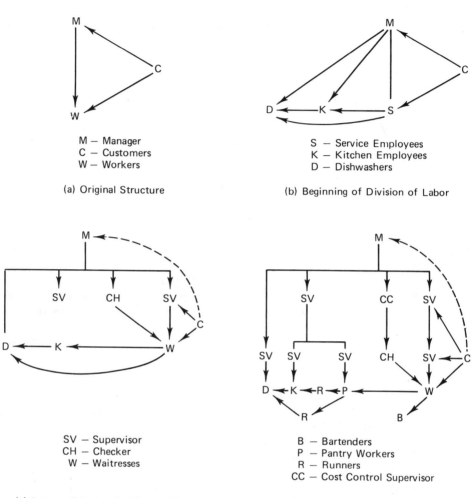

M — Manager
C — Customers
W — Workers

(a) Original Structure

S — Service Employees
K — Kitchen Employees
D — Dishwashers

(b) Beginning of Division of Labor

SV — Supervisor
CH — Checker
W — Waitresses

(c) Intermediate Level of Supervision

B — Bartenders
P — Pantry Workers
R — Runners
CC — Cost Control Supervisor

(d) Third Level of Supervision

Figure 13-3. *Elaboration of Structure in Tom Jones' Restaurant*
(from Whyte, 1969, pp. 572-73)

on it right away." In the large organization, "such informal controls necessarily break down. Jones had to build up a system of cost control, and the old employees had to learn new ways."

Typical of the organizations that have made this type of transition into the bureaucratic stage are mass production business firms, such as automobile and steel producers (as well as large short-order restaurants), and government agencies that provide mass, standardized services, such as post offices and tax collection agencies. As the Stinchcombe study suggests, American industry began a massive transition to the bureaucratic stage early in the nineteenth century as ownership became separated from management and the proportion of clerks increased.

Stage 3: Divisionalized Structure

In his study of the large American corporation of the early twentieth century, such as Du Pont and General Motors, Chandler (1962) describes how they elaborated their structures and integrated themselves vertically. But as long as they concentrated on one or a few related product lines, they retained the bureaucratic structure in its functional form. As Scott (1971) notes, in this stage the focus was on internal operating efficiency more than on market effectiveness. But these organizations grew by diversifying their product lines, and later by expanding geographically. That made their functional bureaucratic structures more and more of a liability. These structures forced an artificial kind of coordination between the activities of the various existing markets, and proved inflexible in absorbing new ones. The organizations required more adaptive structures.

The solution, of course, was the divisionalized structure, the superimposition of the market basis for grouping at the highest level. **Like the amoeba, the overgrown functional bureaucracy split itself into distinct entities, or divisions, each typically a Stage 2 bureaucracy with its own operating core that served its own market. The central "headquarters" coordinated their activities largely through an impersonal performance control system, and occupied itself with the introduction of new divisions to serve new markets and the deletion of old unsuccessful ones.**

Chandler describes this evolution most clearly in his book *Strategy and Structure* (1962). He identifies four "chapters" in the history of the large American enterprise: "the initial expansion and accumulation of resources; the rationalization of the use of resources; the expansion into new markets and lines to help assure the continuing full use of resources; and finally, the development of a new structure to make possible continuing effective mobilization of resources to meet both changing short-term market demands and long-term market trends" (p. 385). Chandler's last chapter is, of course, the transition to divisionalized structure.

Is diversification a stage in organizational aging and growth per se? In other words, do organizations adopt the divisionalized structure just because they age and grow? Stopford and Wells (1972) argue that it is not really size alone but market diversification that drives organizations to divisionalize their structures. Nevertheless, they admit to the influence of size, noting that "large firms are generally much more highly diversified than small firms" (p. 72). We might add that older firms likewise seem to be more highly diversified than younger ones. Apparently, as they age and grow, many organizations start looking around for other things to do. Perhaps time has brought too many competitors into their traditional markets; perhaps their own growth has saturated those markets; perhaps more simply, management has become bored with the old markets and desires new challenges. And other things to do means diversification, which evenually results in divisionalization. In any event, age and size are clearly related to divisionalization, although diversification is obviously the important intermediate variable.[12] Not all older and larger organizations diversify and then divisionalize, but a great many seem to. And so divisionalization takes its place among the stages of structural development, as a natural consequence of aging and growth.

Although the transition to the stage of divisionalized structure is most often discussed in the context of the large business corporation (Chandler, 1962; Wrigley, 1970; Scott, 1971, 1973; Channon, 1973; Franko, 1974; etc.; see Chapter 20), it is certainly not restricted to the private sector. Conditions of large size and diversified markets give rise to pressures that encourage this transition in any kind of organization. Witness, for example, the structure of the Roman Catholic Church or the multicampus university.

Stage 4: Matrix Structure (?) There are hints in some of the more recent literature that divisionalized structure may itself be an intermediate stage before a final transition, to matrix structure. A number of large international corporations have found themselves with competing bases for grouping—geographic, product, sometimes functional as well. The choice to favor any one necessarily involved compromises with the other two.

> Some firms have found that none of the three global structures—area divisions, worldwide product divisions, or a mixture of product and area divisions—is entirely satisfactory. All three structures are based on the principle of unity of command: one man has sole responsibility for a specified part of the business and is accountable to a single superior officer. As a result, barriers to communication between divisions are high, and coordination of the activities of foreign subsidiaries in different divisions is difficult (Stopford and Wells, 1972, p. 27).

Where such problems have proved too costly, some corporations have decided to favor two or more bases for grouping concurrently; in other words, they have made a transition from the divisionalized to the matrix structure, a transition, it should be noted, which drives the organization somewhat back to the organic form. The president of Dow Corning describes such a transition in his firm (Goggin, 1974). Stopford and Wells suggest that these actions may signal the beginning of a trend:

---

[12]The evidence on the relationship between market diversification and structural divisionalization is discussed at length in Chapter 15. In Chapter 20 we discuss at greater length the relationship between size and divisionalization, with market diversification as the intermediate variable.

A few firms have attempted ... to build new structures where managers operate with dual or multiple reporting relationships. Worldwide product divisions
and area divisions are established with shared jurisdiction over the foreign
subsidiaries. The precise nature of this "grid" structure remains unclear, as the
pioneering firms are still in the process of experimentation. There is evidence
that other firms are likely to follow suit in the near future. A [new] phase of
expansion abroad, in which global structures are replaced by new forms, may
thus be emerging (p. 27).

To close our discussion of the contingency factors of age and size, it
should be reemphasized that **structures do not seem to change continuously
or in linear patterns; it seems to be more accurate to describe them as passing through distinct transitions, fundamental changes in the ways their
work is divided and coordinated.** Whereas the very small organization is
able to function with a loose division of labor and personal forms of coordination (whether mutual adjustment or direct supervision), the larger one
seems to require a finer division of labor and a greater reliance on direct
supervision as well as standardization for coordination. First it grows a
managerial hierarchy, then a technostructure, and later, like the amoeba, it
splits into divisions. Eventually, perhaps, it is driven to the more complex
matrix form of structure.

We might also note in closing that our discussion of this first set of
contingency factors has made it quite clear that they together with all the
others form a nice thick soup. We have been able to isolate some of the
effects of age and size on structure, but never have we been free of the nag-
ging influence of the other factors. Clearly, the interrelationships among
them are complex indeed. With this in mind, let us proceed to our discussion
of the second set of contingency factors.

14

Technical System

It has been difficult to keep from discussing technology as a factor in organization design up to this point. It crept into our discussion at the outset, when we reviewed the Trist and Bamforth study of the British coal mines; later we saw it clearly in Crozier's study of the power of the maintenance men in the French tobacco plants; and it reappeared repeatedly in our discussion of organizational size. Technology is clearly a major factor in the design of organizational structures.

We would expect technology to be primarily a phenomenon of the operating core—to have a great influence on the design of the structure there. What influence it has elsewhere is, as we shall soon see, a contentious issue in the literature of organizational theory.

DIMENSIONS OF TECHNOLOGY

To operationalize the variable called technology—to decide what to measure and how—has proved a great problem in the research. As John Child (1974) notes, "The term technology is employed in almost as many different senses as there are writers on the subject" (p. 14). Perhaps the most helpful discussion is presented by John Hunt (1972, Chapter 6). Hunt notes that "The concept of technology is too broad for useful research" (p. 105).

So he focuses instead on *technical system,* the "collective instruments" used by the operators to do their work. Hunt distinguishes three dimensions: the flexibility of the technical system, that is, "the degree of member choice the instruments permit" (p. 100); the complexity of the technical system; and the complexity of the technology itself, including the skills required in the organization (what Hickson et al., 1969, refer to as "knowledge technology"). Hunt carefully distinguishes between these last two forms of complexity, noting for example that a complex technical system—that is, complex instruments—may, in fact, be easy to operate (most people drive automobiles without knowing what goes on under the hood), while a simple technical system may require very complex technology—that is, complex knowledge and skills (as in the case of the surgeon's scalpel).

In fact, **a good deal of the confusion seems to fall aside when we focus exclusively on technical system, what is sometimes called "operations technology"—the instruments used by the operators to transform the inputs into outputs—and consider the broader aspects of complexity of work elsewhere** (in Chapter 15, where we deal with the environment as a contingency factor).[1] In this chapter we shall use Hunt's two technical system dimensions, although we shall rename them *regulation* and *sophistication.* (Two other dimensions of the technical system are also better left to the next chapter: its *rate of change,* because that is dictated by the characteristics of the environment, and its *divisibility*—how easily it can be divided into smaller technical systems—because that ties in with our discussion of environmental diversity.)

The regulation dimension describes the influence of the technical system on the work of the operators. In Hunt's term, it relates to the "locus of control" of the work, the extent to which the operators' work is controlled, or regulated, by their instruments. With little regulation—say, in the case of the surgeon's scalpel or the writer's pen—the operator sets his own pace, determines his own procedures, and, in general, controls his own work; the instruments are almost an adjunct to what he does. With extreme regulation—as in the case of highly mechanized machinery—the operator has almost no discretion in his work. Of course, all technical systems are somewhat regulating, including the surgeon's scalpel and the writer's pen. As I write these words, my thoughts come faster than my simple technical system allows me to get them down on paper. Typing might be faster, but it would also be more regulating: it would not allow me, for example, to change most of my words a few moments after I write them, as I now do.

---

[1]Pennings (1975) mentions the problems that have arisen in confusing technical system with environment, while Stanfield (1976) discusses the inclusion of measures of structure itself in ill-defined technology dimensions.

In the main Aston study (Pugh et al., 1968), four technology variables[2] reduced to a single scale they called "workflow integration," which corresponds to our regulation dimension. "Among organizations scoring high, with very integrated, automated, and rather rigid technologies, were an automobile factory, a food manufacturer, and a swimming baths department. Among those scoring low, with diverse, nonautomated, flexible technologies, were retail stores, an education department, and a building firm" (p. 103).

The sophistication dimension describes the complexity or intricateness of the technical system, namely how difficult it is to understand. This dimension links to the intermediate variable of the comprehensibility of the work, but not the work of the operator of the technical system. As noted earlier, some very sophisticated technical systems can be operated very simply, as in the case of the automated oil refinery with its control panel. The problems of comprehensibility arise rather in the design of the technical system, and in its subsequent maintenance. These tasks fall, in large part, outside the operating core, many in the support units where the technical experts—researchers, systems designers, engineers—are found. Thus, we would expect the highly sophisticated technical system to require an elaborate support staff. Nonoperating specialists abound in the chemical company; they are few in the distillery.

With these two dimensions of technical system in mind, we can turn to a discussion of the influence of the technical system on structure. We begin with a review of one major study, now more than two decades old yet still one of the pillars in the field of organizational theory. Then we conclude with three basic hypotheses.

WOODWARD'S STUDY OF UNIT, MASS, AND PROCESS PRODUCTION

In Chapter 13 we saw the value of treating the relationship between size and structure as a discontinuous one, in terms of distinct stages of development. We also saw that these stages represented the evolution, not only of single organizations, but of whole societies of organizations over the course of recent history. We shall now see the same phenomenon in our discussion of technical systems.

---

[2]These were: work-flow rigidity (the adaptability of the technology to different outputs), automaticity mode and range (two measures of the extent of automation), and interdependence of work-flow segments (the linkage between operations).

As John Hunt (1972, pp. 101–102) notes, technical systems may be considered to have evolved in a series of stages, as follows. In the "modern craft age," skilled craftsmen, supported by assistants, produced individual goods of wood, iron, and bronze with their hands. The "machine age," associated with Watt's eighteenth-century invention of the steam engine, introduced factory mass production and led to a decline in skilled labor. And with the development of electricity in the 1870s came the power age, which freed factories from the need to locate near power sources, enabled production to be automated, and hastened the trend toward continuous-flow systems of production.[3] In general, the trend over these three ages has been toward the development of technical systems of increasing regulation and sophistication.

Organizations of all three ages remain with us, and they are reflected in a study of the 1950s that still stands as the most perceptive probe into the relationship between technical system and structure. In the mid-1950s, Joan Woodward (1965) selected a particular region of England and studied about half of all the manufacturing firms located there. Spending anywhere from a half day to a week in each firm, the Woodward team recorded various measures of structure, including the span of control at different levels, the extent of formalization, and the administrative ratio. They also recorded general information on the firm's background and its commercial success. To operationalize their key independent variable—technology—Woodward categorized the firm's production systems into one or more of eleven categories, which fell into three broad groupings—essentially *unit, mass,* and *process* production—each corresponding roughly to one of Hunt's stages in the development of technical systems:

- Unit (including small-batch) production
  —Production of units to customers' requirements
  —Production of prototypes
  —Fabrication of large equipments in stages
  —Production of small batches to customers' orders
- Mass (including large-batch) production
  —Production of large batches
  —Production of large batches on assembly lines
  —Mass production
- Process production
  —Intermittent production of chemicals in multiprocess plant
  —Continuous-flow production of liquids, gases, and crystalline substances

[3]Hunt also discusses a fourth stage in the development of technical systems, which he calls the nuclear age.

Woodward treated this list, in the order presented, as a scale of technological complexity—in our terms, technical system sophistication. She also noted some of its features. First, it was unrelated to the size of firms—there were unit production firms with many employees and process production firms with few. Second, as noted above, it reflected chronological development, from the oldest form of manufacturing to the newest. And third, the scale was one of regulation, from the least in unit production to the most in process production.

A number of reviewers have commented on the Woodward scale. R. G. Hunt (1970; not to be confused with John Hunt) took issue with the complexity label, pointing out that unit production can sometimes be as complex as process production. Harvey (1968) agreed with this, and preferred to view the scale as one of product change or "technical diffuseness," from the wide range of products in unit production to the rather fixed outputs of process production.[4] In a reconsideration of her own findings a number of years later, Woodward and a coauthor (Reeves and Woodward, 1970) described the scale as one of increasing impersonalization of control, from personal control by administrators in unit production to impersonal control by technocratic systems in mass production to mechanical control by machines in process production. Research by Pugh et al. (1968), Child (1972b), and Khandwalla (1974a) supported the relationship between the Woodward scale and the impersonalization of control. Starbuck (1965) depicted the scale as primarily one of "smoothness of production"—from the ad hoc irregularity of unit production (characterized by the job shop), to the regularity of the discrete outputs of mass production (as in an assembly line), to the complete continuousness or smoothness of process production (as in the oil refinery). Most subsequent reviewers have favored the Starbuck interpretation.

We, too, accept the Starbuck interpretation, but also see some justification in Woodward's claims. Unit production systems, in general but with exceptions, seem to be the least regulating and sophisticated; mass production systems are typically very regulating but of varying sophistication and with more impersonal control; while process production systems are usually highly regulating, frequently to the point of being automated, and often, although not always, the most sophisticated of the three.

---

[4]Harvey used as the measures of his independent variable the number of product changes during the last ten years and the average of the number of different kinds of products offered during the last ten years. However, it is one thing to suggest a relationship between changefulness of products and technical system used, quite another to label product change as technology. No acceptable definition of technology can be that wide! (It might also be noted that Woodward describes unit producers as changing their products virtually on a daily basis, in the sense that the outputs are not standard. What happens when the Harvey measures are applied to these firms?)

Woodward found a number of linear relationships between her scale and structure. Specifically, in moving along the scale from unit to mass to process production:

- The span of control of the chief executive increased (from an average of four to seven to ten).
- The span of control of middle managers decreased.
- The ratio of managers to nonmanagers increased (from an average of one to twenty-three, to one to sixteen, to one to eight); also their qualifications rose (process organizations had more graduates, more managerial training, as well as more promotion from within).
- The ratio of clerical and administrative personnel to production personnel (indirect salaried to hourly paid) increased (from one to one, to four to one, to nine to one; in other words, the A/P was here found to be a function of the technical system, not size).
- The number of levels of management in the production department increased.

In addition, Woodward found some curvilinear relationships, namely that:

- The span of control of the first-line supervisors was highest in mass production firms (about forty-eight, compared with about thirteen in process firms and twenty-three in unit production firms).
- The mass production firms had the smallest proportion of skilled workers.
- The mass production firms were bureaucratic in structure while the process and unit production firms tended to be organically structured.

But what distinguishes this study from the others is not these random observations but the way Woodward uses them to paint an integrated picture of three distinctly different organizational structures associated with the three technical systems.

Unit Production   The firms that manufactured individual units, prototypes, and large equipment in stages exhibited a number of characteristics in common. Most important, **because their outputs were ad hoc or nonstandard, the unit producers' operating work could likewise not be standardized or formalized, and so their structures were organic.** Any coordination that could not be handled by mutual adjustment among the operators themselves was resolved by direct supervision by the first-line managers. **Being directly responsible for production, the first-line managers**

worked closely with the operators, typically in small work groups. This resulted in a narrow span of control at the first level of supervision. (The spans of control for the three different structures at three levels in the hierarchy are shown symbolically in Figure 14–1.) The first-line supervisors' involvement in the operations necessitated high technical competence, "of the kind acquired by long practical experience ... based on 'know-how' rather than professional training. It was interesting to find that in this type of production, supervisors and managers were on average about ten years older than their counterparts elsewhere" (p. 64).

Woodward characterizes unit production as craft in nature, with the structure built around the skills of the workers in the operating core. Starbuck and Dutton (1973) explain why:

> Large [variable production] plants also include a few high-speed machines, but the generally small lot sizes make elaborate set-ups uneconomical, and preference is given to equipment that sets up quickly and cheaply. Since men can be set up very quickly, [these] plants are labour intensive. Even large [ones] operate predominantly as job shops. They install simple, basic machines that are easily adaptable to many uses, because specialized machines are liable to be made obsolete by changing customers' orders. However, this adaptability depends on two things: buffer inventories between machines to accommodate varying machine speeds, and highly skilled machine operators, who can understand the requirements of different products and understand basic machines to different purposes (p. 25).

These characteristics, in turn, meant little elaboration of the administrative structure. **With most of the coordination in the unit production firms**

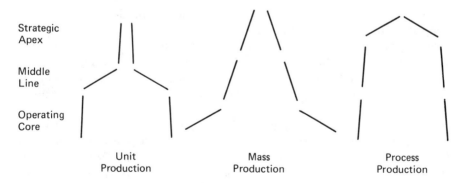

Note: Shapes denote narrow, intermediate, and wide spans of control as Woodward described them.

Figure 14–1. *Spans of Control at Three Levels in Three Technical Systems (based on the findings of Woodward, 1965)*

being ad hoc in nature, handled by mutual adjustment among the operators or direct supervision by the first-line managers, there was little need for an elaborate managerial hierarchy above them or a technostructure beside them. Thus, of the three forms of production, the unit type had the smallest proportion of managers and, as can be seen in Figure 14-1, the widest span of control at the middle levels.

At the strategic apex, however, the span of control tended to be narrow, a reflection perhaps of the ad hoc nature of the business. Not assured of a steady stream of orders, as in more routine production, the top managers had to spend more time with customers and so could not supervise as many people.

Woodward describes the flow of functions in unit production firms as being from marketing to development to production. Marketing had to come first: production could be based only on committed orders (with the result that there could be little activity planning). And the sales personnel had to be technically competent, because the orders they secured, being nonstandard, required them to work closely with the product development people. Likewise, the product developers had to work closely with the production people to ensure that the nonstandard products were produced according to customer specifications. In other words, there had to be close and continuous integration of the three functions. Thus, Woodward found little narrow functionalism, or differentiation, in the unit production firms, as well as a close-knit management group, a high frequency of personal contacts, and organic structure. Woodward makes the convincing case that every one of these characteristics stemmed directly from the technical system used by these firms.

Mass Production   If the structures of the unit production firms were shaped by the nonstandard nature of their technical systems, those of the mass producers were shaped by the standard nature of theirs. Here mass standardized production led to formalized behavior, which led to all the characteristics of the classic bureaucracy. Operating work was routine, unskilled, and highly formalized. Such work required little direct supervision, resulting in wide spans of control for the first-line supervisors. The administration contained a fully developed technostructure to formalize the work. Woodward notes that the mass producers, unlike the other two, conformed to all the patterns of the traditional literature—clearly defined work duties, emphasis on written communication, unity of command, span of control at top levels often in the five-to-seven range, a rigid separation of line and staff, and considerable activity planning, long range at the strategic apex (due to the long product development cycles), short range at lower levels (primarily to deal with sales fluctuations).

Woodward (1965) describes the flow of functions in these mass production firms as being from development to production to marketing. These firms first developed their products, then manufactured them, and finally sold them from inventory. However, the three functions were sharply differentiated, with communication between them being largely of a formal nature, since development took place well in advance of production, and production and marketing were decoupled by buffer inventories. In contrast to the closely knit groups found in unit production, "In two firms, the middle managers on the sales side did not even know the names of the managers at a similar level in the production and research departments" (p. 144) despite the fact that they all ate regularly in the same canteen. Woodward, in fact, argues that these structures worked better when the functions were physically detached from one another.

Woodward considers production to be the prime function in the mass production organizations, the key to success in her view being to keep the costs of manufacturing down. But she does not believe that it was the elite function. That distinction she gives to the technostructure, the part of the organization that rationalized production.

In general, **Woodward found the structures of the mass production firms to be the most segmented of the three and the most riddled with hostility and suspicion. She identifies three major points of conflict: (1) between the technical and social systems of the operating core, which gives rise to conflict that Woodward considers fundamentally irreconcilable, even in the well-run mass production organization; (2) between the short-range focus of the lower-level managers and the long-range focus of the senior managers; (3) and between the line and staff groups in the administrative structure, one with authority, the other with expertise.** Again Woodward describes all these characteristics as deriving directly from the organization's technical system, namely its standardized, mass production.

R. G. Hunt (1970, pp. 171–172) refers to this second Woodward group as "performance" organizations, in contrast to the other two, which he calls "problem-solving" organizations. In Hunt's view, whereas the unit producers handled only exceptions and the process firms were concerned only with exceptions, the mass producers experienced fewer exceptions, these were of a less critical nature, and many of them could be handled by formal routines. These mass production performance organizations spent their time fine-tuning their bureaucratic machines.

Process Production   In firms built for the continuous production of fluid substances, Woodward found another structure again. What would cause these firms to be different from the mass producers? And why should R. G. Hunt describe them as problem solvers, concerned only with exceptions?

The answer seems to lie in a metamorphosis of structure when a technical system becomes so regulating that it approaches the state of automation. Mass production is often highly mechanized, but if Woodward's findings are a fair guide, seldom to the point of automation. The result is work that is highly regulated—simple, routine, and dull—requiring a large staff of unskilled operators. And this, in turn, breeds an obsession with control in the administrative structure: supervisory, especially technocratic, staff are required to watch over and standardize the work of disinterested operators. With automation—which Woodward's findings suggest to be more common in process production—comes a dramatic reduction in the number of unskilled operators tied directly to the pace of production. The giant oil refinery, for example, is operated by six people, and even they only serve as monitors; the technical system runs itself.

With this change in the operating work force comes a dramatic change in structure: the operating core transcends a state of bureaucracy—in a sense it becomes totally bureaucratic, totally standardized, but without the people—and the administration shifts its orientation completely. The rules, regulations, and standards are now built into machines, not workers. As Perrow (1972) notes with a simple example: "A typewriter eliminates the need for rules about the size and clarity of script and the way letters will be formed. Rules on these matters were common before the appearance of typewriters. Any machine is a complex bundle of rules that are built into the machine itself" (p. 24).

And machines never become alienated, no matter how demeaning their work. So out goes the need for direct supervision and technocratic standardization and with it the obsession with control. And in comes a corps of technical specialists, to design the technical system and then maintain it. In other words, **automation brings a replacement in the operating core of unskilled workers directly tied up to the technical system by skilled workers to maintain it, and in the middle levels of the structure a replacement of managers and technocratic staff who control the work of others by a support staff of professional designers who control their own work. And these changes dissolve many of the conflicts of the mass production firms.** Alienated operators no longer resist a control-obsessed management. Even at the strategic apex, "the company executives are increasingly concerned not with running today's factory, but with designing tomorrow's" (Simon, 1977, pp. 22–23). And staff need no longer battle line. This classical distinction—between those who advise and those who choose—becomes irrelevant when it is the control of machines that is at stake. Who gives orders to a machine, its staff designer or its line supervisor? Logically, decisions are taken by whomever has the specialized knowledge needed to make them, whether they be called line or staff.

With these points made, the Woodward findings about the process production firms fall neatly into place, at least assuming they are highly automated.[5] She found that **the process producers' structures were generally**

---

[5]This assumption does not always appear to hold. For example, steel companies in process production require large operating work forces. In these cases, as we shall see later, the struc-

organic in nature.[6] Their operating cores consisted mostly of skilled, indirect workers, such as the service people who maintained the equipment. As in the unit production firms, the first-level supervisory spans of control were narrow, again a reflection of the need for skilled operators to work in "small primary working groups." This led to a "more intimate and informal" relationship between operator and supervisor than in the mass production firms, "probably a contributing factor to better industrial relations" (p. 60).

Of Woodward's three types, **the process producers relied most on training and indoctrination, and had the highest administrative ratios, a reflection of the extensive use of support staff who designed the technical systems and also carried out functions such as research and development.** They, too, tended to work in small groups—teams and task forces—hence the finding of narrow spans of control at middle levels as well.

Woodward also found that **the line/staff distinction was blurred in the process firms,** it being "extremely difficult to distinguish between executive and advisory responsibility" (p. 65). In some firms, the staff specialists were incorporated into the line structure, while in others "the line of command seemed to be disintegrating, executive responsibility being conferred on specialist staff. Eight of the twelve firms in which the status and prestige of the specialists were so high that it was impossible, in practice, to distinguish between advice, service, and control on the one hand, and executive responsibility on the other, were process production firms" (p. 65). But Woodward suggests that it made little real difference whether the firm opted for a line or a staff orientation: in any event, the line managers had training and knowledge similar to that of the staff specialists, and the two in fact interchanged jobs regularly.

In the process firms, the functional work flowed from development to marketing to production. First, products and processes had to be developed, and then markets had to be assured before production could begin. With high capital costs and continuous production flows, the outputs had

---

tures take on the form of the mass producers. So the Woodward findings really seem to hold for automated production, not for process production per se, although that is where automation is most common.

[6]Keller, Slocum, and Susman (1974) support this finding. They found that organic structures were significantly more successful than bureaucratic ones for process firms, although the relationship held more strongly for nonautonomous firms than for autonomous ones. (They explain this by the fact that nonautonomous firms tended to be purer process firms; that is, the manufacturing function was always tied to the firm, whereas the other functions—nonprocess and nonautomated—such as marketing, were sometimes contained elsewhere in the parent organization. Also the nonautonomous firms tended to have longer production runs, hence again were more purely "process" in nature.) Keller et al. also note that structure in process firms is influenced primarily by task uncertainty, not environmental uncertainty, a finding that casts doubt on Harvey's (1968) use of product changefulness as a measure of technology. (See footnote 4.) Keller et al., in fact, refute the implication in the Harvey study that process firms have bureaucratic structures.

to be steadily absorbed; without assured markets, these firms could be literally drowned in inventory.

Such a development cycle led to a very long-range planning orientation. (Woodward cites the example of a butane plant which was thought to require twenty years to recover the capital investment.) **The development cycle also led to a sharp separation between development and operations in the process firms, resulting in a structure with two independent parts: an inner ring of operators with fixed facilities, short-range orientation, and rigid control built into the machinery, and an outer ring of development— both product and process—with a very long-range orientation, loose control, and an emphasis on social relations:**

> [The research laboratories] were remote from the day-to-day activities of the factory, knew very little about what managers and supervisors in other departments did, and certainly did not involve themselves in factory politics. The atmosphere was very like that in university research laboratories or other research organizations. ... There was very little co-ordination even in the exchange of information between this stage of product development and other factory activities (p. 146).

This two-part structure served to reduce conflict, for two reasons. First it detached the technical and social systems from one another, unlike mass production, which put them into direct confrontation. In process production, one part of the structure concerned itself with machines, the other with people. People could be free while machines were tightly controlled. Second, the two-part structure served to decouple the long- and short-range orientation. Another major source of conflict in the mass production firms was further reduced with the blurring of the line/staff distinction.

At the strategic apex of the process production firms, Woodward found a tendency to use "management by committee" instead of by single decision makers: "Twenty of the twenty-five process production firms had management committees or executive boards, whereas the figures for large batch and mass production were ten out of thirty-one, and for small batch and unit production three out of twenty-four" (p. 53). Yet she also found wide spans of control at the strategic apex, a finding that might be explained by the ability of the specialists lower down to make many key decisions, thereby freeing up the top managers to supervise a large number of people. Perhaps the high-level committees served primarily to ensure coordination, by authorizing the choices made lower down.

To conclude, **the dominant factor in the process production firms Woodward studied seems to have been the automation of their technical systems. Automation appears to place an organization in a "postbureaucratic" state: the technical system is fully regulating, but of machines not people, while the social system—largely outside the operating core—need**

not be controlled by rules and so can emerge as an organic structure, using mutual adjustment among the experts, encouraged by the liaison devices, to achieve coordination. Thus, the real difference between Woodward's mass and process producers seems to be that while both sought to regulate their operating work, only the latter could automate it. In having to regulate people, the mass producers developed a control mentality that led to all kinds of conflict; in regulating machines, the process producers experienced no such conflict.

THREE HYPOTHESES ABOUT TECHNICAL SYSTEM

We can draw Woodward's conclusions together with some others to present three basic hypotheses about the relationship between structure and the sophistication and regulation of the technical system.

Hypothesis 6: The more regulating the technical system, the more formalized the operating work and the more bureaucratic the structure of the operating core. This hypothesis concerns the operating core only. As the technical system becomes more regulating, the operating work becomes more routine and predictable; as a result, it can more easily be specialized and formalized. Control becomes more impersonal, eventually mechanical, as staff analysts who design the work flow increasingly take power over it away from the workers who operate it and the managers who supervise them.

We saw this relationship clearly in the Woodward study. In the unit producer firms, with nonregulating technical systems, control of the operating work remained with the skilled craftsman of the operating core and their direct supervisors. The structure remained organic. In the mass production firms, with highly regulating technical systems, control over the execution of the operating work passed out of the operating core to the technostructure. That control was more formalized and impersonal, and the structure was consequently more bureaucratic. What about process production? As Woodward described it, the technical system was almost completely regulating, that is automated. Yet she describes the structures of these firms as organic. But she means the administrative structure, where the people were found. Their operating cores were, in a sense, perfectly bureaucratic; that is, at least in production (not maintenance) their operating work was perfectly standardized; it just did not involve people.[7]

[7]We can also describe this in Thompson's terms, viewing the Woodward scale as one of increasing insulation of the operating core. Whereas unit producers must respond continually to new customer requests, mass producers are able to insulate their operating cores to a large degree,

Other support for Hypothesis 6 comes from the various Aston studies (Pugh et al., 1968; Hickson et al., 1969; Inkson et al., 1970; and Child and Mansfield, 1973), which found a positive relationship between "workflow integration" and the structuring (or formalization) of work in the operating core.

It should be noted that Hypothesis 6 is presented without mention of the sophistication dimension. Bureaucratic structure in the operating core reflects not the sophistication of the technical system but its designers' ability to break it down into routine, simple, specialized, and above all regulating tasks that can be executed by unskilled operators or by machines.

Hypothesis 7: The more sophisticated the technical system, the more elaborate the administrative structure, specifically the larger and more professional the support staff, the greater the selective decentralization (to that staff), and the greater the use of liaison devices (to coordinate the work of that staff).

In Chapter 13 mention was made of a debate between those who favor size as the contingency factor that most influences structure and those who favor technical system. Woodward is, of course, the chief proponent of the latter case, attributing virtually all the structural differences she found to the technical system the firm used, and explicitly dismissing the influence of size. Then along came the Aston group, which found size to be the more important influence. They specifically rejected what they called Woodward's "technological imperative," arguing that the influence of the technical system is restricted primarily to the design of the structure in or near the operating core (e.g., the proportion of employees in maintenance or the span of control of first-line supervisors). The Aston group sought to dismiss Woodward's broader findings with the claim that the firms in her sample were mostly small, with the result that all their activities were close to the operating core and therefore influenced by its technical system.

Subsequent research by Hall, Khandwalla, and others has produced a more plausible conclusion, namely that both size and technical systems influence administrative structure but in different ways. Hall (1972, p. 119), for example, found that size was a key factor given a narrow range of variation in the technical system. He also found that the relationship between size and both behavior formalization and structural elaboration held only for routine technical systems.

Khandwalla (1974a) confirmed the Woodward finding that the size of a firm was not significantly correlated with the technical system it used, but

---

although they do modify them continuously in order to cut costs. Process producers seal off their operating cores almost perfectly: they build single-purpose, highly insulated plants, a change in process often requiring a whole new plant. And the more insulated the operating core, the more easily work there can be regulated, standardized, and formalized.

13

Age and Size

Do the structures of older organizations differ from those of younger ones? Do the structures of larger organizations differ from those of smaller ones? Does the rate of organizational growth affect structure? These are important questions in our society, as obsessed as it is with organizational growth for its own sake. In fact, we have a considerable body of evidence on the effects of age and size on structure, most of which we can capture in five hypotheses, two concerning age and three size. After discussing each hypothesis, we shall see that we can clarify and synthesize the five of them by looking at organizational aging and growth, not as a set of linear progressions, but as a sequence of distinct transitions between "stages of development."[1]

Hypothesis 1: The older the organization, the more formalized its behavior.[2] Here we encounter the "we've-seen-it-all-before" syndrome, as in the case of the tenured college professor whose students follow his lecture

---

[1]Kimberly (1976) reviews incisively 80 empirical studies of the relationship between size and structure, but in terms of the methodologies used rather than the results obtained.

[2]Hypotheses of this type—which will be used in each of the four chapters of this section—are presented as descriptions of reality supported in the research. Considering the findings of Woodward, Khandwalla, and others, as discussed in Chapter 12, all the hypotheses presumably describe the behavior of high-performance organizations more accurately than low-performance ones. We could, in fact, reword all the hypotheses in Thompson's (1967) terms, for example: "Under norms of rationality, as organizations age, they seek increasingly to formalize their behavior."

word for word from the notebook of a previous student, or the government clerk who informs you that your seemingly unique problem is covered in Volume XXII, Page 691, Paragraph 14, a precedent set in 1915. As organizations age, all other things being equal, they repeat their work, with the result that it becomes more predictable, and so more easily formalized. Thus, when the Aston group replicated its study four to five years later (Inkson et al., 1970), it found that 13 of the 14 organizations in both samples had increased in the measure of formalization of activities. Samuel and Mannheim (1970) also found statistically significant evidence that the older Israeli plants they studied were the more impersonal ones.[3] As Starbuck (1965) notes:

> New organizations tend to have vague definitions of their tasks. They are not sure which task segments are important or necessary, and they are not sure how the overall tasks should be factored. . . . As an organization gets older, it learns more and more about coping with its environment and with its internal problems of communication and coordination. . . . the normal organization tries to perpetuate the fruits of its learning by formalizing them. It sets up standard operating procedures; it routinizes reports on organizational performance . . . (p. 480).

Hypothesis 2: Structure reflects the age of founding of the industry. This curious hypothesis is supported in the research of Arthur Stinchcombe (1965). He found that ". . . organizational types generally originate rapidly in a relatively short historical period, to grow and change slowly after that period. The time at which this period of growth took place is highly correlated with the present characteristics of organizations of the type" (p. 168). Specifically, Stinchcombe found that the age of the industry related inversely to job specialization and the use of trained professionals in staff positions (two aspects of what we refer to under the next hypothesis as "structural elaboration").

Stinchcombe studied the proportion of different workers—family, self-employed, clerical, and professionals—in industries founded in four different periods. Prefactory organizations—farms, construction firms, retail stores, and the like—today maintain some of their original structural characteristics; specifically, they rely more than others on unpaid family workers and self-employed owners instead of unpaid clerks. They retain, in effect, a *craft* structure. Industries that established themselves in the early nineteenth century—apparel, textiles, banking, and others—consistently

[3]Interestingly, in their first study, the Aston group found "no relationship between age and structuring of activities ($r=0.09$)" (Pugh et al., 1968, p. 95). This discrepancy suggests that a longitudinal study of the same organization over time is far more reliable than a cross-sectional one with a heterogeneous mixture of organizations. Samuel and Mannheim had a better-defined sample.

he also confirmed the Aston finding that size had a strong influence on structure, specifically on decentralization and the use of sophisticated controls. Khandwalla concluded that the technical system affects structure selectively. In their literature review, Child and Mansfield (1972) describe some of these selective effects: size better predicted formalization and centralization, while technical system better predicted organizational shape, namely the spans of control and the number of levels in the hierarchy.[8]

Our seventh hypothesis describes one of these selective effects on the administrative structure, proposing that sophisticated technical systems require elaborate administrative structures to support them. If an organization is to use complex machinery, it must hire staff specialists who can understand that machinery, who can design, purchase, and modify it. It must give them considerable power to make decisions concerning that machinery. They, in turn, must work in teams and task forces to make those decisions.

In other words, we would expect organizations with sophisticated technical systems to exhibit high administrative ratios, to rely heavily on the liaison devices at middle levels, to favor small units there, and to decentralize selectively, that is, give the support staff power over the technical decisions. All these conclusions are, of course, suggested in the Woodward study, specifically, in the absence of elaborate administrative structure in the unit production firms, generally with the least sophisticated technical systems, and in the presence of all these features in the process firms, generally with the most sophisticated technical systems.

Others support this hypothesis, too. As the technical system becomes more complex or sophisticated, Udy (1959), R. G. Hunt (1970), and Hickson et al. (1969) found that the span of control narrowed or the number of hierarchical levels increased, Udy (1965) found that professionals gained in influence, and John Hunt (1972, pp. 234–235) found that some decisional power was driven down from the strategic apex and up from the operating core to the middle levels, where the staff specialists resided. And Khandwalla (1974a) presents a path diagram based on his research, reproduced in Figure 14-2, which shows a positive relationship between the Woodward scale of

[8]Aldrich (1972) used path analysis to reexamine the Aston data and developed a "plausible" theory from it, which showed technical system to be a major independent variable. He considered its rejection by the Aston group "to be ill-advised and premature" (p. 40), concluding that the problem lay with a weak theoretical foundation and cross-sectional data. Blau et al. (1976) compared the technological imperative with what we might call Aston's "size imperative": treating the Woodward list as a single linear continuum, Blau et al. rejected her imperative (and a number of her hypotheses) in favor of that of the Aston group; however, when they treated unit, mass, and process production systems independently, (or curvilinearly), "the consistency of the pattern [was] impressive" (p. 29): the general thrust of the Woodward findings that related administrative structure to the three technical systems held up well, independent of the size of the firm. Blau et al. also found that office automation—the use of computers—had many of the same effects on structure as process production in the plant.

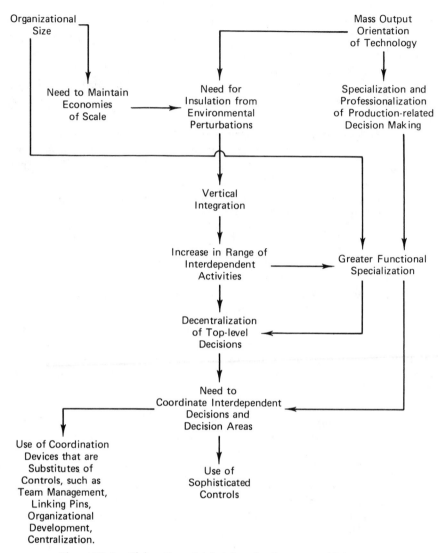

Figure 14-2. *Elaboration of Administrative Structure with Increasing Technical System Sophistication (from Khandwalla, 1974a, p. 95)*

technology and professionalism, specialization, decentralization, and the use of the liaison devices.

Hypothesis 8: The automation of the operating core transforms a bureaucratic administrative structure into an organic one. We have already discussed this hypothesis at some length in our discussion of Woodward's process producers. The key point there was that the automation of routine production appears to introduce a major discontinuity in the Woodward scale, reversing a trend toward bureaucratization in the administrative structure of the organization. Organizations dominated numerically by unskilled operators doing routine work are riddled with interpersonal conflicts. As Woodward notes, these stem largely from the inherent incompatability of the social and technical systems: often what is good for production simply is not good for the producer. That is, extreme routinization of work often proves efficient, even taking into account the costs of work alienation. A spot-welder in an automobile assembly plant provides a poignant illustration:

> One night a guy hit his head on a welding gun. He went to his knees. He was bleeding like a pig, blood was oozing out. So I stopped the line for a second and ran over to help him. The foreman turned the line on again, he almost stepped on the guy. That's the first thing they always do. They didn't even call an ambulance. The guy walked to the medic department—that's about half a mile—he had about five stitches put in his head (quoted in Terkel, 1972, p. 167).

As a result of these conflicts, as noted earlier, **mass production firms develop an obsession with control—a belief that the workers must be constantly watched and pushed if they are to get their work done.** Of course, this is a self-fulfilling prophecy, as we saw in our discussion in Chapter 4 of the vicious circle of administrative control in the traditional bureaucratic structure. Thus, the control mentality feeds on itself. Moreover, **the control mentality spills over the operating core and affects all levels of the hierarchy, from the first level of supervision to the strategic apex.** Control becomes the watchword of the organization. Top managers watch over middle managers, middle managers watch over operators and staff specialists, and staff specialists design systems to watch over everyone.[9]

Automation does not simply bring about more regulation of the activities of the operating core; it causes a fundamental change in the social relationships through the structure. **Automation of routine tasks, as Woodward[10] so clearly showed, eliminates the source of many of the social conflicts, throughout the organization.** No longer do first-line supervisors have to squeeze work out of bored operators. Nor are analysts needed to standardize their work. Both are, in effect, replaced by technical specialists—whether these be designated line or staff—who control their own work. So the major sources of conflict disappear—between controlling managers and controlled operators, and between line managers with authority and staff specialists with knowledge. And with them goes the control mentality. The

---

[9]This point is developed at greater length in Chapter 18.

[10]See also Simon (1977, p. 91) and Peterson (1975).

result is a massive reduction throughout the structure in the rules and regulations that are required to keep a lid on the conflicts.[11]

Moreover, drawing on our last hypothesis, automated technical systems, typically being the most sophisticated, require the largest proportion of staff specialists in the administrative structure. These people tend to communicate among each other informally and to rely for coordination on the liaison devices. And these, of course, are the most flexible of the design parameters. Thus, automation of the operating core breeds all kinds of changes in the administrative structure which drive it to the organic state.

This leads us to an interesting social implication: that one apparent solution to the problems of impersonal bureaucracy is not less regulation of operating tasks but more, to the point of automating them. Automation seems to humanize the traditional bureaucratic structure, something that democratization proves unable to do.[12]

To conclude our discussion of the technical system as a contingency factor, although it may have its greatest influence on the structure of the operating core, we have seen that it also has fundamental, if selective, influence on the structure of the middle levels as well. A regulating technical system bureaucratizes the operating core; a sophisticated one elaborates the support staff structure; and an automated one *de*bureaucratizes the structure above the operating core.

---

[11]New conflicts, however, arise in the organization with an automated operating core, as we shall see in Chapter 21, notably among the different specialists. But these do not regenerate the control mentality; rather, they arise in the absence of it.

[12]According to Blau et al.'s (1976) findings, that should include office automation as well, namely the use of computers. But we might ask whether automation has the opposite effect for the clients, further standardizing and impersonalizing the products and services they receive.

15

Environment

We have so far discussed the influence on structure of factors intrinsic to the organization itself—its age, its size, and the technical system it uses in its operating core. But every organization also exists in a milieu—a set of "domains," formally called—to which it must respond when designing its structure. In the next two chapters we look at contingency factors associated with this milieu; in this one, the characteristics of its general environment, in the next one, some specific aspects of the system of power it faces.

DIMENSIONS OF THE ENVIRONMENT

What does the word *environment* really mean? The dictionary is as vague as the literature of organizational theory: "the aggregate of surrounding things, conditions, or influences ..." (*Random House Dictionary*). So environment comprises virtually everything outside the organization—its "technology" (i.e., the knowledge base it must draw upon), the nature of its products, customers and competitors, its geographical setting, the economic, political, and even meteorological climate in which it must operate, and so on. What the literature does do, however, is focus on certain characteristics of organizational environments, four in particular. Each is introduced briefly below together with its associated intermediate variables.

1. *Stability*   An organization's environment can range from *stable* to *dynamic*, from that of the wood carver, whose customers demand the same pine sculptures decade after decade, to that of the detective squad, which never knows what to expect next. A variety of factors can make an environment dynamic, including unstable government; unpredictable shifts in the economy; unexpected changes in customer demand or competitor supply (or, for that matter, rapid changes in the size of the organization itself[1]); client demands for creativity or frequent novelty, as in an advertising agency, job shop, newspaper, or TV network; a rapidly changing technology, or knowledge base, as in the case of an electronics manufacturer; even weather that cannot be forecasted, as in the case of farms and open-air theater companies. Notice that dynamic is not being defined here as synonomous with "variable." Regular economic cycles, steady growth of demand, even expected changes in the weather, because all of these can be predicted, are easily coped with. The real problems are caused by changes that occur unexpectedly, for which no patterns could have been discerned in advance. That is what we mean by dynamic.[2] Thus, the stability dimension affects the structure through the intermediate variable of the predictability of the work to be done. In other words, a dynamic environment makes the organization's work uncertain or unpredictable.

2. *Complexity*   An organization's environment can range from *simple* to *complex*, from that of the manufacturer of folding boxes who produces his simple products with simple knowledge to that of the space agency which must utilize knowledge from a host of the most advanced scientific fields to produce extremely complex outputs. Clearly, the complexity dimension affects structure through the intermediate variable of the comprehensibility of the work to be done. In other words, an environment is complex to the extent that it requires the organization to have a great deal of sophisticated knowledge about products, customers, or whatever. It becomes simple, however, when that knowledge can be rationalized, that is broken down into easily comprehended components (Heydebrand and Noell, 1973). Thus, automobile companies face relatively simple product environments by virtue of their accumulated knowledge about the machine they produce.

3. *Market Diversity*   The markets of an organization can range from *integrated* to *diversified*, from that of an iron mine that sells its one

---

[1]As noted in Chapter 13, a high rate of internal growth may affect the contingency factor of organizational size, but it also introduces instability into the structure.

[2]On this point, and for a thorough operationalization of the stability dimension, see Hinnings et al. (1974).

commodity to a single steel mill to those of a trade commission that seeks to promote all of a nation's industrial products all over the world. Market diversity may result from a broad range of clients, as in the case of a computer service bureau; or of products or services, as in the case of a toy manufacturer or a general hospital; or of geographical areas in which the outputs are marketed, as in the case of a national supermarket chain. Clearly, market diversity affects the structure through a third intermediate variable, the diversity of the work to be done.

4. *Hostility* Finally, an organization's environment can range from *munificent* to *hostile*, from that of a prestige surgeon who picks and chooses his patients, through that of a construction firm that must bid on all its contracts, to that of an army fighting a war. Hostility is influenced by competition, by the organization's relationships with unions, government, and other outside groups, as well as by the availability of resources to it. The hostility dimension could be subsumed under the stability one, in the sense that hostile environments are typically dynamic ones. But we shall distinguish it because extreme hostility has a special effect on structure. Hostility affects structure through the intermediate variables of the predictability of the work, in that hostile environments are unpredictable ones. But of greater interest is its relationship with the intermediate variable of speed of response, since very hostile environments generally demand fast reactions by the organization.

Five hypotheses about environment will be presented in this chapter. But before discussing them, a number of points should be noted about "environment." First, we are not interested in the environment as an independent entity, but in its specific impact on the organization. In other words, it is not the environment per se that counts but the organization's ability to cope with it—to predict it, comprehend it, deal with its diversity, and respond quickly to it. That is why, for example, when discussing the complexity dimension we noted that if the organization was able to rationalize what seemed to be a complex product into a system of simple components, its product environment could be called simple. Thus, a good deal of the discussion in this chapter will focus on the intermediate variables.[3]

Second, although we may be interested in the organization's ability to cope with its environment, we are not primarily interested in its perceptions of that environment. What concerns us is the real environment to which the organization must respond, not the one the president happens to describe

---

[3]This point was not stressed in Chapters 13 and 14 since age, size, and technical system impact on the organization more directly. Growth in output, for example, simply and directly requires more people and/or more machinery.

on the abstract seven-point scales of the questionnaires mailed to him. Most of the research has relied on such questionnaires—it is by far the easiest way to collect data. But as noted earlier (see Figure 12-4), we should not confuse convenience with correctness. Where possible in the discussion that follows, we try to rely on the studies of actual environmental conditions. Unfortunately, that is not always possible.

Third, while it is convenient to discuss an organization's environment as uniform—a single entity—the fact is that every organization faces multiple environments. The products may be complex but the marketing channels simple, the economic conditions dynamic but the political ones stable, and so on. Often, however, it is a reasonable approximation to treat the environment as uniform along each of its dimensions, either because some of its more placid aspects do not really matter to the organization or, alternatively, because one aspect is so dominant that it affects the entire organization. We shall proceed under this assumption in the first four of the five hypotheses presented below, taking up the case of disparities on the environment in the fifth.

HYPOTHESES ABOUT THE ENVIRONMENT

Five hypotheses are presented below. The first four consider, in turn, the overall effect of each of the four dimensions of the environment—stability, complexity, market diversity, and hostility—on the design parameter it most influences. The fifth then considers the effect of dimensions that impose contradictory demands on the structure.

Hypothesis 9: The more dynamic the environment, the more organic the structure. In peacetime, or well back from the battlefield in wartime, armies tend to be highly bureaucratic institutions, with heavy emphasis on planning, formal drills, and ceremony, close attention being paid to discipline. On the battlefield, at least the modern one, there is the need for greater flexibility, and so the structure becomes less rigid. This is especially so in the dynamic conditions of guerrilla warfare. As Feld (1959) notes, "The rational direction of large masses requires planning, and planning requires a high degree of stability and calm" (p. 17). As a result, "The chain of command and responsibility is nowhere more clear [than at headquarters]. Men here know precisely who their superiors and subordinates are, and know also what is required of them and what sort of assistance they can expect" (p. 16). In sharp contrast, "The conditions of combat are fluid and haphazard in the extreme" (p. 17).

It stands to reason that **in a stable environment, an organization can predict its future conditions and so, all other things being equal, can easily** insulate its operating core and standardize its activities there—establish rules, formalize work, plan actions—or perhaps standardize its skills instead. But this relationship also extends beyond the operating core. In a highly stable environment, the whole organization takes on the form of a protected, or undisturbed system, which can standardize its procedures from top to bottom (Duncan, 1973). As Ansoff (1974) notes with some amusement about years (and environments) gone by, "DuPont managers, in terms which sound quaint today, classified their product lines into those which had been 'standardized' and those yet to become standardized" (p. 30).

Alternatively, faced with uncertain sources of supply, unpredictable customer demand, frequent product change, high labor turnover, unstable political conditions, rapidly changing technology (knowledge), or a high rate of internal growth, the organization cannot easily predict its future, and so it cannot rely on standardization for coordination. It must use a more flexible, less formalized coordinating mechanism instead—direct supervision or mutual adjustment. In other words, it must have an organic structure.

Thus, a group of McGill University students who studied a weekend rotogravure magazine explained its highly organic structure (no clear departmental lines, open communication vertically as well as laterally) in terms of the following conditions, most of them dynamic: tight deadlines requiring fast, free-flowing, informal communication ("If a problem arises, the editor must resolve it as quickly as possible if the magazine is ever to get to the presses"); a small editorial staff working in a single, intimate office; a large proportion of free-lancers among writers and photographers; creativity as an essential feature of the work; and, perhaps most important, an ever-changing product: "The magazine resembles a new company because [it] is always changing. Different ideas, different problems and solutions are tackled with each new week. Thus no matter what the age of the company, the product [continues to change]."[4]

There is a considerable amount of empirical evidence to support this hypothesis. In fact, Burns and Stalker (1966) first introduced the notion of "organic" structure to describe the response of organizations to dynamic environmental conditions. In their words: "Organic systems are adapted to unstable conditions, when problems and requirements for action arise which cannot be broken down and distributed among specialist roles within a clearly defined hierarchy" (pp. 5–6).

More support comes from a variety of other studies, concerning other aspects of dynamic environments. Burns (1967) found that the ordering of seven manufacturing firms according to the percentage of time management spent on spoken communication (as opposed to the more formal, written

[4]From a paper by Dan Lichtenfeld, Arthur Aron, David Saltzman, and Mike Glazer, submitted to the author in Management 420, McGill University, 1970.

kind) corresponded to ordering of their investment in research, namely "their susceptibility to environmental (technological and market) change" (p. 160). Stinchcombe (1959–60) found that the seasonality of employment in construction firms bore a strong negative relationship to the number of clerks in their labor force, an indication of the presence of bureaucratic systems, leading him to conclude that "instability decreases bureaucratization" (p. 179). Harvey (1968), who analyzed the frequency of product change, found that while the more bureaucratic firms could better make day-to-day routine decisions, the organically structured ones made innovative decisions—those demanded of a dynamic environment—faster, with less conflict, and with greater success. Chandler and Sayles (1971) describe NASA's organic structure as "designed to cope with an endless series of unpredictable problems"; they argue that "structure impedes change; stability works against adaptation" (p. 180). An indication of just how organic was this structure is Litzinger et al.'s (1970, p. 7) comment that NASA's Manned Spaceflight Center went through seventeen reorganizations in the first eight years of its existence!

Other researchers have looked across units within the same organization and have found their degree of bureaucratization to vary with the stability of those aspects of the environment they dealt with. In general, research departments, dealing with dynamic knowledge and requiring extensive innovation, tended to be the least bureaucratic, and production departments, best protected from environmental uncertainty, the most (Harvey, 1968; Lawrence and Lorsch, 1967).[5]

As a final point, the reader is asked to note the wording of Hypothesis 9: dynamic environments lead to organic structures, instead of stable environments leading to bureaucratic ones. This wording was chosen to highlight the asymmetrical nature of the relationship—that dynamic conditions have more influence on structure than static ones. Specifically, there is evidence to suggest that **a dynamic environment will drive the structure to an organic state despite forces of large size and regulating technical system that act in the opposite direction, whereas a stable environment will not override the other contingency factors—the structure will be bureaucratic to the extent called for by these other factors.** Child (1974) makes this case for the size variable as does John Hunt (1972, p. 107) for the technical system.[6]

[5]Van de Ven and Delbecq (1974) provide a three-part framework, supported by considerable empirical evidence, to describe the relationship between task variability and the extent of work formalization in a unit.

[6]Hunt, in fact, suggests that a very dynamic environment may affect the choice of technical system, the organization seeking to avoid investment in inflexible ones. It is worth reiterating at this point that while we are emphasizing one type of causation in this section of the book—from contingency factor to structural parameter—the opposite one has equal validity: organic

Hypothesis 10: The more complex the environment, the more decentralized the structure. Before proceeding with discussions of this hypothesis, it will be useful to clarify the distinction between environmental stability and complexity.

Conceptually, it is not difficult to distinguish between these two dimensions of environment. The dice roller easily comprehends his game, yet he cannot predict its outcome. His environment is simple but dynamic. So, too, is that of the dress manufacturer, who easily comprehends his markets and technologies yet has no way to predict style or color from one season to the next. In contrast, the clinical surgeon spends years trying to learn his complicated work, yet he undertakes it only when he is rather certain of its consequences. His environment is complex but stable. Much like that of Nana Mouskouri. I was struck by this at the second concert of her's that I attended. Everything was absolutely standardized—even the jokes were exactly the same ones I had heard in the first concert. Yet this was no simple operation, but a highly complex, professional performance involving years of training and months of rehearsing.

In his research, Duncan (1972) was able to show that, at least in terms of managerial perceptions, the two dimensions are distinct. The uncertainty managers perceived related to the stability dimension but not to the complexity one:

> The data ... indicate that the static-dynamic dimension of the environment is a more important contributor to uncertainty than the simple-complex dimension. Decision units with dynamic environments always experience significantly more uncertainty in decision making regardless of whether their environment is simple or complex (p. 325).

In a good deal of the other research, however, this distinction has not been made. Because these two dimensions often move in tandem—the environment of many organizations being either complex and dynamic or simple and static—researchers have tended to mix them together, and so have been unable to distinguish their individual effects on structure. Lawrence and Lorsch's (1967) plastics firms faced complex, dynamic environments, while their container firms faced simple, stable ones, with less market diversity to boot. Likewise, the Boeing Company, on which Galbraith (1973) based his conclusions, faced an environment which appeared at one and the same time to be complex, dynamic, and rather diversified. Galbraith used the amount of information to be processed as his key intermediate variable, and then equated it with "uncertainty" (whereas we

---

structures create dynamic environments by virtue of their innovations; bureaucracies use their power to stabilize their environments; and so on.

would have been inclined to equate it with complexity). He then listed as factors that contribute to this uncertainty technological change (related to our stability dimension) and diversified product lines (related to our market diversity dimension).[7] Both researchers found evidence of decentralization as well as organic structure in the complex, dynamic environments—at least for the high-performance firms—findings consistent with our Hypotheses 9 and 10. But they were unable to sort out the relationships between the two sets of two variables.

Our tenth hypothesis suggests that the complexity dimension has a very different effect on structure from the stability one. Whereas the latter affects bureaucratization, the former affects decentralization. This comes out most clearly in the research of Hage and Aiken (1967), who examined the distribution of power in sixteen health and welfare organizations. They conclude:

> Participation in decision making about the allocation of organizational resources and the determination of organizational policy was strongly related to the degree of complexity as measured by (1) the number of occupational specialties, (2) the amount of professional training, and (3) the amount of professional activity and was weakly related to the degree of formalization as measured by the degree of job codification and the amount of rule observation (p. 72).

Further evidence, ironically, comes from the work of Pennings (1975). In his study of forty branch offices of a single brokerage firm, he found few correlations between various environmental variables and the design parameters he measured. But one important exception was complexity, which showed some significant correlations with measures that amount to decentralization. (In contrast, the stability measures showed very low correlations with the decentralization ones.) But because Pennings made no conceptual distinction between his environmental variables—he viewed them all, as did Galbraith, as "characterized by uncertainty" (p. 394)—instead of concluding some support for the relationship of Hypothesis 10, he rejected the notion of a goodness of fit or congruency hypothesis between the contingency factors and design parameters altogether.[8]

---

[7]In contrast, Thompson (1967, p. 69) distinguished clearly between diversity and stability in his description of two firms, one high, the other low on both dimensions. Curiously, however, he did not mention the complexity dimension, even though his source of information on these two firms, Dill (1957–58), explicitly mentioned complexity (of inputs) as one of the factors influencing them.

[8]It should be added that Pennings' measures of stability showed almost zero correlations with "structural lateral communication," his closest measure to bureaucratization, which amounts to an absence of support for Hypothesis 9. No explanation for this is evident, other than the fact that forty branch offices of one firm in one industry amounts to a very narrow sample

One of the problems in disentangling Hypotheses 9 and 10, aside from the fact that the two environmental variables often move in tandem, is that the most bureaucratizing of the coordinating mechanisms—the standardization of work processes—also tends to be rather centralizing, while one of the most organic—mutual adjustment—tends to be the most decentralizing.[9] The relationship between the five coordinating mechanisms and bureaucratization was discussed in Chapter 5, that between the mechanisms and decentralization, in Chapter 11. Figure 15-1 summarizes these two discussions, with the coordinating mechanisms of increasing bureaucratization shown along the ordinate and those of increasing decentralization along the abcissa (the latter is, in fact, a replication of Figure 11-4).

We can draw on an argument of Galbraith to use the coordinating mechanisms as shown in Figure 15-1 to disentangle the two hypotheses, and thereby to develop more support for each. Galbraith argues that coordination is most easily achieved in one brain. Faced, therefore, with a simple

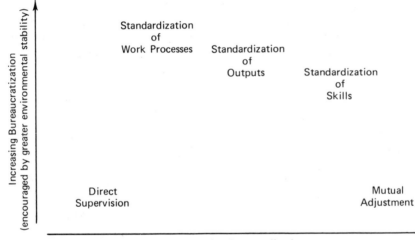

Figure 15-1. *Coordinating Mechanisms on Scales of Decentralization and Bureaucratization*

(despite claims of "considerable variations in structure," p. 400). To add further to the confusion, Pennings' complexity measures may actually be ones of market diversity: his descriptions are ambiguous on this point.

[9]Thus, Galbraith (1973, Chap. 2) presents a continuum of coordination devices along which the organization moves as it is required to process more and more information. The continuum begins with rules and programs and ends with the liaison devices. Hage et al. (1971, p. 86) find a significant relationship between environmental complexity and the use of mutual adjustment, especially across different departments at the same level in the hierarchy.

environment, the organization will tend to rely on one brain to make its key decisions; in other words, it will centralize. Should that environment also be stable, according to Hypothesis 9, it will be in the organization's best interests to standardize for coordination, in other words, to bureaucratize. As can be seen in Figure 15-1, the organization will select the standardization of work processes for coordination, the mechanism that enables it to maintain the tightest centralization within a bureaucratic structure. But should its simple environment be dynamic instead of stable, the organization can no longer bureaucratize but must, rather, remain flexible—organic. So, as can be seen in Figure 15-1, it will rely on direct supervision for coordination, the one mechanism of the five that enables it to have a structure that is both centralized and organic.

What about the organization faced with a complex environment? This introduces problems of comprehensibility. In Galbraith's terms, one brain can no longer cope with the information needed to make all the decisions, strategic, administrative, and operating. It becomes overloaded. So the set of decisions to be made must be carved up into subsets, each of which can be comprehended by a single brain (or a team of brains). Even in the simplest organization, a manager may have to restrict himself to administrative decisions, leaving control of operating ones to the specialists, as in a small laboratory, where the researchers make all the technical decisions. In other words, the organization must decentralize: the top manager, unable to know everything, must give up a good deal of his power to others—other managers, staff specialists, sometimes operators as well. Now should that complex environment be stable, Hypothesis 9 would lead us to expect a bureaucratic structure, in other words, one that relies on standardization for coordination. In that case, the problem becomes to find a coordinating mechanism that allows for standardization with decentralization. And the solution emerges with a quick glance at Figure 15-1: the organization chooses the standardization of skills. Should the complex environment instead be dynamic, the organization seeks a coordinating mechanism that is both decentralizing and organic. Mutual adjustment is the obvious choice.

What emerge from this discussion are two kinds of bureaucratic and two kinds of organic structures, in each case a centralized one for simple environments and a decentralized one for complex environments. That, in fact, corresponds exactly to the conclusion that emerged repeatedly in our discussion of the design parameters. There, for example, we encountered two fundamentally different bureaucracies, a centralized one for unskilled work, a decentralized one for professional work. Now we see that the former operates in a simple environment, the latter in a complex one, in both cases stable.

Lawrence and Lorsch's container firms—or at least the high performer —typify the first bureaucracy, centralized with unskilled work. Operating in stable, simple environments, they standardized their products and proc-

esses, introduced change slowly, and coordinated at the top of the hierarchy, where, as Lawrence and Lorsch note, information could easily be
consolidated and understood. In fact, the container firm that tried to use the
liaison devices—the design parameters of mutual adjustment—exhibited
low performance. Its use just confused a simple situation, not unlike four
people in a car all trying to decide which route to take downtown.

Typical of the bureaucracy that must decentralize because its stable
environment is complex is the university or general hospital. Because its
work is rather predictable, it can standardize. And because that work is
difficult to comprehend, it must decentralize. Power must flow to the highly
trained professionals of the operating core who understand the complex but
routine work. In Chapter 11 we discussed the relationship between professionalism and decentralization at some length, concluding, to use Hall's
(1972) words, that "the control of the individual employee's behavior is left
much more to his own discretion when he is an expert" (p. 154). Here we
can see that, because professionalism results from environmental complexity, the support we presented for that relationship in Chapter 11 also supports Hypothesis 10 here.[10]

As for the two kinds of organic structures associated with dynamic
environments, typical of the one found in the simple environment is the
entrepreneurial firm. That firm seeks a niche in the market which is simple
to understand, yet dynamic enough to keep out the bureaucracies. In such a
place, the entrepreneur can maintain tight personal control (by direct supervision), without having to share his power even with a technostructure.
And typical of the organic structures found in complex yet dynamic environments are those of Lawrence and Lorsch's plastics firms, of the Boeing
Company of Galbraith's study, and of the NASA of the Chandler and
Sayles study. (Notice, in Stinchcombe's terms, that all are organizations of
our age.) The plastics firms, for example, differentiated their structures
extensively and coordinated their work outside the chain of authority, using
the liaison devices liberally to encourage mutual adjustment.[11]

[10]We can, therefore, take issue with the conclusion of Beyer and Lodahl (1976) that "If the
knowledge taught at the university were a fixed commodity that changed little from year to
year, centralization of authority and bureaucratic decision making would be as efficient and
effective for universities as for other organizations with stable environments and technologies"
(p. 109). Bureaucratic yes, centralized no. Even a university that taught only Latin, Ancient
Greek, and Sanskrit would not centralize. These three bodies of knowledge are stable, but
together they are too much for central administrators to comprehend. Thus, to the extent that
universities teach stable bodies of knowledge—and most of the time, even scientific knowledge
remains relatively stable, as Kuhn (1970) argues in *The Structure of Scientific Revolutions*—
they bureaucratize and decentralize.

[11]Khandwalla (1973b) supports the Lawrence and Lorsch conclusion with a larger sample,
finding that, particularly for the high performance firms, there was a strong covariation between the use of uncertainty reduction devices, differentiation, and the emphasis on certain
integration devices. The successful firms were either high, moderate, or low on all three factors.

Hypothesis 11: The more diversified the organization's markets, the greater the propensity to split it into market-based units (given favorable economies of scale). Here we propose a relationship between a third environmental variable—market diversity—and a third design parameter—the basis for grouping units. Hypothesis 11 indicates that the organization that can identify distinctly different markets—products or services, geographical regions, or clients—will be predisposed to split itself into high-level units on this basis, and to give each control of a wide range of the decisions affecting its own markets. This amounts to what we called in Chapter 11 limited vertical decentralization, a good deal of the decision-making power being delegated to the managers of the market units. As Thompson (1967) notes, "organizations facing heterogeneous task environments seek to identify homogeneous segments and establish structural units to deal with each" (p. 70). Or, more simply, diversification breeds divisionalization. Thompson cites as examples the international organization organized into regional divisions, the public school system divided into groupings of elementary and high schools, the transport firm with separate divisions for passenger and cargo traffic.

There is, however, one key impediment to divisionalization, even when markets are diverse, and that is the presence of a common technical system or critical function that cannot be segmented. In divisionalization, each market unit requires its own distinct operating core. This it cannot have when economies of scale dictate a single, unified technical system. Some technical systems can be split up even though of very small scale, while others must remain intact despite massive size. A bakery operating in two states with total sales of, say, $2 million, may find it worthwhile to set up a division with its own plant in each, whereas an aluminum producer with sales 100 times as great may, despite a diversity of customers in all fifty states and a variety of end products (foil, sheets, construction components, etc.), be forced to retain a functional structure because it can only afford one smelter.

Likewise, the presence of a function critical to all the markets in common impedes true divisionalization, as in the case of purchasing in the retail chain or investment in the insurance business (Channon, 1975, 1976). The organization still splits itself into market-based units, but it concentrates the critical function at headquarters. This reduces the autonomy of the market units, leading to an incomplete form of divisionalization, what Channon calls the "functional/divisional hybrid." In fact, as we shall see in a more extended discussion of this phenomenon in Chapter 20, this is most common when the diversity is based on client or region rather than on product or service, common outputs giving rise to important interdependencies among the different clients or regions.

Most of the research in support of Hypothesis 11 comes from the business sector, notably manufacturing, where divisionalization is most common. Best known is Chandler's (1962) study of the emergence of the structure of divisionalization in U.S. industry, which he finds to have been a direct result of the strategy of diversification:

> While the strategy of diversification permitted the continuing and expanded use of a firm's resources, it did not assure their efficient employment. Structural reorganization became necessary.... It became increasingly difficult to coordinate through the existing structure the different functional activities to the needs of several quite different markets.
>
> Channels of communication and authority as well as the information flowing through these channels grew more and more inadequate. The wants of different customers varied, and demand and taste fluctuated differently in different markets. ... In time, then, each major product line came to be administered through a separate, integrated autonomous division. Its manager became responsible for the major operating decisions involved in the coordination of functional activities to changing demand and taste (p. 393).

Subsequent research has indicated that product and regional diversification has spread the divisionalized form of structure to most of the giant American corporations, as well as to many of these in Europe. For example, Wrigley (1970) categorized a random sample of 100 of the 500 largest U.S. corporations in 1967 (the "Fortune 500") according to their degree of diversification. Only six fell into his "single product" category, and all had functional structures. Another fourteen fell into the "dominant product" group (70 percent or more of the sales attributable to one product), and nine of these had divisionalized structures. Of the sixty that had diversified into "related businesses," all but three had divisionalized structures. All of the remaining twenty which had diversified into "unrelated products" had divisionalized structures. These findings were supported by Rumelt (1974), who sampled the Fortune 500 in 1949, 1959, and 1969. As can be seen in Figure 15-2, the increase in diversification over the years was marked, as was that of divisionalization. In 1949, 20 percent had product division structures; in 1969 that figure jumped to 76 percent. Related studies in the United Kingdom, France, Germany, and Italy (Channon, 1973; Dyas and Thanheiser, 1976; and Paven, 1974; see also Scott, 1973) revealed the same trends, although they lagged those in the United States. All of this suggests that the third stage in the development of organizational structure, discussed in Chapter 13, is evoked directly by market diversification, although it is closely related to organizational age and size.

What of the large corporations that did not divisionalize? The studies show that many were in businesses with enormous economies of scale, such

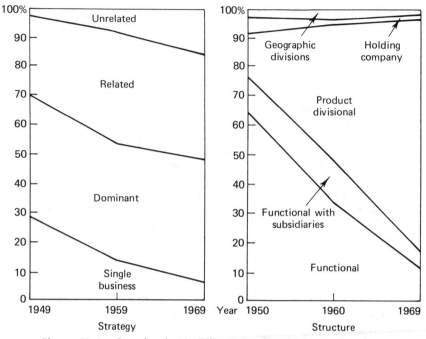

Figure 15-2. *Growth of Diversification and Divisionalization among the Fortune 500 (from Scott, 1973, p. 139, based on study by Rumelt)*

as automobile production and petrochemicals. Others apparently had diversified but had not yet divisionalized. As suggested in the Chandler quote above—and indicated in the longitudinal studies—there is clearly a time lag between diversification and divisionalization, sometimes as long as twenty or thirty years (Scott, 1973, p. 14). It takes time, once a firm has diversified, to realize that its functional structure is inadequate. (Cross-sectional samples would naturally pick up corporations that had already diversified but had not divisionalized.)

In fact, Franco (1974) suggests that this lag is extended by a lack of competition. He found that certain European firms operating under market arrangements such as cartels retained their functional structures despite extensive diversification. It was presumably the absence of competition that enabled these firms to remain viable despite inappropriate structures. Competitive ones had to respond more quickly to the demands of their environments (Scott, 1973, p. 141).[12]

[12]Of course, the same argument about competition could be raised in discussing any of the hypotheses: for example, in the absence of competition, large organizations can retain organic structures, or those operating in dynamic environments can bureaucratize. Recall that our congruence or goodness-of-fit hypothesis refers only to "effective structuring."

We can explain Hypothesis 11 in terms similar to those used to explain Hypothesis 10. The organization that must comprehend information about many different aspects of its market environment eventually finds it convenient to segment that environment into distinct markets if it can and to give individual units control over each. In this way it minimizes the coordination of decision making that must take place across units. As Galbraith (1973) notes, "a diversity of product lines tends to overload [the] decision process of functional organizations" (p. 115).

Unlike Galbraith, however, we make a clear distinction between environmental diversity and complexity, even though both increase the informational load on the decision makers and thereby encourage some kind of decentralization. A simple environment can be very diverse, as in the case of a conglomerate firm that operates a number of simple businesses, say, the manufacture of containers, the growing of wheat, and the serving of fast food. Alternatively, a complex environment may focus on an integrated market, as in the case of the NASA of the 1960s that had one overriding mission—to put a man on the moon before 1970.[13] As Chandler and Sayles (1971) note, in this kind of complex endeavor, with its sophisticated technology, "It is very difficult to segregate activities and create semi-autonomous islands of activity. Everything appears to depend upon everything else" (p. 179). In fact, for reasons that we shall discuss in Chapter 20, divisionalization appears to be better suited to simple diversified markets than to complex ones.

Hypothesis 12: Extreme hostility in its environment drives any organization to centralize its structure temporarily.[14] Hamblin (1958) formed groups of college and high school students in the laboratory and then imposed crisis conditions on some of them. (The college groups began to lose to the high school ones against whom they were competing.) The crisis groups immediately centralized their structures and subsequently changed their leaders when the crises remain unresolved.

We can explain this phenomenon in terms of our coordinating mechanisms. Direct supervision is the fastest and tightest means of coordination —only one brain is involved. All members of the organization know exactly where to send information; no time is wasted in debate; authority for action is clearly defined; one leader makes and coordinates all the decisions. We saw support for this line of reasoning in the communication net studies, discussed in Chapter 11. The more centralized networks organized themselves more quickly and required less communication to make decisions.

[13]NASA, of course, had other missions, for example to launch weather satellites. But the Apollo project was dominant in the 1960s.

[14]It seems reasonable to hypothesize further that extreme hostility drives the organization to organic structure as well, in that hostile environments are unpredictable ones, requiring flexible responses. However, no evidence was found regarding this relationship.

When an organization faces extreme hostility—the sudden loss of its key client or source of supply, severe attack by the government, or whatever— its very survival is threatened. Since it must respond quickly and in an integrated fashion, it turns to its leader for direction.

But what of the organization in a complex environment that faces extreme hostility? The complexity requires it to decentralize in order to comprehend the environment, yet the hostility demands the speed and coordination of a centralized response. Forced to choose, the organization presumably centralizes power temporarily, in order to survive. This enables it to respond to the crisis, even if without due regard for its complexity. With some luck, it may be able to ride it out. But should the crisis persist, the organization may simply be incapable of reconciling the two opposing forces. Thus, in times of deep, chronic hostility, such as during an economic depression or war, a great many organizations simply do not survive. They may centralize power and hang on for a time, but once their slack resources are used up, they simply expire.

Hypothesis 13: Disparities in the environment encourage the organization to decentralize selectively to differentiated work constellations. No organization has ever existed in an environment uniformly dynamic, complex, diverse, or hostile across its entire range. But no organization need respond to every contingency in its environment either. Some are exigent, demanding responses; others are placid, requiring none. Dynamic economic conditions may require organic structure even though the political environment is stable; hostility from the union in an otherwise munificent environment may require temporary centralization followed by a return to decentralization. But what happens when one contingency does not dominate, when disparities in the environment call for different responses in the design of the structure? Take the case of mixed competition—a form of hostility—as Perrow (1974) describes it in the large oil company:

> Mobil Oil and Exxon may compete furiously at the intersection of two streets in any American town, but neither of them is really threatened by this marginal competition. They work very closely together in the important matter of oil depletion allowances, our foreign policy about the Mideast, federal tax policies, the pollution issues, and private transit-versus-mass transit. ... Where, then, is the furious rate of competition? At the lower levels in the organization—the levels of the regional manager who moves prices up and down a fraction and the station manager who washes the windshields and cleans the rest rooms (p. 41).

What this example suggests is that disparities in the environment encourage the organization to differentiate its structure, to create pockets— what we earlier referred to as work constellations—to deal with different aspects of the environment (different "subenvironments").[15] Each constellation is located according to the impact of its subenvironment on the organization—near the top if the impact is universal, farther down if it is local. The managers at the top of the oil company can attend to cooperation while those in the regions deal with the competition. Each work constellation is given power over the decisions required in its subenvironment, and each is allowed to develop the structure its decision processes require. One constellation of an organization may be organically structured to handle dynamic conditions, while others, operating in stable subenvironments, may be structured bureaucratically. We saw this earlier in the case of the new venture teams isolated from the rest of their structures (Hlavacek and Thompson, 1973). Or one constellation may rely on support staff specialists to make its decisions—that is, decentralize horizontally—because these decisions are technologically complex, while another may centralize power in a single line manager because its decisions are simple to comprehend. In other words, disparities in the environment encourage the organization to differentiate its structure and to use what we called in Chapter 11 selective decentralization in both the vertical and horizontal dimensions.

This is clearly illustrated by the McGill MBA group study of the Canadian subsidiary of a European recording company. There were two sharply differentiated constellations here. One, at the strategic apex, comprised the top managers sent from the European headquarters. They handled liaison with it, the financial affairs of the company, and some of the production problems, all relatively stable and simple issues. (The technical system of recording was common to all the subsidiaries.) But the marketing decisions—in particular, what Canadian stars and songs to record—required intimate knowledge of the local scene, of the tastes of the Canadian consumers, both English and French, and of Canadian entertainment personalities. It also required a very different orientation to decision making. With a product life cycle of three months ("there is nothing quite so dead as yesterday's number one hit on the hit parade") and with the most dynamic of supply markets (recording artists being "notoriously hard to get along with"), marketing required a free-wheeling style of decision making, in sharp contrast to that of the rather straitlaced European executives. Thus, a second work constellation was created below the first and given complete and undisputed power over marketing decisions. It worked in a structure for which the word "organic" seemed an understatement.[16]

---

[15]This is, of course, akin to the tendency to divisionalize when markets are diverse, except that here the disparities cut across different environmental dimensions, and the response is to differentiate the structure along functional (and often vertically), instead of market, lines (and horizontally).

[16]From a paper submitted to the author by Alain Berranger and Philip Feldman in Management Policy 276–661, McGill University, November 1972.

Ansoff (1974) discusses in conceptual terms what this example tells us by way of illustration. He argues that decisions are driven up the hierarchy to the level at which coordination can take place naturally: "Thus a natural level for a pricing decision is above manufacturing and marketing; and for a new product decision above these two, as well as above research and development" (p. 41). Ansoff finds that "the competitive intensity [which] gathered momentum in the second half of the mass-production era" (p. 41) has encouraged centralization:

> Increasingly, higher managerial levels, particularly top management, are becoming the only point at which both the resources, the visibility and the impartiality are to be found for making certain momentous enterprise-affecting competitive decisions and enterprise-changing strategic decisions (p. 41).

But Ansoff goes on to note that "paradoxically, in another sense, the trend is also for further decentralization" (p. 42). He cites two reasons for this, the demand for job enrichment and the need for competitive responsiveness in the marketplace. About the second reason, he points out that the "intuitive feel" of the manager, his special knowledge of the customer as well as the competition and the local culture, political developments, and social trends, all "are difficult to code for transmission to a centralized decision point" and to be understood in these "remote and detached" head offices, "beset with competing problems" (p. 42).

And so Ansoff then puts these two competing forces together and comes to the same conclusion as Hypothesis 13. The "apparent anomaly" of "compelling trends toward both centralization and decentralization" is resolved by the "different placement for different decisions ... it is necessary to 'centralize' and 'decentralize' at the same time when the volume and complexity of decisions is rapidly growing as it is now" (p. 43).

A formal case for Hypothesis 13, especially when the organization experiences conflicting pressures of a competitive kind, is made by Khandwalla (1973a). In his study of U.S. manufacturing firms, he found that those in noncompetitive environments tended to centralize all decisions in parallel, while those facing product competition and to a lesser extent price competition, but not marketing competition, tended to decentralize selectively. The reason would seem to lie in the disparity between product competition on the one hand and marketing and price competition on the other along the dimension of environmental complexity. Only product competition would seem to involve major complexity—specifically, the necessity to do research and development—which requires decentralization. Beating the competitor's price or putting a nicer towel in the soap box is not the same as having to design a new product to attract customers. Thus, Khandwalla found that the firms that faced product competition decentralized their product design, development, and marketing decisions while they centralized their pricing, finance, and acquisition ones.[17]

These findings receive support in the Lawrence and Lorsch (1967) study. Presumably, both the container and plastics firms faced competition, but of a decidedly different nature. The container firms sold standardized products, and so competed largely on price and perhaps on marketing as well. In sharp contrast, the plastics firms competed on product design. And so while the container firms centralized all decisions in parallel, the plastics firms decentralized selectively: research decisions—the most complex— farthest down, marketing decisions—requiring knowledge of customer needs—in the middle, and production decisions—perhaps the simplest but requiring the most coordination—closest to the top.

FOUR BASIC ORGANIZATIONAL ENVIRONMENTS

Our discussion of the environment again supports our contention that we learn more by focusing on distinct types of structures found under specific conditions than by tracing continuous relationships between structural and contingency variables. Hypotheses 11, 12, and 13 each describe a specific structural characteristic that emerges from some environmental condition. Although Hypotheses 9 and 10 were initially stated in terms of continuous relationships, they proved more powerful when taken together to generate specific types of structures found in specific kinds of environments. In particular, four basic types emerge from that discussion. (Similar ones were, in fact, first suggested by Perrow, 1970.[18]) They can be shown in matrix form, as follows:

[17]The inclusion of marketing decisions among those decentralized perhaps reflects the convenience of including them with the product decisions. Khandwalla also found that the more competitive firms made more extensive, but more selective, use of performance controls, presumably to monitor the selective decentralization. They also made greater use of various devices to deal with uncertainty, such as marketing research and forecasting techniques. (See also Khandwalla, 1972.)

[18]Perrow's matrix uses as independent our intermediate variables of comprehensibility (how analyzable are decision search procedures) and predictability (how many exceptions the organization encounters). Perrow names organizations in the lower left quadrant "routine," those in the upper left "craft," those in the lower right "engineering," and those in the upper right "non-routine." He then fleshes out his matrix with a number of examples from the manufacturing and service sectors. Van de Ven and Delbecq (1974) present a similar but more elaborate matrix with many other examples and citations of support from the literature.

	Stable	Dynamic
Complex	Decentralized Bureaucratic (standardization of skills)	Decentralized Organic (mutual adjustment)
Simple	Centralized Bureaucratic (standardization of work processes)	Centralized Organic (direct supervision)

Simple, stable environments give rise to centralized, bureaucratic structures, the classic organizational type that relies on standardization of work processes (and the design parameter of formalization of behavior) for coordination. Examples are Woodward's mass production manufacturing firms, Lawrence and Lorsch's container companies, and Crozier's tobacco monopoly. Complex, stable environments lead to structures that are bureaucratic but decentralized. These organizations coordinate by standardizing skills; in effect, they become bureaucratic by virtue of the standard knowledge and procedures learned in formal training programs and imposed on the organization by the professional associations. These organizations are decentralized in both the vertical and horizontal dimensions, their power passing to professionals of the operating core (and out to the professional associations). Typical examples are general hospitals and universities.

When its environment is dynamic but nevertheless simple, the organization requires the flexibility of organic structure but its power can remain centralized. Direct supervision becomes its prime coordinating mechanism. This is the structure characteristic of the entrepreneurial firm, where the chief executive maintains tight, personal control. When the dynamic environment is complex, the organization must decentralize to managers and specialists who can comprehend the issues, yet allow them to interact flexibly in an organic structure so that they can respond to unpredictable changes. Mutual adjustment emerges as the prime coordinating mechanism, its use encouraged by the liaison devices. Lawrence and Lorsch's plastics firms, the Boeing Company studied by Galbraith, and the NASA of the Chandler and Sayles study all fit this description.

Market diversity, as discussed in Hypothesis 11, can be viewed as a third dimension, in effect, as a separate condition superimposed on the two-dimensional matrix. These four types of structures will tend to be functional if the markets are integrated, market-based (at least at the highest level of grouping) if they are diversified (assuming favorable economies of scale and an absence of critical functions). Since, as we saw in Chapter 9, coordination in the market-based structure is achieved by the standardization of outputs, effected through performance control systems, we are able to account for our fifth and last coordinating mechanism in this third dimension.

Similarly, Hypothesis 12 can be viewed as imposing another special condition on the two-dimensional matrix. Extreme hostility drives each of the four types to centralize its structure temporarily, no matter what its initial state of decentralization.

All these conditions assume uniform environments, or at least ones that can be treated as uniform, owing to the dominance of a single characteristic. They are either complex or simple, stable or dynamic, integrated or diversified, extremely hostile or not. Uniformity, in turn, produces consistent use of the design parameters in the structure. Hypothesis 13 drops the assumption of uniformity, indicating that disparities in the environment encourage the organization to respond with a differentiated structure. It sets up work constellations, decentralizes power selectively to them, locates each according to the impact of its decisions on the organization, and allows it to design its internal structure according to the demands of its particular subenvironment.

To conclude this chapter, we have seen that the environmental variables can have a profound effect on structure, often overriding those of age, size, and technical system. Thus, while the other factors may be paramount in stable environments, dynamic environments seem to drive the structure to an organic state no matter what its age, size, or technical system. Likewise, complex conditions seem to require decentralization, and conditions of extreme hostility, centralization, no matter what other contingency factors are present.

The environmental variables also seem to be the most important ones at, and near, the strategic apex. They describe the boundary conditions of the organization, and so it is natural that they should influence most those parts which must be responsive to the milieu, namely the strategic apex and upper levels of the middle line, as well as the gatekeeping staff functions (such as research, public relations, long-range planning, and forecasting), most of which are found near the strategic apex. Among those aspects of structure most strongly influenced by the environmental contingency factors are the amount of decision-making power that must rest at the strategic apex, the speed and flexibility of the organization's strategic responses (i.e., its degree of bureaucratization), and the basis for grouping top-level units. Under certain conditions, the environmental variables have pronounced effects on the other parts of the organization as well, although a prime consideration in the design of the operating core, as Thompson notes, is to try to seal it off from as much direct environmental influence as possible.

16

Power

Organizations do not always adopt the structures called for by their impersonal conditions—their ages and sizes, the technical systems they use, the
stability, complexity, diversity, and hostility of their environments. A number of *power* factors also enter into the design of structure, notably the presence of outside control of the organization, the personal needs of its various
members, and the fashion of the day, embedded in the culture in which the
organization finds itself (in effect, the power of social norms). Three hypotheses describe a number of the findings about these power factors.

Hypothesis 14: The greater the external control of the organization,
the more centralized and formalized its structure. A number of studies have
found a relationship between external control of the organization and the
extent to which it is centralized and/or bureaucratized. Much of this evidence comes from the comparison of public (government-controlled) organizations with private (autonomous) ones. Thus, the government-owned
firms of the Samuel and Mannheim (1970) study used more rules and procedures; the "commonweal" (mostly government) organizations of the Blau
and Scott (1962) study were more centralized than the others (mostly private or institutional) and relied more on written communication; Heydebrand (1973) found more uniform recruiting procedures in publicly owned
than independent hospitals; and Holdaway et al. (1975) found both formalization and centralization to be highest in agricultural colleges and technological institutes, both controlled directly by government departments,

next highest in public colleges, controlled by public boards, and lowest in private colleges, controlled by independent boards.

But other evidence for Hypothesis 14 comes from nongovernmental forms of external control. For example, Strauss and Rosenstein (1970) found that worker participation on boards of directors had the effect of centralizing power within the administrative hierarchy.[1] The Aston group (Pugh et al., 1969b) developed a dimension they called "dependence," which included scales of "impersonality of origin" (founded by a private individual instead of an existing organization) and "public accountability" (the degree to which the parent organization, or the organization itself, if it was autonomous, was subject to public scrutiny; this scale ranged from companies not quoted on the stock exchange, to those that were, to government departments). Dependence related strongly to the Aston dimension of concentration of authority, leading Pugh et al. to conclude: "Dependent organizations have a more centralized authority structure and less autonomy in decision making; independent organizations have more autonomy and decentralize decisions down the hierarchy" (p. 108). Dependence also related strongly to a measure of the standardization of procedures for selection and advancement, but not to their dimension of the structuring of activities. But Reimann (1973), who studied 19 business firms, did find a very strong correlation between measures of dependency and formalization. Finally, as noted in our discussion of the *A/P* studies, Pondy (1969) found a negative relationship between the proportion of owner-managers and the administrative ratio, which suggests that the more ownership resides outside the organization, the more elaborate, and therefore bureaucratic is the administrative structure.

Thus, the evidence indicates that outside control tends to concentrate decision-making power at the top of the organizational hierarchy and to encourage greater than usual reliance on rules and regulations for internal control. All of this, in fact, seems logical enough. **The two most effective means to control an organization from the outside are (1) to hold its most powerful decision maker—namely its chief executive officer—responsible for its actions, and (2) to impose clearly defined standards on it.** The first centralizes the structure; the second formalizes it.

External control groups—specific shareholders, a parent organization, government itself—find it convenient to hold individuals at the top responsible and accountable for organizational actions. "Dependence causes concentration of authority at the apex of publicly owned organizations because pressure for public accountability requires the approval of central committees for many decisions" (Pugh et al., 1969b, p. 112). As Bidwell (1965) notes, school systems, as agents of the public welfare, "must be responsible

---

[1]In this case, the workers participate not as employees within the day-to-day decision-making process, but as outsiders who seek to control the organization from the top.

to the apparatus of government and to a public constituency"; they are held responsible "to use efficiently the public funds from which they are supported"; consequently their administrators are required to ensure a balance of "professional norms and standards, public wishes, and fiscal efficiency" (p. 977).

To extract what they want from the organization, these external groups must establish clearly not only their line of control—through the top management—but also their demands. So it is in their interest to impose tangible standards on the organization, and to ensure that procedures of bureaucratic control are developed to meet them.

Moreover, **external control forces the organization to be especially careful about its actions. Because it must justify its behaviors to outsiders, it tends to formalize them.** Formal, written communication generates records that can be produced when decisions are questioned. Rules ensure fair treatment to clients and employees alike. Thus, government departments develop personnel procedures to govern recruitment so that they cannot be accused of favoritism (such as hiring the minister's niece). They also specify work procedures to ensure that clients are treated equally: "The citizen wants equality of treatment from the Civil Service. Questions in the House [of Commons] try to ensure that he gets it, thereby putting pressure on the Civil Servants to administer strictly in accordance with the rules, so that no questions will be asked" (Stewart, 1963, p. 10). Stewart notes further that demands by the British unions for equality of treatment of the employees of nationalized industries have produced national rules that make little allowance for local needs. These have led to "increasing bureaucracy" (p. 11). Earlier, we saw the same phenomenon in France, in Crozier's (1964) study of the government-owned clerical agency and tobacco monopoly. Employee demands for fair treatment resulted in rules to protect them from their bosses, which made the structures significantly more bureaucratic than they would otherwise have been.

External control can also act to bureaucratize the structure by imposing on it more sweeping demands than usual for rationalization. For example, whereas the autonomous firm can deal with its suppliers and clients in the open market, the subsidiary may be informed by headquarters that it must purchase its supplies from a sister subsidiary, and moreover that the two subsidiaries must sit down together to plan the transfers in advance so that no surplus or shortages will result. Or a parent organization or government might insist on standards being applied across the whole range of organizations it controls. It may demand anything from the use of a common logo, or corporate symbol, to a common management information system or set of purchasing regulations. Entrepreneurial firms with organic structures that are purchased by larger corporations are often forced to develop organigrams, specify job descriptions and reporting relationships more clearly, and adopt action planning and a host of other systems that bureaucratize their structures.

To conclude, Hypothesis 14 indicates that when two organizations are the same age and size, use the same technical system, and operate in the same environment, the structure of the one with the greater amount of external control—by government, a parent organization, the unions, or whatever—will be more centralized and more formalized. This, of course, raises all kinds of interesting issues in societies that find more and more of their autonomous organizations being gobbled up by giant conglomerations—big business, big government, big labor. **The loss of autonomy means not only the surrender of power to the external controller but also significant changes within the structure of the organization itself, no matter what its intrinsic needs—more power concentrated at its strategic apex, tighter personnel procedures, more standardization of work processes, more formal communication, more regulated reporting, more planning and less adapting. In other words, centralization of power at the societal level leads to centralization of power at the organizational level, and to bureaucratization in the use of that power.**

Hypothesis 15: The power needs of the members tend to generate structures that are excessively centralized. All members of the organization typically seek power, if not to control others at least to control the decisions that affect their own work. As a result, the managers of the strategic apex promote centralization in both the vertical and horizontal dimensions; the managers of the middle line promote vertical decentralization, at least down to their own levels, and horizontal centralization to keep power within the line structure; the analysts of the technostructure and the support staff favor horizontal decentralization, to draw power away from the line managers; and the operators seek vertical and horizontal decentralization, all the way down to the operating core.

But the dice of this power game are loaded. As we saw in Section II, to function effectively, organizations typically require hierarchical structures and some degree of formal control. And these naturally put power in the hands of the line managers, as opposed to the staff specialists or the operators, and aggregate that power at the top of the hierarchy, in the hands of the managers of the strategic apex. This is especially so in business organizations, as William Dill (1965) has noted:

> Business firms traditionally have been more unabashedly authoritarian than many other kinds of organizations. Both in ideology and practice, the main locus of formal power starts with the owners or the owner-manager; even now in companies with diffuse and relatively powerless ownership, it lies with the top executives. Strong central control is assumed necessary in order to achieve

the focusing of action, the coordination of effort, the means of conflict resolution, and the control of results that are required to deal effectively with the organization's external environment (p. 1097).

We have seen that various contingency factors—such as a sophisticated technical system and environmental complexity—call for a sharing of central power. But to the extent that the line managers, notably the senior ones, relish power, the structure can easily become excessively centralized. That is, more power can be concentrated at its top than the factors of age, size, technical system, and environment would normally call for (at least until the resulting inefficiencies catch up with the organization).

The evidence for this hypothesis is anecdotal, but plentiful. In particular, many histories have been written of chief executives who destroyed organizations by retaining too much power. Entrepreneurs often fall prey to this syndrome. They create the organization, and hold the bulk of the power—appropriately enough—through the first stage of development. But then they fail to relinquish some of it as the organization grows larger and moves into the second, bureaucratic stage. The classic example of this is Henry Ford, whose need to control everything and everyone in his later years caused him to centralize power, and to build an internal spy network to consolidate it, to the point of nearly destroying the automobile company he had so carefully built.

Hypothesis 16: Fashion favors the structure of the day (and of the culture), sometimes even when inappropriate. Stinchcombe's research, discussed in Hypothesis 2, suggests that there is such a thing as "the structure of the day," that is, the one favored by industries founded in a given period. But his research also shows that structures transcend periods, in other words, that some organizations retain structures favored in previous periods. The implication of this is that **when a new structure comes along, it is appropriate for some organizations but not for others.**

This point has, apparently, been lost on a good many organizations, for there is considerable evidence in the literature that fashion—the power of the norms of the culture in which the organization finds itself—plays an important role in structural design. We might like to believe that organizations are influenced only by factors such as age, size, technical system, and environment, not by what Jones, Inc., is doing next door. But there is too much evidence to the contrary. In her study, for example, Joan Woodward (1965) noted some cases of "management fashion," coupled with personal ambition:

> In one case a young store-keeper who had attended a materials control course had been able to convince his chief executive that his firm needed a materials control department of which he should be manager. Within six months, three

neighbouring firms also had materials control departments. Industrial engineers were other specialists who were becoming fashionable at the time of the research (p. 22).

Part of the problem lies with the business periodicals and consulting firms eager to promote the latest fad. As Whistler (1975) has noted, "There is still money to be made, and notoriety to be gained, in peddling universal prescriptions. In economic terms, the demand is still there, in the form of executives who seek the gospel, the simple truth, *the one best way*" (p. 4). Paris has its salons of haute couture; likewise New York has its offices of "haute structure," the consulting firms that bring the latest in high structural fashion to their clients—long-range planning (LRP), management information systems (MIS), management by objectives (MBO), organization development (OD). About the last one, for example, Strauss (1974) has written:

> Unfortunately, many OD programs are designed to make the organization less bureaucratic, even in situations where lack of organization, rather than excessive bureaucracy, is the real problem. ... Some OD specialists are aware of these problems, but there are others who prescribe a single solution to the problems of all organizations, large and small (p. 12).

In the 1960s the management media heralded "the coming death of bureaucracy." In an article by that title, Bennis (1966) wrote:

> In these new organizations of the future, participants will be called upon to use their minds more than at any other time in history. Fantasy, imagination, and creativity will be legitimate in ways that today seem strange. Social structures will no longer be instruments of psychic repression but will increasingly promote play and freedom on behalf of curiosity and thought (p. 35).

And many organizations took this seriously, some to their regret. Thus, when Lawrence and Lorsch describe the low-performance container firm that tried to use integrators—one of the very fashionable tools of organic structure—in a simple, stable environment, or when Khandwalla tells of the low performer that sought to introduce participative management under the wrong conditions, we find structural fashion extracting its toll in inappropriate structural designs.

Since Bennis's article, it has become evident that bureaucracies will not die. Not so long, at least, as organizations grow old and large, mass-produce their outputs, and find simple, stable environments to nurture their standards. The fact is that articles would not be published and speakers would not attend conferences to tell of "the one best way" if the printers and airlines were not structured as bureaucracies. Today, few would deny that bureaucracies are alive, if not well.

Throughout this century, the swings between centralization and decentralization at the top of large American corporations have resembled the movements of women's hemlines. But the trend toward the use of divisionalization has been consistent, ever since Du Pont and General Motors first made it fashionable in the 1920s. Thus, Rumelt (1974) found in his data on the Fortune 500 strong support not only for Chandler's well-known proposition that "structure follows strategy" but for another, that "structure also follows fashion" (p. 149). The use of the divisionalized form increased from 20 percent in 1949 to 76 percent in 1969; but not all of it was explained by market diversification, as Hypothesis 11 would have us believe: "until the early 1960s the adoption of product-division structures was strongly contingent upon the administrative pressures created by diversification but ... in more recent years divisionalization has become accepted as the norm and managements have sought reorganization along product-division lines in response to normative theory rather than actual administrative pressure" (p. 77). And according to other data, cited in Chapter 15, European corporations seem to be following close behind.

Of course, fashionable structure need not be inappropriate structure. Fashion reflects new advances in organizational design, advances that suit some organizations with older structures. Once the divisionalized form became established, it was appropriately adopted by most diversified companies that had been structured along functional lines.[2] Indeed, those that failed to were saddled with structures that suddenly became out of date— less effective than the new alternative. Much like the dowager who always dresses as she did in her heyday, so too the organization may cling to a structure appropriate to days gone by. This, in fact, seems to explain the Franko (1974) finding discussed in Chapter 15, that in the absence of competitive pressures, some European companies did not divisionalize even though they were diversified. Placid environments enabled them to retain outdated, ineffective structures.

The Franko finding also suggests that structural fashion is in some sense culture-bound. What is all the rage among the Fortune 500 (the largest U.S. corporations) may simply look odd to the Fortune 200 (the largest non-U.S. corporations). West Virginians and Westphalians may simply have different preferences for structure. This is another way of saying that culture, working through fashion, is another factor that influences structural design.

The literature contains a number of illustrations of the influence of culture on structure, particularly on the use of authority and bureaucracy. Dalton (1959) claims that "the theory of bureaucracy hangs much better on the more stratified and disciplined European societies, as it did also on the

---

[2]In fact, there is reason to argue that the real fashion was the strategy of diversification; divisionalization then became the appropriate structural response.

earlier Persian and Roman monarchies" (p. 264), than it does on American society.[3] Child and Keiser (1978) explicitly reject the "culture-free theories" in their study of British and West German companies. So too, in effect, do Azuni and McMillan (1975), who found that even when other contingency factors were accounted for, Japanese firms emerged as more centralized and, as they grew larger, more formalized than their British counterparts. In an article entitled "Japanese Management: Old Ways Became Modern," Shinoda (1973) explains the relationship between bureaucracy and culture in Japan:

> In Tamano Dockyard of Mitsui Shipbuilding, for instance, one may notice that the flow of work is predetermined to the smallest detail. Trucks carry supplies of materials according to a well-established timetable. As a result, idle time has been completely eliminated in the dockyard or in the steel supply; elsewhere in the world fifteen minutes' waiting time is not considered intolerable.
>
> This reflects a difference between the precision as to time and money coming from the Japanese insularity and the generosity inherent to the continental Europeans.
>
> In Japan, every attempt has always been made to reduce unnecessary motions. In the "No-play" or the "Tea Ceremony," all meaningless motions are eliminated. Just essential motions remain and are highly formalized. Especially in "No-play," this reaches its extreme—where every movement is turned into such pure simplicity that it may appear rather symbolic (p. 393).

In contemporary American culture, we see quite different trends in structural fashion. Coming quickly into vogue, close behind the divisionalized form, is project structure, what Toffler (1970) has called "ad-hocracy"— essentially selectively decentralized organic structure that makes heavy use of the liaison devices. One can hardly pick up a management journal without reading about task forces, integrating managers, matrix structure. Clearly, this structure corresponds well to the calls for the destruction of bureaucracy, to the democratic norms prevalent in American society, and to its increasingly better-educated work force. But although this may be the structure of our age—well-suited to new, "future-shocked" industries such as aerospace and think-tank consulting—it may be wholly inappropriate for most older industries. It, too, is no panacea. Like all the structures before it, themselves once fashionable, it suits some organizations and not others. Hopefully, those others will not opt for project structure, as did one of Lawrence and Lorsch's container firms, just because it is fashionable.

---

[3]An explanation for this put forward by Hage et al. (1971) is that social distance inhibits the use of informal means of communication and favors instead the more detached, formalized means, such as regular reporting systems.

To conclude our discussion of power as a contingency factor, we note that external control, the power needs of the members, and fashion as embedded in a culture all exert significant influence on the design of organizational structure, sometimes encouraging organizations to adopt structures that the contingency factors of age, size, technical system, and environment deem inappropriate.

THE CONTINGENCY FACTORS BY LEVEL IN THE STRUCTURE

To conclude our discussion of the contingency factors, we consider their differential impact on the structure. We have seen that the same design parameter can be influenced by various of the contingency factors we have been discussing in the last four chapters. Formalization of behavior has been shown, for example, to be affected by age, size, regulating and automated technical systems, stability in the environment, outside control, member needs for power, fashion, and culture. But overall, each of the four sets of contingency factors seems to affect the various levels of the structure differentially, as shown in Figure 16–1.

The factors of age and size, although significant at all levels, seem most pronounced in the middle of the structure; that is where, by creating changes in the favored mechanism of coordination, they produce extensive structural elaboration. The technical system, being housed in the operating core, clearly makes its greatest impact there. But it has important selective effects elsewhere as well. For example, at middle levels it requires an extensive support staff when it is sophisticated, and at the strategic apex, where its effect is more selective still, it causes structural changes when it becomes automated. The environmental factors seem to have exactly the opposite effect of the technical system ones. **It is the managers and staff specialists at and near the strategic apex, those who must function continuously at the organization's boundaries, who are most affected by the environmental dimensions. These dimensions also importantly affect the structure in the middle, but have only a selective effect on the operating core, which the rest of the structure in fact tries to seal off from direct environmental influence. Finally, the power factors seem to cut across all levels of the structure, but only on a selective basis.** External control, member needs for power, fashion, and culture sometimes modify the structures that would otherwise result from consideration only of the factors of age, size, technical system, and environment.

One major issue now remains to be cleared up. While the relationships expressed in our hypotheses have shed some light on the design of structures, they have left us in the dark about the effects of different contingency

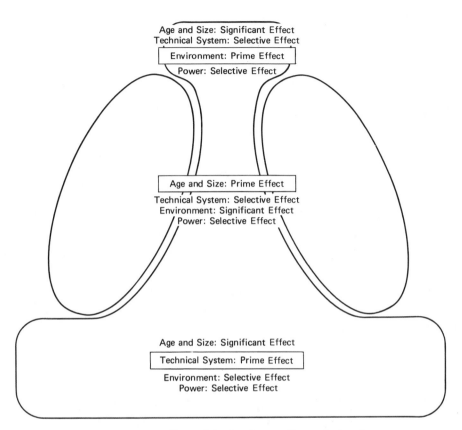

Age and Size: Significant Effect
Technical System: Selective Effect

Environment: Prime Effect

Power: Selective Effect

Age and Size: Prime Effect

Technical System: Selective Effect
Environment: Significant Effect

Power: Selective Effect

Age and Size: Significant Effect

Technical System: Prime Effect

Environment: Selective Effect
Power: Selective Effect

Figure 16-1.   *Effects of the Contingency Factors by Level*

factors on the same design parameter, and about the interrelationships among the design parameters as well as among the contingency factors. Indeed, our discussion of this section of the book has suggested that **we have more to learn from the study of specific types—clusters or configurations of the design parameters and contingency factors together—than from the study of continuous relationships between one variable from each group.** We saw this first in our discussion of the metamorphosis of structure through different stages of development, again in our review of Woodward's three types of technical systems, and finally in our matrix of four distinct structures found in four distinct environments. So, to complete our story of the structuring of organizations, we turn now to the issue of structural types, or configurations.

PART IV

STRUCTURAL CONFIGURATIONS

Throughout this book, ever since the introduction of the five coordinating mechanisms in its first pages, we have seen growing convergences in its findings. For example, the standardization of work processes was seen in Section I to relate most closely to the view of the organization as a system of regulated flows. Then in Section II we saw these two linked up to the design parameter of behavior formalization in particular and the traditional kind of bureaucratic structure in general, where the operating work is highly specialized but unskilled. Later in this section we found that the operating units of such structures are large, and that they tend to be grouped by function as do the units above them in the middle line. At the end of this section, there emerged the conclusion that decentralization in these structures tends to be of the limited horizontal type, where power resides primarily at the strategic apex and secondarily in the technostructure that formalizes everyone else's work. Then in Section III we found that this combination of the design parameters is most likely to appear in rather large and old organizations, specifically in their second stage of development; in organizations that use mass production technical systems, regulating but not automated; in organizations operating in simple, stable environments; and in those subject to external control. Other such convergences appeared in our findings. In effect, **the elements of our study—the coordinating mechanisms, design parameters, and contingency factors—all seem to fall into natural clusters, or configurations.**

It will be recalled that in our discussion of the effective structuring of organizations in Chapter 12, two hypotheses were put forward. The congruence hypothesis, which postulates that effective organizations select their design parameters to fit their situation, was the subject of the last section. In this one, we take up the configuration hypothesis, which postulates that effective organizations achieve an internal consistency among their design parameters, in effect, a structural configuration. It is these configurations that are reflected in the convergences of this book.

How many configurations do we need to describe all organizational structures? The mathematician tells us that p elements, each of which can take on n forms, lead to p^n possible combinations. With our nine design parameters, that number would grow rather large. Nevertheless, we could start building a large matrix, trying to fill in each of the boxes. But the world does not work like that. There is order in the world, but it is a far more profound one than that—a sense of union or harmony that grows out of the natural clustering of elements, whether they be stars, ants, or the characteristics of organizations.

The number "five" has appeared repeatedly in our discussion. First there were five basic coordinating mechanisms, then five basic parts of the organization, later five basic types of decentralization. Five is, of course, no ordinary digit. "It is the sign of union, the nuptial number according to the Pythagoreans; also the number of the center, of harmony and of equilibrium." The *Dictionnaire des Symboles* goes on to tell us that five is the "symbol of man ... likewise of the universe ... the symbol of divine will that seeks only order and perfection." To the ancient writers, five was the essence of the universal laws, there being "five colors, five flavors, five tones, five metals, five viscera, five planets, five orients, five regions of space, of course five senses," not to mention "the five colors of the rainbow." Our modest contribution to this impressive list is five structural configurations. These have appeared repeatedly in our discussion; they are the ones described most frequently in the literature of organizational theory.[1,2]

In fact, the recurrence of the number "five" in our discussion seems not to be coincidental, for it turns out that there is a one-to-one correspondence between all of our fives. In each structural configuration, a different one of the coordinating mechanisms is dominant, a different part of the organiza-

---

[1]Quotes from *Dictionnaire des Symboles,* sous la direction de Jean Chevalier avec la collaboration de Alain Gheerbrant (Editions Robert Laffont, 1969), p. 208; my translation from the French. The obsolescence of most of their fives is not of central concern to us here and now; it simply suggests that we often begin with quintets before we proceed to more elaborate typologies.

[2]Perrow (1970) describes four structures which correspond more or less to four of ours; Segal (1974) and Van de Ven (1976a) describe three; Lawrence and Lorsch (1967) and Pugh et al. (1969a) two; as we shall see, a number of other authors describe one or more of these configurations explicitly.

tion plays the most important role, and a different type of decentralization is used.[3] This correspondence is summarized in the following table:

Structural Configuration	Prime Coordinating Mechanism	Key Part of Organization	Type of Decentralization
Simple Structure	Direct supervision	Strategic apex	Vertical and horizontal centralization
Machine Bureaucracy	Standardization of work processes	Technostructure	Limited horizontal decentralization
Professional Bureaucracy	Standardization of skills	Operating core	Vertical and horizontal decentralization
Divisionalized Form	Standardization of outputs	Middle line	Limited vertical decentralization
Adhocracy	Mutual adjustment	Support staff[4]	Selective decentralization

We can explain this correspondence by considering the organization as being pulled in five different directions, one by each of its parts. (These five pulls are shown in Figure IV–1.) Most organizations experience all five of these pulls; however, to the extent that conditions favor one over the others, the organization is drawn to structure itself as one of the configurations.

Thus, the strategic apex exerts a pull for centralization, by which it can retain control over decision making. This it achieves when direct supervision is relied upon for coordination. To the extent that conditions favor this pull, the configuration called Simple Structure emerges.

The technostructure exerts its pull for standardization—notably for that of work processes, the tightest form—because the design of the standards is its raison d'être. This amounts to a pull for limited horizontal decentralization. To the extent that conditions favor this pull, the organization structures itself as a Machine Bureaucracy.

In contrast, the members of the operating core seek to minimize the influence of the administrators—managers as well as analysts—over their work. That is, they promote horizontal and vertical decentralization. When they succeed, they work relatively autonomously, achieving whatever coordination is necessary through the standardization of skills. Thus, the operators exert a pull for professionalism, that is, for a reliance on outside

[3]At the risk of stretching my credibility, I would like to point out that this neat correspondence was not fabricated. Only after deciding on the five structural configurations was I struck by the correspondence with the five coordinating mechanisms and the five organizational parts. Slight modification in the Chapter 11 typology of decentralization (which rendered it more logical) was, however, suggested by the five configurations.

[4]We shall see in Chapter 21 that there are two basic types of Adhocracies. In the second type— more like the Professional Bureaucracy—the operating core is also a key part.

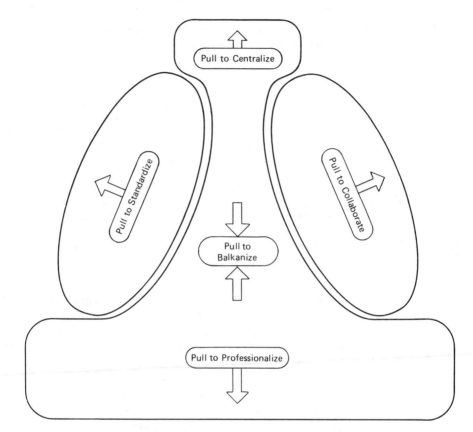

Figure IV-1. *Five Pulls on the Organization*

training that enhances their skills. To the extent that conditions favor this pull, the organization structures itself as a Professional Bureaucracy.

The managers of the middle line also seek autonomy but must achieve it in a very different way—by drawing power down from the strategic apex and, if necessary, up from the operating core, to concentrate it in their own units. In effect, they favor limited vertical decentralization. As a result, they exert a pull to Balkanize the structure, to split it into market-based units which can control their own decisions, coordination being restricted to the standardization of their outputs. To the extent that conditions favor this pull, the Divisionalized Form results.

Finally, the support staff gain the most influence in the organization not when they are autonomous but when their collaboration is called for in decision making, owing to their expertise. This happens when the organization is structured into work constellations to which power is decentralized selectively and which are free to coordinate within and between themselves

by mutual adjustment. To the extent that conditions favor this pull to collaborate, the organization adopts the Adhocracy configuration.

Consider, for example, the case of a film company. The presence of a
great director will favor the pull to centralize and encourage the use of the
Simple Structure. Should there be a number of great directors, each pulling
for their own autonomy, the structure will likely be Balkanized into the
Divisionalized Form. Should the company instead employ highly skilled
actors and cameramen, producing complex but standard industrial films, it
will have a strong incentive to decentralize further and use the Professional
Bureaucracy structure. In contrast, should the company employ relatively
unskilled personnel, perhaps to mass produce spaghetti westerns, it will
experience a strong pull to standardize and to structure itself as a Machine
Bureaucracy. But if, instead, it wishes to innovate, resulting in the strongest
pull to collaborate the efforts of director, designer, actor, and cameraman,
it would have a strong incentive to use the Adhocracy configuration.

These five structural configurations are the subject of this concluding
section of the book. The description of each in the next five chapters serves
two purposes. First, it enables us to propose a fundamental way to categorize organizations—and the correspondences that we have just seen give
us some confidence in asserting that fundamentality. And second, by allowing us to draw together the material of the first sixteen chapters, the descriptions of these last five chapters serve as an excellent way to summarize and,
more important, to *synthesize* the findings of this book.

In describing these structural configurations, we shall be able to clear
up much of the confusion that arose in the last section. The world seems
more ordered, and more easily understood, when we focus on specifics, on
distinct types, instead of on continuous relationships, two variables at a
time. In *general*, it may be impossible to disentangle the effects of size,
technical system, environment, and power on structure; in *particular*, as we
shall see, many of these contingency factors fall neatly into place. In fact,
there seem to be logical configurations of the contingency factors, just as
there are of the design parameters, and the two seem to go together. In so
describing both in this section, we shall, therefore, drop the assumption that
the contingency factors are the independent variables, those which dictate
the choice of the design parameters. Instead, we shall take a "systems"
approach in this section, treating our configurations of the contingency and
structural parameters as "gestalts," clusters of tightly interdependent relationships. There is no dependent or independent variable in a system; everything depends on everything else. Large size may bureaucratize a structure,
but bureaucracies also seek to grow large; dynamic environments may
require organic structures, but organizations with organic structures also
seek out dynamic environments, where they feel more comfortable. Organizations—at least effective ones—appear to change whatever parameters

they can—contingency as well as structural—to maintain the coherence of their gestalts.

Each of the five chapters that follows describes one of the structural configurations, drawing its material from every section of this book. Each chapter begins with a description of the basic structure of the configuration: how it uses the five coordinating mechanisms and the nine design parameters as well how it functions—how authority, material, information, and decision processes flow through its five parts. This is followed by a discussion of the conditions of the configuration—the factors of age, size, technical system, environment, and power typically associated with it. (All these conclusions are summarized in Table 21-1, page 466). Here, also, we seek to identify well-known examples of each configuration, and also note some common hybrids which it forms with other configurations. Finally, each chapter closes with a discussion of some of the more important social issues associated with the configuration. It is here that I take the liberty usually accorded an author of explicitly injecting his own opinions into the concluding section of his work.

One last point before we begin. Parts of this section have an air of conclusiveness about them, as if the five configurations are perfectly distinct and encompass all of organizational reality. That is not true, as we shall see in a sixth and concluding chapter. Until then, the reader would do well to proceed under the assumption that every sentence in this section is an over-statement (including this one!). There are times when we need to caricature, or stereotype, reality in order to sharpen differences and so to better understand it. Thus, the case for each configuration is overstated to make it clearer, not to suggest that every organization—indeed any organization—exactly fits a single configuration. Each configuration is a *pure* type (what Weber called an "ideal" type), a theoretically consistent combination of the contingency and design parameters. Together the five may be thought of as bounding a pentagon within which real structures may be found. In fact, our brief concluding chapter presents such a pentagon, showing within its boundaries the hybrids of the configurations and the transitions between them. But we can only comprehend the inside of a space by identifying its boundaries. So let us proceed with our discussions of the configurations.

17

The Simple Structure

Prime Coordinating Mechanism:	Direct supervision
Key Part of Organization:	Strategic apex
Main Design Parameters:	Centralization, organic structure
Contingency Factors:	Young, small, non-sophisticated technical system, simple, dynamic environment, possible extreme hostility or strong power needs of top manager, not fashionable

Consider an automobile dealership with a flamboyant owner, a brand-new government department, a middle-sized retail store, a corporation run by an aggressive entrepreneur, a government headed by an autocratic politician, a school system in a state of crisis. In most ways, these are vastly different organizations. But the evidence suggests that they share a number of basic structural characteristics. We call the configuration of these characteristics the *Simple Structure*.

The Simple Structure is characterized, above all, by what it is not—elaborated. Typically, it has little or no technostructure, few support staffers, a loose division of labor, minimal differentiation among its units, and a small managerial hierarchy. Little of its behavior is formalized, and it makes minimal use of planning, training, and the liaison devices. It is, above all, organic. In a sense, Simple Structure is nonstructure: it avoids using all the formal devices of structure, and it minimizes its dependence on staff specialists. The latter are typically hired on contract when needed, rather than encompassed permanently within the organization.

Coordination in the Simple Structure is effected largely by direct supervision. Specifically, power over all important decisions tends to be centralized in the hands of the chief executive officer. Thus, the strategic apex emerges as the key part of the structure; indeed, the structure often consists of little more than a one-man strategic apex and an organic operating core. The chief executive tends to have a very wide span of control; in fact, it is not uncommon for everyone else to report to him. Thus a group of management students at McGill University asked the president of a small chain of retail stores they were studying to draw an organigram, since none existed:

> He drew it so that every section of personnel fell below him mainly on one plane. He sees all his employees falling under him and he does not differentiate very clearly between the relative levels of authority. ... He drew his diagram quite unwittingly and it was only when we asked him of their relative positions of authority that he gave us the authority order of the structure.[1]

Grouping into units—if it exists at all—more often than not is on a loose functional basis, with the coordination between units left to the chief executive. Likewise, communication flows informally in this structure, most of it between the chief executive and everyone else. Thus, another McGill student group commented in their study of a small manufacturer of pumps: "It is not unusual to see the president of the company engaged in casual conversation with a machine shop mechanic. These types of specialties enable the president to be informed of a machine breakdown even before the shop superintendent is advised."[2] The work flow too tends to be flexible, with the jobs of the operating core being relatively unspecialized and interchangeable.

---

[1]From a paper submitted to the author in Management 420, McGill University, 1969, by J. Gariepy, R. Miller, G. Nanton, T. Shabrokh.

[2]From a paper submitted to the author in Management Policy 701, McGill University, 1970, by S. Genest and S. Darkanzanli.

Decision making is likewise flexible, with the centralization of power allowing for rapid response. Strategic, administrative and operating decisions can be tightly coordinated since one individual keeps close watch on all of them. Strategy formulation is, of course, the sole responsibility of the chief executive. The process tends to be highly intuitive and nonanalytical, often thriving on uncertainty and oriented to the aggressive search for opportunities. In a word, the organization uses the *entrepreneurial* mode of strategy making (Mintzberg, 1973b). It is not, therefore, surprising that the resulting strategy—seldom made explicit—reflects the chief executive's implicit vision of the place of the organization in its environment. In fact, that strategy is more often than not a direct extrapolation of his personal beliefs, an extension of his own personality.

The disturbance handler and entrepreneur roles are perhaps the most important aspects of the chief executive's work. But considerable attention is also given to the leader role—a reflection of the importance of direct supervision—and to the monitor role—in order to keep himself well informed. In contrast, the more formal aspects of managerial work—for example, those contained in the figurehead role—are of less significance, as are the disseminator and resource allocator roles, since power and information remains in the strategic apex of the Simple Structure.

Figure 17–1 shows the Simple Structure symbolically, in terms of our logo, with a wide span of control at the strategic apex, no staff units, and an insignificant middle line.

Khandwalla (1977) found this simplest of structural forms in his research on Canadian companies. Some of these firms had little R & D and marketing research activities, no training of staff, and rudimentary financial controls. They preferred what Khandwalla labeled the entrepreneurial, power-oriented, conservative, and seat-of-the-pants managerial styles. Pugh et al. (1969a) also allude to this structural form in what they call "implicitly structured organizations," while Woodward (1965) describes such a structure among smaller unit production and single-purpose process firms—

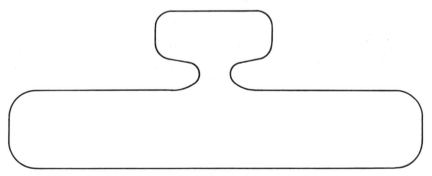

Figure 17-1.   *The Simple Structure*

ones with an absence of formal planning, all coordination by the chief executive, little staff, and organic relationships.

CONDITIONS OF THE SIMPLE STRUCTURE

Above all, the environment of the Simple Structure tends to be at one and the same time simple and dynamic. A simple environment can be comprehended by a single individual, and so enables decision making to be controlled by that individual. A dynamic environment means organic structure: because its future state cannot be predicted, the organization cannot effect coordination by standardization. Another condition common to Simple Structures is a technical system that is both nonsophisticated and nonregulating. Sophisticated ones require elaborate staff support structures, to which power over technical decisions must be delegated, while regulating ones call for bureaucratization of the operating core.

Among the conditions giving rise to variants of the Simple Structure, perhaps the most important is stage of development. The *new organization* tends to adopt the Simple Structure, no matter what its environment or technical system, because it has not had the time to elaborate its administrative structure. It is forced to rely on leadership to get things going. Until it settles down, therefore, it tends to be both organic and centralized. Thus, we can conclude that **most organizations pass through the Simple Structure in their formative years.**

Many small organizations, however, remain with the Simple Structure beyond this period. For them, informal communication is convenient and effective. Moreover, their small size may mean less repetition of work in the operating core, which means less standardization. Of course, some organizations are so small that they can rely on mutual adjustment for coordination, almost in the absence of direct supervision by leaders. They constitute a hybrid we can call the *simplest structure,* a Simple Structure with the open lateral communication channels of the Adhocracy.

Another variant—the crisis organization—appears when extreme hostility forces an organization to centralize, no matter what its usual structure. The need for fast, coordinated response puts power in the hands of the chief executive, and serves to reduce the degree of bureaucratization as well. (Of course, highly elaborated organizations do not eliminate their technostructures and middle lines when faced with a crisis. But they may temporarily set aside their power over decision making.)

James D. Thompson (1967) describes a special case of the crisis organization, what he calls the *synthetic organization.* This is temporary, set up to deal with a natural disaster. The situation is new, and the environment is extremely hostile. Thompson notes that the initial responses to such crises are usually uncoordinated. However, "In a relatively short time, usually, two things happen to change this situation and bring about a synthetic organization: (1) uncommitted resources arrive, with those who possess them seeking places to use them, and (2) information regarding need for additional resources begins to circulate." The headquarters of the synthetic organization becomes established at that place where these supplies and demands meet. And the "authority to coordinate the use of resources is attributed to—forced upon—the individual or group which by happenstance is at the crossroads of the two kinds of necessary information, resource availability and need" (quotes from p. 52). (Of course, permanent organizations that specialize in disaster work, such as the Red Cross, would be expected to develop standardized procedures and so to use a more bureaucratic form of structure.)

Personal needs for power produce another variant, which we call the *autocratic organization*. When a chief executive hoards power and avoids the formalization of behavior as an infringement on his right to rule by fiat, he will, in effect, design a Simple Structure for his organization. The same result is produced in the *charismatic organization*, when the leader gains power not because he hoards it but because his followers lavish it upon him.

Culture seems to figure prominently in both these examples of Simple Structure. The less industrialized societies, perhaps because they lack the educated work forces needed to man the administrative staff jobs of bureaucratic structures, seem more prone to build their organizations around strong leaders who coordinate by direct supervision. Thus, Harbison and Myers (1959) describe the structure of Abboud enterprises, typical of the "great majority of Egyptian-owned private establishments":

> Here the manager is a dominant individual who extends his personal control over all phases of the business. There is no charted plan of organization, no formalized procedure for selection and development of managerial personnel, no publicized system of wage and salary classifications. ... authority is associated exclusively with an individual ... (pp. 40–41).

These forces of autocracy or charisma can sometimes drive even very large organizations toward the Simple Structure, at least when their leaders are skillful in their use of power. Here is how Wilensky (1967) describes the workings of the U.S. government under President Franklin D. Roosevelt:

> Not only did Roosevelt rely heavily on unofficial channels, but he also fostered competition within: he would use one anonymous informant's information to challenge and check another's, putting both on their toes; he recruited strong personalities and structured their work so that clashes would be certain. "His

favorite technique was to keep grants of authority incomplete, jurisdictions uncertain, charters overlapping." In foreign affairs, he gave Moley and Welles tasks that overlapped those of Secretary of State Hull; in conservation and power, he gave Ickes and Wallace identical missions; in welfare, confusing both functions and initials, he assigned PWA to Ickes, WPA to Hopkins; in politics, Farley found himself competing with other political advisers for control over patronage (p. 51; quotation within from A. M. Schlesinger).

Another factor that encourages use of the Simple Structure is owner-management, since this precludes outside control, which encourages bureaucratization. The classic case of the owner-managed organization is, of course, the *entrepreneurial firm*. In fact, **the entrepreneurial firm seems to be the best overall illustration of the Simple Structure, combining almost all of its characteristics—both structural and contingency—into a tight gestalt.** The entrepreneurial firm is aggressive and often innovative, continually searching for the high-risk environments where the bureaucracies fear to tread. Thus, Pareto describes the entrepreneurs as "adventurous souls, hungry for novelty . . . not at all alarmed at change" (quoted in Toffler, 1970, p. 148). But the firm is also careful to remain in market niches that the entrepreneur can fully comprehend. In other words, it seeks out environments that are both dynamic and simple. Similarly, the entrepreneurial firm is careful to remain with a simple, nonregulating technical system, one that allows its structure to remain organic and centralized. The firm is usually small, so that it can remain organic and the entrepreneur can retain tight control. Often, it is also young, in part, because the attrition rate among entrepreneurial firms is high, in part because those that survive tend to switch to a more bureaucratic configuration as they age. The entrepreneur tends to be autocratic and sometimes charismatic as well; typically, he has founded his own firm because he could not tolerate the controls imposed upon him by the bureaucracies in which he has worked (Collins and Moore, 1970). Inside the structure, all revolves around the entrepreneur. Its goals are his goals, its strategy his vision of its place in the world. Most entrepreneurs loath bureaucratic procedures—and the technostructures that come with them—as impositions on their flexibility. So their unpredictable maneuvering keeps their structures lean, flexible, and organic.

This gestalt is almost perfectly illustrated in a small retail firm, which we shall call Chéz Lutin, located in the north of France. It sells notions and novelties in five stores, four of which were opened in a five-year period just before the time of this writing. Both product lines are simple, but the market for novelties is extremely dynamic. Novelties include fashion clothing—turtlenecks, scarves, belts, and the like—that require frequent and rapid response, in high season almost weekly, because of the uncertainty of supply and demand. The technical system—retail selling—is, of course, extremely simple and nonregulating; the only equipment required are cash registers, an automobile that doubles as a truck, and a telephone. Chez Lutin is owned and managed by a husband and wife team—a dual chief executive—the husband looking after control and administration, the wife, purchasing and inventory. Fifty salespeople report directly to the owners, despite the fact that these people are dispersed in the five different stores across a thirty-mile radius. There are no store managers. Instead, the owners visit each store every day. The only other employees—support staff so to speak—are one secretary and one woman who works part-time to balance the inventories among the stores. There is hardly any information system—problems are communicated verbally to the owners during their visits. Sales for each store are, however, reported daily, although overall sales and costs figures generally run about twelve months late. There is no training of salespeople, no differentiation among them (except for the cashiers), no planning, and hardly any rules. Needless to say, Chez Lutin has no organigram, although we drew one up for this book, which is shown in Figure 17–2.

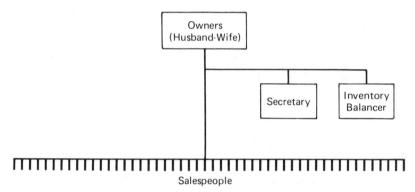

Figure 17-2. *Chez Lutin — The Typical Simple Structure*

SOME ISSUES ASSOCIATED WITH SIMPLE STRUCTURE

In the Simple Structure, decisions concerning strategy and operations are together centralized in the office of the chief executive. **Centralization has the important advantage of ensuring that strategic response reflects full knowledge of the operating core. It also favors flexibility and adaptability in strategic response: only one person need act.** As Hage and Dewer (1973) find in a study of innovation: "... if the leader and the elite favor change, this is much more influential to innovation than decentralizing the power structure" (p. 285)—and this in a study of health and welfare organizations.

But **centralization can also cause confusion between strategic and operating issues.** The chief executive can get so enmeshed in operating problems that he loses sight of strategic considerations. Alternatively, he may become so enthusiastic about strategic opportunities that the more routine operations wither for lack of attention and eventually pull down the whole organization. Both problems occur frequently in entrepreneurial firms. In some, the entrepreneur, always looking for new worlds to conquer, never settles down to consolidate the firm's control over one or two of them. In others, when the creditors finally arrive to close the place down, they find the entrepreneur in back fixing a machine, oblivious to the crisis.

The Simple Structure is also the riskiest of structures, hinging on the health and whims of one individual. One heart attack can literally wipe out the organization's prime coordinating mechanism.

Like all the configurations, restricted to its appropriate situation, the Simple Structure usually functions effectively. Its flexibility is well suited to simple, dynamic environments, to extremely hostile ones (at least for a time), and to young and small organizations. But lacking a developed administration, the Simple Structure becomes a liability outside its narrow range of conditions. Its organic state impedes it from producing the standardized outputs required of an environment having stabilized or an organization having grown large, and its centralized nature renders it ineffective in dealing with an environment having become complex.

Unfortunately, however, when structural changes must come, the only person with the power to make them—the chief executive himself—often resists. The great strength of the Simple Structure—its flexibility—becomes its chief liability. As Strauss (1974) puts it:

> Top management persists in the myth that somehow the company is different from other organizations and that it can avoid the rigidity and bureaucratic coldness of big business. From this comes, at times, an almost pathological aversion to red tape or formalities, whether with regard to purchasing rules, inventory control, or the use of time clocks. . . .
>
> At the very time that staff in one company was trying to introduce what it felt were elements of predictability, a top manager commented, "We have succeeded so far by flying by the seat of our pants. That's our strength. We can turn around on a dime." And another executive in a similar situation bragged, "We aren't held back by organization charts. . . . Everyone pitches in here. We all feel equally responsible for everything that happens" (p. 13).

One great advantage of Simple Structure is its sense of mission. Many people enjoy working in a small, intimate organization, where its leader—often charismatic—knows where he is taking it. As a result, the organization tends to grow rapidly, the world being, so to speak, at its feet. Employees can develop a solid identification with such an organization. Thus, Worthy (1950) writes of the "better integrated social system" of the small organization. Employees can more easily relate to each other and to the chief executive. "There are fewer people, fewer levels in the organizational hierarchy, and a less minute subdivision of labor. It is easier for the employee to adapt himself to such a simpler system and to win a place in it. His work becomes more meaningful ... because he and they can readily see its relation and importance to other functions and to the organization as a whole" (p. 173).

But other people perceive the Simple Structure as highly restrictive. Because one individual calls all the shots, they feel not like the participants on an exciting journey, but like cattle being led to market for someone else's benefit. Thus, Long (1962) writes of the orientation in the literature "which sees management, almost in medieval style, as the head and the rest as body, hands, and feet; or, in Hobbesian terms, which sees management as the sovereign without which there are no alternative to anarchy" (p. 111). No wonder El Salmi and Cummings found that high-level managers reported greater fulfillment of their needs in small organizations, while middle- and lower-level ones reported that kind of fulfillment in larger organizations (cited in Cummings and Berger, 1976, p. 37).

As a matter of fact, the broadening of democratic norms beyond the political sphere into that of organizations has rendered the Simple Structure unfashionable in contemporary society. Increasingly, it is being described as paternalistic, sometimes autocratic, and is accused of distributing organizational power inappropriately. Certainly, our description identifies Simple Structure as the property of one individual, whether in fact or in effect. There are no effective countervailing powers in this structural configuration, which means that the chief executive can easily abuse his authority.

There have been Simple Structures as long as there have been organizations. Indeed, this was probably the only structure known to the men who first discovered the benefits of coordinating their activities in some formal way. But in some sense, Simple Structure had its heyday in the era of the great American trusts of the late nineteenth century, when powerful entrepreneurs personally controlled huge empires. Since then, at least in Western society, the Simple Structure has been on the decline. Between 1895 and 1950, according to one study (cited in Pugh et al., 1963–64, p. 296), the proportion of entrepreneurs in American industry has declined sharply, while that of "bureaucrats" in particular and administrators in general has increased continuously.

Today, many view the Simple Structure as an anachronism in societies that call themselves democratic. Yet it remains a prevalent and important structural configuration, and will, in fact, continue to be so as long as new organizations are created, some organizations prefer to remain small and informal while others require strong leadership despite larger size, society prizes entrepreneurship, and many organizations face temporary environments that are extremely hostile or more permanent ones that are both simple and dynamic.

18

The Machine Bureaucracy

Prime Coordinating Mechanism:	Standardization of work processes
Key Part of Organization:	Technostructure
Main Design Parameters:	Behavior formalization, vertical and horizontal job specialization, usually functional grouping, large operating unit size, vertical centralization and limited horizontal decentralization, action planning
Contingency Factors:	Old, large, regulating, non-automated technical system, simple, stable environment, external control, not fashionable

A national post office, a security agency, a steel company, a custodial prison, an airline, a giant automobile company: all of these organizations appear to have a number of structural characteristics in common. Above all, their operating work is routine, the greatest part of it rather simple and repetitive; as a result, their work processes are highly standardized. These characteristics give rise to the *Machine Bureaucracies* of our society, the structures fine-tuned to run as integrated, regulated machines.

This is the structure that Max Weber first described, with standardized responsibilities, qualifications, communication channels, and work rules, as well as a clearly defined hierarchy of authority. It is the structure that Stinchcombe showed to arise from the Industrial Revolution, the one that Woodward found in the mass production firms, Burns and Stalker in the textile industry, Crozier in the tobacco monopoly, Lawrence and Lorsch in the container firm. It is what the Aston group called "workflow bureaucracy."

DESCRIPTION OF THE BASIC STRUCTURE

A clear configuration of the design parameters has held up consistently in the research: highly specialized, routine operating tasks, very formalized procedures in the operating core, a proliferation of rules, regulations, and formalized communication throughout the organization, large-sized units at the operating level, reliance on the functional basis for grouping tasks, relatively centralized power for decision making, and an elaborate administrative structure with a sharp distinction between line and staff.

The Operating Core The obvious starting point is the operating core, with its highly rationalized work flow. As a result, the operating tasks are simple and repetitive, generally requiring a minimum of skill and little training—often of the order of hours, seldom more than a few weeks, and usually in-house. This leads to a sharp division of labor in the operating core—to narrowly defined jobs, specialized both vertically and horizontally —and to an emphasis on the standardization of work processes for coordination. Thus, formalization of behavior emerges as the key design parameter. Because the workers are left with little discretion in their work, there is little possibility for mutual adjustment in the operating core. The use of direct supervision by first-line managers is limited by the fact that standardization handles most of the coordination. Thus, very large units can be designed in the operating core. (There is, however, as we shall see later, need for another kind of direct supervision, related to the lack of motivation of the operators—not to coordinate their work but simply to ensure that they do it.)

The Administrative Component The tight regulation of the operating work—in effect the sealing off of the operating core from disruptive environmental influence—requires that the administrative structure be highly elaborated. First is the middle line, which is fully developed, especially well above the operating core, and is sharply differentiated into functional units. The managers of this middle line have three prime tasks. One is to handle the disturbances that arise between the highly specialized workers of the operating core. While standardization takes care of most of the operating interdependencies, ambiguities inevitably remain, which give rise to conflicts. These cannot easily be handled by mutual adjustment among the operators, since informal communication is inhibited by the extensive standardization. So they tend to be handled by direct supervision, the orders of first-line managers. And because many of these conflicts arise between operators adjacent to each other in the work flow, the natural tendency is to bring adjacent operators under common supervision, in other words to group the operators into units that deal with distinct parts of the work flow, which results in the functional basis for grouping operating units. The production foreman, for example, heads a unit that deals with conflicts between machine operators who feed each work. For the same reason, this functional grouping gets mirrored all the way up the hierarchy, from the production and maintenance departments, which look to the plant manager to resolve many of their conflicts, to the manufacturing and marketing vice-presidents, who often expect the same of the company president.

A second task of the middle-line managers, which also explains why they are grouped on functional bases, is to work in their liaison role with the analysts of the technostructure to incorporate their standards down into the operating units. Their third task, related to the spokesman, disseminator, and resource allocator roles, is to support the vertical flows in the structure—the aggregation of the feedback information up the hierarchy and the elaboration of the action plans that come back down. All of these tasks of the middle-line managers require personal contacts—with their subordinates, the analysts, and their own superiors—which limit the number of people they can supervise. Hence, units above the operating core tend to be rather small in size and the overall administrative hierarchy rather tall in shape.

The technostructure must also be highly elaborated. In fact, Stinchcombe (1965) identified the birth of the Machine Bureaucracy structure in early nineteenth-century industries such as textiles and banking with the growth of technocratic personnel. **Because the Machine Bureaucracy depends primarily on the standardization of its operating work processes for coordination, the technostructure—which houses the analysts who do the standardizing—emerges as the key part of the structure.** This is so despite the fact that the Machine Bureaucracy sharply distinguishes between line and staff. To the line managers is delegated the formal authority for the operating units; the technocratic staff—officially at least—merely advises. But without the standardizers—the cadre of work study analysts, job description designers, schedulers, quality control engineers, planners, budgeters, MIS designers, accountants, operations researchers, and many, many more—the structure simply could not function. Hence, despite their lack of formal authority, considerable informal power rests with the analysts of the technostructure—those who standardize *everyone else's* work.

The informal power of the technostructure is gained largely at the expense of the operators, whose work they formalize to a high degree, and of the first-line managers, who would otherwise supervise the operators directly. Such formalization institutionalizes the work of these managers, that is, removes much of their power to coordinate and puts it into the systems designed by the analysts. The first-line manager's job can, in fact, become so circumscribed that he can hardly be said to function as a manager at all (that is, as someone who, as we defined earlier, is *in charge* of an organizational unit). The classic case is the foreman on the assembly line. Figure 18-1 shows Paterson's depiction of the manufacturing assembly foreman caught in a tangled web of technocratic and other forces. But this phenomenon is not restricted to manufacturing plants. Consider the constraints Antony Jay (1970) encountered in his job as head of a program production department in the BBC television service:

> ... if I wanted to take on a new production assistant or pay an existing one more money, I had to apply to Establishment Department, if I wanted to promote him to producer I had to apply to Appointments Department, if I wanted a film editor to work on Saturday I had to ask Film Department, if I wanted to change a designer I had to ask Design Department, if I wanted new carpets or an extra office I had to ask Administration Department, if I wanted to change studio rehearsal times I had to apply to Engineering Allocations, if I wanted to tell the press about a programme, I had to do it through the Publicity Officer. There was no question of doing without an extra office so as to pay a producer more—all these budgets were unconnected, and none controlled by me. And none of the heads of these departments worked under the head of my own group, and many did not meet a common boss until three or four levels up the hierarchy; three of them only met in the post of Director-General (p. 66).

The emphasis on standardization extends well beyond the operating core of the Machine Bureaucracy, and with it follows the analysts' influence. As Worthy (1959) explains, "It was all very well," the early proponents of scientific management in manufacturing firms found, "to organize the work of the shop, but no sooner was everything under control there than influences from outside the shop, from other segments of the enterprise (e.g., sales, finance), began to impinge upon and upset their neatly contrived arrangements. Thus the scientific managers soon began to be concerned with the necessity for extending their control to the entire enterprise" (pp. 75-76). Thus, **rules and regulations permeate the entire Machine Bureau-**

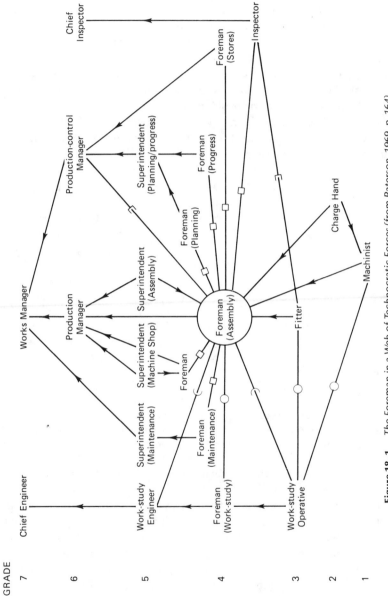

GRADE

7   Chief Engineer   Chief
                                       Inspector

6   Works Manager

5   Work-study   Superintendent
     Engineer   (Maintenance)

4   Foreman
     (Work-study)

3   Work-study
     Operative

2

1   Machinist

Figure 18-1. *The Foreman in a Web of Technocratic Forces (from Paterson, 1969, p. 164)*

cracy structure; formal communication is favored at all levels; decision making tends to follow the formal chain of authority. In no other structural configuration does the flow of information and decision making more closely resemble the system of regulated flows presented in our second overlay (Figure 3-2), with commands amplified down the vertical chain and feedback information aggregated up it. (This is not to suggest that the work of the senior managers is rigid and formalized, but rather that at every hierarchical level, behavior in the Machine Bureaucracy is *relatively* more formalized than that in the other structural configurations.)

A further reflection of this formalization is the sharp divisions of labor all over the Machine Bureaucracy. We have already discussed job specialization in the operating core and the sharp division between line and staff—between the managers with formal authority over the operating work and the analysts who are merely supposed to advise them. Moreover, the administrative structure is sharply differentiated from the operating core. Unlike the Simple Structure, here managers seldom work alongside operators. And the division of labor between the analysts who design the work and the operators who do it is equally sharp. In general, **of the five structural configurations, it is the Machine Bureaucracy that most strongly emphasizes division of labor and unit differentiation, in all their forms—vertical, horizontal, line/staff, functional, hierarchical, and status.**

In general, then, the Machine Bureaucracy functions most clearly in accord with the classical principles of management: formal authority filters down a clearly defined hierarchy, throughout which the principle of unity of command is carefully maintained, as is the rigid distinction between line and staff. Thus, the real error of the classical theorists was not in their principles per se, but in their claim that these were universal; in fact, they apply only to this and another one of the five structural configurations.[1]

The Obsession with Control All of this suggests that **the Machine Bureaucracy is a structure with an obsession, namely control.** A control mentality pervades it from top to bottom. Three quotations illustrate this, each from a different hierarchical level. First, near the bottom, consider how a Ford Assembly Division general foreman describes his work:

> I refer to my watch all the time. I check different items. About every hour I tour my line. About six thirty, I'll tour labor relations to find out who is absent. At seven, I hit the end of the line. I'll check paint, check my scratches and

[1]That other one is, as we shall see, the Divisionalized Form. But to be fair to the classicists, at the time of Fayol's first major statement of his views (1916), one and possibly two of the other three structural configurations hardly existed. The Adhocracy is really a post-World War II structural innovation, and the Professional Bureaucracy developed during this century. We can fault Fayol only for ignoring the Simple Structure, although his followers (some right up to the time of this writing) can be criticized more strongly because they ignored the important structural innovations that were developing all around them.

damage. Around ten I'll start talking to all the foremen. I make sure they're all awake, they're in the area of their responsibility. So we can shut down the end of the line at two o'clock and everything's clean. Friday night everybody'll get paid and they'll want to get out of here as quickly as they can. I gotta keep 'em on the line. I can't afford lettin' 'em get out early.

We can't have no holes, no nothing (quoted in Terkel, 1972, p. 186).

No wonder "There is a German word *Fordismus* which conjures up the epitome of maximum industrial productivity, where everything yields place to the tyranny of economic efficiency" (Parkinson, 1974, p. 60). At the middle level, the issues may be different, but the control mentality remains the same:

> ... a development engineer is not doing the job he is paid for unless he is at his drawing board, drawing, and so on. Higher management has the same instinctive reaction when it finds people moving about the works, when individuals it wants are not "in their place." These managers cannot trust subordinates when they are not demonstrably and physically "on the job." Their response, therefore, when there was an admitted need for "better communication" was to tether functionaries to their posts ... (Burns, 1971, pp. 52–53).

And at the strategic apex:

> When I was president of this big corporation, we lived in a small Ohio town, where the main plant was located. The corporation specified who you could socialize with, and on what level. (His wife interjects: "Who were the wives you could play bridge with.") The president's wife could do what she wants, as long as it's with dignity and grace. In a small town they didn't have to keep check on you. Everybody knew. There are certain sets of rules (quoted in Terkel, 1972, p. 406).

The obsession with control reflects two central facts about these structures. First, **attempts are made to eliminate all possible uncertainty, so that the bureaucratic machine can run smoothly, without interruption.** The operating core must be sealed off from external influence so that the standard outputs can be pumped off the assembly lines without disruption— hence the need for rules from top to bottom. Second, **by virtue of their design, Machine Bureaucracies are structures ridden with conflict: the control systems are required to contain it.** The magnified divisions of labor, horizontal and vertical, the strong departmental differentiation, the rigid distinction between line and staff, the motivational problems arising from the routine work of the operating core, all of these permeate the structure with conflict. As Woodward (1965) notes, in these types of organizations, the ideal social and technical systems simply do not correspond.

It was evident ... that the network of relationships best for production is not necessarily the best for people. If technical ends are well served the result will be a commercial success; if social ends are well served the result is likely to be a satisfactory and co-operative staff. Technical ends may best be served by conflict and pressure. Many of the conflicts that occurred in the firms studied seemed to be constructive by making a contribution to end results, and it was certainly not true to say that the most successful firms were those with the best relationships and closest identification between the staff and the company (p. 45).

Hence, the development of the ubiquitous control mentality: the problem in the Machine Bureaucracy is not to develop an open atmosphere where people can talk the conflicts out, but to enforce a closed, tightly controlled one where the work can get done despite them.

The obsession with control also helps to explain the frequent proliferation of support staff in these structures. Many of the staff services could be purchased from outside suppliers. But that would expose the Machine Bureaucracy to the uncertainties of the open market, leading to disruptions in the systems of flows it so intently tries to regulate. So it "makes" rather than "buys." That is, it envelops as many of these support services as it can within its own boundaries in order to control them, everything from the cafeteria in the factory to the law office at headquarters.

The Strategic Apex **The managers at the strategic apex of these organizations are concerned in large part with the fine tuning of their bureaucratic machines.** As R. G. Hunt (1970) notes, these are "performance organizations," not "problem-solving" ones. Theirs is a perpetual search for more efficient ways to produce given outputs. Thus, the entrepreneur role takes on a very restricted form at the strategic apex.

But all is not strictly improvement of performance. **Just keeping the structure together in the face of its conflicts also consumes a good deal of the energy of top management.** As noted earlier, conflict is not *resolved* in the Machine Bureaucracy; rather it is *bottled up* so that the work can get done. And as in the case of the bottle, the seal is applied at the top: ultimately, it is the top managers who must keep the lid on the conflicts through their role of disturbance handler. Direct supervision is another major concern of top management. Formalization can do only so much at the middle levels, where the work is more complex and unpredictable than in the operating core. The coordination between the highly differentiated middle-level units —for example, between engineering, marketing, and manufacturing in the mass production firm—often requires a flexible mechanism. The obvious choice would seem to be mutual adjustment. But its use is limited by the various blocks to informal communication—status differences between line and staff and between managers at different levels of the hierarchy, sharp differentiation between units at the same level of the hierarchy, and the general emphasis on formal communication and vertical reporting relationships. (In terms of our continuum of Figure 10-5, only the mildest liaison devices tend to be used in these structures, liaison positions and perhaps standing committees but not matrix structure and the like. The latter would destroy the chain of authority and the principle of unity of command, elements of central importance to the basic configuration.) So there remains the need for a good deal of direct supervision. Specifically, the managers of the strategic apex must intervene frequently in the activities of the middle line to effect coordination there through their leader, resource allocator, and disturbance handler roles. The top managers are the only generalists in the structure, the only managers with a perspective broad enough to see all the functions—the means—in terms of the overall ends. Everyone else in the structure is a specialist, concerned with a single link in the chain of activities that produces the outputs.

> In mechanistic systems the problems and tasks facing the concern as a whole are broken down into specialisms. Each individual pursues his task as something distinct from the real tasks of the concern as a whole, as if it were the subject of a sub-contract. "Somebody at the top" is responsible for seeing to its relevance. ... This command hierarchy is maintained by the implicit assumption that all knowledge about the situation of the firm and its tasks is, or should be, available only to the head of the firm. Management, often visualized as the complex hierarchy familiar in organization charts, operates a simple control system, with information flowing up through a succession of filters, and decisions and instructions flowing downwards through a succession of amplifiers (Burns and Stalker, 1966, p. 5).

All of this leads us to the conclusion that **considerable power in the Machine Bureaucracy rests with the managers of the strategic apex.** That is, these are rather centralized structures; in fact, they are second in this characteristic only to the Simple Structure. The *formal* power clearly rests at the top: hierarchy and chain of authority are paramount concepts. But so also does much of the *informal* power, since that resides in knowledge, and only at the top of the hierarchy does the segmented knowledge come together. The managers of the middle line are relatively weak, and the workers of the operating core have hardly any power at all (except, as we shall see later, to disrupt the operations). **The only ones to share any real informal power with the top managers are the analysts of the technostructure, by virtue of their role in standardizing everyone else's work.** Hence, we can conclude that the Machine Bureaucracy is centralized in the vertical dimension and decentralized only to a limited extent in the horizontal one.

Strategy Making   Strategy in these structures clearly emanates from the strategic apex, where the perspective is broad and the power is focused. **The process of strategy making is clearly a top-down affair, with heavy emphasis on action planning.** In top-down strategy making, as described in Chapter 9, all the relevant information is ostensibly sent up to the strategic apex, where it is formulated into an integrated strategy. This is then sent down the chain of authority for implementation, elaborated first into programs and then into activity plans.

Two main characteristics of this strategy-making system should be noted. First, it is intended to be a fully rationalized one, as described in our second overlay of Chapter 3. All the decisions of the organization are meant to be tied into one tightly integrated system. Exceptions flow up the chain of authority, to be handled at the level at which their impact is contained in a single unit, ultimately at the strategic apex if they cut across major functions. In turn, the resulting decisions flow down the chain for implementation in specific contexts. The structure that emerges is not so much one of work constellations, where groups at different levels make different kinds of decisions, as one of a hierarchy of ends and means, where managers at successively lower levels make the same kinds of decisions but with different degrees of specificity. For example, production decisions made at the vice-presidential level may concern what amount should be spent on new machinery, at the plant level, which machines to buy, and at the foreman level, how these machines are to be installed.

Second, unique to this structure is a sharp dichotomy between formulation and implementation in strategy making. The strategic apex formulates and the middle line and operating core implement. We can see this most clearly in the military, where the "high command" plans the grand strategy and the fighting units execute it:

> Military art (or science) recognizes such a dichotomy in its division of the conduct of war under the two headings of strategy and tactics: the one devoted to the general direction of armies, the other devoted to the particular deployment of men and materiel. . . .
>
> Contact between planners and executants is formally limited to the information the latter transmit to the rear. Information, digested and rationalized, is translated into battle plans. Battle plans are submitted to commanders who break them down into specific concrete decisions, and who transmit such decisions as orders to the appropriate subordinates (Feld, 1959, pp. 16, 20).

An Illustration   We can conclude this discussion with a description of the Murray's restaurant chain, operating in central Canada, which may well be the epitome of the Machine Bureaucracy, at least if the article published in the *Weekend Magazine* of September 30, 1972 (as well as this author's own experience) is any guide. First, about Miss Murray, the waitress, shown on the cover suspended from strings like a puppet, author Michael Enright writes:

> She moves easily across the restaurant floor, this Miss Murray, her hair in a bun, the Dr. Scholl's orthopedics muffle-patting on the tiles, moving like a nurse on night rounds. Everything is in place. She is smiling, of course, the apron is crisply white, the bow properly tied according to company directives. . . .
>
> It would be unfair to say that every Miss Murray looks like every other Miss Murray. . . . But there is a feeling in every restaurant that Deanna Durbin is bringing you your supper. She is as wholesome as the rice pudding.

And about the regulated operations:

> The major complaint about Murray's is that the food always and ever tastes the same. And indeed it does. The scrambled eggs with parsley potatoes in Toronto taste the same as the scrambled eggs with parsley potatoes in Sudbury or Ottawa. If you don't like the Strawberry Compote in Montreal, you won't like it in Halifax. This is because of formula cooking and portion control, systems invented and perfected by Murray's. And the Formula is all embracing from the sirloin steak down to the ice in the drinks.
>
> Every Murray's dish devolves from four-by-six inch, carefully printed Formula cards. These cards tell the various Murray's chefs exactly what to use and how to use it. ("Use a 3/16 inch cutter . . . Over-mixing will make the sirloin tough.") As long as the chef can read, he does not have to be cordon bleu. . . . Then there are Formula cards for serving. These cards tell the chefs where to put the parsley and how to scoop the mashed potatoes. Not only does the food taste the same in each Murray's city, it looks the same on the plate. Even the menus are a part of the Formula. The menus run in 21-day cycles . . . The prices are changed only twice a year, despite the fluctuation in wholesale food costs. The planners consider it would be too expensive to reprint thousands of menus that rarely change.

And, so, too, with control and strategic change:

> Every change, every move to tinker with the Murray's formula, is patiently examined and meticulously executed at company HQ, an old red brick building on Montreal's St. Paul Street, next to a ships' outfitters. Supervision over the operation is centred in that building and the lines are tight. Murray's has never expanded out West for that reason; distance could mean loss of control, deviation from the Formula.[2]

Figure 18–2 shows the Machine Bureaucracy symbolically, in terms of our logo, with a fully elaborated administrative and support structure—

[2]From "If You Like John Diefenbaker, Front Page Challenge And Hockey Night In Canada..." by M. Enright, *Weekend Magazine, The Montreal Star,* September 30, 1972. Used with permission.

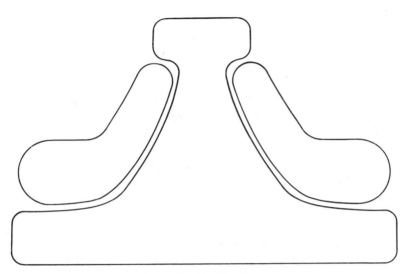

Figure 18-2. *The Machine Bureaucracy*

both staff parts of the organization being focused on the operating core—and large operating units but narrower ones in the middle line to reflect the tall hierarchy of authority.

CONDITIONS OF THE MACHINE BUREAUCRACY

We began our discussion of the basic structure with the point that the work flow of the Machine Bureaucracy is highly rationalized, its tasks simple and repetitive. Now we can see that such **machine bureaucratic work is found, above all, in environments that are simple and stable.** For example, the customers at Murray's "want their food simple, served efficiently without fuss, at a reasonable restaurant price. Allegiance to tradition is as much a part of Murray's as the food, and change comes painfully slow." The work of complex environments cannot be rationalized into simple tasks, while that of dynamic environments cannot be predicted, made repetitive, and so standardized.

In addition, **the Machine Bureaucracy is typically found in the mature organization, large enough to have the volume of operating work needed for repetition and standardization, and old enough to have been able to settle on the standards it wishes to use.** This is the organization that has seen it all before and has established a standard procedure to deal with it. Machine Bureaucracies are clearly the second stage of structural development, as we described in Chapter 13, the consequences of Simple Structures that grow and age.

Machine Bureaucracies tend also to be identified with regulating technical systems, since these routinize work and so enable it to be standardized. These technical systems range from the very simple to the moderately sophisticated, but not beyond. Highly sophisticated technical systems require that considerable power be delegated to staff specialists, resulting in a form of decentralization incompatible with the machine bureaucratic structure. Nor can the technical system be automated, for that would do away with routine operating work, and so debureaucratize the structure, leading to another configuration. Thus, while the organization may make heavy use of mechanization and computers because its work is standardized, it remains a Machine Bureaucracy only so long as these do not displace a work force dominated by unskilled operators.

Mass production firms are perhaps the best known Machine Bureaucracies. Their operating work flows form integrated chains, open at one end to accept raw material inputs, after that functioning as closed systems that process the inputs through sequences of standardized operations until marketable outputs emerge at the other end. These horizontal operating chains are typically segmented into links, each of which forms a functional department that reports up the vertical chain of authority. Figure 18-3, for example, shows the operating chain segmented into purchasing, fabricating, assembling, and selling, which result in three high-level functional departments—purchasing, manufacturing, and marketing. Even in some enormously large mass production firms, the economies of scale are such that functional structures are maintained right up to the top of the hierarchy. Likewise, in process production, when the firm is unable to automate its operations but must rely on a large work force to produce its outputs, it tends to adopt a functional machine bureaucratic structure.[3] Figure 18-4 shows the organigram of a large steel company, functional right to its top level of grouping.

In the case of the giant Machine Bureaucracies, an interesting shift occurs in the relationship between environmental stability and structural formalization: the former becomes the dependent variable. These organizations have great vested interests in environmental stability; without it, they cannot maintain their enormous technical systems. So whereas once upon a time they may have bureaucratized because their environments were stable, as they grew large they found themselves having to stabilize their environments because they were bureaucratic. As Worthy (1959) notes, the early proponents of scientific management no sooner made some headway in regulating the administrative structure than they turned their attention to the environment. "... there were external pressures on the enterprise itself

---

[3]The contradiction with Woodward here, who describes the structure of process production firms as organic, appears to stem from an assumption in her work that process technical systems are always largely automated.

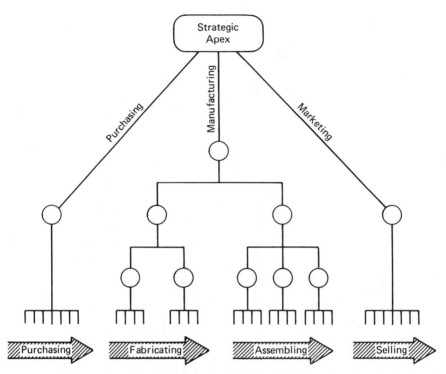

Figure 18-3. *The Operating Chain Segmented into Functional Departments in the Mass Production Firm*

that had to be organized and controlled before scientific management could come into its own" (p. 76). And so giant firms in industries such as transportation, tobacco, and metals are well known for their attempts to control the forces of supply and demand—through the use of advertising, the development of long item supply contacts, sometimes the establishment of cartels, and, as noted earlier, the envelopment of support services. They also adopt strategies of "vertical integration"; that is, they extend their production chains at both ends, becoming their own suppliers and customers. In this way, they are able to bring some of the forces of supply and demand within their own planning processes, and thereby regulate them. The big steel firm develops its own iron mines to ensure a steady source of raw materials at prices it controls, and it establishes a construction subsidiary to market its own steel. In effect, when it gets large enough, the Machine Bureaucracy can extend its control into its environment, seeking to regulate whatever out there can disturb its routine operations.

Of course, the Machine Bureaucracy configuration is not restricted to large, or manufacturing, or even private enterprise organizations. Many small manufacturers—for example, certain producers of discount furniture

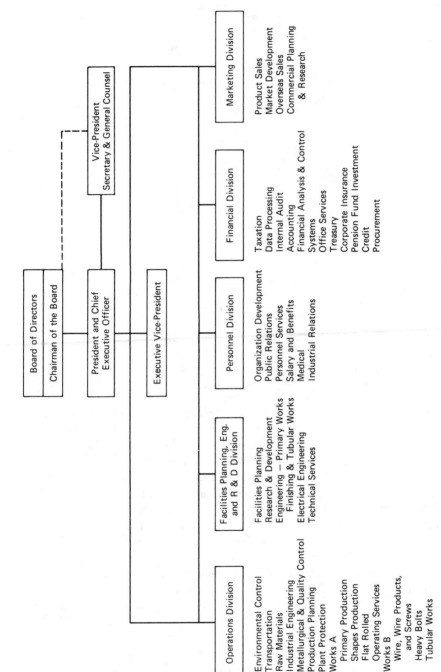

Figure 18-4. *Organigram of a Large Steel Company*

and paper products—prefer this structure because their operating work is simple and repetitive. Many service firms—what we can call *white-collar bureaucracies*—use it for the same reason, even though their operations are not integrated into single chains. Strings of assembly line workers are replaced in the insurance company by grids of office clerks, in the telephone company by rooms of switchboard operators, in the bank by rows of tellers. The outputs of these service firms may differ from those of the factories—as does the color of their workers' collars—but their operating work, being equally routine and nonprofessional, is no less amenable to formalization.

One McGill team of MBA students studied a 600-room downtown hotel, the most machinelike organization encountered in any of these studies. The operating work was very routine and repetitive, hence highly formalized. For example, as a cleaning woman completed her work in a room and pulled the key out of the lock, a signal was automatically flashed at the front desk indicating that the room was available for let. Records were kept on guests; when a regular one appeared, a basket of fruit was immediately dispatched to the room. Figure 18–5 shows the organigram for this hotel.

Large downtown hotels lend themselves to the machine bureaucratic form because their structures are tied right into their permanent physical facilities. Once the hotel is built, its location and size, as well as the nature of its rooms (in effect, its product-market strategy) is largely fixed. Thereafter, its success depends primarily on how effectively it can regulate its operations to the satisfaction of its customers. Those customers have definite expectations—not for surprise but for stability. At the time of this writing, one of the giant hotel chains is running a series of print advertisements under the theme: "At every Holiday Inn, the best surprise is no surprise." In one, George J. Fryzyan III, business insurance consultant, exclaims: "The room was clean. The TV worked. Everything worked. Amazing." After more praise, he adds, "It's got something to do with those 152 standards at every Holiday Inn. ..." Machine Bureaucracies are well suited to ensuring that nothing can possibly go wrong.

Another McGill MBA group studied a security agency with 1,200 part-time guards and nine full-time managers. The guards, paid at or near the minimum wage, were primarily older, retired men. Their work was extremely routine and simple, for example guarding school crossings and patrolling buildings after hours. Correspondingly, everything was absolutely routinized and the structure was remarkably bureaucratic. Uniforms were worn, ranks were used, a tight code of discipline was in force, a manual specified general regulations in minute detail while each job also had its own equally specific regulations. And this formalization of behavior was not restricted to the guards. When the firm embarked on an acquisition campaign, it drew up a procedure to evaluate candidates that seemed like a page out of its operations manual.

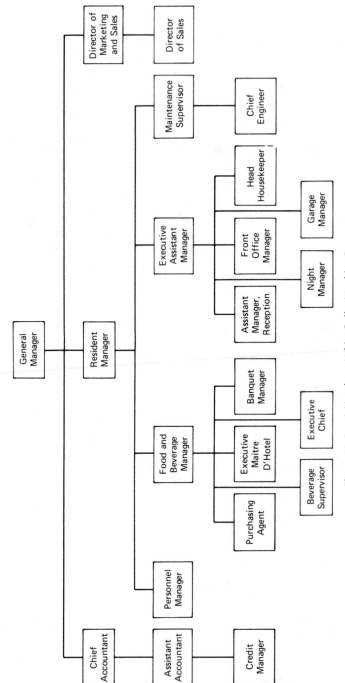

Figure 18-5. *A Hotel as a White Collar Machine Bureaucracy*

This organization was not a Machine Bureaucracy in the pure sense, since it lacked an elaborate administrative hierarchy. There were few middle managers and almost no analysts. The fact is that the tasks of this organization were so simple and so stable that management itself could work their procedures out and then leave them be, almost in perpetuity. Hence, there was no need for a technostructure. The structure was really a hybrid between Simple Structure and Machine Bureaucracy, which we might call the *simple bureaucracy:* centralized, highly bureaucratic, but with no elaboration of the administrative structure. Crozier's (1964) clerical agency seems to be of the same type. He describes its highly bureaucratic procedures and its managers' "relentless drive for control," but notes that its hierarchy was "uncomplicated ... pure line organization, with no staff function at all, at least at the branch level" (p. 14). His explanation: "The technology of the Agency's work is simple and it has remained basically unchanged for thirty-five years" (p. 14). So **given extremely simple and almost perfectly stable work, the Machine Bureaucracy can shed most of its administrative component.**

Another condition often found with Machine Bureaucracy is external control. Hypothesis 14 indicated that the more an organization is controlled externally, the more its structure is centralized and formalized, the two prime design parameters of the Machine Bureaucracy. External control is often most pronounced in government agencies, giving rise to a common example of this configuration which we can call the *public machine bureaucracy.* Many government agencies—such as post offices and tax collection departments—are bureaucratic not only because their operating work is routine but also because they are accountable to the public for their actions. Everything they do must seem to be fair, notably their treatment of clients and their hiring and promotion of employees. So they proliferate regulations. The Aston group distinguishes "workflow bureaucracies," bureaucratic because their work is structured, and "personnel bureaucracies," bureaucratic because their personnel procedures are formalized. They then describe "full bureaucracies," bureaucratic for both reasons, and note that these are "typically government-owned organizations" (Inkson et al., 1970, p. 323; see also Pugh et al., 1969a).

Since control is the forte of the Machine Bureaucracy, it stands to reason that organizations in the business of control—regulatory agencies, custodial prisons, police forces—are drawn to this structural configuration, sometimes in spite of contradictory conditions.[4] These constitute a variant we call the *control bureaucracy.* As Loevinger (1968) notes about regulatory agencies, "There are bureaucracies which are engaged in tasks other than

---

[4]In Chapter 19 we shall see that many police forces, which by all other intents and purposes seem like they should be structured as Professional Bureaucracies, in fact are drawn toward Machine Bureaucracy because of the control orientation and the need for public accountability.

regulation; but it is impossible to imagine regulation operating without a bureaucracy. Typically, bureaucracy is the structure and regulation is the function and each implies the other" (p. 15). Likewise, McCleery (1957) describes the "authoritarian prison," obsessed with its custodial (rather than rehabilitation) mission: "It was totalitarian in the sense that all processes necessary to sustain life within its walls were subject to regulation in detail" (p. 10). These prisons, in fact, exhibited a great many of the characteristics of the classic Machine Bureaucracy: a "disciplined" hierarchy, with a clear chain of authority, from guard through sergeant, watch officer, and senior captain on upward; power vested clearly in office, not function; sharp status distinctions within the custodial hierarchy as well as within the inmate population itself; the exclusive upward flow of information, "leaving each superior better informed than his subordinate and limiting the information on lower levels on which discretion could be based" (p. 13); very close control of those at the bottom of the structure, including "hour-by-hour reports on the location and movement of men" (p. 11); the strict sealing off of the operating core ("a careful censorship of all contacts with the free world," p. 15); and clear centralization of strategy making power, "The Warden and his Deputy [being] the only policy-making officials" (p. 10).

Another condition that drives the organization to the machine bureaucratic structure is the special need for safety. Organizations that fly airplanes or put out fires must minimize the risks they take. Hence, these *safety bureaucracies* formalize their procedures extensively to ensure that these are carried out to the letter. Few people would fly with an airline that had an organic structure, where the maintenance men did whatever struck them as interesting instead of following precise checklists, and the pilots worked out their procedures for landing in foggy weather when the need arose. Likewise, a fire crew cannot arrive at a burning house and then turn to the chief for orders or decide among its members who will connect the hose and who will go up the ladder. The environments of these organizations may seem dynamic, but in fact most of their contingencies are predictable—they have been seen many times before—and so procedures for handling them have been formalized. (Of course, an unexpected contingency forces the crew to revert to organic structure.)

We can also call organizations such as fire departments *contingency bureaucracies.* They exist not to provide routine services, but to stand ready in the event of the need for nonroutine ones. But because these services are critical, the organizations must plan elaborate procedures to respond quickly and efficiently to every contingent event that can be ancitipated. Their operators then spend their time practicing these procedures and waiting around for an event to occur, hopefully one of the contingencies anticipated.

Finally, we note that fashion is no longer a condition that favors the Machine Bureaucracy configuration. This structure was the child of the

Industrial Revolution. Over the course of the last two centuries—particularly at the turn of this one—it emerged as the dominant structural configuration (Rogers, 1975, p. 83). But the Machine Bureaucracy is no longer fashionable. As we shall soon see, it is currently under attack from all sides.

SOME ISSUES ASSOCIATED WITH MACHINE BUREAUCRACY

No structure has evoked more heated debate than the Machine Bureaucracy. As one of its most eminent students has noted:

> On the one hand, most authors consider the bureaucratic organization to be the embodiment of rationality in the modern world, and, as such, to be intrinsically superior to all other possible forms of organization. On the other hand, many authors—often the same ones—consider it a sort of Leviathan, preparing the enslavement of the human race (Crozier, 1964, p. 176).

Weber, of course, emphasized the first point of view; in fact, the word "machine" comes directly from his writings:

> The decisive reason for the advance of bureaucratic organization has always been its purely technical superiority over any other form of organization. The fully developed bureaucratic mechanism compares with other organizations exactly as does the machine with the non-mechanical modes of production.
> Precision, speed, unambiguity, knowledge of the files, continuity, discretion, unity, strict subordination, reduction of friction and of material and personal costs—these are raised to the optimum point in the strictly bureaucratic administration . . . (Gerth and Mills, 1958, p. 214).

A machine is certainly precise; it is also reliable and easy to control; and it is efficient—at least when restricted to the job it has been designed to do. These are the reasons why many organizations are structured as Machine Bureaucracies. In fact, these structures are the prime manifestations of our societies' high degree of specialization; moreover, they are the major contributors to our high material standards of living. Without Machine Bureaucracies, automobiles would be reserved for the rich and travelers would fly at their own peril. No structure is better suited to mass production and consistent output, none can more efficiently regulate work. Our society —such as it is—simply could not function without these structures. **When an integrated set of simple, repetitive tasks must be performed precisely and consistently by human beings, the Machine Bureaucracy is the most efficient structure, indeed the only conceivable one.**

But in these same advantages of machinelike efficiency lie all the disadvantages of these structures. Machines consist of mechanical parts; organizational structures also include human beings—and that is where the analogy breaks down. First, we shall discuss the human problems that arise in the operating core when people see themselves as more than just mechanical factors of production. Second, we shall discuss the coordination problems that arise in the administrative center when conflicts cannot be resolved by standardization. But in another sense, the machine analogy holds up and helps us to define the third set of problems we shall discuss—those of adaptability at the strategic apex. Machines are designed for specific purposes; they are extremely difficult to modify when conditions change.

Human Problems in the Operating Core   James Worthy (1959), when an executive of Sears, Roebuck, wrote a penetrating and scathing criticism of Machine Bureaucracy in his book *Big Business and Free Men.* Worthy traces the root of the human problems in these structures to the "scientific management" movement that swept America and later the Soviet Union[5] in the first third of this century. He sees its founder, Frederick W. Taylor, as the epitome of the personality drawn to the Machine Bureaucracy.

> His virtual obsession to control the environment around him was expressed in everything he did: in his home life, his gardening, his golfing; even his afternoon stroll was not a casual affair but something to be carefully planned and rigidly followed. Nothing was left to chance if in any way chance could be avoided. . . .
>
> From his writings and his biography one gets the impression of a rigid, insecure personality, desperately afraid of the unknown and the unforseen, able to face the world with reasonable equanimity only if everything possible has been done to keep the world in its place and to guard against anything that might upset his careful, painstaking plans (pp. 74–75).[6]

[5]There it had its "fullest flowering," encouraged by Lenin "as a means for accelerating industrial production" (p. 77). Worthy notes further the "interesting parallels between communism and scientific management. In both cases workers are seen as means rather than ends, doers rather than planners or initiators; to be manipulated—by persuasion if possible, by coercion if necessary—in other interests and for other needs than their own" (p. 78). Worthy also makes the link in the other direction, from regulated structure to centralized government. Writing of the American distrust for national planning, he comments: "But let there be a serious downturn in business, let the present smooth functioning of markets collapse under the blows of economic adversity, and the habit of mind that thinks in terms of mechanistic organization of the enterprise will make it easy to think in terms of mechanistic organization of the economy" (p. 79).

[6]Worthy traces the spread of the same mentality in Taylor's followers, from the plant floor, into the administrative structure, out to the organization's own environment, finally to society itself, culminating in Gantt's 1916 proposal for "a fantastic organization, called 'The New Machine' . . . apparently some form of corporate state, dimly foreseen, whose economic system would consist largely of public service corporations—managed, of course, by engineers trained in the skills of scientific management" (pp. 76–77).

Worthy acknowledges Taylor's contribution to efficiency, narrowly defined. Worker initiative did not, however, enter into his efficiency equation. Taylor "visualized the role of people within the organization in precisely the same manner as he visualized the component parts of a mechanism. 'A complicated and delicately adjusted machine' was a favorite figure of speech" (pp. 65–66). So efficient organizations came to be described as "smoothly running machines," the organigrams as "blueprints," and the time-and-motion study analyst's role as "human engineering" (pp. 66–67).

The problem was that "the methods of engineering have proved inappropriate to human organization" (p. 67). The assumption, as Emery (1971) has put it, that "we'll get the engineering system straight and simply tie the social system to it" (p. 186), created its own set of difficulties. Taylor's pleas to remove "all possible brain work" (Worthy, p. 67) from the shop floor also removed all possible initiative from the people who worked there. "... the machine has no will of its own. Its parts have no urge to independent action. Thinking, direction—even purpose—must be provided from outside or above. To those who have inherited Taylor's point of view, human nature' is something annoying—unavoidable, perhaps, but regrettably so, and to be kept in bounds so far as possible" (p. 79). **Treating people as "means," as "categories of status and function rather than as individuals," had the "consequence of destroying the meaning of work itself" (p. 70).**

That has been "fantastically wasteful for industry and society," failing "to recognize and utilize properly management's most valuable resource: the complex and multiple capacities of people" (pp. 70, 69). Organizations have paid dearly for these attitudes in the various forms of worker resistance —absenteeism, high turnover rates, sloppy workmanship, strikes, even outright sabotage (Björk, 1975).

Studs Terkel's (1972) fascinating book, *Working,* in which "people talk about what they do all day and how they feel about what they do" provides chapters of evidence on workers' responses to Machine Bureaucracies. Here is how a spot-welder in a Ford assembly plant in Chicago describes his job:

> I stand in one spot, about two- or three-feet area, all night. The only time a person stops is when the line stops. We do about thirty-two jobs per car, per unit. Forty-eight units an hour, eight hours a day. Thirty-two times forty-eight times eight. Figure it out. That's how many times I push that button. ...
>
> It don't stop. It just goes and goes and goes. I bet there's men who have lived and died out there, never seen the end of that line. And they never will— because it's endless. It's like a serpent. It's just all body, no tail. It can do things to you. ...
>
> Repetition is such that if you were to think about the job itself, you'd slowly go out of your mind (pp. 159–160).

And a steelworker expressed similar frustrations, but in a more poetic way:

I don't know who the guy is who said there is nothing sweeter than an unfinished symphony. Like an unfinished painting and an unfinished poem. If he creates this thing one day—let's say, Michelangelo's Sistine Chapel. It took him a long time to do this, this beautiful work of art. But what if he had to create this Sistine Chapel a thousand times a year? Don't you think that would even dull Michelangelo's mind? Or if da Vinci had to draw his anatomical charts thirty, forty, fifty, sixty, eighty, ninety, a hundred times a day? Don't you think that would even bore da Vinci? (p. xxxvii)

Undoubtedly. Unless he had the temperament of Babe Secoli, a checker in a Chicago supermarket with a very different perspective on machine bureaucratic work:

We sell everything here, millions of items. From potato chips and pop—we even have a genuine pearl in a can of oysters. It sells for two somethin'. Snails with the shells that you put on the table, fanciness. There are items I never heard of we have here. I know the price of every one. Sometimes the boss asks me and I get a kick out of it. There isn't a thing you don't want that isn't in this store.

You sort of memorize the prices. It just comes to you. I know half a gallon of milk is sixty-four cents; a gallon, $1.10. You look at the labels. A small can of peas, Raggedy Ann. Green Giant, that's a few pennies more. I know Green Giant's eighteen and I know Raggedy Ann is fourteen. ... You just memorize. On the register is a list of some prices, that's for the part-time girls. I never look at it.

I don't have to look at the keys on my register. I'm like the secretary that knows her typewriter. The touch. My hand fits. The number nine is my big middle finger. The thumb is number one, two and three and up. The side of my hand uses the bar for the total and all that.

I use my three fingers—my thumb, my index finger, and my middle finger. The right hand. And my left hand is on the groceries. They put down their groceries. I got my hips pushin' on the bottom and it rolls around on the counter. When I feel I have enough groceries in front of me, I let go of my hip. I'm just movin'—the hips, the hand, and the register, the hips, the hand, and the register ... (As she demonstrates, her hands and hips move in the manner of an Oriental dancer.) You just keep goin', one, two, one, two. If you've got that rhythm, you're a fast checker. Your feet are flat on the floor and you're turning your head back and forth. ...

I'm a couple of days away, I'm very lonesome for this place. When I'm on a vacation, I can't wait to go, but two or three days away, I start to get fidgety. I can't stand around and do nothin'. I have to be busy at all times. I look forward to comin' to work. It's a great feelin'. I enjoy it somethin' terrible (pp. 282, 286).

The difference between the da Vincis in the steel mills and the Secolis in the supermarkets is that some people take to routine work while others abhor it. Some simply appreciate regularity in their work, perhaps, like

Secoli, because it gives them a chance to get to know it well, or perhaps because it satisfies a need for order and security. But others, either because their need is to do creative, self-actualizing work or because they dislike being told what to do, cannot tolerate the work offered them in Machine Bureaucracies.

As long as everybody can find the work that best suits them, there is no problem. But apparently they cannot. There appear to be more jobs in the Machine Bureaucracies of our society than people happy to fill them, too few in the more popular structures. Thus, one study in an automobile assembly plant found that 69 percent of the workers complained of monotony, 87 percent wanted to find a job with higher skills, and more responsibility, variety, and freedom; most claimed they stayed because of what they could earn, only 6 percent because they liked the work (cited in Melcher, 1976, p. 85).

And time is not on the side of the Machine Bureaucracy. Rising educational levels raise work asperations, that is, bring out the need for self-actualization at the expense of the need for security. Moreover, the welfare system has taken care of certain security needs, giving the worker the option of doing nothing without starving. "The fear of drudgery has replaced the fear of unemployment" (Morris Abrams, quoted in Baughman et al., 1974, p. 473). The result is that today's Machine Bureaucracies are experiencing more and more resistance from people who simply do not want to be there. (Not only in the operating core. Successful middle-aged executives—no longer tolerant of the control mentality—seem also to be quitting in increasing numbers, after years of struggling to get to where they are.) Clearly, in the view of a growing portion of the work force, Machine Bureaucracies are becoming unacceptable places to spend their working lives.

Taylor was fond of saying: "In the past the man has been first; in the future the system must be first" (quoted in Worthy, 1959, p. 73). Prophetic words, indeed. Modern man seems to exist for his systems: many of the organizations he created to serve him have come to rule him. The consumer seems able to find cheap goods in the marketplace on Saturday only if he is willing to squander his talents as a producer from Monday to Friday. Mass consumption in return for dreary production.

But even the consumption is affected, by what Victor Thompson (1961) has referred to as the "bureaupathologies"—the dysfunctional behaviors of these structures, which lead to higher prices, shoddy workmanship, and indifferent or rude treatment of customers. Sometimes the consequences are bizarre. A story in the December 17, 1971 issue of *Time* magazine tells what happens when specialization drives workers to displace ends in favor of means. Firemen in Genoa, Texas, set fire to abandoned buildings because they were bored. Explained one: "We'd hang around the station on the night shift without a thing to do. We just wanted to get the red light flashing and the bells clanging."

As we saw in Chapter 5, the various bureaupathologies reinforce each other to form vicious circles. The displacement of ends in favor of means, the mistreatment of clients, the various manifestations of worker alienation, all lead to a tightening of the controls on behavior. The implicit motto of the Machine Bureaucracy seems to be: "When in doubt, control." All problems are to be solved by the turning of the technocratic screws. But since this is what caused the bureaupathologies in the first place, more of it serves only to magnify the problems, which leads to the imposition of further controls, and so on. How far this can go is perhaps best illustrated by a firm that intervened to reverse the process. When Marks and Spencer, the U.K. retail chain, dispensed with inventory replacement cards, sales receipts, time clocks, and other control procedures, the owners estimated that the firm was able to eliminate 8000 of its 28,000 jobs and to save 26 million pieces of paper annually (Becker and Gordon, 1966–67, pp. 331–332).

But not every organization can wipe out most of its control system in one fell swoop. So other means have been tried—by the organization or its workers—to reverse the vicious circles, everything from job enlargement to outright democratization.

If the research discussed in Chapter 4 is any indication, job enlargement (or "enrichment"), where the workers are given a wider variety of tasks to perform and perhaps control over the design of those tasks as well, does not seem to hold a great deal of promise for major improvement of the work. No doubt the engineering orientation has led to excessive specialization in many cases. When the human factor is finally plugged into the performance equation—that is, when the worker's initiative is taken into account—it clearly becomes worthwhile to enlarge many jobs.[7] But the question is: how far? And the answer seems to be: not very. As we have emphasized in this chapter, the nature of the Machine Bureaucracy's work reflects above all the regulating characteristic of the organization's technical system and the stability and simplicity of its environment. The obsession with control is a response to these conditions, albeit often an excessive one. As long as these conditions remain—in essence, **as long as society demands cheap, mass produced goods and services—a great many jobs will remain pretty much as they are now, that is, minimally affected by job enlargement.** Braverman (1974) puts it rather brutally: "Taylorism dominates the world of production; the practitioners of 'human relations' and 'industrial psychology' are the maintenance crew for the human machinery" p 87).

If the human problems in the operating core of Machine Bureaucracy cannot be solved by job enlargement, what are the prospects for democrati-

---

[7]See Simon (1973a, b) and Argyris (1973a, b) for an interesting debate on the need for structures that promote "rational" efficiency versus those that promote self-actualization.

zation instead? Here, too, the evidence (discussed in Chapter 11) is discouraging, and for the same reason: **democratization does not eliminate the fundamental conflict in the Machine Bureaucracy between engineering efficiency on the one hand and individual satisfaction on the other.** Giving the workers the right to vote for directors periodically does not change the realities of their everyday work. (It might, however, somewhat change their attitudes to that work, infusing a dose of ideology into an otherwise utilitarian situation. A sense of ownership might reduce the feelings of alienation.) As we saw in Chapter 11, such democratization seems to centralize the structure further, which "may tend to bypass middle management, to weaken the staff function, and to inhibit the development of staff professionalism" (Strauss and Rosenstein, 1970, p. 171). Indeed, these effects can be predicted from our Hypothesis 14, since in electing the directors, the workers constitute a force for external control. That hypothesis indicated that external control not only centralizes a structure but also bureaucratizes it.

Nowhere is this result clearer than in Crozier's (1964) description of another kind of democracy—a judicial type—where the workers impose rules in order to dilute their bosses' control over them. This turns out to be a perverse kind of democracy, indeed. With the bosses constrained by the rules, power passes up the hierarchy, and the structure becomes significantly more centralized. And with workers' rules countering managers' rules, the structure also becomes more bureaucratic, at everybody's expense. The workers end up being locked into an even tighter straightjacket, albeit of their own design. The clients lose, too. Those of the ordinary Machine Bureaucracy can at least take solace in the fact that the rules are for their benefit—to encourage more efficient production. The additional rules of the bureaucracies Crozier describes have nothing to do with efficiency; they serve to protect the worker. As we shall soon see, like all rules, they act to inhibit innovation and adaptation. Where the workers are organized to fight the intrusions of management, change becomes well-nigh impossible. Judicial democratization catches the client in a tug of war between worker and manager. The organization burns up more of its energy in its own conflicts, with less left over to produce outputs for the clients.

The discouraging conclusion is that the Machine Bureaucracy creates major human problems in the operating core, ones for which no solutions are apparent. Job enlargement holds little promise and democratization seems only to augment the bureaupathologies. Joan Woodward had it right when she argued that in these structures there is an irreconcilable conflict between the technical and social systems. What is good for production simply is not good for people. Fundamental change will apparently have to come, not through the front door of direct confrontation or legislation, but through the back door of changed conditions to which the organization must respond. Specifically, nothing short of automation of the technical system (or of an environment becoming more complex or dynamic) seems able to alleviate the social problems of the Machine Bureaucracy.

We do, of course, have one other choice as a society: to reduce our demand for cheap, mass produced goods and services. As we shall see in Chapter 19, craft organizations, structured as Professional Bureaucracies, can sometimes produce the same outputs as Machine Bureaucracies but with less social turmoil and much higher quality. The question is whether we are prepared to pay the price: stoneware dishes replaced every generation instead of plastic ones replaced every year, an occasional dress handwoven in a studio instead of a frequent one mass produced in a factory, a Ferrari every twenty years instead of a Ford every two. Of course, should the vicious circles intensify to the point where life in the Machine Bureaucracy becomes so intolerable that nobody will work there, we shall have no other choice. Perhaps the system will end up serving man after all, despite himself.

Coordination Problems in the Administrative Center   Since the operating core of the Machine Bureaucracy is not designed to handle conflict, many of the human problems that arise there spill over into the administrative structure. Again, Worthy (1959) says it best:

> The organization was set up like a machine and it had to be operated like a machine. But because its components were human rather than mechanical, the task of controlling and directing it taxed the ingenuity of the scientific managers. The elaborate contrivances of the modern industrial organization, the masses of paper work and red tape, the layers on layers of supervision, the luxuriant growth of staff—all these are evidence of the difficulty of controlling human organizations in terms of mechanistic principles (p. 72).

It is one of the ironies of the Machine Bureaucracy that to achieve the control it requires, it must mirror the narrow specialization of its operating core in its administrative structure. "By his sweeping redivision of labor as between workers and management, Taylor so increased the burden on management that a considerable further division of labor within management became essential" (pp. 67–68). And this administrative division of labor, in turn, leads to a sharp differentiation of the administrative structure and narrow functional orientations. "... the individual 'works on his own,' functionally isolated; he 'knows his job,' he is 'responsible for seeing it's done' ... the accountant 'dealing with the costs side,' the works manager 'pushing production' ..." (Burns and Stalker, 1966, p. 124). And that means problems of communication and coordination. For example, Bennett (1977) has written a case describing the three years of convoluted effort

General Motors went through, with no sign of success, just to coordinate the purchase of work gloves across its units.

The fact, as noted earlier, is that the administrative structure of the Machine Bureaucracy is ill-suited to the use of mutual adjustment. All the communication barriers in these structures—horizontal, vertical, status, line/staff—impede informal communication. "Each unit becomes jealous of its own perogatives and finds ways to protect itself against the pressure or encroachments of others" (Worthy, 1950, p. 176).

Narrow functionalism not only impedes coordination, but it also encourages the building of private empires, much as Parkinson (1957) decribed. In such structures, it is difficult to associate any particular function with overall output or performance. Hence, when a manager calls for more personnel—more cost analysts, more clerks, more sales managers—no one can be quite sure whether or not the claim is legitimate. So there emerges a competition among the managers to build bigger and more powerful units, a competition stimulated by the bureaucratic rule that associates salary with number of subordinates. This encourages the building of top-heavy organizations, often more concerned with the political games to be won than the clients to be served. A Machine Bureaucracy free of market forces—for example, a government regulatory agency with an ensured budget and vague performance goals—can become virtually a closed system, responsible to no one and producing nothing, forever spinning its administrative wheels in great busyness.

But if mutual adjustment does not work—generating more political heat than cooperative light—how does the Machine Bureaucracy resolve its coordination problems? Instinctively, by trying standardization.

> ... the ideology of formal bureaucracy seemed so deeply ingrained in industrial management that the common reaction to unfamiliar and novel conditions was to redefine, in most precise and rigorous terms, the roles and working relationships obtaining within management along orthodox lines of "organization charts" and "organization manuals," and to reinforce the formal structure (Burns and Stalker, 1966, p. ix).

But standardization is not suited to handling the nonroutine problems of the administrative center. Indeed, it only makes them worse. The standards undermine "the line organization for benefit of the staff," they impair its flexibility and adaptability, and they generate conflict by forcing managers to "make a good showing" independent of the other departments with which they must coordinate (Worthy, 1950, p. 176).

So **to reconcile the coordination problems that arise in its administrative center, the Machine Bureaucracy is left with only one coordinating mechanism, direct supervision.** Specifically, nonroutine coordination problems between units are "bumped" up the line hierarchy for reconciliation, until they reach a common level of supervision. The conflict that arises between two salesperons, say over the allocation of territory, is resolved by the sales manager; the one between that manager and the advertising manager, over the timing of a campaign, goes up to the marketing vice-president; and the conflict between the latter and the manufacturing vice-president, over the design of a new product, may have to be resolved by the president.

This bumping-up process of course results in the centralization of power for decision making at the upper levels of the hierarchy, ultimately at the strategic apex. With the top managers handling all the important coordination problems, they become, as we noted earlier in the chapter, solely responsible for strategy formulation, for the making and interrelating of the important decisions of the organization. And that results in a host of new problems. In effect, **just as the human problems in the operating core become coordination problems in the administrative center, so too do the coordination problems in the administrative center become adaptation problems at the strategic apex.**

Adaptation Problems at the Strategic Apex   As long as its environment remains perfectly stable, the Machine Bureaucracy faces no great difficulty. Its standard procedures handle the routine problems of coordination, and nonroutine ones do not arise.

But no organization can expect that much stability. Environments inevitably change, generating new nonroutine problems. When these become frequent in the Machine Bureaucracy, the managers at the strategic apex quickly become overloaded. "There can, and frequently does, develop a system by which a large number of executives find—or claim—that they can get matters settled only in direct consultation with the head of the concern" (Burns and Stalker, 1966, p. ix). Every organigram—and our logo as well—shows a narrowing of the middle line as it approaches the strategic apex. The propensity to pass nonroutine problems up the line hierarchy causes a bottleneck at the top during times of change, which forces the senior managers to make their decisions quickly. But how can they do so when these are decisions that arose elsewhere in the organization, in places where the top managers lack intimate contact?

In theory, the Machine Bureaucracy is designed to account for this problem. It has a management information system (MIS) which aggregates information up the hierarchy, presenting the people at the top with concise summaries of what goes on down below—the perfect solution for the overloaded top manager. Except that much of the information is the wrong kind.

A number of problems arise in the MIS. For one thing, there are natural losses whenever information is transmitted through a long chain. In one laboratory experiment, a line drawing of an owl was redrawn successively by eighteen individuals to emerge as a recognizable cat (cited in Williamson, 1967, p. 126); in World War I, "Word-of-mouth communication along the trenches in the British sector during a period when the field telephone was out of order is reputed to have resulted in the message 'Send reinforcements: we are going to advance' from the front line being relayed to headquarters as 'Send three-and-fourpence: we are going to a dance'" (Stopford and Wells, 1972, p. 13). In the tall administrative structure of the Machine Bureaucracy, information must pass through many levels before it reaches the top. Losses take place at each one. Not only natural losses. The fact that the transfers are vertical—between people on different status levels of the hierarchy—means that intentional distortions of information also occur. Good news gets highlighted and bad news blocked on its way up. In 1941, United States staff experts tried to warn their officers of the impending Japanese attack on Pearl Harbor. The latter ignored them as "mere data collectors." So the

> ... subordinate officers in subordinate intelligence and research units tried to communicate their more urgent interpretations directly to the chief of Army and Navy war plans. "But their efforts were unsuccessful because of the poor repute associated with Intelligence, inferior rank, and the province of the specialist, or long-hair." (Wilensky, 1967, p. 44; quotation from Roberta Wholstetter).

Probably a greater problem is the MIS's emphasis on "hard" (quantitative), aggregated information. A good deal of evidence suggests that it is not this kind of information top managers need to make their strategic decisions as much as soft, specific information, in Neustadt's (1960) words, not "bland amalgams" but "tangible detail" (pp. 153–154; see also Aguilar, 1967, p. 94; Mintzberg, 1973a, pp. 69–70; Wrapp, 1967, p. 92).

Often the MIS data are too late as well. It takes time for events to get reported as official "facts," more time for these to get accumulated into reports, and more time still for these to pass up the hierarchy until they finally reach the top manager's desk. In a perfectly stable environment, he can perhaps wait; in a changing one, he cannot. A military commander wants to know about the enemy's movements as they are taking place, not later, when they are reflected in some official measure like casualties in a battle. Likewise, the corporate president wants to be told that his most important customer was seen playing golf yesterday with his major competitor; he does not want to find out about it six months later in the form of a negative variance on a sales report. Gossip, hearsay, speculation—the softest kinds of information—warn the manager of impending problems; the MIS all too often records for posterity that these problems have long since arrived. Moreover, a good deal of important information never even gets into the MIS. The mood in the factory, the conflict between two managers, the reasons for a lost sale—this kind of rich information never becomes the kind of fact that the traditional MIS can handle.

So **the information of the MIS, by the time it reaches the strategic apex —after being filtered and aggregated through the levels of the administrative hierarchy—is often so bland that the top manager cannot rely on it.** He who tries to is forced to subsist on a "diet of abstractions, leaving the choice of what he eats in the hands of his subordinates" (Wrapp, 1967, p. 92). In a changing environment, that manager finds himself out of touch.[8]

The obvious solution for the top managers is to bypass the MIS and set up their own informal information systems, ones that can bring them the rich, tangible information they need, quickly and reliably. Specifically, top managers establish their own networks of contacts and informers, both inside and outside the organization, and they expose themselves to as much first-hand information as possible (Aguilar, 1967; Mintzberg, 1973a).

But getting such information takes time. And that, of course, was the problem in the first place—the bottleneck at the strategic apex of the Machine Bureaucracy in a changed environment. So **a fundamental dilemma faces the top managers of the Machine Bureaucracy as a result of the centralization of the structure and the emphasis on reporting through the chain of authority. In times of change, when they most need to spend time getting the "tangible detail," they are overburdened with decisions coming up the hierarchy for resolution. They are, therefore, reduced to acting superficially, with inadequate, abstract information.**

The essential problem lies in one of the major tenets of the Machine Bureaucracy, that strategy formulation must be sharply differentiated from strategy implementation. The first is the responsibility of top management, the second is to be carried out by everyone else, in hierarchical order. Nowhere in practice is this dichotomy sharper than in the military, with "strategy" focusing on the general direction of armies and "tactics" on the particular deployment of men and materiel. And nowhere in the literature are the problems of this dichotomy more clearly described than in the paper by Feld (1959) on military organization.

> Ideally speaking, military operations are painstakingly planned and then carried out with unquestioning resolution. The one operation requires conditions of orderliness and calm, the other creates an environment of disorderliness and confusion. Planners are therefore in the rear, while executors constitute in themselves the scene of battle. . . .
>
> The professional soldier operates within a bureaucratic framework. . . . Officers responsible for the drawing up of plans, then, have higher status than those responsible for their execution. . . .

[8]This discussion on impediments in the use of MIS is drawn largely from Mintzberg (1975).

The superiority of planners is based on the assumption that their position serves to keep them informed about what is happening to the army as a whole, while that of the executor limits knowledge to personal experience. This assumption is supported by the hierarchical structure of military organization which establishes in specific detail the stages and the direction of the flow of information. In terms of this hierarchy, the man who receives information is superior to the man who transmits it. ... By virtue of his position in the organizational structure, the superior is the best informed and, therefore, the best equipped to give orders. ... A plan of operations once decided must therefore be carried out even if reports from the scene of combat indicate that it is unrealistic. Determination of this kind is regarded as essential if the military structure of rank and authority is to be preserved (p. 22).

That preservation has sometimes proved to be costly indeed. In the infamous battle of Passchendaele of World War I, where 300,000 British troups went over the trenches to become casualties, "No senior officer from the Operations Branch of the General Headquarters, it was claimed, ever set foot (or eyes) on the Passchendaele battlefield during the four months that battle was in progress. Daily reports on the condition of the battlefield were first ignored, then ordered discontinued. Only after the battle did the Army chief of staff learn that he had been directing men to advance through a sea of mud" (p. 21).

The formulation-implementation dichotomy presupposes two fundamental conditions in order to work effectively: (1) the formulator has full information, or at least information as good as that available to the implementor, and (2) the situation is sufficiently stable or predictable to ensure that there will be no need for *re*formulation during implementation. The absence of either condition should lead to a collapse of the dichotomy, to proceeding with formulation and implementation concurrently, in an adaptive rather than a planning mode (Braybrooke and Lindblom, 1963; Mintzberg, 1973b).

If the top manager cannot get the information he needs, he simply cannot formulate a sensible strategy. The Machine Bureaucracy is designed on the questionable assumption that even in times of change the MIS will bring the necessary information up the hierarchy to him. The conditions of the mud are only the most literal example of the inability of the MIS to handle soft information. As Crozier (1964) described in the case of the French government agencies, the problem in these structures is that the power to formulate strategy rests at a different place then the information needed to do so.

The design of the Machine Bureaucracy also assumes that a strategy formulated in one place can later be implemented in another. That is a reasonable assumption under conditions of stability—as long as the world holds still (or at least undergoes predicted changes) while the plan unfolds. Unfortunately, all too often the world refuses to hold still; it insists on changing in unpredictable ways. This imposes the need to adapt, to alter the strategy as it is being implemented. "The rational direction of large masses requires planning, and planning requires a high degree of stability and calm. The conditions of combat are fluid and haphazard in the extreme" (Feld, 1959, p. 17). Under such fluid conditions, either the formulator must implement his own strategy so that he can reformulate it en route—which is what happens in the Simple Structure, which faces a simple, dynamic environment—or else the implementors must take responsibility for the formulation and do it adaptively—which is what happens in the Adhocracy, which decentralizes power for strategy making in the face of a complex, dynamic environment.

We emerge from this discussion with two conclusions. First, strategies must be formulated outside the machine bureaucratic structure if they are to be realistic. Second, the dichotomy between formulation and implementation ceases to have relevance in times of unpredictable change. Together these conclusions tell us that Machine Bureaucracies are fundamentally nonadaptive structures, ill-suited to changing their strategies. But that should come as no surprise. After all, machines are designed for special purposes, not general ones. So, too, are Machine Bureaucracies.

These are, as R. G. Hunt (1970) noted, performance not problem-solving organizations. Strategic diagnosis is simply not part of their repertoire of standard operating procedures. Machine Bureaucracies work best in stable environments because they have been designed for specific, predetermined missions. Efficiency is their forte, not innovation. An organization cannot put blinders on its personnel and then expect peripheral vision. The managers of the Machine Bureaucracy are rewarded for improving operating efficiency, reducing costs, finding better controls and standards; not for taking risks, testing new behaviors, encouraging innovation. Change makes a mess of the standard operating procedures. In the Machine Bureaucracy, everything is nicely coupled, carefully coordinated. Change a link and the whole operating chain must be redesigned; change an element in an integrated strategy and it disintegrates.

Thus, steel companies and post offices are not noted innovators, and the automobile of today is hardly different from that of Henry Ford's day. (Compare the generations of computers or airplanes of the last twenty-five years—products of very different structures, as we shall see in Chapter 21—with the automobiles of the last fifty.) As Hlavacek and Thompson (1973) note:

> At one extreme the need or problems of innovation is not recognized; no special structure is provided; new product innovation is not an important condition for survival. The automobile industry is an example of this extreme. New product changes are superficial; the appearance of change is largely the result

of massive advertising expenditures claiming uniqueness. The innovation problem is given no organizational expression; bureaucracy reigns supreme (p. 365).

When Machine Bureaucracies must change their strategies, their top managers tend to act idiosyncratically: they are not in the habit of making such changes, their MISs have obscured the kind of change that is needed, and their structures are ill-suited to receiving whatever change is eventually proposed (Normann, 1971, p. 214). The top managers seem to succeed only when they are strong enough to cast aside their bureaucratic information and control systems and take matters into their own hands. In other words, ironically, **the top managers succeed in changing the Machine Bureaucracy only by reverting temporarily to the leaner, more flexible Simple Structure.**

To conclude, the Machine Bureaucracy is an inflexible structural configuration. As a machine, it is designed for one purpose only. It is efficient in its own limited domain, but cannot easily adapt itself to any other. Above all, it cannot tolerate an environment that is either dynamic or complex. Nevertheless, the Machine Bureaucracy remains a dominant structural configuration—probably *the* dominant one in our specialized societies. As long as we demand standardized, inexpensive goods and services, and as long as people remain more efficient than automated machines at providing them—and remain willing to do so—the Machine Bureaucracy will remain with us.

19

The Professional Bureaucracy

Prime Coordinating Mechanism:	Standardization of skills
Key Part of Organization:	Operating core
Main Design Parameters:	Training, horizontal job specialization, vertical and horizontal decentralization
Contingency Factors:	Complex, stable environment, nonregulating, nonsophisticated technical system, fashionable

We have seen evidence at various points in this book that organizations can be bureaucratic without being centralized. Their operating work is stable, leading to "predetermined or predictable, in effect, standardized" behavior (our definition of bureaucracy in Chapter 3), but it is also complex, and so must be controlled directly by the operators who do it. Hence, the organization turns to the one coordinating mechanism that allows for standardization and decentralization at the same time, namely the standardization of skills. This gives rise to a structural configuration sometimes called *Professional Bureaucracy*, common in universities, general hospitals, school systems, public accounting firms, social work agencies, and craft production firms. All rely on the skills and knowledge of their operating professionals to function; all produce standard products or services.

THE BASIC STRUCTURE

The Work of the Operating Core   Here again we have a tightly knit configuration of the design parameters. Most important, **the Professional Bureaucracy relies for coordination on the standardization of skills and its associated design parameter, training and indoctrination. It hires duly trained and indoctrinated specialists—professionals—for the operating core, and then gives them considerable control over their own work.** In effect, the work is highly specialized in the horizontal dimension, but enlarged in the vertical one.

Control over his own work means that the professional works relatively independently of his colleagues, but closely with the clients he serves. For example, "Teacher autonomy is reflected in the structure of school systems, resulting in what may be called their structural looseness. The teacher works alone within the classroom, relatively hidden from colleagues and superiors, so that he has a broad discretionary jurisdiction within the boundaries of the classroom" (Bidwell, 1965, pp. 975–976). Likewise, many doctors treats their own patients, and accountants maintain personal contact with the companies whose books they audit.

Most of the necessary coordination between the operating professionals is then handled by the standardization of skills and knowledge, in effect, by what they have learned to expect from their colleagues. "... the system works because everyone knows everyone else knows roughly what is going on" (Meyer quoted in Weick, 1976, p. 14). During an operation as long and as complex as open-heart surgery, "very little needs to be said [between the anesthesiologist and the surgeon] preceding chest opening and during the procedure on the heart itself: lines, beats and lights on equipment are indicative of what everyone is expected to do and does—operations are performed in absolute silence, particularly following the chest-opening phase" (Gosselin, 1978). The point is perhaps best made in reverse, by the cartoon that shows six surgeons standing around a patient on the operating table with one saying, "Who opens?" Similarly, the policy and marketing courses of the management school may be integrated without the two professors involved ever having even met. As long as the courses are standard, each knows more or less what the other teaches.

Just how standardized complex professional work can be is illustrated in a paper read by Spencer (1976) before a meeting of the International Cardiovascular Society. Spencer notes that "Becoming a skillful clinical surgeon requires a long period of training, probably five or more years" (p. 1178). An important feature of that training is "repetitive practice" to evoke "an automatic reflex" (p. 1179). So automatic, in fact, that Spencer keeps a series of surgical "cookbooks" in which he lists, even for "complex" operations, the essential steps as chains of thirty to forty symbols on a single sheet, to "be reviewed mentally in sixty to 120 seconds at some time during the day preceding the operation" (p. 1182).

But no matter how standardized the knowledge and skills, their complexity ensures that considerable discretion remains in their application. No two professionals—no two surgeons or teachers or social workers—ever apply them in exactly the same way. Many judgments are required, as Perrow (1970) notes of policemen and others:

> There exist numerous plans: when to suspend assistance, when to remove a gun from its holster, when to block off an area, when to call the FBI, and when to remove a child from the home. The existence of such plans does not provide a criterion for choosing the most effective plan. . . . Instead of computation the decision depends upon human judgment. The police patrolman must decide whether to try to disperse the street corner gang or call for reinforcements. The welfare worker must likewise decide if new furniture is an allowable expense, and the high school counselor must decide whether to recommend a college preparatory or vocational program. Categories channel and shape these human judgments but they do not replace them (p. 216).

Training and indoctrination is a complicated affair in the Professional Bureaucracy. The initial training typically takes place over a period of years in a university or special institution. Here the skills and knowledge of the profession are formally programmed into the would-be professional. But in many cases that is only the first step, even if the most important one. There typically follows a long period of on-the-job training, such as internship in medicine and articling in accounting. Here the formal knowledge is applied and the practice of the skills perfected, under the close supervision of members of the profession. On-the-job training also completes the process of indoctrination, which began during the formal teaching. Once this process is completed, the professional association typically examines the trainee to determine whether he has the requisite knowledge, skills, and norms to enter the profession. That is not to say, however, that the individual is "examined for the last time in his life, and is pronounced completely full," such that "After this, no new ideas can be imparted to him," as humorist and academic Stephen Leacock once commented about the Ph.D., the test to enter the profession of university teaching. The entrance examination only tests the basic requirements at one point in time; the process of training continues. As new knowledge is generated and new skills develop, the professional upgrades his expertise. He reads the journals, attends the conferences, and perhaps also returns periodically for formal retraining.

The Bureaucratic Nature of the Structure All of this training is geared to one goal—the internalization of standards that serve the client and coordinate the professional work. In other words, **the structure of these organizations is essentially bureaucratic, its coordination—like that of the Machine Bureaucracy—achieved by design, by standards that predetermine what is to be done.** How bureaucratic is illustrated by Perrow's (1970) description of one well-known hospital department:

> ... obstetrics and gynecology is a relatively routine department, which even has something resembling an assembly (or deassembly?) line wherein the mother moves from room to room and nurse to nurse during the predictable course of her labor. It is also one of the hospital units most often accused of impersonality and depersonalization. For the mother, the birth is unique, but not for the doctor and the rest of the staff who go through this many times a day (p. 74).

But the two kinds of bureaucracies differ markedly in the source of their standardization. **Whereas the Machine Bureaucracy generates its own standards—its technostructure designing the work standards for its operators and its line managers enforcing them—the standards of the Professional Bureaucracy originate largely outside its own structure, in the self-governing associations its operators join with their colleagues from other Professional Bureaucracies.** These associations set universal standards which they make sure are taught by the universities and used by all the bureaucracies of the profession. **So whereas the Machine Bureaucracy relies on authority of a hierarchical nature—the power of office—the Professional Bureaucracy emphasizes authority of a professional nature—the power of expertise** (Blau, 1967-68). Thus, although Montagna (1968) found internal as well as external rules in the large public accounting firms he studied, the latter proved more important. These were imposed by the American Institute of Certified Public Accountants and included an elaborate and much revised code of ethics, a newly codified volume of principles of accounting, and revised auditing standards and procedures.

> These rules serve as a foundation for the firms' more specific internal rules, a few of which are more stringent, others of which merely expand on the external rules. Nearly to a man, the total sample [of accountants questioned] agreed that compared with internal rules, the external rules were the more important rules for their firms and for the profession as a whole (p. 143).

Montagna's findings suggest that the other forms of standardization are difficult to rely on in the Professional Bureaucracy. The work processes themselves are too complex to be standardized directly by analysts. One need only try to imagine a work study analyst following a cardiologist on his rounds or observing a teacher in a classroom in order to program their work. Similarly, the outputs of professional work cannot easily be measured, and so do not lend themselves to standardization. Imagine a planner trying to define a cure in psychiatry, the amount of learning that takes place in the classroom, or the quality of an accountant's audit. Thus, Professional Bureaucracies cannot rely extensively on the formalization of professional work or on systems to plan and control it.

Much the same conclusion can be drawn for the two remaining coordinating mechanisms. Both direct supervision and mutual adjustment impede the professional's close relationships with his clients. That relationship is predicated on a high degree of professional autonomy—freedom from having not only to respond to managerial orders but also to consult extensively with peers. In any event, the use of the other four coordinating mechanisms is precluded by the capacity of the standardization of skills to achieve a good deal of the coordination necessary in the operating core.

The Pigeonholing Process   To understand how the Professional Bureaucracy functions in its operating core, it is helpful to think of it as a repertoire of standard programs—in effect, the set of skills the professionals stand ready to use—which are applied to predetermined situations, called contingencies, also standardized. As Weick (1976) notes of one case in point, "schools are in the business of building and maintaining categories" (p. 8). The process is sometimes known as *pigeonholing*. In this regard, the professional has two basic tasks: (1) to categorize the client's need in terms of a contingency, which indicates which standard program to use, a task known as diagnosis, and (2) to apply, or execute, that program. Pigeonholing simplifies matters enormously. "People are categorized and placed into pigeonholes because it would take enormous resources to treat every case as unique and requiring thorough analysis. Like stereotypes, categories allow us to move through the world without making continuous decisions at every moment" (Perrow, 1970, p. 58). Thus, a psychiatrist examines the patient, declares him to be manic-depressive, and initiates psychotherapy. Similarly, a professor finds 100 students registered in his course and executes his lecture program; faced with 20 instead, he runs the class as a seminar. And the management consultant carries his own bag of standard acronymical tricks—MBO, MIS, LRP, PERT, OD. The client with project work gets PERT, the one with managerial conflicts, OD. Simon (1977) captures the spirit of pigeonholing with his comment that "The pleasure that the good professional experiences in his work is not simply a pleasure in handling difficult matters; it is a pleasure in using skillfully a well-stocked kit of well-designed tools to handle problems that are comprehensible in their deep structure but unfamiliar in their detail" (p. 98).

It is the pigeonholing process that enables the Professional Bureaucracy to decouple its various operating tasks and assign them to individual, relatively autonomous professionals. Each can, instead of giving a great deal of attention to coordinating his work with his peers, focus on perfecting his skills. As Spencer (1976) notes in the case of vascular surgery, "with precise diagnosis and expert operative technique excellent results could almost always be obtained" (p. 1177).

The pigeonholing process does not deny the existence of uncertainty in servicing a client. Rather, it seeks to contain it in the jobs of single professionals. As Bidwell (1965) notes, "The problem of dealing with variability in student abilities and accomplishments during a school year ... is vested in the classroom teacher, and one important component of his professional skill is ability to handle day-to-day fluctuations in the response to instruction by individual students and collectively by the classroom group" (p. 975). The containment of this uncertainty—what Simon characterizes as unfamiliarity in detail in the job of the single professional—is one of the reasons why the professional requires considerable discretion in his work.

In the pigeonholing process, we see fundamental differences among the Machine Bureaucracy, the Professional Bureaucracy, and the Adhocracy. The Machine Bureaucracy is a single-purpose structure: presented with a stimulus, it executes its one standard sequence of programs, just as we kick when tapped on the knee. No diagnosis is involved. In the Professional Bureaucracy, diagnosis is a fundamental task, but it is circumscribed. The organization seeks to match a predetermined contingency to a standard program. Fully open-ended diagnosis—that which seeks a creative solution to a unique problem—requires a third structural configuration, which we call Adhocracy. No standard contingencies or programs exist in that structure.

Segal (1974) refers to these three as "chain-structured," "mediatively-structured," and "adaptively-structured" organizations. The chain-structured organization relates to only a small part of the environment and accepts inputs only at one end; once ingested, these are processed through a fixed sequence of operations. The mediatively-structured organization—our Professional Bureaucracy—is designed "to channel external dissimilarity into uniform organizational categories" (p. 215). Segal cites the example of the welfare department:

> A glance at the telephone numbers individuals must call to initiate contact with the welfare department indicates that the potential client cannot simply need help, he must need help as defined by the organization—aging, adoption, children in trouble, landlord-tenant complaints, etc. (p. 215).

In other words, the welfare department leaves part of the diagnosis to the client. The adaptively-structured organization, or Adhocracy, "is not structured to screen out heterogeneity and uncertainty" (p. 217). It adapts to its client's individual problem rather than trying to fit it into one of its own categories. Segal provides an example of each of these three types of organizations from the field of mental health:

> 1. The chain-structured custodial unit responds to the pressure in the environment to keep mental patients out of the public eye and in physical captivity. The chain-structured custodial unit is thus designed to achieve the singular purpose of custodial behavior.
> 2. The individual treatment structure responds to other pressure in the environment by arranging its units and care to help each patient to fit into a *category* of behavior defined by society. This facility is thus categorically responsive as staff attempts to change patients' behavior so that it fits their own standards of "normality."
> 3. The adaptively-structured milieu treatment ward responds to a more relativistic environmental pressure. In this instance, units and roles are arranged so that the very definition of normality is a product of interaction between staff and patients (p. 218).[1]

It is an interesting characteristic of the Professional Bureaucracy that its pigeonholing process creates an equivalence in its structure between the functional and market bases for grouping. **Because clients are categorized— or, as in the case of the welfare recipients above, categorize themselves—in terms of the functional specialists who serve them, the structure of the Professional Bureaucracy becomes at the same time both a functional and a market-based one.** Two illustrations help explain the point. A hospital gynecology department and a university chemistry department can be called functional because they group specialists according to the knowledge, skills, and work processes they use, or market-based because each unit deals with its own unique types of clients—women in the first case, chemistry students in the second. Thus, the distinction between functional and market bases for grouping breaks down in the special case of the Professional Bureaucracy.

Focus on the Operating Core   All the design parameters that we have discussed so far—the emphasis on the training of operators, their vertically enlarged jobs, the little use made of behavior formalization or

---

[1]For an excellent related example—a comparison of the prison as a Machine Bureaucracy (custodial-oriented) and as a Professional Bureaucracy (treatment-oriented)—see Cressey (1958; or 1965, pp. 1044-1048). Van de Ven and Delbecq (1974) also discuss this trichotomy in terms of "systematized" programs, which specify both means and ends in detail, "discretionary" programs, which specify ends and a repertoire of means but require the operator to select the means in terms of the ends, and "developmental" programs, for highly variable tasks, which may specify general ends but not the means to achieve them.

planning and control systems—suggest that **the operating core is the key part of the Professional Bureaucracy. The only other part that is fully elaborated is the support staff, but that is focused very much on serving the operating core.** Given the high cost of the professionals, it makes sense to back them up with as much support as possible, to aid them and have others do whatever routine work can be formalized. For example, universities have printing facilities, faculty clubs, alma mater funds, building and grounds departments, publishing houses, archives, bookstores, information offices, museums, athletics departments, libraries, computer facilities, and many, many other support units.

The technostructure and middle line of management are not highly elaborated in the Professional Bureaucracy. In other configurations (except Adhocracy), they coordinate the work of the operating core. But in the Professional Bureaucracy, they can do little to coordinate the operating work. The need for planning or the formalizing of the work of the professionals is very limited, so there is little call for a technostructure (except, as we shall see, in the case of the nonprofessional support staff). In McGill University, for example, an institution with 17,000 students and 1200 professors, the only units that could be identified by the author as technocratic were two small departments concerned with finance and budgeting, a small planning office, and a center to develop the professors' skills in pedagogy (the latter two fighting a continual uphill battle for acceptance).

Likewise, the middle line in the Professional Bureaucracy is thin. With little need for direct supervision of the operators, or mutual adjustment between them, the operating units can be very large, with few managers at the level of first-line supervisor, or, for that matter, above them. The McGill Faculty of Management at the time of this writing has fifty professors and a single manager, its dean.

Thus, Figure 19-1 shows the Professional Bureaucracy, in terms of our logo, as a flat structure with a thin middle line, a tiny technostructure, and a fully elaborated support staff. All these features are reflected in the organigram of McGill University, shown in Figure 19-2.

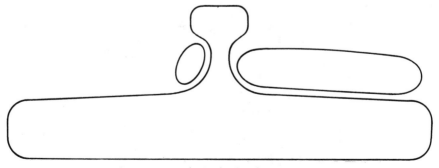

Figure 19-1. *The Professional Bureaucracy*

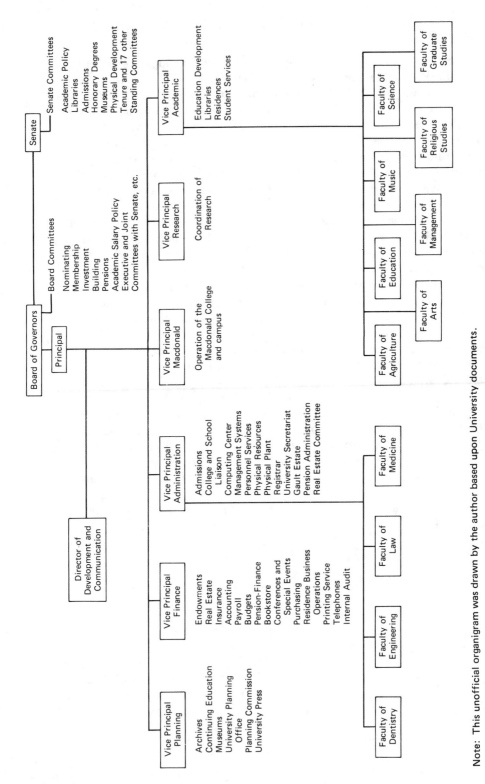

Note: This unofficial organigram was drawn by the author based upon University documents.

Figure 19-2. *Organigram of McGill University (circa 1978, used permission)*

Decentralization in the Professional Bureaucracy Everything we have seen so far tells us that the Professional Bureaucracy is a highly decentralized structure, in both the vertical and horizontal dimensions. A great deal of the power over the operating work rests at the bottom of the structure, with the professionals of the operating core. Often each works with his own clients, subject only to the collective control of his colleagues, who trained and indoctrinated him in the first place and thereafter reserve the right to censure him for malpractice.

The professional's power derives from the fact that not only is his work too complex to be supervised by managers or standardized by analysts, but also that his services are typically in great demand. This gives the professional mobility, which enables him to insist on considerable autonomy in his work. The professional tends to identify more with his profession than with the organization where he practices it. Thus, Perrow (1965, p. 959) talks of the "stronger grip" of the medical profession on its members than the specific hospital, while Beyer and Lodahl (1976) note in academia that "Many faculty members receive an important part of their rewards—recognition—from their scientific communities, and this reward is only secondarily reinforced by their universities" (p. 124). In these organizations, even "promotion is not related to the climbing of an administrative ladder but to professional progress, or the ability to handle more and more complex professional problems" (SIAR, 1975, p. 62). Thus, when the professional does not get the autonomy he feels he requires, he is tempted to pick up his kit bag of skills and move on.

One is inclined to ask why professionals bother to join organizations in the first place. There are, in fact, a number of good reasons. For one thing, professionals can share resources, including support services, in a common organization. One surgeon cannot afford his own operating theater, so he shares it with others, just as professors share laboratories, lecture halls, libraries, and printing facilities. Organizations also bring professionals together to learn from each other, and to train new recruits.

Some professionals must join the organization to get clients. The clients present themselves to an organization that houses many different kinds of professionals, depending on it to diagnose their problem and direct them to the individual professional who can best serve them. Thus, while some physicians have their private patients, others receive them from the hospital emergency department or from in-patient referrals. In universities, students select the department where they wish to study—in effect, diagnosing their own general needs—but that department, in turn, helps direct them into specific courses given by individual professors.

Another reason professionals band together to form organizations is that the clients often need the services of more than one at the same time. An operation requires at least a surgeon, an anesthesiologist, and a nurse;

an MBA program cannot be run with less than about a dozen different specialists. Finally, the bringing together of different types of professionals allows clients to be transferred between them when the initial diagnosis proves incorrect or the needs of the client change during execution. When the kidney patient develops heart trouble, that is no time to change hospitals in search of a cardiologist. Similarly, when a law student finds his client needs a course in moral ethics, or an accountant finds his client needs tax advice, it is comforting to know that other departments in the same organization stand ready to provide the necessary service.

The Administrative Structure   What we have seen so far suggests that the Professional Bureaucracy is a highly democratic structure, at least for the professionals of the operating core. In fact, **not only do the professionals control their own work, but they also seek collective control of the administrative decisions that affect them,** decisions, for example, to hire colleagues, to promote them, and to distribute resources. Controlling these decisions requires control of the middle line of the organization, which professionals do by ensuring that it is staffed with "their own." Some of the administrative work the operating professionals do themselves. Every university professor, for example, carries out some administrative duties and serves on committees of one kind or another to ensure that he retains some control over the decisions that affect his work. Moreover, full-time administrators who wish to have any power at all in these structures must be certified members of the profession, and preferably be elected by the professional operators or at least appointed with their blessing. What emerges, therefore, is a rather democratic administrative structure. The university department chairmen, many of them elected, together with the deans, vice-presidents, and president—all of them necessarily academics— must work alongside a parallel hierarchy of committees of professors, many of them elected, ranging from the departmental curriculum committee to the powerful university senate (shown with its own subcommittees in Figure 19-2). This can be seen clearly in Figure 19-3, the organigram of a typical university hospital. The plethora of committees is shown on the right side, reporting up from the medical departments through the Council of Physicians and Dentists directly to the Board of Trustees, bypassing the managerial hierarchy entirely. (Notice also the large number of support services in the organization and the relative absence of technocratic units.)

The nature of the administrative structure—which itself relies on mutual adjustment for coordination—indicates that the liaison devices, while uncommon in the operating core, are important design parameters in the middle line. Standing committees and ad hoc task forces abound, as was seen in Figure 19-3; a number of positions are designated to integrate the administrative efforts, as in the case of the ward manager in the hospital;

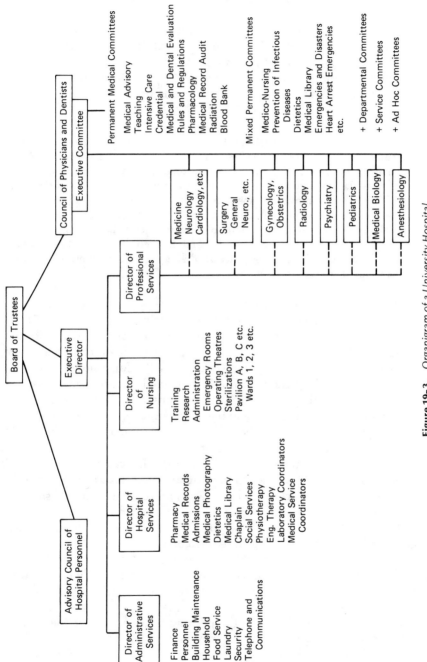

Figure 19-3. *Organigram of a University Hospital*

Board of Trustees

Advisory Council of Hospital Personnel

Council of Physicians and Dentists

Executive Director

Executive Committee

Director of Administrative Services

Finance
Personnel
Building Maintenance
Household
Food Service
Laundry
Security
Telephone and Communications

Director of Hospital Services

Pharmacy
Medical Records
Admissions
Medical Photography
Dietetics
Medical Library
Chaplain
Social Services
Physiotherapy
Eng. Therapy
Laboratory Coordinators
Medical Service Coordinators

Director of Nursing

Training
Research
Administration
Emergency Rooms
Operating Theatres
Sterilizations
Pavilion A, B, C etc.
Wards 1, 2, 3 etc.

Director of Professional Services

Medicine
Neurology
Cardiology, etc.

Surgery
General
Neuro., etc.

Gynecology, Obstetrics

Radiology

Psychiatry

Pediatrics

Medical Biology

Anesthesiology

Permanent Medical Committees

Medical Advisory
Teaching
Intensive Care
Credential
Medical and Dental Evaluation
Rules and Regulations
Pharmacology
Medical Record Audit
Radiation
Blood Bank

Mixed Permanent Committees

Medico-Nursing
Prevention of Infectious Diseases
Dietetics
Medical Library
Emergencies and Disasters
Heart Arrest Emergencies
etc.

+ Departmental Committees
+ Service Committees
+ Ad Hoc Committees

and some Professional Bureaucracies even use matrix structure in administration.

Because of the power of their operators, Professional Bureaucracies
are sometimes called "collegial" organizations. In fact, some professionals
like to describe them as inverse pyramids, with the professional operators at
the top and the administrators down below to serve them—to ensure that
the surgical facilities are kept clean and the classrooms well supplied with
chalk. Thus comments Amitai Etzioni (1959), the well-known sociologist:

> ... in professional organizations the staff-expert line-manager correlation,
> insofar as such a correlation exists at all, is reversed. ... Managers in profes-
> sional organizations are in charge of secondary activities; they administer
> *means* to the major activity carried out by experts. In other words, if there is a
> staff–line relationship at all, experts constitute the line (major authority) struc-
> ture and managers the staff. ... The final internal decision is, functionally
> speaking, in the hands of various professionals and their decision-making
> bodies. The professor decides what research he is going to undertake and to a
> large degree what he is going to teach; the physician determines what treat-
> ment should be given to the patient (p. 52).

Etzioni's description may underestimate the power of the *professional*
administrator—an issue we shall return to shortly—but it seems to be an
accurate description of the nonprofessional one, namely the administrator
who manages the support units. For the support staff—often much larger
than the professional one, but charged largely with doing nonprofessional
work—there is no democracy in the Professional Bureaucracy, only the
oligarchy of the professionals. Support units, such as housekeeping
or kitchen in the hospital, printing in the university, are as likely as not to be
managed tightly from the top. They exist, in effect, as machine bureaucratic
constellations within the Professional Bureaucracy.

**What frequently emerge in the Professional Bureaucracy are parallel
administrative hierarchies, one democratic and bottom up for the professionals, and a second machine bureaucratic and top down for the support
staff.** As Bidwell (1965) notes: "The segregation of professional and nonprofessional hierarchies in school systems presumably permit this differentiation of modes of control" (p. 1016; see also Blau, 1967–68).

In the professional hierarchy, power resides in expertise; one has
influence by virtue of one's knowledge and skills. In other words, a good
deal of power remains at the bottom of the hierarchy, with the professional
operators themselves. That does not, of course, preclude a pecking order
among them. But it does require the pecking order to mirror the professionals experience and expertise. As they gain experience and reputation,
academics move through the ranks of lecturer, and then assistant, associate,
and full professor; and physicians enter the hospital as interns and move up
to residents before they become members of the staff.

In the nonprofession hierarchy, power and status reside in administrative office; one salutes the stripes, not the man. The situation is that Weber originally described: "each lower office is under the control and supervision of a higher one" (cited in Blau, 1967–68, p. 455). Unlike the professional structure, here one must practice administration, not a specialized function of the organization, to attain status.

But "research indicates that a professional orientation toward service and a bureaucratic orientation toward disciplined compliance with procedures are opposite approaches toward work and often create conflict in organizations" (Blau, 1967–68, p. 456). Hence, these two parallel hierarchies are kept quite independent of each other. The two may come together at some intermediate level, as when a university dean oversees both the professional and secretarial staff. But often, as shown in Figure 19-4, they remain separate right up to the strategic apex. The hospital medical staff, as shown in Figure 19-3, does not even report to the executive director—the chief executive officer—but directly to the board of trustees. (Indeed, Charns [1976] reports that 41 percent of physicians he surveyed in academic medical centers claimed they were responsible to no one!)

The Roles of the Professional Administrator Where does all this leave the administrators of the professional hierarchy, the executive directors and chiefs of the hospitals and the presidents and deans of the universities? Are they as powerless as Etzioni suggests? Compared with their peers in the Simple Structure and the Machine Bureaucracy, they certainly lack a good deal of power. But that is far from the whole story. While the professional administrator may not be able to control the professionals directly, he does perform a series of roles that gives him considerable indirect power in the structure.

First, **the professional administrator spends much time handling disturbances in the structure.** The pigeonholing process is an imperfect one at best, leading to all kinds of jurisdictional disputes between the professionals.

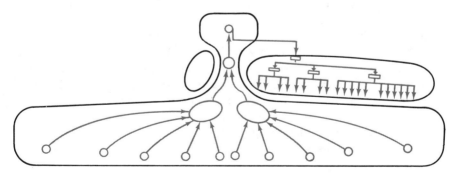

Figure 19-4. *Parallel Hierarchies in the Professional Bureaucracy*

Who should teach the statistics course in the MBA program, the mathematics department or the business school? Who should perform mastectomies in hospitals, surgeons who specialize in operations or gyneocologists who specialize in women? Seldom, however, can a senior administrator *impose* a solution on the professionals or units involved in a dispute. Rather the unit managers—chiefs, deans, or whoever—must sit down together and *negotiate* a solution on behalf of their constituencies. Coordination problems also arise frequently between the two parallel hierarchies, and it often falls to the professional administrator to resolve them.

Second, **the professional administrators—especially those at higher levels—serve key roles at the boundary of the organization, between the professionals inside and interested parties—governments, client associations, and so on—on the outside.** On one hand, the administrators are expected to protect the professionals' autonomy, to "buffer" them from external pressures. "The principal is expected to 'back the teacher up'—support her authority in all cases of parental 'interference'" (Melcher, 1976, p. 334). So, too, the executive director of the hospital is supposed to keep the government or the trustees from interfering in the work of the physicians. On the other hand, the administrators are expected to woo these outsiders to support the organization, both morally and financially. ". . . teachers consider it a prime responsibility of the administrator to secure for them the greatest possible amount of resources" (Hills, quoted in Melcher, 1976, p. 333), as do professors in universities and physicians in hospitals. Thus, the external roles of the manager—maintaining liaison contacts, acting as figurehead and spokesman in a public relations capacity, negotiating with outside agencies—emerge as primary ones in the job of the professional administrator.

Some view the roles professional administrators are called upon to perform as signs of weakness. Like Etzioni, they see these people as the errand boys of the professionals, or else as pawns caught in various tugs of war—between one professional and another, between support staffer and professional, between outsider and professional. In fact, however, these roles are the very sources of administrator power. Power is, after all, gained at the locus of uncertainty. And that is exactly where the professional administrators sit. The administrator who succeeds in raising extra funds for his organization gains a say in how these are distributed. Similarly, the one who can reconcile conflicts in favor of his unit or who can effectively buffer the professionals from external influence becomes a valued—and therefore powerful—member of the organization. The professionals well know that "Without the 'superb politician,' metropolitan school systems, urban governments, universities, mental hospitals, social work systems, and similar complex organizations would be immobilized" (Thompson, 1967, p. 143).

Ironically, **the professional becomes dependent on the effective administrator.** The professional faces a fundamental dilemma. Frequently, he abhors administration, desiring only to be left alone to practice his profession. But that freedom is gained only at the price of administrative effort —raising funds, resolving conflicts, buffering the demands of outsiders. This leaves the professional two choices: to do the administrative work himself, in which case he has less time to practice his profession, or to leave it to administrators, in which case he must surrender some of his power over decision making. And that power must be surrendered, it should further be noted, to administrators who, by virtue of the fact that they no longer wish to practice the profession, probably favor a different set of goals. Damned if he does and damned if he doesn't. Take the case of the university professor oriented to research. To ensure the fullest support for research in his department, he should involve himself in committees where questions of the commitment to teaching versus research are decided. But that takes time, specifically time away from research. What is the use of spending time protecting what one has no time left to do? So the professor is tempted to leave administration to full-time administrators, those who have expressed a disinterest in research by virtue of seeking full-time administrative office.

We can conclude that **power in these structures does flow to those professionals who care to devote the effort to doing administrative instead of professional work**—a considerable amount of power, in fact, to those who do it well, especially in complex professional organizations, such as the modern hospital (Perrow, 1967). **But that, it should be stressed, is not laissez-faire power: the professional administrator keeps his power only as long as the professionals perceive him to be serving their interests effectively.** The managers of the Professional Bureaucracy may be the weakest among those of the five structural configurations, but they are far from impotent. *Individually*, they are usually more powerful than individual professionals —the chief executive remaining the single most powerful member of the Professional Bureaucracy—even if that power can easily be overwhelmed by the *collective* power of the professionals.

Strategy Formulation in the Professional Bureaucracy   A description of the strategy formulation process in the Professional Bureaucracy perhaps best illustrates the two sides of the professional administrator's power. At the outset it should be noted that strategy takes on a very different form in these kinds of organizations. Since their outputs are difficult to measure, their goals cannot easily be agreed upon. So **the notion of a strategy—a single, integrated pattern of decisions common to the entire organization—loses a good deal of its meaning in the Professional Bureaucracy.**

Given the autonomy of each professional—his close working relation-ships with his clients, and his loose ones with his colleagues—it becomes sensible to think in terms of a personal strategy for each professional. In many cases, each selects his own clients and his own methods of dealing with them—in effect, he chooses his own product-market strategy. But professionals do not select their clients and methods at random. They are significantly constrained by the professional standards and skills they have learned. That is, the professional associations and training institutions outside the organization play a major role in determining the strategies that the professionals pursue. Thus, to an important extent all organizations in a given profession exhibit similar strategies, imposed on them from the out-side. These strategies—concerning what clients to serve and how—are inculcated in the professionals during their formal training and are modified as new needs emerge and the new methods developed to cope with them gain acceptance by the professional associations. In medicine, for example, researchers develop new forms of treatment and test them experimentally. They publish their results in the medical journals, these publications leading to more experimentation and elaboration until the methods are considered sufficiently safe to pass into standard practice—that is, to become part of the repertoire of programs of all hospitals. And this whole process is over-seen by the professional associations, which pass judgments on acceptable and unacceptable practices, and through whose journals, newsletters, con-ferences, and training programs information on new practices is dissemi-nated. This control of strategy can sometimes be very direct: in one of the McGill studies, a hospital that refused to adopt a new method of treatment was, in effect, censured when one of the associations of medical specialists passed a resolution declaring failure to use it tantamount to malpractice.

We can conclude, therefore, that **the strategies of the Professional Bureaucracy are largely ones of the individual professionals within the organization as well as of the professional associations on the outside.** Largely, but not completely. There are still degrees of freedom that allow each organization within the profession to adapt the basic strategies to its own needs and interests. There are, for example, mental hospitals, women's hospitals, and veterans' hospitals; all conform to standard medical practice, but each applies it to a different market which it has selected.

How do these organizational strategies get made? It would appear that **the Professional Bureaucracy's own strategies represent the cumulative effect over time of the projects, or strategic "initiatives," that its members are able to convince it to undertake**—to buy a new piece of equipment in a hospital, to establish a new degree program in a university, to develop a new specialty department in an accounting firm. Most of these initiatives are proposed by members of the operating core—by "professional entrepreneurs" willing to expend the efforts needed to negotiate the acceptance of new projects through the complex administrative structure (and if the method is new and controversial, through outside professional associations as well, and also through outside funding agencies if the project is an expensive one). A proposal for a new Ph.D. program in management at McGill University was worked out by an ad hoc committee and then approved within the Faculty of Management by its Graduate Program Committee, Academic Committee, and Faculty Council; from there it went to the Executive Committee and the Council of the Faculty of Graduate Studies; then it moved on to the Academic Policy Committee of the Senate of the University and then to the full Senate itself; from there it went to the University Programs Committee of the Quebec government Ministry of Education and then into the Ministry itself, and then back and forth between these bodies and the university administration a few more times until it was finally approved (as a joint program of four universities).

What is the role of the professional administrator in all this? Certainly far from passive. As noted earlier, administration is neither the forte nor the interest of the operating professional (for good reason, as should be clear from the example above!). So he depends on the full-time administrator to help him negotiate his project through the system. For one thing, the administrator has time to worry about such matters—after all, administration is his job; he no longer practices the profession. For another, the administrator has a full knowledge of the administrative committee system as well as many personal contacts within it, both of which are necessary to see project through it. The administrator deals with the system every day; the professional entrepreneur may promote only one new project in his entire career. Finally, the administrator is more likely to have the requisite managerial skills, for example, those of negotiation and persuasion.

But the power of the effective administrator to influence strategy goes beyond helping the professionals. Every good manager seeks to change his organization in his own way, to alter its strategies to make it more effective. In the Professional Bureaucracy, this translates into a set of strategic initiatives that the administrator himself wishes to take. But in these structures—in principle bottom up—the administrator cannot impose his will on the professionals of the operating core. Instead, he must rely on his informal power, and apply it subtly. Knowing that the professionals want nothing more than to be left alone, the administrator moves carefully—in incremental steps, each one hardly discernible. In this way, he may achieve over time changes that the professionals would have rejected out of hand had they been proposed all at once.

To conclude, we have seen again that while the weak administrator of the Professional Bureaucracy may be no more than the errand boy of the professionals, the strong one—a professional himself, politically adept and fully aware of the power system of his organization—can play a major role in changing its strategies.

CONDITIONS OF THE PROFESSIONAL
BUREAUCRACY

This third structural configuration appears wherever the operating core of an organization is dominated by skilled workers—professionals— who use procedures that are difficult to learn yet are well defined. This means an environment that is both complex and stable—complex enough to require the use of difficult procedures that can be learned only in extensive formal training programs, yet stable enough to enable these skills to become well defined, in effect, standardized. Thus, the environment is the chief contingency factor in the use of the Professional Bureaucracy.

In contrast, the factors of age and size are of less significance. Larger professional organizations tend to be somewhat more formalized (Hold-away et al., 1975; Bidwell, 1965, p. 1017)[2] and to have more fully developed staff support structures (Bidwell, 1965, p. 977). But that does not preclude the existence of small Professional Bureaucracies, or, for that matter, of young ones as well. The Machine Bureaucracy has a start-up time because the standards need to be worked out within the organization. Thus, it passes through a period of Simple Structure before its procedures become routinized. In the Professional Bureaucracy, in contrast, the skilled employees bring the standards into the organization with them when they join. So there is little start-up time. Put a group of doctors in a new hospital or a group of lawyers in a new law office and in no time they are functioning as if they had been there for years. Size would seem to be a relatively minor contingency factor for the same reason, and also because the professionals to a large extent work independently. One accountant working on his own adheres to the same professional standards as 2000 working in a giant firm. Thus, Professional Bureaucracies hardly pass through the stage of Simple Structure in their formative years.

[2]Boland (1973) finds them also to be more democratic, which seems to stem from their being more formalized: "The faculty in the larger institutions are much more likely to develop a strong faculty government. Those in the smaller institutions, on the other hand, are more often subject to the decrees of administrative officials" (p. 636). This seems akin to the situation Crozier described, where the operators of large bureaucratic organizations force in rules to protect their interests. But that seems to work more to the operators' advantage in Professional rather than in Machine Bureaucracies, in the former case the rules setting up the means for true self-government, in the latter, serving only to protect the workers from the arbitrary whims of their bosses.

Technical system is an important contingency factor, at least for what it is not in the Professional Bureaucracy—neither highly regulating, sophisticated, nor automated. The professional operators of this structural configuration require considerable discretion in their work. It is they who serve the clients, usually directly and personally. So the technical system cannot be highly regulating, certainly not highly automated. As Heydebrand and Noell (1973) point out, the professional resists the rationalization of his skills—their division into simply executed steps—because that makes them programmable by the technostructure, destroys his basis of autonomy, and drives the structure to the machine bureaucratic form.

Nor can the technical system be sophisticated. That would pull the professional into a closer working relationship with his colleagues and push him to a more distant one with his clients, driving the organization toward another structural configuration—the adhocratic form. The surgeon uses a scalpel, the accountant a pencil. Both must be sharp, but are otherwise simple and commonplace instruments; yet both allow their users to perform independently what can be exceedingly complex functions. More sophisticated instruments—such as the computer in the accounting firm or the coronary care unit in the hospital—reduce the professional's autonomy by forcing him to work in multidisciplinary teams, as he does in the Adhocracy. These teams are concerned in large part with the design, modification, and maintenance of the equipment; its operation, because that tends to be regulating, and often automated, impersonalizes the relationship between the professional and his clients. Thus, **in the pure form of the Professional Bureaucracy, the technology of the organization—its knowledge base—is sophisticated but its technical system—the set of instruments it uses to apply that knowledge base—is not.**

Thus, the prime example of the Professional Bureaucracy is the *personal service organization*, at least the one with complex, stable work. Schools and universities, consulting firms, law and accounting offices, social work agencies all rely on this structural configuration as long as they concentrate not on innovating in the solution of new problems, but on applying standard programs to well-defined ones. The same is true of hospitals, at least to the extent that their technical systems are simple. (In those areas that call for more sophisticated equipment—apparently a growing number, especially in teaching institutions—the hospital is driven toward a hybrid structure, with characteristics of the Adhocracy. The research function would also seem to drive it, and the university as well, toward the same hybrid, research being oriented more than clinical practice and teaching to innovation.[3] The same effect results from dynamic environmental condi-

---

[3]However, Kuhn's (1970) description of the practice of scientific research gives the distinct impression that most of the time—namely during periods of what he calls "normal" science,

tions—again increasingly common in teaching hospitals. But all these forces are strongly mitigated by the hospital's overriding concern with safety. Only the tried and true can be used on regular patients. Institutions entrusted with the lives of their clients have a natural aversion to the looser, organic structures such as Adhocracy.)

A good deal of the service sector of contemporary society in fact applies standard programs to well-defined problems. Hence, the Professional Bureaucracy structure tends to predominate there. And with the enormous growth of this sector in the last few decades, we find that the Professional Bureaucracy has emerged as a major structural configuration.

So far, all of our examples have come from the service sector. But Professional Bureaucracies are found in manufacturing too, notably where the environment demands work that is complex yet stable, and the technical system is neither regulating nor sophisticated. This is the case of the *craft enterprise,* an important variant of the Professional Bureaucracy. Here the organization relies on skilled craftsmen who use relatively simple instruments to product standard outputs. The very term "craftsman" implies a kind of professional who learns traditional skills through long apprentice training and then is allowed to practice them free of direct supervision. Craft enterprises seem typically to have tiny administrations—no technostructures and few managers, many of whom, in any event, work alongside the craftsmen.

Many craftsmen were eliminated by the Industrial Revolution. Their jobs—for example, the making of shoes—were rationalized, and so control over them passed from the workers who did them to the analysts who designed them. Small craft enterprises metamorphosed into large Machine Bureaucracies. But some craft industries remain, for example, fine glasswork and handmade pottery, portrait photography, and gastronomic cuisine.[4] In fact, as these examples indicate, the term "craft" has today come to be associated with functional art, handmade items that perform a function but are purchased for their aesthetic value.

There is at least one major industry that has remained largely in the craft stage, and that is construction. In a paper entitled "Bureaucratic and Craft Administration of Production: A Comparative Study," Stinchcombe (1959–60) contrasts mass production and construction firms, describing the latter much as we have described Professional Bureaucracy. He notes that "professionalization of the labor force in the construction industry serves the same functions as bureaucratic administration in mass production

---

when the researchers are essentially elaborating and perfecting a given "paradigm"—the professional bureaucratic structure might be equally appropriate. Only during scientific "revolutions" should the adhocratic one clearly be more relevant.

[4]Restaurants can be viewed as falling into the manufacturing or service sectors, depending on whether one focuses on the preparation of the food or on the serving of it.

industries" (p. 169). In construction, "work processes [are] governed by the worker in accordance with the empirical lore that makes up craft principles" (p. 170). As a result, few clerks are needed (20 percent of the administrative personnel, versus 53 percent in mass production, where they are used, Stinchcombe explains, to effect machine bureaucratic control), the communication system is less formalized, and less emphasis is placed on the hierarchy of authority. Stinchcombe also cites another study of the construction industry that noted "the low development of distinctly bureaucratic production control mechanisms, such as cost accounting, detailed scheduling, regularized reporting of work process, and standardized inspection of specific operations" (p. 182).[5]

The markets of the Professional Bureaucracy are often diversified. As noted earlier, these organizations often bring together groups of professionals from different specialties who serve different types of clients. The hospital includes gynecologists to serve women, pediatricians to serve children, and so on, while the university has its philosophy professors to teach those interested in general knowledge and its management professors for those in search of specific career skills. Hypothesis 11 would lead us to the conclusion that such market diversity encourages the use of the market basis for grouping the professionals. In fact, we have already seen this to be the case (although we also saw that the market basis for grouping turns out to be equivalent to the functional one in Professional Bureaucracies, as a result of the way in which professional services are selected).

Sometimes the markets of Professional Bureaucracies are diversified geographically, leading to a variant we call the *dispersed professional bureaucracy*. Here the problem of maintaining loyalty to the organization becomes magnified, since the professionals do their autonomous work in remote locations, far from the administrative structure. The Royal Canadian Mounted Police, for example, were dispersed across the Canadian west and north late last century to bring order to what were then lawless districts of the country. Once sent out, each Mountie was on his own. The same situation exists today in intelligence (spy) agencies, forest ranger services, and international consulting firms. As a result, these organizations must rely extensively on training and indoctrination, especially the latter. The employees are selected carefully, trained extensively, and indoctrinated heavily—often by the organization itself—before they are sent out to the remote areas to perform their work. Thus, even on their own, the Mounties carried the norms and skills of the R.C.M.P. with them and so served it resolutely. Moreover, the employees of the dispersed professional bureaucracy are frequently brought back to the central headquarters for a fresh

---

[5]Stinchcombe also ascribes some of these structural characteristics to the dynamic nature of the construction industry's environment, which pushes the firms to adopt the organic features of Simple Structure or Adhocracy.

dose of indoctrination, and they are often rotated in their jobs to ensure that their loyalty remains with the organization and does not shift to the geographical area they serve. The U.S. Forest Rangers, for example, are recruited largely from the forestry schools—having already demonstrated a commitment to forests and a love of the outdoors—and are then further trained and indoctrinated, and, once on the job, are rotated from post to post. Both the rotation and indoctrination "facilitate communication between headquarters and the field by keeping loyalties and career interests centrally directed" as well as keeping "the foresters independent of private interests in the regions or communities in which they serve . . ." (Wilensky, 1967, pp. 59–60; see also Kaufman, 1960).

This chapter has stressed the role of training in the Professional Bureaucracy more than indoctrination. Indoctrination only emerged as important in this last variant. But there is another variant, the *missionary organization*—common in religious orders, charitable foundations (Sills, 1957), and the like, and sometimes found also in business firms (Perrow, 1970, pp. 166–170)—where indoctrination replaces training as the key design parameter. Because this organization has an attractive mission, and perhaps a distinguished history as well, its members also share a strong ideology—a set of norms about the goals and strategies the organization pursues. The members may come by this naturally, or they may have been indoctrinated into the ideology when they first joined. In any event, because every member of the organization can be trusted to pursue its main goals and strategies, there can be an extensive decentralization to the level of the single individual, resulting in a structure that in some ways resembles the Professional Bureaucracy.

The Professional Bureaucracy is also occasionally found as a hybrid structure. In our discussion of hospitals earlier, we alluded to a possible combination with characteristics of the Adhocracy which we can call the *professional bureau/adhocracy*. Another hybrid—the *simple professional bureaucracy*—occurs when highly trained professionals practicing standard skills nevertheless take their lead from a strong, sometimes even autocratic, leader, as in the Simple Structure. Consider, for example, the following description of a symphony orchestra, an organization staffed with highly skilled musicians who play standard repertoires:

> An orchestra is not a democracy but a dictatorship. The interpretation and presentation of this complex repertoire cannot be pieced together as a kind of consensus among the musicians.
>
> Such a system has been tried out, notably in Russia in the 1920's, but the famous conductorless orchestra, Persimfans, lasted only a few years. There were countless long rehearsals while the musicians argued about the treatment of every passage, and any one of the members was given the democratic right, in turn, to lay down his instrument and listen to the effect from the hall.

It was finally decided that it would be much more efficient, and less costly, to allow one man of recognized ability to impose his ideas upon the rest of the orchestra, a conclusion the rest of the European orchestras had reached more than a century earlier. . . .

I think it was one of Szell's musicians who was quoted as saying: "He's a sonovabitch, but he makes us play beyond ourselves."[6]

Finally, we might note briefly the effects of the contingency factors of power, notably fashion and the influence of the operators. Professionalism is a popular word among all kinds of identifiable specialists today; as a result, **Professional Bureaucracy is a highly fashionable structure**—and for good reason, since it is a very democratic one. Thus, it is to the advantage of every operator to make his job more professional—to enhance the skills it requires, to keep the analysts of the technostructure from rationalizing those skills, and to establish associations that set industry-wide standards to protect those skills. In these ways, the operator can achieve what always escapes him in the Machine Bureaucracy—control of his work and the decisions that affect it.

SOME ISSUES ASSOCIATED WITH PROFESSIONAL BUREAUCRACY

The Professional Bureaucracy is unique among the five structural configurations in answering two of the paramount needs of contemporary men and women. It is democratic, disseminating its power directly to its workers (at least those who are professional). And it provides them with extensive autonomy, freeing them even of the need to coordinate closely with their peers, and all of the pressures and politics that entails. Thus, the professional has the best of both worlds: he is attached to an organization, yet is free to serve his clients in his own way, constrained only by the established standards of his profession.

As a result, professionals tend to emerge as responsible and highly motivated individuals, dedicated to their work and the clients they serve. Unlike the Machine Bureaucracy that places barriers between the operator and the client, this structure removes them, allowing a personal relationship to develop. Here the technical and social systems can function in complete harmony.

Moreover, **autonomy allows the professionals to perfect their skills, free of interference.** They repeat the same complex programs time after time, forever reducing the uncertainty until they get them just about perfect, like the Provençal potter who has spent his career perfecting the glazes he

[6]From "MSD Crisis Plus ça change" by E. McLean, Canada Wide Feature Service in the *Montreal Star*, December 4, 1976. Used with permission.

applies to identical pots. The professional's thought processes are "convergent"—vascular surgeon Spencer (1976) refers to them as deductive reasoning. Spencer quotes approvingly the bridge aficionado who stood behind champion Charles Goren during a three-day tournament and concluded: "He didn't do anything I couldn't do, except he didn't make any mistakes" (p. 1181). That captures nicely the secure feelings of professionals and their clients in Professional Bureaucracies. The Provencal potter expects few surprises when he opens his kiln; so, too do Dr. Spencer's patients when they climb on to his operating table. They know the program has been executed so many times—by this surgeon as well as by the many whose experiences he has read about in the journals—that the possibility of mistakes has been minimized. Hospitals do not even get to execute new programs on regular patients until they have been thoroughly tested and approved by the profession. So the client of the Professional Bureaucracy can take satisfaction in the knowledge that the professional about to serve him will draw on vast quantities of experience and skill, will apply them in a perfected, not an experimental procedure, and will likely be highly motivated in performing that procedure.

But in these same characteristics of democracy and autonomy lie all the major problems of the Professional Bureaucracy. For **there is virtually no control of the work outside the profession, no way to correct deficiencies that the professionals themselves choose to overlook.** What they tend to overlook are the major problems of coordination, of discretion, and of innovation that arise in these structures.

Problems of Coordination   The Professional Bureaucracy can coordinate effectively only by the standardization of skills. Direct supervision and mutual adjustment are resisted as direct infringements on the professional's autonomy, in one case by administrators, in the other by peers. And standardization of work processes and of outputs are ineffective for this complex work with its ill-defined outputs. But **the standardization of skills is a loose coordinating mechanism at best, failing to cope with many of the needs that arise in the Professional Bureaucracy.**

There is, first of all, the need for coordination between the professional and the support staff. To the professional, that is simply resolved: he gives the orders. But that only catches the support staffer between two systems of power pulling in different ways, the vertical power of line authority above him, and the horizontal power of professional expertise to his side.

Perhaps more severe are the coordination problems between the professionals themselves. Unlike Machine Bureaucracies, Professional Bureaucracies are not integrated entities. They are collections of individuals who join to draw on the common resources and support services but otherwise want to be left alone. As long as the pigeonholing process works effectively, they can be. But that process can never be so good that contingencies do not fall in the cracks between the standard programs. The world is a continuous intertwined system. Slicing it up, although necessary to comprehend it, inevitably distorts it. Needs that fall at the margin or that overlap two categories tend to get forced—artificially—into one category or another. In contemporary medicine, for instance, the human body is treated not so much as one integrated system with interdependent parts, as a collection of loosely coupled organs that correspond to the different specialties. For the patient whose malady slots nicely into one of the specialties, problems of coordination do not arise. For others—for example, the patient who falls between psychiatry and internal medicine—it means repeated transfers in search of the right department, a time-consuming process when time is critical. In universities the pigeonholing process can be equally artificial, as in the case of the professor interested in the structure of production systems who fell between the operations and organizational behavior departments of his business school and so was denied tenure.

The pigeonholing process, in fact, emerges as the source of a great deal of the conflict of the Professional Bureaucracy. Much political blood is spilled in the continual reassessment of contingencies, imperfectly conceived, in terms of programs, artificially distinguished.

Problems of Discretion   The assumption underlying the design of the Professional Bureaucracy is that the pigeonholing process contains all of the uncertainty in single professional jobs. As we saw above, that assumption often proves false to the detriment of the organization's performance. But even where it works, problems arise. For it focuses all the discretion in the hands of single professionals, whose complex skills, no matter how standardized, require the exercise of considerable judgment. That is, perhaps, appropriate for professionals who are competent and conscientious. Unfortunately not all of them are; and **the professional bureaucratic structure cannot easily deal with professionals who are either incompetent or unconscientious.**

No two professionals are equally skilled. So the client who is forced to choose among them—to choose in ignorance, since he seeks professional help precisely because he lacks the specialized knowledge to help himself—is exposed to a kind of Russian Roulette, almost literally so in the case of medicine, where single decisions can mean life or death. But that is inevitable: little can be done aside from using the very best screening procedures for applicants to the training schools.

Of greater concern is the unconscientious professional—the one who refuses to update his skills after graduation, who cares more for his income than his clients, or who becomes so enamored with his skills that he forgets about the real needs of his clients. This last case represents a means–ends inversion common in Professional Bureaucracies, different from that found in Machine Bureaucracies but equally serious. In this case, the professional confuses the needs of his clients with the skills he has to offer them. He simply concentrates on the program that he favors—perhaps because he does it best or simply enjoys doing it most—to the exclusion of all the others. This presents no problem as long as only those clients in need of that favorite program are directed his way. But should other clients slip in, trouble ensues. Thus, we have the psychiatrists who think that all patients (indeed, all people) need psychoanalysis, the consulting firms prepared to design the same planning system for all their clients, no matter how dynamic their environments, the professors who use the lecture method for classes of 500 students or 5, the social workers who feel the compulsion to bring power to the people even when the people do not want it.

Dealing with this means–ends inversion is impeded by the difficulty of measuring the outputs of professional work. When psychiatrists cannot even define the words "cure" or "healthy," how are they to prove that psychoanalysis is better for manic-depressives than chemical therapy would be? When no one has been able to measure the learning that takes place in the classroom, how can it be demonstrated with reliability that lectures are better or worse than seminars or, for that matter, than staying home and reading. That is one reason why the obvious solution to the problems of discretion—censure by the professional association—is seldom used. Another is that professionals are notoriously reluctant to act against their own, to wash their dirty linen in public, so to speak. In extreme cases, they will so act—certain behavior is too callous to ignore. But these instances are relatively rare. They do no more than expose the tip of the iceberg of misguided discretion.

Discretion not only enables some professionals to ignore the needs of their clients; it also encourages many of them to ignore the needs of the organization. Professionals in these structures do not generally consider themselves part of a team. To many, the organization is almost incidental, a convenient place to practice their skills. They are loyal to their profession, not to the place where they happen to practice it. But the organization has need for loyalty, too—to support its own strategies, to staff its administrative committees, to see it through conflicts with the professional association. Cooperation, as we saw earlier, is crucial to the functioning of the administrative structure. Yet, as we also saw earlier, professionals resist it furiously. Professors hate to show up for curriculum meetings; they simply do not wish to be dependent on each other. One can say that they know each other only too well!

Problems of Innovation   In these structures, major innovation also depends on cooperation. Existing programs can be perfected by individual specialists. But new ones necessarily cut across existing specialties—in essence, they require a rearrangement of the pigeonholes—and so call for interdisciplinary efforts. As a result, the reluctance of the professionals to work cooperatively with each other translates itself into problems of innovation.

Like the Machine Bureaucracy, the Professional Bureaucracy is an inflexible structure, well suited to producing its standard outputs but ill-suited to adapting to the production of new ones. All bureaucracies are geared to stable environments; they are performance structures designed to perfect programs for contingencies that can be predicted, not problem solving ones designed to create new programs for needs that have never before been encountered.

The problems of innovation in the Professional Bureaucracy find their roots in convergent thinking, in the deductive reasoning of the professional who sees the specific situation in terms of the general concept. In the Professional Bureaucracy this means that new problems are forced into old pigeonholes. The doctoral student in search of an interdisciplinary degree— for, after all, isn't the highest university degree meant to encourage the generation of new knowledge—inevitably finds himself forced back into the old departmental mode. "It must be a D.B.A. or a D.Ed.; we don't offer educational administration here." Nowhere are the effects of this deductive reasoning better illustrated than in Spencer's (1976) comments that "All patients developing significant complications or death among our three hospitals ... are reported to a central office with a narrative description of the sequence of events, with reports varying in length from a third to an entire page," and that six to eight of these cases are discussed in the one-hour weekly "mortality-morbidity" conferences, including presentation of it by the surgeon and "questions and comments" by the audience (p. 1181). An "entire" page and ten minutes of discussion for cases with "significant complications"! Maybe enough to list the symptoms and slot them into pigeonholes; hardly enough even to begin to think about creative solutions. As Lucy once told Charlie Brown, great art cannot be done in half an hour; it takes at least forty-five minutes!

The fact is that great art and innovative problem solving require *inductive* reasoning, that is, the induction of new general concepts or programs from particular experiences. That kind of thinking is *divergent*—it breaks away from old routines or standards rather than perfecting existing ones. And that flies in the face of everything the Professional Bureaucracy is designed to do.

So it should come as no surprise that Professional Bureaucracies and the professional associations that control their procedures tend to be conservative bodies, hesitant to change their well-established ways. Whenever an entrepreneurial member takes up the torch of innovation, great political clashes inevitably ensue. Even in the Machine Bureaucracy, once the managers of the strategic apex finally recognize the need for change, they are able to force it down the hierarchy. In the Professional Bureaucracy, with operator autonomy and bottom-up decision making, and in the professional association with its own democratic procedures, power for strategic change is diffuse. Everybody must agree on the change, not just a few managers or professional representatives. So change comes slowly and painfully, after much political intrigue and shrewd maneuvering by the professional and administrative entrepreneurs.

As long as the environment remains stable, the Professional Bureaucracy encounters no problem. It continues to perfect its skills and the given system of pigeonholes that slots them. But dynamic conditions call for change—new skills, new ways to slot them, and creative, cooperative efforts on the part of multidisciplinary teams of professionals. And that calls for another structural configuration, as we shall see in Chapter 21.

Dysfunctional Responses   What responses do the problems of coordination, discretion, and innovation evoke? Most commonly, **those outside the profession—clients, nonprofessional administrators, members of the society at large and their representatives in government—see the problems as resulting from a lack of external control of the professional, and his profession. So they do the obvious: try to control the work with one of the other coordinating mechanisms. Specifically, they try to use direct supervision, standardization of work processes, or standardization of outputs.**

Direct supervision typically means imposing an intermediate level of supervision, preferably with a narrow "span of control"—in keeping with the tenets of the classical concepts of authority—to watch over the professionals. That may work in cases of gross negligence. The sloppy surgeon or the professor who misses too many classes can be "spoken to" or ultimately perhaps fired. But specific professional activities—complex in execution and vague in results—are difficult to control by anyone other than the professionals themselves. So the administrator detached from the work and bent on direct supervision is left nothing to do except engage in bothersome exercises. As in the case of certain district supervisors who sit between one Montreal school board and its schools and, according to the reports of a number of principals, spend time telephoning them at 4:59 on Friday afternoons to ensure they have not left early for the weekend. The imposition of such intermediate levels of supervision stems from the assumption that professional work can be controlled, like any other, in a top-down manner, an assumption that has proven false again and again.

Likewise, the other forms of standardization, instead of achieving control of the professional work, often serve merely to impede and discourage the professionals. And for the same reasons—the complexity of the work and the vagueness of its outputs. Complex work processes cannot be formalized by rules and regulations, and vague outputs cannot be standardized by planning and control systems. Except in misguided ways, which program the wrong behaviors and measure the wrong outputs, forcing the professionals to play the machine bureaucratic game—satisfying the standards instead of serving the clients. Back to the old means–ends inversion. Like the policeman in Chicago who described to Studs Terkel (1972) the effects of various such standards on his work:

> My supervisor would say, "We need two policy arrests, so we can be equal with the other areas." So we go out and hunt for a policy operator. . . .
>
> A vice officer spends quite a bit of time in court. You learn the judges, the things they look for. You become proficient in testifying. You change your testimony, you change the facts. You switch things around 'cause you're trying to get convictions. . . .
>
> Certain units in the task force have developed a science around stopping your automobile. These men know it's impossible to drive three blocks without committing a traffic violation. We've got so many rules on the books. These police officers use these things to get points and also hustle for money. The traffic law is a fat book. He knows if you don't have two lights on your license plate, that's a violation. If you have a crack in your windshield, that's a violation. If your muffler's dragging, that's a violation. He knows all these little things. . . .
>
> So many points for a robbery, so many points for a man having a gun. When they go to the scene and the man with the gun has gone, they'll lock up somebody anyway, knowing he's not the one. The record says, "Locked up two people for UUW"—unlawful use of weapons. The report will say, "When we got there, we saw these guys and they looked suspicious." They'll get a point even if the case is thrown out of court. The arrest is all that counts (pp. 137–140).

Graphic illustrations of the futility of trying to control work that is essentially professional in nature. Similar things happen when accountants try to control the management consulting arms of their firms—"obedience is stressed as an end in itself because the CPA as administrator is not able to judge the non-accountant expert on the basis of that expert's knowledge" (Montagna, 1968: 144). And in school systems when the government technostructure believes it can program the work of the teacher, as in that of East Germany described proudly to this author by a government planner, where each day every child in the country ostensibly opens the same book to the same page. The individual needs of the students—slow learners and fast, rural and urban—as well as the individual styles of the teachers have to be subordinated to the neatness of the system.

The fact is that complex work cannot be effectively performed unless it comes under the control of the operator who does it. Society may have to control the overall expenditures of its Professional Bureaucracies—to keep the lid on them—and to legislate against the most callous kinds of professional behavior. But too much external control of the professional work itself leads, according to Hypothesis 14, to centralization and formalization of the structure, in effect driving the Professional Bureaucracy to Machine Bureaucracy. The decision-making power flows from the operators to the managers, and on to the analysts of the technostructure. The effect of this is to throw the baby out with the bathwater. Technocratic controls do not improve professional-type work, nor can they distinguish between responsible and irresponsible behavior—they constrain both equally. That may, of course, be appropriate for organizations in which responsible behavior is rare. But where it is not—presumably the majority of cases—**technocratic controls only serve to dampen professional conscientiousness.** As Sorensen and Sorensen (1974) found, the more machine bureaucratic the large public accounting firms, the more they experienced conflict and job dissatisfaction.

Controls also upset the delicate relationship between the professional and his client, a relationship predicated on unimpeded personal contact between the two. Thus, Cizanckas, a police chief, notes that the police officer at the bottom of the pecking order in the "paramilitary structure" is more than willing, in turn, to vent his frustration on the lawbreaker" (paraphrased by Hatvany, 1976, p. 73). The controls remove the responsibility for service from the professional and place it in the administrative structure, where it is of no use to the client. It is not the government that teaches the student, not even the school system or the school itself; it is not the hospital that delivers the baby, not the police force that apprehends the criminal, not the welfare department that helps the distraught family. These things are done by the individual professional. If that professional is incompetent, no plan or rule fashioned in the technostructure, no order from an administrator can ever make him competent. But such plans, rules, and orders can impede the competent professional from providing his service effectively. At least rationalization in the Machine Bureaucracy leaves the client with inexpensive outputs. In the case of professional work, it leaves him with impersonal, ineffective service.

Furthermore, the incentive to perfect, even to innovate—the latter weak in the best of times in professional bureaucracy—can be reduced by external controls. In losing control over their own work, the professionals become passive, like the operators of the Machine Bureaucracy. Even the job of professional administrator—never easy—becomes extremely difficult with a push for external control. In school systems, for example, the government looks top-down to the senior managers to implement its standards, while the professionals look bottom-up to them to resist the standards. The strategic apex gets caught between a government technostructure hungry for control and an operating core hanging on to its autonomy for dear life. No one gains in the process.

Are there then no solutions to a society concerned about its Professional Bureaucracies? Financial control of Professional Bureaucracies and legislation against irresponsible professional behavior are obviously necessary. But beyond that, must the professional be left with a blank check, free of public accountability? Solutions are available, but they grow from a recognition of professional work for what it is. **Change in the Professional Bureaucracy does not sweep in from new administrators taking office to announce major reforms, nor from government technostructures intent on bringing the professionals under control. Rather, change seeps in, by the slow process of changing the professionals—changing who can enter the profession, what they learn in its professional schools (ideals as well as skills and knowledge), and thereafter how willing they are to upgrade their skills.** Where such changes are resisted, society may be best off to call on the professionals' sense of responsibility to serve the public, or, failing that, to bring pressures on the professional associations rather than on the Professional Bureaucracies.

20

The Divisionalized Form

Prime Coordinating Mechanism:	Standardization of outputs
Key Part of Organization:	Middle line
Main Design Parameters:	Market grouping, perform-ance control system, limited vertical decentrali-zation
Contingency Factors:	Diversified markets (par-ticularly products or ser-vices), old, large, power needs of middle managers, fashionable

Like the Professional Bureaucracy, the Divisionalized Form is not so much an integrated organization as a set of quasi-autonomous entities coupled together by a central administrative structure. But whereas those "loosely coupled" entities in the Professional Bureaucracy are individuals—profes-sionals in the operating core—in the Divisionalized Form they are units in the middle line. These units are generally called *divisions*, and the central administration, the *headquarters*. The Divisionalized Form is most widely used in the private sector of the industrialized economy—the vast majority of the Fortune 500, America's largest corporations, are so organized. But it is also found in other sectors as well. The multiversity—the multiple campus institution such as the University of California—uses a variant of this configuration, as does the hospital system comprising a number of specialized hospitals, and the socialist economy, where state enterprises serve as divisions and the economic agencies of the central government, the headquarters.

The Divisionalized Form differs from the other four structural configurations in one important respect. It is not a complete structure from the strategic apex to the operating core, but rather a structure superimposed on others. That is, each division has its own structure. As we shall see, however, divisionalization has an effect on that choice—the divisions are drawn toward the Machine Bureaucracy configuration. But the Divisionalized Form configuration itself focuses on the structural relationship between the headquarters and the divisions, in effect, between the strategic apex and the top of the middle line.

THE BASIC STRUCTURE

The Design Parameters Most important, **the Divisionalized Form relies on the market basis for grouping units at the top of the middle line.** Divisions are created according to markets served and are then given control over the operating functions required to serve these markets. Thus, in Figure 20-1, a typical organigram for a divisionalized manufacturing firm, each division contains its own purchasing, engineering, manufacturing, and marketing activities. **This dispersal (and duplication) of the operating functions minimizes the interdependence between divisions, so that each can operate as a quasi-autonomous entity, free of the need to coordinate with the others.** To use Weick's (1976) term, the system is "loosely coupled"— "tied together either weakly or infrequently or slowly or with minimal interdependence" (p. 5). This, in turn, allows a large number of divisions to be grouped under the headquarters—in other words, **the span of control at the strategic apex of the Divisionalized Form can be rather wide.**

This structural arrangement naturally leads to pronounced decentralization from the headquarters: each division is delegated the powers needed to make the decisions concerning its own operations. But **the decentralization called for in the Divisionalized Form is highly circumscribed: not necessarily more than the delegation from the few managers at headquarters to the few more managers who run the divisions. In other words, the Divisionalized Form calls for decentralization of the parallel, limited vertical variety.** In fact, divisionalized structures can turn out to be rather *centralized* in nature. The division managers can hold the lion's share of the power, pre-

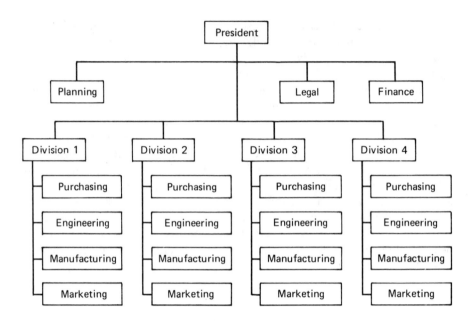

Figure 20-1. *Typical Organigram for a Divisionalized Manufacturing Firm*

cluding further vertical decentralization (down the chain of authority) or horizontal decentralization (to staff specialists and operators). As the president of one conglomerate firm—an organization that inevitably uses the Divisionalized Form—commented:

> Our whole philosophy revolves around where profit responsibility is placed— the divisional general manager. I don't want anyone in this organization to have any doubts that the general manager is boss. This is where the entrepreneurial atmosphere begins (quoted in Lorsch and Allen, 1973, p. 55).

Of course, in theory divisionalization does not preclude the further decentralization of power *within* the divisions. Different divisional structures, in fact, call for different distributions of internal power. But as we shall see as soon as we discuss control in the Divisionalized Form, other of its characteristics drive the divisions to centralize more power than they would if they were independent organizations.

Were the headquarters to delegate *all* of its power to the division managers, it would cease to exist, and each division would, in fact, emerge as an independent organization. So some form of control or coordination is required between headquarters and the divisions. The question then becomes: how can the headquarters maintain control while allowing each division sufficient autonomy to manage its own operations? And the answer lies in one specific design parameter: the performance control system. **In general, the headquarters allows the divisions close to full autonomy to make their own decisions, and then monitors the results of these decisions.** This monitoring is done after the fact, in specific quantitative terms, in the case of the business corporations by measures of profit, sales growth, and return on investment. As Ackerman (1975) notes:

> Accounting reports are not immune to misinterpretation but they relieve the reviewer of the need to sift through and comprehend operating data from diverse businesses. Ironically, but perhaps inevitably, as large corporations become more complex, the gauges used to control them become simpler. . . .
>
> Most important, financial controls are result-oriented. They monitor the actual and expected outcomes and not the process used to secure them (p. 49).

By the use of these systems, headquarters maintains control in the face of divisional autonomy. So **the prime coordinating mechanism in the Divisionalized Form is the standardization of outputs, and a key design parameter, the performance control system.**

This coordinating mechanism and the three design parameters so far discussed determine the basic structure: market-based units at the top of the middle line, parallel, vertical decentralization to those units (but not necessarily within them), and reliance on standardization of the outputs of these units through the use of performance control systems to effect headquarters' control of the divisions. These form an ideal configuration. The market basis for grouping allows for autonomy of the divisions, which encourages decentralization to them and it also allows for easy identification of their outputs, which can then be coordinated through performance control systems.

But other coordinating mechanisms and design parameters also have roles to play in this structural configuration, although they are not the primary ones.

The standardization of work processes is not used by headquarters as a coordinating mechanism because that would interfere with divisional autonomy. So little of the division's behavior is formalized by headquarters. Likewise, action planning is avoided because that, too, would impose decisions on the divisions that they need to make themselves. Mutual adjustment between the divisions, as well as the liaison devices that encourage it, are also precluded in this structure by the absence of interdependence between the divisions.

There is, however, a limited role for the two coordinating mechanisms that remain—standardization of skills and direct supervision. The Divisionalized Form is dependent for its success on the competence of the divisional managers, to whom much of the decision-making power is delegated. Whereas the managers at the top of the middle line of the other structural configurations tend to have functional orientations and limited freedom to act independently, those of the Divisionalized Form are "mini-general managers," who run their own operations. That is why the middle line emerges as the key part of this structure. But this characteristic puts the onus on the headquarters to train these division managers as well as it can (in effect, to standardize their managerial skills). Thus, after the Hungarian government "decentralized" its economy in 1968—that is, reduced its reliance on action planning in favor of greater autonomy of the state enterprises—the training of the managers of those enterprises emerged as a major government preoccupation. When the enterprises were under close control, with decisions imposed on them by the action plans, their managers merely carried out the orders of the government. With a shift to a purer form of divisionalization, they became true general managers who had to make their own decisions.[1] Likewise, indoctrination is used to ensure that the division managers pursue the broader goals of the headquarters instead of the parochial goals of the divisions. Divisional managers are brought back to headquarters periodically for conferences and meetings with the central administrators, and they are sometimes rotated around the different divisions to develop a broad perspective of the organization.

Direct supervision serves as a backup mechanism of coordination in the Divisionalized Form. When a division runs into trouble, the headquarters managers may have to step in, perhaps to replace the division manager. So some knowledge of the operations of the division is required, at least to know when to step in, as well as how. This need for direct supervision reduces the span of control of headquarters managers somewhat.

The Structure of the Divisions   Given an understanding of the means of control of the divisions by headquarters—through performance controls backed up by management training, indoctrination, and direct supervision —we can return to the question of decentralization within the divisions. In theory, the Divisionalized Form can be superimposed on any of the other structural configurations. A multiversity or a national accounting firm with regional offices draws a set of Professional Bureaucracies into the Divisionalized Form; a newspaper chain does the same thing with a set of Adhocracies. And a venture capitalist with equity control of entrepreneurial firms may draw a set of Simple Structures into the Divisionalized Form. The divisions of any one organization may also exhibit a variety of structures as, say, in the case of a municipal government with four "divisions"—a small simple structure antipoverty program, a machine bureaucratic sanita-

---

[1]This account is based on my conversations with Hungarian officials during a 1972 conference in Hungary on management education.

tion service, a professional bureaucratic police force, and an adhocratic urban development group.

But **the Divisionalized Form works best with machine bureaucratic structures in its divisions and, moreover, drives these structures, no matter what their natural inclinations, toward the machine bureaucratic form.** The explanation of this lies in the standardization of outputs, the key to the functioning of the divisionalized structure. The only way that headquarters can retain control, yet protect divisional autonomy, is by after-the-fact monitoring of divisional performance. That requires the establishment of clearly defined performance standards, the existence of which depends on two major assumptions. First, **each division must be treated as a single integrated system with a single, consistent set of goals.** In other words, while the divisions may be loosely coupled with each other, the assumption is that each is tightly coupled within. Second, **those goals must be operational ones, in other words, lend themselves to quantitative measures of performance control.** In the organic structural configurations—Simple Structure and Adhocracy, which exist in dynamic environments—such performance standards are difficult to establish. In the Professional Bureaucracy, as noted in Chapter 19, the complexity of the work precludes the establishment of such standards. Moreover, the Professional Bureaucracy is not one integrated system but a collection of individuals with a wide range of goals. That leaves only one configuration which satisfies the assumptions: the Machine Bureaucracy. In other words, the Divisionalized Form is best superimposed on the Machine Bureaucracy, the only structure that is integrated and has operational goals.

Now, what happens when the Divisionalized Form is superimposed on one of the other three structural configurations? To make it work, the assumptions must be made to hold. That is, each division must be made to function as a single integrated system, on which one set of performance measures can be imposed. The division manager, to whom power is delegated from the headquarters, must be able to impose the measures on his division; in other words, he must treat it as a top-down, regulated system. For the professional bureaucratic and adhocratic structures—in large part bottom-up and nonregulated—that amounts to a pressure to centralize. Moreover, when the division is organized on a functional basis—as it typically is in the Simple Structure, Machine Bureaucracy, and Adhocracy—the division manager is forced to use an action planning system to ensure that division personnel pursue the performance goals. Action planning imposes ever more specific standards concerning decisions and actions on personnel down the line. That amounts to pressure to formalize (and bureaucratize) the structure of the division, especially the Simple Structure and Adhocracy, which are organic to begin with. So the Divisionalized Form drives the divisions to be more centralized and more formalized than they would be as independent organizations. (That is, of course, the affect predicted from Hypothesis 14, since the headquarters is a specific form of external control of the division.) And these are the two distinguishing characteristics of the Machine Bureaucracy. So we conclude that divisionalization drives the structure of the divisions, no matter what their natural inclinations, toward the machine bureaucratic form. The performance control system of the Divisionalized Form weakens the organic nature of the Simple Structure and the Adhocracy; and it upsets the notion of operator autonomy in the Professional Bureaucracy.[2] Only in the Machine Bureaucracy does divisionalization mean no fundamental change in structure.

Why, then, is "divisionalization" treated in much of the literature as synonymous with "decentralization" (and implicitly with debureaucratization). The answer seems to lie in the origins of the configuration. As certain machine bureaucratic corporations in America grew and diversified their markets early in this century, they became increasingly unwieldly—too centralized and too bureaucratic. The development of the Divisionalized Form—in Du Pont in 1921 (Chandler, 1962)—came as a godsend. Instead of one integrated functional structure, a set of them could be designed, one for each market. This eased the bottleneck at the strategic apex, allowing for less centralization and less formalization. So, compared with the Machine Bureaucracy structure—that is, with *one* overall Machine Bureaucracy for all markets—the Divisionalized Form, by creating many smaller and more focused Machine Bureaucracies, reduced the overall centralization of the structure.

But is the Divisionalized Form inherently decentralized, or, to be specific, more decentralized than the other structural configurations? Than the Simple Structure, with all power concentrated in a single office: certainly. Than the Machine Bureaucracy (operating in one market, as it is designed to do): not clear. Who is to say which structure distributes its power more widely—the one with limited *horizontal* decentralization, where the few analysts of the technostructure share power with the managers of the strategic apex, or the one with limited *vertical* decentralization,

---

[2]Indeed, it could not be otherwise. If the divisions remained as Professional Bureaucracies, for example, the professional operators would retain their usual power, and so their control of the administrative structure would naturally extend beyond the divisions into the headquarters; as a result, the position of divisional manager would have no special relevance, and the entire organization would emerge as a single Professional Bureaucracy. What makes a structure divisionalized is *managerial* or *unit* autonomy, not professional autonomy. Alternatively, giving a great deal of power to department managers of a single Professional Bureaucracy drives the structure toward the Divisionalized Form. This apparently happened when deans and department heads assumed much power in the German universities early in this century, and apparently happens to a lesser extent in the British universities today for the same reason (Beyer and Lodahl, 1976, p. 110).

where the few managers at the top of the middle line share that power? And than the Professional Bureaucracy or Adhocracy, with their extensive decentralization deep into the line structure and out to a large number of operating or staff specialists: certainly not.

Moreover, there is another, more logical alternative to the Divisionalized Form—complete fragmentation of the organization—which is also more decentralized. It is a rather small step from quasi-autonomous divisions controlled by one central headquarters to fully autonomous organizations, each controlled by its own board of directors. In fact, the Divisionalized Form often results not from the "decentralization" of a Machine Bureaucracy operating in many markets, but from the "centralization" of a set of independent organizations operating in different markets. They consolidate themselves into a single "federation" with a Divisionalized Form structural configuration, in the process surrendering some of their powers to a new central headquarters.

Ironically, this is what happened in the most famous example of divisionalization, the one most frequently touted as "decentralization"—Alfred P. Sloan's restructuring of General Motors in the 1920s. It was this example that set off the first waves of divisionalization among the Fortune 500. Yet no example better illustrates the fallacy of the "divisionalization means decentralization" relationship. For while Sloan may have divisionalized General Motors, by no stretch of the imagination did he decentralize it. As a well-known student of his actions commented, "If any *one* word is needed to describe the management *structure* of General Motors as it was recast by Sloan and the brilliant group around him, then that word is not decentralization, but *centralization*" (Harold Wolff, quoted in Perrow, 1974, p. 38). As Chandler (1962) and even Sloan (1963) himself tell it, William C. Durant put General Motors together as a holding company, but failed to consolidate it into a single entity. Sloan was brought in to do that job. He instituted central controls, which reduced the power of the unit managers by subjecting their performance to headquarters' control. In other words, Sloan consolidated the structure to the Divisionalized Form, and thereby centralized it. (Later in this chapter we shall see that this process of centralizing power in General Motors has apparently continued unabated to the present day, so that the current structure of the automotive component of the company can no longer be called divisionalized.)[3]

---

[3]Perrow (1974, pp. 37–38) claims that first Peter Drucker, then Ernest Dale, then Alfred Chandler (though more "circumspect"), and finally Sloan himself all gave the impression in their books that Sloan decentralized General Motors: "Sloan himself takes a characteristically ambiguous position about decentralization. His book opens with praise for decentralization in General Motors; a bit later, though, he criticizes Durant, his predecessor, for allowing General Motors to be too decentralized; and still later he calls for a happy medium between centralization and decentralization" (p. 38).

The Powers of the Divisions and the Headquarters   Both communication and decision flows in the Divisionalized Form reflect one central fact: there is a sharp division of labor between the headquarters and the divisions. Communication between the two is, for example, circumscribed and largely formal, in good part restricted to the transmission of performance standards down to the divisions and of performance results back up. This is supplemented by personal interchanges between the managers at the two levels, but that is carefully limited. Too much detailed knowledge at the headquarters level can invite meddling in the decisions of the divisions, thereby defeating the very purpose of divisionalization, namely divisional autonomy. Even communication between managers and their outside environments is quite different at the two levels of the structure. As Allen (1970) notes:

> ... corporate and divisional executives focused their attention on different segments of their firms' task environments. Corporate contacts with external groups and organizations centered mainly around stockholders, the financial community, potential merger candidates, and governmental agencies. By way of contrast, top level division personnel were concerned mainly with the external groups which affected their ability to develop, sell, and produce goods and services in their particular industries (pp. 22–23).

Lorsch and Allen (1973) found that these different patterns of behavior led to rather different cognitive orientations and working styles. Corporate headquarters' units were less formal in their structures, exhibited a longer time perspective, and placed a greater emphasis on financial goals (p. 23).

In the Divisionalized Form, the divisions are given the power to run their own businesses. They control the operations and determine the strategies for the markets that fall under their responsibility. Thus, in the conglomerate Textron, "the divisions are required to formulate their own product strategy ... to determine how [they] will compete in the market place, the prices to be charged for products, delivery schedules, channels of distribution, and product design and initiation"; they "are quite free to determine their own sources of supply"; and they must solve their own engineering and marketing problems (Wrigley, 1970, p. V-96). Their chiefs, therefore, emerge as full-fledged managers who perform all the usual managerial roles (with a special emphasis on spokesman and negotiator to represent their divisions at headquarters and extract from it as much capital as possible).

What powers, then, are retained by the headquarters? Holden et al. (1968) posed the question to the top managers of large American divisionalized corporations. They received unanimous responses on the following items: setting corporate objectives, strategic planning, determination of basic policies, finance, accounting systems, basic research, consummation of mergers or acquisitions, approval of capital expenditures over prescribed limits, setting of executive salaries and bonuses above certain levels, and selection of individuals for positions down to specific echelons in the organization. In our discussion, we shall focus on six headquarters functions in particular.

The first of the powers retained by headquarters, related to the managerial role of entrepreneur, is the formation of the organization's overall product-market *strategy*. Whereas the divisions determine the strategies for *given* product markets, the headquarters decides which ones will be given. In effect, **the headquarters manages the strategic portfolio**, establishing, acquiring, selling, and closing down divisions in order to change its mix of products and markets. This clear separation between the management of the strategic portfolio at headquarters and of the particular product-market strategies in the divisions was one of the major reasons why the Divisionalized Form developed in the first place.

> In September, 1921, the Du Pont Company put into effect this new structure of autonomous, multidepartmental divisions and a general office with staff specialists and general executives. Each division had its functional departments and its own central office to administer the central departments.
>
> Unencumbered by operating duties, the senior executives at the general office now had the time, information, and more of a psychological commitment to carry on the entrepreneurial activities and make the strategic decisions necessary to keep the over-all enterprise alive and growing and to coordinate, appraise, and plan for the work of the divisions (Chandler, 1962, p. 111).

Second among the powers it retains, **headquarters allocates the overall financial resources.** Only pooled coupling exists among the divisions. That is, they do not pass their work back and forth but do share common financial resources. It is clearly the responsibility of the headquarters to manage these resources—to draw excess funds from the divisions that do not need them, to raise additional funds in the capital markets when necessary, and to allocate available funds among the divisions that do need them. As the chief executive of Textron commented, "Number one in the keys to this operation [is] to keep a tight rein on the finances and to control the expansion of the divisions" (quoted in Wrigley, 1970, p. V-82). That meant:

> All division receipts were deposited into a central Textron account. Disbursements to the divisions account were made by the treasurer at corporate office on an agreed upon schedule. Opening and closing bank accounts, changing the authorized signers on bank accounts, assigning receivables, and other activities connected with financing of activities, required the authorization of the corporate treasurer (p. V-78).

Headquarters' power over resource allocation also includes the authorization of those divisional capital projects large enough to affect the overall capital budget of the organization. The need to seek such authorization may constitute some interference with the autonomy of the divisions, but that is an interference necessary to ensure the balanced allocation of funds. In general, however, the assessment by headquarters of divisional capital projects is purely financial in nature—concerned only with questions of risk and availability of funds, not with those of product-market strategy.

The key to the control of the divisions in this structural configuration is the performance control system. Hence, as its third major power, **the headquarters designs the performance control system.** The managers there, with the aid of their own technostructure, set up the system: they decide on performance measures and reporting periods, establish formats for plans and budgets, and design an MIS to feed performance results back to headquarters. They then operate the system, setting targets for each reporting period, perhaps jointly with the divisional managers, and reviewing the MIS results.

What happens when the MIS signals that a division has run into trouble, that it can no longer meet its performance targets? The management at headquarters must first decide whether the problem lies in conditions beyond the control of the division manager or in the manager himself. If he is perceived as competent—that the problem lies in an economic downturn, the arrival of new competition, or whatever—headquarters basically has the choice of divesting itself of the division or carrying it financially to ride out the trouble. In other words, it acts in terms of one of its first two powers, the management of the strategic portfolio or the allocation of financial resources. But if the problem is perceived to lie with the divisional manager, then headquarters draws on its fourth major power. **The headquarters replaces and appoints the managers of the divisions.** This is a crucial power in the Divisionalized Form, because the structure precludes the direct interference by the headquarters managers in the operating affairs of the divisions; the closest they can come is to determine who will run the divisions. To an important extent, therefore, success in the Divisionalized Form depends on this fourth power, on selecting the right people—general managers with the confidence and ability to run quasi-autonomous operations effectively, yet in accordance with the goals of the overall organization.

The performance control system may signal a problem in a division, but it is of little help in determining whether that problem is rooted in adverse conditions or incompetent management. Moreover, there are times when the performance control system fails to do a proper job of reporting problems. Being dependent on quantitative historical data, the MIS sometimes misses the nuances that signal imminent problems. The MIS can also be manipulated by the divisional management, as when an advertising or research budget is cut to show better short-term profit at the expense of long-run profitability. So, although the headquarters depends on the MIS to monitor divisional behavior, it cannot rely exclusively on that system. This leads to the fifth function. **The headquarters monitors divisional behavior on a personal basis.** Here coordination reverts partly back to direct supervision as a supplement to the standardization of outputs. Headquarters managers visit the divisions periodically to "keep in touch," to get to know them well enough to be able to foresee problems. Such knowledge also enables the headquarters managers to assess requests by divisions for large capital expenditures, and it gives them knowledge of the people in the divisions when replacements must be made. Thus, Textron, like many divisionalized corporations, uses the "group executive," what it calls "an extension of the president." Stationed at headquarters, he is more often than not away from it, "spending, perhaps, three days each week traveling and visiting the plants of the divisions under his charge. Thompson [the chief executive] has said 'I don't like surprises,' and the group executive was taken as the means of 'minimizing surprises'" (quotes from Wrigley, 1970, pp. V-73, 85). Wrigley elaborates on the job:

> The role of the group executive was not confined ... to determining the viability of divisional plans. He had also to act as a "general business consultant" when a particular division in his charge was in trouble. And he had a major responsibility to ensure that the divisional managers were up to their jobs, or of seeking a replacement for them if the need arose. Moreover, he had a key role in determining that the divisional plans, as agreed, were, in fact, properly implemented, specifically, that the formal reports on overall results did reflect reality. He had, also, to anticipate what these results might be, particularly in cases likely to hold unpleasant surprises. All this being said, the central thrust of his work was to recommend to corporate management in which of the four or five divisions under his charge it might well, on the basis of the divisional plans, put its money—allocate the resources at its disposal (p. 87).

But too much direct supervision defeats the purpose of the Divisionalized Form, namely providing autonomy to the units in the middle line. So in normal times, the headquarters managers stand on a tightrope between being ignorant of division problems and becoming so familiar with them that they are tempted to interfere in their solution. Some divisionalized organizations try to achieve the right balance by restricting the size of the headquarters. In Textron in 1970, for example, with sales of more than $1.5 billion from thirty different divisions, the headquarters staff numbered only thirty executives and administrators, and the group vice presidents had no assistants or private technocratic staff, just one secretary each (Wrigley, 1970, p. V-77).

As its sixth and final power, the **headquarters provides certain support services common to the divisions.** The location of support services—their concentration in headquarters or dispersal to the divisions—is a major design issue for the Divisionalized Form.[4] Services that must be geared to the needs of single divisions, those that must be located in physically convenient places, and those that are relatively easy to duplicate—as in the cases of a marketing research group, a cafeteria, and a public relations unit, respectively—are typically dispersed to the divisions (and are sometimes duplicated at headquarters as well). But coordinated services that must be offered across the range of divisions, or those that must be provided at the common strategic apex, are concentrated in single units at headquarters.

Stieglitz (1971, pp. 316–317) studied the headquarters and divisional staff units in eighty-two companies and found that those most predominately represented at the headquarters level were finance (with 100 percent representation), legal-secretariat (100 percent), personnel (95 percent), research and development (80 percent), and public relations (70 percent). All of these reflect the global orientation of the headquarters, except perhaps for research and development, which may indicate the very high costs of research facilities as well as general interdependencies among the divisions (in other words, an impure form of divisionalization). The finance units support the headquarters role of resource allocation, look after income tax, insurance, pension matters, and the like common to the different divisions; moreover, they are often the home for the technocratic staffers concerned with the performance control system. The legal-secretariat and public relations departments provide support on corporate-wide relations with the environment, while the personal function (technocratic in nature) helps in the identification, training, and indoctrination of future division managers, as well as the remuneration of current ones. Stieglitz found that the personnel function was, in fact, shared between the two levels of the structure, as did Wrigley (1970, p. VI-12), who notes that the headquarters concerns itself with management manpower planning and general salary scales and the like, while the divisions apply these in their own contexts. Again, however, any organization that wishes to be divisionalized must severely limit the number of support services it provides at headquarters. Each one imposes decisions on the divisions, thereby curtailing their autonomy.

To conclude our discussion of the basic structure, Figure 20-2 shows the Divisionalized Form represented symbolically in terms of our logo. Headquarters is shown in three parts—a small strategic apex of top managers, a small technostructure to the left, concerned with the design and operation of the performance control system as well as some of the management development programs, and a slightly larger staff support group to the right. Four divisions are shown below the headquarters, with a bulge put in

---

[4]See Chapter 7 for a discussion of the concentration and dispersal of staff units.

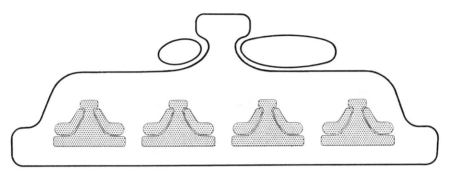

Figure 20-2. *The Divisionalized Form*

at the level of division manager to indicate that the middle line is the key part of the organization. All four divisions are represented as Machine Bureaucracies to illustrate our point that divisionalization encourages the divisions to use this structural configuration.

CONDITIONS OF THE DIVISIONALIZED FORM

Market Diversity One contingency factor above all drives the organization to use the Divisionalized Form—market diversity. The organization faced with a single integrated market simply cannot split itself into autonomous divisions; the one with distinct markets, however, has an incentive to create a unit to deal with each. That enables the organization to manage its strategic portfolio centrally, while giving each component of that portfolio the undivided attention of one unit.

Thus, Child (1977) describes two high-performance airlines which "shared many contingencies"—they operated in similar environments, were even direct competitors on some routes, had similar fleets, used similar technologies, faced almost identical operating decisions, and were both large. The only major difference: one had a more diversified and geographically less compact route system. And that one used the Divisionalized Form, while the other retained an integrated functional structure.

> [The first] airline had divisionalized by region and by major resource area. It had attached full profit responsibility to its cost centres. It delegated authority on expenditure, staffing and other decisions to its divisions. It employed a highly formalized approach to financial and resource management using sophisticated controls. It planned ahead to a relatively long time horizon, using a powerful corporate planning group to provide co-ordination and review. In short, this company was consistent in employing all the main elements of a structure which most authorities would say is appropriate to a large or-

ganization having a geographic spread of operations and a range of resource areas (p. 179).

This relationship between diversification and divisionalization receives a great deal of support in the literature, as we noted in Chapter 15. Chandler (1962) described the advent of the Divisionalized Form in the corporate setting as a direct response to product diversification. Later, Wrigley (1970) and Rumelt (1974) documented its spread to most other large American corporations subsequent to their diversification, while Channon (1973) described its later but similar spread in England, Paven (1974) in Italy, and Dyas and Thanheiser (1976) in France and Germany.

In our discussion of the conditions surrounding the other structural configurations, we noted that not only do the contingency factors influence the choice of the design parameters, but the design parameters also influence the "choice" of the contingency factors. In other words, the contingency factors form a part of the configurations we are discussing. Here we have an excellent example of this. Chandler argued that structure follows strategy, that structural divisionalization results from strategic diversification. But the opposite relationship seems to hold as well, that **divisionalization encourages further diversification** (Rumelt, 1974, pp. 76–77; Fouraker and Stopford, 1968). The ease with which headquarters can add new divisions in this structure encourages it to do so; moreover, divisionalization generates a steady stream of general managers who look for more and larger divisions to run.

> . . . the divisional structure becomes a built-in "school of management", training middle level general managers in the problems and opportunities associated with economic responsibility. As a result, this form of organization provides a pool of trained talent from which to draw, a pool from which a new group may be formed in a few days or weeks to take over and manage a new activity. Both the structure and the internal "schooling" facilitate *rapid* and *profitable* exploitation of new ideas, a key element in the growth strategies of the [divisionalized] firms (Scott, 1971, p. 14).

This seems to explain why Fouraker and Stopford found that the more diversified American firms on the domestic scene were the ones most likely to develop international operations: when new products ran out at home, the aggressive young managers could be satisfied with foreign subsidiaries to manage.

In Chapter 7 we discussed three kinds of market diversity—product and service, client, and region. In theory, all three can lead to divisionalization. Physically dispersed markets, for example, create communication problems that give the organization an incentive to set up geographical divisions to deal with each region, as in retail chains, post offices, and railroads serving large areas. Add to this high transportation costs—as in the

case of cement manufacturers—and there is further incentive to divisionalize on a regional basis.

And yet, **based on client or regional diversification in the absence of
product or service diversification, divisionalization often turns out to be
incomplete.** With identical products or services in each region or for each
group of clients, the headquarters is encouraged to centralize a good deal of
decision making and concentrate a good deal of support service at the center,
to ensure common operating standards for all the divisions. This centralization and concentration of certain functions—some of them critical in formulating product-market strategies—seriously reduces divisional autonomy.
In effect, the structure is driven toward integrated Machine Bureaucracy,
but with one difference: its operations are divided into distinct market-
based units.

In his research on service industries, Channon (1975, 1976) finds this
kind of structure—which he calls a "functional/divisional hybrid" or a
"critical function structure"—to be common. That is "perhaps not as surprising as it might appear at first sight since service industry firms have no
'manufacturing' operation to provide a central focus, but rather the major
assets are located in the 'selling' or distribution function" (1975, p. 16). The
clients must be served where they are—in the bank branch, retail store,
insurance agency. Channon found, for example, that insurance companies
(some of which had product as well as regional divisions) concentrated the
critical function of investment. In retailing, the critical function was purchasing. Headquarters controlled sources of supply, product range, pricing
and volume terms, as well as site and property development and merchandising. Day-to-day operations of the retail stores were left to the store
managers, who were supervised by a regional hierarchy. Channon found
that even the department store chains that grew up as holding companies
through acquisition were moving to this type of structure.

We shall use the term *carbon-copy bureaucracy* for this hybrid of
Divisionalized Form and Machine Bureaucracy, the structure that results
when an organization sets up identical regional divisions and then concentrates certain critical functions at headquarters. Each division is a replica—a
carbon copy—of all the others, performing the same activities in the same
ways, unique only in its location. The carbon-copy bureaucracy is, in fact,
found in all the examples given above of regional divisionalization, but is
probably most common in retailing—the supermarket chain with fifty
identical stores, the post office with duplicated facility in each city of the
nation, the motel or fast-food franchise, where, once inside, customers can
hardly tell whether they are in Driggs, Idaho, or Dublin, Ireland.[5] Consider,
for example, the following description of the McDonald's hamburger chain:

[5]The fire department and Murray's restaurants, discussed in Chapter 18 as Machine Bureaucracies, are actually carbon-copy bureaucracies.

The integrative mechanisms employed by McDonald's, for example, not only include a detailed organizational structure but also continual service, through bookkeeping systems, company troubleshooters, and advertising, to ensure that the franchise manager conforms to McDonald's rules and regulations. The company's operations manual consists of 385 pages of details covering the most minute facet of operating an outlet. It spells out, for example, what equipment (such as cigarette, gum, candy, and pinball machines) is not permitted on store premises.

The franchise manager is visited monthly by one of thirty field service managers. The franchise sends weekly financial reports to the company, and the manager must attend a three-week intensive training at the so-called "Hamburger U." in Elk Grove, Illinois. . . .

These managers also learn the strict standards for personal grooming, the few variations allowed in types of food because of regional tastes, and how to deal with college students as customers and employees. The company also provides the franchise manager with a different maintenance reminder for each day of the year, such as "Lubricate and adjust potato-peeler belt" or "Contact snow removal company". . . .

Fred Turner, McDonald's president since 1968, says: "In an age when so many Americans are on the move, one of our main assets is our consistency and uniformity. It's very important that a man who's used to eating at a McDonald's in Hempstead, Long Island, knows he can get the same food and service when he walks into one in Albuquerque or Omaha."[6]

Without any doubt: the classic Machine Bureaucracy . . . in divisionalized clothing.[7]

Lourenço and Glidewell (1975) describe in some detail a local television station owned and tightly controlled along with four others by a New York network. Much to the frustration of the personnel, who presumably preferred Professional Bureaucracy or Adhocracy, the station was, according to the authors' account, a division in a carbon-copy bureaucracy. Thus, its manager commented to new employees on one occasion: "I object to being a puppet, moving with a string" (p. 492). The authors elaborate: "Not only did the New York network office select, produce and air the prime programs, it also kept close tabs on day-to-day operations" (pp. 494–495). All discrepancies—for example, "anything off the air for more than one minute" (p. 495)—had to be reported to New York. Even local marketing and labor relations came under the close surveillance of headquarters.

[6] From A. Lucas, "As American as McDonald's Hamburger on the Fourth of July," *New York Times Magazine*, July 4, 1971. Used with permission.

[7] An interesting feature of restaurants is that they can adopt such different structural configurations. Here we have a hybrid of Machine Bureaucracy and Divisionalized Form. The gastronomic restaurant leans toward the Professional Bureaucracy, with its focus on the skills of its highly trained chefs. In contrast, the small, single, fast-food restaurant (such as the classic "greasy-spoon") has been described by Whyte (1969) as a Simple Structure.

The carbon-copy bureaucracy is also found in the manufacturing sector, where a simple and stable environment and standard products drive the structure toward Machine Bureaucracy, but dispersed markets coupled with either high transportation costs or perishable products encourage the organization to replicate its production facilities in different regions. Common examples are bakeries, breweries, cement producers, and soft drink bottlers. They produce and market their products in each city of any size, subject to tight standards set and enforced by the central headquarters. (The recent introduction of a small oven in our local bread store—part of a chain operating exclusively in the Montreal area—suggests that manufacturing carbon-copy bureaucracies can exist on small scales indeed.)

The giant multinational enterprise with identical product lines in various national markets also tends to resemble the carbon-copy bureaucracy. A division or "subsidiary" is created in each market to manufacture and distribute the products subject to the dictates of headquarters. In other words, certain critical functions—most notably product development—are retained by the central administration. Of course, the more foreign the subsidiary, the more it needs the power to adapt the products and marketing techniques to its local conditions; in other words, the greater is the pull to pure divisionalization. But the multinational enterprise can avoid that pull by concentrating on products that can be standardized throughout the world (Coca-Cola being the classic example), and by avoiding very foreign markets. Thus, the American corporations have typically expanded first into Canada—close, convenient, and minimally foreign—then into Europe, later perhaps beyond, but not frequently to the cultures most foreign to the West.

In Canada, in fact, the phenomenon of the headless subsidiary—one with no control over its main strategies—is so common that it has merited a special name: the *miniature replica effect*. It is set up in Canada to produce products designed in the United States according to American specifications on production lines engineered by the American technostructure. Of course, the reason these subsidiaries were established in the first place, instead of the Canadian market having been supplied directly from the American factories, was the presence of the Canadian tariff on manufactured goods. It is interesting how often these firms have reacted to recent attacks by Canadian nationalists with the claim that all their employees but one are Canadian nationals. That one is, of course, the president, placed on the shoulders of the subsidiary to receive the orders from its brain in New York.

Technical System   What of the role of the other contingency factors —besides market diversity—in the use of the Divisionalized Form? In a sense, technical system is one factor, specifically its economies of scale. **Divisionalization is possible only when the organization's technical system**

can be efficiently separated into segments, one for each division. For example, whereas a geographically diversified cement company can duplicate its processing facilities many times across the face of the nation, a likewise diversified aluminum company with the same sales volume may be unable to because it cannot afford more than one smelter. And so the aluminum company retains a functional structure. But even in the case of the cement producer, divisionalization is incomplete: geographical diversification, as noted above, leads to the functional divisional hybrid, often the carbon-copy bureaucracy. But when it is the product lines rather than the geographical regions that are diversified, separation of the technical system usually takes place naturally, no matter what the economies of scale: different product lines require different technical systems to begin with.

There is, however, evidence of a more important, although indirect, relationship between economies of scale and divisionalization. Organizations that must devote huge capital resources to very high fixed-cost technical systems—as in the case of steel and aluminum producers and other "heavies" of American industry—tend not to diversify their product lines in the first place, and so do not divisionalize (Rumelt, 1974; Wrigley, 1970). (To be more precise, as a group they show little enthusiasm for "horizontal" diversification—into parallel or unrelated product lines. They do diversify "vertically," moving into the product lines at the two ends of their production chains, thereby becoming their own suppliers and customers. But as we shall see later in this chapter, the strong interdependencies between product lines in the same production chain leads to an incomplete form of divisionalization.)

Environment In respect to the factors of environment, the Divisionalized Form differs fundamentally from the other four structural configurations. Each of those has its own particular environment, specifically one of the four boxes of the static–dynamic, simple–complex matrix discussed in Chapter 15. In other words, **whereas it is primarily the broad environmental dimensions of stability and complexity that position the other configurations, it is another, more restricted environmental dimension—market diversity, in particular, product diversity—that positions the Divisionalized Form. That narrows its range of application considerably compared with the other four configurations.**

Nevertheless, the Divisionalized Form does have a preferred environment, which it shares with the Machine Bureaucracy. That is because of another condition prerequisite to the use of the Divisionalized Form—outputs (specifically performance criteria) that can be standardized. As we saw in Chapter 19, complex environments lead to vague outputs that cannot be measured or standardized. Likewise, in dynamic environments, outputs and performance standards cannot easily be pinned down. So **the Divisionalized Form works best in environments that are neither very complex nor very dynamic, in fact the very same environments that favor the Machine Bureaucracy.** This leads to a rather precise specification of the conditions that most commonly give rise to this structural configuration: **the Divisionalized Form is the structural response to an integrated Machine Bureaucracy, operating in a simple, stable environment (typically without huge economies of scale) that has diversified its product or service lines horizontally.**

However, when an organization attempts to force divisionalization on units operating in other kinds of environments—complex or dynamic ones —where the outputs cannot be measured by performance controls, a hybrid structure normally results. In effect, the headquarters must rely on some mechanism other than the standardization of outputs to control the divisions. If it turns to rules and regulations—in effect, the imposition of standards that control decisions and work processes directly in the divisions— then a hybrid results with Machine Bureaucracy, similar to the carbon-copy bureaucracy. If, instead, the headquarters managers increase their personal surveillance (direct supervision) of the divisions, through more frequent contact with their managers, then a hybrid with Simple Structure results, which we can call the *personalized divisionalized form.* Alternatively, should they seek to control the behavior of the divisions primarily through socialization—in effect appointing only managers they can trust fully because these have been through an extensive program of indoctrination or simply because they enter the organization with a very strong identification with it—then a hybrid with some characteristics of Professional Bureaucracy emerges which we can call the *socialized divisionalized form.*

Competition is another variable that has been suggested as an environmental determinant of the Divisionalized Form. In particular, Franko (1974) concludes in his study of European multinational firms that the absence of competition may delay the adaption of the Divisionalized Form despite product diversification. He found that European companies operating in cartels and the like tended to maintain their functional structures long after they diversified. Likewise, Scott (1973, p. 141) finds the most rapid spread of divisionalization in America during periods when competitive pressures were maintained by antitrust legislation and economic conditions, and in Europe when competitive pressures were generated by the Common Market and by supply catching up with demand in the 1960s.

This argument makes sense, but it is not unique to the Divisionalized Form. It is the need for efficiency that drives all organizations to make sure their structures match their conditions. (That was the point of the congruence hypothesis presented in Chapter 12.) Structural change always lags situational change; the length of that lag is affected by the pressures to be efficient. Competitive pressures figure prominently among these, not only forcing a shift to the Divisionalized Form soon after product diversification, but also presumably forcing a quick shift back to the functional form should the organization later consolidate its product lines.

Age and Size   What about the factors of age and size? Stopford and Wells (1972) argue that "absolute size by itself does not have a direct relationship with [divisionalized] structure," that it is the strategy of diversification that causes the shift to this structural configuration (p. 72). But in the context of the extended *configuration* hypothesis—that all the variables are locked together in an integrated system, with the same ones often being both dependent and independent—that argument can be questioned. Surely, it is not coincidental that in 1968, according to Wrigley's data, ninety-nine of America's 100 largest corporations used some version of the Divisionalized Form, and 430 of the largest 500. The fact is that **as organizations grow large, they become prone to diversify and then to divisionalize.** One reason is protection: large manufacturing firms tend to be organized as Machine Bureaucracies, structures that, as we noted in Chapter 18, try to avoid risks. Diversification spreads the risk. Also, the larger a firm becomes vis-à-vis its competitors, the more it comes to dominate its traditional market. Eventually, it simply runs out of room for expansion (because there is no market share left or because its dominance has come to the attention of the antitrust regulators), and so it must find further growth opportunities elsewhere. Thus it diversifies, and later must divisionalize. Moreover, as noted earlier, divisionalization creates a cadre of aggressive general managers who push for further diversification and further growth. So we must conclude that there is, in fact, an important relationship between size and divisionalization, with diversification the intermediate variable. The giant corporations —with the few exceptions that remain in one business because of enormously high fixed-cost technical systems—not only require divisionalization but were also able to reach their giant size only because of it.

In fact, many corporations have grown so large and diversified that the simple Divisionalized Form is not sufficient for them. They make use of a variant we call the *multiple-divisionalized form,* with divisions on top of divisions. For example, regional divisions may be superimposed on product divisions, as shown in Figure 7–8, or broad product divisions ("groups") may be superimposed on narrower ones, as in the case of General Electric, shown later in this chapter in Figure 20–8.

Like size, age is also associated with the Divisionalized Form. In larger organizations, the management runs out of places to expand in the traditional markets; in older ones, the managers sometimes get bored with the traditional markets and find diversion through diversification. In other cases, time brings new competitors into old market niches, forcing the management to look for new ones with better potential. Thus, with divisionalization most common among the largest and oldest corporations, the Divisionalized Form emerged in Chapter 13 as the third stage of structural development, following Machine Bureaucracy.

The Divisionalized Form need not, however, always follow other structural configurations at a late stage of development. Some organizations, in fact, begin their lives with it. They divisionalize from without, so to speak; that is, they agglomerate rather than diversify. Independent organizations that join together to form new alliances—perhaps to benefit from economies of operating scale, or the sharing of financial resources or support services—but are intent on guarding as much of their previous autonomy as possible, naturally prefer the Divisionalized Form. These alliances, generally known as associations or *federations*, occur when farmers create cooperatives to market their produce, when small construction firms do likewise to countervail such actions by unions or to meet the market power of larger competitors. Of course, not all agglomerations are voluntary: stock market operators take over corporations in proxy fights and force them into federations, as do governments when they nationalize them to pool their resources for purposes of national planning or the development of the scale needed to meet foreign competition. When the federated organizations produce common products or services, strong pressures naturally arise to consolidate their activities into tighter structures—specifically to concentrate critical functions at the administrative headquarters—and their divisionalized structures tend to be driven to integrated machine bureaucratic ones.

Power   These last points introduce our final set of contingency factors, those related to power, which also play a role in the Divisionalized Form configuration. We have just seen that power can explain federation: small organizations need to band together to match the power of the bigger ones, and governments or owners use their power to force unwilling partners to federate. We also saw earlier the role of power within the structure, that of the division managers who encourage growth, diversification, and divisionalization to enhance their own positions. Even in the functionally structured organization, the drive by the aggressive middle manager for more autonomy amounts to a pull to divisionalize at his level of the hierarchy. And in the case of the top manager, the Divisionalized Form is by far the most effective structure for him to increase the power of the overall organization, since it enables units to be added with relatively little effort and disruption. (Internally, the top manager must, of course, share much of that increased power with the divisional managers.) Indeed, the waves of conglomerate diversification in U.S. industry appear to be a giant power game, with corporate chief executives vying with each other to see who can build the largest empire.

These same factors of power have hardly been absent in other spheres as well, helping to explain the growth in popularity of the Divisionalized Form in unions, school systems, universities, and especially governments. Thus, we have the story of the president of a multiversity—one among six public universities in a Canadian province—who justified his attempt to take over the two smallest ones with the argument that it would be more "convenient" for the government to negotiate with four administrations instead of six. No mention of augmenting his power, no mention of the costs of his administration having to negotiate with two new campuses, no mention of the effects on those small Professional Bureaucracies of the introduction of another intermediate layer of supervision.

As government grows larger—itself often spurred on by similar "convenient" power grabs—it is forced more and more to revert to a kind of Divisionalized Form. That is, the central administrators, being unable to control all the agencies and departments (divisions) directly, settle for granting their managers considerable autonomy and then try to control their performance. One can, in fact, view the entire government as a giant Divisionalized Form (admittedly an oversimplification, since all kinds of interdependencies exist among the departments), with its three main coordinative agencies corresponding to three main forms of control used by the headquarters of the divisionalized organization. The budgetary agency, technocratic in nature, concerns itself with performance control of the departments; the public service commission, also partly technocratic, concerns itself with the recruiting and training of government managers; and the executive (or Privy Council) office reviews the major proposals and initiatives of the departments. Perhaps this concept of the government as a giant Divisionalized Form is taken to its natural conclusion in the communist government, where public corporations and other agencies are tightly regulated by planning and control systems operated by a powerful central technostructure.

Finally, there is fashion, not an insignificant contingency factor in the popularity of the Divisionalized Form. Our comments above suggest that this structural form is becoming increasingly popular in the public and institutional sectors. In the private sector, divisionalization became fashionable after the restructuring of Du Pont and General Motors in the 1920s. Since that time American corporations have undergone a number of waves of such structural change. Much of this was, as noted, stimulated by diversification. But not all. As Rumelt (1974) notes in looking at his data, "structure also follows fashion" (p. 149). In more recent years, some managements have reorganized "in response to normative theory rather than actual administrative pressure" (p. 77). We have seen that in Europe, until recently,

the Divisionalized Form was unfashionable, with many diversified corporations resisting its use. Now the pendulum seems to be swinging the other
way, and no doubt some corporations with integrated markets will be
carried along, to their eventual regret.

STAGES IN THE TRANSITION TO
THE DIVISIONALIZED FORM

We have a good deal of research on the transition of the corporation
from the functional to the Divisionalized Form, much of it from the Harvard
Business School, which has shown a special interest in the structure of the
large corporation.[8] Figure 20–3 and the discussion that follows borrows
from these results to describe four stages of that transition.

**We begin with the large corporation that produces all of its products
through one chain and so retains what we call the integrated form—a pure
functional structure, a Machine Bureaucracy or perhaps an Adhocracy. As
the corporation begins to market some of the intermediate products of its
production processes, it makes the first shift toward divisionalization, called
the by-product form. Further moves in the same direction, to the point
where the by-products become more important than end products although
a central theme remains in the product-market strategy, lead to a structure
closer to the divisionalized one, which is called the related product form.
And finally, the complete breakdown of the production chain, to the point
where the different products have no relationship with each other, takes the
corporation to the conglomerate form, a pure divisional structure. While
some corporations may move through all these stages in sequence, we shall
see that others stop at one stage along the way because of very high fixed-
cost technical systems (typical in the case of the integrated form), operations
based on a single raw material (typical in the case of the by-product form),
or focus on a core technology or market theme (typical in the case of the
related product form).**

The Integrated Form   At the top of Figure 20–3 is the pure functional
form, used by the corporation whose production activities form one integrated, unbroken chain. Only the final output is sold to the customers. The
tight interdependencies of the different activities make it impossible for such

[8]This includes Wrigley (1970), Salter (1970), Scott (1971, 1973), Lorsch and Allen (1973), and
Rumelt (1974), all of whom focused on the American corporation; Fouraker and Stopford
(1968), who focused on international diversification; Channon (1973), who studied divisionalization in Britain, and later followed this up with a study of the service industries there (1975,
1976); Paven (1974), who studied divisionalization in Italy; Dyas and Thanheiser (1976), who
did likewise in France and Germany; and Franko (1972, 1974), who studied the European multinational firms in general. The Scott (1973) paper reviews the results of a number of these studies.

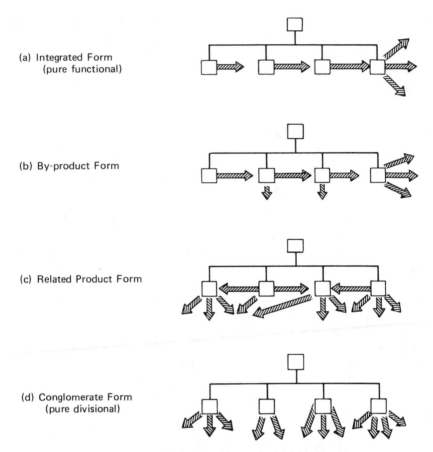

(a) Integrated Form
    (pure functional)

(b) By-product Form

(c) Related Product Form

(d) Conglomerate Form
    (pure divisional)

Figure 20-3. *Stages in the Transition to the Divisionalized Form*

corporations to use the Divisionalized Form—that is, to grant autonomy to units performing any of the steps in the chain—and so they organize themselves as functional Machine Bureaucracies (or Adhocracies if they face complex, dynamic environments). They typically produce a single product line, or at least one line dominates. Large firms using this structure also tend to be vertically integrated and capital-intensive (Fouraker and Stopford, 1968; Salter, 1970; Stewart, 1970, pp. 37–38). Units responsible for different steps in the production chain are sometimes called "divisions," and may in fact produce products similar to those of the true divisions of other corporations—for example, iron ore in the case of a vertically integrated steel company as compared with the mining division of a conglomerate company. But in recalling from Chapter 7 that grouping is defined according to the "ultimate markets served by the organization," these units can be seen to be based on function—on the *means* to reach the end products and markets rather than on these *ends* themselves. These units have no choice but to buy from or sell to their sister units in the same corporation, and so they lack the autonomy of true divisions.

Ironically, despite its reputation as the very model of divisionalization, General Motors seems to fit best into this category. That is, aside from its nonautomotive activities, which are relatively small (under 10 percent of total sales), the corporation seems not to be truly divisionalized at all, despite its use of that term. Earlier we saw that Sloan consolidated the structure of General Motors in the 1920s, converted a holding company into a divisionalized one. In fact, he continued to consolidate it throughout his tenure as chief executive officer. As Perrow (1974) notes:

> When Sloan came in, he radically and continuously centralized the organization. He introduced inventory-control and production-control devices and internal pricing, allotted markets to the various units, controlled capital outlays, centralized advertising and personnel, standardized parts, and routinized innovation. At every step the divisions lost autonomy (p. 38).

And that process of consolidation has apparently continued unabated to the present day (Perrow, 1974, p. 38; Scott, 1971, p. 24). Wrigley (1970) documents the result. He describes General Motors' production process as one integrated "closed system" (p. VI-23), shown in Figure 20-4. For example, "neither G.M. Assembly nor Fisher Body can be permitted to sell their facilities to the market, nor the car divisions [Chevrolet, Pontiac, Buick, Oldsmobile, Cadillac] to buy the kind of facilities [they need] from the open market" (p. V-5). No break is allowed in the chain. The central office controls labor relations, market forecasting, research, engineering, quality control, styling, pricing, production scheduling, inventory levels, product range, and dealer relations; it decides what plants are to be. built, and what cars; it styles them (all must have "a General Motors look," p. V-29), and it tests them at the corporate Proving Ground. "It is of note that

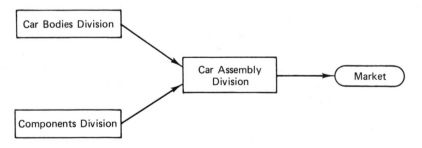

Figure 20-4. *General Motors' Simplified Automotive Production System (from Wrigley, 1970, VI-23)*

the Engineering Policy Group of General Motors does not include divisional managers" (p. V-33).

One is tempted to ask what decisions are left for the car divisions to make. By Wrigley's account, not much more than marketing and distribution ones,[9] and even those are circumscribed by a central office that sets prices, determines the number of dealers each may have in the major metropolitan areas, establishes guidelines for granting franchises, and organizes the committee that arbitrates disputes on the withdrawal of franchises. By way of conclusion, Wrigley quotes Sloan (1963) on how the division managers "make almost all of the divisional operating decisions," and then comments on the decisions he found they really did make:

> ... all this is in the realm of routine operations. It certainly does not justify the characterization of "General Management" work, still less of "entrepreneurial" activity. It is quite clear that in no significant sense of the term are the automotive divisions of General Motors "autonomous" or "independent businesses," nor are their managers "Presidents of small businesses" (even allowing that Chevrolet is a small business). The role of the automotive division is to follow corporate goals through corporate determined means. They have little autonomy (pp. V-37–V-38).

The By-product Form   As the integrated firm seeks wider markets, it may choose to diversify its end product lines and shift all the way over to the pure divisional structure. A less risky alternative, however, is to start by marketing its intermediate products on the open market. This introduces small breaks in its processing chain, which in turn calls for a measure of divisionalization in its structure, what can be called the *by-product form.* Each link in the processing chain can now be given some autonomy in order to market its by-products, although it is understood that most of its outputs will be passed on internally to the next link in the chain.

Many of the organizations that fall into this category are vertically integrated ones that base their operations on a single basic material, such as wood, oil, or aluminum, which they process to a variety of consumable end products. Figure 20–5 shows the processing chain for Alcoa in 1969, which earned 69 percent of its revenue from fabricated aluminum end products, such as cookware and auto parts, and 27 percent from intermediate by-products, including cargo space, chemicals, bauxite, and pit and ingot aluminum. (Real estate development—a horizontally diversified service—accounted for the remaining 4 percent.)

[9]They also control some of the purchasing from external sources, the hiring, firing, and promoting of their own personnel ("up to a certain level," p. V-37), and the allocation of work between plants under their jurisdiction.

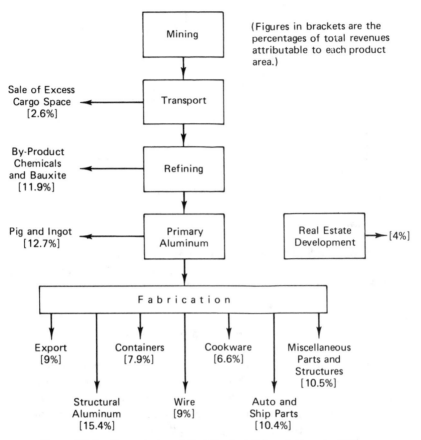

Figure 20-5. *By-product and End Product Sales of Alcoa in 1969 (from Rumelt, 1974, p. 21; prepared from data in company's annual reports)*

In the by-product form, because the processing chain remains more or less intact, headquarters retains considerable control over strategy formulation and some aspects of operations as well. Specifically, it relies on action planning to manage the interdependencies between the divisions. Figure 20-6 shows Lorsch and Allen's (1973) depiction of the relationship between divisions and headquarters in a vertically integrated paper company, with one by-product and two end product markets. Here the headquarters and divisions shared responsibility for the planning and scheduling of mill capacity, the headquarters scheduling department took responsibility for balancing the demands of the converting divisions with the supplies of the mills, and the headquarters planning department played an important role in developing the expansion projects of the mills. "Executives ... indicated

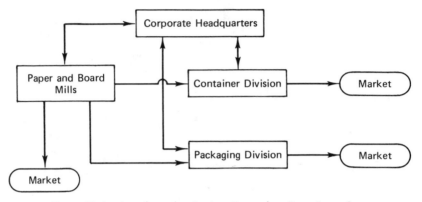

Figure 20-6. *Interdependencies in a By-product Form Paper Company (from Lorsch and Allen, 1973, p. 117)*

that, while the mill organization was heavily involved in determining the nature of future facilities to be built, it was the corporate planning function which had the market information necessary to justify an expansion" (p. 126).

The Related Product Form   Some corporations continue to diversify their by-product markets, further breaking down their processing chains until what the divisions sell on the open market becomes more important than what they supply to each other. The organization then moves to the *related product form.* For example, a firm manufacturing washing machines may set up a division to produce the motors. Eventually, the motor division may become so successful on its own that the washing machine division is no longer the dominant customer. A more serious form of divisionalization is then called for, to reflect the greater independence of the divisions. Thus, Wrigley found that 85 percent of the firms he categorized as "related product" diversified had what he considered divisionalized structures.

What typically holds the divisions of these firms together is some common thread among their products, sometimes a core skill or technology, sometimes a central market theme. The divisions often sell to many of the same outside customers as well. In effect, the firm retains a semblance of an integrated product-market strategy. Rumelt (1974) describes the diversification of the Carborundum company between 1949 and 1969 in steps from one related business to another. The before and after product lines are shown in Figure 20-7(a) and (b).

In 1949, all of Carborundum's businesses were closely related to the firm's basic strengths: the efficient production of high quality grains of silicon carbide and aluminum oxide, and the competence in the materials sciences necessary to engineer these materials to various uses. . . .

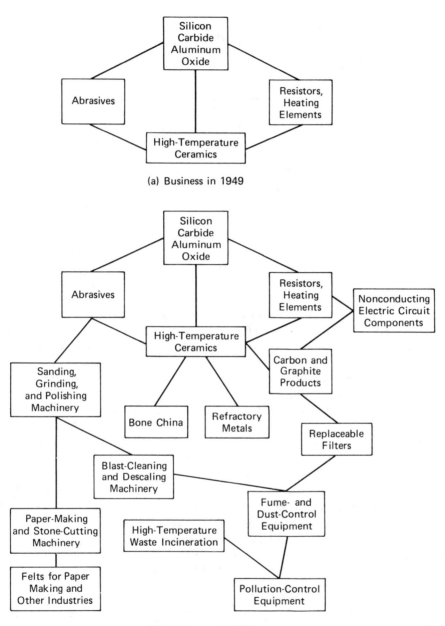

(a) Business in 1949

(b) Businesses in 1969

Figure 20-7. *The Related Product Diversification of Carborundum, Inc. (from Rumelt, 1974, pp. 17, 19; prepared from data in company's annual reports)*

During the 1950s, however, Carborundum began to produce a line of grinding, cutting, and polishing machines to complement its line of abrasives. Then, beginning in 1962 ... [the] skills acquired in manufacturing abrasive machines were applied to other types of industrial machinery, and nonabrasive cleaning and descaling equipment was added. Ceramics technology led to ceramic electrical components and carbon and graphite materials, which in turn provided a base for expansion into filtering media. High temperature technology led to the refractory metals business. Recently, the company's activities in filtering media, cleaning machinery, general industrial machinery, and high temperature technology have been brought together through a position in the solid waste disposal and pollution control fields (pp. 17–19).

Central planning at the headquarters in the related product form must be less constraining than in the by-product form, more concerned with measuring performance than prescribing actions. A good deal of the control over the specific product-market strategies must revert to the divisions. But the interdependencies around the central product-market theme encourage the headquarters to retain functions common to the divisions, for example, research and development in the case of a core technology. Thus, Wrigley found the headquarters staffs in the related product firms to be large but specialized in the core areas. These central functions are, of course, the "critical" ones for the corporation, so Channon's functional/divisional hybrids—specifically, the ones with *product* or *service* divisions, such as insurance companies that centralized the critical investment function—would fall into this grouping.

Wrigley (1970, pp. V-40–V-69) describes at some length the structure of General Electric as an example of the related product form. He notes that some products, such as artificial diamonds, are sold mainly to users outside the company, while others, such as appliance components and small motors, are sold both inside and outside. The structure is divisionalized—in fact, multiple-divisionalized, with groups over divisions, as can be seen in its organigram (circa 1975) reproduced in Figure 20–8. In many ways its structure is typical of the Divisionalized Form, except that the "spearhead" of its "massive" research and development effort—employing some 650 scientists and engineers and 1200 support personnel at the time of Wrigley's study—is attached to the headquarters (p. V-54). Research and development is apparently a critical function at General Electric. Moreover, included in the central support staff, in addition to the usual functions found at the headquarters of divisionalized firms, are labor relations (with line responsibility for major negotiations), market forecasting, and engineering and marketing (these two provided on a consulting basis). According to Wrigley, the divisional managers are given little control over management development and supplies, two other functions apparently viewed as critical. Otherwise, in line with the performance standards imposed on them, they have consider-

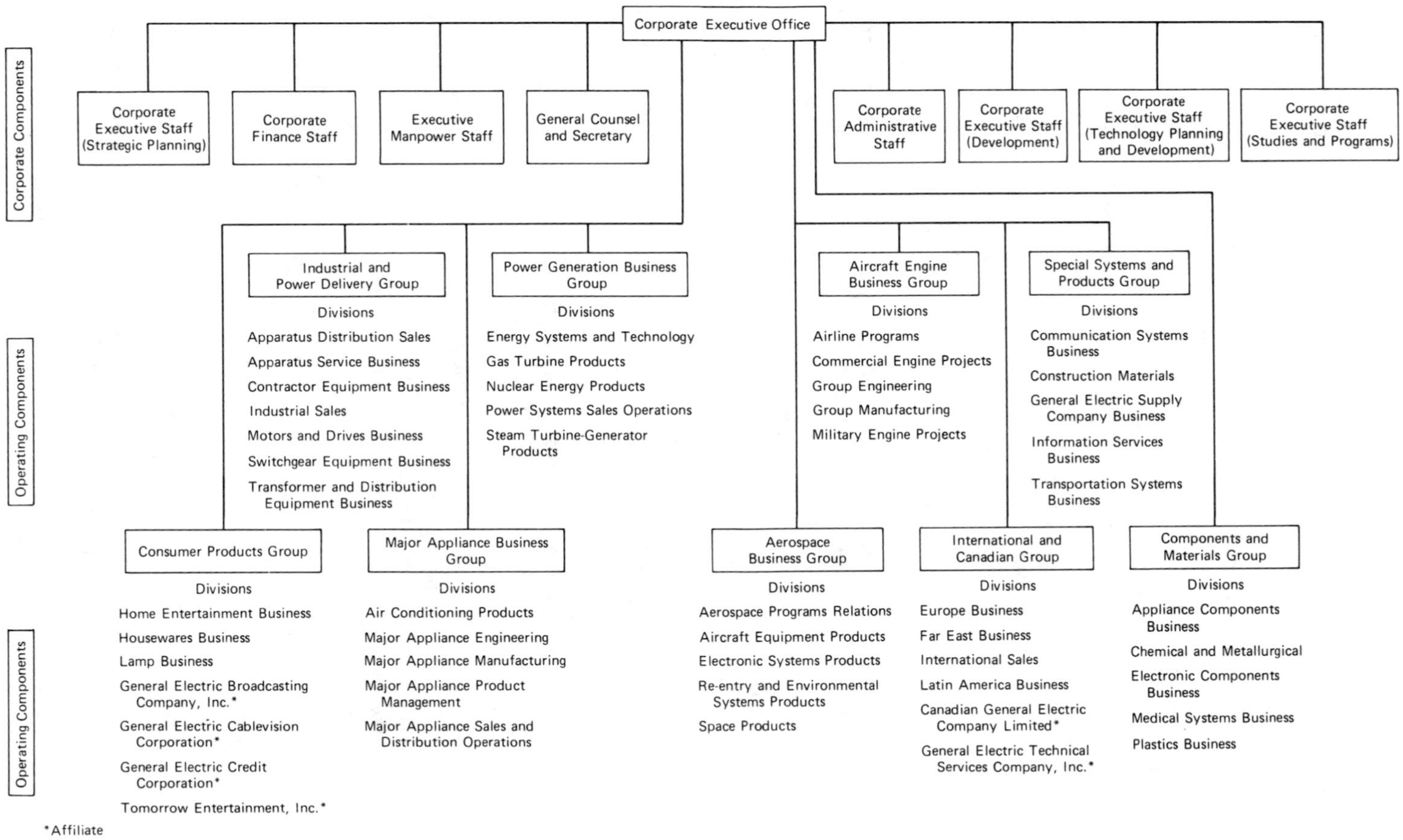

Figure 20-8. Organigram of General Electric (circa 1975, used with permission)

*Affiliate

Corporate Components

Operating Components

Operating Components

411

able autonomy to run their own operations and formulate their own product-market strategies.

The Conglomerate Form   As the related product firm expands into new markets or acquires other firms, with less and less regard for a central strategic theme, the organization moves to the *conglomerate form*[10] and adopts a pure divisionalized structure, the one we described earlier in this chapter as the basic structure. Each division serves its own markets, producing product lines unrelated to those of the other divisions—thumbtacks in one, steam shovels in a second, funeral services in a third. In the conglomerate, there are no important interdependencies among the divisions, save for the pooling of resources. As a result, the headquarters planning and control system becomes simply a vehicle for regulating performance, specifically financial performance:

> The goals have become not only more financially oriented, but more abstract. And these two changes, the increasing abstractness and increasingly financial nature of the goals, lend themselves to increased tolerance for deviations from tradition—so long as such deviations give promise of adequate financial returns. The test of a new idea is not so much how it fits with tradition as what its potential pay-off is likely to be in a competitive environment (Scott, 1971, p. 33).

Wrigley (1970) found that the conglomerates (which he refers to as "unrelated product" companies) tend to have small headquarters' staffs and strong divisions. He quotes a chief executive of Textron—where the staff of thirty executives and administrators oversaw thirty divisions doing more than $1.5 billion of sales volume:

> A key concept is that we have a minimum of home staff. It consists almost entirely of line managers and clerical personnel, with virtually no staff helping the line managers. We have no R and D section or manufacturing section or marketing section, for example. With our collection of businesses, what would they do? Neither do we have any corporate labour relations officer or staff. We want the unions to bargain separately in each of our divisions, and we will not send any corporate representatives to any labour negotiations (pp. V-76–77).

Lorsch and Allen (1973) support Wrigley's conclusions in their study of six corporations, four conglomerates and two more integrated firms.

---

[10]Salter (1970) introduces another stage before this last one, the "single-product firms that are geographically decentralized" (p. 30). But by his definition, these correspond exactly to our carbon-copy bureaucracies. They have been discussed earlier in this chapter because they seem to be a special case of Machine Bureaucracy that does not fit into this continuum of increasing divisionalization.

Table 20–1 shows their results. While the conglomerates, with one exception which we shall come to shortly, had very small headquarters professional and managerial staffs (seventeen, twenty, and twenty-five people), the vertically integrated firms had 250 and 479 people at headquarters. And the conglomerates carried out fewer activities at headquarters, concentrating on financial control, long-range planning, legal services, and industrial relations. The integrated firms had all of these functions as well as research and development (as did one of the conglomerates), central planning and scheduling of outputs, and centralized purchasing.

TABLE 20-1   Basic Characteristics of Corporate Headquarters Units in Six Firms* (from Lorsch and Allen, 1973: 148)

	Conglomerate Firms				Vertically Integrated Firms	
	1	2	3	4	5	6
A. Size—total number of management and professional employees	17	20	25	230	479	250
B. Functions performed in reference to divisions						
1. Financial/control	X_P	X_P	X_P	X_P	$X_{O,P}$	$X_{O,P}$
2. Long-range planning	X_P	X_P	X_P	X_P	$X_{O,P}$	$X_{O,P}$
3. Legal	$X_{O,P}$	$X_{O,P}$	$X_{O,P}$	$X_{O,P}$	$X_{O,P}$	$X_{O,P}$
4. Industrial relations	$X_{O,P}$	$X_{O,P}$	$X_{O,P}$	$X_{O,P}$	$X_{O,P}$	$X_{O,P}$
5. Operations research					X_P	
6. Marketing		X_P	X_P	X_O	X_O	X_O
7. Manufacturing/industrial engineering			X_P	X_P		
8. Planning and scheduling of output					X_O	X_O
9. Purchasing					X_O	X_O
10. Engineering (other than industrial)				X_P		
11. Research and development				$X_{O,P}$	X_O	X_O

*X indicates that certain functions in specified areas are performed by the headquarters unit for the divisions. P indicates that corporate involvement is of a policy-setting nature (i.e., setting policies, advising, providing basic approaches). O indicates an operating responsibility for the headquarters unit (e.g., actually carrying out some purchasing activities for certain divisions).

One thing that can, however, vary widely in the conglomerate form is the tightness of the performance control system, although it always remains financial. At one extreme is the well-known system of ITT, described by one of its executives as follows:

> From our New York office we operate a rigid system of controls on inventories, receivables, debt levels, capital expenditures, G & A expense, profit forecasts, etc., through a highly sophisticated system of reporting. For example, no sub-

sidiary can increase its level of debt over budget without justification to, and prior approval of, the Treasurer's office. It is also characteristic of our continuous attention that we make a worldwide check of the forecast of earnings at each division twice a month. If any of our subsidiaries forecasts a slippage in the approved budget levels in any the areas mentioned above, immediate remedial steps are put into effect either by on-the-spot visits from the appropriate New York staff, or from the appropriate regional staff (Martyn, 1967, p. 17).

In fact, there seems at the time of this writing to be a marked trend toward such tight control systems, at least if Allen's (1978) recent findings are any indication. Seventeen of the thirty companies he surveyed significantly increased "the emphasis they placed on long-range planning systems, monthly budget reviews, monthly narrative reports on operations, formal goal-setting systems, and performance evaluation/incentive compensation systems for division executives" (p. 29). In fact, Conglomerate 4 in Table 20-1, from Allen's book with Lorsch, seems to be just such a firm, the large headquarters staff presumably required to run the tight financial control system.

At the other extreme, although far less fashionable, is the holding company, a federation of businesses so loose that it is probably not even appropriate to think of it as one entity. The holding company typically has no central headquarters and no real control system, save the occasional meeting of its different presidents. This is the logical finale to our discussion of the stages in the transition to the Divisionalized Form—fragmentation of structure to the point where we can no longer talk of a single organization.[11]

SOME ISSUES ASSOCIATED WITH THE DIVISIONALIZED FORM

We begin our discussion of issues by enumerating some of the advantages traditionally claimed for the Divisionalized Form over the more integrated functional forms. Then, from society's perspective, we suggest that the Divisionalized Form should logically be compared with another alternative, that of the divisions constituted as independent organizations. In this context, we reassess its advantages. Both of these discussions consider only the administrative and economic consequences of divisionalization. At that

[11]The holding company may, in fact, be an unstable form, eventually consolidated into a tighter divisionalized structure or split up into separate companies. Chandler (1962, p. 4) reports that the holding companies in the industries he studied tended to consolidate by 1909 into single, centralized, functional organizations. Had the Divisionalized Form been developed by that time, they presumably would have chosen this structure instead.

point we turn to the social consequences, specifically the problems the Divisionalized Form poses for social responsibility and centralization of power in society. All of these discussions focus on the conglomerate form in the private sector—conglomerate because it is the purest form of divisionalization, where the issues are most pronounced, and private sector because, as we shall see toward the end of our discussion, the pure Divisionalized Form turns out to be ill-suited to other sectors. We close our discussion of the issues with a description of the Divisionalized Form as the most vulnerable of the five structural configurations, a structure symbolically on the edge of a cliff.

The Economic Advantages of Divisionalization   The Divisionalized Form offers four basic advantages over the functional structure with integrated operations. First, the Divisionalized Form encourages efficient allocation of capital. Headquarters can choose where to put its money, and so it can concentrate on its strongest markets, milking the surpluses of some divisions in favor of others. The functional structure has all its eggs in one strategic basket, so to speak. Second, by opening up opportunities to run individual businesses, the Divisionalized Form helps to train general managers. In contrast, the middle-line managers of functional structures are locked into dependent relationships with each other, which preclude individual responsibility and autonomy. Third, the Divisionalized Form spreads its risk. "... if there is a breakdown in one portion of a loosely coupled system then this breakdown is sealed off and does not affect other portions of the organization" (Weick, 1976, p. 7). In contrast, one broken link in the operating chain of the functional structure brings the entire system to a grinding halt. Fourth, and perhaps most important, the Divisionalized Form is strategically responsive. In the words of Ansoff and Brandenburg (1971), the divisionalized structure's "superiority over the functional form is that it combines steady-state efficiency with organizational responsiveness" (p. 722). The divisions can fine-tune their bureaucratic machine while the headquarters concentrates on its strategic portfolio. It can acquire new businesses and divest itself of older, ineffective ones, while the division managers are free to perfect the operation of their businesses.

But is the functional form the correct basis of comparison? Is it the real alternative to the Divisionalized Form? It is, if one wishes to compare diversified with nondiversified organizations. **Strategic diversification, because it leads to structural divisionalization, encourages the efficient allocation of capital within the organization; it trains general managers, reduces risks, and increases strategic responsiveness. In other words, it solves many of the economic problems that arise in the Machine Bureaucracy.** From the perspective of the organization itself, diversification followed by divisionalization offers a number of distinct advantages over remaining nondiversified.

But once an organization is diversified and then divisionalized, there is reason to change the basis of comparison. The real alternative, at least from society's perspective, becomes the one of taking a further step along the same path, to the point of eliminating the headquarters and allowing the divisions to function as independent organizations. Textron, as described by Wrigley, had thirty divisions operating in as many different businesses; Beatrice Foods, described in a 1976 *Fortune* magazine article (Martin, 1976), had 397. The issue is whether either of these corporations was more efficient than thirty or 397 separate corporations. In effect, the perspective shifts from that of the organization to that of society. In this context, we can reconsider the four advantages discussed above.

In the divisionalized organization, headquarters allocates the capital resources among the thirty or 397 divisions. In the case of thirty or 397 independent corporations, the capital markets do the job instead. Which does it better? Two studies suggest that the answer is not a simple one.

Williamson (1975) argues that the Divisionalized Form does the better job. In fact, he describes it as the administrative response to inefficiencies in the capital markets—to idiosyncratic knowledge, opportunistic behaviors, and the like. By virtue of their elaborate performance control systems and their personal contacts, the headquarters managers are better able than the investors to inform themselves of the potential of different businesses, at least a limited number of businesses. "A tradeoff between breadth of information, in which respect the banking system may be presumed to have the advantage, and depth of information, which is the advantage of the specialized firm, is involved. The conglomerate can be regarded as an intermediate form that, ideally, optimizes with respect to the breadth–depth tradeoff" (p. 162). Moreover, the headquarters managers are able to transfer capital between the divisions more quickly and flexibly than can the equivalent market mechanisms. So the Divisionalized Form has "mitigated capital market failures by transferring functions traditionally imputed to the capital market to the firm instead" (p. 136).

Williamson's arguments may, in fact, explain why many conglomerate firms have been able to survive and prosper in the economic system. But Moyer in a 1970 paper suggests that these advantages come at a price, specifically that conglomeration—especially by acquisition, the most common way to achieve it—has proven more costly and, in some ways, *less* flexible than the market mechanisms:

> An acquiring firm normally pays a 15% premium above the market price of the firm to be acquired in order to consummate a merger. Completely diversified mutual funds can be purchased for a selling charge of 7–9% in the case of "load" funds. ... Furthermore, an individual stockholder can diversify his own portfolio with brokerage costs averaging only 1.5% to 3.5% of the value of the stock purchased. ...

Because conglomerate firms have not been required in the past to publish earnings for wholly owned divisions or subsidiaries ... the stockholder is
not in a position to make decisions as to whether subsidiaries which management has seen fit to purchase are enhancing his earning power. An individually
diversified portfolio has substantially more flexibility than a conglomerate
portfolio. The individual can buy and sell with a minimum of effort depending
on the performance of individual stocks. It is a different and more involved
matter for a conglomerate to decide to divest itself of one or more of its subsidiaries (p. 22).

Moyer believes that conglomeration denies the shareholder one of his few
remaining prerogatives, namely the choice of an industry—and a risk level
—in which to put his capital. The choice among stocks of different conglomerate firms amounts to the choice among given portfolios—Beatrice
Foods instead of Dannon Yogurt.

On the issue of management development, the question becomes
whether the division managers receive better training and experience than
they would as company presidents. The Divisionalized Form is able to put
on training courses and to rotate its managers to vary their experiences; the
independent form is limited in these respects. But if, as the proponents of
divisionalization claim, autonomy is the key to management development,
then presumably the more autonomy the better. The division managers
have a headquarters to lean on—and to be leaned on by. In Textron, "The
price of autonomy is plan achievement. If a division cannot for one reason
or another meet its goals, it is subject to close and detailed supervision ..."
(Wrigley, 1970, p. V-91). In contrast, the company president is on his own,
to make his own mistakes and learn from them.

On the third issue, of risk, the argument from the divisionalized perspective is that the independent organization is vulnerable during periods of
internal crisis or economic slump: conglomeration provides it with the
support to see it through such periods. The counterargument is that divisionalization may conceal bankruptcies, that ailing divisions are sometimes
supported longer than necessary, whereas the market bankrupts the independent firm and is done with it. Another point, this one from the perspective of the organization itself, is that just as the Divisionalized Form spreads
its risk, so too does it spread the consequences of that risk. A single division
cannot go bankrupt; the whole organization is legally responsible for its
debts. So a massive-enough problem in one division—say an enormous
increase in the price of nuclear fuel a division has committed itself to buy in
large quantities—can siphon off the resources of the healthy divisions and
even bankrupt the whole organization. *Loose* coupling turns out to be
riskier than *no* coupling!

Finally, there is the issue of strategic responsiveness. The loosely
coupled Divisionalized Form may be more responsive than the tightly

coupled functional form. But the question is: what price even loose coupling? In other words, what effect does conglomeration have on strategic responsiveness? The control system of the Divisionalized Form—which keeps that carrot just the right distance in front of the divisional managers—encourages them to strive for better and better financial performance. At the same time, however, it impedes their ability to innovate. "Textron's management has ... learned that developing new inventions is not one of its strong points" (quoted in Wrigley, 1970, p. V-89). Bower (1970) explains why:

> ... the risks to the division manager of a major innovation can be considerable if he is measured on short-run, year-to-year, earnings performance. The result is a tendency to avoid big risky bets, and the concomitant phenomenon that major new developments are, with few exceptions, made outside the major firms in the industry. Those exceptions tend to be single-product companies whose top managements are committed to true product leadership: Bell Laboratories, IBM, Xerox, and Polaroid. These are the top managements that can make major strategic moves for their whole company. Instead, the diversified companies give us a steady diet of small incremental change (p. 194).

Innovation requires entrepreneurship, and entrepreneurship does not thrive under standardized external control. The entrepreneur takes his own risks to earn his own rewards. No control system managed from a headquarters can substitute for that kind of motivation. In fact, many entrepreneurs set up their own businesses to escape bureaucratic controls (Collins and Moore, 1970), the kind Textron's president described to Wrigley: "Anything out of routine must be analyzed and justified"; he and the chairman "are in more frequent contact with any division that has something especially big in the works" (p. V-90). Such procedures may avert risk, but they also avert the benefits of risk—true innovation as opposed to "small incremental change."

Thus, the independent firm appears to be more strategically responsive than the corporate division, although perhaps less motivated to achieve consistently high economic performance. Indeed, many divisionalized corporations depend on these firms for their strategic responsiveness, since they diversify not by innovating themselves but by acquiring the innovative results of independent entrepreneurs.

The Role of Headquarters   To assess the effectiveness of conglomeration, it is necessary to assess what actual contribution the headquarters makes to the divisions. Since the headquarters function of control is supposed to be performed by the board of directors of the independent firm, the question becomes: What does a headquarters offer to the division that an independent board of directors does not?[12]

One thing that neither the headquarters managers nor the board of directors can offer is the management of the individual business. Both are involved with it only on a part-time basis.[13] The management of it is, therefore, logically left to its full-time managers—they have the required time and information. In fact, one issue that faces the Divisionalized Form more than the independent business, because of the closer links between headquarters and divisional managers, is the tendency to forget this point. **A strong set of forces encourage the headquarters managers to usurp divisional powers, to centralize certain product-market decisions at headquarters and so defeat the purpose of divisionalization.** Headquarters managers may believe they can do better; they may be tempted to eliminate duplication (one advertising department instead of 397); they may simply enjoy exercising the power that is potentially theirs; or they may be lured by new administrative techniques. An enthusiastic technostructure or consulting firm may oversell a sophisticated MIS or a system that suggests product-market decisions can be made according to data on market share or product life cycle.

The trouble with many of these techniques is that they give the illusion of knowledge without giving the knowledge itself. As we noted in Chapter 18 and elsewhere, a good deal of the information needed for formulating strategies is soft and speculative—bits and pieces of impression, rumor, and the like that never get documented or quantified. What the MIS carries back to headquarters are abstracted, aggregated generalizations. But no business can be understood solely from reports on market share, product life cycle, and the like. Such understanding requires soft information which inevitably remains behind in the divisions, whose managers are in personal touch with the specific situations. Even if the MIS could bring back the right information—or the headquarters managers tried to use the telephone to get it verbally—they would lack the time to absorb it. Lack of time to understand many businesses is precisely the reason why organizations are divisionalized in the first place, to give each business the undivided attention of one man-

---

[12]It is interesting that Williamson (1975) ignores the role of the board in control, arguing that "division managers are subordinates: as such, both their accounting records and backup files are appropriate subjects for review. Stockholders, by contrast, are much more limited in what they can demand in the way of disclosure" (p. 146), and that "internal disclosure is affirmatively regarded as necessary to the integrity of the organization and is rewarded accordingly. Disclosure to outsiders, by contrast, commonly exposes the informant to penalties" (p. 147). The shareholders may be outsiders, with limited access to information, but Williamson forgets that they are supposed to be legally represented by the directors, who have no such limitations.

[13]If the directors are full-time, they become, in effect, the management, and there is no formal external control of the firm.

ager and his unit. So the high-speed transmission lines only lure some headquarters managers into making decisions better left in the divisions. As
Antony Jay (1970) notes, things were better when such lines did not exist,
when the headquarters managers could not use direct supervision to control
their subordinates:

> ...one reason why the Roman empire grew so large and survived so long—a
> prodigious feat of management—is that there was no railway, car, aeroplane,
> radio, paper or telephone. Above all, no telephone. And therefore you could
> not maintain any illusion of direct control over a general or a provincial
> governor, you could not feel at the back of your mind that you could ring him
> up, or he could ring you, if a situation cropped up which was too much for
> him, or that you could fly over and sort things out if they started to get into a
> mess. You appointed him, you watched his chariot and baggage train disappear
> over the hill in a cloud of dust, or his trireme recede over the horizon, and that
> was that. If there was a disaster you would know nothing about it until months
> later when a messenger came panting up from the port of Ostia or galloping in
> down the Via Apennina to tell you that an army had been lost or a province
> overrun. There was, therefore, no question of appointing a man who was not
> fully trained, or not quite up to the job; you knew that everything depended
> on his being the best man for the job before he set off. And so you took great
> care in selecting him; but more than that, you made sure that he knew all about
> Rome and Roman government and the Roman army before he went out (p. 69).

Jay later quotes a "disgruntled" British admiral after the Suez operation of
1956: "Nelson would never have won a single victory if there'd been a Telex"
(p. 79).

In this regard, the Swedish SIAR group (1975) describes a "vicious
circle of one way communication" that results when "... all people from
headquarters [of a multinational organization] are regarded (and regard
themselves) as superiors of a kind, with a supervisory function" (p. 10). The
headquarters comes to dominate both language and communication
channels to the divisions, and to set the agendas and determine what issues
are important. But the headquarters is out of touch with local conditions,
coming "to know less and less about what is actually happening in the field"
(p. 13). And so the division personnel lose interest in responding to headquarters initiatives, and headquarters becomes more and more isolated
from "the real thing." The SIAR group believes that "One reason why so
many international conglomerates have been in severe problems during the
last years is no doubt this failure to understand the differences between their
many subsidiaries" (p. 13). Headquarters generates policies "by abstract
deduction or by imitation of other organizations" (p. 15). These get ignored
in the divisions, and so headquarters is encouraged to tighten its control
over the divisions—by formalizing more of its communication to them,
increasing the amount of indoctrination of divisional personnel, and placing

inspectors in the divisions. All of this serves to enlarge the headquarters staff, which aggregates the basic problem of inappropriate centralization. "In one international company that we studied, the table of contents [of the manual for the divisions] was alone as thick as the telephone book of a large city" (p. 16).

So one function of the headquarters managers of the conglomerate diversified corporation is *not* to manage the divisions. The wise ones know what they cannot know.

Among the functions headquarters managers *do* perform are the establishment of objectives for the divisions, the monitoring of their performance in terms of these objectives (an appropriate use for the MIS), the maintenance of limited personal contacts with division managers, and the approval of the major capital expenditures of the divisions. Interestingly, these are also the responsibilities of the board of directors, at least in theory. In practice, however, many boards—notably those of widely held corporations—do these things ineffectively, leaving management carte blanche to do what it likes (Mace, 1971). Here, then, we seem to have a major advantage of the Divisionalized Form. It exists as an administrative arrangement to overcome another major weakness of the free-market system, namely the ineffective board. With the attention the headquarters pays to its formal and personal control systems, it induces divisional managers to strive for better and better financial results.

There is a catch in this argument, however, for conglomerate diversification often serves both to diffuse stock ownership and to render the corporation more difficult to understand and control by its board. For one thing, as we saw earlier, diversified corporations are typically large ones and so typically widely held and difficult to understand in any event. For another, the more businesses an organization operates, the harder it is for part-time directors to know what is going on. And finally, one common effect of conglomerate acquisition is to increase the number of shareholders, and so to make the corporation more widely held:

> In general, the impact of a merger is to increase the diffusion of ownership in the surviving firm. Quasi-ownership capital instruments have been shown to be of great importance in large mergers. The near term effect of the use of these instruments is the surrender of voting power by the acquired firm's stockholders to the stockholders of the acquiring firm. As these instruments are converted, voting power becomes increasingly diffused among a larger and larger group of stockholders (Moyer, 1970, p. 29).

Thus, the Divisionalized Form in some sense only resolves a problem of its own making. Had the corporation remained in one business, it would likely have been more narrowly held and easier to understand, and so its directors could have performed their functions more effectively. Diversification helped create the problem that divisionalization solved. Indeed, it is ironic that many a divisionalized corporation that does such an effective job of monitoring the performance of its divisions is itself so poorly monitored by its own board of directors.[14]

A main purpose of this monitoring is to flag problems and correct them before they emerge as full-fledged crises. A well-known weakness of the independent corporation is that top management can pull the wool over the eyes of its directors, camouflaging serious problems (Mace, 1971). That is harder to do in the divisionalized corporation, with its persistent managers at headquarters. But camouflaging is hardly unknown in the Divisionalized Form either, and for the same reason—the detailed information rests with the full-time managers of each business, not with those who are supposed to control them on a part-time basis. The following story, told by an assistant controller at one headquarters, illustrates this clearly:

> Our top management likes to make all the major decisions. They think they do, but I've just seen one case where a division beat them.
>
> I received for editing a request from the division for a large chimney. I couldn't see what anyone could do with just a chimney, so I flew out for a visit. They've built and equipped a whole plant on plant expense orders. The chimney is the only indivisible item that exceeded the $50,000 limit we put on the expense orders.
>
> Apparently they learned informally that a new plant wouldn't be favorably received, so they built the damn thing. I don't know exactly what I'm going to say (quoted in Bower, 1970, p. 189).

What happens when a problem does get flagged? What can headquarters do about it that a board of directors could not? The chairman of Textron told a meeting of the New York Society of Security Analysts, in reference to the headquarters vice-presidents who oversee the divisions, that "it is not too difficult to coordinate five companies that are well run" (quoted in Wrigley, 1970, p. V-78). True enough. But what about five that are badly run? What can the staff of thirty administrators at Textron headquarters really do to correct problems in the thirty operating divisions? The natural tendency to tighten the control screws does not usually help once the problem has manifested itself, nor does exercising close surveillance. As noted earlier, the headquarters managers cannot manage the divisions. Essentially, that leaves them with two alternatives. They can replace the division manager or they can divest the corporation of the division. Of course, the board of directors can also change the management. Indeed, that seems to be its only real prerogative; the management does everything else. So the question

[14] These points about the power and control of the board of directors are developed at greater length in a forthcoming book in this series entitled *Power In and Around Organizations*.

becomes: Who can better select the manager of a business, a headquarters or a board of directors? The answer to that question is not clear. A headquarters can move faster and it has a pool of managers from other divisions to draw from. But it has to be thinking about the managers of thirty or 397 divisions from time to time, whereas the board of directors need worry about only one. As for divestment, that merely puts the problem in somebody else's lap; from society's perspective, it does not solve it (unless, of course, conglomeration caused the problem in the first place!).

On balance, the case for one headquarters versus a set of separate boards of directors appears to be mixed. It should come as no surprise that one study found that corporations with "controlled diversity" had better profit than those with conglomerate diversity (Rumelt, 1974). Controlled diversity means interdependence among the divisions, which calls for an intermediate, or impure, form of divisionalization, with some critical functions concentrated at headquarters.

Pure divisionalization remedies certain inefficiencies in the capital market, but it introduces new ones of its own; it trains general managers, but then gives them less autonomy than does the independent business; it spreads its risks, but it also spreads the consequences of those risks; it protects vulnerable operations during economic slumps, including some that later prove to have not been worth protecting; its control systems encourage the steady improvement of financial performance yet discourage true entrepreneurial innovation; its headquarters does a better job of monitoring business performance than does the board of the widely held corporation, but its inherent diversification is one of the causes of corporations being widely held and boards being ill-informed in the first place; and in the final analysis, it can do little more than a board of directors to correct the fundamental problems in a business—ultimately, both are reduced to changing the management. Overall, the pure Divisionalized Form (i.e., the conglomerate form) may offer some advantages over a weak system of boards of directors and inefficient capital markets; but most of those advantages would probably disappear if certain problems in capital markets and boards were rectified.[15] And there is reason to argue that society would be better off trying to correct fundamental inefficiencies in its economic system rather than encouraging private administrative arrangements to circumvent them. In fact, as we now turn from the administrative and economic consequences of the Divisionalized Form to its social ones, we shall see two additional reasons to support this conclusion, one related to the social responsibility of the Divisionalized Form, the other to its tendency to concentrate power in society.

[15]For example, Mace (1971) proposes a system of professional directors, individuals who would work full time as directors of perhaps five companies, and so would have the time to get to know each of them well enough to exercise their directorship functions effectively.

The Social Performance of the Performance Control System   The performance control system of the Divisionalized Form is one of its fundamental design parameters and the chief source of its economic efficiency. Yet this system also produces one of its most serious social consequences.

The Divisionalized Form requires that headquarters control the divisions primarily by quantitative performance criteria, and that typically means financial ones—profit, sales growth, return on investment, and the like. The problem is that these performance measures become virtual obsessions, driving out goals that cannot be measured—product quality, pride in work, customers well served, an environment protected or beautified. In effect, the economic goals drive out the social ones. "We, in Textron, worship the god of Net Worth" (quoted in Wrigley, 1970, p. V-86).

That would pose no problems if the social and economic consequences of decisions could easily be separated. Governments would look after the former, corporations the latter. But the fact is that the two are intertwined: every strategic decision involves social as well as economic consequences. As a result, **the control system of the Divisionalized Form drives it to act, at best, socially unresponsively, at worst, socially irresponsibly.** Forced to concentrate on the economic consequences of his decisions, the division manager comes to ignore their social consequences. And it should be remembered that the *specific* decisions of the divisionalized corporation— those with social impact—are controlled by the managers in the divisions, not those at headquarters. Thus, Bower (1970) finds that "The best record in the race relations area are those of single-product [nondivisionalized] companies whose strong top managements are deeply involved in the business" (p. 193).

Robert Ackerman (1975), in a study carried out at the Harvard Business School, tested the proposition that while business leaders "would like to avoid doing what they believe to be irresponsible" (p. 4), the difficulty their firms "were having in satisfying their social critics might be precisely in the organizational innovations that had permitted them to cope effectively with diversification and competitive conditions" (p. vii). Ackerman found that the benefits of social responsiveness—such as "a rosier public image . . . pride among managers . . . an attractive posture for recruiting on campus" (p. 55)—cannot be easily measured. "From the accountant's point of view, they have unfortunate characteristics of being largely intangible, unassignable to the costs of organizational units creating them" (pp. 55–56). In other words, these criteria cannot be plugged into the performance control system, with the result that:

> . . . the financial reporting system may actually inhibit social responsiveness. By focusing on economic performance, even with appropriate safeguards to protect against sacrificing long-term benefits, such a system directs energy and

resources to achieving results measured in financial terms. It is the only game in town, so to speak, at least the only one with an official scorecard (p. 56).

Headquarters managers—concerned about public relations and corporate liability—are tempted to intervene directly in the divisions' responses to new social issues. But they are discouraged by the Divisionalized Form's strict division of labor: divisional autonomy requires no headquarters meddling in specific decisions.

> . . . if the chief executive takes a strong hand in implementation beyond merely issuing a policy statement, he may indeed secure greater responsiveness but at the expense of increased organizational ambiguities. By assuming some of the responsibility for accommodating social issues, he may diminish the extent to which he can hold the divisions accountable for achieving agreed-upon financial results (p. 54).

As long as the screws of the performance control system are not turned too tight, the division manager retains some discretion to consider the social consequences of his actions. But, as we saw earlier, the trend in the divisionalized corporation is the other way, to the imitation of the ITT system of tight controls. That may be why Collins and Ganotis (1974) found in a general survey, "A sense of futility concerning the ability of lower- and middle-level managers to effect corporate social policy and perhaps a related attitude that social goals can best be achieved by individuals working outside their companies" (p. 306). The manager who must submit a balance sheet and income statement each month, as Wrigley found he must in Textron, or worse, send back a "flash report" to headquarters on the tenth day of every month, can hardly worry about the results these reports do not measure. He keeps his attention firmly fixed on financial performance.

When the screws are turned really tight, the division manager intent on achieving the standards, may have no choice but to act irresponsibly. Bower (1970) cites the well-known example of the General Electric price-fixing case of 1962:

> The corporate management of G.E. required its executives to sign the so-called "directive 20.5" which explicitly forbade price fixing or any other violation of the antitrust laws. But a very severely managed system of reward and punishment that demanded yearly improvements in earnings, return, and market share, applied indiscriminately to all divisions, yielded a situation, which was —at the very least—conducive to collusion in the oligopolistic and mature electric equipment markets (p. 193).

The headquarters managers may try to wash their hands of such divisional wrongdoing, proclaiming their ignorance of it, as did Ralph Cordiner, president of General Electric at the time. But they must accept responsibility for designing and exploiting the structure that evoked the behavior in question.

Thus, we conclude, with Bower, that "while the planning process of the diversified [and divisionalized] firm may be highly efficient," at least in the strict economic sense, it may also tend to make the firm "socially irresponsible" (p. 193).

The Problems of the Concentration of Power   Earlier we discussed the relationship between size and the Divisionalized Form, concluding that not only do large organizations tend to divisionalize but also that divisionalization encourages small organizations to grow large, and large organizations to grow larger. The Fortune 500 would count few billion-dollar corporations among its ranks if it were not for the development of the Divisionalized Form.

From society's point of view, we must ask what price bigness. Clearly **there are potential economic costs to bigness, notably the threat to the competitive market.** In *The New Industrial State*, John Kenneth Galbraith (1967) develops the theme that giant corporations use their market power, coupled with their planning and marketing techniques, to subvert competitive conditions. Galbraith's points have been repeatedly attacked by the more conservative economists, but it seems difficult to deny that sheer size can affect competition, for example, through the ability to use massive advertising expenditure to restrict entry to markets. In the case of conglomerate diversification, there is the added danger of what is known as "reciprocity"—"I buy from you if you buy from me" deals between corporations.

But the social costs of bigness may be the most serious ones. For one thing, big means bureaucratic. As noted in Hypothesis 5, the larger an organization, the more formalized its behavior. Moreover, in the case of the Divisionalized Form, as noted earlier in this chapter, the performance control system drives the divisions to be more bureaucratic than they would be as independent corporations. The presence of a headquarters—an agency of external control—also makes them more centralized. So the Divisionalized Form becomes a force for formalization and centralization, in other words, for machine bureaucratization—in a society, as noted in Chapter 18, already burdened with too many such structures.

Moreover, there are forces in the Divisionalized Form that drive it to centralize power not only at the divisional level but also at the headquarters level. In the case of the giant corporation, this results in the concentrating of enormous amounts of power in very few hands.

One of these forces for headquarters centralization, discussed a few pages back, is the illusion that the MIS and other techniques give of providing the information needed to make effective business strategies. (Indeed, should that not prove an illusion, the danger of centralization would be far more serious.) Another force for centralization is the very fact that the divisions are coupled together in a single legal unit under a single name. As noted earlier, no single division can go bankrupt; nor can it keep its bad publicity to itself. It shares its mistakes with its sister divisions, in the name of the corporation. No matter how loosely coupled the system, the whole is liable for the errors of any of the parts. So there are pressures on the headquarters to involve itself in specific divisional decisions—for example, to review long-term contracts that could later drain corporate resources and to oversee social behaviors that could lead to bad publicity. In fact, its control system, by encouraging socially unresponsive or irresponsible behavior, has brought the divisionalized corporation more and more bad publicity, which pushes it to centralize more and more power at headquarters in order to protect itself. In some sense, the giant corporation seems to have a choice between social irresponsibility and power centralization.

Another force for centralization is captured in Lord Acton's famous dictum: "Power tends to corrupt; absolute power corrupts absolutely." With strong chains of authority below and diffused shareholders above, the managers at the headquarters of the giant corporations have enormous amounts of potential power. This raises pressures to centralize for its own sake. Market forces no doubt mitigate these tendencies, discouraging the use of overcentralized structures. But as noted earlier, the bigger the corporation, the less it tends to be subject to market forces.

So far we have seen that divisionalization encourages a concentration of power at the divisional and then at the headquarters level. Paradoxically, **the concentration of power within the corporation also leads to conglomeration, divisionalization, and the concentration of power in spheres outside the corporation. Unions federate and governments add agencies to establish countervailing powers—ones to match those of the corporation.** Government is, in fact, drawn to intervene directly in the affairs of the corporation because of the very issues we have been discussing—the concentration of too much power in too few hands, power exercised free of shareholder, societal, and sometimes even market control, and the tendency toward unresponsive or irresponsible social behavior. Citizens who question the legitimacy of the power base of the giant corporation naturally look to government to intervene.

And it is the supreme irony that the very arguments used in favor of the Divisionalized Form of structure suggest the way to government intervention. Consider Williamson's key point in this regard, that the administrative arrangements are efficient while the capital markets are not. Why should the government worry about interfering with markets that do not work efficiently? And if the administrative arrangements work as well as Williamson claims, why should government not use them too? If Beatrice

Foods really can control 397 divisions, what is to stop Washington from believing that it can control 397 Beatrices? Using the same systems. With a public calling for more and more control of corporate behavior, and with Lord Acton's dictum ever present, what will eventually stop government administrators from being lured by the illusion that an MIS can provide the information they need to control the corporation—whether through nationalization or national planning.

Of course, like the corporation, so too would governments be driven to favor economic goals over social ones, as a result of the nature of the control system they would have to use. This means that government control, while perhaps legitimizing the activities of the corporation, would not solve the fundamental social problems raised by divisionalization and would, in fact, aggravate that of the concentration of power in society.

In general, **the pure Divisionalized Form does not work effectively outside the private sector.** This despite widespread attempts to use it—in school systems, universities, hospitals, government corporations, indeed in all of them together in one giant public sector divisionalized monolith.

One problem is that government and sometimes other institutions cannot divest themselves of divisions, or at least the realities of power are that they seldom do. So there is no vehicle for organizational renewal. Another problem in government is that its civil service regulations on appointments interfere with the concept of managerial responsibility: "If a superior is to have complete confidence in his subordinates, he must have some measure of control over who his subordinates are. He must have a degree of freedom in their selection, their discipline, and if necessary their transfer or dismissal. The federal civil service system, however, places restrictions on such freedom" (Worthy, 1959, p. 113).

But the most serious problem remains that of measurement: the goals governments and most institutions must plug into the performance control system—basically social goals—do not lend themselves to measurement. And without measurement, the pure Divisionalized Form cannot work. Nothing stops them from establishing market-based divisions. But lacking adequate performance measures, they must find other means to control the divisions (or force in artificial measures that fail to capture the spirit of the social goals or that ignore them entirely in favor of economic goals). One is socialization—the appointment of managers who believe in the social goals in question. But that can go only so far, and pressures arise to use other means of control. The obvious ones are direct supervision and standardization of work, the issuing of direct orders and general rules. But both damage divisional autonomy. **So the choices facing the government—and unions, multiversities, and other federated institutions that try to use the Divisionalized Form in the face of nonquantifiable goals—are to forget control beyond the appointment of socialized managers, to control machine bureau-**

cratically, or to force in divisionalized control by the imposition of artificial performance standards.

Examples abound of all three. The press regularly reports on government departments that have run out of control. Perhaps more common is the case of machine bureaucratic control, of government departments that lack the autonomy they need to act because of the plethora of blanket rules governments impose on all of their departments. And so, too, do examples get reported of artificial performance controls, perhaps the best one being Frank's (1958–59) description of the system used by the Soviet government to regulate the performance of its factories. Standards abounded—type, quantity, quality, and mix of production; amount of materials and labor used; wages paid; production norms for workers to achieve; special campaign goals; and many more. The standards were so tight and often contradictory that the managers on the receiving end had no choice but to act irresponsibly, just as do division managers in America who are overcontrolled, as long as they wish to keep their jobs. They lied about their factories' needs; they stockpiled materials; they complied with the letter but not the spirit of the standards, for example, by reducing product quality (which could not easily be measured); they hired the "tolkach," or "influence peddler," to make deals outside the control system.

In the final analysis, perhaps the best that can be done by governments and institutions intent on using some form of divisionalization is to appoint managers and other employees who believe in the social goals to be pursued and then to set up the mechanism for some kind of periodic personal review of their progress (requiring, in effect, the creation of some kind of independent board of directors).

In Conclusion: A Structure at the Edge of a Cliff   Our discussion has led to to á "damned if you do, damned if you don't" conclusion. The pure (conglomerate) Divisionalized Form emerges as a structural configuration symbolically perched on the edge of the cliff, at the end of a long path. Ahead, it is one step away from *dis*integration—breaking up into separate organizations on the rocks below. Behind it is the way back to a more stable integration, perhaps a hybrid structure with Machine Bureaucracy at some intermediate spot along the path. And ever hovering above is the eagle, attracted by its position on the edge of the cliff and waiting for the chance to pull the Divisionalized Form up to more centralized social control, on another, perhaps more dangerous, cliff. The edge of the cliff is an uncomfortable place to be—maybe even a temporary one that must inevitably lead to disintegration on the rocks below, a trip to that cliff above, or a return to a safer resting place on the path behind.

In other words, **we conclude that the Divisionalized Form has the narrowest range of all the structural configurations. It has no real environ-**

ment of its own; at best it piggybacks on the Machine Bureaucracy in the simple, stable environment, and therefore always feels drawn back to that integrated structural form. The pure Divisionalized Form may prove inherently unstable, in a social context a legitimate tendency but not a legitimate structure. The economic advantages it offers over independent organizations reflect fundamental inefficiencies in capital markets and stockholder control systems that should themselves be corrected. And it creates fundamental social problems. Perhaps there is justification only in its intermediate forms —by-product or related product. It is, after all, the interdependencies among its activities that give an organization its justification, its reason to "organize." Perhaps the pure Divisionalized Form, with so few of these interdependencies, really is an "ideal type"—one to be approached but never reached.

21

The Adhocracy

Prime Coordinating Mechanism:	Mutual adjustment
Key Part of Organization:	Support staff (in the Administrative Adhocracy; together with the operating core in the Operating Adhocracy)
Main Design Parameters:	Liaison devices, organic structure, selective decentralization, horizontal job specialization, training, functional and market grouping concurrently
Contingency Factors:	Complex, dynamic, (sometimes disparate) environment, young (especially Operating Adhocracy), sophisticated and often automated technical system (in the Administrative Adhocracy), fashionable

None of the structural configurations so far discussed is capable of sophisticated innovation, the kind required of a space agency, an avant-garde film company, a factory manufacturing complex prototypes, an integrated petrochemicals company. The Simple Structure can certainly innovate, but only in a relatively simple way. Both the Machine and Professional Bureaucracies are performance, not problem-solving, structures. They are designed to perfect standard programs, not to invent new ones. And while the Divisionalized Form resolves the problem of strategic inflexibility in the Machine Bureaucracy, as noted in Chapter 20, it, too, is not a true innovator. A focus on control by standardizing outputs does not encourage innovation.

Sophisticated innovation requires a fifth and very different structural configuration, one that is able to fuse experts drawn from different disciplines into smoothly functioning ad hoc project teams. To borrow the word Alvin Toffler (1970) popularized in *Future Shock,* these are the *Adhocracies* of our society. They appeared repeatedly in our review, in Lawrence and Lorsch's plastics companies, and Burns and Stalker's electronics firms, among Woodward's unit and process producers, in the NASA described by Chandler and Sayles, and the Boeing Company described by Galbraith.

(Before beginning our discussion of the basic structure, we should note that Simple Structure, being almost nonstructure, generated a chapter that was short and simple. Machine and Professional Bureaucracy, as well as the Divisionalized Form, being for the most part highly ordered structures, led to chapters that were highly ordered as well. Adhocracy, in contrast, is the most complex structure of the five, yet is not highly ordered. Moreover, it is the newest of the five, the one about which we know the least. The reader is forewarned that the chapter cannot help reflecting the characteristics of the structure it describes.)

DESCRIPTION OF THE BASIC STRUCTURE

The Design Parameters   In Adhocracy, we have a fifth distinct structural configuration: highly organic structure, with little formalization of behavior; high horizontal job specialization based on formal training; a tendency to group the specialists in functional units for housekeeping purposes but to deploy them in small market-based project teams to do their work; a reliance on the liaison devices to encourage mutual adjustment—the key coordinating mechanism—within and between these teams; and selective decentralization to and within these teams, which are located at various places in the organization and involve various mixtures of line managers and staff and operating experts.

To innovate means to break away from established patterns. So the innovative organization cannot rely on any form of standardization for coordination. In other words, it must avoid all the trappings of bureaucratic structure, notably sharp divisions of labor, extensive unit differentiation, highly formalized behaviors, and an emphasis on planning and control systems. As Goodman and Goodman (1976) find in the case of theater companies: "role clarity" inhibits innovation; "Coordination can no longer be planned but must come through interaction" (pp. 494–495). The structure of the Adhocracy must be flexible, self-renewing, organic, in Hedberg et al.'s (1976) terms, a "tent" instead of a "palace":

> An organizational tent actually exploits benefits hidden within properties that designers have generally regarded as liabilities. Ambiguous authority structures, unclear objectives, and contradictory assignments of responsibility can legitimate controversies and challenge traditions. . . . Incoherence and indecision can foster exploration, self-evaluation, and learning (p. 45).

A tent can be picked up and moved at will; likewise, Toffler (1970) notes that Adhocracies "now change their internal shape with a frequency—and sometime a rashness—that makes the head swim. Titles change from week to week. Jobs are transformed. Responsibilities shift. Vast organizational structures are taken apart, bolted together again in new forms, then rearranged again. Departments and divisions spring up overnight only to vanish in another, and yet another, reorganization" (p. 128). For example, the Manned Space Flight Center of the National Aeronautics and Space Administration (NASA), America's most famous Adhocracy of the 1960s, changed its structure seventeen times in the first eight years of its existence (Litzinger et al., 1970, p. 7). A search for organigrams to illustrate this chapter elicited the following response from one corporation well known for its adhocratic structure: ". . . we would prefer not to supply an organization chart, since it would change too quickly to serve any useful purpose."

As Chandler and Sayles (1971) note, these organizations lack the advantages of those that do repetitive work. Since project work is usually "being done for the first time . . . precedents and policies are somewhat irrelevant" and "it is difficult to draw neat jurisdictional lines" (p. 202). As a result, "the organization *cannot* compartmentalize its activities into the neat boxes the chartists and consultants envision. . . . Responsibilities too clearly compartmentalized can lead to stultification" (p. 201).

Of all the structural configurations, Adhocracy shows the least reverance for the classical principles of management, especially unity of command. The regulated system does not matter much either. In this structure, information and decision processes flow flexibly and informally, wherever they must to promote innovation. And that means overriding the chain of authority if need be. As one NASA executive commented:

To be on the safe side, NASA may err in overcommunicating upward, laterally, and downward. It engulfs anyone who can conceivably influence or implement the decision. It establishes various "management councils" composed of co-equal associates to share progress and problems on a frequent basis. In an unending effort to exchange information in real–time, it uses telephone, hot lines, executive aircraft, datafax, long distance conference hookups by voice and data display and computer data transmissions (quoted in Chandler and Sayles, 1971, p. 20).

The Simple Structure also retains an organic structure, and so is able to innovate as well. But that innovation is restricted to simple environments, ones that can be easily comprehended by a central leader. Innovation of the sophisticated variety takes place in environments not easily understood. So another kind of organic structure is required, one that relies on the application of sophisticated expertise. **The Adhocracy must hire and give power to experts—professionals whose knowledge and skills have been highly developed in training programs.** Thus, Toffler notes in his discussion of Adhocracy "the arrival on the scene of hordes of experts—specialists in vital fields so narrow that often the men on top have difficulty understanding them. Increasingly, managers have to rely on the judgment of these experts. Solid state physicists, computer programmers, systems designers, operation researchers, engineering specialists—such men are assuming a new decision-making function" (p. 140).

But unlike the Professional Bureaucracy, **the Adhocracy cannot rely on the standardized skills of these experts to achieve coordination,** because that would lead to standardization instead of innovation. Rather it must treat existing knowledge and skills merely as bases on which to build new ones.

Moreover, the building of new knowledge and skills requires the combination of different bodies of existing ones. So rather than allowing the specialization of the expert or the differentiation of the functional unit to dominate its behavior, the Adhocracy must instead break through the boundaries of conventional specialization and differentiation. "An electrical specialist can spot a mechanical problem, perhaps in part because he does not know the conventional wisdom, and a bright engineer working in an apparently unrelated field can come up with a solution to a problem that has been frustrating the functional specialists" (Chandler and Sayles, 1971, p. 202). Thus, whereas each professional of the Professional Bureaucracy can operate on his own, in the Adhocracy the professionals must amalgamate their efforts. "Traditional organizations can assume that they know all the problems and the methods. They therefore can assign expertise to a single specialist or compartmentalized, functional group. They also can assume that they know all the interrelationships; thus lateral contacts can be limited to those who have a 'need to know'" (p. 203). In sharp contrast, in Adhocracies the different specialists must join forces in multidisciplinary teams, each formed around a specific project of innovation.

How does the organization cope with the problem of "uprooting the professional yet allowing him to maintain his ties to his field of expertise" (Chandler and Sayles, p. 15)? The solution is obvious: **The Adhocracy tends to use the functional and market bases for grouping concurrently, in a matrix structure.** The experts are grouped in functional units for housekeeping purposes—for hiring, professional communication, and the like—but then are deployed in project teams to carry out their basic work of innovation.

And how is coordination effected in and between these project teams? As noted earlier, standardization is precluded as a major coordinating mechanism. The efforts must be innovative, not standardized. So, too, is direct supervision, because of the complexity of the work. Coordination must be effected by those with the knowledge, the experts who actually do the project work. That leaves mutual adjustment, the prime coordinating mechanism of the Adhocracy. As Khandwalla (1976) notes, "the job of coordination is not left to a few charged with the responsibility, but assumed by most individuals in the organization, much in the way members of a well-knit hockey or cricket team all work spontaneously to keep its activities focused on the goal of winning" (p. 10). And, of course, **with the concentration on mutual adjustment in the Adhocracy comes an emphasis on the design parameter meant to encourage it, namely the set of liaison devices.** Integrating managers and liaison positions are established to coordinate the efforts among and between the functional units and project teams; the teams themselves are established as task forces; and, as noted above, matrix structure is favored to achieve concurrent functional and market grouping. As Sayles (1976) notes, matrix structure "*reuses* old organizations instead of creating new ones for new goals and problems. It forces organizations to keep changing themselves because of conflicting goals, values, and priorities and builds instability into the very structure of the organization" (p. 15).

Thus, **managers abound in the Adhocracy—functional managers, integrating managers, project managers.** The latter are particularly numerous, since the project teams must be small, to encourage mutual adjustment among their members, and each team needs a designated leader, a "manager." That results in a narrow "span of control" for the Adhocracy, by conventional measures. But that measure has nothing to do with "control"; it merely reflects the small size of the work units. Most of the managers do not "manage" in the usual sense, that is, give orders by direct supervision in the leader and resource allocator roles. Instead, they spend a good deal of their time in the liaison and negotiator roles, coordinating the work laterally among the different teams and between them and the functional units.

Many of these managers are, in fact, experts, too, who take their place alongside the others on the project teams.

With its reliance on highly trained experts, the Adhocracy—like the Professional Bureaucracy—is decentralized. But not in the same way, because in the Adhocracy the experts are distributed throughout the structure, notably in the support staff and managerial ranks as well as the operating core. So rather than a concentration of power in the operating core, there is a more even distribution of it in all the parts. **The decentralization of the Adhocracy is what we labeled selective in Chapter 11, in both the horizontal and vertical dimensions. Decision-making power is distributed among managers and nonmanagers at all the levels of the hierarchy, according to the nature of the different decisions to be made.** No one in the Adhocracy monopolizes the power to innovate.

To proceed with our discussion, and elaborate on how the Adhocracy makes decisions, we must at this point divide it into two types—the Operating Adhocracy and the Administrative Adhocracy.

The Operating Adhocracy   The Operating Adhocracy innovates and solves problems directly on behalf of its clients. Its multidisciplinary teams of experts often work directly under contract, as in the think-tank consulting firm, creative advertising agency, or manufacturer of engineering prototypes. In some cases, however, there is no contract per se, as in the filmmaking agency or theater company.

In fact, **for every Operating Adhocracy, there is a corresponding Professional Bureaucracy, one that does similar work but with a narrower orientation.** Faced with a client problem, the Operating Adhocracy engages in creative effort to find a novel solution; the Professional Bureaucracy pigeonholes it into a known contingency to which it can apply a standard program. One engages in divergent thinking aimed at innovation; the other in convergent thinking aimed at perfection. "The investigator's mind dwells on the unknown and puzzling, and his eagerness is often towards displaying doubts and difficulties." In contrast, "The mind of the craftsman dwells on what he knows, and he delights to use and to display his knowledge" (Sir Thomas Lewis, quoted in Carlson, 1951, pp. 112–113). One management consulting firm treats each contract as a creative challenge; another interprets each as the need to divisionalize the client's structure or strengthen its planning system, or both. One theater company seeks out new avant-garde plays to perform; another perfects its performance of Shakespeare year after year. In effect, one is prepared to consider an infinite number of contingencies and solutions; the other restricts itself to a few. The missions are the same, but the outputs and the structures that produce them differ radically. Both decentralize power to their highly trained specialists. But because the

Operating Adhocracy seeks to innovate, its specialists must interact informally by mutual adjustment in organically structured project teams; the Professional Bureaucracy, because it standardizes its services, structures itself as a bureaucracy in which each specialist can function on his own, his work automatically coordinated with the others by virtue of his standardized knowledge and skills.

A key feature of the Operating Adhocracy is that its administrative and operating work tend to blend into a single effort. That is, in ad hoc project work it is difficult to differentiate the planning and design of the work from its actual execution. Both require the same specialized skills, on a project-by-project basis. As a result, the Operating Adhocracy may not even bother to distinguish its middle levels from its operating core. Managers of the middle line and members of what in other organizations would be called the support staff—typically a highly trained and important group in the Operating Adhocracy—may take their place right alongside the operating specialists on the project teams. And even when distinctions are made, a close rapport must develop between the administrative and operating levels, sometimes to the point where they are able to interchange their roles freely. Consider Joan Woodward's (1965) description of the building of engineering prototypes:

> Some products were completed and dispatched to customers direct from the development workshops. There seemed to be no clear-cut line of demarcation between the development and the production workshops. In theory, prototypes of a complicated construction that were developed and fabricated simultaneously were the responsibility of the development workshops. In practice, however, there were a large number of other factors influencing the way in which a job was routed. These included the personal interests of the development engineers, the pressure of work in the development and production workshops respectively, and the nature of the product. Because the more complicated work was done in the development workshops, the fitters employed there had the reputation of being better craftsmen than those employed in the production workshops (p. 133).

Figure 21–1 shows the organigram of the National Film Board of Canada, as we shall see a classic Operating Adhocracy (even though it does produce an organigram—one that changes frequently, it might be added). The "Board" is an agency of the Canadian federal government, and produces mostly short films, many of them documentaries. The organigram shows a large number of support units as well as liaison positions (for example, research, technical, and production coordinators). The operating core can also be seen to include loose, concurrent functional and market groupings (the latter by region as well as type of film produced).

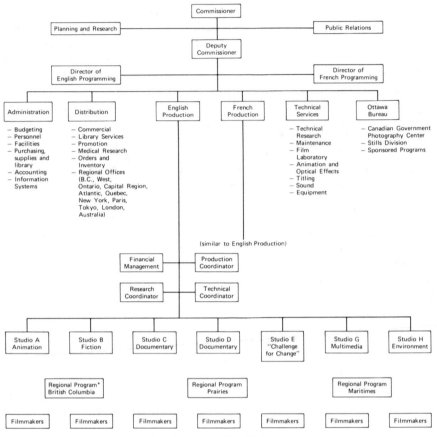

Figure 21-1. *The National Film Board of Canada: An Operating Adhocracy (circa 1975, used with permission)*

The Administrative Adhocracy The second major type of Adhocracy also functions with project teams, but toward a different end. Whereas the Operating Adhocracy undertakes projects to serve its clients, **the Administrative Adhocracy undertakes its projects to serve itself. And in sharp contrast to the Operating Adhocracy, the Administrative Adhocracy makes a sharp distinction between its administrative component and operating core; the operating core is truncated—cut right off from the rest of the organization—so that the administrative component that remains can be structured as an Adhocracy.**

This truncation may take place in a number of ways. First, when an organization has a special need to be innovative, perhaps because of intense product competition or a very dynamic technology, but its operating core must be machine bureaucratic, the operating core may be established as a separate organization. As we saw in Chapter 18, the social tensions at the base of the Machine Bureaucracy overflow the operating core and permeate the administration. The whole organization becomes ridden with conflict and obsessed by control, too bureaucratic to innovate. By truncating the operating core—setting it up apart with its own administration that reports in at the strategic apex—the main administrative component of the organization can be structured organically for innovation.[1] Ansoff and Brandenburg (1971) refer to this kind of structure in corporations as the "innovative form." An innovative group concerns itself with diversification and expansion of the enterprise; it takes projects to full implementation and then turns them over to a current business group that manages them.[2]

Second, the operating core may be done away with altogether, in effect contracted out to other organizations. This leaves the organization free to concentrate on development work. That is what NASA did in the 1960s, when its attention was focused on the Apollo project, whose singular goal was to put an American on the moon before 1970. NASA conducted much of its own development work but contracted production out to independent manufacturing firms. The two functions simply required very different organizational structures (Chandler and Sayles, 1971, p. 180).[3]

A third form of truncation arises when the operating core becomes automated. This amounts to truncation, because an automated operating core is able to run itself, largely free of the need for direct supervision or other direct control from the administrative component. The latter, because it need not give attention to routine operating matters, can structure itself as an Adhocracy, concerned with change and innovation, with projects to bring new operating facilities on line. "The automated factory increasingly . . . runs itself; the company executives are increasingly concerned not with running today's factory, but with designing tomorrow's" (Simon, 1977, pp.

---

[1] The organization that truncates its bureaucratic operating core should not be confused with the one that gets up a venture team, a separate organic pocket for innovation. In that case, the innovative unit is cut off from the rest of the central administration, which remains bureaucratic.

[2] Goodman and Goodman (1976, p. 500) propose a similar structure for theater companies— Adhocracy for planning productions and Professional Bureaucracy for performing them. To the extent that this truncation is possible, the theater company is more appropriately viewed as an Administrative Adhocracy than an Operating one.

[3] A variation of this occurs when it is the developmental work that is contracted out. In effect, one organization becomes the innovating arm for another, or for a consortium of organizations. Here the Administrative and Operating Adhocracies meet, for the development organization is an Operating Adhocracy, doing development work for its clients rather than itself. An example is the "turn-key" project, where a firm sets up a plant on contract, typically in a foreign country, and then hands it over to local authorities to run. Only the key remains to be turned.

32–33). Simon pictures the organization that emerges as a three-layered cake:

> In the bottom layer we have the basic work processes—in a manufacturing organization, the processes that procure raw materials, manufacture the physical product, warehouse it, and ship it. In the middle layer we have the programed decision-making processes—the processes that govern the day-to-day operation of the manufacturing and distribution system. In the top layer we have the nonprogramed decision-making processes, the processes that are required to design and redesign the entire system, to provide it with its basic goals and objectives, and to monitor its performance (p. 110).

Oil companies, because of the high automation of their production process, are in part at least drawn toward the Administrative Adhocracy configuration. Figure 21-2 shows the organigram for one oil company, reproduced exactly as presented by the company (except for modifications to mask its identity, made at the company's request). Note the domination of "Administration and Services," shown at the bottom of the chart; the operating functions, particularly "Production," are lost by comparison. Note also the description of the strategic apex in terms of standing committees instead of individual executives.

The Administrative Component of the Adhocracies   The important conclusion to be drawn from this discussion is that in both types of Adhocracy, the relationship between the operating core and the administrative component is unlike that of any other structural configuration. In the Administrative Adhocracy, the operating core is truncated and becomes a relatively unimportant part of the organization; in the Operating Adhocracy, the two merge into a single entity. In both cases, there is little need for line managers to exercise close direct supervision over the operators. Rather, **the managers become functioning members of the project teams, with special responsibility to effect coordination between them.** But in this capacity they act more as peers than as supervisors, their influence deriving from their expertise and interpersonal skill rather than from their formal position. And, of course, to the extent that direct supervision and formal authority diminish in importance, **the distinction between line and staff blurs.** It no longer makes sense to distinguish those who have the formal power to decide from those who have only the informal right to advise. Power over decision making flows to anyone in the Adhocracy with expertise, regardless of position.

The support staff plays a key role in the Adhocracy. In fact, it is the key part of the Administrative Adhocracy, for that is where this structure houses most of the experts on which it is so dependent. The Operating

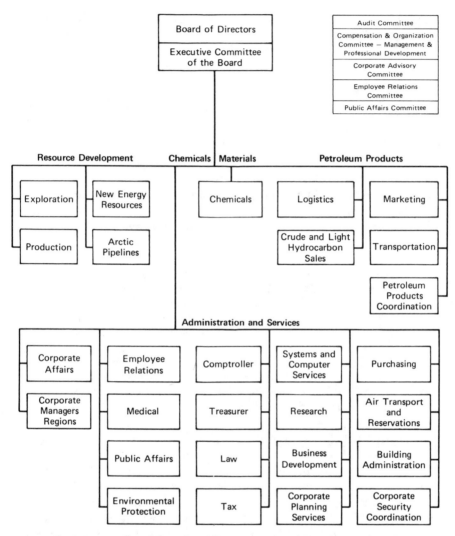

Figure 21-2. *Organigram of an Oil Company: An Administrative Adhocracy*

Adhocracy also depends on experts, but since it retains its operating core, it houses many of them there as well as in the support staff. But in both cases, as noted above, much of the support staff is not sharply differentiated from other parts of the organization, not off to one side, to speak only when spoken to, as in the bureaucratic configurations. Rather, the support staff, together with the line managers (and the operators in the case of the Operating Adhocracy), form part of the central pool of expert talent from which the project personnel are drawn. (There are, of course, exceptions. Some support units must always remain bureaucratic, and apart. Even NASA needs cafeterias.)

Because the Adhocracy does not rely on standardization for coordination, it has little need for a technostructure to develop systems for regulation. The Administrative Adhocracy does employ analysts concerned with adaptation to its external environment, such as marketing researchers and economic forecasters. As we shall see later, it does do some action planning, although of a rather general kind. But these analysts do not design systems to control other people so much as take their place alongside the line managers and the support staffers as members of the project teams.

To summarize, **the administrative component of the Adhocracy emerges as an organic mass of line managers and staff experts (together with operators in the Operating Adhocracy), working together in ever-shifting relationships on ad hoc projects.** As Chandler and Sayles (1971) note in the case of NASA:

> While there may be a number of permanent operations in such projects, much of the work is temporary. People get shifted around and plans get changed in an environment quite different from the tiresome monotony bemoaned by so many in traditional institutions. Projects, task forces, and temporary "teams" also mean that individuals have multiple organizational "homes." A scientist may be part of a university, responsible for the design and testing of an experiment to be flown by a NASA spacecraft, serving as a consultant to an industrial contractor that builds equipment for the agency, and a member of an advisory board that helps shape future science policy for NASA and other government agencies (p. 6).

Figure 21–3 shows the Adhocracy in terms of our logo, with its parts mingled together in one amorphous mass in the middle. In the Operating Adhocracy, this mass includes the middle line, support staff, technostructure, and operating core. The Administrative Adhocracy includes all of these except the operating core, which is kept apart in a truncated, bureaucratic structure, shown by the dotted section below the central mass.[4] The reader will also note that the strategic apex of the figure is shown partly merged into the central mass as well. We shall see why in the discussion of strategy formation that follows.

Strategy Formation in the Adhocracy   In the Professional Bureaucracy, the strategy formulation process is controlled primarily by the professional associations outside the structure, secondarily by the professionals

[4]In their study of the shape of organizations, Kaufman and Seidman found one type that was diamond-shaped, with "concentration of large numbers in middle ranks and small numbers in both higher and lower levels" (1970, p. 442). This appears to describe the Administrative Adhocracy, as shown in Figure 21–3.

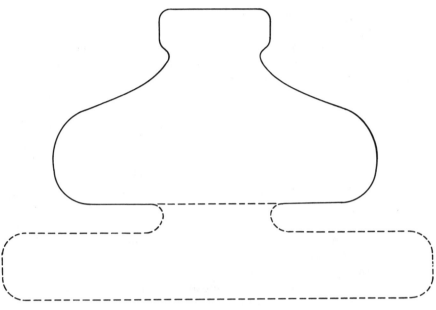

Figure 21-3. *The Adhocracy*

of the operating core themselves, and only after that by the administrative component. In effect, the process is bottom-up, and outside-in. In all the other structural configurations so far discussed, the process is clearly top-down, controlled by the strategic apex (and in the Divisionalized Form, the strategic apexes of the divisions as well). In sharp contrast, **control of the strategy formulation process in the Adhocracy is not clearly placed, at the strategic apex or elsewhere.**

Moreover, the process is best thought of as strategy formation, because strategy in these structures is not so much formulated consciously by individuals as formed implicitly by the decisions they make, one at a time. The concept of the formulation–implementation dichotomy in strategy making—a pillar of the Machine Bureaucracy—loses its meaning in the Adhocracy. It is in the making of specific decisions within and about projects—what would normally be considered implementation—that strategies evolve, that is, are formed, in the Adhocracy. That is because when the central purpose of an organization is to innovate, the results of its efforts can never be predetermined. So it cannot specify a strategy—a pattern or consistency in its stream of decisions—in advance, before it makes its decisions. Such patterns at best emerge after the fact, the results of specific decisions. "... goals continue to emerge as the task is pursued ... a single engine fighter plane may evolve into a twin-engine attack bomber; a funding program for exceptional children may become a strategy for integration; a construction project may become a training program for the unskilled" (Goodman and Goodman, 1976, p. 496).

That is why action planning cannot be extensively relied upon in the Adhocracy. Any process that separates conceptualization from action—planning from execution, formulation from implementation—impedes the flexibility of the organization to respond creatively to its uncertain environment.[5]

Consider the case of the Operating Adhocracy, a structure never quite sure what it will do next. That depends on what projects come along, which in turn depends partly on how well it does in its current projects. So its strategy never really stabilizes, but changes continuously, as projects change. To put this another way, when the strategy does stabilize, the structure ceases to be adhocratic. A stable strategy means that the organization has determined which markets it will serve, and how, in other words, which contingencies it will respond to and with which standard programs. It has, in effect, restructured itself as a bureaucracy, machine if it concentrates on a single program, professional if it remains open to a few.

Now if strategy evolves continuously according to the projects being done, it stands to reason that strategy formation is controlled by whoever decides what projects are done and how. And in the Operating Adhocracy, that includes line managers, staff specialists, and operators, in other words, potentially everyone in the organization.

Take the case of the National Film Board. Among its most important strategies are those related to the content of its films—some about the geography of Canada and the sociology of its peoples, others on pure experimental themes, and so on. So a key to understanding how the Board makes strategy is to understand who decides what films to make. Since the Board concentrates primarily on short, documentary-type films, those choices are made about 100 times each year. Were the Board structured as a Machine Bureaucracy, the word would come down from on high. There would be one stable film strategy, formulated at the strategic apex and implemented lower down. (If the Board were structured as the Divisionalized Form, the word would come down from the head of each film division, one film content strategy for each film market. And the headquarters would open and close divisions according to the markets it wished to be in.) If it were struc-

---

[5]The same conditions of uncertainty apply in the Simple Structure, with the same result, namely that planning cannot be relied upon and that strategy formulation cannot be separated from strategy implementation. But because it innovates in simpler ways, the Simple Structure resolves the issue by focusing control for both at the strategic apex. The chief executive formulates a general vision of direction—a vague strategy—in his head and then implements it, continually reformulating his vision as he receives feedback on his actions. He does not make his strategy explicit, for that would announce it to others and so reduce his flexibility to change it at will (Mintzberg, 1973b).

tured as a Professional Bureaucracy, each filmmaker would have his own standard repertoire of basic film scenarios, which he would repeat year after year, and the organization would have a series of stable film content strategies coming up from the operating core.

In fact, the Board is structured as an Operating Adhocracy, and so it follows none of these procedures. Proposals for new films enter the system in two basic ways. About one-third are sponsored by agencies of the Canadian government. As long as interested filmmakers can be found, these are accepted. To the extent that there is some pattern in the content of these films, we can conclude that part of the film content strategy is imposed on the organization by its clients. But two-thirds of the Board's films are proposed by its own employees, and are funded from its own general budget. Each proposal is submitted to a standing committee—the "Program Committee"—which at the time of this writing consists of four members elected by the filmmakers, two appointed by the Distribution (marketing) Branch, as well as the Director of Production and the Director of Programming. The Commissioner—the chief executive—must approve the Program Committee's choices. Thus, operators, middle-line managers, support staffers, and managers at the strategic apex all get involved in the choices of what films to make.

A few proposals come from the Commissioner and the research coordinator charged with proposing themes for films, but the vast majority are initiated by the filmmakers themselves and the executive producers. Each has his own general preferences, whether those be for animated or experimental films, documentaries, or whatever, but a glance at the Board's catalog invalidates any conclusion about standardization. The filmmakers and executive producers certainly communicate among themselves about their preferences and in so doing influence each other. As a result, certain general themes develop from time to time. They also learn which films fail to meet with the Program Committee's approval. It, in turn, is naturally predisposed to favor the kinds of films with which the Board has had its greatest recent successes. So while there is no stable film content strategy, a dynamic one can be identified, one in a continual state of adaptation.

The Operating Adhocracy's strategy evolves continuously as hundreds of these kinds of decisions are made each year in complicated ways. Each project leaves its imprint on the strategy. It is in the strategy-making process we see most clearly the intertwining of all the Adhocracy's decisions—operating, administrative, and strategic. And to return to the basic point being made, so many people at so many levels are involved in these projects—both in deciding which ones to carry out and then in actually carrying them out—that we cannot point a finger at any one part of the organization and say that is where the strategy is formulated. Everyone who gets involved—and that means top- and middle-level managers, staff specialists, and operators, all combined in various task forces and standing committees—has a hand in influencing the strategy that gets formed.

That is why we concluded earlier that the Operating Adhocracy is decentralized selectively, in both the horizontal and vertical dimensions. The power for decision making is distributed widely, in the most complicated of ways, among managerial and nonmanagerial personnel, at all levels of the hierarchy.

Similar conclusions can be reached about the Administrative Adhocracy, although the strategy-making process is slightly neater there. That is because the Administrative Adhocracy tends to concentrate its attention on fewer projects, which involve more people in interdependent relationships. NASA's Apollo project involved most of its personnel for almost 10 years; similarly, the bringing on line of a new processing plant can involve a good deal of the administrative staff of a petrochemical company for years. Moreover, since it carries out its projects only for itself, not for a range of outside clients, the Administrative Adhocracy tends to have a more concentrated product-market sphere of operations. Through the 1960s, for example, NASA focused on the single goal of landing an American on the moon before 1970.

Larger, more integrated projects and a more focused sphere of operations means that the efforts of the various specialists must be more carefully structured than in the Operating Adhocracy. As a result, **the Administrative Adhocracy structures itself as a system of work constellations, each located at the level of the hierarchy commensurate with the kinds of functional decisions it must make.** We saw a clear example of this in Lawrence and Lorsch's (1967) plastics firm discussed in Chapter 11 (see Figure 11-2, p. 190), with its manufacturing, marketing, and research constellations located at various levels of the hierarchy. Each constellation draws on line managers and staff specialists as necessary, and distributes power to them according to the use of their expertise in the decisions that must be made. Hence, the Administrative Adhocracy is also decentralized selectively in the vertical and horizontal dimensions. And once again we cannot point to any one part of the organization as *the* place where strategy is formulated, although the existence of the work constellations does enable us to identify certain kinds of strategic decisions with certain parts of the organization. As Chandler and Sayles (1971) note of the NASA of the Apollo era:

> ... while it is clear who has the authority to make, and who announces, the final decision (the top administrator of NASA), it is much more difficult to say who, in fact, "makes" the decision. It is the product of a complex process of interation and confrontation in which technical, administrative, and broader political criteria are applied and in which both technical and managerial personnel participate. ... This process illustrates the naivete of endeavoring to dichotomize organizations on the basis of whether decisions are made at the

bottom (presumably in highly technical–professional environments) or at the top (traditional hierarchically functioning organizations). Decision-making is a process in which various organizational levels and interest groups compete for position in a sequence and to make their voice the strongest (pp. 174–176).

The need to structure the efforts of the specialists also suggests a need for action planning in the Administrative Adhocracy. The problem with such planning, however, is that while the end or goal of the organization may clearly be defined, the means for reaching it are not. These must be worked out en route to the goal, by trial and error. So only a general kind of action planning can take place, one that sets out broad, flexible guidelines within which the work constellations can proceed to make their specific decisions. Again, therefore, it is only through the making of specific decisions—namely those that determine which projects are undertaken and how these projects turn out—that strategies evolve. Even in the case of NASA, an organization thought to rely heavily on planning, it is

> ...a rather different function in these large developmental systems where uncertainties predominate. Traditionally, managers are taught to identify their ultimate ends and purposes, set objectives that will help attain these ends, and then develop operational plans. Unfortunately, this comforting and logical sequence gets upset in the real world of large systems. Clear objectives often disguise conflicting purposes reflecting the divergencies among the temporarily allied groups in the federation. ... Planning turns out to be a dynamic, iterative process. This inevitably disperses authority, since a small group of expert, high-level "planners" cannot define strategy (Chandler and Sayles, 1971, p. 7).

The Roles of the Strategic Apex   **The top managers of the strategic apex of the Adhocracy may not spend much time formulating explicit strategies, but they must spend a good deal of their time in the battles that ensue over strategic choices, and in handling the many other disturbances that arise all over these fluid structures.** The Adhocracy combines organic working arrangements instead of bureaucratic ones with expert power instead of formal authority. Together these conditions breed aggressiveness and conflict. But the job of the top managers is not to bottle up that aggressiveness, as in the Machine Bureaucracy—that would be impossible in any event—but to channel it to productive ends. Thus, in performing the leader and disturbance handler roles, the top manager of the Adhocracy (as well as those in its middle line) must be a master of human relations, able to use persuasion, negotiation, coalition, reputation, rapport, or whatever to fuse the individualistic experts into smoothly functioning multidisciplinary teams.

The top managers must also devote a good deal of time to monitoring the projects. Innovative project work is notoriously difficult to control. No MIS can be relied upon to send up complete, unambiguous results. So there must be careful, personal monitoring of projects to ensure that they are completed according to specifications, on schedule, and at the estimates projected (or, more exactly, not excessively late with too great a cost over-run). In NASA:

> In practice top management has served largely a control function: the measurement, primarily after the fact, of the extent to which funds are being spent wisely; schedules are likely to be met; and whether all federal personnel, contracting, and other policies are being adhered to by both program offices and centers (Chandler and Sayles, 1971, p. 173).

But perhaps the most important single role of the top management of Adhocracy (especially Operating Adhocracy) is that of liaison with the external environment. The other structural configurations tend to focus their attention on clearly defined markets, and are more or less assured of a steady flow of work. Not so in the Operating Adhocracy, which lives from project to project, and disappears when it can find no more. Since each project is different, the Operating Adhocracy can never be sure where the next one will come from. Moreover, in the Professional Bureaucracy it is frequently the operators who bring in their own clients. That is less common in the Operating Adhocracy, where the operators work in teams. So that responsibility often falls on the top managers. In the Operating Adhocracy, therefore, the managers of the strategic apex must devote a great deal of their time to ensuring a steady and balanced stream of incoming projects. That means developing liaison contacts with potential customers and negotiating contracts with them.

Nowhere is this more clearly illustrated than in the consulting business, particularly where the approach is innovative and the structure therefore adhocratic. An executive once commented to this author that "Every consulting firm is three months away from bankruptcy." In other words, three dry months could use up all the surplus funds, leaving none to pay the high professional salaries. And so when a consultant becomes a partner in one of these firms—in effect, moves into the strategic apex—he normally hangs up his calculator and becomes virtually a full-time salesperson. It is an unusual characteristic of many an Operating Adhocracy that the selling function literally takes place at the strategic apex.

Project work poses similar problems in the Administrative Adhocracy, with similar results. Reeser (1969) asked a group of managers in three aerospace companies "What are some of the human problems of project management?" Among the common answers were two related to balancing the workload:

- The temporary nature of the organization often necessitates "make work" assignments for its displaced members after the organization has been disbanded, until productive jobs can be found for them. Sometimes the "make work" assignments last so long that the individuals lose initiative.

- Members of the organization who are displaced because of the phasing out of the work upon which they are engaged may have to wait a long time before they get another assignment at as high a level of responsibility (p. 463).

And so the top managers of the Administrative Adhocracy must also devote considerable attention to the liaison and negotiator roles in order to ensure a steady stream of work. As Chandler and Sayles (1971) note in the case of NASA, dependent on government budgets and public support in general, "a good deal of the time of the key top managers was devoted to external relations with various units of the Executive Branch, with Congress, and with key public groups representing private business, universities, the scientific community, and various international interests" (p. 173).

CONDITIONS OF THE ADHOCRACY

Basic Environment   The conditions of the environment are the most important ones for this configuration; specifically, **the Adhocracy is clearly positioned in an environment that is both dynamic and complex.** According to Hypotheses 9 and 10, a dynamic environment calls for organic structure and a complex one calls for decentralized structure. And Adhocracy is the only configuration that is both organic and relatively decentralized. In effect, innovative work, being unpredictable, is associated with a dynamic environment; and the fact that the innovation must be sophisticated means that it is difficult to comprehend, in other words associated with a complex environment. Toffler (1970) in fact, focuses on these two characteristics in his discussion of Adhocracy: "... when change is accelerated, more and more novel first-time problems arise, and traditional forms of organization prove inadequate"; later, it is the "combined demand for *more* information at *faster* speeds that is now undermining the great vertical hierarchies so typical of bureaucracy" (pp. 135, 139).

Toffler suggests that the conditions of the environment dictate the parameters of structure. But as we have noted for all the configurations, organizations that prefer particular structures also try to "choose" environments appropriate to them. This is especially clear in the case of the Operating Adhocracy. As noted earlier, advertising agencies and consulting firms that prefer to structure themselves as Professional Bureaucracies seek out stable environments; those that prefer Adhocracy find environments that are dynamic, where the client needs are unpredictable. In any event, we find Adhocracies wherever the conditions of dynamism and complexity together prevail, in organizations ranging from guerrilla units to space agencies. There is no other way to fight a war in the jungle or put the first man on the moon:

Both the Viet Cong and the Green Berets attempt to maintain ... built-in structural flexibility. Both organizations aspire to be able to enter a village, and, depending upon the circumstances, initiate a health program, establish a civil government, or destroy the enemy. Each of these diverse functions requires structural and role variations. The most medically skilled member of a guerrilla warfare unit might not be the highest ranking individual or the most competent in hand-to-hand combat. Nevertheless, the organization must be able to shift its structure to the needs of the task (Segal, 1974, p. 229).

As for putting a man on the moon, at least for the first time, that proved to be an incredibly complex task, requiring the coordinated application of a multitude of society's most sophisticated sciences. Moreover, the task was unpredictable—having never been tried before—and rendered more dynamic by the fact that it was carried out as a race with the Russians. Under all these conditions, NASA had no choice but to structure itself as an Adhocracy.

Research-based organizations—whether laboratories that do nothing else or corporations in high-technology industries that are heavily influenced by their research efforts—are drawn to the Adhocracy configuration because their work is by its very nature complex, unpredictable, and often competitive. Even hospitals and universities, described in Chapter 19 as closest to Professional Bureaucracy for their routine clinical and teaching work, are drawn to Adhocracy when they do innovative research. Their orientation to convergent, deductive thinking in their routine work precludes real innovation. So, while their professionals are often able to work alone when they apply their *standard* knowledge and skills, they must typically join in organic multidisciplinary teams to create *new* knowledge and skills.

Disparate Forces in the Environment   Hypothesis 13 of Chapter 15 indicated that **disparities in an organization's environment encourage it to decentralize selectively to differentiated work constellations, in other words, to structure itself as an Administrative Adhocracy.** The organization must create different work constellations to deal with different aspects of its environment and then integrate all their efforts.

This seems to have happened recently in the case of a number of multinational firms. For years these firms have been predisposed to using the Divisionalized Form, grouping their major divisions either by region or by product line.[6] But recent changes in their environments have resulted in a near balance of the pressures to adopt each of these two bases of grouping, making the choice of one over the other an agonizing one. The choice of

[6]Some used the multiple-divisionalized form, having both kinds of divisions, but always with one over the other in the hierarchy.

divisionalization by region denied the interdependencies that arose from marketing the same products in different places, resulting, for example, in the duplication of manufacturing faculties in each region. On the other hand, the choice of divisionalization by product line ignored the interdependencies across product lines, requiring, for example, many different marketing units in the same region. Intent on maintaining the Divisionalized Form, these firms traded off one interdependency against the other. Or else they found themselves acting schizophrenically, changing their basis of grouping back and forth in a kind of perpetual game of ping-pong.

With the emergence of matrix structure, however, these firms were presented with a logical solution to their dilemma. They could establish regional *and* product divisions at the same level of the hierarchy, in a permanent matrix structure—as long, of course, as they were prepared to dispense with the principle of unity of command. A product manager in a given region could report to both an all-product regional division manager and an all-region (worldwide) product division manager. What emerged was a hybrid structure we can call the *divisionalized adhocracy*, with characteristics of both the structural configurations from which it derives its name. Its markets are diversified, like all organizations that use the Divisionalized Form, but parts of its environment are more complex and dynamic (in essence, disparate) than the others.

Goggin (1974) describes such a hybrid structure in Dow Corning. The adhocratic nature of the structure was reflected in the matrix design and the large number of high-level task forces and standing committees used to encourage mutual adjustment among the different units. A board existed for each of the businesses, a product management group for each of the product families, and industry marketing teams for the different markets. Moreover, the company used ad hoc task forces to resolve specific problems. But Goggin also notes the emphasis placed on performance control, through the use of management by objectives, profit reporting, and the like—reflections of the Divisionalized Form of structure. Goggin describes this structure as being appropriate for firms "Developing, manufacturing, and marketing many diverse but interrelated technological products and materials," with broad "market interests," in "a rapidly expanding *global* business" and an "environment of rapid and drastic change, together with strong competition" (p. 64).

Knight (1976) and Stopford and Wells (1972, pp. 86–95) discuss other multinational firms that used the divisionalized adhocracy, although the data from a more recent survey by Allen (1978) suggest that there is no general trend in this direction. Those divisionalized companies in his study that increased "the complexity of their coordinative devices" did so through the use of more elaborate performance control systems, not a greater emphasis on "task forces and committees and coordinative roles other than that of group vice president" (pp. 29–30). Be that as it may, there seems little doubt that **among the multinational firms with interdependencies among their different product lines, those facing increasing complexity as well as dynamism in their environment will feel drawn toward the divisionalized adhocracy hybrid.** For them at least, Adhocracy becomes a natural fourth stage of structural development, after Simple Structure, Machine Bureaucracy, and Divisionalized Form.

The divisionalized adhocracy may also have some relevance for non-commercial organizations that face similar conditions. In a thought-provoking study for UNICEF, the Scandinavian Institutes for Administrative Research (SIAR, 1975) propose such a structure for that United Nations agency. They describe the UNICEF structure at the time of their study as a regional Divisionalized Form but with a tendency toward too much headquarters control. That leads to the vicious circle of one-way communication discussed in Chapter 20: the headquarters staff tries to control the regional divisions, which ignore their policies because they are out of touch with the local needs, which leads to further efforts by headquarters to control the divisions until it comes to dominate the communication channels. In the opinion of the SIAR group, UNICEF required a different structure because "the need for learning and adaptation throughout the organization is so extremely high" (p. 17). This was the result of its orientation toward regional service, its intangible tasks, and major unknowns in its future, such as the availability of resources. "... the organization will in many cases have to resolve problems of a size and nature of which it has only limited experience. This will again add to the need for an ability to develop and use its human resources, to transfer knowledge from one area to another and for cooperation and coordination between functions and units" (p. 21).

Essentially UNICEF faced the same dilemma as the multinational corporations we just discussed: the concurrent needs to respect regional knowledge and achieve interregional coordination. That can be resolved in the divisionalized organization not by more standardization and direct supervision from headquarters, which involves a shift of the entire structure toward Machine Bureaucracy, but by more mutual adjustment among divisions, which involves a shift toward Adhocracy. Thus, SIAR proposes what amounts to a divisionalized adhocracy for UNICEF: considerable power should be delegated to the regions, according to their expertise; the headquarters staff should advise rather than supervise; and an interactive or team structure should be used in the field. The result would be a more organic structure, built around flexible projects carried out by work constellations:

> [The] new structure [is] based on the assumption that new ideas for products or policies and techniques can develop anywhere in the international network of the organization, with the result that different centres emerge in different places for different purposes ...

The role of headquarters in the knowledge dimension is mainly to encourage the formation of knowledge networks; to allocate financial and human resources to those knowledge networks (groups of individuals) which take initiatives and develop real knowledge; to encourage inter-office communication, and to prepare or review and approve any recommendations for policy change (pp. 28, 33).

The SIAR report proposes a list of measures to effect the proposed structural change—a list that may, in fact, be practical for any divisionalized organization wishing to move toward Adhocracy. Among the recommendations: the elimination of one tier in the divisionalized hierarchy (such as the group vice-president level in the multiple-divisionalized corporation) in order to reduce the emphasis on direct supervision; the integration of the planning and programming functions at headquarters, which would work with the new knowledge networks; the use of more teamwork at headquarters; a reduction in the use of performance control techniques; in their place, occasional "extended visits" by a headquarters team, with a broad rather than a functional orientation and led by the chief executive; the institution of matrix structure; the encouragement of professionalism in attitude, type of work, career pattern, and training; the reorientation of the job of regional director to professional senior rather than administrative supervisor; and the reorientation of internal communication flows to emphasize dialogue, problem solving, and learning rather than reporting, controlling, and explaining.

Frequent Product Change A number of organizations are drawn toward adhocratic structure because of the dynamic conditions that result from very frequent product change. The extreme case is the *unit producer,* the manufacturing firm that custom-makes each of its products to order, as in the case of the engineering company that produces prototypes. Because each customer order constitutes a new project, the organization is encouraged to structure itself as an Operating Adhocracy. Woodward (1965) describes such a structure in the unit production firms she studied—organic and rather decentralized, but with the middle-level development engineers having considerable power. The main functions of these firms were "not easily separated in time or place," with the result that "Close and continuous co-operation was required between the managers and supervisors responsible for development and marketing respectively; the activities of the various departments had to be integrated at a day-to-day operational level" (p. 134). In the same vein, Samuel and Mannheim (1970) describe the novel case of the union-owned Israeli manufacturing enterprises:

... they have about 20 to 30 workers, produce small batches of custom-made equipment, belong to union-owned enterprises employing around 200 people, and were established about 30 years ago. Their characteristic bureaucratic structure is not clearly delimited: varying intensities of structural control are exercised; the functionalization patterns are all rudimentary—five to six different skilled jobs with most workers concentrated in one or two of them; the superior–subordinate relations are neutral, being limited to the work place in a rather nonintimate but informal climate; few written procedures and even fewer behavioral regulations characterize the regimes (p. 226).

Similar to the unit producer is the small high-technology firm, such as those surrounding Boston on Route 128. For the most part, these firms do sophisticated project work—design and sometimes manufacturing—under direct contract to the U.S. government or to the larger corporations in industries such as defense, aerospace, and atomic energy. Their work being complex and their environments dynamic, these firms are dependent on highly trained experts who work in interdisciplinary project teams. But these firms are also small and owned by individual entrepreneurs who maintain personal control. (They are able to do so, of course, only because they are as highly trained as their employees.) So the structure emerges as a hybrid between Operating Adhocracy and Simple Structure, which we call the *entrepreneurial adhocracy*.

Another variant of the unit producer is the newspaper or magazine. From the editorial point of view, every product—that is, every issue—is different. Moreover, the environment is typically very dynamic and often rather complex, especially in the case of daily newspapers and newsmagazines, which must report a vast world of fast-breaking news with very short deadlines. Moreover, the efforts of all kinds of reporters, photographers, editors, and others must be integrated into a single product. So adhocratic structure is called for in the editorial department. But from the point of view of the printing and distribution functions, there is great repetition—thousands, sometimes millions of copies of the same issue. And the environment is extremely stable—the tasks remain unchanged no matter what the content of the issue. So machine bureaucratic structure is called for in these functions. The need for two different structures is, of course, reconciled by truncation. The different functions are kept well separated, with standard outputs serving as the one interface. The adhocratic editorial department completes its work and then converts it into standardized format—typed copy, page layouts, clipped photographs—which become the inputs to the bureaucratic production process. In the case of the weekend rotogravure magazine studied by a McGill student group, the editorial function (together with newspaper relations and advertising) and the printing function were constituted as separate companies, although jointly owned.

Some manufacturers of consumer goods operate in markets so competitive that they must change their products almost continuously. Here again, dynamic conditions, when coupled with some complexity, drive the structure toward the adhocratic form. An excellent example of what we shall call the *competitive adhocracy* is the pop recording company discussed earlier. Its dramatically short product life cycle and fluid supply of recording talent required extremely fast response based on a great deal of inside knowledge. As the student group that did the study noted: "The product life of a 45 rpm is three months. This is measured from the idea of releasing some song by an artist to the last sale of the single to stores. There is nothing quite so dead as yesterday's number one hit on the hit parade."[7] Other examples of competitive adhocracies are found in the cosmetics, pharmaceuticals, and plastics industries. Lawrence and Lorsch's (1967) successful plastics companies fit the description of the Administrative Adhocracy very closely as, apparently, does a firm like Proctor and Gamble, a well-known leader in the use of the liaison devices.

It should be noted that, according to the findings of Khandwalla (1973a), it is really only product competition that leads to this kind of structure. Competition based on price or marketing is simpler to understand and deal with, and so often can be handled in Simple Structure or Machine Bureaucracy. In contrast, product competition requires more serious innovation and more complex decision making, often based on sophisticated research and development activity. So Adhocracy becomes the favored structure. Those manufacturing firms in Khandwalla's sample that perceived their environments as noncompetitive reported that they centralized or decentralized in parallel, while those that experienced product competition (price competition to a lesser extent and marketing competition not at all) reported that they decentralized selectively, in other words tended to use the Administrative Adhocracy structure. Specifically, they decentralized their product design, development, and marketing decisions, and centralized their finance, pricing, and acquisition decisions. Which is exactly what the student group reported for the pop recording company.

Youth as a Condition of the Adhocracy A number of nonenvironmental conditions are also associated with Adhocracy. One is age—or more exactly youth—since Adhocracy is the least stable form of structure. It is difficult to keep any structure in that state for long periods of time—to keep behaviors from formalizing and to ensure a steady flow of truly innovative, ad hoc projects. **All kinds of forces drive the Adhocracy to bureaucratize itself as it ages.** On the other side of the coin, according to Hypothesis 1, young organizations tend to be structured organically since they are still finding their way and also since they are typically eager for innovative, ad hoc projects on which to test themselves. So we can conclude that **the adhocratic form tends to be associated with youth, with early stages in the development of organizational structures.**

[7]From a paper submitted to the author in Management Policy 276–661, November 1972, by Alain Berranger and Philip Feldman.

The Operating Adhocracy is particularly prone to a short life. For one thing, it faces a risky market, which can quickly destroy it. Unlike the Professional Bureaucracy or Machine Bureaucracy, with its standardized outputs, the Operating Adhocracy can never be sure where its next project will come from. A downturn in the economy or the loss of a major contract can close it down literally overnight.

But if some Operating Adhocracies have short lives because they fail, others have short lives because they succeed. Success—and aging—encourage a metamorphosis in the Operating Adhocracy, driving it to more stable conditions and more bureaucratic structure. Over time, the successful organization develops a reputation for what it does best. That encourages it to repeat certain projects, in effect to focus its attention on specific contingencies and programs. And this tends to suit its employees, who, growing older themselves, welcome more stability in their work. So the Operating Adhocracy is driven over time toward the Professional Bureaucracy to concentrate on the programs it does best, sometimes even toward the Machine Bureaucracy to exploit a single program or invention. The organization survives, but the structural configuration dies.

> For example, the innovating psychiatric clinic gains a reputation and attracts both patients and personnel. Its novel techniques, created by one or a few people, are viewed as the reason for its success. Thus, the same techniques are prescribed for new personnel to follow. As a result, these techniques must be explicated and broken down into steps, and checkpoints must be provided along the way. Soon the new approaches are frozen into convenient dogma, and the clinic has become a factory. . . .
>
> The successful small law firm, blessed with one or two imaginative people and probably some very good connections and publicity, adds staff and clients, and becomes a routinized giant in its field. The greatest threat to successful, small advertising agencies is the need to balance growth with flexibility. Growth can be phenomenal since clients bring in huge advertising programs that will run for a few years. "We grew too fast," is the common complaint. "But we had to; our old accounts would not stay with us unless they were reassured by our getting huge new accounts," is the next line. The inventor of a sophisticated electronic device has but two choices—to sell the invention to a large firm, or to build his own large firm, with volume production (Perrow, 1970, pp. 66–67).

Administrative Adhocracies typically live longer. They, too, feel the pressures to bureaucratize as they age. This leads many to try to stop innovating, or to innovate in stereotyped ways, and thereby to revert to more bureaucratic structure, notably of the machine type. But unlike the Operating Adhocracy, the Administrative Adhocracy typically cannot change its structure yet remain in the same industry. In choosing that industry, it chose a complex, dynamic environment. Stereotyped innovation will eventually destroy the organization. Newspapers, plastics, and pharmaceuticals companies—at least those facing severe competition—may have no choice but to structure themselves as Adhocracies.

In recognition of the tendencies for organization to bureaucratize themselves as they age, a variant has emerged which Goodman and Goodman (1976) call the "temporary system" and Toffler (1970) calls the "disposable" organization—"the organizational equivalent of paper dresses or throw-away tissues" (p. 133). These *temporary adhocracies*, as we shall call them, are created to draw together specialists from different existing organizations to do single projects. Temporary adhocracies are becoming common in a great many spheres of modern society: the production group that performs a single play, the election campaign committee that promotes a single candidate, the guerrilla group that overthrows a single government, the Olympic Committee that plans a single Games. Harris (1975) describes the "overhaul" organization created to clean up an administrative mess in a large Machine Bureaucracy. Clark (1965–66) describes the Physical Science Study Committee of professors and teachers set up with federal and foundation money to revise the teaching of physics in American high schools. It not only developed a host of teaching materials (books, assignments, films, laboratory apparatus, etc.), but also saw to their eventual manufacture and dissemination through teacher training.

A related variant is the *mammoth project adhocracy*, a giant temporary adhocracy which draws on thousands of experts for anywhere from a year to a decade to carry out a single task.

> When Lockheed Aircraft Corporation won a controversial contract to build fifty-eight giant C-5A military air transports, it created a whole new 11,000-man organization specifically for that purpose. To complete the multi-billion-dollar job, Lockheed had to coordinate the work not only of its own people, but of hundreds of subcontracting firms. In all, 6000 companies are involved in producing the more than 120,000 parts needed for each of these enormous airplanes. The Lockheed project organization created for this purpose has its own management and its own complex internal structure. ... the entire imposing organization created for this job had a planned life span of five years (Toffler, 1970, pp. 132–133).

In the same vein, Chandler and Sayles (1971, p. 2) refer to the "polyorganization," wherein existing organizations pool their experts in a consortium to carry out a large, complex project. For example, the Columbia Broadcasting Corporation, other mass-media producers and distributors, electronics firms, and manufacturers of film all joined forces to exploit a new technique for taping television programs.

These last examples suggest that size is a less important condition than age for the Adhocracy. Administrative Adhocracies in particular can grow very large indeed. However, Operating Adhocracies tend to be small or middle-sized, constrained by the projects they do, by the number and size of the multidisciplinary teams they can organize, and by their desire to avoid the pressure to bureaucratize that comes from growing large.

Technical System as a Condition of the Adhocracy   Technical system is another important condition in certain cases of this configuration. While Operating Adhocracies, like their sister Professional Bureaucracies, tend to have simple, nonregulating technical systems, the case for Administrative Adhocracies is frequently quite the opposite. **Many organizations use the Administrative Adhocracy because their technical systems are sophisticated and perhaps automated as well.**

As described in Hypothesis 7, when its technical system is sophisticated, the organization requires an elaborate, highly trained support staff to design or purchase, modify, and maintain it; the organization must give considerable power over its technical decisions to that support staff; and that staff, in turn, must use the liaison devices to coordinate its work. In other words, complex machinery requires specialists who have the knowledge, power, and flexible working arrangements to cope with it. The result is that support staffers emerge as powerful members of the organization, drawing power down from the strategic apex, up from the operating core, and over from the middle line. The organization is drawn to the Administrative Adhocracy configuration.

Automation of a sophisticated technical system evokes even stronger forces in the same direction. "Far from fastening the grip of bureaucracy on civilization more tightly than before, automation leads to its overthrow" (Toffler, 1970, p. 141). As we saw in Chapter 14, the Machine Bureaucracy that succeeds in automating its operating core undergoes a dramatic metamorphosis. The problem of motivating uninterested operators disappears, and with it goes the control mentality that permeates the Machine Bureaucracy; the distinction between line and staff blurs (machines being indifferent as to who turns their knobs), which leads to another important reduction in conflict; the technostructure loses its influence, since control is built into the machinery itself by its designers rather than imposed on workers by the rules and standards of the analysts. Overall, the administrative structure becomes more decentralized and organic, emerging as the type we call the *automated adhocracy*.

Automation is common in the process industries, such as petrochemicals and cosmetics (another reason why firms such as Procter and Gamble would be drawn toward Adhocracy). That is presumably why Joan Woodward's (1965) description of the process producers fits Administrative Adhocracy to a tee. But it should be noted that not all process firms use this structure. Many are, in fact, far from fully automated, and therefore require large operating work forces which draw them toward Machine Bureaucracy.

Steel companies, discussed in Chapter 18, are a case in point. Then there are the process producers that, although highly automated, exhibit strong machine bureaucratic as well as administrative adhocratic tendencies, in some cases because they require large routine work forces for other functions (such as marketing in the oil company with many of its own retail outlets), in others because they exist in high fixed-cost industries with no competition. An example of the latter, reviewed at some length by Perrow (1970, pp. 154–155), is the power utility more intent on lobbying for the support of the government than innovating for the service of the customer. Finally, there are the automated process producers, with such simple environments and technical systems—for example, the small manufacturer of one line of hand creams—that the Simple Structure suffices instead of the Administrative Adhocracy.[8]

Fashion as a Condition of the Adhocracy We come now to the power factors. Power itself is not a major condition of the Adhocracy, except to the extent that the support staff of the Machine Bureaucracy is able to take control of certain technical decisions or the operators of the Professional Bureaucracy care to encourage innovation instead of standardization and thereby drive their structure to Adhocracy. But **fashion most decidedly is a condition of Adhocracy.** Every characteristic of the Adhocracy is very much in vogue today: emphasis on expertise, organic structure, project teams and task forces, decentralization without a single concentration of power, matrix structure, sophisticated and automated technical systems, youth, and environments that are complex and dynamic. Ansoff's (1974) enthusiasm is typical of many of today's "future thinkers":

> . . . in the next ten years the concepts of structure and capability are due for a change as revolutionary as the transition from static trenches to mobile warfare. A vast majority of technology used in design of organizations today is based on a Maginot line concept of "permanent" or at best "semi-permanent" structures. if the reasoning in this paper is only half-correct, the trend is toward the concept of flexible task-responsive "mobile warfare" capabilities (p. 83).

If Simple Structure and Machine Bureaucracy were yesterday's structures, and Professional Bureaucracy and the Divisionalized Form are today's, then Adhocracy is clearly tomorrow's. This is the structure for a population growing ever better educated and more specialized, yet under constant exhortation to adopt the "systems" approach—to view the world as an integrated whole instead of a collection of loosely coupled parts. It is

[8]Perrow (1967), using additional data on the sample provided by Woodward, was able to categorize all but her process producers in his two-by-two matrix (similar to ours presented at the end of Chapter 15 that categorizes all of our configurations except the Divisionalized Form). "Efforts to do so after her book appeared floundered because of lack of data" (p. 207).

the structure for environments becoming more complex and demanding of innovation, and for technical systems becoming more sophisticated and highly automated. It is the only structure now available to those who believe organizations must become at the same time more democratic yet less bureaucratic.

Yet despite our current infatuation with it, Adhocracy is not the structure for all organizations. Like all the other configurations, it too has its place. And that place, as the examples of this chapter make clear, seems to be in the new industries of our age—aerospace, electronics, think-tank consulting, research, advertising, filmmaking, petrochemicals, virtually all the industries that grew up since World War II. Stinchcombe's descendents, should they choose sometime during the twenty-first century to verify his conclusion of 1965 that organizational structure reflects the age of founding of the industry, will no doubt identify Adhocracy as the structural configuration of the last half of the twentieth century.

SOME ISSUES ASSOCIATED WITH ADHOCRACY

There has been little exploration of the issues associated with Adhocracy, the newest of the five structural configurations. Simple Structure is so old that its advantages and disadvantages are by now taken for granted. The issues associated with Machine Bureaucracy have been discussed at great length in the literature, especially those concerning alienation and conflict. There has also been quite a bit of discussion of the issues associated with Professional Bureaucracy, and, more recently, of the Divisionalized Form as well. But all of these structural configurations have been around for some time. In contrast, Adhocracy is new. And every new structure, because it solves problems the old ones could not, attracts a dedicated following—one enamored with its advantages and blind to its problems. With this kind of support, time is required to bring its issues into focus—time to live with the structure and learn about its weaknesses as well as its strengths. Especially in the case of a structure as complex as Adhocracy.

Nevertheless, there has been some discussion of the issues associated with Adhocracy, three in particular: the reactions of people who must live with the ambiguities of Adhocracy, its inefficiencies, and its propensity to make inappropriate transitions to other structures.

Human Reactions to Ambiguity   Many people, especially creative ones, dislike both structural rigidity and concentration of power. That leaves them only one structural configuration. Adhocracy is the one that is both organic and decentralized—so they find it a great place to work. In essence, **Adhocracy is the only structure for those who believe in more democracy with less bureaucracy.**

But not every structure can be adhocratic. The organization's conditions must call for it. Forcing Adhocracy on, say, a simple, stable environment, is as unnatural—and therefore as unpleasant for the participants—as forcing Machine Bureaucracy on a complex, dynamic one. Furthermore, not everyone shares the same vision of structural utopia. As we saw in Chapter 18, there are those who prefer the life of Machine Bureaucracy, a life of stability and well-defined relationships. They, in fact, dislike the relationships of Adhocracy, viewing it as a nice place to visit but no place to spend a career. **Even dedicated members of Adhocracies periodically exhibit the same low tolerance for ambiguity:**

> The organic form by departing from the familiar clarity and fixity of the hierarchic structure, is often experienced by the individual manager as an uneasy, embarrassed, or chronically anxious quest for knowledge about what he should be doing, or what is expected of him, and similar apprehensiveness about what others are doing. ... In these situations, all managers some of the time, and many managers all the time, yearn for more definition and structure (Burns and Stalker, 1966, pp. 122–123).

Earlier we discussed two of the common responses Reeser received when he asked managers in three aerospace companies "What are some of the human problems of project organization?" Of the other eight responses Reeser (1969) reports, six, in fact, relate to structural ambiguities:

- The knowledge that the work upon which their jobs depend is getting close to its eventual phase-out causes anxieties and feelings of frustration on the part of the members of the organization.
- The members of the organization don't feel that they really know who their boss is; they don't know for sure what one individual they should try to please or impress in order to get raises and promotions.
- Individuals who have experienced a series of transfers from one organization to another as a result of contracts phasing-out and other contracts being started may feel a low sense of loyalty to the organization of which they are temporarily members.
- Confusion and ambiguity are common conditions because the jobs in the organization are not clearly defined, authority relationships are obscure, and lines of communication are loose and unorganized.
- The personal development of individuals is random and unplanned because they are seldom under any one manager long enough for him to feel responsible for assuring that they get the training and experience they need in order to mature.
- The work environment is one of intense competition with other organizations for resources, recognition, and rewards. The result is often conflict between the members of the competing organization (pp. 462, 464, 465).

Reeser's last point raises another major problem of ambiguity, the politicization of the structure. **Coupling its ambiguities with its interdependencies, Adhocracy emerges as the most politicized of the five structural configurations.** No structure can be more Darwinian than the Adhocracy—more supportive of the fit, as long as they remain fit, and more destructive of the weak. Structures this fluid tend to be highly competitive and at times ruthless—breeding grounds for all kinds of political forces. The French have a graphic expression for this: *un panier de crabes*—a bucket of crabs, all clawing at each other to get up, or out. Take, for example, matrix structure: as noted in Chapter 10, what it does is establish an adversary system, thereby institutionalizing organizational conflict.[9]

There are conflicts that breed politics in the other configurations, too, as we have noted in each of the last four chapters. But these conflicts are always contained within well-defined ground rules. In the Simple Structure, the politics that do take place are directed at the chief executive. But his close, personal control precludes much of the political activity in the first place. Those who do not like the structure simply get out. And in all of the bureaucratic configurations, conflicts and politics are focused on well-defined issues—the power of line versus staff or professional versus nonprofessional, the resistance of workers to the control mentality, the biasing of information sent up to the central headquarters, the ambiguities of pigeonholing, and so on. In the Professional Bureaucracy, for example, highly trained experts with considerable power are naturally predisposed to do battle with each other, most often over territorial imperatives. But at least these battles are guided by professional norms and affiliations. Their incidence is sharply reduced by the fact that the professionals work largely on their own, often with their own clients. Not so in the Adhocracy, where specialists from different professions must work together on multidisciplinary teams, and where, owing to the organic nature of the structure, the political games that result are played without rules. Adhocracy requires the specialist to subordinate his individual goals and the rules of his profession to the needs of the group, in spite of the fact that he, like his colleague in the Professional Bureaucracy, remains—potentially at least—a strong individualist.

In bureaucracies—especially of the machine type—management must spend a good deal of time trying to bottle up conflict. But in the Adhocracy that must not be done—even if it could be. Such efforts only stifle creativity. "Any anxieties and frictions that might be generated were an inevitable circumstance of life as it is, and one could not 'manage them out of the organization'—not, at least, without neglecting or damaging some more vital

---

[9]See Lindblom's (1965) very detailed discussion of the techniques employed to reach agreement by mutual adjustment, including various forms of negotiation, reciprocation, and manipulation.

interest" (Burns and Stalker, 1966, p. 3). **Conflict and aggressiveness are necessary elements in the Adhocracy; management's job is to channel them toward productive ends.**

Problems of Efficiency   No structure is better suited to solving complex, ill-structured problems than the Adhocracy. None can match it for sophisticated innovation. Or, unfortunately, for the costs of that innovation. Adhocracy is simply not an efficient structure:

> The nonbureaucratic organization loses economies of scale, sacrifices the advantages of specialization in personnel, programs, and equipment, incurs great costs from lack of coordination, and runs the risk of inadequate and untimely accounting information. Such an organization may even be particularly open to the exploitation of positions by managers and to empire building. Where uncertainty is high, controls weak, and performance standards uncertain, staff members have much greater leeway in exercising discretion in favor of non-organizational values and interests. From all these points of view *internal* efficiency is low as compared to the bureaucratic organization (Perrow, 1970, pp. 64–65).

In other words, while it is ideally suited for the one-of-a-kind project, the **Adhocracy is not competent at doing ordinary things.** It is designed for the *extra*ordinary. The bureaucracies are all mass producers; they gain efficiency through standardization. The Adhocracy is a custom producer, unable to standardize and so to be efficient.

The root of its inefficiency is the Adhocracy's high cost of communication (Knight, 1976, p. 126). People talk a lot in these structures; that is how they combine their knowledge to develop new ideas. But that takes time, a great deal. Faced with the need to make a decision in the Machine Bureaucracy, someone up above gives an order and that is that. Not so in the Adhocracy. Everyone gets into the act. First are all the managers who must be consulted—functional managers, project managers, liaison managers. Then are all the specialists who believe their point of view should be represented in the decision. A meeting is called, probably to schedule another meeting, eventually to decide who should participate in the decision. Then those people settle down to the decision process. The problem is defined and redefined, ideas for its solution are generated and debated, alliances build and fall around different solutions, and eventually everyone settles down to hard bargaining about the favored one. Finally, a decision emerges—that in itself is an accomplishment—although it is typically late and will probably be modified later. All of this is the cost of having to find a creative solution to a complex, ill-structured problem.

It should be noted, however, that the heavy costs incurred in reaching a decision are partially recuperated in its execution. Widespread participation in decision making ensures widespread support for the decisions made.

So the execution stage can be smoother in the Adhocracy than in the Machine Bureaucracy or the Simple Structure, where resistance by the operators, not party to the decision, is often encountered.[10]

A further source of inefficiency in the Adhocracy is the unbalanced workloads, as mentioned earlier. It is almost impossible to keep the personnel of a project structure—high-priced personnel, it should be noted —busy on a steady basis. "... the work necessary to solve unfamiliar problems is not well-planned so that there is a need for periods of intensified effort which alternate with periods of unproductive waiting time" (Goodman and Goodman, 1976, p. 495). In January, the specialists are playing bridge for want of work; in March they are working overtime with no hope of completing the project on time.

The Dangers of Inappropriate Transition   Of course, one solution to the problems of ambiguity and inefficiency is to change the structure. Employees no longer able to tolerate the ambiguity and customers fed up with the inefficiency try to drive the structure to a more stable, bureaucratic form.

That is relatively easily done in the Operating Adhocracy, as noted earlier. The organization simply selects the standard programs it does best and goes into the business of doing them. It becomes a Professional Bureaucracy. Or else it uses its creative talent one last time to find a single market niche, and then turns itself into a Machine Bureaucracy to mass produce in that niche.

But **the transition from Operating Adhocracy into bureaucracy, however easily effected, is not always appropriate.** The organization came into being to solve problems imaginatively, not to apply standards indiscriminately. In many spheres, society has more mass producers than it needs; what it lacks are true problem solvers. It has little need for the laboratory that comes up with a modification of an old design when a new one is called for, the consulting firm ready with a standard technique when the client has a unique problem, the medical or university researcher who sees every new challenge in terms of an old theory. The standard output of bureaucracy will not do when the conditions call for the creativity of Adhocracy.

This seems to describe some of the problems of the television networks. Despite their need to be creative, the networks face one irresistible pressure to bureaucratize: the requirement that they produce on a routine basis, hour after hour, night after night, with never a break. One would think they would tend toward professional bureaucratic structures, but Jay's comments on his experiences as a producer for the BBC and Lourenço and Glidewell's comments about the powerlessness of the network stations, reproduced in

[10]In his discussion of mutual adjustment, Lindblom (1965, Chap. 14) elaborates on this point at length. But his discussion of the techniques of mutual adjustment also indicates its very high cost of communication.

Chapters 18 and 20, respectively, suggest strong elements of Machine Bureaucracy. And the results are what one would expect of such structures: stereotyped programming, stale jokes supported by canned laughter, television doctors and detectives that are interchangeable between channels, repetition of the old movies. Interestingly, the two bright spots on TV are the news and the specials, for reasons already suggested in our discussion of Adhocracy. The news department, like the newspaper, faces a truly dynamic environment. The networks can control and therefore stabilize the series, but never the news. Every day is different, and so, therefore, is every program. And the specials really are ad hoc—in this case, by the choice of the networks—and so lend themselves to the creative approach of the Adhocracy. But elsewhere the pressures of the routine neutralize creativity, and the result is standardization.

Other organizations face these same dual pressures—to produce routinely yet also be creative. Universities and teaching hospitals must, for example, serve their regular clients yet also produce creative research. Universities sometimes set up research centers to differentiate the research and teaching activities. These enable the professors with the greatest potential for research—often poor teachers—to do it without interruption. In the absence of such differentiation, the organization risks falling into a schizophrenic state, continually wavering between two kinds of structure, never clearly isolating either to the detriment of both. Thus, Charns et al. (1977) find that hospital physicians blur the perceptions of their roles of clinician, teacher, and researcher.". . . approximately the same organizational arrangements are used for all functions. . . . Given the differences in [these] functions, it is questionable whether the same organizational arrangements are appropriate for all functions" (p. 82). They suggest that a strong differentiation of these roles might prove more effective—for example, by separating them clearly in place or over time.

The Administrative Adhocracy runs into more serious difficulties when it succumbs to the pressures to bureaucratize. It exists to innovate for itself, in its own industry. The conditions of dynamism and complexity, requiring sophisticated innovation, typically cut across the entire industry. So unlike the Operating Adhocracy, the Administrative Adhocracy cannot often select new clients yet remain in the same industry. And so its conversion to Machine Bureaucracy—the natural transition for the Administrative Adhocracy tired of perpetual change—by destroying the organization's ability to innovate, can eventually destroy the organization itself.

To reiterate a central theme of our discussion throughout this book: **in general, there is no one best structure; in particular, there may be, as long as the design parameters are internally consistent and together with the contingency factors form a coherent configuration.** We have delineated five such configurations in this last section of the book; their dimensions are summarized in Table 21–1.

TABLE 21-1. Dimensions of the Five Structural Configurations*

	Simple Structure	Machine Bureaucracy	Professional Bureaucracy	Divisionalized Form	Adhocracy
Key coordinating mechanism:	Direct Supervision	Standardization of work	Standardization of skills	Standardization of outputs	Mutual adjustment
Key part of organization:	Strategix apex	Technostructure	Operating core	Middle line	Support staff (with operating core in Op. Ad.)
Design parameters:					
Specialization of jobs	Little specialization	Much horiz. and vert. spec.	Much horiz. spec.	Some horiz. and vert. spec. (between divisions and HQ)	Much horiz. spec.
Training and indoctrination	Little tr. and indoc.	Little tr. and indoc.	Much tr. and indoc.	Some tr. and indoc. (of div. managers)	Much training
Formalization of behavior, bureaucratic/organic	Little formalization, organic	Much formalization, bureaucratic	Little formalization, bureaucratic	Much formalization (within divisions), bureaucratic	Little formalization, organic
Grouping	Usually functional	Usually functional	Functional and market	Market	Functional and market
Unit size	Wide	Wide at bottom, narrow elsewhere	Wide at bottom, narrow elsewhere	Wide (at top)	Narrow throughout
Planning and control systems	Little pl. and control	Action planning	Little pl. and control	Much perf. control	Limited action pl. (esp. in Adm. Ad.)
Liaison devices	Few liaison devices	Few liaison devices	Liaison devices in administration	Few liaison devices	Many liaison devices throughout
Decentralization	Centralization	Limited horizontal decent.	Horizontal and vertical decent.	Limited vertical decent.	Selective decent.
Functioning:					
Strategic apex	All administrative work	Fine tuning, coordination of functions, conflict resolution	External liaison, conflict resolution	Strategic portfolio, performance control	External liaison, conflict resolution, work balancing, project monitoring
Operating core	Informal work with little discretion	Routine, formalized work with little discretion	Skilled, standardized work with much individual autonomy	Tendency to formalize due to divisionalization	Truncated (in Adm. Ad.) or merged with administration to do informal project work (in Op. Ad.)

Middle line	Insignificant	Elaborated and differentiated; conflict resolution, staff liaison, support of vert. flows	Controlled by professionals; much mutual adjustment	Formulation of div. strategy, managing operations	Extensive but blurred with staff; involved in project work
Technostructure	None	Elaborated to formalize work	Little	Elaborated at HQ for perf. control	Small and blurred within middle in project work
Support staff	Small	Often elaborated to reduce uncertainty	Elaborated to support professionals; Mach. Bur. structure	Split between HQ and divisions	Highly elaborated (esp. in Adm. Ad.) but blurred within middle in project work
Flow of authority	Significant from top	Significant throughout	Insignificant (except in support staff)	Significant throughout	Insignificant
Flow of regulated system	Insignificant	Significant throughout	Insignificant (except in support staff)	Significant throughout	Insignificant
Flow of informal communication	Significant	Discouraged	Significant in administration	Some between HQ and divisions	Significant throughout
Work constellations	None	Insignificant, esp. at lower levels	Some in administration	Insignificant	Significant throughout (esp. in Adm. Ad.)
Flow of decision making	Top down	Top down	Bottom up	Differentiated between HQ and divisions	Mixed, all levels
Contingency factors:					
Age and size	Typically young and small (first stage)	Typically old and large (second stage)	Varies	Typically old and very large (third stage)	Typically young (Op. Ad.)
Technical system	Simple, not regulating	Regulating but not automated, not very sophisticated	Not regulating or sophisticated	Divisible, otherwise typically like Mach. Bur.	Very sophisticated, often automated (in Adm. Ad.); not regulating or sophisticated (in Op. Ad.)
Environment	Simple and dynamic; sometimes hostile	Simple and stable	Complex and stable	Relatively simple and stable; diversified markets (esp. products and services)	Complex and dynamic; sometimes disparate (in Adm. Ad.)
Power	Chief executive control; often owner-managed; not fashionable	Technocratic and external control; not fashionable	Professional operator control; fashionable	Middle-line (control; fashionable (esp. in industry)	Expert control; very fashionable

*Italic type designates key design parameter.

22

A Concluding Pentagon

Do any of these five structural configurations really exist? That is a strange question to raise after more than 150 pages of discussion, filled with illustrations. But it is worth asking, in order to draw a tighter line between the five structural configurations and the reality they purport to describe.

In one sense the structural configurations do not exist at all. After all, they are just words and pictures on pieces of paper, not reality itself. Real structures in all but the most trivial organizations are enormously complex, far more so than any of these five configurations on paper. What they constitute is a theory, and every theory necessarily simplifies and therefore distorts the reality. That was why the reader was warned at the outset to proceed under the assumption that every sentence in this section (including this one) was an overstatement.

But that should not lead to a rejection of the configurations. For the reader's choice is not between theory and reality, so much as between alternative theories. No one carries reality around in his head; no head is that big. Rather, we carry around thoughts, impressions, and beliefs about reality, and measures of it we call facts. But all of this is useless unless it is ordered in some way, just as a library of books is useless unless the books are catalogued. So, most important, we carry around in our heads comprehensible simplifications—concepts or models or theories—that enable us to catalogue our data and experience. The reader's choice then becomes one of alternative systems of cataloging, that is, alternative theories.

The reader can trust the theories he builds himself, based on his own experiences, or else he can select from among those offered in books like this one, based on the experiences of the organizations reported in the research. Or, more realistically, he selects from among them in building up his own models of reality. His choice of theories is normally based on two criteria: how rich is the description, that is, how powerfully it reflects the reality (or, alternatively, how little it distorts the reality), and how simple it is to comprehend. The most useful theories are simple when stated yet powerful when applied, like $E = MC^2$.

And so in another sense—at least if I have done my job well—the configurations do indeed exist, in the reader's mind. The mind is where all knowledge exists. The classical principles of structure existed because people believed in them and so made them part of their reality. So, too, the concept of informal structure exists, and of contingency relationships. The five structural configurations will also exist if they prove to constitute a simple yet powerful theory, more useful in some ways than the others currently available.

To give the theory of the configurations a little push toward that end, this last chapter discusses a number of possible applications of it. First, we discuss it as a set of five pulls acting on almost every organization, second as a set of five pure types that reflect the structures of many organizations, third as the basis for describing hybrid structures, and fourth as the basis for describing structural transitions. Figure 22–1 seeks to capture the spirit of these four discussions. Symbolically, it shows the five structural configurations as forming a pentagon, bounding a reality within which real structures can be found. Each configuration sits at one of the nodes, pulling real structures toward it. The Simple Structure, the first stage for many organizations, sits at the top. At the next level, on either side of it, are the two bureaucracies, Machine Bureaucracy on the left and Professional Bureaucracy on the right. Down at the third, bottom level are the two most elaborate structural configurations, the Divisionalized Form on the left and Adhocracy on the right. Some real structures fall into position close to one node—one of the pure structures—while others fall between two or more, as hybrids, perhaps in transition from one pure form to another.

THE CONFIGURATIONS AS A SET OF BASIC PULLS ON THE ORGANIZATION

To repeat a point made at the start of this section, **the configurations represent a set of five forces that pull organizations in five different structural directions.** These pulls are shown in the pentagon and are listed below:

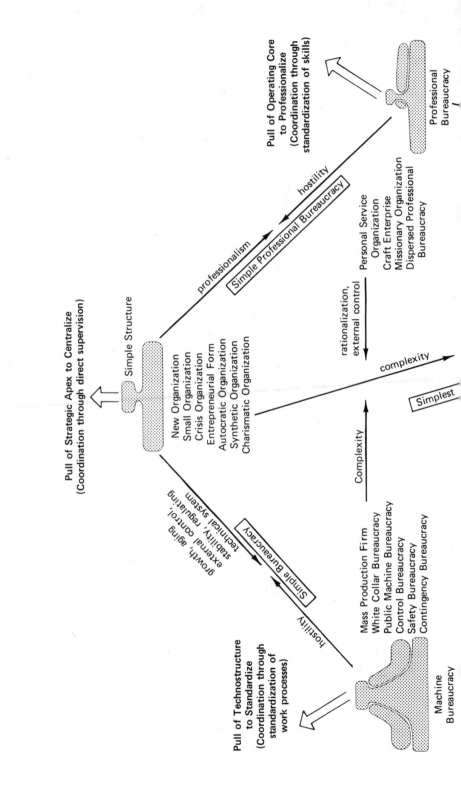

Pull of Strategic Apex to Centralize
(Coordination through direct supervision)

Pull of Operating Core to Professionalize
(Coordination through standardization of skills)

Pull of Technostructure to Standardize
(Coordination through standardization of work processes)

Simple Structure

New Organization
Small Organization
Crisis Organization
Entrepreneurial Form
Autocratic Organization
Synthetic Organization
Charismatic Organization

Professional Bureaucracy

Personal Service Organization
Craft Enterprise
Missionary Organization
Dispersed Professional Bureaucracy

Machine Bureaucracy

Mass Production Firm
White Collar Bureaucracy
Public Machine Bureaucracy
Control Bureaucracy
Safety Bureaucracy
Contingency Bureaucracy

Simple Professional Bureaucracy

professionalism

hostility

rationalization, external control

complexity

Complexity

Simplest

Simple Bureaucracy

growth, aging
external control,
stability, regulating
technical system

hostility

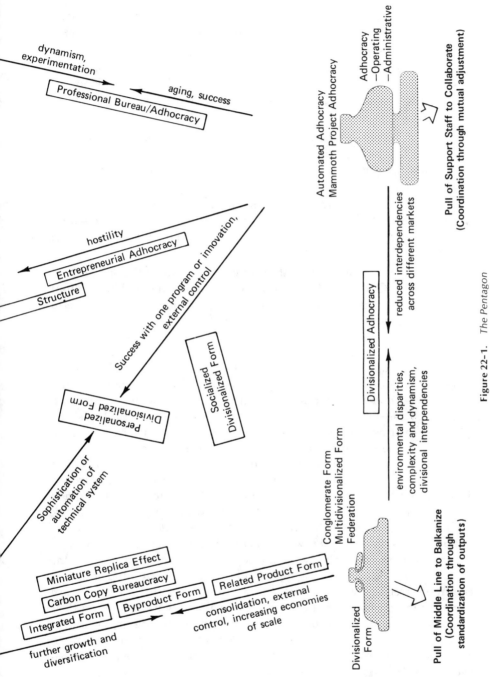

Figure 22-1. The Pentagon

471

- First is the pull exercised by the strategic apex to centralize, to coordinate by direct supervision, and so to structure the organization as a Simple Structure.
- Second is the pull exercised by the technostructure, to coordinate by standardization—notably of work processes, the tightest kind—in order to increase its influence, and so to structure the organization as a Machine Bureaucracy.
- Third is the pull exercised by the operators to professionalize, to coordinate by the standardization of skills in order to maximize their autonomy, and so to structure the organization as a Professional Bureaucracy.
- Fourth is the pull exercised by the middle managers to Balkanize, to be given the autonomy to manage their own units, with coordination restricted to the standardization of outputs, and so to structure the organization as a Divisionalized Form.
- Fifth is the pull exercised by the support staff (and by the operators as well in the Operating Adhocracy), for collaboration (and innovation) in decision making, to coordinate by mutual adjustment, and so to structure the organization as an Adhocracy.

Almost every organization experiences these five pulls; what structure it designs depends in large part on how strong each one is. Take, for example, the case of the theater company, as described by Goodman and Goodman (1972, all quotes from p. 104). They note "the sense of ownership expressed by the directors," also their power "to a certain extent [to] shape a play into their own image," to choose the team to perform that play, and even to limit the creative contributions of members of that team. All of these constitute pulls toward Simple Structure. Of course, put a number of these directors in one organization, and there also emerges a pull toward the Divisionalized Form, where each can maximize his autonomy. Goodman and Goodman also cite the case of one director who kept "a detailed book which he made and used in the production of a large-scale musical comedy." That book constituted a pull toward Machine Bureaucracy. In experimental theater, however, the "ability to do detailed planning diminishes," the director being "less firm in knowing what he wants" and cuts and additions being more frequent. The pull is toward Adhocracy. In most theatrical companies the members are highly professional and work largely on their own, as Goodman and Goodman (1976) note: the "choreographer usually creates a dance sequence to fit music that has already been composed and to fit the space available given the existing set design. The three people need never see or speak to each other and are often working in separate locations ..." (p. 496). The pull is toward Professional Bureaucracy.

Thus, in this first application of the theory, we see the five configurations being used to understand the forces that pull organizations to structure themselves in one way or another.

THE CONFIGURATIONS AS PURE TYPES

In this second application of the theory, **the set of configurations is treated as a typology of ideal or pure types, each one a description of a basic kind of organizational structure and its situation.**

Our examples throughout this section suggest that a great many organizations, being dominated by one of the five pulls, tend to design structures rather close to one of the configurations. No structure matches any one configuration perfectly, but some come remarkably close—like the small entrepreneurial firm controlled by its president in an almost pure Simple Structure or the conglomerate corporation that fits virtually all the characteristics of the pure Divisionalized Form.

In the preceding five chapters, we have, in fact, labeled and discussed a number of examples and variants of each of the pure types. All of these are listed on the pentagon of Figure 22–1, next to their own configuration. Their number gives some justification for treating the configurations as a typology of pure types.

Support for the notion of a pure type comes from the configuration hypothesis, which was introduced together with corroborating evidence in Chapter 12: effective structuring requires an internal consistency among the design parameters. In other words, **the organization is driven toward one of the configurations in a search for harmony in its structure.** It may experience pulls toward different configurations, but it has a tendency to favor one of them. For it, better to be consistent and selective than comprehensive and half-hearted. In fact, we saw in the extended configuration hypothesis of Chapter 12, and in a good deal of evidence presented in the preceding five chapters, that this search for harmony and consistency extends to the contingency factors as well. The organization with an integrated structure also favors an environment, a technical system, a size, even an age and a power system consistent with that structure.

Thus, we sometimes find that different organizations in the same industry prefer different configurations, depending on which pull they decide to respond to. To return to the theater company, one prefers Simple Structure because of a strong-willed director (or Divisionalized Form because of many of them), another Machine Bureaucracy because it chooses to produce musicals by the book, another Professional Bureaucracy in order to perfect its performance of Shakespeare year after year, and a last one Adhocracy to produce experimental plays. And the restaurant can structure itself like a Simple Structure, Machine Bureaucracy, or Professional Bureaucracy, depending on whether it wishes to remain a small, classic greasy-spoon, grow large through the mass distribution of basics, such as steak and lobster, or develop the gourmet skills of its chefs.

THE CONFIGURATIONS AS THE BASIS
FOR DESCRIBING STRUCTURAL HYBRIDS

In this third application of the theory, we see that **the set of five configurations can be treated as the basis for describing structural hybrids.**

We have seen in our discussion that not all organizations choose to be consistent in designing their structures, at least not as we have described consistency. They use what we have called hybrid structures, ones that exhibit characteristics of more than one configuration. **Some of the hybrids we have come across in our discussion seem to be dysfunctional,** indications of organizations that cannot make up their minds or, in wanting the best of more than one world, end up with the worst of many. Consider the organization that no sooner gives its middle managers autonomy subject to performance control, as in the Divisionalized Form, than it takes it away by direct supervision, as in the Simple Structure. In some cases, however, organizations have no choice: contradictory contingency factors over which they have no control force them to adopt dysfunctional hybrids. We saw a good deal of evidence of this in school systems, police forces, and other organizations with trained operators that seem to require Professional Bureaucracy structures, yet are driven by concentrated external control (usually governmental) to take on certain characteristics of Machine Bureaucracy, to the detriment of their performance.

But other hybrids seem perfectly logical, indications of the need to respond to more than one valid force at the same time—like the symphony orchestra, a simple professional bureaucracy discussed in Chapter 19, that hires highly trained musicians and relies largely on their standardized skills to produce its music, yet also requires a strong, sometimes autocratic leader to weld them into a tightly coordinated unit. Or the related product corporation discussed in Chapter 20 that needs to divisionalize yet also must coordinate certain critical functions near the strategic apex as does a Machine Bureaucracy. Or the entrepreneurial adhocracy of Chapter 21, where the chief executive, an expert himself, is able to retain a semblance of central control despite the use of multidisciplinary project teams. All the hybrids discussed in the preceding five chapters are shown on the pentagon of Figure 22–1, each on a line between the two configurations from which it draws its characteristics.

The hybrids of Figure 22–1 all involve two configurations. But nothing precludes a combination of the characteristics of three or more configurations. Thus, one McGill student group described an effective church-run convalescent hospital as being tightly controlled by its chief executive—the students referred to her as the "top nun"—yet having a proliferation of its own work rules, and also being dependent on the skills of its medical staff. Here we have a Simple Structure–Machine Bureaucracy–Professional Bureaucracy hybrid. The students' whimsical representation of it is reproduced in Figure 22–2, with the top nun overlooking everything. Another McGill group described a subsidiary of a Japanese trading company as "a divisionalized professional machine adhocracy." (Good thing it wasn't simple!)

Does the existence of such hybrids negate the theory? It is certainly true that the more common the hybrids, the more they should be called pure types and the configurations treated as the hybrids. But the presence of hybrids in a typology does not negate it. There is always gray between black and white. The theory remains useful so long as it helps us to describe a wide variety of structures, even hybrid ones. That is, what matters is not that the theory always matches the reality, but that it helps us to understand the reality. That is its purpose. If we can better describe the Japanese trading company by using terms such as adhocracy, machine, professional, and divisionalized, then the theory has served us. By identifying its nodes, we are able to map the pentagon.

So far we have talked of the hybrid only as a combination throughout a structure of the design parameters of different configurations. But **there is another kind of hybrid as well, the one that uses different configurations in different parts of the organization.** In this way, there can be consistency in the structure of each part, if not in the overall organization. We saw an example of this in the case of the newspaper, with its editorial function structured like an Adhocracy and its printing function structured like a Machine Bureaucracy.

Is this notion of different structures in different parts of the organization inconsistent with the theme running through the preceding five chapters, that whole organizations can be described in terms of single configurations? Not necessarily. There are forces that drive a great many organizations to favor one configuration overall. But within these organizations, there are always forces that favor different structures in different places. (This point was noted in Chapters 4 to 11, in the concluding discussions of each of the design parameters by part of the organization.) Each part of the organization strives for the structure that is most appropriate to its own particular needs, in the face of pressures to conform to the most appropriate structure for the overall organization, and it ends up with some sort of compromise. NASA's cafeterias are, no doubt, run as bureaucracies, but they may prove to be more organic than most; likewise, General Motors' research laboratories no doubt favor adhocratic structure, but they would probably prove

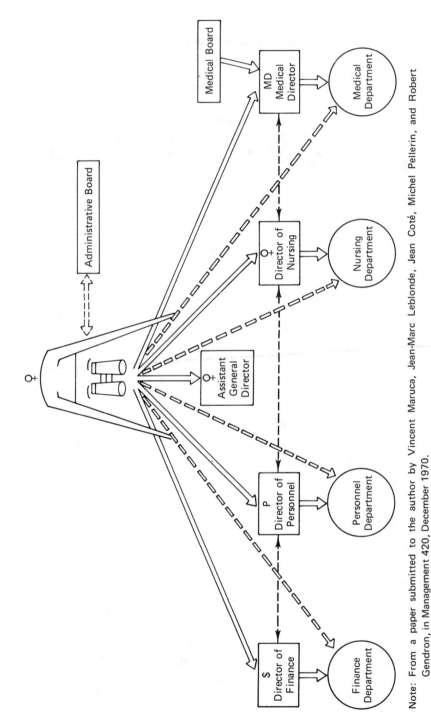

Figure 22-2. *A Simple Structure–Machine Bureaucracy–Professional Bureaucracy Hybrid*

Note: From a paper submitted to the author by Vincent Maruca, Jean-Marc Leblonde, Jean Coté, Michel Pellerin, and Robert Gendron, in Management 420, December 1970.

to be more bureaucratic than those at NASA. And so, while the theory may be a convenient tool to describe a whole organization in terms of a pure type, that description should always be recognized as a simplification, to be followed by deeper probes into the structure of each of its component parts.

In Chapter 19, for example, of the five configurations, we found that Professional Bureaucracy seemed best to describe the overall structure of the general hospital. But in so describing, we also noted that the support staff tended to be structured along the lines of a Machine Bureaucracy. And then in Chapter 21, we noted that the research function might best be described as an Adhocracy. Professional Bureaucracy, in effect, really applied to the clinical mission, albeit the most critical one. But even when we look deeply within this mission, as has Gosselin (1978), we find a range of interdependencies, with resulting variations in the use of the design parameters. Hospitals use incredibly complex structures: to understand them fully, we must look intensively at all their component parts—housekeeping and research and clinical medicine, and obstetrics and radiology and surgery, and plastic surgery and cardiovascular surgery and thoracic surgery.

Again, we conclude by emphasizing that the five configurations are meant to be treated not as five mutually exclusive structures that organizations can use, but as an integrated frame of reference or theory—a pentagon —to guide us in trying to understand and to build complex real-world structures.

THE CONFIGURATIONS AS THE BASIS FOR DESCRIBING STRUCTURAL TRANSITIONS

The theory of the structural configurations can also be used as a basis to help us to understand how and why organizations undertake transitions from one structure to another. Our discussion of the last five chapters has been laced with comments about such transitions, for example from Simple Structure to Machine Bureaucracy as an organization ages and grows, or from Operating Adhocracy to Professional Bureaucracy as an organization tires of innovation and seeks to settle down. All the factors discussed in these chapters that cause a transition from one configuration to another are recorded on the pentagon, along arrows running between them.

Two major patterns have appeared among these transitions, both related to stages in the structural development of organizations. The first pattern applies to organizations that begin in simple environments; it flows around the left side of the pentagon starting at the top. Most organizations begin their lives with something close to the Simple Structure. As they age and grow, and perhaps come under external control, they tend to formalize their behaviors and eventually make a first transition toward Machine Bureaucracy. When these organizations continue to grow, they eventually tend to diversify and later to begin a second structural transition, toward the Divisionalized Form. They may stop along the way with one of the intermediate, hybrid forms—such as the by-product or related product form—or else go all the way to the pure Divisionalized Form. But as we noted in Chapter 20, that may prove to be an unstable structure, and pressures may arise for another transition. In the recognition of divisional interdependencies, the organization may consolidate back toward Machine Bureaucracy or else establish a new hybrid on the way to Adhocracy.

Of course, a number of other forces can intervene to change this sequence. Should the environment of the new organization become complex or its technical system sophisticated, it will find itself drawn toward Adhocracy instead of Machine Bureaucracy. Likewise, should the organization with a structure like Machine Bureaucracy find itself facing more complexity and less stability, perhaps due to product competition or having to use a more sophisticated or even automated technical system, it, too, will tend to shift toward Adhocracy. And should any of the later-stage organizations suddenly find themselves with a hostile environment, they will tend to revert back toward Simple Structure. Should external control instead become a strong force, the transition will be made back toward Machine Bureaucracy.

The second pattern among the transitions applies to organizations that are born in complex environments. This pattern begins at the bottom right side of the pentagon and then moves up and to the left. In this case, organizations begin their lives with Adhocracy structures, eager to develop innovative solutions to wide ranges of contingencies. Sometimes they remain there, perhaps locked in complex, dynamic environments. But among those able to escape, many eventually wish to do so. As they age, these organizations become more conservative. In their search for stability, they begin a transition to bureaucracy. Some concentrate on a few contingencies, at which they can become expert, and structure themselves like Professional Bureaucracies. Others focus on single contingencies and shift toward Machine Bureaucracy. Some organizations, in fact, plan such transitions in line with predictable changes in their functioning. In the theater company described by Goodman and Goodman (1976) or the project organization described by Chandler and Sayles (1971), the development function, organized like an Adhocracy, is followed by the production function, organized like a Professional or Machine Bureaucracy.

Of course, some organizations also begin their lives with Professional Bureaucracy, imitating the structure of other established professional organizations. They often maintain these structures throughout their lives, unless rationalization of the professional tasks or external control eventually drives them toward Machine Bureaucracy, or the desire for more experimentation on the part of their professional operators, perhaps a reflection of a new dynamism in the environment, drives them toward Adhocracy.

It should be noted that **structural transitions often lag the new conditions that evoke them.** Structural change is always difficult, necessitating major rearrangements in established patterns of behavior. So there is a tendency to resist it. Such resistance, in fact, explains many of the dysfunctions found in structures—as in the case of the entrepreneur who hangs on to a Simple Structure even though his organization has grown too large for it, or the organization that continues to formalize even though its environment, having grown complex and dynamic, calls for a structure closer to Adhocracy. Their structures may be internally consistent, but they have outlived the conditions that gave rise to them.

As the need for structural change is finally recognized, the organization begins its transition, perhaps in steps to soften the blow. We saw this in the case of the Machine Bureaucracies that diversify in steps, passing through the by-product and related product hybrids on their way to the Divisionalized Form. But some organizations never complete the transition; they remain in an intermediate, hybrid state because they experience contradictory forces, new ones calling for change, old ones for retention of the current structure. Thus, many corporations remain permanently in the by-product or related product hybrid: they have diversified, but interdependencies remain among their product lines. But when the forces calling for change are unequivocal, the transition is probably best effected quickly and decisively. Wavering between two structures—the old, established one no longer appropriate and the new, uncertain one now necessary—leads to a kind of organizational schizophrenia that may be the most damaging state of all.

To conclude, we have seen in this discussion a fourth application of the theory, as a basis to comprehend structural transitions. It is in these transitions, in fact, that the interrelationships among the five configurations become most evident.

Finally: Is there a sixth structural configuration?   Well, the rainbow still has only five colors.[1] But the planets turned out to number more than five. We even seem to be on the verge of recognizing a sixth sense. So why not a sixth structural configuration. As long, of course, as it maintains the harmony of our theory: it must have its own unique coordinating mechanism, and a new, sixth part of the organization must dominate it.

We do, in fact, have a candidate for the sixth structural configuration, one treated as a variant of the Professional Bureaucracy in Chapter 19 and of the Simple Structure in Chapter 17. Because the operators of the *mission-*

---

[1] In fact, various sources I consulted referred to five, six, and seven colors. I even tried to count, but there was considerable ambiguity in the sample of one I managed to collect. In any event, the rainbow almost certainly has the same number of colors it always did.

ary organization can be trusted to pursue its goals, free of any central control, the structure can be highly decentralized and so we likened it to a Professional Bureaucracy. And because the members of the *charismatic* organization lavish a good deal of power on their leader, we described it as having a Simple Structure. But these two may actually be the same organization, for missionary goals and charismatic leadership typically go together. This suggests a hybrid structure. Moreover, the work of such organizations is often simple and routine, as in the Machine Bureaucracy; its members often work in quasi-autonomous cells or orders, as in the Divisionalized Form; and the members are prepared to cooperate with each other when necessary, as in the Adhocracy. A composite of all five structural configurations should probably be taken as a signal to introduce a sixth.

The *Missionary configuration* would have its own prime coordinating mechanism—socialization, or, if you like, the standardization of norms—and a corresponding main design parameter—indoctrination. Its members would coordinate their behaviors by virtue of the norms they share, in part a result of their indoctrination by the organization. The organization would even have a sixth part, at least one evident to those with that sixth sense. That would be *ideology*, a living, if not animate, part of the missionary organization. The perceptive visitor would "sense" it immediately. Ideology, in fact, represents a sixth important force in every organization, a pull toward a sense of mission. Perhaps our descendants, no longer content with five traditional configurations in their "postadhocratic" age, will turn increasingly toward ideology and the Missionary configuration in the structuring of their organizations.

And so it should be told that one day in her aging years, when Ms. Raku came down from her fifty-fifth story office to preside at the groundbreaking ceremony of Ceramico's largest-ever factory, she slipped on her shovel and fell in the mud. Her sense of revulsion at having dirtied her dress was suddenly replaced by one of profound nostalgia, for she realized that this was her first real contact with the earth since her days in the studio. There came the sudden revelation that making pots was more important than making money. And so the organization took on a new mission—the hand-making of beautiful yet functional pots—and it developed a new structure to reflect its new ideology. As her last act as president, Ms. Raku changed the name of the organization one last time—to Potters of the Earth.

Bibliography

ACKERMAN, R. W., *The Social Challenge to Business* (Harvard University Press, 1975).

AGUILAR, F. J., *Scanning the Business Environment* (Macmillan, 1967).

ALDRICH, H. E., Technology and Organizational Structure: A Reexamination of the Findings of the Aston Group, *Administrative Science Quarterly* (1972: 26–43).

————, Reaction to Donaldson's Note, *Administrative Science Quarterly* (1975: 457–459).

ALLEN, L. A., The Line–Staff Relationship, *Management Record* (September 1955: 346–349, 374–376).

ALLEN, S. A. III, Organizational Choices and General Management Influence Networks in Divisionalized Companies, *Academy of Management Journal* (September, 1978).

ALLEN, T. J., and COHEN, S. I., Information Flow in Research and Development Laboratories, *Administrative Science Quarterly* (1969: 12–19).

ANDERSON, T. R., and WARKOV, S., Organizational Size and Functional Complexity: A Study of Administration in Hospitals, *American Sociological Review* (1961: 23–28).

ANSOFF, H. I., *Corporate Structure: Present and Future* (Working Paper, European Institute for Advanced Studies in Management, Brussels, 1974). Used with permission.

ANSOFF, H. I., and BRANDENBURG, R. G., A Language for Organization Design: Part II, *Management Science* (1971: B717–731).

ARGYRIS, C., "Excerpts from Organization of a Bank," in A. H. Rubenstein and C. J. Haberstroh (eds.), *Some Theories of Organization* (Irwin-Dorsey, 1966).

———, Some Limits of Rational Man Organizational Theory, *Public Administration Review* (1973a: 253–267).

———, Organization Man: Rational *and* Self-Actualizing, *Public Administration Review* (1973b: 354–357).

AZUNI, K., and MCMILLAN, C. J., Culture and Organizational Structure: A Comparison of Japanese and British Organizations, *International Studies of Management and Organization* (1975: 35–47).

BAUGHMAN, J. P.; LODGE, G. C.; and PIFER, H. W., *Environmental Analysis for Management* (Irwin, 1974).

BAVELAS, A., Communication Patterns in Task-Oriented Groups, *Journal of the Acoustical Society of America* (1950: 725–730).

BECKER, S. W., and GORDON, G., An Entrepreneurial Theory of Formal Organizations Part I: Patterns of Formal Organizations, *Administrative Science Quarterly* (1966–67: 315–344).

BEER, S., *Brain of the Firm* (London: Penguin, 1972). Used with permission.

BENNETT, R. C., *General Motors (F): Organizing a Corporate Purchase Agreement* (Case Study, copyright by the President and Fellows of Harvard College, Harvard Business School, 1977).

BENNIS, W. G., The Coming Death of Bureaucracy, *Think Magazine* (November–December 1966: 30–35).

BERGMANN, A. E., Industrial Democracy in Germany—The Battle for Power, *Journal of General Management* (1975: 20–29).

BEYER, J. M., and LODAHL, T. M., A Comparative Study of Patterns of Influence in United States and English Universities, *Administrative Science Quarterly* (1976: 104–129).

BIDWELL, C. E., "The School as a Formal Organization," in J. G. March (ed.), *The Handbook of Organizations* (Rand McNally, 1965), Chapter 23.

BJORK, L. E., An Experiment in Work Satisfaction, *Scientific American* (March 1975: 17–23).

BLAU, P. M., The Hierarchy of Authority in Organizations, *American Journal of Sociology* (1967–68: 453–467).

———, A Formal Theory of Differentiation in Organizations, *American Sociological Review* (1970: 201–218).

BLAU, P. M.; FALBE, C. M.; MCKINLEY, W.; and TRACY, D. K., Technology and Organization in Manufacturing, *Administrative Science Quarterly* (1976: 20–40).

BLAU, P. M., and SCHOENHERR, P. A., *The Structure of Organizations* (Basic Books, 1971).

BLAU, P. M., and SCOTT, R., *Formal Organizations* (Chandler, 1962).

BOLAND, W. R., "Size, Eternal Relations, and the Distribution of Power: A Study of Colleges and Universities," in W. V. Heydebrand (ed.), *Comparative Organizations* (Prentice-Hall, 1973), 428–441.

BONINI, C. P., *Stimulation of Information and Decision Systems in the Firm* (Prentice-Hall, 1963). Used with permission.

BOS, A. H., Development Principles of Organizations, *Management International Review* (1969: 17–30).

BOULDING, K. E., *Conflict and Defense* (Harper & Row, 1962).

BOWER, J. L., Planning Within the Firm, *The American Economic Review* (1970: 186–194).

BRAVERMAN, H., *Labor and Monopoly Capital: The Degradation of Work in the Twentieth Century* (Monthly Review Press, 1974).

BRAYBROOKE, D., and LINDBLOM, C. E., *A Strategy of Decision* (Free Press, 1963).

BUCHELE, R., B., *Business Policy in Growing Firms* (Chandler, 1967).

BURNS, J., "Effective Management of Programs," in J. W. Lorsch and P. R. Lawrence (eds.), *Studies in Organization Design* (Irwin–Dorsey, 1970).

BURNS, T., The Directions of Activity and Communication in a Departmental Executive Group, *Human Relations* (1954: 73–97).

————, Management in Action, *Operational Research Quarterly* (1957: 45–60).

————, "The Comparative Study of Organizations," in V. Vroom (ed.), *Methods of Organizational Research* (University of Pittsburgh Press, 1967).

————, "Mechanistic and Organismic Structures," in D. S. Pugh (ed.), *Organization Theory* (Penguin, 1971).

BURNS, T., and STALKER, G. M., *The Management of Innovation,* 2nd ed. (Tavistock, 1966). Used with permission.

CAPLOW, T., "Rumors in War," in A. H. Rubenstein and C. J. Haberstroh (eds.), *Some Theories of Organization* (Irwin–Dorsey, 1966).

CARLSON, S., *Executive Behaviour: A Study of the Workload and the Working Methods of Managing Directors* (Stockholm: Strombergs, 1951).

CARTER, E. E., The Behavioral Theory of the Firm and Top Level Corporate Decisions, *Administrative Science Quarterly* (1971: 413–428).

CARZO, R., JR., and YANOUZAS, J. N., Effects of Flat and Tall Organization Structure, *Administrative Science Quarterly* (1969: 178–191).

CHANDLER, A. D., *Strategy and Structure* (MIT Press, 1962).

CHANDLER, M. K., and SAYLES, L. R., *Managing Large Systems* (Harper & Row, 1971). Used with permission.

CHANNON, D. F., *The Strategy and Structure of British Enterprise* (Division of Research, Harvard Graduate School of Business Administration, 1973).

————, *The Strategy, Structure and Financial Performance of the Service Industries* (Working Paper, Manchester Business School, 1975). Used with permission.

————, "Corporate Evolution in the Service Industries 1950–1974," in L. Hannah (ed.), *Corporate Strategy and Management Organization* (London: Macmillan, 1976).

CHAPPLE, E. D., and SAYLES, L. R. *The Measure of Management* (Macmillan, 1961). Used with permission.

CHARNS, M. P., Breaking the Tradition Barrier: Managing Integration in Health Care Facilities, *Health Care Management Review* (Winter, 1976: 55–67).

CHARNS, M. P., LAWRENCE, P. R., and WEISBORD, M. R., Organizing Multiple-Function Professionals in Academic Medical Centers, in *TIMS Studies in the Management Sciences* (5, 1977: 71–88).

CHILD, J., Organizational Structure, Environment, and Performance: The Role of Strategic Choice, *Sociology* (1972a: 1–22).

————, Organization Structure and Strategies of Control: A Replication of the Aston Study, *Administration Science Quarterly* (1972b: 163–177).

————, Parkinson's Progress: Accounting for the Number of Specialists in Organizations, *Administrative Science Quarterly* (1973: 328–349).

————, What Determines Organization? *Organizational Dynamics* (Summer 1974: 2–18).

————, Comments on Donaldson's Note, *Administrative Science Quarterly* (1975: 456).

————, Organizational Design and Performance—Contingency Theory and Beyond, *Organization and Administrative Sciences* (Summer-Fall 1977: 169–183).

CHILD, J., and KEISER, A., "Organization and Managerial Roles in British and West German Companies—An Examination of the Culture-Free Thesis," in C. J. Lamers and D. J. Hickson (eds.), *Organisations Alike and Unlike* (Routledge and Kegan Paul, 1978).

CHILD, J., and MANSFIELD, R., Technology, Size, and Organization Structure, *Sociology* (1972: 369–393).

CLARK, B. R., Interorganizational Patterns in Education, *Administrative Science Quarterly* (1965–66: 224–237).

COLLINS, J. W., and GANOTIS, G. G., "Managerial Attitudes Toward Corporate Social Responsibility," in S. P. Sethi (ed.), *The Unstable Ground: Corporate Social Policy in a Dynamic Society* (Melville, 1974).

COLLINS, O., and MOORE, D. G., *The Organization Makers* (Appleton-Century-Crofts, 1970).

CONRATH, D. W., Communications Environment and Its Relationship to Organizational Structure, *Management Science* (1973: 586–602). Used with permission.

CRESSEY, D. R., Achievement of an Unstated Organizational Goal: An Observation of Prisons, *The Pacific Sociological Review* (Fall 1958: 43–49).

————, "Prison Organizations," in J. G. March (ed.), *Handbook of Organizations* (Rand McNally, 1965), Chapter 24.

CROZIER, M., *The Bureaucratic Phenomenon*, English translation (University of Chicago Press, 1964). Used with permission.

CUMMINGS, L. L., and BERGER, C. J., Organization Structure: How Does It Influence Attitudes and Performance? *Organizational Dynamics* (Autumn 1976: 34–49).

CYERT, R. M., and MARCH, J. G., *A Behavioral Theory of the Firm* (Prentice-Hall, 1963).

DALTON, M., *Men Who Manage* (Wiley, 1959). Used with permission.

DAVIS, K., Management Communication and the Grapevine, *Harvard Business Review* (September–October 1953: 43–49).

————, Success of Chain-of-Command Oral Communication in a Manufacturing Management Group, *Academy of Management Journal* (1968: 379–387).

DAVIS, L.; CANTER, R. R.; and HOFFMAN, J., Current Job Design Criteria, *Journal of Industrial Engineering* (March–April 1955: 5–8, 21–23).

DELBECQ, A., and FILLEY, A. C., *Program and Project Management in a Matrix Organization: A Case Study* (Monograph No. 9, Graduate School of Business, Bureau of Business Research and Service, University of Wisconsin, Madison, 1974). Used with permission.

DESSLER, G., *Organization and Management: A Contingency Approach*, Prentice-Hall, 1976.

DILL, W. R., Environment as an Influence on Managerial Autonomy, *Administrative Science Quarterly*, 1957–58: 409–443.

————, "Business Organizations," in J. G. March (ed.), *Handbook of Organizations* (Rand McNally, 1965), Chapter 25.

DONALDSON, L., Organizational Status and the Measurement of Centralization, *Administrative Science Quarterly* (1975: 453–456).

DOWNEY, H. K.; HELLRIEGEL, D.; and SLOCUM, J. W., JR., Reply to Tinker, *Administrative Science Quarterly* (1976: 508–510).

DRIVER, M. J., and STREUFERT, S., Integrative Complexity: An Approach to Individuals and Groups as Information-Processing Systems, *Administrative Science Quarterly* (1969: 272–285).

DUNCAN, R. B., Characteristics of Organizational Environments and Perceived Environmental Uncertainty, *Administrative Science Quarterly* (1972: 313–327).

————, Multiple Decision-Making Structures in Adapting to Environmental Uncertainty: The Impact on Organizational Effectiveness, *Human Relations* (1973: 273–291).

DYAS, G. P., and THANHEISER, H. T., *The Emerging European Enterprise: Strategy and Structure in French and German Industry* (Macmillan of London, 1976).

EMERY, F. E., Democratization of the Work Place: A Historical Review of Studies, *International Studies of Management and Organization* (1971: 181–201).

EMERY, F. E., and TRIST, E. L., "Socio-Technical Systems," in C. W. Churchman and M. Verhulst (eds.), *Management Science Models and Techniques, Vol. 2,* (Pergamon, 1960), 83–97.

EMERY, J., *Organizational Planning and Control Systems* (Macmillan, 1969).

ETZIONI, A., Authority Structure and Organizational Effectiveness, *Administrative Science Quarterly* (1959: 43–67).

————, *A Comparative Analysis of Complex Organizations* (Free Press, 1961).

FAYOL, H., *General and Industrial Management* (Pitman, 1949); first published in French in 1916.

FELD, M. D., Information and Authority: The Structure of Military Organization, *American Sociological Review* (1959: 15–22). Used with permission.

FIEDLER, F. E., "The Contingency Model: A Theory of Leadership Effectiveness," in H. Proshansky and B. Seidenberg (eds.), *Basic Studies in Social Psychology* (Holt, Rinehart, and Winston, 1966).

FILLEY, A. C., and HOUSE, R. J., *Managerial Process and Organizational Behaviour* (Scott, Foresman, 1969); also second edition with S. Kerr, 1976.

FOURAKER, L. E., and STOPFORD, J. M., Organizational Structure and the Multinational Strategy, *Administrative Science Quarterly* (1968: 47–64).

FRANK, A. G., Goal Ambiguity and Conflicting Standards: An Approach to the Study of Organization, *Human Organization* (Winter 1958–59: 8–13).

FRANKO, L. G., Strategy + Structure − Frustration = The Experiences of European Firms in America, *The Business Quarterly* (Autumn 1972: 70–83).

———— The Move Toward a Multidivisional Structure in European Organizations, *Administrative Science Quarterly* (1974: 493–506).

GALBRAITH, J. K., *The New Industrial State* (Houghton Mifflin, 1967).

GALBRAITH, J. R., Matrix Organization Designs, *Business Horizons* (February 1971: 29–40).

————, *Designing Complex Organizations* (Addison-Wesley, 1973). Used with permission.

GALBRAITH, J. R., and EDSTROM, A., "Creating Decentralization Through Informal Networks: The Role of Transfer," in R. H. Kilmann, L. R. Pondy, and D. P. Slevin (eds.), *The Management of Organization Design, Volume II* (Elsevier, 1976), 289–310.

GERTH, H. H., and MILLS, C. W. (eds.), *From Max Weber: Essays in Sociology* (Oxford University Press, 1958). Used with permission.

GLANZER, M., and GLASER, P., Techniques for the Study of Group Structure and Behavior: Empirical Studies of the Effects of Structure in Small Groups, *Psychological Bulletin* (1961: 1–27).

GOGGIN, W. C., How the Multidimensional Structure Works at Dow Corning, *Harvard Business Review* (January-February 1974: 54–65). Copyright by the President and Fellows of Harvard College. Used with permission.

GOODMAN, L. P., and GOODMAN, R. A., Theater as a Temporary System, *California Management Review* (Winter 1972: 103–108).

GOODMAN, R. A., and GOODMAN, L. P., Some Management Issues in Temporary Systems: A Study of Professional Development and Manpower—Theater Case, *Administrative Science Quarterly* (1976: 494–501).

GOSSELIN, R., *A Study of the Interdependence of Medical Specialists in Quebec Teaching Hospitals* (Ph.D. Thesis, Faculty of Management, McGill University, 1978). Used with permission.

GREENWOOD, R., and HININGS, C. R., A Research Note: Centralization Revisited, *Administrative Science Quarterly* (1976: 151–155).

GREINER, L. E., Evolution and Revolution as Organizations Grow, *Harvard Business Review* (July-August 1972: 37–46).

GUETZKOW, H., "Communications in Organizations," in J. G. March (ed.), *Handbook of Organizations* (Rand McNally, 1965), Chapter 12.

GUETZKOW, H., and SIMON, H. A. The Impact of Certain Communication Nets Upon Organization and Performance in Task-Oriented Groups, *Management Science* (1954–55: 233–250). Used with permission.

GULICK, L. H., and URWICK, L. F. (eds.), *Papers on the Science of Administration* (Columbia University Press, 1937).

GUSTAVSEN, B., Redefining the Role of the Board, *Journal of General Management* (Spring 1975: 35–44).

HAGE, J., and AIKEN, M., Relationship of Centralization to Other Structural Properties, *Administrative Science Quarterly* (1967: 72–92).

HAGE, J., and DEWER, R., Elite Values versus Organizational Structure in Predicting Innovation, *Administrative Science Quarterly* (1973: 279–290).

HAGE, J.; AIKEN, M., and MARRETT, C. B., Organization Structure and Communications, *American Sociological Review* (1971: 860–871).

HAIRE, M., "Biological Models and Empirical Histories of the Growth of Organizations," in M. Haire (ed.), *Modern Organization Theory* (Wiley, 1959), 272–306. Used with permission.

————, *Psychology in Management* (McGraw-Hill, 1964).

HALL, R. H., Intraorganizational and Structural Variation: Application of the Bureaucratic Model, *Administrative Science Quarterly* (1962: 295–308).

————, The Concept of Bureaucracy: An Empirical Assessment, *American Journal of Sociology* (1963: 32–40).

————, Professionalization and Bureaucratization, *American Sociological Review* (1968: 92–104).

————, *Organizations: Structure and Process* (Prentice-Hall, 1972).

HALL, R. H.; HASS, J. E.; and JOHNSON, N. J., Organizational Size, Complexity, and Formalization, *American Sociological Review* (1967: 903–912).

HAMBLIN, R. L., Leadership and Crises, *Sociometry* (1958: 322–335).

HAMPDEN-TURNER, C., "Synergy as the Optimization of Differentiation and Integration by the Human Personality," in J. W. Lorsch and P. R. Lawrence (eds.), *Studies in Organization Design* (Irwin–Dorsey, 1970), 187–196.

HARBISON, E., and MYERS, C. A., *Management in the Industrial World* (McGraw-Hill, 1959).

HARRIS, K. L., Organizing to Overhaul a Mess, *California Management Review* (Spring 1975: 40–49).

HARRISON, F., The Management of Scientists: Determinants of Perceived Role Performance, *Academy of Management Journal* (1974: 234–241).

HARVEY, E., Technology and the Structure of Organizations, *American Sociological Review* (1968: 247–259).

HATVANY, N. G., Review of "A Profile of Tomorrow's Police Officer and his Organization" by Victor Cizanckas, in A. M. Jaeger (ed.), *Seminars on Organizations* (Stanford University, Winter and Spring, 1976: 72–74).

HEDBERG, B. L. T.; NYSTROM, P. C.; and STARBUCK, W. H., Camping on Seesaws: Prescriptions for a Self-Designing Organization, *Administrative Science Quarterly* (1976: 41–65).

HELLRIEGEL, D., and SLOCUM J. W., JR., Organizational Design: A Contingency Approach, *Business Horizons* (April 1973: 59–68).

HERZBERG, F., One More Time: How Do You Motivate Employees? *Harvard Business Review* (January-February 1968: 53–62).

HEWES, J. E., JR., *From Root to McNamara: Army Organization and Administration, 1900–1963* (Center of Military History, United States Army, Washington, D.C., 1975).

HEYDEBRAND, W. V., "Autonomy, Complexity, and Non-bureaucratic Coordination in Professional Organizations," in W. V. Heydebrand (ed.), *Comparative Organizations* (Prentice-Hall, 1973) 158–189.

HEYDEBRAND, W. V., and NOELL, J. J., "Task Structure and Innovation in Professional Organizations," in W. V. Heydebrand (ed.), *Comparative Organizations* (Prentice-Hall, 1973) 294–322.

HICKSON, D. J., A Convergence in Organization Theory, *Administrative Science Quarterly* (1966–67: 224–237).

HICKSON, D. J.; PUGH, D. S.; and PHEYSEY, D. C., Operations Technology and Organization Structure: An Empirical Reappraisal, *Administrative Science Quarterly* (1969: 378–379).

HININGS, C. R.; HICKSON, D. J.; PENNINGS, J. M.; and SCHNECK, R. E., Structural Conditions of Intraorganizational Power, *Administrative Science Quarterly* (1974: 22–44).

HLAVACEK, J. D., and THOMPSON, V. A., Bureaucracy and New Product Innovation, *Academy of Management Journal* (1973: 361–372).

HOLDAWAY, E. A.; NEWBERRY J. F.; HICKSON, D. J.; and HERON, R. P., Dimensions of Organizations in Complex Societies: The Educational Sector, *Administrative Science Quarterly* (1975: 37–58).

HOLDEN, P. E.; PEDERSON, C. A.; and GERMANE, G. E., *Top Management* (McGraw-Hill, 1968).

HOLSTEIN, W. K., and BERRY, W. L., Work Flow Structure: An Analysis for Planning and Control, *Management Science* (1970: B324–336). Used with permission.

HULIN, C. L. and BLOOD, M. R., Job Enlargement, Individual Differences, and Worker Responses, *Psychological Bulletin* (1968: 41–55).

HUNT, J. W., *The Restless Organization* (Wiley International, 1972).

HUNT, R. G., Technology and Organization, *Academy of Management Journal* (1970: 235–252).

INDIK, B. P., The Relationship Between Organization Size and Supervision Ratio, *Administrative Science Quarterly* (1964: 301–312).

INKSON, J. H. K.; PUGH, D. S.; and HICKSON, D. J., Organization, Context and Structure: An Abbreviated Replication, *Administrative Science Quarterly* (1970: 318–329).

IVANCEVICH, J. M., and DONNELLY, J. H., JR., Relation of Organizational Structure to Job Satisfaction, Anxiety-Stress, and Performance, *Administrative Science Quarterly* (1975: 272–280).

JACOBSON, E., and SEASHORE, S. E., Communication Practices in Complex Organizations, *Journal of Social Issues* (1951: 28–40).

JAY, A., *Management and Machiavelli* (Penguin, 1970). Used with permission.

JENNERGREN, L. P., *Decentralization in Organizations* (Working Paper, International Institute of Management, West Berlin, 1974); preliminary version of chapter to be published in *Handbook of Organizational Design,* W. H. Starbuck and P. Nystrom (eds.).

KAST, E. E., and ROSENZWEIG, J. E., *Organization and Management: A Systems Approach* (McGraw-Hill, 1970).

KATZ, D., and KAHN, R. L., *The Social Psychology of Organizations* (Wiley, 1966).

KAUFMAN, H., *The Forest Ranger: A Study in Administrative Behavior* (Johns Hopkins Press, 1960).

KAUFMAN, H., and SEIDMAN, D., The Morphology of Organization, *Administrative Science Quarterly* (1970: 439–445).

KELLER, R. T.; SLOCUM, J. W., JR.; and SUSMAN, G. J., Uncertainty and Type of Management System in Continuous Process Organizations, *Academy of Management Journal* (1974: 56–68).

KHANDWALLA, P. N., *Report on the Influence of the Techno-Economic Environment on Firms' Organization* (Report of research findings presented to participating corporations in a study of organizational structure, McGill University, 1971). Used with permission.

———, The Effect of Different Types of Competition on the Use of Management Controls, *Journal of Accounting Research* (1972: 275–285).

———, Effect of Competition on the Structure of Top Management Control, *Academy of Management Journal* (1973a: 285–295).

———, Viable and Effective Organizational Designs of Firms, *Academy of Management Journal* (1973b: 481–495).

———, Environment and "Optimal" Design of Organizations, *Productivity* (1973c: 540–552).

———, Mass Output Orientation of Operations Technology and Organizational Structure, *Administrative Science Quarterly* (1974: 74–97). Used with permission.

———, Organizational Design for Change, *Learning Systems, Conceptual Reading 5* (New Delhi, India, 1976).

———, *The Design of Organizations* (Harcourt Brace Jovanovich, 1977).

KIMBERLY, J. R., Organizational Size and the Structuralist Perspective: A Review, Critique, and Proposal, *Administrative Science Quarterly* (1976: 571–597).

KLAHR, D., and LEAVITT, H. J., "Tasks, Organization Structures, Computers, Programs," in C. A. Myers (ed.), *The Impact of Computers on Management* (MIT Press, 1967).

KLATZKY, S. P., Relationship of Organizational Size to Complexity and Coordination, *Administrative Science Quarterly* (1970: 428–438).

KNIGHT, K., Matrix Organization: A Review, *The Journal of Management Studies* (1976: 111–130).

KOCHEN, M., and DEUTSCH, K. W., Toward a Rational Theory of Decentralization: Some Implications of a Mathematical Approach, *American Political Science Review* (1969: 734–749).

———, Decentralization by Function and Location, *Management Science* (1973: 841–855).

KOVER, A. J., Reorganization in an Advertising Agency: A Case Study of a Decrease in Integration, *Human Organization* (1963–64: 252–259).

KUHN, T. S., *The Structure of Scientific Revolutions,* 2nd ed. (University of Chicago Press, 1970).

LANDSBERGER, H. A., The Horizontal Dimension in Bureaucracy, *Administration Science Quarterly* (1961–62: 299–332).

LAWRENCE, P. R., *The Changing of Organizational Behavior Patterns* (Riverside Press, 1958).

LAWRENCE, P. R., and LORSCH, J. W., *Organization and Environment* (Irwin, 1967).

LEAVITT, J. H., Some Effects of Certain Communication Patterns on Group Performance, *Journal of Abnormal and Social Psychology* (1951: 38–50).

LIKERT, R., *New Patterns of Management* (McGraw-Hill, 1961).

LINDBLOM, C. E., *The Intelligence of Democracy: Decision Making Through Mutual Adjustment* (Free Press, 1965).

LITTERER, J. A., *The Analysis of Organizations* (Wiley, 1965); also 2nd ed., 1973. Used with permission.

LITZINGER, W.; MAYRINAC, A.; and WAGLE, J., The Manned Spacecraft Center in Houston: The Practice of Matrix Management, *International Review of Administrative Sciences* (1970: 1–8).

LOEVINGER, L., The Sociology of Bureaucracy, *The Business Lawyer* (November 1968: 7–18).

LONG, N. E., "The Administrative Organization as a Political System," in S. Mailick and E. Van Ness (eds.), *Concepts and Issues on Administrative Behavior* (Prentice-Hall, 1962).

LORSCH, J. W., and ALLEN, S. A. III, *Managing Diversity and Interdependence* (Division of Research, Graduate School of Business Administration, Harvard University, 1973.) Used with permission.

LOURENCO, S. V., and GLIDEWELL, J. C., A Dialectical Analysis of Organizational Conflict, *Administrative Science Quarterly* (1975: 489–508).

MACE, M. L., *Directors: Myth and Reality* (Division of Research, Harvard Business School, 1971).

MANNS, C., Review of "Formalization and Centralization: The Case of Polish Industry," by Lena Kolarska, in A. M. Jaeger (ed.), *Seminars on Organizations* (Stanford University, Winter and Spring 1976: 64–66).

MANSFIELD, R., Bureaucracy and Centralization: An Examination of Organizational Structure, *Administrative Science Quarterly* (1973: 477–488).

MARCH, J. G., and SIMON, H. A., *Organizations* (Wiley, 1958). Used with permission.

MARTIN, L. G., How Beatrice Foods Sneaked Up on $5 Billion, *Fortune* (1976: 188–121, 124, 126, 129).

MARTIN, N. H., Differential Decisions in the Management of an Industrial Plant, *The Journal of Business* (1956: 249–260).

MARTYN, H., Effects of Multi-national Affiliation on Local Management, *Michigan Business Review* (March 1967: 15–20).

MASLOW, A. H., *Motivation and Personality* (Harper & Row, 1954).

MCCLEERY, R. H., *Policy Change in Prison Management* (Michigan State University Press, 1957).

MCWHINNEY, W. H., On the Geometry of Organizations, *Administrative Science Quarterly* (1965: 347–362).

MELCHER, A. J., *Structure and Process of Organizations: A Systems Approach* (Prentice-Hall, 1976).

MERTON, R. K., *Social Theory and Social Structure* (Free Press, 1957).

MEYER, M. W., The Two Authority Structures of Bureaucratic Organizations, *Administrative Science Quarterly* (1968: 211–228).

MILLER, E. J., Technology, Territory and Time: The Internal Differentiation of Complex Production Systems, *Human Relations* (1959: 243–272). Used with permission.

———, Socio-Technical Systems in Weaving, 1953–1970: A Follow-up Study, *Human Relations* (1975: 349–388).

MINTZBERG, H., *The Nature of Managerial Work* (Harper & Row, 1973a).

———, Strategy-making in Three Modes, *California Management Review* (Winter 1973b: 44–53).

———, *Impediments to the Use of Management Information* (National Association of Accountants Monograph, 1975).

———, Patterns in Strategy Formation, *Management Science* (1978: 934–948).

MINTZBERG, H.; RAISINGHANI, D.; and THÉORÊT, A., The Structure of "Unstructured" Decision Processes, *Administrative Science Quarterly* (1976: 246–275).

MONTAGNA, P. D., Professionalization and Bureaucratization in Large Professional Organizations, *The American Journal of Sociology* (1968: 138–145).

MORRIS, D., *The Naked Ape* (McGraw-Hill, 1967).

MOYER, R. C., Berle and Means Revisited: The Conglomerate Merger, *Business and Society* (Spring 1970: 20–29).

NEUSTADT, R. E., *Presidential Power* (Wiley, 1960).

NORMANN, R., Organizational Innovativeness: Product Variation and Reorientation, *Administrative Science Quarterly* (1971: 203–215).

OUCHI, W. G., and DOWLING, J. B., Defining the Span of Control, *Administrative Science Quarterly* (1974: 357–365).

OUCHI, W. G., and MCGUIRE, M. A., Organizational Control: Two Functions, *Administrative Science Quarterly* (1975: 559–569).

PALUMBO, D., Power and Role Specificity in Organization Theory, *Public Administration Review* (1969: 237–248).

PARKINSON, C. N., *Parkinson's Law* (John Murray, Ltd., and Houghton Mifflin, 1957). Used with permission.

———, *Big Business* (Weidenfeld and Nicolson, 1974).

PATERSON, T. T., *Management Theory* (Business Publications Ltd., 1969). Used with permission.

PAVEN, R. J., *Diversification and Divisional Structure in Italy* (Paper presented at the Annual Meeting of the Academy of Management, Seattle, 1974).

PENNINGS, J. M., The Relevance of the Structural-Contingency Model for Organizational Effectiveness, *Administrative Science Quarterly* (1975: 393–410).

PERROW, C., "Hospitals: Technology, Structure, and Goals," in J. G. March (ed.), *Handbook of Organizations* (Rand McNally, 1965), Chapter 22.

———, A Framework for the Comparative Analysis of Organizations, *American Sociological Review* (1967: 194–208).

———, *Organizational Analysis: A Sociological Review* (Wadsworth, 1970). Used with permission.

———, *Complex Organizations: A Critical Essay* (Scott, Foresman, 1972).

———, The Short and Glorious History of Organizational Theory, *Organizational Dynamics* (Summer 1973: 2–15).

———, Is Business Really Changing? *Organizational Dynamics* (Summer 1974: 31–44).

PETERSON, R. B., The Interaction of Technological Process and Perceived Organizational Climate in Norwegian Firms, *Academy of Management Journal* (1975: 288–299).

PETTIGREW, A. M., Information Control as a Power Resource, *Sociology* (1972: 188–204).

PFEFFER, J., and LEBLEBICI, H., The Effect of Competition on Some Dimensions of Organizational Structure, *Social Forces* (1973–74: 268–279).

PFIFFNER, J. M., Administrative Rationality, *Public Administration Review* (1960: 125–132).

PFIFFNER, J. M., and SHERWOOD, F., *Administrative Organization* (Prentice-Hall, 1960). Used with permission.

PIERCE, J. L., and DUNHAM, R. B., Task Design: A Literature Review, *Academy of Management Review* (October 1976: 83–97).

PONDY, L. R., Effects of Size, Complexity, and Ownership on Administrative Intensity, *Administrative Science Quarterly* (1969: 47–60).

PORTER, L. W., and LAWLER, E. E., The Effects of "Tall" vs. "Flat" Organization Structures on Managerial Job Satisfaction, *Personnel Psychology* (1964: 135–148).

PRICE, J. L., The Impact of Departmentalization on Interoccupational Cooperation, *Human Organization* (1968: 362–368).

PUGH, D. S.; HICKSON, D. J.; and HININGS, C. R., An Empirical Taxonomy of Structures of Work Organizations, *Administrative Science Quarterly* (1969a: 115–126).

PUGH, D. S.; HICKSON, D. J.; HININGS, C. R.; MACDONALD, K. M.; TURNER, C.; and LUPTON, T., A Conceptual Scheme for Organizational Analysis, *Administrative Science Quarterly* (1963–64; 289–315).

PUGH, D. S.; HICKSON, D. J.; HININGS, C. R.; and TURNER, C., Dimensions of Organization Structure, *Administrative Science Quarterly* (1968: 65–105).

PUGH, D. S.; HICKSON, D. J.; HININGS, C. R.; and TURNER, C., The Context of Organization Structures, *Administrative Science Quarterly* (1969b: 91–114).

REESER, C., Some Potential Human Problems of the Project Form of Organization, *Academy of Management Journal* (1969: 459–467).

REEVES, T. K., and WOODWARD, J., "The Study of Managerial Control," in J. Woodward (ed.), *Industrial Organization: Behaviour and Control* (Oxford University Press, 1970).

REIMANN, B. C., On the Dimensions of Bureaucratic Structure: An Empirical Reappraisal, *Administrative Science Quarterly* (1973: 462–476).

RICE, A. K., Productivity and Social Organization in an Indian Weaving Shed, *Human Relations* (1953: 297–329).

ROETHLISBERGER, F. J., and DICKSON, W. J., *Management and the Worker: An Account of a Research Program Conducted by the Western Electric Company, Hawthorne Works, Chicago* (Harvard University Press, 1939).

ROGERS, D. C., *Essentials of Business Policy* (Harper & Row, 1975).

RUMELT, R. P., *Strategy, Structure, and Economic Performance* (Division of Research, Graduate School of Business Administration, Harvard University, 1974). Used with permission.

RUSHING, W. A., The Effects of Industry Size and Division of Labor on Administration, *Administrative Science Quarterly* (1967–68: 273–295).

———, Two Patterns of Industrial Administration, *Human Organization* (1976: 32–39).

SALTER, M. S., Stages of Corporate Development, *Journal of Business Policy* (Autumn 1970: 23–37).

SAMUEL, Y., and MANNHEIM, B. F., A Multidimensional Approach Toward a Typology of Bureaucracy, *Administrative Science Quarterly* (1970: 216–228).

SAYLES, L. R., Matrix Organization: The Structure with a Future, *Organizational Dynamics* (Autumn 1976: 2–17). Used with permission.

SCHARPF, F. W., "Does Organization Matter? Task Structure and Interaction in the Ministerial Bureaucracy," in E. H. Burack and A. R. Negardhi, *Organization Design: Theoretical Perspectives and Empirical Findings*, (Kent State University Press, 1977: 149–167).

SCHEIN, E. H., Organizational Socialization and the Profession of Management, *Industrial Management Review* (Winter 1968: 1–16).

SCOTT, B. R., *Stages of Corporate Development, Part I* (Working Paper, Harvard Business School, 14–371–294; BP993, 1971).

———, The Industrial State: Old Myths and New Realities, *Harvard Business Review* (March–April 1973: 133–148). Copyright by the President and Fellows of Harvard College. Used with permission.

SCOTT, W. G., Organization Theory: An Overview and an Appraisal, *Academy of Management Journal* (1961: 7–26).

SEGAL, M., Organization and Environment: A Typology of Adaptability and Structure, *Public Administration Review* (1974: 212–220).

SHINODA, Y., "Japanese Management: Old Ways Become Modern," in B. Taylor and K. Macmillan (eds.), *Top Management* (Longman, 1973).

SIAR, *Management Survey of UNICEF*, (Stockholm: Scandinavian Institutes for Administrative Research, 1975). Used with permission.

SILLS, D. L., *The Volunteers* (Free Press, 1957).

SIMON, H. A., *Administrative Behavior*, 2nd ed. (Macmillan, 1957). Used with permission.

———, The Future of Information Processing Technology, *Management Science* (1968: 619–624).

———, *The Sciences of the Artificial* (MIT Press, 1969).

———, Applying Information Technology to Organization Design, *Public Administration Review* (1973a: 268–278).

———, Organization Man: Rational or Self-Actualizing, *Public Administration Review* (1973b: 346–353).

———, *The New Science of Management Decision*, rev. ed. (Prentice-Hall, 1977).

SLOAN, A. P., *My Years at General Motors* (Doubleday, 1963).

SMITH, A., *The Wealth of Nations* (London: Dent, 1910).

SORENSEN, J. E., and SORENSEN, T. L., The Conflict of Professionals in Bureaucratic Organizations, *Administrative Science Quarterly* (1974: 98–106).

SPENCER, F. C., Deductive Reasoning in the Lifelong Continuing Education of a Cardiovascular Surgeon, *Archives of Surgery* (1976: 1177–1183).

STANFIELD, G. G., Technology and Organization Structure as Theoretical Categories, *Administrative Science Quarterly* (1976: 489–493).

STARBUCK, W. H., "Organizational Growth and Development," in J. G. March (ed.), *Handbook of Organizations* (Rand McNally, 1965), Chapter 11.

———, *Organizational Growth and Development* (Penguin, 1971).

STARBUCK, W. H., and DUTTON, J. M., Designing Adaptive Organizations, *Journal of Business Policy* (Summer 1973: 21–28).

STEWART, R., *The Reality of Management* (Heinemann, 1963).

———, *The Reality of Organisations* (Macmillan of London, 1970).

STIEGLITZ, H., "Organization Structures—What's Been Happening," in H. E. Frank (ed.), *Organization Structuring* (McGraw-Hill, 1971).

STINCHCOMBE, A. L., Bureaucratic and Craft Administration of Production: A Comparative Study, *Administrative Science Quarterly* (1959–60: 168–187).

———, "Social Structure and Organizations," in J. G. March (ed.), *Handbook of Organizations* (Rand McNally, 1965), Chapter 4.

STOPFORD, J. M., and WELLS, L. T., JR., *Managing the Multinational Enterprise: Organization of the Firm and Ownership of the Subsidiaries* (Basic Books, 1972).

STRAUSS, G., Tactics of Lateral Relationship: The Purchasing Agent, *Administrative Science Quarterly* (1962–63: 161–186).

———, Adolescence in Organization Growth: Problems, Pains, Possibilities, *Organizational Dynamics* (Spring 1974: 3–17).

STRAUSS, G., and ROSENSTEIN, R., Worker Participation: Critical View, *Industrial Relations* (1970: 197–214).

SUTTON, H., and PORTER, L. W., A Study of the Grapevine in a Governmental Organization, *Personnel Psychology* (1968: 223–230).

TAYLOR, F. W., *Scientific Management* (Harper & Row, 1947, first published in 1911).

TERKEL, S., *Working* (Pantheon, 1972, and Wildwood House, 1975). Used with permission.

TERRIEN, F. W., and MILLS, D. L., The Effect of Changing Size upon the Internal Structure of Organizations, *American Sociological Review* (1955: 11–13).

THOMASON, G. F., Managerial Work Roles and Relationships, Part I, *The Journal of Management Studies* (1966: 270–284).

————, Managerial Work Roles and Relationships, Part II, *The Journal of Management Studies* (1967: 17–30).

THOMPSON, J. D., *Organizations in Action* (McGraw-Hill, 1967).

THOMPSON, V. A., *Modern Organizations* (Knopf, 1961).

TINKER, A. M., A Note on "Environmental Uncertainty" and a Suggestion for our Editorial Function, *Administrative Science Quarterly* (1976: 506–508).

TOFFLER, A., *Future Shock* (Bantam Books, 1970).

TOPOFF, H. R., The Social Behavior of Army Ants, *Scientific American* (November 1972: 71–79).

TRIST, E. L., and BAMFORTH, K. W., Some Social and Psychological Consequences of the Long-Wall Method of Coal-Getting, *Human Relations* (1951: 3–38).

UDY, S. H., JR., *Organization of Work* (New Haven, Conn.: HRAF Press, 1959).

————, "The Comparative Analysis of Organizations," in J. G. March (ed.), *Handbook of Organizations* (Rand McNally, 1965), Chapter 16.

URWICK, L. F., The Manager's Span of Control, *Harvard Business Review* (May–June 1956: 39–47).

VAN DE VEN, A. H., A Framework for Organizational Assessment, *Academy of Management Review* (1976a: 64–78).

————, A Panel Study of Determinants of Authority Structures Within Organizational Units, *Proceedings of the National Meeting of the Academy of Management* (1976b: 256–262).

VAN DE VEN, A. H., and DELBECQ, A. L., A Task Contingent Model of Work-Unit Structure, *Administrative Science Quarterly* (1974: 183–197).

WALKER, A. H., and LORSCH, J. W., "Organizational Choice: Product Versus Function," in J. W. Lorsch and P. R. Lawrence (eds.), *Studies in Organization Design* (Irwin–Dorsey, 1970), 36–53.

WEICK, K. E., Educational Organizations as Loosely Coupled Systems, *Administrative Science Quarterly* (1976: 1–19).

WHISLER, T., *Organizational Research and the Strategist* (speech presented at conference on "Strategy and Structure," Stanford University, December, 1975). Used with permission.

WHYTE, W. F., *Organizational Behavior: Theory and Application* (Irwin-Dorsey, 1969). Used with permission.

WILD, R., Mass Production Work, *Journal of General Management* (Spring 1976: 30–40).

WILENSKY, H. L., *Organizational Intelligence* (Basic Books, 1967).

WILLIAMSON, O. E., Hierarchical Control and Optimum Firm Size, *The Journal of Political Economy* (1967: 123–138).

————, *Markets and Hierarchies: Analysis and Antitrust Implications* (Free Press, 1975).

WOODWARD, J., *Industrial Organization: Theory and Practice* (Oxford University Press, 1965). Used with permission.

WORTHY, j. C., Organizational Structure and Employee Morale, *American Sociological Review* (1950: 169–179).

————, *Big Business and Free Men* (Harper & Row, 1959). Used with permission.

WRAPP, H. E., Good Managers Don't Make Policy Decisions, *Harvard Business Review* (September–October 1967: 91–99).

WREN, D. A., Interface and Interorganizational Coordination, *Academy of Management Journal* (1967: 69–81).

WRIGLEY, L., *Diversification and Divisional Autonomy* (D.B.A. thesis, Harvard Business School, 1970). Used with permission.

Index

Note: Because of the nature of the synthesis of this book, terms introduced throughout the early chapters—such as direct supervision, support staff, and specialization—are used increasingly in the later chapters. Some are used hundreds of times, in virtually every combination with the other terms. It was, therefore, decided to index such terms only when they are introduced and thereafter only when they are discussed at some length or in an important way. Also, the decision was made not to index the examples—whether industries (e.g., hospitals or oil companies) or specific organizations (e.g., Corborundum or Murray's Restaurants)—in order to avoid focusing special attention on them; they have been included only to illustrate the concepts.